PRINCIPLES OF CYE

PRINCIPLES OF CYBERCRIME

JONATHAN CLOUGH

Faculty of Law, Monash University

CAMBRIDGE
UNIVERSITY PRESS

CAMBRIDGE UNIVERSITY PRESS

Cambridge, New York, Melbourne, Madrid, Cape Town, Singapore,
São Paulo, Delhi, Dubai, Tokyo

Cambridge University Press
The Edinburgh Building, Cambridge CB2 8RU, UK

Published in the United States of America by Cambridge University Press, New York

www.cambridge.org
Information on this title: www.cambridge.org/9780521728126

First published 2010

Printed in the United Kingdom at the University Press, Cambridge

A catalogue record for this publication is available from the British Library

ISBN 978-0-521-89925-3 Hardback
ISBN 978-0-521-72812-6 Paperback

CONTENTS

PREFACE

The idea for this book arose several years ago when I was teaching my cybercrime class for the first time. In compiling materials, I was struck by two things: first, that the challenges of cybercrime were being faced simultaneously by all developed and, increasingly, developing countries; second, that much of the academic writing in the area was criminological in nature, with relatively little doctrinal analysis. It was in this context that I first proposed to write this book: a comparative doctrinal analysis of cybercrime laws. While some time has passed between idea and fruition, in this case delay has ultimately been beneficial. The last few years in particular have seen increased legislative and judicial activity in the area of cybercrime, creating a considerable body of law in this relatively new field. As this book amply demonstrates, the criminal law has well and truly arrived in cyberspace.

This book is intended for anyone who wishes to gain a deeper understanding of the legal principles which are applied to 'cybercrimes', whether they be academics, legal practitioners, law enforcement officers or students. Aside from jurisdictional issues, it does not address the law of criminal investigation, procedure or evidence. The unique feature of this book is that the various offences are analysed across four major common-law jurisdictions: Australia, Canada, the United Kingdom and the United States. These jurisdictions were chosen for a number of reasons. First, they share a common law heritage. Second, they are each advanced developed countries that have dealt extensively with the challenges of cybercrime. Third, Canada, the United Kingdom and the United States are all signatories to the Council of Europe Convention on Cybercrime, the most significant international instrument in this area. Together these jurisdictions provide a wealth of information on the nature of cybercrime and the ways in which it may be addressed. This collective experience is of interest not only to readers from these respective countries, but from any country seeking to understand the challenges of cybercrime.

Each chapter begins with a background to the offence type, followed by an overview of the legislative environment in each jurisdiction. The key principles which are found within each offence are then analysed drawing upon the law of each jurisdiction. In some cases, there is considerable overlap, while in others quite distinct approaches are adopted. Where possible, guidance is provided in the text pointing out these similarities and differences. In this way, it is hoped that the book can be read by a reader focusing on their own jurisdiction, while also facilitating comparisons with other jurisdictions. I have endeavoured to state the law to at least March 2009, although some material was being added right up to the submission of the manuscript. Any errors are of course my own.

This book has been some time in the making and there are many people to thank: Inspector Peter Wilkins, Victoria Police, for his early support in my endeavours in the field; Jill Henry, who first put me in touch with Cambridge University Press; Finola O'Sullivan, for commissioning the book and her ongoing support, and the team at Cambridge for their hard work throughout the process; the Monash Law Faculty for a small grant which helped with research assistance, but more importantly for the friendship and support of my colleagues; Jennie Avery for her early research assistance; and Dr Russell Smith, Principal Criminologist, Australian Institute of Criminology, and Professor Susan Brenner, NCR Distinguished Professor of Law, University of Dayton, USA, for their encouragement and comments on draft chapters. A particular debt of gratitude is owed to my research assistant, Natalia Antolak-Saper, who has demonstrated skill, patience and attention to detail above and beyond the call of duty. Last, but not least, a big thank you to my family and friends who are a constant source of love, support and encouragement.

Jonathan Clough
Melbourne, June 2009

ACKNOWLEDGEMENTS

Sections of Chapter 10 were previously published in J. Clough, 'Now you see it, now you don't: Digital images and the meaning of "possession"' (2008) 19 *Criminal Law Forum* 209. Reproduced with kind permission of Springer Press.

The use of data from the 2008 CSI Computer Crime and Security Survey is with kind permission of the Computer Security Institute.

ABBREVIATIONS

AHTCC	Australian High Tech Crime Centre
AIC	Australian Institute of Criminology
AOL	America Online
APIG	All Party Parliamentary Internet Group
ATM	Automatic Teller Machine
BBS	Bulletin Board System
CFAA	Computer Fraud and Abuse Act
CPU	Central Processing Unit
DDoS	Distributed Denial of Service (attack)
DNS	Domain Name Server
DoS	Denial of Service (attack)
ECPA	Electronic Communications Privacy Act
EFTPOS	Electronic Fund Transfer (at) Point of Sale (Aus/NZ)
GPS	Global Positioning System
HTTP	Hypertext Transfer Protocol
ICANN	Internet Corporation For Assigned Names And Numbers
ICMP	Internet Control Message Protocol
IP	Internet Protocol
ISP	Internet Service Provider
LAN	Local Area Network
MCCOC	Model Criminal Code Officers Committee
MDA	Mail Delivery Agent
MMS	Multimedia Messaging Service
MUA	Mail User Agent
p2p	peer-to-peer
PDA	Personal Digital Assistant
PIN	Personal Identification Number
RIPA	Regulation of Investigatory Powers Act 2000 (UK)
SCA	Stored Communications Act
SMS	Short Messaging Service
SMTP	Simple Mail Transfer Protocol
URL	Uniform Resource Locator
USB	Universal Serial Bus
VDU	Video Display Unit
VOIP	Voice over Internet Protocol

TABLE OF CASES

Canada

New Zealand

United Kingdom

TABLE OF LEGISLATION

Australia

Commonwealth

Queensland

South Australia

New Zealand

United Kingdom

United States

Federal

State legislation

International instruments

PART I

Introduction

Cybercrime

1. The evolution of cybercrime

> It is known of all men that the radical change in transportation of persons and goods effected by the introduction of the automobile, the speed with which it moves, and the ease with which evil-minded persons can avoid capture, have greatly encouraged and increased crimes.[1]

What could be said of the automobile in the 1920s is equally apposite of digital technology today. It is trite, but nonetheless true, to say that we live in a digital age. The proliferation of digital technology, and the convergence of computing and communication devices, has transformed the way in which we socialise and do business. While overwhelmingly positive, there has also been a dark side to these developments. Proving the maxim that crime follows opportunity, virtually every advance has been accompanied by a corresponding niche to be exploited for criminal purposes.

The magic of digital cameras and sharing photos on the Internet is exploited by child pornographers. The convenience of electronic banking and online sales provides fertile ground for fraud. Electronic communication such as email and SMS may be used to stalk and harass. The ease with which digital media may be shared has led to an explosion in copyright infringement. Our increasing dependence on computers and digital networks makes the technology itself a tempting target; either for the gaining of information or as a means of causing disruption and damage.

The idea of a separate category of 'computer crime' arose at about the same time that computers became more mainstream. As early as the 1960s there were reports of computer manipulation, computer sabotage,

---

1 *Brooks* v. *US*, 267 US 432, 438–9 (1925).

computer espionage and the illegal use of computer systems.[2] While the
1970s saw the first serious treatments of 'computer crime',[3] the relatively
limited role of computers in daily life meant that such offences typically
related to theft of telecommunication services and fraudulent transfer
of electronic funds.[4] In subsequent decades, the increasing networking
of computers and the proliferation of personal computers transformed
computer crime and saw the introduction of specific computer crime
laws.

The evolution of such legislation followed successive waves, reflecting changing concerns surrounding the misuse of computers.[5] Initial concerns which related to unauthorised access to private information expanded into concern that computers could also be used for
economic crimes. As computers became more and more central, the
concern was to protect against unauthorised access to computer data
per se. Increasing connectivity not only magnified these concerns; it
gave rise to new problems, such as remote attacks on computers and
networks, and gave new life to old offences such as infringement of
copyright, the distribution of child pornography and global fraudulent
schemes.

Rapid technological development continues, and will continue, to
present new challenges. The increasing uptake of broadband allows many
home users to leave their computers connected to the Internet, thus making them more vulnerable to external attack.[6] Peer-to-peer technology
may not only be used to transfer illegal content, but also to orchestrate
Denial of Service ('DoS') attacks and disseminate malware.[7] The convergence of telecommunications and computing has transformed mobile
phones into miniature networked computers, with attendant potential
for criminality.

2 U. Sieber, *Legal Aspects of Computer-Related Crime in the Information Society*, COMCRIME
  Study, European Commission (1998), p. 19.
3 See, e.g., G. McKnight, *Computer Crime* (London: Joseph, 1973) and D. B. Parker, *Crime
  by Computer* (New York: Scribner, 1976).
4 M. D. Goodman and S. W. Brenner, 'The emerging consensus on criminal conduct in
  cyberspace' (2002) *UCLA Journal of Law and Technology* 3, 12.
5 Sieber, *Legal Aspects of Computer-Related Crime*, pp. 25–32, 39.
6 S. Morris, *The Future of Netcrime Now: Part 1 – threats and challenges*, Home Office Online
  Report 62/04 (2004), p. 20.
7 *Ibid.*, p. 21. The nature of this technology is discussed at p. 222.

2. The challenges of cybercrime

[W]e live in a society exquisitely dependent on science and technology, in which hardly anyone knows anything about science and technology.[8]

It has been said that there are three factors necessary for the commission of crime: a supply of motivated offenders, the availability of suitable opportunities and the absence of capable guardians.[9] On all three counts, the digital environment provides fertile ground for offending. While specific impacts will be discussed in subsequent chapters, it is useful to summarise briefly some of the key features of digital technology which facilitate crime and hamper law enforcement.

A. Scale

Unlike more traditional forms of communication, the Internet allows users to communicate with many people, cheaply and easily. The estimated 1.6 billion people on the Internet, approximately 24 per cent of the world's population,[10] provide an unprecedented pool of potential offenders and victims. This acts as a 'force multiplier', allowing offending to be committed on a scale that could not be achieved in the offline environment.[11] The ability to automate certain processes further amplifies this effect.

B. Accessibility

Not so long ago, computers were large, cumbersome devices utilised primarily by government, research and financial institutions. The ability to commit computer crimes was largely limited to those with access and expertise. Today, the technology is ubiquitous and increasingly easy to use, ensuring its availability to both offenders and victims.

---

8 Dr Carl Sagan, cited in *In the Matter of the Application of the United States of America for an Order Authorizing the Installation and Use of a Pen Register and a Trap & Trace Device on E-Mail Account*, 416 F Supp 2d 13, 14 (D DC 2006).

9 L. Cohen and M. Felson, 'Social change and crime rate trends: A routine activity approach' (1979) 44 *American Sociological Review* 588, 589.

10 Internet World Stats, *Internet Usage Statistics: The Internet big picture – world Internet users and population stats* (2009), www.internetworldstats.com/stats.htm.

11 Model Criminal Code Officers Committee of the Standing Committee of Attorneys-General, *Chapter 4: Damage and Computer Offences, Final Report* (2001), p. 95.

In 2007–8, 67% of Australians had access to a computer at home,[12] while in 2006, 70% had used the Internet[13] and 82% a mobile phone.[14] In 2003, 64% of Canadian households had at least one member who used the Internet regularly[15] and in 2006, 67% of households reported having a mobile phone.[16] In 2003, 75% of adults in the UK had a mobile phone,[17] while in 2007 61% of households could access the Internet from home.[18] In the United States, the percentage of households with computers rose from 8.2% in 1984 to 61.8% in 2003,[19] while those with access to the Internet increased from 18% in 1997 to 54.7% in 2003.[20] The ubiquitous 'Internet café' also provides a ready source of connectivity.

For those activities that may be beyond the skills of the individual, the Internet provides easy access to those who will do it for you, or tell you how. Offenders who might otherwise be isolated in their offending, can now find like minds, forming virtual communities to further their offending.[21]

C. Anonymity

Anonymity is an obvious advantage for an offender, and digital technology facilitates this in a number of ways. Offenders may deliberately conceal their identity online by the use of proxy servers, spoofed email or IP addresses or anonymous emailers. Simply opening an email account which does not require identity verification provides a false identity. Confidentiality may be protected by the use of readily available encryption technology, while traces of digital evidence may be removed using commercially available software.

---

12 Australian Bureau of Statistics, *Household Use of Information Technology, Australia 2007–08*, Cat. no. 8146.0 (2008).

13 Australian Government, Department of Broadband, Communications and the Digital Economy, *Online Statistics* (2008), www.archive.dbcde.gov.au/2008/01/statistical_benchmarking/online_statistics.

14 *Ibid.*

15 Statistics Canada, *Household Internet Use Survey-Microdata User's Guide 2003*, Cat. no. 56M0002GIE (2004), p. 7.

16 Statistics Canada, *Residential Telephone Service Survey*, The Daily (2007), www.statcan.gc.ca/daily-quotidien/070504/dq070504a-eng.htm.

17 National Statistics, *Adult Mobile Phone Ownership or Use: By age, 2001 and 2003*, Social Trends 34 (2009), www.statistics.gov.uk/STATBASE/ssdataset.asp?vlnk=7202.

18 National Statistics, *First Release: Internet access 2007: Households and individuals* (2007), p. 1, www.statistics.gov.uk/pdfdir/inta0807.pdf.

19 US Census Bureau, *Computer and Internet Use in the United States 2003* (2005), p. 1, www.census.gov/prod/2005pubs/p23–208.pdf.

20 *Ibid.*   21 Morris, *The Future of Netcrime*, p. 18.

The networked nature of modern communications in itself means that data will routinely be routed through a number of jurisdictions before reaching its destination, making tracing of communications extremely difficult and time sensitive. Accessing wireless networks, with or without authorisation, may conceal the identity of the actual user even if the location can be identified. Data may be stored deliberately in jurisdictions where regulation and oversight is lax.

D. Portability and transferability

Central to the power of digital technology is the ability to store enormous amounts of data in a small space, and to replicate that data with no appreciable diminution of quality. Storage and processing power which would once have occupied rooms, will now fit into a pocket. Copies of images or sound may be transmitted simply and at negligible cost to potentially millions of recipients. The convergence of computing and communication technologies has made this process a seamless one, with the ability to take a digital image with a mobile phone and then upload it to a website within seconds.

E. Global reach

Criminal law is traditionally regarded as local in nature, being restricted to the territorial jurisdiction in which the offence occurred. Modern computer networks have challenged that paradigm. As individuals may now communicate overseas as easily as next door, offenders may be present, and cause harm, anywhere there is an Internet connection. Whether it be a fraudulent scheme, a DoS attack or the distribution of child pornography, there is no need for offenders and victims to be in the same jurisdiction. Not only does this provide, literally, a world of opportunity for offenders, it presents enormous challenges to law enforcement and harmonisation.

F. Absence of capable guardians

An important factor which may affect offending behaviour is the perceived risk of detection and prosecution. In this respect, digital technology presents law enforcement with a range of challenges. The volatile nature of electronic data requires sophisticated forensic techniques to ensure its retrieval, preservation and validity for use in a criminal trial. Apart from the sheer volume of users, the networked nature of modern communications makes surveillance extremely difficult. Much of the infrastructure is privately owned, meaning that law enforcement agencies must deal with a number of different entities. Communications will routinely be routed through multiple jurisdictions, necessitating the assistance of local law enforcement agencies. Even if the assistance of local authorities can be obtained, data retention may be limited or non-existent. If the defendant is present in another jurisdiction, can he or she be extradited? The complexity and cost of such investigations necessarily means they will not be undertaken lightly.

As in the offline environment, it is neither practical nor desirable that police be everywhere. The role of 'guardian' must be shared with others across the community, whether it be parents monitoring their children's use of the Internet, financial institutions looking for suspicious transactions or system administrators detecting network intrusions. All play an important guardianship role, as do industry groups and government regulators. ISPs are particularly significant, being effectively the gatekeepers of data on the Internet.

Effective regulation requires a broad range of responses, addressing the four modalities of constraint identified by Lessig: the law, architecture, social norms and the market.[22] The focus of this book is on one component of the regulatory mix, namely the application of the substantive criminal law to the digital environment. Such 'tertiary crime prevention' operates not only through deterrence and incapacitation, but also influences social norms as to what is, and what is not, acceptable behaviour in the online environment.[23]

3. Defining cybercrime

The range of technology-enabled crime is always evolving, both as a function of technological change and in terms of social interaction with new technologies.[24]

---

22 L. Lessig, *Code and Other Laws of Cyberspace* (New York: Basic Books, 1999), pp. 85–99. See generally, N. K. Katyal, 'Criminal law in cyberspace' (2001) 149 *University of Pennsylania Law Review* 1003; O. S. Kerr, 'Virtual crime, virtual deterrence: A skeptical view of self help, architecture and civil liability' (2005) *Journal of Law, Economics and Policy* 197; S. W. Brenner, 'Toward a criminal law for cyberspace: Distributed security' (2004) 10 *Buffalo Journal of Science and Technology* 1; and M. E. O'Neill, 'Old crimes in new bottles: Sanctioning cybercrime' (2000) 9 *George Mason Law Review* 237.

23 R. G. Smith, P. Grabosky and G. Urbas, *Cyber Criminals on Trial* (Cambridge: Cambridge University Press, 2004), p. 2.

24 G. Urbas and K. R. Choo, *Resource Materials on Technology-Enabled Crime*, Technical and Background Paper no. 28 (AIC, 2008), p. 5.

There are almost as many terms to describe cybercrime as there are cybercrimes. Early descriptions included 'computer crime', 'computer-related crime' or 'crime by computer'.[25] As digital technology became more pervasive, terms such as 'high-technology' or 'information-age' crime were added to the lexicon.[26] The advent of the Internet brought us 'cybercrime' and 'Internet' or 'net' crime.[27] Other variants include 'digital', 'electronic' (or 'e-'), 'virtual', 'IT', 'high-tech' and 'technology-enabled' crime.

If taken literally, each term suffers from one or more deficiencies. Those definitions that focus on 'computers' may not incorporate networks. Others such as 'cybercrime' or 'virtual crime' may be seen as focusing exclusively on the Internet.[28] Terms such as 'digital', 'electronic' or 'high-tech' crime may be seen as so broad as to be meaningless. For example, 'hi-tech crime' may go beyond networked information technology to include other 'hi-tech' developments such as nanotechnology and bioengineering.[29]

Such terms should not, however, be approached literally, but rather as broadly descriptive terms which emphasise the role of technology in the commission of crime. Although it is still the case that no one term has become truly pervasive, with many being used interchangeably, 'cybercrime' has been adopted in this book for a number of reasons. First, it is commonly used in the literature.[30] Secondly, it has found its way into common usage.[31] Thirdly, it emphasises the importance of networked computers.[32] Fourthly, and most importantly, it is the term adopted in the Council of Europe Convention on Cybercrime.[33]

---

25 House Of Commons Standing Committee On Justice And Legal Affairs, *Computer Crime*, Final Report (1983), p. 12; Sieber, *Legal Aspects of Computer-Related Crime* and Parker, *Crime by Computer*.

26 S. W. Brenner, 'Cybercrime metrics: Old wine, new bottles?' (2004) 9 *Virginia Journal of Law and Technology* 1, n. 4.

27 Morris, *The Future of Netcrime*, p. vi.

28 According to the *Oxford English Dictionary*, in later usage the prefix 'cyber' has come to be used to form terms relating to the Internet.

29 Morris, *The Future of Netcrime*, p. vi.

30 It also (rarely) appears in legislation; see, e.g., the Cybercrime Act 2001 (Cth).

31 The *Oxford English Dictionary* defines 'cybercrime' as 'crime or a crime committed using computers or the Internet'.

32 Although the term 'cyber' is technically limited to crimes involving the Internet, it is used more broadly to refer to crimes committed using stand-alone computers; P. Grabosky, *Electronic Crime* (New Jersey: Pearson Prentice Hall, 2007), p. 2.

33 See p. 21.

For all the variations in terminology, there is now a broad consensus as to what these terms encompass. This involves a three-stage classification, as summarised by the US Department of Justice:

1. Crimes in which the computer or computer network is the target of the criminal activity. For example, hacking, malware and DoS attacks.
2. Existing offences where the computer is a tool used to commit the crime. For example, child pornography, stalking, criminal copyright infringement and fraud.
3. Crimes in which the use of the computer is an incidental aspect of the commission of the crime but may afford evidence of the crime. For example, addresses found in the computer of a murder suspect, or phone records of conversations between offender and victim before a homicide. In such cases the computer is not significantly implicated in the commission of the offence, but is more a repository for evidence.[34]

We therefore see a tripartite classification of computer crimes, computer-facilitated crimes and computer-supported crimes.[35] This form of classification, or a variant of it, has also been used in Australia,[36] Canada,[37] the UK,[38] and at an international level.[39] Our focus is on the first two categories of cybercrime, with computer-supported crimes raising issues of procedural and evidentiary law which are beyond the scope of this book.[40]

This classification also addresses the question of whether cybercrime is an entirely new form of offending, with no analogues in the offline environment, or whether it is simply old crimes committed in new ways.[41] The answer is both. The majority of cybercrimes discussed in this book

34 Computer Crime and Intellectual Property Section, US Department of Justice, *The National Information Infrastructure Protection Act of 1996*, Legislative Analysis (1996), www.cybercrime.gov/1030analysis.html.
35 This latter term is adopted in Canada: M. Kowalski, *Cyber-Crime: Issues, data sources, and feasibility of collecting police-reported statistics*, Cat. no. 85–558, Canadian Centre for Justice Statistics (2002), p. 6.
36 Urbas and Choo, *Technology-Enabled Crime*, p. 5.   37 Kowalski, *Cyber-Crime*, p. 6.
38 National Criminal Intelligence Service, *Project Trawler: Crime on the information highways* (1999), www.cyber-rights.org/documents/trawler.htm; and Morris, *The Future of Netcrime*, p. 3.
39 A. Rathmell et al., *Handbook of Legislative Procedures of Computer and Network Misuse in EU Countries*, Study for the European Commission Directorate-General Information Society (2002), p. 16.
40 See Smith, Grabosky and Urbas, *Cyber Criminals on Trial*; Computer Crime and Intellectual Property Section, US Department of Justice, *Manual on Prosecuting Computer Crime* (2007), www.cybercrime.gov/ccmanual/01ccma.pdf.
41 Brenner, 'Cybercrime metrics', 15.

are existing offences committed in new ways. The true 'cybercrimes', in the sense of offences that would not exist at all without computing, are those against computers and computer networks themselves.

4. Cyberterrorism

> Without a great deal of thought about security, the Nation shifted the control of essential processes in manufacturing, utilities, banking, and communications to networked computers.[42]

Reliance on digital technology, particularly networked communications, has now become so pervasive that it is regarded as part of the critical infrastructure.[43] Consequently, another motivation for attacks on computer networks is to further a political, religious or ideological cause – so-called 'cyberterrorism'. Such attacks have the potential to cause considerable harm, possibly disrupting essential services such as water, power, hospitals, financial systems, emergency services, air/shipping control and the like.

Although, to date, the threat has been more potential than real, studies suggest that there has been an increase in the number of cyber-attacks against critical infrastructure, including Supervisory Control And Data Acquisition systems (SCADA), namely computer systems which are relied upon to automatically monitor and adjust critical infrastructure.[44] Attacks against networked infrastructure may also be used to 'leverage' physical attacks, for example by hampering the ability of emergency services to respond.[45] It is therefore important to clarify what is meant by this emotive and imprecise term.

Given differing views on the meaning of 'terrorism', it is not surprising that the term 'cyberterrorism' is ill-defined.[46] It may, however, broadly

---

42 The White House, *The National Strategy to Secure Cyberspace* (2003), p. 5, www.dhs.gov/xlibrary/assets/National_Cyberspace_Strategy.pdf.

43 See for example, Organisation for Economic Co-Operation and Development, *OECD Guidelines for the Security of Information Systems and Networks: Towards a culture of security* (OECD, 2002); Parliamentary Joint Committee on the Australian Crime Commission, *Cybercrime* (Parliament of the Commonwealth of Australia, 2004), Ch 5.

44 C. Wilson, *Computer Attack and Cyberterrorism: Vulnerabilities and policy issues for Congress*, Congressional Research Service Report for Congress, (Congressional Research Service, 2005), pp. 8–10.

45 The White House, *The National Strategy to Secure Cyberspace*, p. 7.

46 S. Keith, 'Fear-mongering or fact: The construction of "cyber-terrorism" in US, UK, and Canadian news media', Paper presented at Safety and Security in a Networked World: Balancing cyber-rights and responsibilities, sponsored by the Oxford Internet Institute, Oxford, England, 8–10 September, 2005, pp. 1–2.

be divided into two categories. The first, and broadest, simply describes those situations where technology is used to facilitate the activities of terrorists.[47] For example, DoS attacks may be used against government websites or servers. Anonymous email accounts and encryption may be used to conceal terrorist communications. Websites may be used to spread propaganda or recruit members. The Internet can also be used as a way of gathering intelligence or instructions on weapons or weapons training.[48] Technology may also be utilised in raising finance, for example through identity crime or as a vehicle for laundering money.

In this sense, 'cyberterrorism' simply ascribes a motivation for other forms of cybercrime.[49] Such conduct may be punished under the relevant criminal offences, or may fall within some of the broader terrorism offences.[50] It should, however, be distinguished from cyberterrorism in the narrower sense of 'the use of computer network tools to harm or shut down critical national infrastructures (such as energy, transportation, government operations)'.[51] Such a view sees cyberterrorism as terrorism in the narrower legal sense of actual or threatened harm to persons, property or essential services, usually with a political, religious or ideological motive, with the intention of intimidating the public and/or influencing government action.[52]

> Cybercrime and cyberterrorism are not coterminous. Cyberspace attacks must have a 'terrorist' component in order to be labelled cyberterrorism. The attacks must instil terror as commonly understood (that is, result in death and/or large-scale destruction), and they must have a political motivation . . . Terrorist use of computers as a facilitator of their activities, whether for propaganda, recruitment, data mining, communication, or other purposes, is simply not cyberterrorism.[53]

---

47 C. Walker, 'Cyber-terrorism: Legal principle and law in the United Kingdom' (2006) *Pennsylvania State Law Review* 625, 635–42.
48 See, e.g., *R v. Lodhi* [2006] NSWSC 584.
49 A distinction is sometimes drawn between cyberterrorism and so-called 'hacktivism', that is the use of hacking by political activists: G. Weimann, 'Cyberterrorism: The sum of all fears?' (2005) *Studies in Conflict and Terrorism* 129, 135.
50 E.g., possession of materials in preparation for a terrorist act; Criminal Code Act 1995 (Cth) s. 101.4 and Terrorism Act 2000 (UK) s. 57.
51 Weimann, 'The sum of all fears?', 130.
52 Criminal Code Act 1995 (Cth) s. 100.1, Criminal Code (Can) s. 83.01, Terrorism Act 2000 (UK) s. 1 and 18 USC § 3077.
53 Weimann, 'The sum of all fears?', 132–3. Also see D. E. Denning, *Cyberterrorism: Testimony before the Special Oversight Panel on Terrorism Committee on Armed Services*, US House of Representatives, 23 May 2000, www.cs.georgetown.edu/~denning/infosec/cyberterror.html.

However, traditional definitions of terrorism tend to focus on the use of violent action. For example, one US federal definition states that 'terrorism' is 'premeditated, politically motivated violence perpetrated against non-combatant targets by subnational groups or clandestine agents'.[54] The use of the term 'violence' may exclude activities 'which might not be violent in themselves but which can have a devastating impact'.[55] Accordingly, modern definitions of 'terrorism' incorporate attacks on electronic infrastructure. For example, s. 1 Terrorism Act 2000 (UK) includes action that 'is designed seriously to interfere with or seriously to disrupt an electronic system'. Similarly, the definition of 'terrorist act' under the Australian federal provisions specifically includes conduct which seriously interferes with, disrupts or destroys an 'electronic system', which includes, but is not limited to, a telecommunications system.[56]

To date, cyberterrorism in this sense is in the realm of speculation, with no reported instances of 'true' cyberterrorism. The closest example is perhaps an incident in the Australian state of Queensland where the defendant used wireless access to hack into a Queensland sewerage system, causing millions of litres of untreated sewage to spill into rivers and parks.[57] Although the defendant in this case was a disgruntled employee rather than terrorist, it serves to illustrate the potential damage that can be caused by attacks on critical infrastructure.

5. The scale of the problem

The lack of reliable statistical cybercrime data has been noted for some time. In 1988, the UK Law Commission commented that there was insufficient evidence of the scale and consequences of computer misuse to conclude that it required prompt legislative action.[58] More than twenty years on and the situation has not improved greatly.[59] Although such statistics as are available will be discussed in relation to specific offence types, it is useful to consider those factors that continue to make accurate data collection difficult.

---

54 22 USC § 2565f(d). Also see the offence of terrorism under 18 USC § 2331.
55 Walker, 'Cyber-terrorism', 631.
56 Criminal Code Act 1995 (Cth) s. 100.1(2)(f). Also see Criminal Code (Can) s. 83.01(1).
57 R v. Boden [2002] QCA 164.
58 Law Commission, Computer Misuse, Working Paper no. 110 (1988), [6.18].
59 See, for example, K. Hyde-Bales, S. Morris and A. Charlton, The Police Recording of Computer Crime, Development and Practice Report (Home Office, 2004).

First, the lack of consensus as to the meaning of 'cybercrime' means that it may not be included within official crime statistics. Even where there is a specific cybercrime, it may be concealed within other statistics. For example, unauthorised access to a computer under the Computer Misuse Act is recorded as 'other fraud' in the British Crime Survey.[60]

Secondly, many so-called 'cybercrimes' are in fact existing offences that are facilitated by technology. Consequently, although the offence itself, such as stalking, will be recorded in crime statistics, the use of technology by offenders may not. However, care must also be taken in incorporating the use of computers within crime statistics. For example, in the United States the Uniform Crime Reporting Program allows reporting crime officers to indicate whether a computer was the object of the crime or was used to perpetrate the crime.[61] While this is a useful development, it may skew results as theft of laptops or other computers is therefore included within 'computer crime' statistics.[62]

Thirdly, the level of actual offending may not accurately be reflected in crime statistics due to under-reporting. According to the 2008 CSI/FBI *Computer Crime and Security Survey*, only 27 per cent of incidents were reported to law enforcement, with 23.9 per cent of incidents not reported at all.[63] In the equivalent Australian survey, 69 per cent of respondents did not report attacks to any external party.[64] Common reasons for organisations not reporting include the fear of negative publicity or a belief that reporting is futile as the perpetrators are unlikely to be caught.[65] Many ordinary computer users may not even realise that the conduct has taken place or even if aware that it is an offence.

Fourthly, police may not have the expertise and/or resources to detect or investigate cybercrime, while the range of agencies involved may also hamper accurate recording.

---

60 C. Kershaw, S. Nicholas and A. Walker, *Crime in England and Wales 2007/08*, Home Office Statistical Bulletin (2008), p. 177.

61 Federal Bureau of Investigation, *National Incident-Based Reporting System*, i: *Data collection guidelines* (US Department of Justice, 2000), pp. 19–20.

62 The most recent version of the survey (UCR2.1) includes a data element for recording any fraud that involves the unauthorised use of a computer or use of a computer for illegal means: Kowalski, *Cyber-Crime*, p. 17.

63 R. Richardson, *CSI Computer Crime and Security Survey* (Computer Security Institute, 2008), pp. 22–3.

64 AusCERT, *Australian Computer Crime and Security Survey* (2006), p. 35, www.auscert. org.au/crimesurvey.

65 *Ibid.*

Finally, media reporting of cybercrime may present a distorted picture.[66] As with other forms of crime, it is tempting to focus on the novel and/or the sensational rather than the mainstream, and stories of computer misuse may be uncritically accepted and repeated.

6. Online/offline consistency

Our discussion is limited to breaches of the criminal law rather than computer 'misuse' or 'abuse'; these terms being used to refer more broadly to 'unethical or unauthorized behaviour in relation to the use of computers, programs, or data'.[67] Of course, what is criminal is a fluid concept, and decisions will be made as to whether particular online conduct should be criminalised. Relevant to this question is the principle of 'online/offline consistency'; that is, so far as possible, online conduct should be regulated in the same way as any other conduct and existing laws relied upon.[68] This results in a 'half-way' approach to reform, creating wholly new offences only where absolutely necessary, and amending existing offences in order to address specific problems.[69]

Such an approach helps to ensure that the online environment is not less regulated than the offline environment and hence more attractive to criminals.[70] It also seeks to avoid the false dichotomy that the 'online/offline' distinction sometimes presents:

> Treating the cyberworld as if it is 'out there' . . . encourages us to look for new, separate solutions to Internet problems without first determining whether we might already have useful experiences or tools in the 'real' world that could help.[71]

Where conduct is already criminalised in the offline environment, the question then becomes whether the law requires modification to ensure

---

66 M. Wasik, *Crime and the Computer* (Oxford: Clarendon Press, 1991), pp. 3–4.

67 *Ibid.*, p. 3.

68 President's Working Group on Unlawful Conduct on the Internet, *The Electronic Frontier: The challenge of unlawful conduct involving the use of the Internet* (2000), www.usdoj.gov/criminal/cybercrime/unlawful.htm; Law Commission, *Computer Misuse* (1988), [1.6]; Model Criminal Code Officers Committee, *Computer Offences* (2001), p. 94.

69 Law Commission, *Computer Misuse* (1988), [4.5].

70 Katyal, 'Criminal law in cyberspace', 1005–7.

71 V. Nash and M. Peltu, *Rethinking Safety and Security in a Networked World: Reducing harm by increasing cooperation*, Oxford Internet Institute Forum, Discussion Paper no. 6 (2005), p. 11.

it may be prosecuted in the online environment. Rarely, if ever, would it be the case that conduct which may be prosecuted offline should not be criminal online. Conversely, where conduct is not criminalised in the offline environment, the question is whether technology has had such an impact on the nature of the conduct or its prevalence that it necessitates criminalisation.

In such cases, the decision to criminalise is no different to criminalisation in the offline environment, and is subject to the same guiding principles. These include, that the conduct should be so serious that it cannot properly be dealt with on the bases of compensation and should impact on the public interest. Secondly, criminal sanctions should be reserved for behaviour which other, less drastic means of control would be ineffective, impracticable or insufficient. Thirdly, the new offence should be enforceable. In particular, it should be clear in its scope and effect.[72] The principle of online/offline consistency simply adds the question of whether such criminalisation should be formally limited to the online environment. In most, if not all, cases this should be avoided.

7. Virtual crimes?

The increasing popularity and sophistication of online 'worlds' has reinvigorated debate as to whether there are such things as 'virtual crimes'. Such forums have evolved from relatively basic, text-based virtual communities, through hugely popular graphics-based online role-playing games such as 'World of Warcraft'[73] to 'virtual worlds' such as 'Second Life'.[74] Given the millions of people participating in such online forums, what may broadly be described as antisocial behaviour is inevitable. The question then becomes: what role, if any, does the criminal law play in regulating such online communities?

This issue first came to prominence some years ago in an online community known as 'LambdaMOO'.[75] LambdaMOO was, and is, a text-based virtual community where members create their online world and interact via text-based commands. It was in this context that a character

---

72 Law Commission, *Computer Misuse* (1988), [1.11].   73 www.worldofwarcraft.com.

74 www.secondlife.com. For a history of the evolution of such forums, see S. W. Brenner, 'Fantasy crime: The role of criminal law in virtual worlds' (2008) 11 *Vanderbilt Journal of Entertainment and Technology Law* 1, 9–24.

75 www.lambdamoo.info. According to the website, a multi-user dungeon ('MUD') is '[a]n interactive text based, or 3D vector graphic virtual world', while a MUD object orientated ('MOO') is a MUD with the 'ability to "program", or create interactive objects'.

known as 'Mr Bungle' 'spoofed several players in a public space, forcing them to engage in violent sex acts and making it appear that they were acting voluntarily'.[76] Those players were outraged that 'they' had been forced to perform sexual acts against their will, and debate ensued within the LambdaMOO community as to what should be done about Mr Bungle.[77] Before a formal resolution could be achieved, Mr Bungle's online presence was terminated by another player.[78]

This incident gave rise to debate as to whether such conduct represented a 'virtual crime'; a crime committed in 'cyberspace'. This debate in fact reveals two distinct issues. First, is the question of where such crimes occur. Do they occur in 'cyberspace'? This issue arose out of broader debates as to whether cyberspace represents a distinct 'place' which should be subject to its own distinct regulatory regime.[79]

Whatever merits such arguments may have in other contexts, they have gained little traction in the criminal law. In large part this is because the criminal law is grounded in physical conduct. For an offence to be committed, there must be physical conduct engaged in by the defendant, accompanied by the requisite mental state, if any. Accordingly, 'online offending' must necessarily be reduced to the physical, as what matters to the criminal law is the harm caused and the conduct leading to it, both of which occur in the offline world.[80]

No matter how realistic an online world feels to its users, the relevant conduct for the purposes of the criminal law is always the same; the transmission of electronic communications via computer networks producing graphics and/or audio on another's computer.

> What matters is what actually happens from a physical perspective instead of what a virtual world user perceives ... misconduct that draws social significance from its meaning in virtual reality normally will have no resonance with criminal statutes.[81]

---

76 J. L. Mnookin, 'Virtual(ly) law: The emergence of law in LambdaMOO' (1996) 2 *Journal of Computer-Mediated Communication*. A full account of the incident can be found in J. Dibbell, 'A rape in cyberspace: How an evil clown, a Haitian trickster spirit, two wizards, and a cast of dozens turned a database into a society', *The Village Voice* 23 December 1993, http://juliandibbell.com/texts/bungle_vv.html.

77 Brenner, 'Fantasy crime', 75–7.   78 *Ibid.*

79 See, e.g., D. R. Johnson and D. Post, 'Law and borders: The rise of law in cyberspace' (1996) 48 *Stanford Law Review* 1367 and J. Goldsmith, 'Against cyberanarchy' (1998) *University of Chicago Law Review* 1199.

80 Brenner, 'Fantasy crime', 26.

81 O. S. Kerr, 'Criminal law in virtual worlds' (2008) *University of Chicago Legal Forum* 415, 418.

The difference in perception neatly illustrates the distinction between what has been termed 'internal' and 'external' perspectives of online conduct.[82] An 'internal perspective' is the perspective of the computer user who perceives that he or she has entered an online world which is distinct from the geographical location in which they are physically sitting.[83] An 'external perspective', on the other hand, adopts the viewpoint of the outsider observing the functioning of the computer in the physical world rather than the perceptions of the user.[84]

Adopting an internal perspective, the person controlling their avatar would consider that their conduct occurred in that online world. The victims of Mr Bungle, for example, perceive that their avatars have been raped. An external perspective would state that what has really occurred is that electronic communications have passed between the various participants; it is, at most, a description of a rape. This is not to say that such communications do not have consequences; the victims may indeed feel real distress. But it is the distress of a person who has read a distressing communication, not the distress of someone who has been raped.

Once we have established that these alleged crimes occur in the offline world, the second question is whether that particular communication is an offence in the jurisdiction in which it is sent or received. More precisely, did it cause a recognised harm, or occur in proscribed circumstances, such that it constitutes a criminal offence? If yes, then it may be prosecuted. If not, then other methods of resolution must be sought. Online conduct which is commonly discussed as potentially giving rise to criminal sanction generally falls into one of three categories.

The first is offences against the person, the 'virtual rape' in LambdaMOO being an example. Other examples include 'virtual murder', as with the Japanese woman who hacked into a computer and 'killed' her virtual husband after he divorced her in the online game 'Maple Story'.[85] Of course, no physical harm is done to victims in such cases. The relevant harms are the distress of the victim and interference with their use of the game. In terms of the distress caused to the victim, this could only be prosecuted if it fell within threat, harassment or stalking statutes. This will

---

82 O. S. Kerr, 'The problem of perspective in Internet law' (2003) *Georgetown Law Journal* 357. Alternatively referred to as the perspective of 'virtual reality' and 'physical reality'; Kerr, 'Virtual crime', 201–7.

83 Kerr, 'The problem of perspective', 359–60.   84 *Ibid.*, 360.

85 'Woman in jail over virtual murder', *BBC News Online* (Asia-Pacific), 24 October 2008, http://news.bbc.co.uk/2/hi/asia-pacific/7688091.stm.

primarily depend upon the reaction of the 'victim' and the mental state of the alleged offender. In relation to interference with the game itself, the appropriate criminal law response, if any, would be offences relating to unauthorised access and/or modification of data. This would largely depend on whether the person was authorised to carry out the relevant function.

In some cases, avatars may 'consent' to be tortured and murdered.[86] In such cases, there is presumably no harm to the victim, although it may be prosecuted under obscenity or similar laws if others are able to view what occurs. The mental state of the offender may also cause difficulties. Did he or she know the offline identity of the person? Did they intend, or were they reckless as to causing that harm?[87] In some cases it cannot even be presumed that there is a person operating the avatar, as in World of Warcraft where some people employ bots to play the game for them while they are away from the keyboard.[88]

The second variant is offences against property. In some online forums there is currency that can officially or unofficially be traded for cash. For example, Second Life has its own currency, the 'Linden Dollar' which can be purchased using real currency. Members of Second Life may trade in goods that they create or trade 'virtual property' that they own. It is therefore possible for one person to take an item belonging to another that is of actual value.

For example, a teenager in the Netherlands was arrested for 'stealing' €4,000 of virtual furniture from a social networking site known as 'Habbo Hotel'.[89] Users of the site create avatars and are able to decorate rooms using credits which are bought with real money. Using phishing techniques[90] the defendant created a false website and tricked victims into providing their usernames and passwords. He then moved the furniture of other players into his own room.[91] Other examples include the 'fencing' of stolen 'virtual property',[92] unauthorised copying of online creations or

---

86 Brenner, 'Fantasy crime', 41.
87 C. Reed, *Why Must You Be Mean to Me?: Crime, punishment and online personality*, School of Law Working Paper Series, Queen Mary University of London (2008), p. 14.
88 *MDY Industries, LLC* v. *Blizzard Entertainment, Inc. and Vivendi Games, Inc.*, 2008 US Dist LEXIS 53988 (D Ariz 2008).
89 www.habbo.com   90 See p. 192.
91 '"Virtual theft" leads to arrest', BBC News Online, (Asia-Pacific), 14 November 2007, http://news.bbc.co.uk/2/hi/technology/7094764.stm.
92 F. G. Lastowka and D. Hunter, 'Virtual crimes' (2004–5) *New York Law School Law Review* 293, 302.

property damage. There is also the potential for Second Life to be utilised for money laundering.[93]

Although those affected by such conduct may understandably feel that their property rights have been violated, whether the criminal law is able to intervene presents a number of difficulties. While the Habbo Hotel example is similar to the prosecution of fraudulent use of credit cards or ATMs, the suggestion that it is an 'actual theft'[94] requires further analysis. It cannot be assumed that property offences translate readily to the online environment.[95]

For example, although purchased with real money the 'furniture' may fall outside the concept of 'property' in some criminal statutes. Whether the ability to move and use the furniture is a 'financial advantage' within the terms of fraud statutes is another interesting question. Unauthorised copying of designs would be protected, if at all, by intellectual property laws. Damage to another person's online property may fall within computer crime statutes, although query whether it is permitted within the terms of the game.[96] Further, the use of phishing techniques to obtain identifying information may be a breach of identity theft laws.[97]

The third category is sexual activity. As avatars may be programmed to engage in depictions of sexual activity, it is not surprising that this would give rise to misconduct. However, as with offences against the person, these are depictions of sex, rather than actual sex. For example, virtual prostitution could not be prosecuted under prostitution laws, but under obscenity and related laws, if at all.[98] More challenging are those who act out paedophilic and incest fantasies. Again, such images may fall within child pornography laws, although virtual child pornography presents particular challenges in the United States.[99]

There are some who have focused on virtual worlds as 'games' and suggested that the application of the criminal law in the online environment depends upon whether the rules of the game allow the conduct. For example, combat is allowed in some areas of Second Life but not in others.[100] Consequently, it is suggested that if the rules of the game allow for the conduct to occur, then the criminal law has no role to play. In the context of property offences, the argument goes that if the game

---

93 Brenner, 'Fantasy crime', 28.   94 Kerr, 'Criminal law in virtual worlds', 425–6.
95 See p. 41.
96 For example, 'stealing' is not permitted under the terms of use for Habbo Hotel, www.habbo.com/papers/termsAndConditions.
97 See p. 207.   98 Brenner, 'Fantasy crime', 32.   99 See p. 271.
100 Brenner, 'Fantasy crime', 17.

allows the item to be stolen it cannot be theft.[101] An analogy is drawn with basketball where the 'stealing' of a ball during the course of the game would not be prosecuted. 'Instead, the available self-help remedy must be perfected consistent with the rules of the game, *which prohibit state intervention in disputes over ball ownership.*'[102]

However, the rules of the game in no way prohibit state intervention, nor do they 'supercede the standard rules of society'.[103] The rules of the game are simply one relevant factor in the application of the criminal law. In the basketball example, the police do not intervene for a number of reasons. First, assuming the ball is to be returned to its rightful owner it has not been stolen; merely borrowed. Secondly, the conduct is trivial and not worthy of police intervention. Thirdly, and relatedly, the parties can be expected to settle the dispute themselves.

8. A global problem: the Convention on Cybercrime

Since the early 1980s a series of surveys and reviews carried out by international bodies, including the OECD, UN, Council of Europe, G8 and Interpol, have led to near global awareness of the challenges presented by cybercrime.[104] Given the global nature of cybercrimes, it is apparent that some degree of harmonisation between countries is vital if effective regulation is to be achieved.[105] Greater harmonisation facilitates the exchange of information and knowledge between governments and industry, and is crucial for co-operation between law enforcement agencies. Dual criminality, for example, is often a precondition of both mutual assistance and extradition laws.

Although desirable, true consensus is unachievable. Countries are understandably protective of their right to impose their own standards under their domestic criminal law, particularly when we consider the myriad of interests that come into play when seeking to regulate the Internet and other new technologies. While some level of consensus may

---

101 Lastowka and Hunter, 'Virtual crimes', 305.
102 *Ibid.*, 306 (emphasis added).   103 *Ibid.*
104 For a summary of these early activities, see Goodman and Brenner, 'Emerging consensus', 14–19 and S. Schjølberg and A. M. Hubbard, *Harmonizing National Legal Approaches on Cybercrime*, Background Paper, International Telecommunications Union (2005), pp. 6–10.
105 *United Nations Manual on the Prevention and Control of Computer Related Crime*, International Review of Criminal Policy nos. 43 and 44 (1999), [116]; and United Nations, *Resolution on Combating the Criminal Misuse of Information Technologies* GA Res 55/63, UN GA, 55th sess., 81st plen. mtg, UN Doc. A/RES/55/63 (2001).

be achieved in respect of offences against the person and property, crimes against the state and crimes against morality are more problematic.[106] Some countries may even see opportunities to establish themselves as 'data havens', providing maximum privacy and minimal regulation of content hosted there.[107] For others, particularly in the developing world, cybercrime may simply not be a priority.

What may be achieved, however, is a broad consensus which can then be built upon in the future for those areas where there is less international agreement.[108] This is the approach adopted by the Council of Europe Convention on Cybercrime,[109] the first, and so far the only, multinational instrument to address issues of cybercrime.[110]

The Cybercrime Convention was opened for signature in November 2001, and came into force on 1 July 2004. In addition to forty-two European signatories (including the UK) a number of non-member countries such as Canada[111] have also signed.[112] Of particular significance, the US government was involved in the drafting of the Convention. It was ratified by President Bush on 22 September 2006 and entered into force for the United States on 1 January 2007. To date, twenty-four European countries have ratified, although not the UK.[113]

The Cybercrime Convention represents a comprehensive international response to the problems of cybercrime. It is divided into four chapters, encompassing issues of substantive and procedural law, as well as

---

106 Goodman and Brenner, 'Emerging consensus', 20–1.
107 J. N. Geltzer, 'The new Pirates of the Caribbean: How data havens can provide safe harbors on the internet beyond governmental reach' (2004) *Southwestern Journal of Law and Trade in the Americas* 433. One of the more bizarre examples must be 'HavenCo Ltd' hosted by the 'Principality of Sealand', an inhabited former anti-aircraft platform just outside Britain's territorial waters, www.sealandgov.org.
108 For example, the Additional Protocol to the Convention on Cybercrime, concerning the criminalisation of acts of a racist or xenophobic nature committed through computer systems came into force on 1 March 2006.
109 European Treaty Series no. 185 ('Cybercrime Convention').
110 A 'Model Law on Computer and Computer Related Crime' based on the Convention was recommended for endorsement by Law Ministers from the Commonwealth in October 2002, www.thecommonwealth.org/shared_asp_files/uploadedfiles/ %7BDA109CD2–5204–4FAB-AA77–86970A639B05%7D_Computer%20Crime.pdf.
111 As a permanent observer to the Council of Europe, Canada was invited to participate in the negotiation of the Convention: Department of Justice Canada, *Lawful Access-Consultation Document* (Department of Justice, Industry Canada, and Solicitor General Canada, 2002), p. 5.
112 http://conventions.coe.int/Treaty/Commun/ChercheSig.asp?NT=185&CM=8&DF= &CL=ENG.
113 *Ibid.*

international co-operation. Chapter I defines certain terms used in the Convention. Chapter II is divided into two sections. Section 1, 'Substantive Criminal Law', is the focus of this book. Section 2 is concerned with procedural law and contains requirements designed to address the challenges of electronic evidence gathering. For example, provision is made for the expedited preservation of stored computer data (Title 2) as well as the real-time collection of both traffic and content data (Title 5). Chapter III is concerned with international co-operation, particularly in the areas of extradition and mutual assistance, while Chapter IV addresses a range of procedural matters including territorial application, reservations, dispute settlement and the like.

As noted above, it is Chapter II Section 1 that is the focus of this book. Aside from provisions concerned with ancillary and corporate liability and sanctions,[114] the Cybercrime Convention provides for four broad categories of offence. The first, found in Title 1, is 'Offences against the confidentiality, integrity and availability of computer data and systems.' These offences are true 'cybercrimes' in that it is the computer or computer data which is the target of the offence. They are further divided into illegal access (Art. 2) illegal interception (Art. 3), data and system interference (Arts. 4 and 5) and misuse of devices (Art. 6).

Title 2, 'Computer-related Offences' would suggest all offences where the computer is used to facilitate the commission of an offence. While in practice this could take in a range of offences, the Convention provides for only two: computer-related forgery (Art. 7) and computer-related fraud (Art. 8). Title 3 is concerned with content-related offences, and focuses on the most significant offence type in this category: child pornography. Finally, Title 4 deals with offences related to copyrighting infringement and related rights.

This book will broadly follow this taxonomy though with some modifications. As noted above, the Cybercrime Convention reflects those offences on which international agreement could be reached. There are a number of others not encompassed by the Convention but which nonetheless fall within the definition of 'cybercrime'. As with the Convention, we begin with those offences where the computer is the target of the offence in Part II. Part III is concerned with fraud and the loosely related offences of criminal copyright infringement and the regulation of 'spam'. Part IV focuses on child pornography as the primary example of a content-related offence. Part V is concerned with a category of offence

---

114 Cybercrime Convention, Title 5.

not encompassed by the Convention, that of offences against the person, including stalking, grooming and voyeurism. We conclude in Part VI with a discussion of jurisdictional principles which are particularly significant given the global nature of cybercrimes.

The approach adopted in this book is comparative, drawing upon the substantive laws of four major common-law jurisdictions: Australia, Canada, the United Kingdom and the United States. In addition to sharing a common-law heritage, each is an advanced developed economy which has undergone significant reform of their laws in relation to cybercrime. In this constantly developing area of the law, there is much to be learned from the experience of each of these countries in addressing the challenges of cybercrime. In Australia, Canada and the United States, each of which is a federation, our focus is on federal offences.[115] In the UK, all legislative references are to England and Wales unless otherwise specified.[116]

---

115 For a general summary of state initiatives in the US, see J. Audal, Q. Lu and P. Roman, 'Computer crimes' (2008) *American Criminal Law Review* 233, 267–70. Also see A. H. Scott, *Computer and Intellectual Property Crime: Federal and state law* (Washington DC: The Bureau of National Affairs, Inc., 2001).

116 In the UK, Scotland and Northern Ireland are separate jurisdictions, although many offences, including those found under the Computer Misuse Act 1990 (UK), apply to all of the UK.

PART II

Computer as target

2

Computer as target

1. Introduction

We turn now to consider the first distinct category of cybercrimes: those offences where a computer is itself the target. Such offences are colloquially referred to as 'hacking',[1] and cover a broad range of conduct arising from an equally broad range of motivations. Given the ubiquitous presence of computers in modern life, and the dependency of modern commerce on computer networks, such offences have potentially serious consequences.

We are not here concerned with those offences where a computer is physically taken or damaged. Although some surveys include offences such as theft of a computer within the definition of cybercrime, such conduct falls comfortably within the scope of existing property offences. Rather, our focus is on '[o]ffences against the confidentiality, integrity and availability of computer data and systems'.[2] In essence, the conduct which these offences seek to address is:

1. the gaining of unauthorised access to a computer or computer system
2. causing unauthorised damage or impairment to computer data or the operation of a computer or computer system
3. the unauthorised interception of computer data.

Such conduct ranges from the technically sophisticated to the decidedly low-tech. While the sophisticated hacker is a very real threat, these offences may equally be committed by a disgruntled employee who steals a password or exceeds his or her authorised level of access. Any criminal law response must be capable of responding to this broad spectrum of offending conduct.

---

1 For convenience, 'hack' and its variants will be used to describe unauthorised access to computers and computer systems. While acknowledging that a distinction is sometimes drawn between unauthorised access carried out for noble ('hacking') as opposed to ignoble ('cracking') purposes, aside from sentencing such issues of motivation have little legal relevance, and in popular usage the distinction is rarely observed.
2 Cybercrime Convention, Ch. II, Section I, Title 1.

The history and phenomenon of 'hacking' has been extensively dis-cussed elsewhere.[3] For our purposes it will suffice to provide an outline of the key forms of conduct which potentially fall within this class of offence. At the outset it must be acknowledged that these categories are neither mutually exclusive nor fixed. One of the great challenges of draft-ing cybercrime laws is ensuring that they can adapt to a broad range of overlapping and constantly evolving threats. Nonetheless, the three main categories of conduct are:

1. unauthorised access to computers or computer systems
2. malicious software
3. denial of service attacks.

A. Unauthorised access to computers or computer systems

At a basic level, unauthorised access to a computer may be obtained simply by logging on without permission. At the more sophisticated level, it may involve hackers using networks to gain remote access, sometimes via computers in a number of jurisdictions. Such hacks may be 'user level', where the hacker has the same access to the system as an ordinary user of the system, or 'root level' or 'god' access, where the hacker has the same rights as the system administrator and can view or modify data at will.[4] The rapid pace with which software is developed means that 'bugs' in software are inevitable, with hackers seeking to exploit these vulnerabilities before they are rectified.[5]

The reasons for gaining unauthorised access to computers are as varied as the data found in those computers. Nonetheless, some categorisation of offender motivation is important in further refining precisely what conduct falls within the broad umbrella of unauthorised 'access' to a computer. It is suggested that there are essentially three motivations:

1. access to information
2. modification of data
3. use of a computer.

---

3 See, for example, M. Yar, *Cybercrime and Society* (London: Sage Publications, 2006), Ch. 2; and D. S. Wall, *Cybercrime* (Cambridge: Polity, 2007) Ch. 4.
4 E. J. Sinrod and W. P. Reilly, 'Cyber-crimes: A practical approach to the application of federal computer crime laws' (2000) 16 *Santa Clara Computer and High Tech Law Journal* 177, 205–7, 210–12.
5 Australian High Tech Crime Centre, *Malware: Viruses, worms, Trojan horses*, High Tech Crime Brief no. 10 (AIC, 2006), p. 1.

Access to information

Given the wealth of information that is stored on computers and in computer networks, access to that information is an obvious motivation for gaining access. Typical reasons for unauthorised access to data include obtaining confidential commercial or government information (e.g. trade secrets, intellectual property, defence secrets) or personal information (e.g. medical records, credit card or social security numbers or credit history). For example, in *US* v. *Levine*[6] the defendant and others used decryption software to gain access to the database of a corporation that was a repository for customer information for other companies and downloaded more than 1 billion personal records.

In other cases, the purpose is to interrogate the computer for possible open connections or other vulnerabilities. For example, 'port scanning' is a technique by which requests are sent to networked computer ports in order to ascertain whether particular machines have vulnerabilities; the electronic equivalent of 'rattling doorknobs'.[7] Such conduct is commonly a precursor to further intrusions, but may itself be a form of unauthorised access.

Modification of data

A defendant may not only wish to gain access to data in a computer; he or she may modify that data in some way. Again, the motivations for such behaviour are many and varied. The defendant may wish to delete valuable data, or alter that data so that it is misleading and/or worthless. In *US* v. *Middleton*[8] the defendant, a former employee of an ISP, used a program called 'Switch User' to switch his account to that of the company's receptionist. He then used his unauthorised access to create, delete and modify accounts, alter the computer's registry and delete the entire billing system and two internal databases. In another example, a former employee programmer of an Internet dating agency altered the company's website so that clients would be diverted to a pornographic website.[9]

Modification of data may also be used to obtain a financial or other advantage, for example by increasing a line of credit.[10] Hackers will

---

6 *US* v. *Levine* (ED Ark 2006) US Department of Justice, Press Release, 22 February 2006, www.cybercrime.gov/levineSent.htm.
7 *US* v. *Phillips*, 477 F 3d 215, 217 (5th Cir 2007).   8 231 F 3d 1207 (9th Cir 2000).
9 *YourNetDating LLC* v. *Mitchell*, 88 F Supp 2d 870 (ND Ill 2000).
10 *US* v. *Marles*, 408 F Supp 2d 38 (D Maine 2006).

commonly take steps to conceal their presence; for example, by modifying system logs, webpages may be defaced or malicious software installed. The list goes on and on.

Use of a computer

An obvious form of computer misuse is where a person uses computer time to which he or she is not entitled. In many cases, the use will be of negligible value and impact and is hardly worth prosecuting. The use of a work computer for non-work purposes, for example, is generally better dealt with as a matter of employment law rather than criminal law. There are, however, circumstances where unauthorised use of a computer may be more significant. Unauthorised access to, and use of, commercial databases may allow the hacker to obtain valuable services for free. Hackers may gain access to more powerful computers in order to run programs that require high-levels of processing power. In one reported example, hackers accessed Cray Inc. supercomputers in order to run password-cracking programs.[11] A hacker may also use a computer as part of the practice of 'weaving', that is the hacker gains access to a succession of computers using them as 'stepping stones' in order to conceal his or her identity and/or location.[12]

An increasingly significant example is so-called 'wardriving'[13] or 'wireless hacking', that is using a wireless network without authorisation. This is a product of the proliferation of 'Wi-fi' networks allowing wireless network access. In addition to the roaming wireless access provided by telecommunications companies, individual homes or businesses may set up local networks allowing wireless access to their network within a limited radius. Access is straightforward; any computer that is wireless-enabled can be used to detect networks by simply viewing available networks.

11 Computer Crime and Intellectual Property Section, *The National Information Infrastructure Protection Act of 1996*, Legislative Analysis (US Department of Justice, 1996), www.cybercrime.gov/1030analysis.html. Also see *US* v. *Phillips*, 477 F 3d 215, 218 (5th Cir 2007).
12 Computer Crime and Intellectual Property Section, *The online world and law enforcement*, US Department of Justice, www.fpd-fln.org/online_world_and_law_enforcement.htm.
13 The practice and term are an extension of 'wardialing', made famous in the film 'War Games', in which, amongst other things, a computer is programmed to dial a sequence of numbers in an attempt to gain access to a modem and thereby facilitate access to the associated computer: P. S. Ryan, 'War, peace, or stalemate: Wargames, wardialing, wardriving, and the emerging market for hacker ethics' (2004) 9 *Virginia Journal of Law and Technology* 7, 11. See, e.g., *State of Kansas* v. *Allen*, 260 Kan 107 (SC Kansas 1996).

In some contexts, networks are deliberately left open in order to attract customers with free use of wi-fi. For those who wish to restrict access the use of encryption, passwords and firewall protection will generally deter all but the determined hacker.[14] However, the default setting of many networks allows for open access and, as many people do not change the security settings, they are then providing open network access to anyone in range. While specific tools for detecting and interrogating networks are readily available, and have legitimate use for testing the security of networks, many computers are configured to automatically access any open network within range so that access may occur without the user being aware. This may give rise to arguments of implied authorisation to access the network and or lack of *mens rea* on the part of the person accessing.

The unauthorised use of a wireless network gives rise to a number of potentially criminal scenarios. First, there is the use of a service to which the person is not entitled. Although in some cases this practice will have no appreciable impact on the 'victim', if the authorised user is paying for the service according to the amount of data download, the cost of such unauthorised use may be significant. It may also reduce download speed for authorised users.

Secondly, use of another person's network may allow a defendant to conceal other illegal activities such as accessing child pornography or the sending of spam, particularly public wireless access points that do not require a subscription or collect an IP address.[15] For example, a Canadian man was charged after being caught viewing in his car child pornography, which he was downloading from open networks.[16]

Thirdly, a wireless network may provide a point of entry for unauthorised access to a computer system. For example, eleven defendants were recently charged with using the wireless networks of major department stores to gain access to the computer systems and install sniffer programs, allowing them to obtain more than 40 million credit and debit card numbers as well as password and account information.[17]

---

14 A. Ramasastry, J. K. Winn and P. Winn, 'Will wi-fi make your private network public? Wardriving, criminal and civil liability, and the security risks of wireless networks' (2005) 1 *Shidler Journal of Law, Commerce and Technology* 9, 10.

15 S. Morris, *The Future of Netcrime Now: Part 1 – threats and challenges*, Home Office Online Report 62/04 (2004), p. 24.

16 Ryan, 'Wargames', 18–19.

17 US Department of Justice, 'Retail hacking ring charged for stealing and distributing credit and debit card numbers from major US retailers', Press Release, 5 August 2008, www.usdoj.gov/opa/pr/2008/August/08-ag-689.html.

Fourthly, it is possible to intercept communications transmitted over wireless networks. For example, tools for cracking the commonly used WEP encryption keys are readily available. Another way of achieving this is to establish a 'base-station clone' by creating a duplicate wireless Internet access point close to a legitimate access point. The illegitimate source has a stronger signal than the legitimate source but mimics the legitimate settings. The unsuspecting user therefore accesses the hacker's network, allowing him or her to monitor all communications over that network.[18]

B. Malicious software

The second category is where the defendant disseminates malicious software ('malware') such as viruses, worms and/or Trojans. While traditionally used to cause unauthorised modification and impairment of data, malware is increasingly being used to access confidential information to facilitate fraud and other offences, so-called 'blended threats',[19] for example gaining access to confidential data and communications,[20] creating false accounts[21] or obtaining false identification documents.[22]

Whether software is malicious may depend upon the purpose for which it was installed. For example, software such as adware and spyware is often used to provide advertising for products or to collect information for commercial purposes. While most applications of this nature fall within the realm of 'unwanted' rather than 'malicious', they may be used for malicious purposes such as gathering personal information for the purposes of fraud, or discovering computer vulnerabilities that may be exploited.[23]

Malware may be disseminated directly, for example by inserting an infected disk, or, more commonly, via the Internet or other computer network via executable files. The main categories of malware are:

---

18 S. McDonald, 'Wireless hotspots: The truth about their evil twins' (2006) 9 *Internet Law Bulletin* 13.
19 G. Urbas and K. R. Choo, *Resource Materials on Technology-Enabled Crime*, Technical and Background Paper (AIC, 2008), p. 5.
20 *US* v. *Kwak* (D DC 2006) US Department of Justice, Press Release, 12 May 2006, www.cybercrime.gov/kwakSent.htm.
21 *US* v. *An Unnamed Juvenile II* (D Mass 2005) US Department of Justice, Press Release, 8 September 2005, www.cybercrime.gov/juvenileSentboston.htm.
22 *Hull* v. *WA* [2005] WASCA 194.
23 Australian High Tech Crime Centre, *Malware*, p. 1.

1. viruses and worms
2. Trojans
3. bots
4. spyware.

Viruses and worms

Although technically distinct, the line between viruses and worms is increasingly blurred. Both are programs that infect a computer by being copied and then performing a programmed function. These functions can vary from the very simple, such as displaying a message on a particular date, to deletion or modification of data or installation of other malware such as Trojans or bots. Some malware, known as 'logic bombs', is programmed to activate on a certain event occurring, such as a specific date or when a particular program is loaded.

The distinction between viruses and worms is that a virus must infect another program. For example, the infamous 'Melissa' virus was first posted on an Internet newsgroup 'Alt.Sex.' in 1999. Visitors to the newsgroup were tempted to download the document which promised passwords to adult websites. Once the file was executed, the victim's computer was infected. The virus targeted Windows operating systems and altered Microsoft word processing programs so that any document created using Word would also be infected. The virus was then able to replicate itself via Microsoft Outlook by causing computers to send emails to the first fifty addresses in the victim's address book. Each email contained the message 'Here is that document you asked for . . . don't show anyone else;-).' Opening the document of course infected the computer, which in turn caused more emails to be sent. Because each infected computer could infect fifty additional computers, which in turn could infect another fifty computers, the virus proliferated rapidly and exponentially, resulting in substantial impairment of computer networks.[24]

Worms are similar to viruses but are self-replicating; that is, they do not need to infect another application. In one of the earliest cybercrime prosecutions the defendant, a graduate student at Cornell University, programmed a computer worm that he released to the fledgling Internet via a computer at the Massachusetts Institute of Technology.[25] The worm was intended to test security and other weaknesses in the Internet, which

---

24 *US* v. *Smith* (D NJ 2002) US Department of Justice, Press Release, 2 May 2002, www.cybercrime.gov/melissaSent.htm.
25 *US* v. *Morris*, 928 F 2d 504 (2nd Cir 1991).

at that time was 'a group of national networks that connect university, governmental, and military computers around the country'.[26] Although the defendant took a number of steps to reduce the impact of the worm, he miscalculated the speed with which it would replicate and a large number of computers crashed as a result.

Trojans

Like the legendary Trojan horse after which they are named, Trojans are programs which appear to be innocent but contain a hidden function. Such programs may be embedded in software, email attachments or websites. In one example, a spam email was used to circulate a URL which linked to a website with a fraudulent domain name similar to a legitimate domain name. A user visiting the site would have a Trojan installed on his or her computer which was then able to capture data transmitted by the user, as well as password information stored on the computer. It also deleted the update function on anti-viral software to prevent future detection. The captured data was then transmitted to a logging server in Russia.[27]

Other Trojans may install a 'back door' allowing access by a hacker. For example, 'Back Orifice 2000' (BO2K) was a Trojan which once installed on the victim's computer allowed the hacker to perform system commands, redirect network traffic and reconfigure the victim's computer. If the computer is networked, then the hacker may gain access to that network.[28]

Because they allow remote operation of a computer unknown to the authorised user, the possible presence of malware may also be used as a 'defence' in some cases. That is, the defendant asserts that the conduct was in fact caused by malware installed on his or her computer of which the defendant was unaware.[29] This argument has been used successfully in cases involving possession of child pornography on the basis that the images may have been transferred to the computer via a Trojan.[30]

---

26 *Ibid.*, 505.
27 AusCERT, *Australian Computer Crime and Security Survey* (2006), p. 24, www.auscert. org.au/crimesurvey.
28 Sinrod and Reilly, 'Cybercrimes', 223–4.
29 S. W. Brenner, B. Carrier and J. Henninger, 'The Trojan horse defense in cybercrime cases' (2004) 21 *Santa Clara Computer and High Technology Law Journal* 1.
30 M. Kotadia, 'Trojan horse found responsible for child porn', ZDNet.co.uk, 1 August 2003, http://news.zdnet.co.uk/security/0,1000000189,39115422,00.htm.

Bots

A bot is a program which infects a targeted computer and allows it to be controlled remotely. The attacker exploits security weaknesses, generally in a computer connected to the Internet, to place small programs called daemons which run in the background of the host computer, unknown to the third party. These computers are often referred to as 'zombies' or 'bots' and are controlled remotely. These 'botnets' can then be instructed to perform co-ordinated tasks, typically launching a DoS attack on a target computer(s).[31] Increasingly, peer-to-peer networks are being used to launch such attacks, making it harder to shut down as there is no single point of control.[32]

In *US* v. *Clark*, the 21-year-old defendant pleaded guilty to launching a computer attack against the Internet auction site eBay. The defendant accumulated approximately 20,000 bots by using a worm program that took advantage of a computer vulnerability in the Windows operating system. The bots were then directed to a password-protected Internet relay chat (IRC) server, where they connected, logged in, and waited for instructions. When instructed to do so, the bots launched DoS attacks at computers or computer networks connected to the Internet.[33]

Botnets may also be used to send unsolicited email or SMS,[34] place adware on target computers or to act as proxies for malicious websites, allowing the IP addresses for those sites to be rotated to evade discovery.[35] Access to botnets may also be sold for these purposes. In one case, the defendant admitted taking more than US$107,000 in exchange for downloading adware to more than 400,000 infected computers that he controlled.[36] Such activities can also have potentially serious unintended consequences. In *US* v. *Maxwell*, while searching for additional computers for the purpose of installing adware, the defendant's 'botnet' caused

---

31 Sinrod and Reilly, 'Cybercrimes', 194–7.
32 C. Biever, 'New hacking tool hijacks file-sharing networks', New Scientist.com News Service, 19 March 2004, www.newscientist.com/article/dn4799-new-hacking-tool-hijacks-filesharing-networks.html.
33 *US* v. *Clark* (ND Cal 2005) US Department of Justice, Press Release, 28 December 2005, www.cybercrime.gov/cccases.html.
34 Morris, *The Future of Netcrime*, p. 23.
35 Federal Trade Commission, *Spam summit: The next generation of threats and solutions* (Federal Trade Commission, 2007), p. 12.
36 *US* v. *Ancheta* (CD Cal 2006) US Department of Justice, Press Release, 8 May 2006, www.cybercrime.gov/anchetaSent.htm.

computer malfunctions at a hospital and also damaged military computers in the United States and overseas.[37]

Spyware

The term 'spyware' is a generic description for a range of programs that in
some way monitor computer use. This ranges from adware that generates
'pop-ups', to programs that communicate information about an Internet
user's activities to a remote system without his or her knowledge.[38] These
include 'sniffer' programs, which intercept passwords; keyloggers, which
record the user's keystrokes; 'cookies', which record the user's Internet
viewing habits;[39] and 'web bugs', which are embedded in webpages or
email and collect information as to the date/time of access and the IP
address and browser type of the accessing computer. A 'browser hijacker',
often associated with pornography websites, is malware which can change
browser settings (such as the default start page), produce pop-up ads, add
bookmarks or redirect users to unwanted websites.

In *US* v. *Perez*[40] the defendants allegedly created and marketed a
spyware program called 'Loverspy' via a website. Prospective purchasers
could access the program for a fee, and then select from a menu an electronic greeting card to send to up to five different email addresses. Once
the recipient opened the card, 'Loverspy' secretly installed itself on their
computer. It would then monitor all activities on the computer, including emails sent and received, websites visited, and passwords entered.
These details were then sent to the purchaser. The purchaser was also able
to remotely control the victim's computer, including accessing files and
turning on web-enabled cameras. It was alleged that there were over 1,000
purchasers in the United States and internationally with more than 2,000
victims.

Another form of spyware, which has given rise to civil litigation in the
United States, is a 'web crawler', also known as 'web spider', 'web robot'

---

37 *US* v. *Maxwell* (WD Wash 2006) US Department of Justice, Press Release, 4 May 2006,
www.cybercrime.gov/maxwellPlea.htm.

38 All Party Parliamentary Internet Group, *Revision of the Computer Misuse Act: Report of
an Inquiry by the All Party Internet Group* (2004), [49].

39 See generally, M. R. Siebecker, 'Cookies and the common law: Are Internet advertisers trespassing on our computers?' (2003) 76 *Southern California Law Review* 893,
895–9.

40 *US* v. *Perez* (SD Cal 2005) US Department of Justice, Press Release, 26 August 2005,
www.cybercrime.gov/perezIndict.htm.

or 'web scraper'. This is a 'computer program which operates across the Internet to perform searching, copying and retrieving functions on the web sites of others'.[41] Such programs may be used by spammers, seeking to harvest email addresses, or by businesses seeking pricing and other commercial information from their competitor's websites.[42]

C. Denial of service attacks

A DoS attack exploits the way in which networked computers communicate in order to overwhelm a network and thereby 'deny service'. A similar effect may be observed when a website is unable to cope with the number of requests it is receiving, for example when tickets go on sale for a popular concert and the system is overwhelmed by the number of simultaneous requests. A DoS attack replicates this effect intentionally, and can target a single computer, server, website or network.

Such attacks are common, with one estimate in the UK put at approximately 4,000 per week, although these of course vary considerably in terms of scale and impact.[43] Some are concerted attacks, as when an ISP which offered a gaming server facility was subjected to DoS attack on forty-three occasions, preventing thousands of users from accessing the servers.[44] In other attacks, well-known websites, including Yahoo.com, Amazon.com, eBay.com and Buy.com were temporarily disabled as a result of such attacks.[45]

There are a number of ways in which DoS attacks may be achieved. Network routers may be disabled[46] or wireless access points reprogrammed so that others cannot access the network. Another form of DoS attack is known as 'mail bombing' where the attacker uses specialist software to send large volumes of email to a single address in an effort to overwhelm the mail server. Denial of service may also result from a replicating program such as a virus overwhelming the network.

The functioning of a computer may also be impaired where it is used for significant processing such as brute-force cracking. In *US* v. *Phillips*[47] the

---

41 *eBay, Inc.* v. *Bidder's Edge, Inc.*, 100 F Supp 2d 1058, 1060 (ND Cal 2000).
42 *Ibid.* Also see *EF Cultural Travel BV* v. *Zefer Corporation and Explorica*, Inc., 318 F 3d 58 (1st Cir 2003).
43 APIG, *Computer Misuse Act*, [58].   44 AusCERT, *Computer Crime Survey*, p. 28.
45 Computer Crimes and Intellectual Property Section, *The online world and law enforcement*.
46 *Ibid.*   47 477 F 3d 215 (5th Cir 2007).

defendant's use of a brute-force program to send thousands of requests to a university computer increased the usual monthly number of unique requests from approximately 20,000 to as many as 1,200,000, causing the system to crash several times.

More sophisticated DoS attacks utilise Internet protocols to overwhelm the target computer(s). A networked system such as the Internet relies upon protocols to allow computers to communicate with one another and to ensure that the data requested arrives at its destination. The client computer sends a request to the server, which then responds and identifies itself. Once the client computer receives this identification, data can be transferred.[48]

A number of techniques may be utilised to overwhelm this process. For example, the server may be overwhelmed with requests. As the server can only handle a certain number of requests, they are put into a queue. Eventually, there is no room in the queue and no further requests will be received. This is analogous to overwhelming the staff of a store with bogus inquires until they cannot respond to legitimate customers who form a queue and block the entrance to the store further denying access to legitimate customers.[49] Alternatively, the attacker may use a spoofed address to send the request to the server. The server duly identifies itself and waits to hear back. However, it will never hear back because it has been given the wrong or a non-existent address. If enough messages are sent the server is paralysed by waiting.[50]

Another variation is an ICMP flood. 'Pings' are small signals that are sent to other computers to see if they are available and connected to the same network, and to check for network problems. An ICMP attack involves sending a large number of forged ping requests to a third party server. The ping requests have the return address of the victim which is then flooded with responses to the pings from the server. This can cause both server and victim to crash.[51]

In a 'distributed denial of service attack' (DDoS attack) the attacker enlists other computers to attack the target computer or network. In one example, the defendant ran two web-based companies, which sold sportswear. He enlisted the help of a sixteen-year-old man, Jasmine Singh, to conduct a DDoS attack on his competitors' websites. Singh had infected some 2,000 personal computers and, using his home computer, instructed these 'bots' to access the targeted website all at once. The attack not only

---

48 The process is described in detail in Sinrod and Reilly, 'Cybercrimes', 190–1.
49 *Ibid.*, n. 60.   50 *Ibid.*, 192.   51 *Ibid.*, 193.

overloaded the server hosting the websites, it also caused harm to other sites hosted by the server, having impacts as far away as Europe.[52]

2. The prevalence of cybercrime

The difficulty in obtaining meaningful statistics on cybercrime generally has already been noted. The problem is particularly acute in the context of true cybercrimes, which are often not recorded in official crime statistics.[53] In other cases, computer crimes may be punished under other provisions. For example, British Telecom has in the past indicated a preference for pursuing hackers for 'fraudulent use of telecommunication system'[54] rather than the provisions of the Computer Misuse Act.[55]

The most comprehensive ongoing survey of computer security trends is the CSI/FBI *Computer Crime and Security Survey*, now in its thirteenth year.[56] As the survey is based on the responses of computer security professionals, the results are likely to be quite different to those that would be obtained from a more general community survey. Further, the definition of 'computer crime' is very broad, and includes such offences as theft of laptops. Nonetheless, it provides an ongoing snapshot of cybercrime trends.

One of the key findings of the latest survey is that most forms of computer crime have been consistently declining over recent years.[57] The most common incidents were viruses (50%), insider abuse of access (44%), laptop theft (42%) and unauthorised access (29%).[58] In terms of losses caused, the most expensive type of incident was financial fraud, followed by dealing with 'bot' computers within the organisation's network.[59] However, as noted in the survey, these figures must be treated with caution as relatively few respondents were prepared to disclose financial information.

---

52 *US* v. *Arabo* (D NJ 2006) United States Department of Justice, Press Release, 25 August 2006, www.cybercrime.gov/araboSent.htm.

53 E.g., computer misuse offences are not recorded in the Home Office Crime Statistics for England and Wales; see 'Crime type definitions' at www.crimestatistics.org.uk/output/page70.asp.

54 Telecommunications Act 1984 (UK), s. 42. This provision has now been repealed and replaced by the offence of dishonestly obtaining electronic communication services under s. 125 Communications Act 2003 (UK).

55 APIG, *Computer Misuse Act*, [106].

56 R. Richardson, *2008: CSI Computer Crime and Security Survey* (Computer Security Institute, 2008), www.gocsi.com.

57 *Ibid.*, p. 14.   58 *Ibid.*, p. 15.   59 *Ibid.*, p. 16.

The equivalent Australian survey is produced by the Australian High
Tech Crime Centre (AHTCC), in collaboration with federal, state and
territory police.[60] According to the 2006 survey, only 22 per cent of respondents experienced electronic attacks, the lowest level in four years.[61] Of
those that reported attacks, 83 per cent reported external attacks while
only 29 per cent reported internal attacks.[62]

In previous years the most common category of attack was virus, worm
or Trojan infections (64 per cent in 2005). In 2006 the survey split this
category into two new categories, 'virus or worm infections' and 'Trojan
or rootkit infections': forty-five per cent of respondents experienced virus
or worm infections, 21 per cent experienced Trojan or rootkit infections
while 18 per cent experienced both. The relatively high level of attack
by Trojans and rootkits reflects a broader trend of such malware being
utilised for ID theft and the creation of botnets.[63]

Although limited, prosecution statistics also indicate that this type of
offending is significant. For example, in Canada in 2000–1, the most common computer-related offence was theft of a telecommunication service,
with 270 charges disposed of, followed by unauthorised use of computer
(58) and mischief in relation to data (16).[64] In the same year, there were 83
computer-related prosecutions in England and Wales, although in 70 per
cent of those cases the computer offence was not the principal offence.[65] In
the United States in 2007 there was a total of 108 completed prosecutions
under the principle cybercrime provision (18 USC § 1030).[66]

3. The legislative environment

Prior to the enactment of specific cybercrime offences, prosecutors looked
to existing offences to deal with this new form of offending. For example,
unauthorised access could be seen as analogous to trespass. Other parallels
to impairment of data could be found in criminal damage.[67] Such an

---

60 AusCERT, *Computer Crime Survey*.   61 *Ibid.*, p. 17.
62 *Ibid.*, p. 19.   63 *Ibid.*, p. 21.   64 Kowalski, *Cyber-Crime*, p. 16.
65 Internet Crime Forum Legal Subgroup, *Reform of the Computer Misuse Act 1990* (Internet
    Crime Forum, 2003), Appendix B.
66 Bureau of Justice Statistics, Federal Justice Statistics Resource Center, http://fjsrc.
    urban.org/tsec.cfm. There is no systematic recording of cybercrime prosecutions under
    state law; O. S. Kerr, 'Cybercrime's scope: Interpreting "access" and "authorization" in
    computer misuse statutes' (2003) 78 *New York University Law Review* 1596, n. 86.
67 S. W. Brenner, 'Is there such a thing as "virtual crime"?' (2001) 4 *California Criminal Law
    Review* 1, 71–3, 82–4.

approach had the advantage of being seen as an extension of the law rather than a radical overhaul.[68]

Although property offences provided a ready analogy, such efforts were complicated by the application of traditional notions of property to computer data.[69] For example, at common law, confidential information is generally not regarded as 'property' for the purposes of theft.[70] Applying this same principle to computer data, a person who accesses but does not modify data will not generally be liable for theft as there is no taking away of property.[71]

In other contexts, courts had difficulty in determining whether computer data constitutes property at all; the success or failure of the prosecution largely depending upon the wording of the particular statute. For example, in *US* v. *Brown*[72] it was held that a computer program was not 'goods, wares, merchandise, securities, or moneys' for the purposes of transporting stolen property.[73] In contrast, in *US* v. *Collins*[74] it was held that the offence of converting government property contrary to 18 USC § 641 was not limited to tangible property and could apply to unauthorised use of a government computer. Other prosecutions focused on the use of the computer without authorisation as being theft of a telecommunication service,[75] fraud[76] or criminal damage.[77]

While convictions were sometimes obtained by utilising existing offences, there was 'recurrent (and understandable) difficulty in explaining to judges, magistrates and juries how the facts fit in with the present

---

68 M. Wasik, *Crime and the Computer* (Oxford: Clarendon Press, 1991), p. 69.

69 *Ibid.*, pp. 95–102 and Kerr, 'Cybercrime's scope', 1603–13.

70 *Oxford* v. *Moss* (1978) 68 Cr App R 183. Also see *R* v. *Stewart* [1988] 1 SCR 963.

71 *Ward v Superior Court of Alameda County*, 3 Computer L Serv Rep (Callaghan) 206 (Cal Super Ct 1972). Cf. *Hancock v Texas*, 402 SW 2d 906 (CCA Tex 1966) where the computer programs were in written form. Also see *R* v. *Alexander* [2006] OJ no 3173 at [60] per Ducharme J.

72 925 F 2d 1301, 1308–9 (10th Cir 1991). Cf. *US* v. *Farraj*, 142 F Supp 2d 484 (SD NY 2001).

73 Under the National Stolen Property Act, 18 USC §§ 2314, 2315.

74 56 F 3d 1416 (DC Cir 1995). Also see *State of Oregon* v. *Schwartz*, 173 Ore App 301, 317 (2001) where it was held that password files could be the subject of theft under the Oregon statute.

75 *R* v. *McLaughlin* [1980] 2 SCR 331.

76 In the United States, the 'Wire Fraud Statute' (18 USC § 1343) was often used to prosecute computer offences prior to the enactment of the Computer Fraud and Abuse Act; A. V. Gross, 'Criminal liability for theft of, interference with, or unauthorized use of, computer programs, files, or systems' (2003) 51 *ALR* 4th 971. See, e.g., *US* v. *Schreier*, 908 F 2d 645 (10th Cir 1990).

77 *R* v. *Whitely* (1991) 93 Cr App R 25; *Cox* v. *Riley* (1986) 83 Cr App R 54; and *Re Turner* (1984) 13 CCC (3d) 430.

law'.[78] One particularly tortured example was *R* v. *Gold, R* v. *Schifreen*,[79] described by the House of Lords as a 'Procrustean attempt to force these facts into the language of an Act not designed to fit them'.[80]

The defendants were charged, under s. 1 Forgery and Counterfeiting Act 1981 (UK), with making a false instrument. By obtaining the identification numbers and passwords of authorised users, the defendants gained unauthorised access to a computer database. They then accessed information, made unauthorised alterations to data and caused unauthorised charges to be made to account holders. The House of Lords rejected the prosecution argument that the user segment of the computer into which the identification numbers and passwords were entered was a device 'on or in which information is recorded or stored by . . . electronic means' within the definition of 'instrument' in the Act. Although the section contemplates that information may be recorded or stored by electronic means, the ordinary and natural meaning of the words 'recorded' and 'stored' connote the preservation of the thing recorded or stored for an appreciable time with the object of subsequent retrieval or recovery.[81] The entering of false numbers was not sufficient as the impulses were stored only for a very brief time while they were verified.

While it may be thought that a simple remedy would be to amend the definition of 'property' to incorporate computer data,[82] such an approach has not been adopted for a number of reasons. First, it is not only the concept of 'property' which is problematic. Similar difficulties arise in respect of other elements such as whether there has been an appropriation[83] or whether the defendant had an intention to permanently deprive.[84] Such offences also fail to encompass new forms of offending such as DoS attacks, which suppress rather than modify or delete data.

Secondly, it confers upon information stored within a computer the status of property, which does not generally apply to information stored in other forms. By simply defining data to be property, the need for

---

78 Law Commission, *Computer Misuse*, Final Report no. 186 (1989), [2.31].
79 [1988] AC 1063.   80 *Ibid.*, at 1071 per Lord Brandon of Oakbrook.
81 *Ibid.*, at 1073. For a more detailed discussion, see Law Commission, *Computer Misuse*, Working Paper no. 110 (1988), [3.15]–[3.21].
82 D. B. Parker, *Fighting Computer Crime* (New York: Scribner, 1983), p. 240; J. McConvill, 'Contemporary comment: Computer trespass in Victoria' (2001) 25 *Criminal Law Journal* 220, 224; and J. M. Olivenbaum, '<CTRL> <ALT> <DEL>: Rethinking federal computer crime legislation' (1997) 27 *Seton Hall Law Review* 574, 638.
83 *Lund* v. *Commonwealth*, 217 Va 688 (SC Va 1977).
84 *State* v. *McGraw*, 480 NE 2d 552 (SC Ind 1985).

criminalisation is assumed to be the same as that which applies to tangible property. This avoids a thorough analysis of the underlying criminality of such conduct.

Thirdly, continued reliance on existing laws is a reactive response to a constantly evolving problem. Even if property and related offences may be utilised in the context of domestic prosecutions, those offences may not have analogues in other jurisdictions, thereby hampering international co-operation in the investigation and prosecution of cybercrimes. Computers and computer networks are simply too important for their protection to be dependent on the adaptation of often arcane doctrine.

Accordingly, each jurisdiction has enacted specific cybercrime provisions. Under the Cybercrime Convention, such offences are classified as offences against the confidentiality, integrity and availability of computer data and systems.[85]

A. Australia

In Australia, criminal law is primarily a matter of state and territory responsibility, with the Commonwealth limited to areas within its constitutional power. Despite this, the Commonwealth has had a considerable influence in the area of cybercrime for two reasons.

First, the Commonwealth has been instrumental in the wholesale review of Australian criminal laws. Although the earliest Australian legislative reforms relating to cybercrime occurred in the Northern Territory in 1983,[86] more widespread reform did not occur until the recommendations of the Attorney-General's Department's Review of Commonwealth Criminal Law in 1988.[87] These were in turn overtaken by the project to develop a uniform Criminal Code, a task carried out by the Model Criminal Code Officers Committee (MCCOC).[88] This resulted in the current

---

85 Cybercrime Convention, Ch. II, Section I, Title 1.

86 S. 222 of the Criminal Code Act (NT); see S. Bronitt and M. Gani, 'Shifting boundaries of cybercrime: From computer hacking to cyberterrorism' (2003) 27 *Criminal Law Journal* 303, 307.

87 Attorney-General's Department, *Review of Commonwealth Criminal Law: Interim report, computer crime* (1988). For a discussion of early Australian computer crime laws, see C. Sullivan, 'The response of the criminal law in Australia to computer abuse' (1988) 12 *Criminal Law Journal* 228, 239–46.

88 See generally MCCOC, *Chapter 4: Damage and Computer Offences*, Discussion Paper (2000); and *Chapter 4: Damage and Computer Offences*, Final Report (2001).

computer offence provisions found in Part 10.7 Criminal Code Act 1995 (Cth).[89]

Although based to a large extent on the English reforms discussed below, the committee was also influenced by the Cybercrime Convention, which at the time was in draft form.[90] Part 10.7 contains a range of offences concerned with unauthorised access, modification and impairment of data. These offences are further divided into serious computer offences (Division 477) and other computer offences (Division 478). The interception of communications is dealt with in separate legislation.[91] Although intended to provide a model for all jurisdictions, the Criminal Code has not been widely adopted. Consequently, Australian cybercrimes are a patchwork of jurisdictions with some based on Part 10.7,[92] some adopting their own approaches[93] while others do both.[94]

Secondly, the Commonwealth's legislative power in relation to telecommunications gives it a wide legislative mandate in this area.[95] The most extreme example is found in s. 474.14. Under this provision it is an offence to connect equipment to, or use equipment connected[96] to, a telecommunications network intending to commit, or to facilitate the commission of, a serious offence.[97]

There is no limitation on the nature of the serious offence; that is, it need not be concerned with telecommunications. So long as the network is used to facilitate or commit such an offence, the offence is made out. Nor is there a need to prove that the serious offence was actually facilitated; in fact, the offence may be made out even where committing the serious offence

---

89 'Criminal Code (Cth)'. See generally, A. Steel, 'Vaguely going where no-one has gone: The expansive new computer access offences' (2002) 26 *Criminal Law Journal* 72. These reforms replaced the previous federal computer offence provisions which were found in Part IVA Crimes Act 1914 (Cth).

90 MCCOC, *Computer Offences* (2001), p. 89.   91 See Ch. 6.

92 Criminal Code 2002 (ACT), Part 4.2, Crimes Act 1900 (NSW), Part 6 and Crimes Act 1958 (Vic), Division 3(6).

93 Criminal Code Act 1899 (Qld), s. 408D, Criminal Code Act 1924 (Tas), Ch. XXVIIIA and Criminal Code Act Compilation Act 1913 (WA), s. 440A.

94 Criminal Code (NT), Part VII, Division 10 and Summary Offences Act 1953 (SA), s. 4 and Criminal Law Consolidation Act 1935 (SA), Part 4A.

95 For a range of offences associated with telecommunications, see Division 474 Criminal Code (Cth).

96 'Connected' in relation to a telecommunications network is defined to include 'connection otherwise than by means of physical contact (for example, a connection by means of radiocommunication)': Criminal Code (Cth), s. 473.1.

97 Either against a law of the Commonwealth, a state or a territory or a foreign law: s. 474.12(1)(b). Both offences are punishable by a penalty not exceeding the penalty applicable to the serious offence: s. 474.14(3).

is impossible.[98] It is enough that the defendant *intended* to facilitate the offence. It therefore punishes preparatory conduct that may fall far short of the law of attempts.[99]

This represents an extraordinary expansion of Commonwealth power, which not only potentially overlaps with state laws (although it is unlikely that the Commonwealth has evinced an intention to cover the field) but may displace more targeted Commonwealth offences such as those concerned with unauthorised access to computers with intention to commit a serious offence.[100] These problems are further exacerbated by its application to foreign laws.[101]

B. Canada

Reform of the Criminal Code (Can) to address problems of computer misuse arose largely as a result of the Supreme Court's decision in *McLaughlin*.[102] A bill[103] was referred to the House Standing Committee on Justice and Legal Affairs, which tabled its report on 29 June 1983. The Committee rejected the idea of a specific cybercrime statute on the basis that such a statute would take too long to draft, and that cybercrime should not be treated differently from other types of crime.[104] The Committee therefore recommended amendments to the Criminal Code, adopting a two-tier approach, with an offence of unauthorised access and one of unauthorised alteration or destruction of computer data.[105] These amendments came into force on 4 December 1985,[106] and were supplemented in 1997 by the Criminal Law Improvement Act, which introduced an offence of trafficking in computer passwords and devices used to commit cybercrimes.[107]

---

98 S. 474.14(5).

99 It is not, however, an offence to attempt to commit these offences: s. 474.14(6).

100 Urbas and Choo, *Technology-Enabled Crime*, p. 23.

101 'Serious offence against a foreign law' means an offence against a law of a foreign country constituted by conduct that, if it had occurred in Australia, would have constituted a serious offence against a law of the Commonwealth, a state or a territory: s. 473.1.

102 See p. 41.

103 Bill C-667, 'An Act to Amend the Criminal Code and the Canada Evidence Act in respect of Computer Crime', (1982).

104 House of Commons Standing Committee On Justice And Legal Affairs, *Computer Crime*, Final Report (1983), pp. 15–16.

105 *Ibid.*, p. 16.

106 Criminal Law Amendment Act 1985 (Can). See M. Hébert and H. Pilon, *Computer Crime* (Department of Justice Canada, 1991).

107 An Act to amend the Criminal Code and certain other Acts, S. C 1997, c. 18, s. 18.

C. The United Kingdom

Once commenced, reform in the UK occurred rapidly. The Law Commission published both its Working Paper[108] and Final Report[109] on 'Computer Misuse' within a year of each other. This was followed in 1990 by the enactment of the Computer Misuse Act 1990 (UK).[110] The Act initially penalised two forms of conduct: 'unauthorised access to computer material' (ss. 1 and 2) and 'unauthorised modification of computer material' (s. 3). Following a review by the All Party Parliamentary Internet Group (APIG)[111] some important reforms were made by Part 5 of the Police and Justice Act 2006 (UK). These amendments attempted to address some of the specific problems that had arisen under the existing law, particularly in relation to DoS attacks, and also to conform with the Cybercrime Convention and the EU Framework Decision.[112] The amendments also introduced a new offence dealing with trafficking in 'hacking devices'.

D. The United States

The first US computer crime statute was enacted in Florida in 1978, with all fifty states now having followed suit.[113] Although federal legislation had been proposed earlier,[114] the first federal Act was the Counterfeit Access Device and Computer Fraud and Abuse Act of 1984. However, its narrow scope and lack of clarity meant it was soon superseded by the Computer Fraud and Abuse Act of 1986 (CFAA), codified at 18 USC § 1030. This remains the principal federal computer-crime statute, although its reach has been significantly expanded to include 'protected computers', the dissemination of malicious code and trafficking in computer passwords.[115]

---

108 Law Commission, *Computer Misuse* (1988).
109 Law Commission, *Computer Misuse* (1989). The Scottish Law Commission had published its report two years earlier: Scottish Law Commission, *Report on Computer Crime*, no. 106 (1987).
110 'Computer Misuse Act'.   111 APIG, *Computer Misuse Act.*
112 Explanatory Notes, Police and Justice Act 2006 (UK), [301].
113 Kerr, 'Cybercrime's scope', 1615. For a summary of state computer crime statutes see M. D. Goodman and S. W. Brenner, 'The emerging consensus on criminal conduct in cyberspace' (2002) *UCLA Journal of Law and Technology* 44.
114 J. Roddy, 'The Federal Computer Systems Protection Act' (1979) 7 *Rutgers Journal of Computers Technology and the Law* 343.
115 For a history of US efforts to address computer crime prior to this act see Goodman and Brenner, 'Emerging consensus', 12–13.

Importantly, the CFAA also allows for civil remedies.[116] In recent years, this appears to have been the greatest contributor to jurisprudence in this area, and has, arguably, led to more expansive interpretations than might occur in the criminal courts.[117]

We now turn to consider the specific offence categories. Chapter 3 is concerned with unauthorised access to computers, while Chapter 4 focuses on unauthorised impairment of data. Also relevant to this category of offending are those offences relating to the misuse of devices which may be used to facilitate the commission of these offences (Chapter 5) and unauthorised interception of data (Chapter 6).

---

116 18 USC § 1030(g).
117 O. S. Kerr, 'Lifting the "fog" of Internet surveillance: How a suppression remedy would change computer crime law' (2003) 54 *Hastings Law Journal* 805, 829–36. Note that US courts generally apply civil precedents in the criminal context unless there is evidence that Congress did not intend the same standard to govern: *US* v. *Bigham*, 812 F 2d 943, 948 (5th Cir 1987).

3

Access offences

1. Introduction

This first category of offence is concerned with intentional and without-right access to the whole or part of a computer system.[1] It is intended to provide the basic offence of 'dangerous threats to, and attacks against, the security . . . of computer systems and data'.[2] Given the potential breadth of such an offence, parties may require that the offence be 'committed by infringing security measures, with the intent of obtaining computer data or other dishonest intent, or in relation to a computer system that is connected to another computer system'.[3]

A. Australia

We have seen that the Australian provisions are classified according to whether they are 'serious computer offences' or 'other computer offences'.[4] In the context of access, the serious computer offences are found in ss. 477.1(1)(a)(i) and 477.1(4)(a)(i) of the Criminal Code (Cth). Both provisions are in the same terms but with different jurisdictional nexus; s. 477.1(1) applies to access by means of a carriage service,[5] while s. 477.1(4) applies where there is an intention to commit a serious Commonwealth offence. Both provisions make it an offence for a person to cause any unauthorised access to data held in a computer, knowing the access is unauthorised, and by that access intending to commit, or facilitate

---

1 Cybercrime Convention, Ch. II, Section I, Art. 1.
2 Council of Europe, 'Convention on Cybercrime: Explanatory Report', ETS no. 185, [44].
3 Cybercrime Convention, Ch. II, Section I, Art. 1.   4 See p. 44.
5 In the Dictionary to the Code, 'carriage service' has the same meaning as in the Telecommunications Act 1997 (Cth). Absolute liability applies to this aspect of the offence. That is, the prosecution does not need to prove that the person knew it was caused by means of a telecommunications service: s. 477.1(2).

the commission, of a serious offence.[6] These offences are punishable by a penalty not exceeding the penalty for the relevant serious offence.[7] A person may be guilty of these offences even if committing the serious offence is impossible, but it is not an offence to attempt to commit these offences.[8]

In relation to 'other computer offences' it is an offence under s. 478.1(1) Criminal Code (Cth) for a person to intentionally cause any unauthorised access to 'restricted data', knowing that the access is unauthorised.[9] The significant feature of this provision is that it punishes simple access to data, with no requirement of an intent to commit or facilitate the commission of another offence. The federal offence is also limited by the jurisdictional requirement that the data must be held in a Commonwealth computer,[10] be held on behalf of the Commonwealth, or the access is caused by means of a 'carriage service'.[11]

B. Canada

The Canadian provisions are classified as 'Offences against Rights of Property' under Part IX Criminal Code (Can). Unlike the other jurisdictions, these provisions focus on obtaining the use of a computer, rather than access to the computer. Under s. 342.1(1) it is an offence where a person fraudulently and without colour of right:

> (a) obtains, directly or indirectly, any computer service . . .
> (c) uses or causes to be used, directly or indirectly, a computer system with intent to commit an offence under paragraph (a) or (b)[12] or an offence under s. 430 in relation to data or a computer system.[13]

C. The United Kingdom

The UK offences concerned with access to data are found in ss. 1 and 2 Computer Misuse Act. Following the recommendation of the Law

---

6 A 'serious offence' means an offence against a law of the Commonwealth, a state or a territory that is punishable by imprisonment for life or a period of 5 or more years: s. 477.1(9).

7 S. 477.1(6).   8 S. 477.1(7)(8).

9 Maximum penalty 2 years' imprisonment: s. 478.1.

10 Defined as a computer owned, leased or operated by a Commonwealth entity: s. 476.1.

11 S. 478.1(1)(d).

12 The offence under s. 342.1(1)(b) Criminal Code (Can) is discussed at p. 140.

13 Maximum penalty on indictment is 10 years' imprisonment: s. 342.1. The offence of 'mischief' under s. 430, so far as it relates to data, is dicussed at p. 104.

Commission, there is a basic offence which applies to all forms of hacking, whether fraudulent or malicious or not, with more serious cases addressed by a separate provision requiring proof of an intent to commit a specified offence.[14]

Under s. 1(1), a person is guilty of an offence if:

(a) he causes a computer to perform any function with intent to secure access to any program or data held in any computer;
(b) the access he intends to secure is unauthorised; and
(c) he knows at the time when he causes the computer to perform the function that that is the case.[15]

It is not necessary for the prosecution to prove that access to the computer has been achieved. It is sufficient that the defendant intended to secure access. Under the 2006 amendments, it was proposed that the offence would extend to intent to 'enable such access to be secured'.[16] This was intended to make it clear that the offence would apply where the defendant seeks to enable another person to access the computer, or to enable himself or herself to access the computer at a later time.[17] However, this provision has since been repealed.[18]

The reference to 'any program or data held in *any* computer' (emphasis added) means that the computer which performs the function may also be the computer to which access is sought. There need be no second computer involved.[19] Equally, the computer which performs the function and the computer into which access is sought need not be the same.[20] Further, 'program or data held in any particular computer' includes 'any program or data held in any removable storage medium which is for the time being in the computer; and a computer is to be regarded as containing any program or data held in any such medium'.[21] So, for example, a defendant may distribute malware unaware of the precise computers he or she is targeting, or intend to gain access but be unaware of precisely what data, if any, will be on the computer. In both of these cases, the offence may still be made out.

---

14 Law Commission, *Computer Misuse*, Final Report no. 186 (1989), [3.9].
15 Maximum penalty 2 years' imprisonment; s. 1(3).
16 Police and Justice Act 2006 (UK), s. 35(2).
17 Explanatory Notes, Police and Justice Act 2006 (UK), [295].
18 Serious Crime Act 2007 (UK), s. 61.
19 *Attorney General's Reference (No. 1 of 1991)* [1993] QB 94 at 97 per Lord Taylor.
20 Computer Misuse Act, s. 1(2).
21 S. 17(6). Difficulties associated with this definition are discussed in the context of the equivalent Australian provision at pp. 61–2.

Section 2(1) is a more serious offence where a s. 1 offence is committed with an intention to commit a specified offence.[22] The offence also includes the facilitation of a specified offence by the defendant or any other person, for example the person who accesses financial information in order to facilitate a fraud by another person.[23] It is immaterial whether the further offence is to be committed on the same occasion or in the future,[24] or whether the commission of the further offence is impossible.[25] It is therefore both a preliminary offence and an aggravated form of the basic offence.[26]

This offence was particularly aimed at those cases where the conduct is engaged in with the intention of committing a further offence, in circumstances where the conduct is not sufficiently proximate to the completed offence to constitute an attempt, for example the hacker who accesses a bank's computer system intending to fraudulently transfer funds but who is unable to get past further security systems; or the person who hacks into a computer in order to gain personal information for the purposes of blackmail.[27]

D. The United States

As noted above, the principal US federal computer crime statute is the CFAA. The offence provisions are based upon accessing a computer without authorisation or exceeding authorised access, with additional elements then built upon this central concept to create a range of offences.[28]

Rather than considering each provision in detail, we will now consider the key elements of these offences:

1. 'computer'
2. 'access'
3. 'unauthorised'
4. fault elements
5. additional elements.

---

22 Maximum penalty 5 years' imprisonment; s. 2(5). The Law Commission felt that although it would typically be offences of dishonesty, it would not be prudent to try to draw up a list of offences to which access to a computer might be preparatory: Law Commission, *Computer Misuse* (1989), [3.55]–[3.56].
23 *Ibid.*, [3.49], [3.58].   24 Computer Misuse Act, s. 2(3).
25 Computer Misuse Act, s. 2(4).
26 Law Commission, *Computer Misuse* (1989), [3.49].   27 *Ibid.*, [3.52]–[3.53].
28 Although our focus is on the federal provisions, the state provisions generally follow a similar model: O. S. Kerr, 'Cybercrime's scope: Interpreting "access" and "authorization" in computer misuse statutes' (2003) 78 *New York University Law Review* 1615.

2. The meaning of 'computer'

In the context of computer crimes, the meaning of the term 'computer' is obviously central. Although a word of common usage, its meaning varies according to context and audience.[29] Equally, with technology evolving so rapidly, our conception of what is a 'computer' is constantly challenged. Mobile phones now have the processing power once reserved for mainframes occupying whole rooms, while more and more domestic appliances and other everyday items include some degree of processing capacity. There are essentially two responses to these challenges. The first, which has been adopted in Australia, Canada and the UK, is to leave the term undefined. The other, and that which is adopted in the United States, is to attempt a comprehensive definition of computer.

The Cybercrime Convention is of little assistance in this regard, adopting something of both approaches. Although the term 'computer' is not defined, 'computer system' is defined as 'any device or a group of interconnected or related devices, one or more of which, pursuant to a program, performs automatic processing of data'.[30] Therefore, by implication, a 'computer' is a device which, pursuant to a program, performs automatic processing of data. The Convention therefore does not expressly address the issue, neither advocating for a particular definition nor leaving the term completely undefined.

At the same time, there is a need not to over-criminalise conduct simply because a computer was involved. The dangers of over-breadth are well illustrated by the early Australian computer offences which sought to protect the 'confidentiality and integrity of data or programs stored in Commonwealth computers'.[31] Although punishing simple unauthorised access, at least in the Commonwealth sphere this definition was limited to Commonwealth computers. However, in those states which adopted it without any such limitation, unauthorised access to any computer became an offence. Not only did this extend protection to computer data that did not apply to data recorded in paper form, the scope of the provision was so

---

29 *R* v. *McLaughlin* [1980] 2 SCR 331 at 338 per Estey J.

30 Cybercrime Convention, Ch. I, Art. 1(a). 'Computer data' is defined to mean 'any representation of facts, information or concepts in a form suitable for processing in a computer system, including a program suitable to cause a computer system to perform a function': Art. 1(b).

31 S. Bronitt and M. Gani, 'Shifting boundaries of cybercrime: From computer hacking to cyberterrorism' (2003) 27 *Criminal Law Journal* 307.

broad that it would apply to any unauthorised function of the computer or its programs at all:[32]

> The explosive growth in the number of people using computers, the variety of uses to which they are put, coupled with the intractable problems of defining what is and what is not a computer, should preclude blunderbuss prohibitions of this nature. One might just as well argue for offences of impeding the lawful use of a television set or record player.[33]

A. Australia, Canada and the United Kingdom

In Australia, Canada and the UK, the term 'computer' is undefined. In Australia and the UK, this approach was specifically recommended by law reform agencies. The Law Commission made its recommendation on the basis that any definition was likely to be both under-inclusive, because it might not keep up with technology, and over-inclusive, because it might encompass items such as household appliances, calculators, digital watches and the like.[34] The Commission also rejected a compromise of leaving the term undefined but specifying certain items which are not computers for these purposes, as such an approach would still encounter the same problem in defining those exceptions in such a way that they are not rapidly outdated:

> In view of the nature of the proposed hacking offence, especially the *mens rea* required . . . we cannot think that there will ever be serious grounds for arguments based on the ordinary meaning of the term 'computer'. By contrast, all the attempted definitions that we have seen are so complex, in an endeavour to be all-embracing, that they are likely to produce extensive argument, and thus confusion for magistrates, juries and judges . . .[35]

Although influenced in part by the Law Commission's recommendations, the Australian committee was less sanguine, noting that this approach was perhaps more manageable when it was first proposed. The increasing computerisation of many household appliances and other everyday items presents a real danger of over-criminalisation. For example, if unauthorised access to a computer is made an offence, then it could conceivably extend to use of a computer game without permission:

32 *Ibid.*, 308.   33 MCCOC, *Computer Offences* (2001), p. 91.
34 Law Commission, *Computer Misuse* (1989), [3.39].
35 *Ibid.* Also see M. Wasik, *Crime and the Computer* (Oxford: Clarendon Press, 1991), pp. 4–5.

> Rapid expansion of the functions assigned to computers has eroded, to an uncertain extent, confidence that the limits of computer crime legislation can be determined in this way. The decision to refrain from definition, which seemed reasonable at the beginning of the decade, begins to assume the aspect of an extensive delegation of legislative responsibility to courts.[36]

Nonetheless, the Committee took the view that problems of over-criminalisation would not be addressed by defining the term 'computer'. First, it is simply not possible to provide a definition which excludes unauthorised access to a pocket calculator but not a laptop computer.[37] The Committee also rejected the idea of defining 'computer' subject to a power to exclude by regulation any machine or other item from the definition.[38]

More broadly, both the Law Commission and the MCCOC took the view that problems of over-criminalisation are best addressed by the scope of the offence itself, rather than attempting to define the term 'computer'. If the limits of the offence are properly described, it will not matter that various items may be described as 'computers' as the relevant conduct will fall outside the scope of the offence. It is only if the offence itself is drafted too broadly that problems of over-criminalisation will arise. Prosecutorial discretion may also be relied upon to avoid the more absurd application of such provisions.

The Canadian provisions do not refer to a 'computer' as such, but rather to a 'computer service' or 'computer system'. 'Computer service' is defined to include 'data processing and the storage or retrieval of data'.[39] A 'computer system' is:

> a device that, or a group of interconnected or related devices one or more of which,
> (a) contains computer programs or other data, and
> (b) pursuant to computer programs,
>   i. performs logic and control, and
>   ii. may perform any other function . . .[40]

---

36 MCCOC, *Computer Offences* (2001), p. 125.
37 *Ibid.*, p. 127. For a contrasting approach, see the US provisions at p. 56.
38 Such a proposal had been put forward by the Tasmanian Law Reform Commission, *Report on Computer Misuse*, Report no. 47 (1986), p. 12.
39 Criminal Code (Can), s. 342.1(2).
40 S. 342.1(2). 'Function' includes logic, control, arithmetic, deletion, storage and retrieval and communication or telecommunication to, from or within a computer system: s. 342.1(2).

Therefore in each of these jurisdictions the term 'computer' is left undefined and must be given its ordinary meaning. While there is merit in this approach, it provides a trial judge with no guidance as to whether a particular item is, or is not, a computer. It therefore only superficially avoids the problem of over-inclusion as a trial judge is likely to take the view that a computer is an ordinary word to be given its commonly understood meaning, albeit seen in its statutory context. Such definitions tend to be capable of very broad application.

For example, the *Oxford English Dictionary* defines 'computer' as '[a] calculating-machine; esp. an automatic electronic device for performing mathematical or logical operations'. Similarly, the Supreme Court of Canada, although not deciding the issue, has cited two dictionary definitions of 'computer' as 'a calculator esp. designed for the solution of complex mathematical problems; specific: a programmable electronic device that can store, retrieve, and process data' or 'a mechanical or electronic apparatus capable of carrying out repetitive and highly complex mathematical operations at high speeds'.[41] Such definitions are capable of applying to a wide variety of domestic appliances and other items that would not ordinarily be expected to be subject to computer-offence provisions. For example, the act of triggering a burglar alarm or driving a car may both cause a computer to execute a function.[42]

In its review of the Computer Misuse Act, APIG received a number of submissions arguing that 'computer' should be defined in the Act; in particular, that it should specifically incorporate items such as PDAs, palmtop devices and network components such as routers.[43] However, APIG noted that it had received considerable evidence indicating that the lack of definition had not given rise to problems in practice, and that the courts had consistently applied a broad definition. Consequently, it was recommended that no change be made in this regard.[44]

In some cases, this approach of leaving terms undefined is also adopted in relation to terms such as 'data' and 'program', their meaning being left to the courts to determine, guided by the 'evolving common understanding of those terms modified, where appropriate, by their statutory context'.[45]

---

41 *R* v. *McLaughlin* [1980] 2 SCR 331 at 339 per Estey J citing *Webster's Third New International Dictionary* (1976) and *Random House Dictionary of the English Language* (1973) respectively.

42 MCCOC, *Computer Offences* (2001), p. 135.

43 All Party Parliamentary Internet Group, *Revision of the Computer Misuse Act: Report of an Inquiry by the All Party Internet Group* (2004), [13].

44 *Ibid.*, [17].   45 MCCOC, *Computer Offences* (2001), p. 129.

For example, in the UK the term 'data' is not defined, the Law Commission being of the view that its ordinary meaning is 'information or facts stored or held in a computer' and does not require a technical definition.[46] In contrast, the Canadian provision defines 'data' to mean 'representations of information or of concepts that are being prepared or have been prepared in a form suitable for use in a computer system'.[47]

B. The United States

In contrast to the other jurisdictions, the CFAA contains an exhaustive definition of 'computer'. Under 18 USC § 1030(e)(1) 'computer' is defined to mean:

> an electronic, magnetic, optical, electrochemical, or other high speed data processing device performing logical, arithmetic, or storage functions, and includes any data storage facility or communications facility directly related to or operating in conjunction with such device, but such term does not include an automated typewriter or typesetter, a portable hand held calculator, or other similar device.

The main advantage of a precise definition is certainty, in particular clarifying the status of certain devices which might otherwise be ambiguous. For example, this provision specifically includes a data-storage or communications facility associated with the computer. It may therefore encompass devices such as USB sticks and wireless routers so long as they are 'directly related to or operating in conjunction with' a computer. However, in such a rapidly evolving area certainty is difficult to achieve and generally short-lived. Any definition must be sufficiently precise to provide the desired certainty, but flexible enough to be adaptable to changing technologies. This then raises problems of over-inclusiveness. For example, the CFAA definition would seem to include mobile telephones, portable calculators, PDAs, electronic games, mp3 players and even domestic appliances such as fridges, DVD players or the computer systems in cars which all contain processing capacity.

The dangers of an over-broad definition were clearly recognised in the drafting of the CFAA, which specifically excludes 'an automated typewriter or typesetter, a portable hand held calculator, or other

---

46 Law Commission, *Computer Misuse* (1989), [3.30].
47 Criminal Code (Can), s 342.1(2). Also see the definition of 'data' in the Australian provisions at p. 61.

similar device'. However, this wording immediately dates the provision and perfectly illustrates the dangers of technically specific language:

> a calculator today can be programmable and be as powerful as a minicom-
> puter with limited storage. Tomorrow it could be equivalent to some of the
> largest computers in use today and be able to store millions and billions
> of bits of data.[48]

As technology develops, it becomes necessary to determine whether a particular device falls within terms such as a 'portable calculator'. To remain current, the provision may require legislative amendment. For example, previous concern that the definition was potentially under-inclusive as not encompassing non-electronic computers[49] has been addressed by reference to 'an electronic, magnetic, optical, electrochemical, or other high speed data processing device'.

However, the problem of over-inclusion is not limited to specific definitions such as this. As we have seen in relation to other jurisdictions, dictionary definitions are equally susceptible to broad application. As in those jurisdictions, the important limitation is found not in the definition itself, but in the additional elements of the offence, particularly the fault elements. Many of the more extreme possible applications of the section do not arise because these additional elements are missing. If they are present, there is no reason that such conduct should not be punished merely because the device would not, in ordinary usage, be described as a computer.

This point is well illustrated by the decision of the Seventh Circuit in *US v. Mitra*.[50] The defendant used radio hardware and computer equipment to monitor communications over the Smartnet II system, a computer-based radio system for emergency communications. He then sent powerful signals that prevented the computer from receiving essential data, leaving emergency services unable to co-ordinate their activities. Alternatively, the defendant would leave the communication channels open and would append a sound, such as a woman's sexual moan, to the end of each communication.

The defendant was convicted under 18 USC § 1030(a)(5). The prosecution argued that Smartnet II was a 'computer' within the meaning of the section as it contained a chip that performs high-speed processing, and is a 'communications facility directly related to or operating in conjunction'

---

48 D. B. Parker, *Fighting Computer Crime* (New York: Scribner, 1983).
49 MCCOC, *Computer Offences* (2001), p. 123.   50 405 F 3d 492 (7th Cir 2005).

with that computer chip. The defendant contended that the statute was intended to apply to more traditional examples of 'hacking' such as stealing financial information from banks, erasing data or disseminating worms or viruses. It was not intended to apply to situations such as this where all he did was 'gum up a radio system'. If the radio system was a computer, then '[e]very cell phone and cell tower is a "computer" . . . ; so is every iPod, every wireless base station in the corner coffee shop, and many another gadget'.[51]

The court rejected the defendant's argument. While Congress may not have contemplated or intended this particular application, that is precisely why some statutes are written in general terms. The section provides exceptions for 'automatic typewriters, typesetters, and handheld calculators' which demonstrates that other devices with embedded processors and software are covered by the definition:

> As more devices come to have built-in intelligence, the effective scope of the statute grows. This might prompt Congress to amend the statute but does not authorize the judiciary to give the existing version less coverage than its language portends . . . What protects people who accidentally erase songs on an iPod, trip over (and thus disable) a wireless base station, or rear-end a car and set off a computerized airbag, is not judicial creativity but the requirements of the statute itself: the damage must be intentional, it must be substantial . . . and the computer must operate in interstate or foreign commerce.[52]

In contrast to some other jurisdictions, the CFAA refers only to a computer, and not to computer networks. However, the definition of 'computer' makes clear that it includes a 'communications facility associated with the computer'. It therefore seems clear that not only the computers on a network in a traditional sense, but the associated communications facilities such as routers would also fall within the meaning of 'computer network'. An attack against a network must, however, be particularised as offences against particular computers in that network, as opposed to an attack on the network per se.

3. Access

Under the Cybercrime Convention, '"[a]ccess" comprises the entering of the whole or any part of a computer system (hardware, components, stored data of the system installed, directories, traffic and content-related data)'.[53] It also:

---

51 *Ibid.*, 495.   52 *Ibid.*, 495–6.
53 Cybercrime Convention, Explanatory Report, [46].

includes the entering of another computer system, where it is connected via public telecommunication networks, or to a computer system on the same network, such as a LAN (local area network) or Intranet within an organisation. The method of communication (e.g. from a distance, including via wireless links or at a close range) does not matter.[54]

The use of the word 'access' immediately imports a concept that has developed in the physical environment and applies it to a digital context. Such terminology evokes images of being 'inside' or 'outside' the computer. Consistent with 'computer trespass' being amongst the earliest cybercrimes,[55] the computer is seen as similar to a 'box', a repository of information, and it is unauthorized entry to the box which is prohibited. Such an approach reflects an 'internal perspective'; that is, the perspective of the computer user who sees access as metaphorically getting 'inside' the computer, rather like entering a building.[56]

Such an analogy makes some sense in the archetypal situation of the person who logs on to a computer without permission, or the hacker who bypasses security measures in order to gain access. However, the days when our interactions with computers were primarily governed by passwords and logins are long passed. There are myriad ways in which a person may interact with a computer, and new ways are constantly evolving.[57] This creates an environment in which it is difficult to conceptualise the meaning of access utilising the 'trespass' paradigm.

Adopting an 'external' rather than an 'internal' perspective' produces a very different picture. An 'external perspective' adopts the viewpoint of the outsider observing the functioning of the computer in the physical world rather than the perceptions of the user.[58] From this perspective we see that access to a computer necessarily involves access to data. For example, it is possible to modify data without, in the colloquial sense, gaining access to the computer. As a matter of ordinary language if a person tried to guess a password to enter a computer, but failed, we would say that person had not accessed the computer. However, the person has, in fact, caused the computer to respond, and in the process modified data, albeit not in the way intended.[59] Even the act of attempting to view a file which then requests a password could be seen as 'accessing' even if no password is entered.[60]

---

54 *Ibid.*   55 For example, the now-repealed s. 9A Summary Offences Act 1966 (Vic).

56 O. S. Kerr, 'The problem of perspective in Internet law' (2003) *Georgetown Law Journal*, 359–60.

57 Kerr, 'Cybercrime's scope', 1647–8.   58 Kerr, 'The problem of perspective', 360.

59 Kerr, 'Cybercrime's scope', 1620–1.   60 *Ibid.*, 1621.

Similar complexities arise with something as apparently simple as view-ing a webpage. If we do not have permission to view the page, or the page we are looking for is not available, then in a general sense we have not 'accessed' that page. We have, nonetheless, sent a communication to var-ious computers along the way, each of which has performed a function in response to our request.[61]

From this perspective it is more accurate to describe 'use' of a com-puter rather than 'access' to a computer.[62] The primary concern of these offences therefore becomes access to the data itself rather than access to the 'computer'. Rather than 'trespass', the appropriate metaphor is 'information-as-thing' whereby the data is seen as the object of the access and the 'thing' which is to be protected.[63] Against this background, we now turn to consider the meaning of 'access' in each jurisdiction.

A. Australia

The Australian provisions avoid using 'access' as a verb, the relevant conduct being to 'cause' any unauthorised access rather than 'to access'.[64] 'Access to data held in a computer' is defined to mean:

  (a) the display of the data by the computer or any other output of the data from the computer; or
  (b) the copying or moving of the data to any other place in the computer or to a data storage device; or
  (c) in the case of a program – the execution of the program.[65]

Although this is an exhaustive definition, it is extremely broad. In essence, 'access' is synonymous with 'use' of the data as essentially any interaction with the data which causes the computer to respond will constitute access, whether by local or remote use of the computer. There is no requirement that the access be 'successful'. So, for example, entering an incorrect pass-word nonetheless causes the execution of a program and so could be said to constitute access to data held in that computer. There are, however, some limitations.

---

61 *Ibid.*   62 *Ibid.*, 1641.
63 M. J. Madison, 'Rights of access and the shape of the Internet' (2003) *Boston College Law Review* 433, 442.
64 MCCOC, *Computer Offences* (2001), p. 135.
65 Criminal Code (Cth), s. 476.1(1). In contrast to the UK provisions, terms such as 'output' are not defined, the committee being of the view that the UK definitions of 'output' and 'use' were unduly complex: MCCOC, *Computer Offences* (2001), p. 135.

First, the defendant must actually cause the access to occur.[66] So, for example, simply viewing data on a screen will not constitute access unless the defendant actually caused the display to occur. Secondly, the access must be caused, whether directly or indirectly, by the execution of a function of a computer.[67] This was intended to exclude from the provision the use of a physical device, for example a screwdriver, to gain 'access' to a computer. Such situations are more appropriately dealt with as criminal damage.[68]

Data held in a computer

Each of these offences requires that the access be to data held in a computer. 'Data' is defined in the Dictionary to the Code to include:

(a) information in any form
(b) any program (or part of a program).

Clearly, data which is stored within the internal memory of a computer will fall within the terms of the section. There is no need to show that the data is part of the operating system of the computer, and the definition includes data which is entered into the computer for reference or use.[69]

Further, 'data held in a computer' is defined to include:

(a) data held in any removable data storage device for the time being held in a computer
(b) data held in a data storage device on a computer network of which the computer forms a part.

'Data storage device' is in turn defined to mean 'a thing (for example, a disk or file server) containing, or designed to contain, data for use by a computer'.[70] Consequently, the unauthorised access offences apply to data which is held in a data storage device such as a USB memory stick, external memory or CD-Rom, so long as it is held 'in' the computer at the relevant time. If it is not held in the computer, the relevant offences relate to damage to the data.[71]

---

66 Criminal Code (Cth), s. 476.2(3).
67 S 476.1(2). This formulation was preferred over the potentially narrower 'use of a computer' to cause access: MCCOC, *Computer Offences* (2001), p. 133.
68 MCCOC, *Computer Offences* (2001), p. 133.
69 *Ibid.*, p. 121. The original proposed definition specifically referred to data 'entered or copied into the computer': p. 122. The current formulation is the same as that found in the now repealed s. 76A Crimes Act 1914 (Cth).
70 Criminal Code (Cth), Dictionary.   71 See p. 114.

On a literal interpretation, it may be argued that an external storage device, connected via a USB cable or Bluetooth, is not held 'in' the computer for these purposes. However, the definition is inclusive and merely reflects common terminology at the time. The definition should be broad enough to extend to data storage devices which are external to the computer but available to it electronically, via cable or wireless connection.[72] 'The offence extends to impairment of data held on discs or other removable data storage devices. Once the device is electronically accessible by a computer, the data held on the device comes within the protective scope of the provisions.'[73]

The definition also extends to data held in a data storage device on a computer network of which the computer forms part. This is the only context in which the term 'computer network' is used and the term is undefined. It must therefore be given its ordinary meaning, defined in the *Oxford English Dictionary* as a 'network of interconnected computers'. Consequently, any computers that are interconnected form a computer network.

Where the storage device is part of a network, it is enough that the data is electronically accessible by the computer via a network. It does not have to be held in the computer itself, so long as the computer forms part of the network. This would encompass such situations as where the computer forms part of a LAN and data on that network is accessed from a computer. It would also seem to extend to any computer that is accessed via the Internet. That is, data on any server is data which is held on a data storage device on a computer network of which the computer forms a part.

B. *The United Kingdom*

A broad concept of access is also apparent in the UK provisions which make it an offence to cause a computer to perform any function with intent to secure or enable access. The Law Commission specifically rejected the approach of 'obtaining unauthorised access to a computer'. Although the definition of 'to access' includes to gain access to data held in a computer, it was felt that such terminology may nonetheless prove problematic. First, it may be thought to encompass obtaining physical access to a computer. Secondly, it could be thought to extend to obtaining a hard copy of data stored in a computer. Thirdly, it was felt that such an offence

---

72 MCCOC, *Computer Offences* (2001), p. 120.   73 *Ibid.*, p. 121.

might apply to electronic eavesdropping and thereby go beyond protecting the integrity of computers to protecting the confidentiality of data.[74] In contrast, the term 'causes a computer to perform any function' covers any manipulation and is likely to withstand technological change. It also excludes mere physical access and mere scrutiny of data where there is no interaction with the computer.[75]

The phrase is extremely broad as there is no limitation on the manner in which the defendant causes the computer to perform any function. Simply switching a computer on, or attempting to enter a password would both be encompassed by the terms of the section.[76] Equally, the person who tries to access a computer remotely will invariably cause it to perform a function. In fact, any input to a computer will cause that computer to function at some level. So long as it is accompanied by the relevant intent, it may also apply to the sending of malware as the installation of such programs necessarily requires the computer to perform a function. It may even apply to the interception of data as the person is causing the computer to function with the intention of securing access to data which he or she is not authorised to access.[77]

C. Canada

In contrast, under the Canadian provisions it is an offence where a person 'obtains, directly or indirectly, any computer service' or 'uses or causes to be used, directly or indirectly, a computer system' with intent to commit a specified offence.[78]

The scope of this offence was considered by the Alberta Provincial Court in *R* v. *Forsythe (R)*.[79] The defendant was found to be in possession of hard-copy printouts of criminal records obtained from the Royal Canadian Mounted Police and the Edmonton Police Service. The printouts had been obtained by two others, Curtis and Wagner. Curtis was a civilian employee of the police service who had obtained the printouts directly from the computer at the request of Wagner.

It was held that there was insufficient evidence on which a jury could convict the defendant of obtaining a computer service under s. 342.1(1)(a). The verb 'obtains' is used in its active sense of gaining or attaining possession, rather than the passive action of having or

---

74 Law Commission, *Computer Misuse* (1989), [3.22]–[3.25].   75 *Ibid.*, [3.26].
76 *Ibid.*, [3.19].   77 Wasik, *Crime and the Computer*, pp. 91–2.
78 Criminal Code (Can), s. 342.1(1)(a)(c).   79 1992 A. R. LEXIS 4568.

possessing, and is modified by the adverbs 'directly or indirectly' and the phrase 'fraudulently and without colour of right'.[80] On these facts it could be said that Curtis obtained the service directly, and Wagner did so indirectly (and in fact pleaded guilty). However, the defendant in this case was merely in possession of the printouts. It was held that the word 'indirectly' does not encompass merely being in possession of the products of a computer service. The offence only extends to those who actively obtain the service, directly or indirectly, fraudulently and without right.[81]

It therefore seems that 'obtaining' for these purposes requires that the defendant must have been able to 'gain' something. This is consistent with its classification as a property offence, the gravamen of the offence being the 'taking' or use of the service without authorisation.[82] Consequently, attempting to guess a password but failing would not be within the offence as the person had not in fact obtained a service.

Such a limitation arguably does not apply to the offence of using or causing to be used, directly or indirectly, a computer system with intent to commit a specified offence.[83] This section would appear to be aimed primarily at the use of computer networks with the intention that one of the other specified offences be committed. There is no need to establish that the other offence has been committed, only that the system was used with that intention. It may therefore be argued that any 'use' of the computer accompanied by the relevant intention should be an offence, irrespective of whether the use was 'successful' or not.

Alternatively, if 'use' is given its ordinary meaning of to 'employ or make use of (an article, etc.), especially for a profitable end or purpose; to utilize, turn to account',[84] then the scope of the offence may be limited to those circumstances where the defendant has used the computer in a qualitative rather than literal sense.

This interpretation of the word 'use' was adopted by the House of Lords, albeit in the context of use of data rather than a computer. In *R* v. *Brown*[85] the defendant, a police officer, was alleged to have accessed the national police computer for improper purposes. He had not accessed the computer personally, but had asked another officer to do so and then read the information off the screen. The question for the court was whether this

---

80 *Ibid.*, at [4] per Ketchum PCJ.   81 *Ibid.*, at [9].
82 This view was expressed in relation to a similar Western Australian offence which is also
    found amongst property offences: *Hull* v. *WA* [2005] WASCA 194 at [4] per Wheeler JA.
83 Criminal Code (Can), s. 342.1(1)(c).   84 *Oxford English Dictionary*.
85 [1996] AC 543.

constituted 'use' of that data within the meaning of s. 5 Data Protection Act 1984 (UK).

Their Lordships approved of the interpretation given by the Court of Appeal that before a person can be said to have 'used' the data it is first necessary to do something to it, and not merely to access it.[86] As the word 'use' is not defined, it must be given its natural and ordinary meaning. Synonyms of the verb 'use' are to 'make use of', or to 'employ for a purpose'.[87] Here the word is used in relation to 'data', and a distinction may be drawn between retrieval of data and the use of it. 'Retrieving data from a computer seems to me a use of the computer rather than a use of the data.'[88] Although information in a computer-readable form is data for the purposes of the act, in all but the most exceptional case such information must first be retrieved. 'In such a case, the retrieval is not the use; it is simply a prerequisite of the use.'[89]

D. The United States

In the United States, the term 'access' is undefined and there is surprisingly little federal authority on point.[90] It does appear that 'access' is used in its active sense of 'to gain access to', or 'to exercise the freedom or ability to make use of something',[91] and so receiving information does not constitute gaining access to a computer.

A narrow view of 'access' was applied by the Supreme Court of Kansas in *State of Kansas* v. *Allen*.[92] The defendant was alleged to have used his computer and modem to call various modems belonging to the telecommunications company Southwestern Bell. The computer was programmed to dial random numbers and to determine whether the call was answered by a person or a modem. Ordinarily, this practice is engaged in to facilitate further attempts at unauthorised access. In this case it seems to have been done out of curiosity. The defendant did not interfere with data on the system, cause it to perform any function or interfere with its operation. Nor was there any evidence that he had attempted to enter a password when prompted. All of the calls but one lasted less than one minute.

---

86 *Ibid.*, at 548–9 per Lord Goff of Chieveley.   87 *Ibid.*
88 *Ibid.*, at 561 per Lord Hoffman, with whom Lord Browne-Wilkinson agreed.
89 *Ibid.*, 549 per Lord Goff of Chieveley.
90 This is apparently also the case with most US computer crime statutes: Kerr, 'Cybercrime's scope', 1621.
91 *Role Models Am., Inc.* v. *Jones*, 305 F Supp 2d 564, 567 (D Maryland 2004).
92 260 Kan 107 (SC Kans 1996).

The defendant was charged with intentionally and without authorisation gaining or attempting to gain access to a computer.[93] Although 'access' was defined in the statute,[94] the court held that this definition was void for vagueness and instead applied the plain and ordinary meaning of the word. 'Access' is defined in Webster's dictionary as 'freedom or ability to obtain or make use of'.[95] Applying this definition, it was held that until the defendant went beyond the initial prompts indicating that connection had been made, and entered appropriate passwords, he did not have the ability to make use of the computers or to obtain anything and so could not be said to have gained access as that term is commonly understood.[96]

A more expansive view was adopted by the Supreme Court of Washington in *State of Washington* v. *Riley*.[97] The defendant used his computer to obtain long-distance phone calls without payment. The placement of calls was controlled by a computer switch, and it was accepted that this switch was a 'computer' within the terms of the statute.[98] Legitimate users of the phone service would need to dial a six-digit access code before they could use the service. The defendant's computer was programmed to dial six randomly selected numbers followed by a long-distance number. By noting which calls were connected, the defendant could determine that the six numbers matched the access code of a legitimate user.

The defendant was convicted, inter alia, of two counts of computer trespass. This offence required proof that he had, without authorisation, intentionally gained access to a computer system.[99] The court rejected the defendant's argument that his conduct was equivalent to making a telephone call. 'Access' is defined in the section as 'to approach . . . or otherwise make use of any resources of a computer, directly or by electronic means'.[100] By causing the computer to dial the numbers he was 'approach[ing]' or 'otherwise mak[ing] use of any resources of a computer'.[101] It was irrelevant that he had not entered, read, inserted or copied data from that computer.

In reaching this conclusion, the court did not appear to have the same difficulty as others with the term 'approach', apparently interpreting the

93 KSA 21–3755(b)(1).
94 KSA 21–3755(a)(1). This definition is similar to that used in a number of state statutes: Kerr, 'Cybercrime's scope', n. 105.
95 *Webster's New Collegiate Dictionary* (1977), p. 7.
96 *State of Kansas* v. *Allen*, 260 Kan 107, 114 (SC Kans 1996).
97 *State* v. *Riley*, 846 P 2d 1365 (SC Wash 1993).   98 *Ibid.*, 1373.
99 RCW 9A.52.110.   100 RCW 9A.52.010(6).
101 *State of Washington* v. *Riley*, 846 P 2d 1365, 1373 (SC Wash 1993).

word as referring to an electronic rather than physical approach.[102] It is not clear, however, whether the defendant's actions were seen as an approach or 'making use' of the computer, the court simply accepting that the defendant had accessed the computer on either or both of these bases.

The issue was considered in a federal, albeit civil, context in *America Online Inc.* v. *National Health Care Discount Inc.*[103] The plaintiff, AOL, alleged that the defendant had employed another organisation to send bulk emails advertising its services and to harvest email addresses from newsgroups and other sources. It was argued that the harvesting of AOL email addresses and the sending of unsolicited emails to AOL subscribers was in violation of AOL's terms of service and constituted unauthorised access to AOL's computers contrary to 18 USC § 1030(a)(5)(C). At the time, this provision related to 'intentionally accessing a protected computer without authorization, and as a result of such conduct, causing damage'.[104]

In denying the plaintiff's motion for summary judgment, the court held that in harvesting the email addresses of AOL members, and sending bulk emails to AOL members, the emailers exercised the freedom or ability to make use of AOL's computers. They had therefore accessed those computers:

> For purposes of the CFAA, when someone sends an e-mail message from his or her own computer, and the message then is transmitted through a number of other computers until it reaches its destination, the sender is making use of all of those computers, and is therefore 'accessing' them.[105]

The same argument may be made in relation to a port scan or other electronic attempt to communicate with a computer in order to gain access. Even if such an attempt is 'unsuccessful', the scan will nonetheless elicit a response from the computer and, in the same way as a failed

102 Cf the court in *Allen* which noted more general criticisms of the use of 'approach' in a definition of 'access'. In particular, the US Department of Justice had commented that if taken literally it could apply to any unauthorised physical proximity to a computer: *State of Kansas* v. *Allen*, 260 Kan 107, 113 (SC Kans 1996).
103 121 F Supp 2d 1255 (ND Iowa 2001).
104 AOL's computers were clearly protected computers as they were used in interstate or foreign commerce; *ibid.*, 1272.
105 *Ibid.*, cited with approval in *Four Seasons Hotels & Resorts B.V.* v. *Consorcio Barr, S.A.*, 267 F Supp 2d 1268, 1322–3 (SD Flor 2003). This is contrary to the view expressed in the Cybercrime Convention that access 'does not include the mere sending of an e-mail message or file to that system': Cybercrime Convention, Explanatory Report, [46].

password attempt, may be argued to constitute access. For example, in *Moulton and Network Installation Computer Services, Inc. v. VC3*[106] the plaintiff had performed an unauthorised port scan[107] and throughput test[108] on the defendant's servers. The plaintiff brought actions under both the Georgia Computer Systems Protection Act and the CFAA, claiming that such tests could slow down a network.

Both actions failed on the basis that damage could not be made out, it being conceded that any impact was negligible at best and would not be noticeable to the company or its customers.[109] However, putting questions of damage to one side the court specifically stated that the defendant may nonetheless have been subject to criminal prosecution under the Georgia statute.[110] In the context of the CFAA, the element of access appears to have been assumed, the court focusing solely on the question of damage. It therefore seems arguable that a port scan or throughput test, even if 'unsuccessful', nonetheless constitutes access.

Given differences in jurisdiction and statutory terms it is difficult to distil a general principle of 'access' from these cases. Professor Kerr argues that they illustrate both internal and external perspectives of this issue. *Allen* may be seen as reflecting an internal perspective, whereby access is only gained once the person is able to 'enter' and gain access to the files 'inside' the computer.[111] In contrast, *AOL* and *Riley* reflect an external perspective whereby an email passing though a computer or simply dialling and making contact with the computer is sufficient to constitute access.

While this analysis is helpful, there seems to be a more fundamental distinction at play, based on the degree to which the defendant is able to 'use' the computer. It may be noted that each of the definitions considered, dictionary or statutory, refer to 'making use' of a computer. In applying this concept, a qualitative distinction seems to be drawn between two different meanings of 'use'.

The first is 'use' in the literal sense, where any interaction with the computer by way of inputs is a 'use' of that computer. This broader perspective is illustrated by *Riley* as in that case the dialling of the numbers

---

106 2000 US Dist LEXIS 19916 (ND Ga).   107 See p. 29.
108 A throughput test sends information across a network to test the speed with which a computer processes data: *Moulton and Network Installation Computer Services, Inc. v. VC3*, 2000 US Dist LEXIS 19916, [3]–[4] (ND Ga).
109 *Ibid.*, [19]–[21].   110 *Ibid.*, [18]–[20].   111 Kerr, 'Cybercrime's scope', 1625–8.

was sufficient to constitute access. It did not matter that the defendant did not go further and access data or programs in the way that an authorised user could. The input of the numbers caused the computer to respond, and in doing so he had made use of, and therefore accessed, the computer. Under this approach, a failed password attempt or a hacker who endeavours to secure full access but fails would nonetheless have 'accessed' the computer.

Under the second approach, 'access' or 'use' is used in a more figurative sense whereby the defendant must be able to 'make use' of the computer in the sense of obtain the use of programs or data. For example, in *Allen* it seems that use is determined by whether the defendant acquires one or more of the rights and privileges of the authorised user. There must be some utility in the action performed, so that a failed password attempt is not access as although the computer may have responded, the defendant was not able to obtain the use of the computer. *AOL* can be interpreted either way as the passing of the email 'through' the computer would arguably constitute use in both the literal and figurative senses.

The broader perspective is advocated by Professor Kerr, who proposes that access should be defined as 'any successful interaction with the computer'.[112] Importantly, the measure of 'success' is objective; the defendant's subjective intention is irrelevant. The question is simply whether the command did what it was intended to do.[113] Consequently, calling up a login prompt would constitute access, even where an incorrect password is used. In refusing 'access', the program is doing what it was intended to do, even if from the defendant's perspective the attempt was 'unsuccessful'. Sending an email to a computer, viewing a webpage, all would constitute access. In effect, access becomes synonymous with use in its broad sense.

It is suggested that such an approach is correct. Convergence of technology, the use of ADSL and broadband, wireless, internet and the imprecise nature of networks all create an environment in which it is more accurate to describe 'use' of a computer rather than access to a computer.[114] Adopting a broad definition helps to avoid technical and often arbitrary arguments about what constitutes access, and appropriately focuses on the remaining elements, which determine whether the alleged conduct is in fact criminal. It is these elements that determine the criminality of the conduct and help avoid over-breadth. It is also consistent with the

112 *Ibid.*, 1646–7.   113 *Ibid.*, n. 226.   114 *Ibid.*, 1641.

approach adopted in other jurisdictions, most notably Australia and the UK, where the conduct element of the offence is defined very broadly.

While such an approach is arguably preferable, there are aspects of the federal provision that could indicate otherwise. In particular, the provision specifically provides that it is an offence to attempt to commit these offences.[115] It may be thought that if 'use' is interpreted broadly there is little, if any, conduct that would constitute an attempt to access. One situation may be the defendant who is caught at the keyboard about to type in the password but is stopped before a keystroke is made. Even assuming such a situation could be proved, it comes very close to the criticised element of 'approaching' a computer.[116] Alternatively, there is the person who tries to gain remote access but for technical reasons is unable to communicate with the target computer at all. Even on a broad interpretation, such a person has not accessed the computer but has nonetheless attempted to do so.

The role of attempt in this context is, however, more significant than may be first thought, so long as it is remembered that what is punished is an attempt to commit the completed offence, not an attempt to access the computer. Therefore, the person who gains access, in the broad sense, but fails to obtain information for example, is guilty of an attempt, not the completed offence. This seems consistent with the statutory scheme where most provisions require an additional element to be proved rather than simple access. The exception is § 1030(a)(4) which may punish simple access to government computers.[117] Any interaction without authorisation could be an offence under this provision, and there would seem little role for the offence of attempt other than the person who tries to gain access but is stopped before he or she has any interaction with the computer.

4. Unauthorised

Central to all of these offences is a requirement that the access was 'unauthorised'. Under the Cybercrime Convention, there is no offence where the conduct is 'authorised by the owner or other right holder of the system or part of it (such as for the purpose of authorised testing or protection of the computer system concerned)'.[118] Although the precise terminology varies, the essential concept is the same in each jurisdiction.

---

115 18 USC § 1030(b).   116 See n. 101.   117 See p. 99.
118 Cybercrime Convention, Explanatory Report, [47].

In Australia, the provision specifically states that access to data held in a computer is unauthorised if the person is not entitled to cause that access.[119] In Canada, the equivalent requirement is that the offence must be committed 'fraudulently and without colour of right'.[120] 'Without colour of right' is a general term which describes those situations where the defendant held an honest belief in a state of facts which, if it actually existed, would at law justify or excuse the act done.[121] Where such a belief is held, it is therefore necessary to determine whether the defendant would have been entitled to perform the relevant act.

In the UK, access of any kind by any person to any program or data held in a computer is unauthorised if:

(a) he is not himself entitled to control[122] access of the kind in question to the program or data and

(b) he does not have consent to access by him of the kind in question to the program[123] or data from any person who is so entitled.[124]

In relation to an offence under s. 3, an act done in relation to a computer is unauthorised if:

> the person doing the act (or causing it to be done):
>
> (a) is not himself a person who has responsibility for the computer and is entitled to determine whether the act may be done; and
>
> (b) does not have consent to the fact from any such person.[125]

Although the term 'without authorisation' is not defined in the US provision, it has been held that 'authorisation' is 'of common usage, without any technical or ambiguous meaning' and accordingly there is no need to instruct the jury as to its meaning.[126] Other cases have looked to the dictionary definition of 'authorise': 'to empower; to give a right or authority to act. To endow with authority or effective legal power, warrant, or

---

119 Criminal Code (Cth), s. 476.2(1).
120 The meaning of fraudulently is discussed below at p. 94.
121 R v. DeMarco (1973) 13 CCC (2d) 369 at 362 per Martin JA.
122 The word 'control' is not used in the physical sense of the ability to operate or manipulate the computer: R v. Bow Street Metropolitan Stipendiary Magistrate and anor, ex parte Government of the United States of America [2000] 2 AC 216 at 225 per Lord Hobhouse of Woodborough.
123 Note that 'program' includes part of a program; s. 17(10).
124 Computer Misuse Act, s. 17(5).
125 Computer Misuse Act, s. 17(8), as inserted by Police and Justice Act 2006, Sch. 14, [29(4)]. The s. 3 offence is discussed at p. 104.
126 US v. Morris, 928 F 2d 504, 511 (2nd Cir 1991).

right. To permit a thing to be done in the future.'[127] Consequently, to act without authorisation is to act without a lawful entitlement to engage in the relevant conduct.

In each jurisdiction it is clear that these provisions are not aimed solely at outsiders gaining unauthorised access, but also insiders who exceed authorised access.[128] It is, however, important to consider the question of authorisation in relation to the conduct which is prohibited under the section.

In Australia and the UK, the question of authorisation relates to access to the relevant data or program. In these jurisdictions the focus is therefore on the program or data that is accessed and whether that access is authorised. The access to data is not limited to initial access to the computer and may be committed subsequent to an authorised access. The same approach is adopted in Canada where it is the obtaining/use of the computer service/system which must be without right.

For example, a computer data operator accesses his or her computer for legitimate purposes with no intent to secure unauthorised access to data. However, he or she subsequently forms the intention to access unauthorised data and is aware that such access is unauthorised. Once the defendant causes the computer to function in order to affect that access the offence is committed notwithstanding the initial authorised access.

In contrast, the US provisions focus on access to a *computer*. This is an important distinction as the focus is on the defendant's interaction with the computer rather than with specific data. It may therefore be argued that once the defendant has authorised access to a computer, he or she cannot be liable for subsequent access to data even if that access is unauthorised. Such access would be of data, not of a computer.

For example, in *Briggs* v. *State of Maryland*[129] the defendant was a computer programmer and systems administrator for an investment company. He was entrusted with the management of the entire computer system and, as part of his responsibilities, entered data in the computer system and placed passwords on the files to secure the data. Following a dispute, Briggs resigned and shortly afterwards the company realised that a

---

127 *Briggs* v. *State of Maryland*, 704 A 2d 904, 909 (CA MD 1998), citing *Black's Law Dictionary*, 6th edn (1990), pp. 133–4. Also see *State of Washington* v. *Olson*, 735 P 2d 1362, 1364 (CA Wash 1987), citing *Webster's Third New International Dictionary* (1981), p. 146.

128 *DPP* v. *Murdoch* [1993] 1 VR 406 at 409 per Hayne J; Law Commission, *Computer Misuse* (1989), [3.5]; *US* v. *Morris*, 928 F 2d 504, 510–11 (2nd Cir 1991).

129 704 A 2d 904 (CA MD 1998).

number of files had been secured by passwords known only to the defendant. It was alleged that Briggs had changed the passwords and moved the files to a folder entitled 'ha-ha he-he' two days before a meeting to discuss his employment.

Briggs was charged, inter alia, with computer trespass under the Maryland Code.[130] This offence required the prosecution to prove that the defendant: (1) intentionally and wilfully accessed a computer or computer system; (2) that the access was without authorisation; and (3) the access was with the intent to interrupt the operation of the computer services. The evidence was that Briggs was authorised to access the computer within the terms of the statute. In particular he was authorised to enter data and place passwords on files. 'The statute makes no reference to authorized users who exceed the scope of their authority. If the Legislature intended the statute to cover employees who exceeded the scope of their authority or who misused their authority, it could have done so explicitly.'[131] His conviction was therefore reversed.

Similar issues arose in the federal context in *US* v. *Morris*,[132] the facts of which were outlined above.[133] Morris argued that his access was not unauthorised as he was authorised to access several federal interest computers at Cornell, Harvard and Berkeley. At most, he had exceeded authorised access which at the time was not specifically punished by the section. The court found that there were some computers accessed by the defendant that he was clearly not authorised to access. In other cases where he was merely exceeding authorised access, the worm which was disseminated by Morris was designed to, and did, access computers that he was clearly not authorised to access.[134]

The matter was subsequently put beyond doubt by the amendment of 18 USC § 1030 to include 'exceeding authorized access', the meaning of which is discussed below.[135]

Unauthorised

Despite the variations in terminology, it can be seen that each jurisdiction requires an analysis of whether the defendant was authorised to engage in the relevant conduct. A clear example of authorised access would be where

---

130 Art. 27, § 146(c)(2).
131 *Briggs* v. *State of Maryland*, 704 A 2d 904, 910 (CA MD 1998).
132 928 F 2d 504 (2nd Cir 1991).   133 See pp. 33–4.
134 *US* v. *Morris*, 928 F 2d 504 (2nd Cir 1991). Also see *People* v. *Lawton*, (1996) 48 Cal App 4th Supp 11.
135 See p. 85.

the defendant was acting under a warrant or similar legal authority.[136] More commonly, the conduct will have been authorised by the owner or other right holder, or the computer is generally accessible to the public.[137] Of course, a person who obtains authorisation by force or fraud would obviously be acting without authorisation.

There are broadly two ways in which authorisation may be restricted or denied: by code and by contract.[138] Regulation by code is where the owner[139] places some form of technical barrier which restricts access to the computer, for example an account which requires the entering of a username and password. Where the defendant bypasses such a restriction, by guessing the password or by using technical means to circumvent it, the resulting access will be unauthorised.

In some cases, the restriction by code may malfunction, allowing access to otherwise restricted data. In *Healthcare Advocates, Inc. v. Harding, Earley, Follmer & Frailey*,[140] the defendants were able to access archived images from the defendant's website using an ordinary search engine. They did this by using a website called the 'Wayback Machine', operated by an organisation called the Internet Archive which allowed the user to see what a prior version of a public website looked like. Ordinarily, the material on the plaintiff's website would not have been able to be viewed but, due to a server malfunction, the defendants were able to access what should have been protected information. It was held that they had not exceeded authorised access as the machine allowed them to receive the images. 'The Harding firm got lucky, because the servers were malfunctioning, but getting lucky is not equivalent to exceeding authorized access.'[141]

Regulation by contract is where the owner imposes terms and conditions on access:

> To use a physical-world analogy, the difference between regulation by code and regulation by contract resembles the difference between keeping a stranger out by closing and locking the door and keeping a stranger out by putting up a sign in front of an open front door saying 'strangers may not enter'.[142]

136 Criminal Code (Cth), s. 476.2(4).
137 Cybercrime Convention, Explanatory Report, [47].
138 Kerr, 'Cybercrime's scope', 1644–6.
139 Owner is used generically to refer to any person who has lawful authority to restrict access to the computer.
140 497 F Supp 2d 627, 647 (ED Pa 2007).   141 *Ibid.*, 649 (ED Pa 2007).
142 Kerr, 'Cybercrime's scope', 1646.

Such conditions may be formal or informal, express or implied. Common examples include employment contracts,[143] IT 'acceptable use' policies,[144] a formal agreement entered into with an ISP or 'terms of use' that the user accepts before entering a website.[145] For example, in *America Online, Inc. v LCGM, Inc.*[146] the defendant had an AOL email account and used it, together with special software, to harvest the email addresses of AOL subscribers. Such conduct was specifically prohibited by AOL's terms of service and hence was unauthorised for the purposes of 18 USC § 1030.

An example of the use of § 1030 in relation to breach of terms of use arose in the infamous case of Lori Drew, the 49-year-old mother who adopted a false online persona on the 'MySpace' website. Pretending to be sixteen-year-old 'Josh Evans', Drew led thirteen-year-old Megan Meier to believe that 'Josh' was romantically interested in her. After the 'boy' spurned her, saying amongst other things that 'the world would be a better place without you', the girl hanged herself. Drew was convicted on three misdemeanour counts of accessing a protected computer without authorisation.[147] Her convictions were subsequently overturned by the District Court, the judge noting that otherwise anyone who had ever been in violation of the social networking site's terms of service would be guilty of a misdemeanour.[148]

Authorisation may also be governed by a software licence agreement. For example, access of a program by someone other than the licensee, or access in breach of the license agreement may be unauthorised.[149] In *North Texas Preventive Imaging, LLC v. Harvey Eisenberg MD*,[150] the plaintiffs were a medical diagnostic company that had purchased a computer system from the defendant. Following a dispute over the licensing agreement, the defendants sent an update disk to the plaintiffs, which they duly installed. Unknown to them, the disk contained a disabling code or 'time bomb', which caused the software to become inoperable at a set date and time. The plaintiffs alleged, inter alia, that this was a breach of the CFAA.

---

143 *Hewlett-Packard Co. v. Byd:Sign, Inc.*, 2007 US Dist LEXIS 5323 at [40].
144 *US* v. *Phillips*, 477 F 3d 215 (5th Cir 2007). Also see *Australian Municipal Administrative Clerical and Services Union* v. *Ansett Australia* (2000) 175 ALR 173.
145 So-called 'click through' agreements: Madison 'Rights of access', 447–64.
146 46 F Supp 2d 444, 448 (ED Va 1998).
147 J. Steinhauer, 'Verdict in MySpace suicide case', *New York Times*, 26 November 2008.
148 Associated Press, 'Lori Drew cleared of MySpace cyber-bullying', *The Age*, 3 July 2009.
149 S. Singleton, 'Comment: Computer Misuse Act 1990 – Recent developments' (1993) 57 *Journal of Criminal Law* 181, 182. Also see APIG, *Computer Misuse Act*, [46]–[47].
150 1996 US Dist LEXIS 19990.

Whether or not the use of disabling codes would be in breach of the CFAA was addressed during debate over the 1994 amendments, in response to the concern of software manufacturers that legitimate use of disabling codes may fall within the terms of the section. The senator sponsoring the amendment stated that such use would not be criminalised where they were authorised under a licensing agreement. Although the senator did not state that it would criminalise such codes if not specificied in a lawful licensing agreement, 'this is certainly a reasonable implication of the statement'.[151] Consequently, the provisions of the CFAA could apply to disabling codes where their use was unauthorised and accompanied by the necessary intent.[152]

Of course, contractual limitations will only bind those who are parties to the contract. In *America Online Inc.* v *National Health Care Discount Inc.*,[153] although emailers had accessed AOL's computers by making use of them, it was not clear that violation of AOL's terms of service would render that access unauthorised. The court raised two questions but had heard insufficient argument to answer them.[154] First, although AOL members clearly have authority to access the AOL network, does their access become unauthorised if they do so but then breach the terms of service?[155]

The answer to this question would seem to depend on the approach taken in the particular jurisdiction. In those jurisdictions where the focus is on access to data then the question of authorisation must be asked in relation to each access. Even where the initial access is authorised, the subsequent conduct that breaches the terms of conduct is clearly unauthorised. In the United States where the prohibition relates to access of a computer, it would seem that subsequent breach of the terms of service does not render the initial access unauthorised. Such circumstances must, as in this case, be treated as 'exceeds authorised access'.[156]

The second question is what impact do the AOL terms of service have on the use of AOL by non-members?[157] As to use of the network by non-members, it would seem that if the terms of service are not binding on non-members, then they will have no impact on the question of autho-risation under either perspective. The issue is not so much whether the terms of service are binding on non-members, but the fact that they are

---

151 *Ibid.*, at [15].   152 *Ibid.*, at [16].
153 121 F Supp 2d 1255 (ND Iowa 2001). The facts of this case are discussed at p. 67 above.
154 *Ibid.*, 899.   155 *Ibid.*, 1273.
156 *Ibid.*, 1276. The concept of 'exceeds authorised access' is discussed below at p. 85.
157 *Ibid.*, 1273.

not directed at non-members. In such cases there is no express authori-- sation/prohibition of the particular conduct.

Contractual limitations will also depend upon the express or implied terms of the limitation. In *Register.com Inc.* v. *Verio Inc.*,[158] the plaintiff was a domain-name registrar, but also offered customers other related services. All accredited domain-name registrars are required to enter into an agreement with the Internet Corporation for Assigned Names and Numbers (ICANN) agreeing to provide an online, interactive database containing the names and contact information of customers who regis-ter domain names through the registrar. The database was made freely accessible to the public, subject to terms and conditions for use, which stated that the data could be used for any lawful purpose except spam or to enable high-volume, automated, electronic processes. Verio Inc. was a competitor of the plaintiff and, in order to market more effectively, used a 'robot' to access the database and collect the contact information of customers who had recently registered a domain name.

In determining the plaintiff's claim under the CFAA, the court held that the use of the search robot did not breach the terms and conditions. Although the robot was involved in harvesting the information, it did not use it, nor did it engage in 'high-volume, automated, electronic processes'. It simply deposited the information in a database. The court held that the use of the robot was nonetheless unauthorised as since the date of the lawsuit it was clear that Register.com did not consent to Verio's use of a search robot and Verio was on notice of that fact.[159]

In other cases, it may be questionable whether the restriction on access has been effectively communicated. For example, in *CompuServe Inc.* v. *Cyber Promotions, Inc.*,[160] the plaintiffs had notified the defendants that they were prohibited from using its computer equipment to process and store unsolicited email. This restriction was communicated by an online notice denying unauthorised parties the use of CompuServe equipment to send unsolicited electronic mail messages. Although the court consid-ered that it was arguable that this policy statement may be insufficiently communicated when merely posted online, in this case the invitation had been specifically revoked in relation to the defendants who were expressly notified that they were no longer entitled to use CompuServe's equipment for those purposes.[161]

---

158 126 F Supp 2d 238, 238–49 (SD NY 2000).
159 *Ibid.*, 249–51. Also see *Register.com Inc.* v. *Verio Inc.*, 356 F 3d 393, 404–5 (2nd Cir 2004).
160 962 F Supp 1015 (SD Oho 1997).   161 *Ibid.*, 1024.

It is suggested that there are two separate issues here. The first is whether the access was in fact authorised. The notice in such a case is clear evidence that the access was unauthorised. The second issue is whether the defendant was aware that it was unauthorised. This is addressed in the context of the fault element, and is an important limitation on the breadth of the offence.[162]

Authorisation may relate to certain equipment, but not others. In *Ellis* v. *DPP*,[163] the defendant was a former university student. It was personally explained to him that as a graduate member of the university library he was entitled to use only open-access university computers. Nonetheless, on three occasions he browsed the Internet using non-open-access university computers that had not been logged-off by their previous users. Although admitting that he did not have a password, he claimed he had done nothing wrong and drew an analogy with reading a discarded newspaper. The defendant's convictions under s.1 Computer Misuse Act were upheld. He had caused a computer to perform a function with intent to secure access to any programme or data held in any computer, he was not authorised to do so and he was aware that he was not authorised to do so.

In other cases, authorisation is granted by reference to particular circumstances. For example, authorisation may be granted only while the person has a particular status. In *Shurgard Storage Centers, Inc.* v. *Safeguard Self Storage, Inc.*,[164] the plaintiff and defendant were competitors in the self-storage business. The plaintiff alleged that the defendant had engaged in a systematic scheme to lure away several of the plaintiff's key employees in order to obtain the plaintiff's trade secrets. In particular, one employee, a Mr Leland, while employed by the plaintiff but acting as an agent for the defendant, emailed various trade secrets and proprietary information of the plaintiff to the defendant. It was held that 'the authority of an agent terminates if, without knowledge of the principal, he acquires adverse interests or if he is otherwise guilty of a serious breach of loyalty to the principal'.[165] So, on these facts the conduct of the employee was without authorisation once he was acting as an agent of the defendant.

The concept of authorisation is particularly difficult when many computers are openly accessible via the Internet. Although the maintenance

162 See p. 92.
163 [2002] EWHC 135. Also see *Ellis* v. *DPP* [2001] EWHC Admin 362.
164 119 F Supp 2d 1121 (WD Wash 2001).
165 *Ibid.*, 1125, citing the *Restatement (Second) of Agency*, § 112 (1958).

of a public website implies consent to access by other users, it has been held that the fact that a login page may be viewed by the public does not amount to a general authorisation to the public to access all material on that site. Access to restricted sections of the website must be given by those who administer the site.[166]

More difficult is the question of consent to receiving unsolicited communications. In *R v. Lennon*,[167] the defendant was charged under the earlier version of s. 3(1) Computer Misuse Act with causing an unauthorised modification to a computer belonging to his former employer with intent to impair the contents of the computer.[168] The prosecution case was that the defendant used a 'mail-bombing' program downloaded from the Internet to send approximately 5 million emails to his employer. Most of the emails purported to come from the company's HR manager, and were copied to a number of other employees.

The prosecution case was that by sending the emails the defendant caused unauthorised modifications by adding data to the computers. He was aware that he was not authorised to cause these modifications and intended to hinder or prevent access to the computers by overwhelming them with the emails.[169] The defendant admitted sending the emails in order to cause a 'bit of a mess up' in the company, but did not intend to cause damage to the company.

The trial judge dismissed the charge on the basis that the sending of the emails was not unauthorised. The Divisional Court allowed the appeal and remitted the case to the trial judge. At the time, s. 17(8) provided that a modification is unauthorized if the person whose act causes it is not himself entitled to determine whether the modification should be made, and he does not have consent to the modification from any person who is so entitled.[170] Clearly the defendant did not have authority to authorise the modification, but did he have the consent of another person who was so entitled?

It was accepted that ordinarily the owner of a computer that is able to receive emails is taken to impliedly consent to the sending of emails to the computer.[171] An analogy may be drawn with the implied consent by a householder to members of the public to walk up the path to his or her door when they have a legitimate reason for doing so, or to using a private mail box. However, such implied consent is not without limitations. 'The

---

166 *US v. Phillips*, 477 F 3d 215, 220–1 (5th Cir 2007).   167 [2006] EWHC 1201.
168 The current offence is discussed at p. 104.   169 *Ibid.*, at [5] per Jack J.
170 The current wording of s. 17(8) is found at p. 71 above.   171 *Ibid.*, at [9].

householder does not consent to a burglar coming up his path. Nor does he consent to having his letterbox choked with rubbish.'[172]

In the computer context, without defining the precise limits of the implied consent, it was held that such consent does not extend to emails that are not sent for the purpose of communication with the owner, but that are sent for the purpose of interrupting the proper operation and use of the computer system:

> I, for my part, see a clear distinction between the receipt of e-mails which the recipient merely does not want but which do not overwhelm or otherwise harm the server, and the receipt of bulk e-mails which do overwhelm it. It may be that the recipient is to be taken to have consented to the receipt of the former if he does not configure the server so as to exclude them. But, in my judgment, he does not consent to receiving e-mails sent in a quantity and at a speed which are likely to overwhelm the server. Such consent is not to be implied from the fact that the server has an open, as opposed to a restricted, configuration.[173]

The court went on to state that in determining implied consent, the defendant's conduct must be considered as a whole, and not on an email-by-email basis. The defence submitted that if there was some point at which the sending of emails became unauthorised by reason of their number, then there could be no certainty in the law because that point could not be sufficiently identified.[174] The court rejected this argument as here the emails were unauthorised from the beginning and so the issue did not arise.

Although his Honour Justice Jack went on to say that even if the circumstances were different, he would not have accepted this submission, no analysis was given. Therefore, the issue of at what point the sending of emails become unauthorised was avoided. If the previous reasoning was accepted, presumably we imagine at what point the owner would say 'enough, no more!' Another approach might be the point at which it caused impairment to the owner's computer – although the offence does not require impairment to be caused, only modification accompanied by an intention to cause impairment.

Finally, it was held that the emails were unauthorised because they purported to come from a person who had not sent them or authorised sending them. In this context, the court applied the reasoning of the Divisional Court in *Zezev and Yarimaka* v. *Governor of HM Prison Brixton*

---

172 *Ibid.*   173 *Ibid.*, at [14] per Keene LJ.   174 *Ibid.*, at [11] per Jack J.

and anor[175] and held that there was no implied consent to receiving malicious emails purporting to come from the HR manager.[176] However, not all emails which purport to come from one person but in fact come from another are necessarily unauthorised. For example, a joke email sent with no malicious intent might still fall within the implied consent of the owner.[177]

Similar issues have arisen in the United States, primarily in the context of companies trying to prevent spam emails. Prior to the enactment of anti-spam legislation, such cases typically involved actions for trespass to chattels. Such an action must fail if the plaintiff consented to the defendant's actions. Although it has been held that the '"cluster of ideas" associated with common law "trespass" cannot be imported into the CFAA',[178] these cases contain useful observations in relation to the concept of authorisation for unsolicited communications.

In *CompuServe Inc.* v. *Cyber Promotions, Inc.*,[179] it was held that one of the features of an email service is that it allows the receipt of messages from anyone on the Internet. Consequently, 'there is at least a tacit invitation for anyone on the Internet to utilize plaintiff's computer equipment to send e-mail to its subscribers'.[180] It therefore seems that where there is no express or implied limitation, there is a general invitation to communicate with a networked computer, even where that message is unwelcome. As stated in *Intel Corporation* v. *Hamidi*:

> Intel connected its e-mail system to the Internet and permitted its employees to make use of this connection both for business and, to a reasonable extent, for their own purposes. In doing so, the company necessarily contemplated the employees' receipt of unsolicited as well as solicited communications from other companies and individuals. That some communications would, because of their contents, be unwelcome to Intel management was virtually inevitable.[181]

Implicit in this statement is the limitation, already noted in the UK context, that the implied licence does not extend to emails which are sent maliciously or to cause impairment.

---

175 [2002] 2 Cr App R 33. See p. 115 below.
176 *R* v. *Lennon* [2006] EWHC 1201 at [12] per Jack J.   177 *Ibid.*
178 *In re America Online, Inc. Version 5.0 Software Litigation*, 168 F Supp 2d 1359, 1371 (SD Fa 2001) citing *Carter* v. *US* 530 US 255, 265 (2000).
179 962 F Supp 1015 (SD Ohio 1997).   180 *Ibid.*, 1022–4.
181 30 Cal 4th 1342, 1359–60 (Cal SC 2003).

The scope of the implied licence was considered in *EF Cultural Travel BV* v. *Zefer Corporation and Explorica, Inc.*[182] A preliminary injunction was granted against Zefer Corporation to prevent it from using a 'scraper' tool[183] to collect pricing information from the plaintiff's website. The injunction was granted on the basis that this practice breached various provisions of the CFAA, and went beyond the 'reasonable expectations' of ordinary users.[184]

In reviewing the injunction, such a test was rejected by the First Circuit on the basis that the term 'reasonable expectations' is highly imprecise and likely to lead to litigation. Rejection of such a test did not reflect a presumption of open access to Internet information. Public website providers can easily spell out explicitly what is forbidden, for example by placing express statements on the website, including statements precluding the use of scrapers. Lack of authorisation may also be implicit, as where there is password protection.[185] '[W]ith rare exceptions, public website providers ought to say just what non-password protected access they purport to forbid.'[186] The scraper was simply a more efficient way of doing what could be done manually, and there was no suggestion that EF could preclude their competitor's access to their website.

As with any implied licence, it can of course be revoked. Just as a person may put a notice on their driveway prohibiting entry, computer users may prohibit certain conduct in relation to their computers. For example, in *eBay, Inc.* v. *Bidder's Edge, Inc.*,[187] the online auction site eBay brought civil actions against the defendant for unauthorised use of 'robots' on its website.[188] That the use of such devices on eBay's site was prohibited was communicated in three ways. First, users of the eBay site had to register and agree to the eBay User Agreement, which, inter alia, prohibits the use of 'any robot, spider, other automatic device, or manual process to monitor or copy our web pages or the content contained herein without our prior expressed written permission'. Second, the eBay site used 'robot exclusion headers', which is a message, sent to computers programmed to detect and respond to such headers, that eBay does not permit unauthorised robotic activity. Third, eBay expressly told the defendants to cease listing information about eBay auctions on its website.

---

182 318 F 3d 58 (1st Cir 2003).   183 See p. 37.
184 *EF Cultural Travel BV* v. *Zefer Corporation and Explorica, Inc.*, 318 F 3d 58, 62 (1st Cir 2003).
185 *Ibid.*, 62–3.   186 *Ibid.*, 64.   187 100 F Supp 2d 1058 (ND Cal 2000).
188 See pp. 36–7.

The court rejected the defendant's argument that it could not trespass eBay's website because the site is publicly accessible:

> eBay's servers are private property, conditional access to which eBay grants the public. eBay does not generally permit the type of automated access made by BE. In fact, eBay explicitly notifies automated visitors that their access is not permitted.[189]

In any event, 'eBay repeatedly and explicitly notified BE that its use of eBay's computer system was unauthorized'.[190]

Another test of whether particular access was authorised has been described as the 'intended function test'.[191] This asks whether the defendant used the computer according to its intended function. This test was applied in *Morris*, it being held that even in using those computers that he was entitled to access, Morris' conduct was unauthorised as he did not use them according to their intended function. In particular, although Morris was entitled to access some of the computers, his use of the SENDMAIL and 'finger demon' (*sic*)[192] in order to propagate the virus were without authorisation as he 'did not use either of those features in any way related to their intended function'.[193] In a more recent example, the Fifth Circuit held that the use of a brute-force attack program was 'not an intended use of the [university] network within the understanding of any reasonable computer user and constitutes a method of obtaining unauthorized access to computerized data that he was not permitted to view or use'.[194]

Such a test is fraught with difficulties, most notably determining what is the intended function of the particular program. It would appear that the 'intended function' approach must be based on 'expected norms of intended use or the nature of the relationship established between the computer owner and the user'.[195] Given the multitude of purposes for which computer programs are utilised it would be extremely difficult, if not impossible, to determine such norms. It also detracts attention from the real question, which is whether the defendant was authorised to engage in the relevant conduct.

Another interesting challenge in this context is spyware. While malicious programs will constitute unauthorised intrusion, many forms of

---

189 *eBay, Inc.* v. *Bidder's Edge, Inc.*, 100 F Supp 2d 1058, 1070 (ND Cal 2000).
190 *Ibid.*   191 Kerr, 'Cybercrime's scope', 1596.
192 The correct term is daemon: *ibid.*, n. 138.
193 *US* v. *Morris*, 928 F 2d 504, 510 (2nd Cir 1991).
194 *US* v. *Phillips*, 477 F 3d 215, 220 (5th Cir 2007).
195 *Ibid.*, 219. Kerr, 'Cybercrime's scope', 1632.

spyware are a common, if sometimes unwanted, component of the modern computing environment. Adware may be bundled up with other software programs, while many websites routinely use cookies to monitor browsing patterns.

According to the Cybercrime Convention:

> The application of specific technical tools may result in an access under Article 2, such as the access of a web page, directly or through hypertext links, including deep-links or the application of 'cookies' or 'bots' to locate and retrieve information on behalf of communication. The application of such tools per se is not 'without right'... in particular where the rightholder of the accessed system can be considered to have accepted its application, e.g. in the case of 'cookies' by not rejecting the initial instalment or not removing it.[196]

Where the user is given the opportunity to accept the installation of the program then clearly that access is authorised, although query the extent to which such consent is 'informed'.[197] However, in most cases the user does not expressly consent to the placement of cookies unless their browser is configured to do so. In such cases it could be argued that there is implied consent, although a user may disable cookies and this still does not always prevent their installation. Many users would be completely unaware of the presence of cookies and few if any steps are taken by those who place them there to make users' aware.

Finally, it is important to note the distinction between motive and authorisation. For example, some hackers suggest that their activities are intended to assist rather than harm, and indeed some are employed by companies and government in an effort to test the security of computer systems.[198] However, it is for the owner, not the defendant, to determine what conduct is authorised.[199] This equally applies to those who claim to act with noble motives, for example a person who attacks a website promoting holocaust revisionist material, sites hosting child pornography[200] or those who allegedly act in 'self-defence'.[201]

---

196 Cybercrime Convention, Explanatory Report, [48].
197 APIG, *Computer Misuse Act*, [54].
198 P. S. Ryan, 'War, peace, or stalemate: Wargames, wardialing, wardriving, and the emerging market for hacker ethics' (2004) 9 *Virginia Journal of Law and Technology*, 12.
199 Law Commission, *Computer Misuse* (1989), [2.17].
200 S. W. Brenner, 'Is there such a thing as "virtual crime"?' (2001) 4 *California Criminal Law Review*, 28.
201 MCCOC, *Computer Offences* (2001), pp. 108–9.

Exceeding authorised access

A particular challenge, which arises in each jurisdiction, is where access is authorised for a specific purpose and the defendant exceeds that authorisation, for example the tax-office employee who is authorised to access confidential taxpayer information but does so for personal reasons which he knew to be outside the scope of his authority.[202] The crucial issue in such cases is determining the scope of the authorisation. If the defendant is acting within the scope of the authorisation, then the conduct is authorised. If outside the scope of that authorisation, then the access will be unauthorised.

A useful analogy may be found in the law of burglary, which requires that the defendant entered the relevant property as a trespasser. In *Barker v R*[203] the defendant had been asked to keep an eye on his neighbour's house while the neighbour was away, and for this purpose was told where the spare key was hidden. He took this opportunity to steal a large number of items, but claimed that he had removed the items to protect them and that he had subsequently returned them. The neighbour gave evidence that although Barker had authority to enter his house, he had no authority to remove goods. It was, however, conceded that he would have had his authority to do so if it were necessary for the protection of the goods. Barker appealed his conviction for burglary, one of the elements of which was that the defendant must have entered as a trespasser.[204] It was argued that Barker had not entered as a trespasser as he had the authority of the owner to enter the property.

In dismissing the appeal, the High Court of Australia held that whether or not someone enters as a trespasser depends upon their authority to enter the premises. 'If the right or authority to enter is limited in scope then an entry which is unrelated to the right or authority will amount to a trespass.'[205] It is therefore necessary to determine the express or implied scope of the permission to enter. Where a person has permission to enter for a specific purpose, he or she commits a trespass if the entry is for any other purpose.

The precise terms of the permission to enter, either express or implied, is a question of fact to be determined according to the circumstances of the

---

202 *US* v. *Czubinski*, 106 F 3d 1069 (1st Cir 1997).   203 (1983) 153 CLR 338.
204 Crimes Act 1958 (Vic), s. 76.
205 *Barker* v. *R* (1983) 153 CLR 338 at 342 per Mason J; 358 per Brennan and Deane JJ. Also see *Gross* v. *Wright* [1923] 2 DLR 171 at 185 per Anglin J (with whom Davies CJ agreed) and *R* v. *Jones*; *R* v. *Smith* [1976] 3 All ER 54.

particular case. The broader the terms of the permission, the less likely the person enters as a trespasser. In particular, not all permission to enter is determined by reference to purpose. Where the permission is not limited by reference to purpose, entry within the terms of the permission will not be converted to a trespass merely because the defendant entered for an unlawful purpose.[206] Where the defendant enters for two purposes, one of which is authorised while the other is not, whether there is a trespass will depend on the nature of the permission to enter:

> In such a case, if the permission extends to authorize every entry for the particular purpose, it covers the entry for both purposes since the entry satisfies the requirement that it be for the designated purpose: if the permission extends only to authorize an entry which is exclusively for the particular purpose, entry for both purposes does not satisfy that requirement and is beyond its ambit.[207]

Further, the offence of burglary requires not only that the defendant entered as a trespasser, but that he or she knew, or was at least reckless, as to being a trespasser. Consequently, even though the defendant may enter as a trespasser, if he or she has an honest belief in having permission to enter there can be no burglary:[208]

> A person who enters premises with apparent consent but with intent to steal, such as an ordinary shoplifter, is likely to believe at the time he enters the premises that he has the same right of entry as other persons, notwithstanding the criminal purpose for which he enters.[209]

The application of these principles in a digital context was considered by the Supreme Court of Victoria in *DPP* v. *Murdoch*.[210] The defendant was employed in the information systems department of what was then the State Bank of Victoria. He initially worked in the section which was responsible for running the bank's network of ATMs. Although subsequently transferred to another section, he retained his earlier access, including access to the computers controlling the ATMs. The system was programmed in such a way that while the system was 'on host' and able to communicate with the main computer, if a customer attempted to withdraw money from an ATM and they had insufficient funds, the transaction would be declined. However, if the system was for some reason 'off host'

---

206 *Barker* v. *R* (1983) 153 CLR 338 at 365 per Brennan and Deane JJ.
207 *Ibid.*, 365.   208 *Ibid.*, at 366.
209 *Ibid.*, at 371 per Dawson J. This is also relevant to the *mens rea* for access offences, discussed at p. 92 below.
210 [1993] 1 VR 406.

and could not communicate with the main computer, then the ATM would allow the customer to withdraw $200 irrespective of the sufficiency of funds in their account. The defendant used his access to take a specific ATM 'off host' so that he could withdraw money from his account despite having insufficient funds to cover the transaction. He would then return the ATM to 'on host' status. Although he had the necessary access to perform these operations, he clearly was not authorised to do so in order to allow him to overdraw his account.

The defendant was charged with 'computer trespass' under the now repealed s. 9A Summary Offences Act 1966 (Vic). That section made it an offence to 'gain access to, or enter, a computer system or part of a computer system without lawful authority to do so'. Adopting a similar approach to that adopted by the High Court in *Barker* his Honour held that the question is whether the entry was made with lawful authority and where, as here, there is permission to enter, the focus must be on the scope of that permission and whether the particular entry was within the scope of that permission.

If the permission was not subject to some express or implied limitation which excluded the entry from its scope, then the entry will be with lawful justification but if the permission was subject to an actual, express or implied limitation, which excluded the actual entry made, then the entry will be 'without lawful authority to do so'.[211]

His Honour held that there was evidence from which it could be inferred that the defendant had gained entry in excess of the permission that was granted to him:

> In the case of an employee the question will be whether that employee had authority to effect the entry with which he stands charged. If he has a general and unlimited permission to enter the system then no offence is proved. If however there are limits upon the permission given to him to enter that system, it will be necessary to ask was the entry within the scope of that permission? If it was, then no offence was committed; if it was not, then he has entered the system without lawful authority to do so.[212]

This decision was applied in *Gilmour* v. *DPP (Cth)*.[213] The defendant was convicted on nineteen counts of intentionally and without authority or lawful excuse inserting data into a Commonwealth computer, contrary to the now repealed s. 76C Crimes Act 1914 (Cth). The appellant was an employee of the Australian Taxation Office with limited authority to

---

211 *Ibid.*, at 409 per Hayne J.　　212 *Ibid.*, at 409–10.　　213 (1995) 43 NSWLR 243.

input data in relation to individuals' tax returns. In particular, he was not authorised to grant tax relief and could not enter what was known as relief code '43' unless relief had in fact been granted. On the occasions charged the appellant entered the relief code despite the fact that relief had not been granted, and knowing that he was not authorised to do so. It was alleged that he made no financial gain but was motivated by a desire to expedite the process, a heavy workload and concern about suggested inconsistencies in determinations of applications for relief.

The question of law for determination by the New South Wales Court of Criminal Appeal was whether the appellant had 'authority' to insert the data in a Commonwealth computer. It was argued that the appellant was not authorised to insert the relief code '43' without the specific permission of his employer. Citing *Murdoch* and *Barker*, it was held that the charges did not relate to gaining access to the computer, which was authorised, but with entering the relief codes on the specified occasions. It was the entry of *that* data which had to be authorised.[214] On the facts it was clear that the applicant had a limited authority to make such entries and by going outside those limitations he was acting without authority.[215]

In drafting the Australian provisions the MCCOC took the view that liability should not be imposed merely because the authorisation was misused.[216] Accordingly, the code provides that access is not unauthorised merely because the person has an ulterior purpose for causing it.[217] Consistent with comments in *Barker*, the mere fact that the person acts with an ulterior purpose is not of itself sufficient to render that conduct unauthorised. If, however, access is expressly or impliedly limited to access for a particular purpose, then access for another purpose will be unauthorised. The broader the permission, the less likely that the defendant was not entitled to access the data.

This is an important reminder of the importance of putting clear limitations in place in organisations to ensure that employees and others are aware of the limitations placed on access. For example, in *State of Washington* v. *Olson*,[218] the defendant was convicted of computer trespass under the Washington Revised Code,[219] under which it is an offence to intentionally gain access to a computer system or electronic database of another without authorisation. The defendant in this case was a police officer with

214 *Ibid.*, at 247 per Dunford J, with whom Hunt CJ and Allen J agreed.
215 *Ibid.*, at 248.   216 MCCOC, *Computer Offences* (2001), p. 141.
217 Criminal Code (Cth), s 476.2(2).   218 735 P 2d 1362 (CA Wash 1987).
219 RCW 9A.52.110.

the University of Washington who accessed a computer database and printed out pictures of young female university students. These were for his own personal purposes and were not connected to any police investigation.

The Washington Court of Appeals reversed his conviction. Although the defendant had clearly accessed the computer, he was authorised to do so. 'While the evidence shows that certain uses of retrieved data were against departmental policy, it did not show that permission to access the computer was conditioned on the uses made of the data.'[220] While there could of course be situations where conditions are attached to access, for example that access was not permitted for personal use, this was not the case on these facts.[221]

The concept of authorisation in the context of the UK provisions was considered by the House of Lords in *Bow Street Metropolitan Stipendiary Magistrate and anor, ex parte Government of the United States of America*.[222] This case involved the extradition of a Mr Allison to the United States. It was alleged that Mr Allison had conspired with a Ms Ojomo and others to secure unauthorised access to the American Express computer system with intent to commit theft, forgery and to cause unauthorised modification to the contents of that system.

Ms Ojomo worked as a credit analyst for American Express. While she was able to access all customers' accounts, she was only authorised to access those accounts that were assigned to her. Nonetheless, she accessed 189 accounts not assigned to her and gave confidential information to Mr Allison and others. This information was then used to encode other credit cards and supply PINs, which were in turn used to fraudulently obtain large sums of money from ATMs, allegedly defrauding American Express of approximately US$1million.

Ms Ojomo's alleged lack of authority was an essential element of the offences charged and in the context of proceedings challenging her extradition, the Divisional Court[223] certified a question of law of general public importance:

> Whether on a true construction of section 1 (and thereafter section 2) of the Computer Misuse Act 1990 a person who has authority to access data of the kind in question nonetheless has unauthorised access if: (a) the

220 *State of Washington v. Olson*, 735 P 2d 1362, 1365 (CA Wash 1987).
221 *Ibid.*, 1364. Also see *US v. Czubinski*, 106 F 3d 1069 (1st Cir 1997), *US v. Rice*, US App LEXIS 9562 (4th Cir 1992) and *Edge v. Professional Claims Bureau Inc.*, 64 F Supp 2d 115, 119 (ED NY 1999).
222 [2000] 2 AC 216.   223 [1999] QB 847.

access to the particular data in question was intentional; (b) the access in question was unauthorised by a person entitled to that particular data; (c) knowing that the access to that particular data was unauthorised.[224]

In dismissing the application, the Divisional Court had felt constrained by its earlier decision in *DPP v Bignell*.[225] In that case, the defendants were police officers who were alleged to have, without authorisation, caused a police computer operator to obtain for them for their own private purposes information about the ownership and registration of two cars from the Police National Computer. It was common ground that the access secured was for non-police purposes, and that such access involved giving a false 'Reason Code' in contravention of police instructions. The appeal against conviction was allowed by the Crown Court, which accepted the defendants' submission that the use of the computer, even if for private purposes, was not unauthorised under s. 1 Computer Misuse Act.

The question for the court in *Bignell* was whether a person who is authorised to cause a computer to perform a function to secure access to any program or data held in a computer nonetheless commits an offence if he or she intends to secure access for unauthorised purposes. In this case, was it an offence for a police officer to secure access to the Police National Computer for purposes other than for policing?

The court held that in those circumstances there was no offence as the defendants were authorised to access the computer at the level at which they did. That is, they were authorised to, and did, use the data or cause an output of data.[226] In contrast, they did not have authorisation to, and did not, alter, erase, copy or move data.[227] The ability to 'control access' for the purposes of s. 17(5) was not limited to the Police Commissioner, but included the authority the respondents had over the computer operator who accessed data on their behalf.[228] They therefore had authority to access even though they did not do so for an authorised purpose and the Crown Court had been correct to allow the appeal.

On appeal to the House of Lords in *Bow Street*, although describing the Divisional Court's decision in *Bignell* as 'probably right',[229] their Lordships were critical of some aspects of the judgment. In particular, Astill J had introduced a number of glosses which are not present in the Act itself. The concept of control was changed from that of being entitled to authorise,

---

224 *Ibid.*, at 862–3 per Kennedy LJ and Blofeld J.   225 [1998] 1 Cr App R 1.
226 Computer Misuse Act, s. 17(2)(c)(d).   227 S. 17(2)(a)(b).
228 *DPP* v. *Bignell* [1998] 1 Cr App R 1, 8–9 per Astill J.
229 *Bow Street Metropolitan Stipendiary Magistrate and anor, ex parte Government of the United States of America* [2000] 2 AC 216 at 225 per Lord Hobhouse of Woodborough.

to authorised to cause the computer to function. The concept of access to a program or data was changed to access to the computer at a particular 'level'.[230] This led the Divisional Court to error in the present case.

The reference in the certified question to 'authority to access data of the kind in question' confuses kinds of access and kinds of data. Section 1 is concerned with authority to access the actual data involved. Even though an offence can be committed without actually accessing any data, the access to that data still has to be unauthorised.[231] This led the Divisional Court to conclude that Ms Ojomo was entitled to control access of the kind in question to the program or data, so the access was not unauthorised even though she misused the information she obtained.[232] The error is in treating the phrase 'entitlement to control' as if it related to the control of the computer as opposed to the entitlement to authorise operators to access the data in question.

Section 17(5) identifies the two ways in which authority may be acquired: either being the person entitled to authorise or by being a person who has been authorised by a person entitled to authorise.[233] The authority must relate not simply to the data or program but also to the actual kind of access secured. For example, authority to view data may not extend to authority to copy or alter that data.[234] However, for access to be authorised it must be authorised to the relevant data or relevant program or part of a program. Authority to access one piece of data is not treated as authority to access other pieces of data 'of the same kind'.[235] The intention referred to in s. 1 is an intent to secure unauthorised access to any program or data. 'These plain words leave no room for any suggestion that the relevant person may say: "Yes, I know that I was not authorised to access that data but I was authorised to access other data of the same kind."'[236]

In the United States, 'exceeds authorised access' is defined to mean 'to access a computer with authorization and to use such access to obtain or alter information in the computer that the accesser is not entitled so to obtain or alter'.[237] While it has been said that the 'difference between "without authorization" and "exceeding authorized access" is

---

230 *Ibid.*, at 225.   231 *Ibid.*, at 225–6.

232 *Bow Street Metropolitan Stipendiary Magistrate and anor, ex parte Government of the United States of America* [1999] QB 847 at 857 per Kennedy LJ.

233 *Bow Street Metropolitan Stipendiary Magistrate and anor, ex parte Government of the United States of America* [2000] 2 AC 216 at 224 per Lord Hobhouse.

234 *Ibid.*   235 *Ibid.*

236 *Ibid.* Note that similar issues arise in the application of s. 17(8) to a s. 3 offence, discussed at pp. 80–1 above.

237 18 USC § 1030(e)(6).

paper thin . . . but not quite invisible',[238] the purpose behind the distinction is clear. It is to ensure that those who are granted some level of access
to a computer do not abuse that right and commit further abuse under
cover of the initial authorised access. The first question is whether the
initial access to the computer was unauthorised. If the answer is 'yes', then
clearly there is an offence subject to the additional elements. If it is authorised, whether his or her subsequent conduct exceeds authorised access
depends upon whether he or she was authorised to obtain or alter the
relevant information. The focus then moves to authorisation to obtain or
alter particular information in the computer rather than the computer
itself.

The question of 'exceeding authorised access' was considered in *International Airport Centers, LLC* v. *Citrin*.[239] The defendant, a former
employee of the plaintiff, was loaned a laptop computer for work purposes. After deciding to resign and go into business for himself, he not
only deleted all of the data on the laptop but also used a secure-erasure
program to prevent their recovery. Although clearly no longer authorised
to access the computer as agent, he was authorised under his employment
contract to 'return *or destroy*' data in the laptop when he ceased being
employed by the plaintiff.[240] However, this authorisation was only on a
limited basis and certainly not the type of data which he did destroy. He
had therefore exceeded his authorised access.[241]

5. Fault element

In addition to lack of authorisation, another significant limitation on the
scope of these offences is found in the fault element. It is these requirements which help to avoid the offences becoming a 'catch-all' for all forms
of irregular conduct involving a computer.[242] Non-intentional conduct
may reflect 'carelessness, stupidity or inattention' and may be the subject of disciplinary sanctions, but should not be the subject of a criminal
offence.[243] A requirement that the defendant knew his or her conduct
was unauthorised also provides an incentive for computer operators to
lay down clear practices as to the scope of authority of employees and
managers in relation to access to computers.[244]

---

238 *International Airport Centers, LLC* v. *Citrin*, 440 F 3d 418, 420 (7th Cir 2006).
239 *Ibid.*
240 *Ibid.*, 420. Also see *Shurgard Storage Centers, Inc.* v. *Safeguard Self Storage, Inc.*, 119 F
    Supp 2d 1121, 1125 (2001).
241 *Ibid.*, 421.   242 Law Commission, *Computer Misuse* (1989), [3.27].
243 *Ibid.*, [3.36].   244 *Ibid.*, [3.37].

In Australia, the serious computer offences require that the accused both knew that the access was unauthorised, and by that access intended to commit, or facilitate the commission of, a serious offence.[245] In relation to 'other computer offences' it must be proved that the defendant intentionally caused any unauthorised access to 'restricted data', knowing that the access was unauthorised.[246]

This is also the position in the UK where the prosecution must prove that the defendant both intended to secure access and knew that it was unauthorised. The prosecution is not required to prove that the defendant intended to access any particular program or data, a program or data of any particular kind, or a program or data held in any particular computer.[247] In the context of the more serious offences under s. 2 Computer Misuse Act, there must also be an intention to commit a specified offence.

In R v. Lennon[248] the Court of Appeal suggested that an appropriate test for determining the defendant's knowledge that the conduct was unauthorised might be to consider how the company would have responded to a request for permission to engage in the impugned conduct:

> If Mr Lennon had telephoned Ms Rhodes and requested consent to send her an e-mail raising a point about the termination of his employment, she would have been puzzled as to why he bothered to ask and said that of course he might. If he had asked if he might send the half million e-mails he did send, he would have got a quite different answer.[249]

The danger of adopting such a test is that it introduces an objective standard into a subjective test. The question is whether the defendant had actual knowledge that the conduct was unauthorised. Although the unreasonableness of that belief may be a factor in determining whether it was honestly held, it remains a subjective test.

Such an approach also seems to adopt the following reasoning:

> Use of a computer that causes harm to its owner is use that the owner would not want; use that an owner would not want is access that the owner implicitly has forbidden; and access that an owner implicitly forbids is access without authorization.[250]

This looks at the conduct after the event, rather than asking whether the defendant knew the conduct was unauthorised at the time it occurred.

---

245 Criminal Code (Cth), ss. 477.1(1)(a)(i) and 477.1(4)(a)(i). As to the meaning of intention in an earlier Commonwealth offence, see *Gilmour* v. *DPP (Cth)* (1995) 43 NSWLR 243.
246 Criminal Code (Cth), s. 478.1(1).   247 Computer Misuse Act, s. 1(2).
248 [2006] EWHC 1201.   249 *Ibid.*, at [9] per Jack J.
250 Kerr, 'Cybercrime's scope', 1642.

In Canada, the offences must be committed 'fraudulently and without colour of right'. Whether the defendant acted 'fraudulently' depends on whether his or her conduct was dishonest according to the standards of reasonable people.[251]

In the United States the fault element associated with these offences is generally either 'knowingly' or 'intentionally'.[252] However, the drafting is such that the precise scope of the fault element is often unclear. The variants are: 'knowingly accessed a computer without authorization or exceeding authorized access',[253] 'intentionally accesses a computer without authorization or exceeds authorized access',[254] 'intentionally, without authorization to access . . . accesses such a computer'[255] and 'knowingly and with intent to defraud, accesses a protected computer without authorization, or exceeds authorized access'.[256]

The fault element of 18 USC § 1030(a)(5)(A), as it then was, was considered in *US* v. *Morris*.[257] At the time, the offence required proof that the defendant intentionally accessed, without authorisation, a 'federal interest computer' and damaged or prevented authorised use of information in that computer, causing loss of US$1,000 or more. It was held that the intention requirement applied only to the 'access' element, and not the damage.[258] Consequently, a person could be guilty of an offence where he or she intentionally gained unauthorised access but inadvertently or recklessly caused damage.

However, this case leaves unresolved the question of whether the defendant must merely intend the access, or whether he or she must intend/know that the access is unauthorised/exceeding authorised access. This is in contrast to some state provisions which make clear that the defendant must have acted 'with knowledge that such use is without authority'.[259]

Finally, it is important to emphasise the distinction between motive and intention/knowledge. While motive may be relevant to the question of whether the defendant had the necessary intention/knowledge, they

---

251 *R* v. *Zlatic* (1993) 79 CCC (3d) 466 at 477 per McLachlin J. The requirement of 'without colour of right' is discussed at p. 71 above.

252 The fault elements have changed considerably with the various amendments to the Act: see H. Hong, 'Hacking through the Computer Fraud and Abuse Act' (1997) 31 *UC Davis Law Review* 283, 290–301.

253 18 USC § 1030(a)(1).   254 18 USC § 1030(a)(2).

255 18 USC § 1030(a)(3).   256 18 USC § 1030(a)(4).

257 928 F 2d 504 (2nd Cir 1991); cert. denied, *Morris* v. *US*, 502 US 817 (1991). The facts of this case are discussed at pp. 33–4 above.

258 *Ibid.*, 509, followed in *US* v. *Sablan*, 92 F 3d 865, 868 (9th Cir 1996).

259 OCGA § 16–9–92 (11), considered in *Fugarino* v. *State*, 243 Ga App 268 (2000).

are not synonymous. For example, in the UK a nineteen-year-old student was charged with conspiracy under the Computer Misuse Act. The alleged conduct involved hacking into academic, government and commercial computers and modifying data. The defendant argued that he was addicted to computing and called expert evidence to this effect. It was argued that his addiction was such that he could not form the necessary intent to commit the offence.[260]

Although the defendant was acquitted, such cases must be approached with caution. First, one may query whether such evidence was in fact relevant to the defendant's intention. Secondly, if it were, then this is the basis on which he should have been acquitted. As the trial judge directed the jury, obsession and dependence are not defences.[261]

6. Additional elements

Those jurisdictions that do not wish to criminalise unauthorised access where no danger was posed by the access may require proof of damage or an intention to cause harm or commit additional offences.[262] Typically, such additional elements take one of three forms. The first is to punish access where it is accompanied by an intent to commit a more serious offence, for example fraud.[263]

The second is to limit the offence by the type of information which is accessed. Such restrictions must be carefully drafted to ensure that they accurately define the data to be protected, without being over broad. For example, in *Snell* v. *Pryce*[264] the defendant was charged with unlawfully abstracting confidential information from a computer with intent to use it to obtain an advantage for another.[265] The court held that the charge was not made out, drawing a distinction between confidential information and information which is imparted in confidence. In this case the information accessed, such as names and addresses, was not 'confidential information' even though it was held in a confidential database.

The third limitation is to protect data where it is subject to some form of access restriction, or only where the computer is part of a networked

260 A. Charlesworth, 'Legislating against computer misuse: The trials and tribulations of the Computer Misuse Act 1990' (1993) 4 *Journal of Law and Information Science* 80, 87–92.

261 *Ibid.*   262 Cybercrime Convention, Explanatory Report, [49].

263 Cybercrime Convention, Ch. II, Section 1, Art. 1; Law Commission, *Computer Misuse* (1989), [3.28].

264 (1990) 99 FLR 213.   265 S. 222 Criminal Code Act (NT).

computer system.[266] For example, under the Cybercrime Convention, a party may require that the offence be committed by infringing security measures or in relation to a computer system that is connected to another computer system.[267] This last option allows parties to exclude access to a stand-alone computer, and to limit the offence 'to illegal access to networked computer systems (including public networks provided by telecommunication services and private networks, such as Intranets or Extranets)'.[268]

A particularly interesting example is found in s. 478.1(1) Criminal Code (Cth), which makes it an offence to intentionally cause any unauthorised access to 'restricted data' knowing that the access is unauthorised. The significant feature of this provision is that it punishes simple access to data, with no requirement of an intent to commit or facilitate the commission of another offence. It is the concept of 'restricted data' which limits the application of this provision.[269]

'Restricted data' is defined in s. 478.1(3) to mean data that is held in a computer and to which access is restricted by an access control system associated with a function of the computer.[270] 'Access control system' is not defined, but is intended to refer primarily to password protection and other similar programs which limit access to data.[271]

The access control system must be to restrict access to the data, not just the computer generally. So, for example, a password requirement at log-in would arguably make all data held in that computer 'restricted data'. If, however, it is possible to access the computer without a password, only data or groups of data to which password or similar restrictions were in place would be 'restricted data'. The section also makes clear that the access restriction device must be associated with a function of the computer. This is intended to distinguish password protection from, for example, a mechanical lock on a computer. It is arguable that biometric identification devices, if associated with a function of the computer, would constitute an access control system.

---

266 Cybercrime Convention, Explanatory Report, [50]. Given that the majority of computers are connected to the Internet, this provides little in the way of limitation.
267 Ch. II, Section 1, Art. 1.   268 Cybercrime Convention, Explanatory Report, [50].
269 Such a provision was specifically rejected by The Scottish Law Commission, in part because it would discriminate unfairly against those who do not employ a security system: Scottish Law Commission, *Report on Computer Crime*, Final Report no. 106 (1987), [4.15].
270 Also see s. 408D Criminal Code 1989 (Qld) and s. 440A Criminal Code Act Compilation Act 1913 (WA).
271 MCCOC, *Computer Offences* (2001), p. 187.

Although the concept of 'restricted data' provides some limitation to the scope of the offence, a plain reading of the section indicates that it is the presence of the restriction, rather than the bypassing of it, that is central to the offence. All that is required is that the access to the data is restricted by an access control system. There is no requirement that the defendant bypassed that system in accessing the data. That is, once data is designated as restricted because of the presence of an access control system, any access or modification of that data with the necessary fault element is an offence, notwithstanding that the defendant has not bypassed the device.

For example, imagine that a co-worker of the defendant has left her computer on. The defendant goes up to the computer, opens 'Word', and reads the last document to be opened on that program. The defendant has clearly accessed data held in that computer. If there is no password or similar protection on that computer, then the data is not restricted and there is no offence under this provision. If there is an access control system and the defendant knows the co-worker's password and uses it without permission, then he or she has accessed or modified restricted data. However, even if the co-worker has left the computer logged in, the data is still restricted data so long as access to it is restricted by an access control system, notwithstanding it did not have to be bypassed in order to access the data. This scenario was one of the reasons offered by the Scottish Law Commission for rejecting such a provision.[272] In such cases, the fault element assumes particular significance as it must be shown not only that the defendant intentionally accessed the data, but also that he or she knew that the access was unauthorised.

In the United States, the CFAA provides for a number of additional elements which focus on 'harmful intent and resultant harm, rather than on the technical concept of computer access'.[273] In many cases these provisions will overlap and this is intended to ensure that it has maximum application without the debates that may arise if they are mutually exclusive.[274] These additional elements are where the defendant:

272 Scottish Law Commission, *Computer Crime*, [4.15].
273 *North Texas Preventative Imaging, LLC* v. *Harvey Eisenberg MD*, 1996 US Dist LEXIS 19990 at [13], quoting the sponsor of the 1994 amendment, Senator Leahy.
274 Computer Crime and Intellectual Property Section, *The National Information Infrastructure Protection Act of 1996, Legislative analysis* (US Department of Justice 2003), www.cybercrime.gov/1030analysis.html.

(a) knowingly accesses a computer without authorisation or exceeds authorised access and by means of that access obtains and wilfully communicates specified protected information.[275]

There was some concern expressed by the Department of Justice that the term 'obtains' in relation to information would require that there had been some physical asportation.[276] However, the Senate Committee at the time of drafting made clear that 'obtaining information' in this context 'includes mere observation of the data. Actual asportation, in the sense of physically removing the data from its original location, or transcribing the data, need not be proved.'[277]

(b) intentionally accesses a computer without authorisation or exceeds authorised access and thereby obtains specified financial information, information from any US department or agency or information from any protected computer if the conduct involved an interstate or foreign communication.[278]

According to the Senate Report regarding the 1996 amendments, this section 'is intended to protect against the interstate or foreign theft of information by computer [and] would ensure that the theft of intangible information by the unauthorized use of a computer is prohibited in the same way theft of physical items are protected'.[279] It could apply, for example, to downloading password files. It has also been held, in a civil case, that email addresses were 'information' for these purposes.[280]

Although a number of civil cases have held that intentionally placing cookies on the plaintiff's computer and retrieving data for the purpose of monitoring the plaintiffs' web activity would satisfy the fault elements of 18 USC §§ 1030(a)(2)(C) and 1030(a)(5)(A),[281] all failed to demonstrate

275 18 USC § 1030(a)(1).
276 Computer Crime and Intellectual Property Section, *The National Information Infrastructure Protection Act.*
277 G. Roach and W. J. Michiels, 'Damages is the gatekeeper issue for federal computer fraud' (2006) 8 *Tulane Journal of Technology & Intellectual Property* 61, 64.
278 18 USC § 1030(a)(2).
279 *Shurgard Storage Centers Inc.* v. *Safeguard Self Storage Inc.*, 119 F Supp 2d 1121, 1128 (WD Wash 2001).
280 *America Online* v. *LCGM, Inc.*, 46 F Supp 2d 444, 450–1 (ED Va 1998). Also see *America Online Inc.* v. *National Health Care Discount Inc.*, 174 F Supp 2d 890, 899 (ND Iowa 2001).
281 *In re Intuit Privacy Litigation*, 138 F Supp 2d 127 (2001); *In re Toys R Us, Inc. Privacy Litigation*, Dist LEXIS 16947 (ND Calif 2001); *Chance* v. *Avenue A Inc.*, 165 F Supp 2d 1153(WD Wash 2001); *In re DoubleClick Inc., Privacy Litigation*, 154 F Supp 2d

US$5,000 loss resulting from a single act. While the limit on aggregation does not apply to criminal prosecutions, authorities are unlikely to prosecute in the context of commercial cookies without additional evidence of fraud or similar aggravating circumstances. It may, however, be applied to other forms of spyware.

(c) intentionally accesses, without authorization, a non-public computer of a US department or agency that is exclusively for the use of the US Government or, if not for its exclusive use, is used by or for the US Government and such conduct affects that use.[282]

This section punishes simple access if the computer is for the exclusive use of the department or agency, but if not exclusive, then it must be shown that the access affected its use by the department or agency. Note that the requirement that the defendant's conduct 'adversely' affect its use was removed so that the defence cannot argue that the unauthorised access was benign.[283] The insertion of the term 'non-public' was intended to make it clear that a person who has no authority to access any non-public computer of a department or agency may be convicted under (a)(3) even though permitted to access publicly available computers.[284]

(d) knowingly and with intent to defraud, accesses a protected computer without authorization, or exceeds authorized access, and thereby furthers the intended fraud and obtains anything of value.[285]

Fraud in this context simply means 'wronging one in his property rights by dishonest methods or schemes' and does not require proof of the common-law elements of fraud.[286] For example, in US v. DeMonte,[287] the

497 (SD NY 2001) and In re Pharmatrack Inc., Privacy Litigation, 220 F Supp 2d 4 (D Mass 2002). For a general discussion of these cases, see M. R. Siebecker, 'Cookies and the common law: Are Internet advertisers trespassing on our computers?' (2003) 76 Southern California Law Review 893.
282 18 USC § 1030(a)(3).
283 Computer Crime and Intellectual Property Section, The National Information Infrastructure Protection Act.
284 Ibid.
285 18 USC § 1030(a)(4). The section does not apply if the object of the fraud and the thing obtained consists only of the use of the computer and the value of such use is not more than US$5,000 in any 1 year period.
286 Shurgard Storage Centers Inc. v. Safeguard Self Storage Inc., 119 F Supp 2d 1121, 1125 (WD Wash 2001), citing US v. Czubinski 106 F 3d 1069, 1078 (1st Cir 1997).
287 US App LEXIS 11392 (6th Cir 1992).

defendant was a supervisory accountant with the Department of Veterans' Affairs. Through numerous false computer entries he caused payments in excess of US$46,000 to be made to a company, which he had established for the purpose. This provision may also apply where the defendant obtains the use of computer services, for example processing power.

Impairment of data

1. Introduction

The previous chapter was concerned with those offences which punish access to data. In this chapter, we look at those situations where the defendant interferes with the data in some way. In the past, such conduct was prosecuted, with some success, as criminal damage.[1] However, criminal damage does not fully encompass the range of conduct which may arise in this context, and is based on notions of property, the application of which to data was often 'more ingenious than practical'.[2] Accordingly, each jurisdiction has specific offences concerned with the impairment of data.

Such offences are encompassed by Arts. 4 and 5 of the Cybercrime Convention, relating to data and system interference respectively. 'Data interference' offences are those which relate to the intentional and without right 'damaging, deletion, deterioration, alteration or suppression of computer data'.[3] These offences are intended to protect computer data from intentional damage, protecting the integrity, 'proper functioning or use of computer data or computer programs'.[4] Of course, simply executing a program will cause an alteration of data. Accordingly, the Convention allows parties to reserve the right to require that the conduct resulted in serious harm before such conduct is criminalised.[5]

While Art. 4 is concerned with intentional damage to the data itself, Art. 5 relates to 'system interference' where there is the intentional and without right 'serious hindering . . . of the functioning of a computer system by inputting, transmitting, damaging, deleting, deteriorating, altering or suppressing computer data'. Although hindering the functioning of a

---

1 *R* v. *Whiteley* (1991) 93 Cr App Rep 25; *Cox* v. *Riley* (1986) 83 Cr App Rep 54; and *Re Turner* (1984) 13 CCC (3d) 430. See generally M. Wasik, *Crime and the Computer* (Oxford: Clarendon Press, 1991), pp. 136–42.
2 MCCOC, *Computer Offences* (2001), p. 159.
3 Cybercrime Convention, Ch. I, Title 1, Art. 4.
4 Cybercrime Convention, Explanatory Report, [60].   5 *Ibid.*

computer system will commonly occur due to modification of data, it may also occur where there is no modification of data but access to the computer is prevented or its functioning restricted; for example, a DoS attack. Hence, these offences apply to intentionally hindering the use of a computer system (which includes telecommunications facilities) by 'using or influencing' computer data.[6]

Although similar in rationale to offences of criminal damage, it is important that a distinction be maintained between physical damage to a computer and damage caused by the operation of a computer.[7] Further, there is a strong argument for parity between penalties for physical damage and those for impairment of data. 'There is no reason why smashing a computer cabinet should carry twice the penalty which can be visited on an offender who impairs computer data – an offence which may result in catastrophic economic loss or disruption.'[8]

2. Legislative provisions

A. Australia

The Australian federal provisions may be divided according to whether the offence relates to modification of data, or to impairment of communication to or from a computer.

Modification of data

There are three offences concerned with modification of data, the first two being 'serious computer offences'. Under s. 477.1(1)[9] Criminal Code (Cth) a person is guilty of an offence if he or she causes any unauthorised modification of data held in a computer knowing the modification is unauthorised, and by that modification intending to commit, or facilitate the commission of a serious offence, whether by that person or another person.[10]

Further, under s. 477.2(1) a person is guilty of an offence if:

    (a) the person causes any unauthorised modification of data held in a computer; and
    (b) the person knows the modification is unauthorised; and

---

6 Cybercrime Convention, Explanatory Report, [65].
7 MCCOC, *Computer Offences* (2001), p. 157.   8 *Ibid.*, p. 165.
9 S. 477.1(4) is a mirror provision which relates to an intention to commit a federal offence.
10 The elements of this offence other than modification are discussed in Ch 3. The maximum penalty for this offence is determined by reference to the maximum penalty for the relevant serious offence; s. 477.1(6).

(c) the person is reckless as to whether the modification impairs or will impair:

    i. access to that or any other data held in any computer; or

    ii. the reliability, security or operation, of any such data.

In addition, one of the jurisdictional nexus set out in (d) must apply.[11]

The third offence is found in s. 478.1(1) Criminal Code (Cth) which provides that it is an offence for a person to intentionally cause any unauthorised modification of 'restricted data', knowing that the access is unauthorised.[12]

A related offence is found in s. 478.2(1) which provides that it is an offence for a person to intentionally cause any unauthorised impairment of 'the reliability, security or operation of data held' on a computer disk, credit card or 'another device used to store data by electronic means' knowing that the impairment is unauthorised.[13]

Impairment of communication

Under s. 477.1(1) Criminal Code (Cth),[14] a person is guilty of an offence if he or she causes any unauthorised impairment of electronic communication to or from a computer knowing the impairment is unauthorised and by that impairment intending to commit, or facilitate the commission of a serious offence, whether by that person or another person.[15]

Further, under s. 477.3(1) a person is guilty of an offence if:

(a) the person causes any unauthorised impairment of electronic communication to or from a computer; and

(b) the person knows that the impairment is unauthorised.

In addition, one or both of the jurisdictional nexus in (c) applies.[16]

---

11 Absolute liability applies to these jurisdictional requirements: s. 477.2(2). Maximum penalty 10 years' imprisonment. This offence is an alternative verdict to an offence against s. 477.3 (unauthorised impairment of electronic communication): s. 477.2(4).

12 Maximum penalty 2 years' imprisonment. The meaning of 'restricted data' is discussed at p. 96.

13 Maximum penalty 2 years' imprisonment. For jurisdictional reasons, the computer disk, credit card or other device must be owned or leased by a Commonwealth entity: s. 478.2(1)(d). Absolute liability applies to this element of the offence: s. 478.2(2).

14 S. 477.1(4) of the Criminal Code (Cth) is a mirror provision which relates to an intention to commit a federal offence.

15 Other elements of this offence are discussed in Ch 3.

16 Maximum penalty 10 years' imprisonment. This offence is an alternative verdict to s. 477.2, 'unauthorised modification of data to cause impairment'. Absolute liability applies to the jurisdictional elements of the offence: s. 477.3(2).

B. *Canada*

The equivalent Canadian offence is that of 'mischief in relation to data'. Under s. 430(1.1) Criminal Code (Can) it is an offence where a person:

(a) destroys or alters data
(b) renders data meaningless, useless or ineffective
(c) obstructs, interrupts or interferes with the lawful use of data
(d) obstructs, interrupts or interferes with any person in the lawful use of data or denies access to data to any person who is entitled to access thereto.[17]

C. *The United Kingdom*

Under s. 3 Computer Misuse Act, a person is guilty of an offence if he or she does any unauthorised act in relation to a computer, knowing that it is unauthorised, and either intends by doing the act to do any of the following, or is reckless[18] as to whether the act will:

(a) impair the operation of any computer
(b) prevent or hinder access to any program or data held in any computer
(c) impair the operation of any such program or the reliability of any such data.[19]

The fault element is an important limitation on the breadth of this offence. It is not intended to cover unauthorised use of a computer, even though that may cause a modification, unless there is intention or foresight of impairment or impact on accessibility. Mere use is unlikely to have any impact on the operability of a computer and hence will not fall within the section.[20]

D. *The United States*

The principal federal offence relating to 'damage' to computers is found in 18 USC § 1030(a)(5).[21] There are three limbs to this offence. The

---

17 Maximum penalty is 10 years' imprisonment: s. 430(5).
18 There is some debate in the UK as to the form of recklessness which applies in this context; see S. Fafinski, 'Computer misuse: The implications of the Police and Justice Act 2006' (2008) 72 *Journal of Criminal Law* 53, 58.
19 Computer Misuse Act, (UK), s 3(1)–(3). These offences are punishable on indictment by a maximum penalty of 10 years' imprisonment: s 3(6).
20 Law Commission, *Computer Misuse*, Final Report no. 186 (1989), [3.77].
21 18 USC § 1030(a)(3) punishes access to a non-public government computer which is not used exclusively for government use where that conduct *affects* the use of the computer (emphasis added). The punishment for these offences is set out in 18 USC § 1030(c).

first is concerned with 'transmission of a program information, code or command', and punishes the intentional causing of damage.[22] The second and third limbs are both concerned with intentional unauthorised access, where damage, or damage and loss, is caused, either recklessly or inadvertently.[23] Each offence requires proof that the conduct was unauthorised, and that damage, or damage and loss, was caused.

The fault element of these provisions is significant. In the first the transmission must be caused knowingly and the damage intentional. This helps to avoid the situation where a person knowingly transmits a code, information or command but does not mean to cause the resultant damage. Under the second and third limbs the defendant must intentionally access the computer. Under the former, the damage must be caused recklessly while in the latter damage and loss must be caused inadvertently.[24]

Each of these offences must also occur 'without authorization', although none apply where the person exceeds authorised access.[25] It is important to note, however, that this requirement applies only to one aspect of the offence. Under subs. (A) it is the causing of damage which must be without authorization, rather than the transmission.[26] Therefore even where the transmission is authorised the defendant may still be liable if the damage caused is not.[27] In contrast, in the case of subss. (B) and (C), it is the access that must be without authorisation.

However, the wording of the sections does not make clear whether the defendant must also know that the transmission/access is unauthorised. While in many cases the defendant will clearly be aware that his or her conduct is unauthorised, one can imagine, for example, a former employee intentionally deleting data in the belief that he or she was authorised to do so. This issue was recently considered by the Fifth Circuit Court of Appeals, which held that these offences require proof that the defendant acted with knowledge that the damage/access was unauthorised.[28]

It is also an offence to, 'with intent to extort from any person any money or other thing of value', transmit 'in interstate or foreign commerce any communication containing any threat to cause damage to a protected computer'.[29] This section was enacted to address concerns that existing offences may not apply to threats directed against computer systems as it

22 § 1030(a)(5)(A).   23 § 1030(a)(5)(B)(C).
24 US v. Phillips 477 F 3d 215, 223 (5th Cir 2007).
25 For a discussion of the distinction, see p. 85.
26 Lloyd v. US 2005 US Dist. LEXIS 18158, 24.
27 Lockheed Martin Corp. v. Speed, 2006 US Dist. LEXIS 53108 at 21.
28 US v. Phillips, 477 F 3d 215, 223 (5th Cir 2007).   29 18 USC § 1030(a)(7).

was not clear whether a threat to impair the operation or availability of a computer was a threat to 'property'.[30]

Many aspects of these offences have already been discussed in the preceding chapter. This chapter will focus on two new elements:

1. the nature of the conduct causing modification or impairment
2. the meaning of modification or impairment.

3. Conduct causing modification or impairment

A. Australia

The Australian provisions simply require that the defendant cause any unauthorised modification or modification. As with unauthorised access, the modification or impairment must be caused, directly or indirectly, 'by the execution of a function of a computer'.[31]

B. Canada

The Canadian provision does not specify any particular conduct other than the prohibited results. Although there is no reference to computer in the provision, the meaning of 'data' is the same as in s. 342.1, that is 'representations of information or of concepts that are being prepared or have been prepared in a form suitable for use in a computer system'.[32] While the section protects data in electronic form, and is sufficiently broad to encompass a wide range of conduct directed against computers, it does not require that the mischief be caused by the function of a computer. On a strict reading it would seem that the section would apply equally to damage to data caused by physical means, for example physically destroying a disk or by erasing data using a magnet.

Similar criticisms were made of an early provision in the Australian State of New South Wales. Under what was then s. 310 Crimes Act 1900 (NSW), it was an offence for a person to intentionally and without authority or lawful excuse:

(a) destroy, erase or alter data stored in or insert data into a computer
(b) interfere with or interrupt or obstruct the lawful use of a computer.

---

30 Computer Crime and Intellectual Property Section, *The National Information Infrastructure Protection Act.*
31 Criminal Code (Cth), s. 476.1(2). See p. 61.
32 Criminal Code (Can), s. 430(8). See p. 56.

As with the Canadian provision, the first limb was liable to cover potentially trivial conduct. The act of 'altering' data potentially encompasses a broad range of conduct which, without more, should not be the subject of criminal sanction. The second limb does not require that the interference, interruption or obstruction be caused by the operation of a computer. It could equally apply to locking a cabinet containing the computer.[33]

Although both forms of mischief under the Canadian provisions may be punished summarily, there is a stark difference in the maximum penalties that apply where the offence is charged on indictment. Where mischief is directed at property other than data, the maximum penalty is two years, whereas mischief in relation to data carries a maximum penalty of ten years.[34] To paraphrase the criticism of a similar discrepancy in the New South Wales provision: 'The penalty of 10 years' imprisonment for unauthorised interference with a computer is [five times] the penalty for destroying it entirely, under the criminal damage provisions . . .'.[35]

C. The United Kingdom

In the UK, the relevant conduct is any 'act in relation to a computer'. This term replaced 'unauthorised modification' as a result of the 2006 amendments.[36] As originally drafted, the term 'unauthorised modification' was intended to cover such conduct as erasing or altering data, distributing malware and adding a password without authorisation to restrict access to a file.[37] DoS attacks were not envisaged, and the APIG had noted that there was some debate about the applicability of s. 3 to such attacks. It was therefore suggested that a new offence of 'impairing access to data' should be enacted.[38]

Although the case of *Lennon*,[39] decided after these recommendations, made clear that s. 3 may apply to a DoS attack, the APIG's concerns remained valid. While in many cases a DoS attack will involve modification to a computer, in some cases all the attack does is fill a nearby communication link with data. That is, there is excessive traffic but it is not directed at the particular computer. In such cases there would be no

---

33 MCCOC, *Computer Offences* (2001), p. 161.   34 Criminal Code (Can), ss. 430(4)–(5).
35 MCCOC, *Computer Offences* (2001), p. 161.
36 Explanatory Notes, Police and Justice Act 2006 (UK), [298]–[301].
37 Law Commission, *Computer Misuse* (1989), [3.65].
38 All Party Parliamentary Internet Group, *Revision of the Computer Misuse Act: Report of an Inquiry by the All Party Internet Group* (2004), [60]–[62], [75].
39 Discussed at p. 79.

offence as no data would have been modified.[40] The term 'unauthorised act' makes clear that it is no longer necessary to prove that there has been an unauthorised modification, only that there has been an unauthorised act 'in relation to' a computer. It is the intended or foreseen consequences of the act, which all relate to a computer, that provide the limiting factor.

This phrase is sufficiently broad to encompass a wide range of conduct, and references to 'doing an act' includes causing an act to be done, while references to 'act' includes a series of acts.[41] Accessing a computer, either directly or remotely, may constitute an act 'in relation to' a computer, as would the installation of malware or the sending of messages in an attempt to overwhelm a computer. The provision also applies to 'any computer' or 'any program or data held in any computer'. This therefore addresses concerns that the earlier provision did not apply, for example, to data held in a data storage device.[42]

If read literally, the conduct does not have to be an act which involves a function of a computer, as ss. 1 and 2 do, and could therefore include physical damage. Such conduct is, however, more likely to be charged as criminal damage. For the purposes of the Criminal Damage Act 1971 (UK), a modification of the contents of a computer 'shall not be regarded as damaging any computer or computer storage medium unless its effect on that computer or computer storage medium impairs its physical condition'.[43]

D. The United States

The US provisions apply to two forms of conduct: transmission of a program, information, code, or command, and intentional access to a protected computer.

Transmission of a program, information, code, or command

Under 18 USC § 1030(a)(5)(A)(i) it is an offence to knowingly cause the transmission of a program, information, code, or command and, as a

40 APIG, *Computer Misuse Act*, [65].   41 Computer Misuse Act, s. 3(5)(a)(b).
42 MCCOC, *Computer Offences* (2001), p. 163. See the discussion in relation to the Australian provision at p. 61.
43 Computer Misuse Act, s. 3(6). Also see the Law Commission, *Computer Misuse* (1989), [3.78].

result of such conduct, intentionally cause damage without authorisation to a protected computer.

The critical element in this offence is the word 'transmission'. While clearly applicable to the transmission of malicious code from an external source, the word 'transmission' has been interpreted much more broadly. In *Lloyd* v. *US*[44] the defendant planted a 'time bomb' in the computers of his employer, which deleted massive amounts of data after he left the organisation. The court rejected the defendant's argument that 'transmission' in this context was intended to apply only to transmission through 'remote access', that is transmission by a telecommunication device between two computers. The ordinary meaning of 'transmission' is 'to cause to go or be conveyed to another person or place'.[45] Neither this definition, nor the act, makes any distinction between remote and direct access as the source of the transmission. Therefore it makes no difference whether the computer was infected via telecommunication lines or by direct input.

A similar approach was adopted by the Seventh Circuit in the civil case of *International Airport Centers, LLC* v. *Citrin.*[46] In response to the plaintiff's claim under 18 USC § 1030(a)(5)(A)(i) the defendant argued that merely erasing a file from a computer is not a 'transmission'. Although accepting that pressing a delete or erase key does transmit a command to the computer, the court considered that 'it might be stretching the statute too far . . . to consider any typing on a computer keyboard to be a form of "transmission" just because it transmits a command to the computer'.[47] However, in this case the defendant did more than press a delete key; he installed the secure-erase program to the computer. For the purposes of this section, it does not matter whether the program was downloaded directly on to the computer from the Internet, or copied from a storage device.

> Congress was concerned with both types of attack: attacks by virus and worm writers, on the one hand, which come mainly from the outside, and attacks by disgruntled programmers who decide to trash the employer's data system on the way out (or threaten to do so in order to extort payments), on the other.[48]

44 2005 US Dist LEXIS 18158.
45 *Ibid.*, 22–3 citing Webster's Third New International Dictionary. Also see *Shaw* v. *Toshiba America Information Systems Inc.*, 91 F Supp 2d 926, 933 (ED Texas 1999); and *North Texas Preventive Imaging LLC* v. *Harvey Eisenberg MD*, 1996 US Dist LEXIS 19990.
46 440 F 3d 418 (7th Cir 2006). The facts of this case are outlined at p. 92.
47 *Ibid.*, 419.   48 *Ibid.*, 420.

The court was clearly concerned that the provision would be too broad if any keystroke on a computer was a 'transmission', particularly as this provision has penal as well as civil consequences. However, it is difficult to see how such an arbitrary distinction can be drawn. If it is accepted that the introduction of a program via an external storage device is a 'transmission', or that as in *Lloyd* the direct entry of code into a computer is also a transmission, then the pressing of a function key must also be a transmission. There would seem to be no logical difference between the entering of code manually and pressing a delete key where the destructive command is pre-programmed. In both cases the command is transferred, via circuitry, from the keystroke to the processor. Given that the section applies to transmission of 'information', even the act of typing and overwriting data could fall within the provision so long as the necessary damage was caused.

As the court noted in *Citrin*, it can be difficult to maintain any cogent distinction between different forms of transmission. For example, any apparent distinction between downloading from the Internet and the insertion of a disk is removed if the storage device is connected to the computer via a cable or wireless connection.[49] If the use of a wireless keyboard to enter information constitutes a transmission, then the fact that a keyboard is connected to the computer, or in the case of a laptop is embedded in the body of the computer itself, does not negate the fact that there is still a 'transmission', however small.

It therefore seems that 'transmission' in this context is essentially synonymous with 'input', raising the possibility of considerable overlap with the remaining two sections.[50] However, this interpretation must be understood in its legislative context. As noted above, the three limbs of this section punish, respectively, intentional, reckless and inadvertent damage. It is only transmission which relates to intentional damage. Therefore, unless transmission is interpreted broadly, the first limb would not apply to the 'insider' cases, which would have to be charged, if at all, with the lesser offences of intentional access and reckless or inadvertent damage. An alternative would be to amend the section to include a provision relating to intentional access *and* intentional damage.

The prosecution must, of course, prove that the defendant caused the transmission. In some cases, the defendant may point to the fact that some other person had access to the computer or passwords, or that the system is not secure. Such assertions will often be refuted by circumstantial evidence

---

49 *Ibid.*, 419–20.   50 *US* v. *Phillips*, 477 F 3d 215, 222 (5th Cir 2007).

such as computer logs indicating the defendant's use of the computer at relevant times, expertise, motive, and the like.[51]

Intentionally access a protected computer

Under 18 USC § 1030(a)(5)(A)(ii) it is an offence to intentionally access a protected computer without authorisation, and as a result of such conduct, recklessly cause damage. Subsection (iii) is in the same terms but applies where the defendant inadvertently causes damage.[52] As noted above, given the broad interpretation of access, there is potential for overlap between these provisions and 18 USC § 1030(a)(5)(A)(i). For example, 'spoofing' involves forging an IP address so that when a computer receives a data packet or communication it believes it is coming from somewhere else. This practice provides anonymity to the person seeking access, or may allow access where access is restricted to an IP address within a certain valid range. It may also impair the availability of the spoofed computer.[53] Such conduct may constitute both transmission or attempted access, as may a DoS attack.[54] The key distinction then becomes the relevant fault element in respect of the damage caused.

4. Modification or impairment

As noted above, the Cybercrime Convention envisages two categories of offence. The first relates to the 'damaging, deletion, deterioration, alteration or suppression' of computer data.[55] While 'damaging' and 'deteriorating' are concerned with alteration of the integrity of data, 'deletion' is the equivalent of destroying an object.[56] 'Suppressing' of computer data refers to 'any action that prevents or terminates the availability of the data to the person who has access to the computer or the data carrier on which it was stored'.[57] The term 'alteration' means the modification of existing data.[58]

---

51 *US* v. *Shea*, 493 F 3d 1110, 1115 (9th Cir 2007).
52 The meaning of 'access' and 'protected computer' are discussed at pp. 65 and 409 respectively.
53 *Four Seasons Hotels & Resorts B.V. v. Consorcio Barr, S.A.*, 267 F Supp 2d 1268, 1298 (SD Fl 2003).
54 *Ibid.*, 1322–3.   55 Cybercrime Convention, Ch. I, Title 1, Art. 4.
56 Cybercrime Convention, Explanatory Report, [61].   57 *Ibid.*
58 In the context of a US statute, it has been held that the ordinary meaning of 'alter' is 'to cause to become different in some particular characteristic . . . without changing into something else': *State of Oregon* v. *Schwartz*, 173 Ore App 301, 312–13 (CA Oregon, 2001) citing *Webster's Third New Int'l Dictionary*.

The second category is 'system interference', that is the intentional and without right 'serious hindering . . . of the functioning of a computer system by inputting, transmitting, damaging, deleting, deteriorating, altering or suppressing computer data'.[59] The focus is therefore on the impaired functioning of the system as a result of data interference.

A. Australia

The key phrase in the context of the Australian provisions is 'unauthorised modification of data held in a computer'.[60] 'Modification', in the context of data held in a computer, means:

(a) the alteration or removal of the data or
(b) an addition to the data.[61]

This is apt to cover a range of conduct such as deletion of data, installation of malware or changing of data such as IP addresses. Where the defendant intends to commit or facilitate a serious offence, or the modified data is restricted data, there is no further requirement of impairment. However, in the case of s. 477.2(1), the prosecution must prove that the defendant was reckless as to whether the modification impaired or would impair:

(i) access to that or any other data held in any computer or
(ii) the reliability, security or operation, of any such data.[62]

'Impair' is not defined in this context, and is presumably to be given its ordinary meaning of 'to make worse, less valuable, or weaker; to lessen injuriously; to damage, injure'.[63] Access to data may be impaired by preventing access or by slowing access down. A program (which falls within the definition of 'data') may be less reliable or its operation impaired if it is unable to function normally, for example malware causing Internet browsers to redirect to unwanted websites. Security may be impaired where access control systems are overridden.

---

59 Cybercrime Convention, Ch. I, Title 1, Art. 5.
60 The concepts of 'data held in a computer' and 'unauthorised' have already been discussed in Ch. 3.
61 Criminal Code (Cth), s. 476.1(1).
62 As to similar wording in the UK provisions, see p. 115.
63 *Oxford English Dictionary*. Further discussion of the meaning of 'impairment' is found in the context of the US provisions at p. 117.

A person may be guilty of an offence against this section even if there is or will be no actual impairment.[64] For example, data may be modified by a logic bomb designed to 'detonate' at a future date. There is no need to prove that the modification caused impairment, only that the defendant caused the modification and was reckless as to the risk of impairment.[65] The data which is impaired may be held in *any* computer, not necessarily the one in which the data was modified.

Sections 477.1(1) and 477.3(1) Criminal Code (Cth) are both concerned with 'impairment of electronic communication to or from a computer'. This is defined to include:

(a) the prevention of any such communication
(b) the impairment of any such communication on an electronic link or network used by the computer.

But this does not include a mere interception of any such communication.[66]

'Electronic communication' means a communication of information in any form by means of guided or unguided electromagnetic energy.[67]

These sections encompass impairment which results from modification of data, such as alteration of IP addresses or removal of a network connection. However, they may also apply to DoS attacks and other techniques which impair communication by a computer without necessarily modifying data on that computer. Because the modification/impairment must be caused by the execution of a function of a computer, it would not, for example, apply to severing a network cable.

The Committee deliberately avoided the use of the term 'computer systems' in this context, preferring the impairment of electronic communication 'to or from' a computer. This was 'meant to ensure that liability for offences of unauthorised impairment of data is not limited by the spatial location of the tangible components of a data processing system'.[68] This was particularly prescient given the increasing 'networking' of devices, including appliances. Rather than requiring a determination as to whether linked computers are part of a computer system, the section focuses on impairment of communication to or from individual computers.[69]

---

64 Criminal Code (Cth), s. 477.2(3).   65 MCCOC, *Computer Offences* (2001), p. 165.
66 Criminal Code (Cth), s. 476.1(1). Interception offences are discussed in Ch. 6.
67 *Ibid.*   68 MCCOC, *Computer Offences* (2001), p. 129.   69 *Ibid.*, p. 131.

Finally, s. 478.2(1) Criminal Code (Cth) punishes unauthorised impairment of the 'reliability, security or operation of data held on a computer disk, credit card or another device used to store data by electronic means'.[70] This provision may apply to a range of data-storage devices including CD-ROM, USB sticks and the like. In addition to credit cards, which are expressly mentioned, this provision may also encompass the many cards used in daily life which contain embedded data, either in the form of magnetic stripe and/or microchip.

Unlike the other sections, there is no limitation that the impairment must be caused by operation of a computer.[71] It could therefore apply to causing physical damage to a device, or impairing its operation, for example by the use of a strong magnetic field or an electronic pulse. It could also be argued that the security of devices such as credit cards is impaired by the use of card-skimming devices. However, although the security of the *account* may be compromised, the security of the *data* on the original card remains unchanged.

B. Canada

The forms of conduct enumerated in s. 430(1.1) Criminal Code (Can) are apt to cover the forms of impairment most commonly encountered. 'Destroy or alter data' clearly applies to the person who accesses the data, remotely or directly, and deletes or otherwise modifies the data. Rendering data 'meaningless, useless or ineffective' may be brought about by adding additional data which renders existing data unintelligible, or by adding false data which means that the original data cannot be relied upon.

The remaining two limbs which apply to obstructing, interrupting or interfering with the lawful use of data, or denying access to data, are apt to cover those situations where there is no modification of the data but access or use is denied, for example a DoS attack[72] or a person who encrypts or places a password on data, thereby denying access to others.

C. The United Kingdom

Under s. 3 Computer Misuse Act, the defendant must intend or be reckless as to whether his or her conduct will:

---

70 Maximum penalty 2 years' imprisonment.
71 S. 476.1(2) Criminal Code (Cth) only applies to 'impairment of an electronic communication to or from a computer'.
72 *R* v. *Geller*, 2003 WCBJ LEXIS 324 at [7].

(a) impair the operation of *any* computer

(b) prevent or hinder access to any program or data held in any computer

(c) impair the operation of any such program or the reliability of any such data.[73]

As with ss. 1 and 2 Computer Misuse Act, there is no requirement that these effects actually be caused, only that the person act with the necessary intention or recklessness. The intention or recklessness need not relate to any particular computer, program or data, or to any particular kind of program or data.[74]

The term 'impairment' is undefined and is presumably to be given its ordinary meaning.[75] Some concern has been expressed that it may apply too broadly,[76] particularly as impairment may be only temporary.[77] For example, it has been noted that 'cyber-protest' groups sometimes seek to shut down websites for a short period. 'Where such protesters are simply fetching web pages using standard browsers we can see significant dangers in creating a framework for criminalising their behaviour.'[78]

However, if the impairment is sufficiently great so as to be detected and reported to police, coupled with the necessary *mens rea*, it is not clear why such conduct should not be prosecuted. Prosecutorial discretion may be relied upon to exclude trivial matters, and defences may be provided to allow for justifiable instances of intentional or reckless impairment of computers. The alternative of providing a quantitative definition of impairment may be unrealistic and lead to its own complications, as seen by the US experience.[79]

The meaning of impairing the reliability of data was considered in *Zezev and Yarimaka* v. *Governor of HM Prison Brixton and anor.*[80] That case concerned an application for habeas corpus by the two applicants in response to an order that they be extradited to the United States. Zevev had been employed by Kazkommerets Securities, a company located in Kazakhstan. That company subscribed to services provided by Bloomberg LP which provided news and financial information. The applicants gained unauthorised access to the Bloomberg computer system in New York and were able to access the email accounts of Mr Bloomberg (founder and director of the company) and the head of security of the company. Zezev

---

73 References to enabling such conduct, inserted by Police and Justice Act 2006, s. 36, were subsequently repealed by the Serious Crime Act 2007, s. 61.

74 Computer Misuse Act, s. 3(4).   75 See p. 117.

76 Fafinski, 'Computer misuse', 59.   77 Computer Misuse Act, s. 5(5)(c).

78 APIG, *Computer Misuse Act*, [70].   79 See p. 119.   80 [2002] 2 Cr App R 33.

sent a series of emails to Mr Bloomberg demanding money or he would
disclose that the system had been compromised.

Extradition proceedings were based on a number of charges: the most
relevant for our purposes being conspiracy to gain unauthorised access
and to cause unauthorised modification to Bloomberg's computer system.
There was evidence that Zezev would use the computer so as to record
the arrival of information that did not come from the purported source.
In other words, the information would appear to come from person A,
when in fact it had come from person B.

It was submitted for the defence that the purpose of s. 3 is confined to
those who damage the computer so that it does not record the information
that is fed into it. If information is accurately fed into the computer but the
information is untrue, that does not impair the operation of the computer
because it is meant to record the information as inputted and has done
so. Nor is anyone prevented or hindered from accessing that data. This
argument was rejected.

Under (c), the requisite intent can exist if it impairs the operation
of any such program or the 'reliability' of any such data. Although it
appears from the evidence of the Law Commission's report that such
conduct was not intended to fall within the section, the language of
the section is clear.[81] 'If a computer is caused to record information
which shows that it came from one person, when it in fact came from
someone else, that manifestly affects its reliability.'[82] Consequently, all
of the elements of the offence were present. The placing of the bogus email
in the files of the computer was an unauthorised addition to the data which
the defendant clearly intended and which impaired the reliability of the
data.[83]

Finally, the defendant must have intended or foreseen *impairment*,
not merely that data would be altered or modified. So, for example, a
defendant who installs keylogging software may argue that he or she
did not intended or foresee that this would impair the operation of any
computer or program nor the reliability of any data. Such conduct must
then be punished, if at all, as unauthorised access.

81 *Ibid.*, at [16] per Lord Woolf CJ, citing Law Commission, *Computer Misuse* (1989),
    [3.62].
82 *Ibid.*, at [18].
83 *Ibid.*, at [22] per Wright J. Cf *Attorney General's Reference (No.1 of 1991)* [1993] QB 94 at
    100 per Lord Taylor where it was queried, without deciding, whether it would necessarily
    impair the reliability of data in the computer 'that you feed in something which will
    produce a result more favourable to a customer than the store holder intended'.

D. The United States

In addition, to the conduct described above, in all cases it must be proved that the defendant caused 'damage' and, in some cases, loss. This requirement is an important limitation on the reach of the section, seeking to strike a balance between punishing significant damage to computers while not over-criminalising less-serious conduct.[84] It has also proved to be an important restraint on the numerous civil cases involving the placing of cookies on computers.[85]

Damage

Under the first limb the damage must be to a protected computer. In the second and third limbs, while there must be access to a protected computer, there is no express requirement that the damage caused was to a protected computer. So long as the damage was caused as a result of access to a protected computer, the damage need not relate to that computer.[86]

'Damage' is defined to mean any 'impairment to the integrity or availability of data, a program, a system, or information.'[87] These are ordinary words capable of being given their ordinary meaning. 'Impairment' is defined as 'something that damages or makes worse by diminishing in some material respect', while integrity means 'unimpaired, sound, complete, without corruption'. 'Availability' is the 'state of being present or ready for immediate use; accessible'.[88]

The concept of 'damage' clearly applies to circumstances where data is modified or deleted, including where the data has been restored. 'Integrity', in the context of data, contemplates maintaining the data in a protected state.[89] For example, an unauthorised intruder may alter login files in order to retrieve passwords, and then restore the files to their original condition. Such conduct nonetheless falls within the meaning of

---

84 G. Roach and W. J. Michiels, 'Damages is the gatekeeper issue for federal computer fraud' (2006) 8 *Tulane Journal of Technology & Intellectual Property*, 62.

85 See the discussion at p. 98.

86 *Healthcare Advocates, Inc.* v. *Harding, Earley, Follmer & Frailey*, 497 F Supp 2d 627, 647 (ED Pa 2007). As to the meaning of protected computer see p. 409.

87 18 USC § 1030(e)(8).

88 *America Online, Inc.* v. *National Health Care Discount, Inc.*, 121 F Supp 2d 1255, 1274 (ND Iowa 2000) citing *Merriam-Webster's Collegiate Dictionary*.

89 *Shurgard Storage Centers Inc.* v. *Safeguard Self Storage Inc.*, 119 F Supp 2d 1121, 1127 (WD Wash 2001).

'damage' as, although the data has not been physically changed or erased, its integrity has been impaired.[90]

Equally, the provisions are intended to encompass damage to the integrity *or* availability of data. Therefore, encrypting data may be said to 'damage' the data because its availability is impaired even though the underlying data is unchanged.[91] Similarly, a DoS attack may also constitute damage as the availability of the data is restricted even though the data itself is unaffected.[92]

There is limited civil authority that 'damage' may encompass disclosure of trade secrets, notwithstanding the data remains unaltered.[93] However, it is submitted that such a view should not be followed, particularly in a criminal context.[94] The damage that is proscribed by the section is damage to a computer. While a trade secret may have lost some or all of its value through disclosure, its integrity remains intact except on the broadest interpretation of the word. This is yet another example of the CFAA being used as a vehicle for litigation in respect of trade secrets rather than damage to computers as such.[95]

A potentially significant limitation is the requirement of causation. In each case the damage must be 'as a result of' the relevant conduct. So, in relation to subs. (A), the damage must occur as a result of the transmission of the program, information, code or command. Obviously this will be made out where the program or code is designed to cause the damage. However, the entering of a password, for example, may not cause damage, even though it may allow the defendant to cause damage. Similarly, in the case of subss. (B) and (C), it is the intentional access which must cause the damage. On a strict reading of the section it does not apply to damage caused after access has been obtained, but only to damage which results from the access itself.

In some cases, it may be argued that the damage caused is so minimal that it should not fall within the scope of the section. For example,

---

90 *Ibid.*, cited with apparent approval in *Thurmond* v. *Compaq Computer Corp*, 171 F Supp 2d 667, 678 (ED Tex 2001).

91 Computer Crime and Intellectual Property Section, *The National Information Infrastructure Protection Act.* Cf refusing to decode a program: *State of Arizona* v. *Moran*, 162 Ariz 524 (CA Ariz 1989).

92 *Four Seasons Hotels & Resorts B.V.* v. *Consorcio Barr, S.A.*, 267 F Supp 2d 1268, 1323 (SD Flor 2003).

93 *Shurgard Storage Centers Inc.* v. *Safeguard Self Storage Inc.*, 119 F Supp 2d 1121, 1126 (WD Wash 2001).

94 *Lockheed Martin Corp.* v. *Speed*, 2006 US Dist LEXIS 53108 at 25–6.

95 See the discussion at pp. 98–9.

in *Moulton and Network Installation Computer Services, Inc.* v. *VC3*[96] it was held that although a throughput test or ping flood can slow down a network, in this case the slow-down was negligible at best, and not noticeable to the company or its customers. It therefore did not constitute 'interfering' with the defendant's network within the meaning of the Georgia Computer Systems Protection Act.[97]

This decision is, however, ambiguous in that the court then went on to say that the defendant could still be open to prosecution under the Act. This suggests that there was in fact 'interference', but without sufficient damage to warrant a civil claim.[98] Such a view seems preferable. The consequential harm caused is the appropriate limitation on the reach of the section, rather than the courts engaging in debate as to whether a particular interference is *de minimis*.

Loss

An additional requirement under § 1030(a)(5)(C) is that the defendant's conduct must have caused damage *and* loss. 'Loss' is defined as:

> any reasonable cost to any victim, including the cost of responding to an offense, conducting a damage assessment, and restoring the data, program, system, or information to its condition prior to the offense, and any revenue lost, cost incurred, or other consequential damages incurred because of interruption of service.[99]

This allows for the fact that even where there may have been no obvious 'damage' to the computer, the victim may nonetheless suffer because, for example, passwords have been compromised and the system must be re-secured.[100] For example, in *US v. Phillips*[101] over US$122,000 was spent assessing the damage and $60,000 notifying victims that their personal information had been compromised.

While loss in this sense includes costs that were a 'natural and foreseeable result' of the defendant's conduct, that were 'reasonably necessary' and that would 'resecure' the computer to avoid further damage, it does not extend to creating a better or more secure system than existed prior to the impairment.[102]

---

96 2000 US Dist LEXIS 19916 (ND Ga).   97 *Ibid.*, 18–19.
98 *Ibid.*, 19.   99 18 USC § 1030(e)(11).
100 *Shurgard Storage Centers Inc.* v. *Safeguard Self Storage Inc.*, 119 F Supp 2d 1121, 1126 (WD Wash 2001).
101 477 F 3d 215, 218 (5th Cir 2007).
102 *US* v. *Middleton*, 231 F 3d 1207, 1213 (9th Cir 2000).

5

Misuse of devices

1. Introduction

The offences discussed in previous chapters may require a level of technical sophistication to commit. Certainly, gaining unauthorised access to computer systems, or writing malicious code, often requires a level of expertise not possessed by most people. At the other end of the spectrum, all that is required in some cases is access to the relevant password. In either case, the need for a means of access creates an incentive to acquire items which facilitate that process, and may create a black market in passwords and other information that may facilitate computer misuse.[1] For example, a person may make available on the Internet information outlining security weaknesses in a computer system. Another may post malicious code. Yet another may simply trade in passwords. 'Rootkits', which disguise a person's presence on a compromised computer, were once the domain of highly skilled hackers. Now, they are freely and widely available and increasingly easy to use.[2]

While such conduct may be prosecuted under existing offences such as conspiracy to defraud[3] or incitement,[4] there is an arguable need for offences which specifically relate to trafficking in items that facilitate the commission of computer offences. The aim of these inchoate offences is to restrict access to specific items that are used to commit the relevant offences.[5]

Under Art. 6 of the Cybercrime Convention, each party shall adopt such legislative and other measures as may be necessary to establish as criminal offences under its domestic law, when committed intentionally and without right:

---

1 Cybercrime Convention, Explanatory Report, [71].
2 AusCERT, *Australian Computer Crime and Security Survey* (2006), p. 23, www.auscert. org.au/crimesurvey.
3 *R* v. *Hollinshead and ors* [1985] 2 All ER 769.
4 *R* v. *Maxwell-King* [2001] 2 Cr App R(S) 136.
5 Cybercrime Convention, Explanatory Report, [71].

(a) the production, sale, procurement for use, import, distribution or otherwise making available of:
  i. a device, including a computer program, designed or adapted primarily for the purpose of committing any of the offences established in accordance with ... Articles 2 through 5;
  ii. a computer password, access code, or similar data by which the whole or any part of a computer system is capable of being accessed,
(b) with intent that it be used for the purpose of committing any of the offences established in Articles 2 through 5; and
(c) the possession of an item referred to in paragraphs (a)(i) or (ii) above, with intent that it be used for the purpose of committing any of the offences established in Articles 2 through 5.[6]

The Convention allows parties to opt out of these provisions other than in respect of 'sale, distribution or otherwise making available'.[7] This allows a party not to criminalise the production or importation of such items, but each Party must criminalise conduct that may potentially release such material into the broader community. Although a country may argue that it should be permitted to allow for sale or distribution within its national boarders, the inability to effectively restrict the transmission of data out of the jurisdiction arguably makes it necessary to curb sale and distribution at source.

There are a number of points to emphasise about this provision that should be borne in mind when considering the various offences discussed in this chapter. First, a distinction is drawn between passwords and other data used to access computer systems, and devices which may be used to commit other computer offences. Both should be addressed by the relevant provisions.

In relation to 'a computer password, access code, or similar data', for completeness the offence should extend to instructions as to how to gain unauthorised access, for example 'exploits' outlining the weaknesses in computer systems. However, the phrase 'or similar data' may cause difficulties in this context. Applying the principle of *ejusdem generis*, the general must be interpreted in light of the specific, in which case it may be argued that such information is not 'similar to' a password or access code.[8]

In relation to 'devices', although the term is not defined, its use in this context would suggest it includes both hardware and software.[9] In

---

6 Cybercrime Convention, Ch. I, Title 1, Art. 6.   7 *Ibid.*, Art. 6(3).
8 See the discussion of this issue in the US context at p. 133.
9 I. Walden, *Computer Crimes and Digital Investigations* (New York: Oxford University Press, 2007), p. 193.

particular, the inclusion of a 'computer program' is intended to encompass malware such as viruses, or programs designed or adapted to gain access to computer systems.[10]

Second, there is a clear tension between restricting the illegitimate use and distribution of such material while allowing for legitimate uses. Many items of this nature are 'dual use', and widely used by security professionals and system administrators. For example, penetration-testing devices are used to detect security weakness, but may also be used by hackers as a way of gaining unauthorised access.[11] Limiting the offence to those devices designed exclusively or specifically for committing offences, while excluding dual-use devices, would lead to potentially insurmountable difficulties of proof, rendering it of marginal application.[12] Conversely, applying the offence to all devices, whether legally produced and distributed or not, would be too broad. The criminality of such conduct would then depend upon proof of the subjective intent to commit a computer offence.[13]

The compromise position was to require specific intent, but only in relation to items which are objectively designed, or adapted primarily, for the purpose of committing an offence. Consequently, authorised testing or protection of a computer system will not satisfy this element.[14] It was considered that in the majority of cases this alone would be sufficient to exclude dual-use devices. In addition, legitimate conduct will also be covered by the requirement that the offence be committed 'without right'. Devices which are produced for the purpose of analysing networks and testing security are produced for a legitimate purpose and would be regarded as 'with right'.[15]

Finally, the focus of these provisions is on what may broadly be described as 'trafficking' – that is, 'the production, sale, procurement for use, import, distribution or otherwise making available of' such items. 'Distribution' relates to actively forwarding data to others, while 'making available' refers to placing devices online, including through the use of hyperlinks.[16] Possession is only an offence where it is accompanied by the specific intent; simple possession is not sufficient. In addition, a party may require that a particular number of items be possessed before criminal

10 Cybercrime Convention, Explanatory Report, [72].
11 P. Sommer, 'Criminalising hacking tools' (2006) 3 *Digital Investigation* 68, 70.
12 All Party Parliamentary Internet Group, *Revision of the Computer Misuse Act: Report of an Inquiry by the All Party Internet Group* (2004), [73].
13 *Ibid.*   14 Cybercrime Convention, Art. 6(2).
15 Cybercrime Convention, Explanatory Report, [77].
16 *Ibid.*, [72]. The meaning of these words is discussed at pp. 293 and 288 respectively.

liability attaches.[17] In any event, the number of devices possessed may be some evidence from which intention may be inferred.[18]

2. Australia

The Australian provisions were specifically drawn from the Convention and most accurately reflect the criteria outlined above.[19] They are divided into two types of offence: possession or control of data and producing, obtaining or supplying data. Both are inchoate offences in that they relate to an intention to commit or facilitate a future offence. Although a person may be found guilty of either offence, even if committing the future offence is impossible, it is not an offence to attempt to commit these offences.[20]

A. Possession or control of data

Under s. 478.3 Criminal Code (Cth), it is an offence for a person to have possession or control of data with the intention that the data be used, by the person or another person, in committing or facilitating an offence against Division 477 ('Serious Computer Offences').[21] As discussed above, data includes information in any form, whether electronic or tangible.[22] The offence is therefore not limited to the possession of passwords, but may extend to malicious code, or even information on how to exploit weaknesses in a computer or computer network.

Possession is defined very broadly to include:

(a) having possession of a computer or data storage device that holds or contains the data. (For example, data contained on a USB drive)[23]
(b) having possession of a document[24] in which the data is recorded. (For example, a book on hacking techniques or virus code in written form)

---

17 Cybercrime Convention, Art. 6(1)(b). This is the position in the US, see p. 130.
18 Cybercrime Convention, Explanatory Report, [75].
19 MCCOC, *Computer Offences* (2001), p. 92.
20 Criminal Code (Cth), ss. 478.3(2)(3) and 478.4(2)(3).
21 Maximum penalty 3 years' imprisonment: s. 478.3(1).   22 See p. 61.
23 The meaning of 'data storage device' is discussed at p. 61.
24 'Document' is defined broadly and includes 'any article or material from which sounds, images or writings are capable of being reproduced with or without the aid of any other article or device': Acts Interpretation Act 1901 (Cth), s. 25(c).

(c) having control of data held in a computer that is in the possession of another person, whether inside or outside Australia (for example, information placed on a website for others to read).[25]

Problems of over-breadth are addressed by the fault element. Consistent with Art. 6(1)(c) of the Convention, the prosecution must prove that the defendant was in possession of the data with the intention that it be used, either by the defendant or another person, in committing or facilitating a serious computer offence. Recklessness does not suffice, nor does an intention to commit or facilitate one of the other computer offences found in Division 478 Criminal Code (Cth).

B. Produce, supply or obtain data

Section 478.4 Criminal Code (Cth) is consistent with Art. 6(1)(a)(b) of the Convention by punishing what can broadly be described as 'trafficking' in such data. Under this provision it is an offence to produce, supply or obtain data with the intention that the data be used, by the person or another person, in committing or facilitating an offence against Division 477.[26] 'Producing, supplying or obtaining data' includes:

(a) producing, supplying or obtaining data held or contained in a computer or data storage device
(b) producing, supplying or obtaining a document in which the data is recorded.[27]

These provisions are therefore broad enough not only to encompass the person who writes and/or disseminates the data, but also the person who obtains it. For example, a person who obtains data, or a document recording the data, from a website would potentially fall within this offence. As with possession, the scope of the offence is considerably limited by the need to prove an intention to commit or facilitate a serious computer offence.

3. Canada

In Canada, there are separate offences relating to passwords and to tangible devices. Under s. 342.1(1)(d) Criminal Code (Can) it is an

---

25 Criminal Code (Cth), s. 478.3(4). The meaning of 'possession' in the context of digital images is discussed at p. 301.
26 Maximum penalty 3 years' imprisonment: s. 478.4(1).
27 Criminal Code (Cth), s. 478.4(4). The meaning of some of these terms is discussed in the context of digital images in Ch. 10.

offence to fraudulently and without right, use, possess, traffic in, or permit another person to have access to a computer password that would enable a person to commit an offence under s. 342.1(1)(a)–(c).[28] The term 'computer password' is further defined to mean 'any data by which a computer service or computer system is capable of being obtained or used'.[29] While the section clearly applies to passwords or other access codes, it could also arguably extend to information outlining weaknesses in computer security or other information facilitating access to a computer. Such information could conceivably be described as 'data by which a computer or computer system is capable of being obtained or used'.

Less clear is whether the provision applies to malicious code which is intended to impair computer systems. Computer mischief under s. 430 is not mentioned specifically as a relevant offence, but falls within the reference to s. 342.1(1)(c). This makes it an offence to use or cause to be used, directly or indirectly, a computer system with intent to commit an offence under s. 430 in relation to data or a computer system. While the dissemination of malicious code would clearly be an offence under this section, it is not clear that the code itself is 'data by which a computer service or computer system is capable of being obtained or used'. It would have to be argued that the code is data by which the target computer is capable of being used, and that this enables a person to commit an offence under subs. (c). Such a reading seems strained, and this provision would benefit from revision to make it clear that it applies to other forms of data other than passwords, and that it specifically applies to s. 430.

A further limitation on this section is that the password must be such that it 'would enable' a person to commit a specified offence. Presumably, if the data is incorrect, for example a false password, then the offence has not been committed and would have to be charged as an attempt. This is in contrast to the wording of s. 342.2 as discussed below.

The relevant conduct in relation to the password is to use, possess, traffic in or permit another person to have access to the password. 'Traffic', in this context, is defined very broadly to mean 'to sell, export from or import into Canada, distribute or deal with in any other way'.[30] The phrase 'permit another person to have access to' is also apt to capture the person who places the password on a website for others to download. In contrast to s. 342.2, it does not apply to the creation of a password. However,

---

28 These offences are discussed at pp. 49 and 140. Maximum penalty 10 years' imprisonment: s. 342.1(1).

29 Criminal Code (Can), s. 342.1(2). The meaning of 'data', 'computer service' and 'computer system' are discussed at pp. 54 and 56.

30 The meaning of some of these concepts in the context of data is considered in Ch. 10.

in many cases the person who creates the password will also necessarily have been in possession of or 'dealt with' the password. The breadth of the offence is limited by the requirement that the conduct is engaged in 'fraudulently and without claim of right'.[31]

While s. 342.1(1)(d) is concerned with trafficking in passwords, under s. 342.2(1) it is an offence to make, possess, sell, offer for sale or distribute, without lawful justification or excuse, any 'instrument or device or any component thereof' the design of which renders it primarily useful for committing any offence under s. 342.1,[32] under circumstances that give rise to a reasonable inference that the instrument, device or component, has been used or is, or was, intended to be used to commit an offence contrary to that section.[33] The wording of this provision is drawn from earlier provisions concerned with possession of housebreaking or similar equipment[34] or devices for obtaining use of a telecommunications facility without payment.[35] Cases relating to these provisions provide the most significant jurisprudence in this area.[36]

The focus of this section is quite different to the previous section. Although the phrase 'instrument or device or any component thereof' suggests that it is aimed at physical items rather than intangible data, it appears that 'devices' in this context is assumed to include computer programs.[37] Further, many such devices may have multiple uses, and so the device must be such that its design renders it 'primarily useful' for committing any of the offences under s. 342.1. This may include card skimmers, or other devices used to obtain passwords or devices designed to intercept data. It would not, however, apply to a computer as a computer is not *primarily* designed for that purpose.

The elements of the offence are in two parts. First, the prosecution must prove that the defendant made, possessed, sold, offered for sale or distributed the relevant instrument. The prosecution must then prove that this occurred in circumstances that gave rise to the necessary inference.[38] There are three distinct inferences which may arise:

31 The meaning of 'fraudulently and without right' is discussed at p. 71.
32 Note that this section does not apply to an offence under s. 430: s. 342.1(1)(c).
33 Maximum penalty 2 years' imprisonment: s. 342.2(1)(a).
34 S. 351 (formerly s. 309).
35 S. 327. This section is aimed primarily at the obtaining of pay-television without charge.
36 It is also an offence under s. 191 to possess, sell or purchase 'any electro-magnetic, acoustic, mechanical or other device or any component thereof knowing that the design thereof renders it primarily useful for surreptitious interception of private communications.'
37 Department of Justice Canada, *Lawful Access-Consultation Document* (2002), p. 14.
38 *R* v. *Holmes* [1988] 1 SCR 914 at 943 per Dickson CJ.

1. that the device has been used for that purpose in the past
2. that it is intended to be used for that purpose
3. that it was intended to be used for that purpose.

This is an interesting provision as it may punish the defendant for his or her present conduct in relation to an item because of what was done or intended to be done with that item in the past. The use or intended use of the device may be by any person, including the defendant. The section therefore applies, for example, to the person who merely stores devices knowing of their intended use.[39] Where the charge relates to the intended use of the item the offence is complete without the need to prove that the device was in fact used for that purpose.[40] The fact that a particular device may be widely available for lawful purposes does not avail the defendant who has it in his or her possession for unlawful purposes.[41]

It may be argued that the phrase 'would give rise to a reasonable inference' requires something less than proof beyond reasonable doubt. For example, given the device must be 'primarily useful' for such an offence, it would seem to flow from mere possession that use for that purpose is 'a' reasonable inference, and that the presence of other inferences does not negate a finding of guilt. However, this argument was rejected by the Supreme Court in the context of a similar provision:

> The words 'reasonable inference' (of guilt) employed in a criminal enactment can mean only an inference which, on the basis of the criminal standard of proof beyond a reasonable doubt, would warrant a conclusion of guilt in the absence of any answer or explanation. An inference of guilt is not reasonable in the criminal context unless it overrides a reasonable doubt.[42]

That is, for the offence to be made out, the inference alleged by the prosecution must be the only reasonable inference in the circumstances.

Finally, the provision is subject to the defence of 'lawful justification or excuse'. Ordinarily, such a provision would make available the defence of 'innocent purpose',[43] for example the person who uses a device in order to test their own network security. However, it has been held that the requirement for the prosecution to prove the circumstances give rise to a

---

39 *R* v. *Fulop*, 1988 OAC LEXIS 551 at 8 per Lacourciere, Goodman and Catzman JJA; upheld by the Supreme Court in *R* v. *Fulop* [1990] 3 SCR 695.
40 *R* v. *Millar*, 2002 BCC LEXIS 4506 at 60 per Clancy J. Also see *R* v. *Holmes* [1988] 1 SCR 914 at 944 per Dickson CJ.
41 *R* v. *Millar* [2004] BCJ no. 828 at 12 per Hall JA.
42 *R* v. *Holmes* [1988] 1 SCR 914 at 944–5 per Dickson CJ.   43 *Ibid.*, at 946.

reasonable inference that the device was used or was intended to be used for a criminal purpose effectively renders the defence superfluous.[44] That is, before the issue of lawful justification or excuse arises, the prosecution must already have proved that it was used or intended to be used for a criminal purpose.

4. The United Kingdom

Until recently, there was no specific offence of this nature in the UK.[45] As recently as 2004 the Home Office stated that the enactment of an offence to criminalise the possession of 'hacking tools' was unlikely.[46] However, in response to concern about a growing market in such material, and to comply with Art. 6(1)(a) of the Cybercrime Convention,[47] s. 37 of the Police and Justice Act 2006 inserted a new s. 3A into the Computer Misuse Act. Under that section, there are in fact three new offences covering a range of conduct, from making or adapting to supplying or offering to supply.[48]

Each offence relates to 'articles' which may be used in the commission of an offence under ss. 1 or 3 of the Computer Misuse Act.[49] 'Article' is defined to include 'any program or data held in electronic form'.[50] This inclusive definition makes clear that although the term may include intangibles such as passwords or malicious code stored on a computer, it is not limited to intangibles. A computer itself is an article which may be used to commit an offence under ss. 1 or 3.

The first offence is to make, adapt, supply or offer to supply any article intending it to be used to commit or to assist in the commission of an offence under ss. 1 or 3.[51] Although the term 'production' as used in the Convention is arguably more appropriate, the ordinary meaning of the terms 'make' and 'adapt' would seem capable of applying to the creation

---

44 *Ibid.*, at 947.
45 Although see the offence of possessing or supplying an apparatus for the purpose of dishonestly obtaining an electronic communications service: Communications Act 2003 (UK), s. 126.
46 APIG, *Computer Misuse Act*, [80].
47 Explanatory Notes, Police and Justice Act 2006 (UK), [303]. Although the notes do not refer to Art. 6(1)(b), it also seems to be covered by the new provision. Art. 6(1)(c) is not complied with as it is not an offence to possess such articles, even with an intention to commit an offence under ss. 1 or 2.
48 Maximum penalty 2 years' imprisonment: s. 3A(5).
49 These offences are discussed in Chs. 3 and 4 respectively.
50 Computer Misuse Act, s. 3A(4).   51 S. 3A(1).

of intangible data, for example writing code. 'Supply' or 'offer to supply' would encompass both the actual dissemination of the article, but also advertising its availability, for example via a website.[52]

While such terms may encompass a broad range of legitimate and illegitimate conduct, in order for an offence to be committed the prosecution must prove that the defendant engaged in the relevant conduct with the intention that the article was intended to be used in, or to assist in the commission of a relevant offence. It is not, however, necessary to prove that it could in fact be used in that way. For example, the supply of incorrect passwords or malicious code that is ineffective could still be an offence under this section so long as the defendant had the necessary intention.

The second offence is to supply or offer to supply any article believing that it is likely to be used to commit, or to assist in the commission of, an offence under ss. 1 or 3.[53] This provision applies a recklessness standard to the fault element for supplying or offering to supply, it presumably being unlikely that a person would make or adapt an article recklessly. This offence clearly applies to the person who posts or otherwise distributes information with no intention of using it, but knowing that it is likely that others will make use of it to commit an offence. The wording of the section indicates that the prosecution must prove an actual belief. It is not sufficient that a reasonable person would have believed it was likely.

However, given the dual-use nature of many devices, this requirement is arguably too broad, particularly as there is no definition of how 'likely' the use must be.[54] Suppliers of legitimate products such as penetration-testing software, network filters and the like may be aware that their product may be used to commit or facilitate the commission of an offence and hence exposed to criminal liability. This is in contrast to the recommendations of the Convention, which not only requires specific intent, but also that the offence be committed 'without right'.

Thirdly, it is an offence to obtain any article with a view to its being supplied for use to commit or to assist in the commission of an offence under ss. 1 or 3.[55] Because possession is not an offence under the Act, even with intent to commit an offence, this provision is aimed at the person

52 The meaning of these terms in a digital context is discussed in Ch. 10.
53 Computer Misuse Act, s. 3A(2).   54 Fafinski, 'Computer misuse', 64–5.
55 Computer Misuse Act, s. 3A(3).

who obtains such articles for the purpose of providing them to others to commit an offence.

5. The United States

The relevant US offences, found in 18 USC §§ 1029 and 1030(a)(6), are both the most complex and the least comprehensive of equivalent provisions.

A. 18 USC § 1029

Section 1029, entitled 'fraud and related activity in connection with access devices', provides for no less than ten separate offences.[56] Rather than consider each provision separately, our focus will be on the meaning of 'access device', which largely determines the scope of these offences.

'Access device'

'Access device' is defined exhaustively as:

> any card, plate, code, account number, electronic serial number, mobile identification number, personal identification number, or other telecommunications service, equipment, or instrument identifier, or other means of account access that can be used, alone or in conjunction with another access device, to obtain money, goods, services, or any other thing of value, or that can be used to initiate a transfer of funds (other than a transfer originated solely by paper instrument).[57]

These provisions were enacted primarily in response to the growing incidence of credit card fraud in the 1980s, and were not aimed at access devices in digital form.[58] At that time, one of the most common forms of credit card fraud involved taking account numbers from the carbon imprints which accompanied credit card transactions. Nonetheless, its legislative history indicates that the term 'access device' was 'intended to be broad enough to encompass technical advances',[59] and the term has been held to apply to credit card account numbers,[60] merchant account

---

56 The penalties for these provisions are provided for in 18 USC § 1029(c).
57 18 USC § 1029(e)(1).   58 *US* v. *Caputo*, 808 F 2d 963, 966 (2nd Cir 1987).
59 *US* v. *Brewer*, 835 F 2d 550, 553 (5th Cir 1987). Also see *US* v. *Dabbs*, 134 F 3d 1071, 1080–1 (11th Cir 1998).
60 *US* v. *Caputo*, 808 F 2d 963, 966 (2nd Cir 1987) and *US* v. *Taylor* 945 F 2d 1050 (8th Cir 1991).

numbers,[61] blank credit cards,[62] access codes for long-distance telephone calls,[63] PINs for ATMs,[64] 'cloned' mobile telephones'[65] as well as mobile phone electronic serial numbers (ESNs) and mobile identification numbers (MINs).[66] Its origin in relation to fraud, however, means that it is not apt to cover other relevant material such as hacking instructions or software.

There is no requirement that the access code be valid in order to form the basis of a charge.[67] However, the numbers must actually correspond to an actual account, and number strings which do not represent an actual account number are not 'access devices' within the meaning of the section.[68]

The phrase 'alone or in conjunction with another access device' extends the definition of access device to 'any means of account access that can be used to obtain goods or services regardless of whether the means of access is alone sufficient to complete the transaction or whether it must be used in conjunction with another access device to do so'.[69] The term 'use in conjunction with' is not defined and is given its ordinary meaning, which includes 'any means of account access that can be brought together with another access device and used in combination therewith for the common purpose of obtaining goods or services'.[70] The fact that another device, not being an access device, is also required does not preclude the application of this provision.

For example, in addition to several cloned mobile telephones, the defendants in *US* v. *Sepulveda*[71] were also found to be in possession of ESNs and MINs, which had not been programmed into phones. While the ESNs and MINs were a 'means of account access', the microchips in the mobile phone were sufficiently analogous to the 'cards' and 'plates' used to store and convey other types of account information to constitute another

---

61 *US* v. *Dabbs*, 134 F 3d 1071 (11th Cir 1998).
62 *US* v. *Nguyen*, 81 F 3d 912 (9th Cir 1996).
63 *US* v. *Brewer*, 835 F 2d 550 (5th Cir 1987).
64 *Ibid.*, 553. Also see *US* v. *Dabbs*, 134 F 3d 1071, 1080–1 (11th Cir 1998).
65 That is, mobile phones programmed with false identifying information allowing unauthorised calls to be charged to a subscriber's account: *US* v. *Sepulveda*, 115 F 3d 882 (11th Cir 1997).
66 *Ibid.*
67 *US* v. *Brewer*, 835 F 2d 550, 554 (5th Cir 1987). Also see *US* v. *Taylor*, 945 F 2d 1050 (8th Cir 1991) in relation to use of valid but unassigned American Express credit card numbers.
68 *US* v. *Humes*, 312 F Supp 2d 893, 898 (ED Mich 2004).
69 *US* v. *Sepulveda*, 115 F 3d 882, 887 (11th Cir 1997).   70 *Ibid.*, 886.   71 *Ibid.*

'means of account access'.[72] These numbers had to be programmed into the mobile phone by the use of specialist software to which the defendants had access. The fact that this process required the use of another device(s) not being an access device(s), did not preclude the means of account access (the microchip) being used 'in conjunction with' the access device (the ESN and MIN).

Counterfeit/Unauthorised access device

'Counterfeit access device' is defined to mean 'any access device that is counterfeit, fictitious, altered, or forged, or an identifiable component of an access device or a counterfeit access device'.[73] The term 'unauthorised access device' means any access device that is lost, stolen, expired, revoked, cancelled or obtained with intent to defraud.[74]

It has been argued that an access device cannot simultaneously be both counterfeit and unauthorised. In *US* v. *Brewer*[75] the defendant placed numerous calls to a long-distance telephone company and entered a series of numbers in an attempt to correctly guess a valid access number. By doing so he accumulated approximately thirty valid access codes and also sold several numbers to an undercover secret service agent. He was convicted under 18 USC § 1029 of possessing and trafficking in counterfeit and unauthorised access devices.

The defendant argued that his convictions for trafficking in counterfeit access devices were inconsistent with his convictions for possessing unauthorized access devices. It was argued that an access device can be counterfeit, that is totally forged or altered; or unauthorised, where it is genuine but possessed without authority; but it cannot be both. This view is arguably supported by subs. (a)(3) which refers to possession of either a counterfeit *or* unauthorised access device.[76]

This argument was rejected. Even if there is a definitional distinction between the two forms of access device, this did not mean that one access device could not fall within both definitions. In this case the access codes were both 'counterfeit' because they were 'fictitious' and 'forged', and 'unauthorised' because they were obtained with an 'intent to defraud'.[77] 'Congress need not have anticipated that technological advances would create the opportunity for conduct that meets both definitions.'[78]

---

72 *Ibid.*, 886.   73 18 USC § 1029(e)(2).   74 18 USC § 1029(e)(3).
75 835 F 2d 550 (5th Cir 1987).   76 *Ibid.*, 553 (emphasis added).
77 *Ibid.*   78 *Ibid.*

The court also rejected the argument that because the defendant had guessed valid codes, that those codes could not be counterfeit. The defendant did not 'obtain' valid codes from the system; he fabricated codes, which happened to match valid codes. 'By analogy, someone who manufactures phony credit cards is no less a "counterfeiter" because he happens to give them numbers that match valid accounts.'[79]

B. 18 USC § 1030(a)(6)

Under 18 USC § 1030(a)(6) it is an offence to knowingly and with intent to defraud, traffic[80] in, any password or similar information through which a computer may be accessed without authorisation, if either (a) such trafficking affects interstate or foreign commerce, or (b) such computer is used by or for the government of the United States.

In contrast to some other jurisdictions, this section applies only to information. Although passwords are specifically referred to, it also extends to 'similar information through which a computer may be accessed without authorization'. While it could be argued that 'information through which a computer may be accessed without authorization' could include software which facilitates such access, or even instructions as to how to gain unauthorised access, such information is arguably not 'similar' to a password. Such an interpretation would arguably be inconsistent with the legislative intent behind the definition, which was 'to sweep within the subsection not only classic, single-word passwords, but also any "longer and more detailed explanations on how to access others'" computers'.[81]

Nonetheless, this definition would seem clearly inapplicable to malicious code which is designed to impair data rather than allow unauthorized access. Nor would it seem to apply to information which purported to allow access but which was in fact false, for example an incorrect password. On a strict reading, such information is not information through which a computer may be accessed without authorisation, and would have to be charged as an attempt.[82]

---

79 *Ibid.*, 554.
80 The term 'traffic' is defined as 'transfer, or otherwise dispose of, to another, or obtain control of with intent to transfer or dispose of': 18 USC § 1029(e)(5).
81 A. H. Scott, *Computer and Intellectual Property Crime: Federal and state law* (Washington DC: The Bureau of National Affairs, Inc., 2001), p. 103.
82 18 USC § 1030(b).

There are two fault elements. The first is that the person must knowingly traffic in the information. The second is that he or she must do so with intent to defraud.[83] This reflects the origin of the provisions in the context of computer fraud, and further limits the potential scope of this provision in its application to other forms of data which may be used to access computers, but without intent to defraud.

83 The meaning of 'intent to defraud' is discussed at pp. 99–100.

6

Interception of data

1. The changing nature of telecommunications

We have seen in previous chapters that offences concerned with unautho-rised 'access' to a computer evolved to being more generally concerned with the protection of data stored in a computer. In this chapter we con-sider the next layer of vulnerability: when the data leaves the computer and is communicated to others. Whether it is an email passing over a telecommunications network, an instant message on a LAN, or images sent over a wireless connection, there is the potential for that data to be intercepted. The unauthorised uses to which such information may be put are as varied as the communications themselves, but include harassment, blackmail, fraud or economic espionage.

Prior to the advent of the Internet, mass communication was still dom-inated by conventional post and telephony. The Internet has transformed the way in which we communicate by allowing large amounts of data to be transferred rapidly and easily, throughout the world, at low cost. Emails, SMS/MMS and instant messaging are increasingly the preferred modes of personal and business communication. VoIP and similar mechanisms compete with conventional telephony by providing real-time audio and visual communication over the Internet. The convergence of technology means that mobile phones are now small networked computers. This increasing connectivity is accompanied by a commensurate increase in opportunities for data to be intercepted.

Offences concerned with the unauthorised interception of communi-cations are not new and are found in each jurisdiction.[1] Such offences

1 The first US federal wiretap offence was created in 1934: 47 USC § 60, cited in O. S. Kerr, 'Internet surveillance law after the USA Patriot Act: The Big Brother that isn't' (2003) 97 *Northwestern University Law Review* 607, 630. The first telephone interception offence in Canada was enacted in 1880: R. W. Hubbard, P. M. Brauti and S. K. Fenton, *Wiretapping and Other Electronic Surveillance: Law and procedure*, (Ontario: Canada Law Book, 2008), pp. 1–2.

5

have generally evolved from provisions concerned with interception of telephone calls over public telecommunication networks, and many of the challenges which arise have been associated with their application to digital communications. Interception was relatively straightforward when the main form of electronic communication was telephone calls, transmitted over copper wires provided by, at most, a handful of providers. In contrast, modern communications may travel over a variety of networks, in different countries and via different media, before reaching their destination. For example, an email sent from a laptop may travel via a wireless network to the router where it is sent over telecommunication networks, via a combination of copper lines, optical fibres and radio waves, to the addressee. Internet communications are automatically routed via the most efficient route, and may pass through a number of servers in different jurisdictions en route to their destination. Over the course of that transmission the communication may, at various points, be stored while awaiting delivery.

To say that this is a complex area of the law would be a considerable understatement. However, much of the complexity, debate and reform in this area relates to the ability of law enforcement to conduct surveillance. In the United States in particular, case law and commentary is dominated by the Fourth Amendment protection against unreasonable search and seizure.[2] As in other chapters, we will (with some relief) not focus on the procedural issues surrounding digital surveillance.[3] Our focus is on the substantive offences punishing unauthorised interception of data as specified in the Cybercrime Convention.

2. The legislative framework

A. The Cybercrime Convention

Offences relating to the interception of data are found in Chapter II, Section 1, Title 1, 'Offences against the confidentiality, integrity and availability of computer data and systems'. Under Art. 3, parties are required to

---

2 These issues are also significant under Art. 8 of the *Canadian Charter of Rights and Freedoms*; Department of Justice Canada, *Lawful Access – Consultation Document* (2002), pp. 15–16.
3 See, generally, O. S. Kerr, 'Searches and seizures in a digital world' (2006) 119 *Harvard Law Review* 531; Computer Crime and Intellectual Property Section, *Searching and Seizing Computers and Obtaining Electronic Evidence in Criminal Investigations* (Criminal Division, United States Department of Justice, 2002); I. Walden, *Computer Crimes and Digital Investigations* (New York: Oxford University Press, 2007), pp. 203–97 and Hubbard, Brauti and Fenton, *Wiretapping and Other Electronic Surveillance.*

provide for offences which relate to 'the interception without right, made by technical means, of non-public transmissions of computer data to, from or within a computer system, including electromagnetic emissions from a computer system carrying such computer data'. The aim of this provision is to protect the right of privacy in all forms of electronic data transfer, similar to that traditionally afforded to telephone conversations.[4] As with other offences, the interception must be committed 'intentionally', and 'without right'. Parties 'may also require that the offence be committed with dishonest intent, or in relation to a computer system that is connected to another computer system'.[5]

There are a number of points which may be noted about this provision. First, it applies to 'non-public' transmissions of computer data. The term 'non-public' qualifies the nature of the transmission process, rather than the nature of the data transmitted.[6] Therefore, the provision may apply to transmission over public networks of data that may be publicly available, so long as the parties wish to communicate the information confidentially.

Secondly, interception by 'technical means' is a 'restrictive qualification to avoid over-criminalisation'.[7] It relates to:

> listening to, monitoring or surveillance of the content of communications, to the procuring of the content of data either directly, through access and use of the computer system, or indirectly, through the use of electronic eavesdropping or tapping devices.[8]

'Technical means' includes technical devices fixed to transmission lines, such as 'packet sniffers', as well as devices to collect and record wireless communications. It may also include the use of software, passwords and codes.[9]

The reference to 'electromagnetic emissions from a computer system carrying such computer data' harks back to the 'early days' of personal computers when there was concern about the use of surveillance devices which could detect the electromagnetic radiation emitted by the VDU of the computer.[10] Although such emissions do not fall within the definition of 'data' in Art. 1, data can be reconstructed from such emissions.[11] While the issue still had some currency at the time the Convention was drafted, it

---

4 Cybercrime Convention, Explanatory Report, [51].
5 Cybercrime Convention, Art. 3.
6 Cybercrime Convention, Explanatory Report, [54].   7 Ibid., [53].
8 Ibid.   9 Ibid.
10 Scottish Law Commission, Report on Computer Crime, no. 106 (1987), [2.10].
11 Cybercrime Convention, Explanatory Report, [57].

is less of a problem now with changes in VDU technology which generally
no longer rely on cathode-ray emissions.

Thirdly, the provision specifically applies to interceptions 'within' a
computer system. The Internet is the most obvious example of a 'computer system', but the provision may equally apply as between two computers belonging to the same person or organisation, for example a LAN
or a home wireless network.[12] However, parties may require, as an additional element, that the communication be transmitted between computer systems remotely connected – that is, not penalise interceptions
within a single computer system or computer systems that are directly
connected.[13]

Further, although the definition of 'computer system' may encompass
radio connections, parties are not required to criminalise the interception
of any non-public radio transmission which takes place in a relatively
open, and easily accessible manner, and can therefore be intercepted.[14]
This limitation has particular relevance in the context of 'Bluetooth' and
other devices using radio waves to communicate data over relatively short
distances.

Finally, to be an offence, an interception must be 'without right'. Examples of interceptions which are not 'without right' include those that are
carried out with the consent of the participants, authorised testing by a
service provider or where duly authorised for the purposes of law enforcement or lawful workplace surveillance.[15]

The Convention therefore provides a broad framework for interception offences. In many cases, these may overlap with unauthorised-access
offences, although it is generally considered desirable to maintain a distinction between the two categories.[16]

B. Australia

In Australia, the key federal provision is s. 7(1) Telecommunications
(Interception and Access) Act 1979 (Cth). This provides that a person
must not intercept, authorise, suffer or permit another person to intercept, or do any act, or thing that will enable him, or her, or another
person to intercept a communication passing over a telecommunications system.[17] Where a communication is no longer passing over a

---

12 Ibid., [55].   13 Ibid.   14 Ibid., [56].   15 Ibid., [58].

16 Ibid., [59]; Law Commission, Computer Misuse, Working Paper no. 110 (1988), [3.32].

17 Maximum penalty 2 years' imprisonment; s. 105. Civil remedies are also provided for
under Part 2–10 of the Act.

telecommunications system, it may become a 'stored communication'. Access to stored communications is governed by Chapter 3 Telecommunications (Interception and Access) Act 1979 (Cth). Under s. 108(1), a person commits an offence if:

    (a) the person:
        (i) accesses a stored communication; or
        (ii) authorises, suffers or permits another person to access a stored communication; or
        (iii) does any act or thing that will enable the person or another person to access a stored communication; and
    (b) the person does so with the knowledge of neither of the following:
        (i) the intended recipient of the stored communication;
        (ii) the person who sent the stored communication.

The circumstances in which an interception is not unlawful include under warrant, lawful operation of service providers and consent.[18]

In a federal system such as Australia, the application of this provision to a telecommunications system is an important basis for federal jurisdiction. Section 51(v) of the Constitution gives the Commonwealth power to legislate in respect of 'postal, telegraphic, telephonic and other like services'. It has been held that the Commonwealth Act covers the field in this regard, displacing any state regulation that seeks to regulate the interception of telecommunications.[19] Although these decisions related to the interception of telephone conversations, it is likely that the interception of any communication while in the course of transmission over a telecommunications network would be governed exclusively by federal law.[20]

C. Canada

The Canadian legislative framework is the least developed in terms of dealing with new communication technologies, and reform in this area has proved difficult, with the last major attempt at reform failing to pass.[21]

---

18 Ss. 7 and 108. Also see Parts 2–2, 2–3, 2–5, 3–2 and 3–3.
19 *Edelsten* v. *Investigating Committee of New South Wales* (1986) 7 NSWLR 222 at 230 per Lee J, citing *Miller* v. *Miller* (1978) 141 CLR 269 at 276 per Barwick CJ.
20 New South Wales Law Reform Commission, *Surveillance: Final Report*, Report 108 (2005), [2.3].
21 Bill C-74, *Modernization of Investigative Techniques Act* (2005). For a critical analysis, see D. Gilbert, I. R. Kerr and J. McGill, 'The medium and the message: Personal privacy and the forced marriage of police and telecommunications providers' (2007) 51 *Criminal Law Quarterly* 469.

The principal telecommunication interception provisions are found in Part VI Criminal Code (Can): 'Invasion of Privacy'. Section 184(1) makes it an offence for a person, by means of any 'electro-magnetic, acoustic, mechanical or other device',[22] to wilfully intercept a 'private communication'.[23]

Also relevant in the cybercrime context is s. 342.1(1)(b) Criminal Code (Can), which is aimed at intercepts that do not involve telecommunications. It provides that it is an offence, fraudulently and without colour of right, by means of an electro-magnetic, acoustic, mechanical or other device, to intercept or cause to be intercepted, directly or indirectly, any function of a computer system.[24]

Some of the circumstances in which an interception will not be 'without colour of right' include under warrant, lawful operations of service providers and consent.[25] There are, however, offences relating to unauthorised disclosure of interceptions under Part VI.[26]

D. The United Kingdom

In the UK, inadequacies in the existing framework led to the enactment of the Regulation of Investigatory Powers Act 2000 (UK) (RIPA) in an attempt to provide a single legal framework for the interception of communications, regardless of the means of communication or at which point the communication is intercepted.[27] Under s. 1(1)–(2) RIPA it is an offence for a person intentionally, and without lawful authority, to intercept at any place in the UK any communication in the course of its transmission by means of a public or private telecommunication system.[28] The circumstances in which an interception may be lawful are

---

22 Defined as 'any device or apparatus that is used or is capable of being used to intercept a private communication, but does not include a hearing aid used to correct subnormal hearing of the user to not better than normal hearing': Criminal Code (Can), s. 183.

23 Maximum penalty 5 years' imprisonment. Section 184.5 Criminal Code (Can) is in the same terms but relates to radio-based telecommunications and requires that the interception be made 'maliciously or for gain'.

24 Maximum penalty 10 years' imprisonment.

25 Criminal Code (Can), ss. 184(2), 184.1, 184.2 and 184.4. For a detailed discussion, see Hubbard, Brauti and Fenton, *Wiretapping and Other Electronic Surveillance*.

26 Criminal Code (Can), ss. 193 and 193.1.

27 See generally, Y. Akdeniz, N. Taylor and C. Walker, 'Regulation of Investigatory Powers Act 2000 (1): BigBrother.gov.uk: State surveillance in the age of information and rights' (2001) *Criminal Law Review* 73.

28 Maximum penalty 2 years' imprisonment: s. 1(7).

under warrant,[29] lawful operation of a service provider[30] and consent of a person who has the right to control the operation or use of the system or has the express or implied consent of such a person.[31]

E. The United States

Surveillance law in the United States has been described by a leading commentator as 'famously complex, if not entirely impenetrable',[32] and by the courts as 'convoluted',[33] 'confusing and uncertain'[34] and an 'evidentiary nightmare'.[35] Major reform of interception laws occurred with the Electronic Communications Privacy Act of 1986 (ECPA), and many of the difficulties arise because 'the ECPA was written prior to the advent of the Internet and the World Wide Web. As a result, the existing statutory framework is ill-suited to address modern forms of communication.'[36] As with the CFAA, the presence of a civil liability provision has provided a fruitful, though often unhelpful, source of jurisprudence in this area.[37] The ECPA amended Title III of the Omnibus Crime Control and Safe Streets Act of 1968 and restructured it into three major sections.[38]

Title I (the Wiretap Act) governs the interception of content.[39] In particular, under 18 USC § 2511(1)(a) it is an offence to intentionally intercept, endeavour to intercept, or procure any other person to intercept or endeavour to intercept, any wire, oral or electronic communication.[40] An 'oral communication' is speech which is uttered in the justifiable expectation that it is not subject to interception,[41] while a 'wire communication' is essentially an oral communication sent over a telecommunication

29 The interception warrant provisions are found in RIPA, ss. 5–11, and 5(1) and s. 3 Wireless Telegraphy Act 1949 (UK).

30 RIPA, s. 3(3).

31 RIPA, ss. 1(6) and 3(1)(2). It has been held that 'right to control' means the right to authorise and forbid, rather than merely the right to access or operate the system'; *R v. Stanford* [2006] EWCA Crim 258 at [20]–[22] per Lord Phillips CJ.

32 O. S. Kerr, 'Lifting the "fog" of Internet surveillance: How a suppression remedy would change computer crime law' (2003) 54 *Hastings Law Journal* 805, 820.

33 *US v. Smith*, 155 F 3d 1051, 1055 (9th Cir 1998).

34 *Konop v. Hawaiian Airlines Inc.*, 302 F 3d 868, 874 (9th Cir 2002).

35 *US v. Councilman*, 245 F Supp 2d 319, 321 (D Mass 2003).

36 *Konop v. Hawaiian Airlines Inc.*, 302 F 3d 868, 874 (9th Cir 2002).

37 18 USC § 2511(5).

38 K. A. Oyama, 'E-mail privacy after United States v. Councilman: Legislative options for amending ECPA' (2006) 21 *Berkeley Technology Law Journal* 499.

39 18 USC §§ 2510–22.

40 The penalties for this offence are found in 18 USC § 2511(4).   41 18 USC § 2510(2).

network.[42] Prior to the introduction of the term 'electronic communication', it was held that interception of computer data did not constitute a
'wire communication'.[43]

Title II (the Stored Communications Act or SCA) governs access to
stored communications.[44] The Act is overwhelmingly concerned with
procedural rules governing disclosure of stored communications, the one
substantive offence provision being 18 USC § 2701(a).[45] This makes it
an offence to intentionally access, without or in excess of authorisation, a
facility through which an 'electronic communication service'[46] is provided
and thereby to obtain, alter or prevent authorised access to a wire or
electronic communication while it is in electronic storage.[47]

Title III (the Pen Register Act) governs access to traffic data.[48] Under 18
USC § 3121(a) there is a general prohibition on the use of a pen register
or a trap and trace device without a court order.[49] A 'pen register' is:

> a device or process which records or decodes dialing, routing, address-
> ing, or signaling information transmitted by an instrument or facility
> from which a wire or electronic communication is transmitted, provided,
> however, that such information shall not include the contents of any
> communication.[50]

On the other hand, a 'trap and trace device' is:

> a device or process which captures the incoming electronic or other
> impulses which identify the originating number or other dialing, rout-
> ing, addressing, and signaling information reasonably likely to identify the
> source of a wire or electronic communication, provided, however, that
> such information shall not include the contents of any communication.[51]

---

42 18 USC § 2510(1).   43 *US* v. *Seidlitz*, 589 F 2d 152, 156 (4th Cir 1978).
44 18 USC §§ 2701–12. For a detailed analysis of the Act, see O. S. Kerr, 'A user's guide to the
Stored Communications Act – and a legislator's guide to amending it' (2004) 72 *George
Washington Law Review* 1701.
45 Kerr, 'Stored Communications Act', 36.
46 Defined as 'any service which provides to users thereof the ability to send or receive wire
or electronic communications': 18 USC § 2510(15), which applies by virtue of 18 USC
§ 2711(1).
47 The penalties for this offence are set out in 18 USC § 2701(b).
48 18 USC §§ 3121–7. Prior to amendments introduced by the PATRIOT Act, there were
some doubt as to whether the Pen Register Statute applied to the Internet, although the
general view was that it did; Kerr, 'Internet surveillance', 632–6.
49 18 USC § 3123. Maximum penalty 1 year's imprisonment: 18 USC § 3121(d). Provisions
relating to authorisation are 18 USC §§ 3122, 3123 and 3125.
50 18 USC § 3127(3). 'Wire communication' and 'electronic communication' have the same
meaning as in 18 USC § 2510 which applies by virtue of 18 USC § 3127(1).
51 18 USC § 3127(4).

In essence, when combined, the devices record addressing information that is incoming (trap and trace) or outgoing (pen register).

There are a number of circumstances in which interceptions or access to stored communications will be lawful. These include under warrant,[52] lawful operation of service providers[53] and the consent of a party.[54]

Rather than reviewing each provision individually, the following discussion focuses on the key principles, which form the basis of interception offences:

1. the meaning of 'telecommunication'
2. the distinction between content and traffic data
3. the distinction between live and stored communications.

3. The meaning of 'telecommunication'

Traditional intercept laws were drafted with public telecommunications networks in mind. Today, private networks are a central feature of modern communications, with the boundary between public and private increasingly blurred. Consequently, intercept laws drafted to apply only to public telecommunications present considerable challenges in the context of Internet communications, which may pass over both public and private networks. Whether a communication is protected from interception will depend upon the type of network over which it was passing at the time it was intercepted, an issue which is not always easy to determine.[55]

A. Australia

The boundary between telecommunications networks and other forms of interception is a confused issue in Australia, despite going to the heart of federal versus state responsibility. It has been said that what s. 51(v) of the Constitution embraces is 'the organized communication of messages from a distance, as well as the communication of messages by an organized means from a distance'.[56] While the power conferred by s. 51(v) is 'not confined to the telephonic and telegraphic services conducted at the

---

52 18 USC § 2701(c). Relevant warrant provisions are found in 18 USC §§ 2703, 2704, 2518, 3123(b)(2), and/or 3124(a)(b).
53 18 USC §§ 2511(2)(a)(i), 2701(c)(1), 3127(3), 3121(b).
54 18 USC §§ 2511(2)(c)(d) and 3121(b)(3).
55 See, e.g., *R* v. *Taylor-Sabori* [1999] 1 All ER 160.
56 *Jones* v. *Cth* (1965) 112 CLR 206 at 219 per Barwick CJ.

time of Federation, nor to services which are like them',[57] the advent of
new forms of communication such as wireless networks presents challenges to the existing framework. This is an issue of some significance,
with the interface with state surveillance legislation producing a 'complex and, at times, confusing web of Commonwealth, State and Territory
laws'.[58]

In order to fall within the scope of the federal interception provisions, the communication must be passing over a 'telecommunications
system'. This is defined as a 'telecommunications network' that is wholly
or partly[59] within Australia and includes equipment,[60] a line[61] or other
facility[62] that is connected to such a network and is within Australia. A
'telecommunications network' is in turn defined to mean a 'system, or
series of systems, for carrying communications by means of guided or
unguided electromagnetic energy or both'.[63] In contrast to the UK position, there is no requirement that the system be part of, or connected to,
public telecommunication systems.[64]

This definition therefore seems broad enough to cover most forms of
private or public networks, including stand-alone networks. The term
'equipment' is defined so broadly that any networked computer forms
part of that network. It also suggests that interception within the device
itself, such as through use of a keylogger, is an interception for these
purposes.

The Act also includes aspects of the network, such as wireless routers,
where communications are carried by unguided electromagnetic energy.
It does not, however, apply to a system for carrying communications

---

57 *Ibid.*   58 NSW Law Reform Commission, *Surveillance*, [2.1].
59 The Act only applies to the extent that the network is in Australia; Telecommunications
   (Interception and Access) Act 1979 (Cth), s. 5(1).
60 'Equipment' means 'any apparatus or equipment used, or intended for use, in or in
   connection with a telecommunications network, and includes a telecommunications
   device but does not include a line': s. 5(1).
61 Defined as 'a wire, cable, optical fibre, tube, conduit, waveguide or other physical medium
   used, or for use, as a continuous artificial guide for or in connection with carrying communications by means of guided electromagnetic energy': Telecommunications (Interception and Access) Act 1979 (Cth), s. 5(1) and Telecommunications Act 1997 (Cth),
   s. 7.
62 Defined as 'any part of the infrastructure of a telecommunications network, or any
   line, equipment, apparatus, tower, mast, antenna, tunnel, duct, hole, pit, pole or other
   structure or thing used, or for use, in or in connection with a telecommunications
   network': Telecommunications (Interception and Access) Act 1979 (Cth), s. 5(1) and
   Telecommunications Act 1997 (Cth), s. 7.
63 S. 5(1).   64 See p. 148.

'solely by means of radiocommunication'.[65] This raises significant questions about the applicability of the Act to wireless networks. Although such networks often interface with other aspects of the telecommunication network, and hence do not carry communications *solely* by means of radiocommunication, an independent wireless network may arguably fall outside the Act.[66] At the very least, this would appear to be the case with systems such as Bluetooth, which utilise radiowaves to transmit data over short distances.[67]

Where data is not 'passing over a telecommunication system' and falls outside the stored communications provisions,[68] its interception would be governed, if at all, by surveillance devices legislation. For example, s. 6 Surveillance Devices Act 2004 (Cth) governs the use of 'data surveillance devices', defined as 'any device or program capable of being used to record or monitor the input of information into, or the output of information from, a computer'.[69] However, in most jurisdictions these Acts govern only the use of these devices by law enforcement officers, there being no general offence against unauthorised use of data surveillance devices.[70] Others do not incorporate data surveillance at all, being limited to listening, optical and/or tracking surveillance.[71] Only in New South Wales is it an offence for any person to utilise a data surveillance device without authorisation.[72]

B. Canada

The Canadian legislation draws a distinction between 'oral communications' and 'telecommunications'. Our focus is on 'telecommunications', defined broadly as 'the emission, transmission or reception of signs, signals, writing, images, sounds or intelligence of any nature by any wire,

---

65 S. 5(1). S. 6(1) Radiocommunications Act 1992 (Cth) defines a 'radiocommunication' as 'radio emission or reception of radio emission for the purpose of communicating information between persons and persons, persons and things or things and things'.

66 A. Blunn, *Report of the Review of the Regulation of Access to Communications* (Australian Government Attorney-General's Department, 2005), [11.4].

67 Although radiocommunications are primarily governed by the Radiocommunications Act 1992 (Cth), that Act does not contain an offence of unlawful interception.

68 See p. 166.

69 Surveillance Devices Act 2004 (Cth), s. 6.

70 Surveillance Devices Act 1999 (Vic), Surveillance Devices Act 2004 (Cth), Surveillance Devices Act 2007 (NT) and Police Powers and Responsibilities Act 2000 (Qld).

71 Listening Devices Act 1992 (ACT), Listening and Surveillance Devices Act 1972 (SA), Listening Devices Act 1991 (Tas) and Surveillance Devices Act 1998 (WA).

72 Surveillance Devices Act 2007 (NSW), s. 10.

cable, radio, optical or other electromagnetic system, or by any similar technical system'.[73] Although clearly drafted in the context of conventional telecommunication intercepts, its broad language seems capable of application to modern communication networks, including wireless applications.

A similar definition of 'telecommunication' was considered by the Supreme Court of Canada in *R* v. *McLaughlin*.[74] The defendant was charged with theft, having used a computer terminal to access a mainframe and obtain data. Under s. 287(1)(b) (as it then was) Criminal Code (Can), a person commits theft who fraudulently, maliciously, or without colour of right uses any telecommunication facility or obtains any telecommunication service. The narrow question for the court was whether a computer was a 'telecommunications facility'. The court accepted that the computer system (consisting of the mainframe, memory, printers and approximately 300 connected terminals) was a 'facility' – that is, 'something built, installed or established to serve a particular function or to accomplish some end or provide a certain service'.[75] The question was whether it was a 'telecommunication facility'.

The definition of 'telecommunication' under s. 287(2) was, to all intents and purposes, the same as applies to s. 183.[76] It was held that although the defendant's conduct clearly involved 'transmission of intelligence from one part of the facility to another, there was no reception by other facilities nor emissions from this facility'.[77] Accordingly, there was no 'telecommunication' as:

> [t]he computer, being a computing device, contemplates the participation of one entity only, namely the operator. In a sense, he communicates with himself, but it could hardly be said that the operator by operating the terminal or console of the computer is thereby communicating information in the sense of transmitting information and hence it stretches the language beyond reality to conclude that a person using a computer is thereby using a telecommunication facility in the sense of the Criminal Code.[78]

Although in a different context, this decision provides some useful insights, in particular that a telecommunication requires transmission

73 Interpretation Act 1985 (Can), s. 35.   74 [1980] 2 SCR 331.
75 *Ibid.*, at 336 per Laskin CJ.
76 The only real difference is that the definition of 'telecommunication' pursuant to s. 35 Interpretation Act 1985 (Can) refers to 'wire, cable . . . or other electromagnetic system, or by any similar technical system', while s. 287(2) Criminal Code (Can), referred to 'electronic or other electromagnetic system'.
77 *R* v. *McLaughlin* [1980] 2 SCR 331 at 336.   78 *Ibid.*, at 341 per Estey J.

or reception of information from an 'outside recipient'. This is consistent with the requirement in s. 183 that there be an originator and an intended recipient.[79]

Where difficulties arise is when data is intercepted internally to the computer, for example the use of a keylogger to monitor keystrokes. Although the internal transfer of data seems to fall within the literal definition of 'telecommunication', applying the reasoning in *McLaughlin* such transfers of data would be regarded as 'data processing' rather than telecommunications.[80] A personal computer, for example, is essentially a miniaturised version of the mainframe described by the court, the components being contained in the one device. The transmission of data to the CPU is not directed to an 'outside recipient', and so there is no originator or intended recipient. It therefore seems that, in contrast to the United States, the Canadian interception provision does not apply to purely internal communications.[81]

As the court acknowledged, the distinction may be a narrow one.[82] For example, imagine a computer user composing an email and the keystrokes are being recorded. At this stage, there is no telecommunication as although the document is intended for a recipient, the data is utilised internally within the computer for the purposes of data processing only. Once the email is sent, however, it is a telecommunication, even if intercepted internally, as it is the transmission of information from an originator to an intended recipient. This would seem to be the case even if the communication was intended for the originator, there being no inherent requirement that the person intended to receive the communication must be someone other than the originator.

Such internal communications would, however, be governed by s. 342.1(1)(b) Criminal Code (Can). This is one aspect of the broader offence of 'unauthorised use of a computer' and applies to the interception of any 'function of a computer system'. The term 'function of a computer' is not defined, but would seem potentially very broad in scope; the ordinary meaning of 'function' being the 'special kind of activity proper to anything; the mode of action by which it fulfils its purpose'.[83] It would therefore seem capable of applying to the interception of any activity of a computer, including those which are purely internal.

---

79 The meaning of these terms is discussed further at p. 156.
80 *R* v. *McLaughlin* [1980] 2 SCR 331 at 336 per Laskin CJ.
81 See pp. 150–1.   82 *R* v. *McLaughlin* [1980] 2 SCR 331 at 332.
83 *Oxford English Dictionary.*

C. *The United Kingdom*

Prior to the enactment of RIPA, the primary legislation governing interception in the UK was the Interception of Communications Act 1985
(UK). However, the scope of this legislation was determined, in part, by
definitions in the Telecommunications Act 1984 (UK). The effect of this
was that the Act applied only to telecommunications carried by the public
telecommunications system and did not extend to communications on
private networks such as those within hotels and workplaces.[84]

The Act also failed to address the increasing use of 'wireless telegraphy',
whereby radio communication is used to transmit data, for example using
wireless routers or other forms of wireless communication such as Bluetooth. Such communications fell outside the Interception of Communications Act 1985 (UK) and were governed by the less rigorous provisions
of the Wireless Telegraphy Act 1949 (UK).[85] Such gaps in the law not only
left some communications potentially unprotected, but could also render
the activities of law enforcement agencies unlawful.[86]

As a result of these inadequacies, the interception provisions under
RIPA expressly apply to both public and private telecommunication
systems.[87] 'Telecommunication system' is defined to mean:

> any system (including the apparatus comprised in it) which exists (whether
> wholly or partly in the United Kingdom or elsewhere) for the purpose of
> facilitating the transmission of communications by any means involving
> the use of electrical or electro-magnetic energy.[88]

This provision makes clear that the Act applies to the interception of
communications whether they are transmitted by guided or unguided
electromagnetic energy. It therefore applies to wireless communications,
although interception of a communication does not include the interception of any communication broadcast for *general* reception.[89] This covers
such things as television and radio signals, but not pager or mobile-phone
signals which are covered by the Act.[90]

Under s. 2 RIPA, a 'public telecommunication system' means 'any
such parts of a telecommunication system by means of which any public telecommunications service is provided as are located in the United

---

84 *R* v. *Effik* [1995] 1 AC 309.   85 Now see the Wireless Telegraphy Act 2006 (UK).
86 *Halford* v. *United Kingdom* [1998] Criminal Law Review 753.
87 Interception Legislation Team, Home Office, *Interception of Communications in the United
    Kingdom*, Consultation Paper, Cm. 4368, (1999), pp. 13–15.
88 RIPA, s. 2(1).   89 RIPA, s. 2(3).
90 Explanatory Notes, Regulation of Investigatory Powers Act 2000 (UK), [29].

Kingdom'. 'Public telecommunication service' means any telecommunications service[91] 'which is offered or provided to, or to a substantial section of, the public in any one or more parts of the United Kingdom'. A 'private telecommunication system' is a telecommunication system which is not a public telecommunication system and is:

> attached, directly or indirectly and whether or not for the purposes of the communication in question, to a public telecommunication system; and ... there is apparatus comprised in the system which is both located in the United Kingdom and used (with or without other apparatus) for making the attachment to the public telecommunication system.[92]

This makes it clear that a system which is attached to the public system also falls within the scope of the legislation, whether or not the particular communication is to be transmitted over the public system.[93] This would apply, for example, to LANs within organisations which are connected to the public system. It would also apply to interception of wireless communications from a wireless router, which is also connected to the public system. It would not, however, apply to a network which was entirely stand-alone and not connected to the public system. Similarly, communications between devices via Bluetooth and similar systems presumably do not fall within the interception provisions of the Act.

Although the offences applicable to public and private systems are in the same terms, the defences which apply to them are not. For example, the consent of the person having the right to control the operation or use of the system is a defence in relation to private systems, but not public.[94] The question of whether a communication was intercepted while being transmitted by a public or private system may therefore be of some significance.

D. The United States

'Electronic communications' are defined as 'any transfer of signs, signals, writing, images, sounds, data, or intelligence of any nature transmitted in whole or in part by a wire, radio, electromagnetic, photoelectronic

---

91 'Telecommunications service' means 'any service that consists in the provision of access to, and of facilities for making use of, any telecommunication system (whether or not one provided by the person providing the service)': RIPA, s. 2(1).
92 RIPA, s 2(1).   93 Cf R v. Effik [1995] 1 AC 309.   94 RIPA, s. 1(3).

or photooptical system that affects interstate or foreign commerce'.[95] According to the House Report relating to the 1986 amendments:

> [t]he term 'electronic communication' is intended to cover a broad range of communication activities . . . As a rule, a communication is an electronic communication if it is neither carried by sound waves nor can fairly be characterized as one containing the human voice (carried in part by wire). Communications consisting solely of data, for example . . . would be electronic communications.[96]

No distinction is drawn between communications passing over telecommunication networks and other forms of data transfer; the scope of the provision being limited by the requirement that the system (not the communication) must affect interstate or foreign commerce. This can, however, give rise to fine distinctions, as illustrated by the decision in *US v. Ropp*.[97] The defendant was alleged to have installed a device known as a 'KeyKatcher' on the desktop computer of a Ms Beck who worked for an insurance company. It was accepted that the device captured the electronic impulses passing from the keyboard to the computer, recording the keystrokes which could later be recovered and converted into text.

In granting the defendant's motion to dismiss his indictment for violation of 18 USC § 2511(1)(a) the court held that the communication in this case was not an 'electronic communication within the meaning of the statute because it is not transmitted by a system that affects interstate or foreign commerce'. In reaching this conclusion, the court considered another keylogger case, *US v. Scarfo*,[98] in which the court considered a motion to suppress evidence obtained through use of a keylogging device installed by the FBI on the defendant's computer. Because the computer was connected to a modem, the keylogger was configured in such a way that keystrokes would only be recorded when there was no activity in any of the communication ports of the computer. It was held that the Act would apply only to those signals transferred through the modem and over a telephone or cable and, therefore, the interceptions should not be suppressed.[99]

---

95 18 USC § 2510(12). This definition is subject to a number of exceptions including wire or oral communications, communications made through a tone-only paging device, tracking devices (as defined in 18 USC § 3117) and certain electronic funds transfer information stored by a financial institution.

96 H.R. Rep. no. 99–647 (1986), p. 35; cited in *US v. Councilman* 418 F 3d 67, 77 (1st Cir 2005).

97 347 F Supp 2d 831 (CD Ca 2004).   98 180 F Supp 2d 572 (D NJ 2001).

99 *US v. Ropp*, 347 F Supp 2d 831, 836 (CD Ca 2004). Also citing *US v. Councilman*, 373 F 3d 197 (1st Cir 2004).

In this case, the relevant 'system' was the computer's hardware (including the keyboard) and software programs. Although connected to a larger system, which did affect interstate or foreign commerce, the transmission in issue did not involve that system and when intercepted 'no more affected interstate commerce than a letter, placed in a stamped envelope, that has not yet been mailed'.[100] The transmissions in this case could equally have been made on a stand-alone computer that had no link at all to the Internet, or any other external network. Consequently, the interception did not fall within the provisions of the Wiretap Act.[101]

The issue of whether unauthorised access to a website can constitute interception of an electronic communication was considered by the Ninth Circuit in the civil case of *Konop* v. *Hawaiian Airlines, Inc.*[102] The plaintiff, an airline pilot, brought an action against his employer, Hawaiian Airlines, under various statutes including the ECPA. The plaintiff maintained a website on which he posted bulletins critical of the airline. Access to the website was controlled by username and password, and the plaintiff created a list of fellow pilots and employees who would be allowed access. The airline president asked one of these people to allow him to use his username to access the site, which he did. One issue for determination was whether accessing a secure website constitutes a breach of either the Wiretap Act or the SCA. More specifically, was the website an 'electronic communication' and, if so, did accessing that website constitute an 'interception'?

The court held that the website fell within the definition of 'electronic communication'.[103] The creation of a website involves the creator sending the relevant documents to a server where they are stored. The person accessing the site sends a request to the server which then transmits a copy of the document to the person requesting:

> When the server sends the document to the user's computer for viewing, a transfer of information from the website owner to the user has occurred. Although the website owner's document does not go directly or immediately to the user, once a user accesses a website, information is transferred from the website owner to the user via one of the specified mediums.[104]

With respect, such a conclusion is correct subject to the clarification that the website itself is not a communication. Rather, it is the uploading or

---

100 *Ibid.*, 835, citing *US* v. *Robinson*, 545 F 2d 301, 304 (2d Cir 1976).   101 *Ibid.*, 837–8.
102 302 F 3d 868 (9th Cir 2002); cert. denied, *Konop* v. *Hawaiian Airlines, Inc.*, 537 US 1193 (2003).
103 *Ibid.*, 876.   104 *Ibid.*

downloading of data, to or from the website, that constitute the electronic communication as it is only then that there is a transfer of data. Until that point, it is simply data stored passively on a server. As the court pointed out, the meaning of 'intercept' in this context requires acquisition contemporaneous with transmission.[105] To simply access data stored on a website is not to intercept data. It is, at most, to access a stored communication. However, where data is being uploaded or download from the website there is an electronic communication which may be intercepted. This is reflected in the court's conclusion that for a website to be 'intercepted' it must be acquired during transmission, not while it is in electronic storage.[106]

One category of data which blurs the distinction between different forms of communication is the transmission of voice over the Internet, for example by VoIP. It appears that such communications fall within the definition of 'wire communication' as being an 'aural transfer made in whole or in part through the use of facilities for the transmission of communications by the aid of wire, cable, or other like connection between the point of origin and the point of reception'.[107]

4. What is a 'communication'? (Content vs. Traffic data)

In considering the interception of communications, it is important to distinguish between the content of the communication, and the information which is necessary for it to reach its destination – so-called 'traffic data'. This is most easily understood in the context of conventional mail. The address and return address, the stamp and postmark are all simply addressing information which allows the letter to reach its destination, or to be returned to the sender. In contrast, the letter inside the envelope is the content of the communication. A similar distinction is made in relation to telephone calls; the addressing information being the number dialled, and the number from which the call is made, as well as the time and duration of the calls.

This broad distinction between content and addressing, or 'envelope', information may equally be applied to Internet communications. For example, while the body and subject line of an email are clearly content,

---

105 *Ibid.*, 878. Also see p. 173.   106 This issue is discussed further at pp. 173–4.
107 18 USC § 2510(1). O. S. Kerr, *Computer Crime Law* (St Paul: Thomson West, 2006), pp. 455–6.

the mail header gives information as to when the email was sent, by and to whom, and the path via which it was routed.

The nature of such addressing information has expanded considerably in an age of networked communications. The Internet is a 'packet-switched' network,[108] meaning that each communication is broken down into small packets of data before being transmitted. Each packet has a 'packet header', which contains the addressing information for that packet including the IP addresses of the sending and receiving computers. It also contains information about the type of packet it is, for example whether is it part of an email, webpage, etc. When it arrives at its destination, the header is discarded and the content or 'payload' delivered.[109]

Therefore email is only one form of communication over the Internet. There are requests to, and responses from, websites, as well as automated communications between the myriad computers which allow the network to function, such as domain name servers.[110] Potential data which may be intercepted includes URLs, email addresses, IP addresses, port numbers and search terms.[111] Mobile-phone data may allow the user's approximate location to be calculated, in real time, through a process of triangulation.[112]

'Traffic data' is defined in the Cybercrime Convention as:

> any computer data relating to a communication by means of a computer system, generated by a computer system that formed a part in the chain of communication, indicating the communication's origin, destination, route, time, date, size, duration, or type of underlying service.[113]

While data such as email and IP addresses are clearly traffic data, the question is more difficult when considering data such as URLs or search terms. On one view these are simply a set of binary instructions allowing the user's computer to retrieve information from other computers. In this respect, it is akin to traffic data. On the other hand, it may be said that it

---

108 This may be contrasted with a 'circuit-switched network' where a dedicated line is created between the two communicating devices: Australian Law Reform Commission, *For Your Information: Australian privacy law and practice*, Report 108 (2008), vol. i, [9.33].

109 Kerr, 'Big Brother', 614.   110 *Ibid.*, 613.

111 For a useful summary of the key data-types associated with Internet activity, see H. Lamb, *Principal Current Data Types* (Internet Crime Forum, 2001), found in Home Office, *Retention of Communications Data Under Part 11: Anti-Terrorism, Crime and Security Act 2001*, Voluntary Code of Practice (2001), Appendix C.

112 S. Morris, *The Future of Netcrime Now: Part 1 – threats and challenges*, Home Office Online Report 62/04 (2004), pp. 22–3.

113 Cybercrime Convention, Chapter II, Section 1, Title 1, Art. 1(d).

is a communication because it communicates something of the person's thoughts in typing in the URL or search term.[114] HTTP requests, for example, may include information such as the email address of the user, the last web page viewed and search terms.[115]

Against this background, we now turn to consider the meaning of 'communication' in each jurisdiction.

A. Australia

In Australia, 'communication' is defined to include 'conversation and a message, and any part of a conversation or message', whether in the form of, inter alia, data, text, visual images, signals or 'in any other form or in any combination of forms'.[116] The reference to conversation clearly applies to conventional telephone conversations. Given that the conversation may be in the form of data or in a combination of forms, it would seem to equally apply to the transmission of oral communications over the Internet, for example by VoIP.[117] More significant for our purposes is the term 'message', which is not otherwise defined. While it would seem clearly to apply to communications such as emails or SMS, less clear is whether it extends to other elements of the communication, such as traffic data.

The ordinary meaning of 'message' is a 'communication transmitted through a messenger or other agency; an oral, written, recorded, or electronic communication sent from one person, group, etc., to another'.[118] On this interpretation, it is arguable that the term 'message' is limited to communications between people, whereas traffic data is a communication between computers, or from a person to a computer. On the other hand, the legislative definition of communication is inclusive, and its reference to 'any part of a conversation or message' would seem sufficiently broad to encompass traffic data associated with the message. Similar to the position in the UK, on that analysis, traffic data would only fall within the provision if it were associated with a message.[119]

Although there are restrictions on the disclosure of 'telecommunications data' by carriers and others involved in the transmission of

114 Kerr, 'Big Brother', 645–6.
115 Australian Law Reform Commission, *For Your Information*, [9.23].
116 Telecommunications (Interception and Access) Act 1979 (Cth), s. 5.
117 This was assumed in the Blunn Report which specifically recommended against VoIP being specifically identified: Blunn, *Access to Communications*, [1.4.2].
118 *Oxford English Dictionary.*   119 See pp. 159–60.

telecommunications,[120] this does not address the issue of interception of traffic data.[121] Nor is 'telecommunications data' defined under the Act. According to the Explanatory Memorandum, in relation to Internet-based communications it includes the IP address and the start and finish time of each session.[122] It does not, however, include content such as the subject line of an email or details of Internet sessions.[123] While the lack of definition has some advantages in terms of technological neutrality,[124] the distinction between content and substance in the context of modern communications is not so easily drawn, and this issue would benefit from clarification as occurred in the UK.[125]

B. Canada

The equivalent term in Canada is 'private communication', defined as:

> any oral communication, or any telecommunication, that is made by an originator who is in Canada or is intended by the originator to be received by a person who is in Canada and that is made under circumstances in which it is reasonable for the originator to expect that it will not be intercepted by any person other than the person intended by the originator to receive it, and includes any radio-based telephone communication that is treated electronically or otherwise for the purpose of preventing intelligible reception by any person other than the person intended by the originator to receive it.[126]

The definition of 'telecommunication', discussed above, is clearly capable of applying to a broad range of network communications.[127] The definition of 'private communication', however, imposes two significant limitations. First, there must be a reasonable expectation of privacy in

120 Telecommunications (Interception and Access) Act 1979 (Cth), Ch. 4.
121 Blunn, *Access to Communications*, [1.5.15]. The report further notes at [1.1.25] that while mobile phone data may provide evidence of location, it is not clear that such data is subject to any regulation.
122 Explanatory Memorandum, Telecommunications (Interception and Access) Amendment Bill 2007 (Cth), p. 6.
123 *Ibid.*, at p. 8.
124 Australian Law Reform Commission, *For Your Information*, [73.33].
125 See pp. 159–60. Also see Standing Committee on Legal and Constitutional Affairs, *Telecommunications (Interception and Access) Amendment Bill 2007* (Canberra, Commonwealth of Australia, 2007), pp. 18–20; and Australian Law Reform Commission, *For Your Information*, [73.30]–[73.32].
126 Criminal Code (Can), s. 183. The reference to radio waves addresses the earlier decision of the Supreme Court in *Maltais* v. *R* [1978] 1 SCR 441.
127 See pp. 145–6.

respect of the communication. This question is considered objectively from the perspective of the 'originator' – that is, the person who made the remark or remarks.[128] In order to establish that the communication was not private, the prosecution must prove, beyond a reasonable doubt, that the originator knew, or ought to have known, that such communications could be intercepted by someone other than the person for whom they were intended.[129]

For example, it has been held that 'an ordinary user of a cellular phone knows or ought to know that a communication transmitted through such a device may be intercepted by someone other than the one for whom it is intended.'[130] For this reason, there is some debate as to whether an email falls within this provision as it may be argued that because such messages are easily intercepted, it is not reasonable for the originator to expect that it will not be intercepted within the terms of the section.[131]

The second limitation is the requirement of an originator and intended recipient.[132] While such a requirement makes sense in the context of conventional communications between people, its application to traffic data is unclear. While the Supreme Court in R v. McLaughlin seemed to accept that the 'activating source' of a telecommunication may be a device rather than a person,[133] the court was there envisaging the use of telex machines or faxes rather than modern packet-switched networks.

This issue was considered by the Ontario Court of Appeal in R v. Fegan.[134] The defendant was alleged to have engaged in indecent, harassing and threatening phone calls. The prosecution sought to admit evidence from a digital number recorder (DNR) utilised by the phone company in investigating complaints related to these calls. The DNR was a device which recorded the number dialled from the appellant's phone, indicating the time of the call and the number to which it was made, but not recording the nature or substance of the conversation.

128 R v. Solomon (1992) 77 CCC (3d) 264 at 276 per Boisvert MCJ.
129 Ibid., at 278.   130 Ibid., at 283.
131 D. Valiquet, Telecommunications and Lawful Access: I. The legislative situation in Canada (Library of Parliament, 2006), pp. 10–11. Limited authority supporting a reasonable expectation of privacy is found in the decision of the Alberta Court of Queen's Bench in R v. Weir (1999) 213 AR 285. This issue is discussed at greater length in the context of the US provisions; see p. 161.
132 Note that the originator or the intended recipient must be in Canada. If neither is in Canada, the communication is not a 'private communication' for these purposes.
133 R v McLaughlin [1980] 2 SCR 331 at 338 per Estey J.   134 (1993) 13 OR (3d) 88.

In considering the admissibility of this evidence, the court held that the DNR signals were not a 'communication' for the purposes of Part VI of the Code:

> 'communication' in the sense of private communication contemplates an exchange of information between persons, whether it be oral or otherwise... it is the message that the originator of the call expects will not be intercepted, not the fact that a means of communication has been engaged.[135]

This same reasoning could be applied to other forms of traffic data. A similar view was expressed by the Canadian Law Reform Commission which stated that pen register and similar devices should not be included within Part VI which is intended to protect the privacy of communications in the sense of a discourse between persons.[136] Equally, the entering of a search term, while having a human originator, does not have a person as its intended recipient. However, such data arguably falls within the meaning of 'function of a computer' and hence would fall within s. 342.1(1)(b).[137]

C. The United Kingdom

In the UK, the meaning of 'communication' was considered by the House of Lords in the context of the now-repealed Interception of Communications Act 1985 (UK). In *Morgans* v. *DPP*[138] the defendant appealed his convictions for various offences under the Computer Misuse Act, as well as fraudulent use of a telecommunications system.[139] The question on appeal related to the admissibility of evidence obtained from a call-logging device. At the request of police, the phone companies used this device to capture data relating to the defendant's phone calls. These data included the time and date on which calls were made, the duration of the calls and the numbers dialled. In determining the admissibility of the evidence, the court needed first to determine whether the information obtained by the logging device was a 'communication' within the terms of the Act.

---

135 *Ibid.*, at 99 per Finlayson JA for the Court. Cf the decisions of the English courts, discussed at pp. 157–9.
136 Canada Law Reform Commission, *Electronic Surveillance*, Working Paper no. 47 (1986), p. 20.
137 See p. 140.   138 [2001] 1 AC 315.
139 Telecommunications Act 1984 (UK), s. 42.

The court rejected the prosecution's submission that the information obtained by the logging devices was 'metering information' only and therefore did not constitute a 'communication'. The prosecution had argued that the logging device merely recorded evidence of phone numbers dialled, both before and after connection, and that these numbers were merely the means by which a communication was to be achieved and not a communication in themselves.[140]

However, the device was able to capture numbers dialled both before and *after* the phone connection was established. The prosecution case was that the purpose of dialling those numbers after the connection was made was to obtain unauthorised access to the network, either to use the network without charge or to access the voicemail of authorised users. It was held that this was more than 'metering information'.

> The numbers which he dialled before making the connection to the network can properly be described as the means by which he intended to make the connection... But the numbers which he dialled after making the connection were in an entirely different category. At this stage he was communicating with the networks to which he had been connected. The numbers which he dialled resulted in the transmission of signals to those networks. They produced the same kind of computer generated response from them as he would have achieved if they had been programmed to respond to the human voice.[141]

The court cited with approval the statement of Lord Oliver in *R* v. *Effik*[142] that:

> 'communication' does not refer to the whole of a transmission or message; it refers to the telephonic communication which is intercepted in fact, and on the evidence... consists of what has been variously described as the electrical impulse or signal which is affected by the interception that is made.[143]

Lord Hope went on to say:

> It is sufficient, to constitute a communication by means of a public telecommunication system for the purposes of the Act, for an electrical impulse or signal to be transmitted from the telephone number from which the impulse or signal is sent to the telephone number with which it has been

140 *Morgans* v. *DPP* [2001] 1 AC 315 at 332 per Lord Hope of Craighead.
141 *Ibid.*, at 332.   142 [1995] 1 AC 309.
143 *Ibid.*, at 320 per Lord Oliver of Aylmerton, himself referring with approval to the statement of Evans LJ in *R* v. *Ahmed*, Court of Appeal (Criminal Division), unreported, 29 March 1994, cited in *Morgans* v. *DPP* [2001] 1 AC 315 at 333.

connected. The sending of an electrical impulse or signal in either direction will do, irrespective of the response which it elicits from the recipient and the length or content of the message which it conveys.[144]

Although any electrical impulse or signal transmitted over the telecommunication system may be a communication for the purposes of the Act, implicit in the judgment is that mere metering information does not constitute a communication. The crucial distinction on these facts was that the intercepted data was a communication by the defendant to the network in order to achieve a particular response. This is distinct from numbers dialled in order to obtain a connection. If the intercepted data had been confined to those numbers, 'it could properly have been described as metering information'.[145]

Applying this reasoning to the networked environment, the dialling of numbers for the purpose of generating an SMS, for example, would be a communication. Similarly, web addresses are intended to elicit a response from the network and would also seem to be communications, as would data entered to populate fields such as passwords or data required for online purposes. IP addresses, on the other hand, are merely the means to generate the connection and, together with other automatically generated routing information, would not constitute a communication.

The issue has now been clarified by s. 2(5)(a) RIPA, which provides that interception of a communication in the course of its transmission does not include:

> any conduct that takes place in relation only to so much of the communication as consists in any traffic data comprised in or attached to a communication (whether by the sender or otherwise) for the purposes of any postal service or telecommunication system by means of which it is being or may be transmitted.[146]

This therefore makes clear that 'communication' in the context of the UK provision relates only to content and not traffic data. Nor does it apply to conduct which gives a person access to so much of the communication as is necessary for the purpose of identifying traffic data so comprised

---

144 *Ibid.*   145 *Ibid.*, at 332.
146 References to traffic data being 'attached' to a communication include references to the data and the communication being 'logically associated' with each other: s. 2(10)(b). This clarifies that the definition includes 'data which may not be transmitted simultaneously with the contents of that communication', e.g., the data which identifies the number of the person making a telephone call (the calling line identifier): Explanatory Notes, RIPA, [35].

or attached.[147] This latter point seems to address the issue raised in the
United States, that with advances in surveillance technology there is a
danger that in accessing traffic data content data would also be accessed.[148]
This section makes clear that access to other aspects of the communication
is not an offence if necessary to identify traffic data.

Under s. 2(9) RIPA, 'traffic data' is defined to mean:

> (a) any data identifying, or purporting to identify, any person, appara-
>   tus or location to or from which the communication is or may be
>   transmitted,
> (b) any data identifying or selecting, or purporting to identify or select,
>   apparatus through which, or by means of which, the communication
>   is or may be transmitted,
> (c) any data comprising signals for the actuation of apparatus used for
>   the purposes of a telecommunication system for effecting (in whole
>   or in part) the transmission of any communication,[149] and
> (d) any data identifying the data or other data as data comprised in or
>   attached to a particular communication.

The Explanatory Notes to the Act explain that (a) and (b) are intended
to cover subscriber and routing information respectively. Paragraph (c)
is intended to address 'dial through fraud', for example 'data entered by
a user seeking to arrange for a telephone call to be accepted and routed
by a telecommunication system'.[150] Finally, paragraph (d) encompasses
'data which is found at the beginning of each packet in a packet switched
network which indicates which communications data attaches to which
communication'.[151]

'Traffic data' also includes data identifying a computer file or computer
program, access to which is obtained, or which is run, by means of the
communication 'to the extent only that the file or program is identified
by reference to the apparatus in which it is stored'.[152] This is intended to
put 'beyond doubt' that 'in relation to internet communications, traffic
data stops at the apparatus within which files or programs are stored, so
the traffic may identify a server but not a website or page'.[153]

---

147 RIPA, s. 2(5)(b).   148 See p. 163.
149 Under RIPA, s. 2(10)(a), in relation to traffic data comprising signals for the actuation
    of apparatus, references to a telecommunication system by means of which a commu-
    nication is being or may be transmitted include references to any telecommunication
    system in which that apparatus is comprised.
150 Explanatory Notes, RIPA, [33].   151 *Ibid.*   152 RIPA, s. 2(9).
153 Explanatory Notes, RIPA, [34].

Although traffic data falls outside the definition of interception, the acquisition and disclosure of 'communications data' is governed by Chapter II of the Act. That Chapter applies to any conduct in relation to a telecommunication system for obtaining communications data, other than the interception of communications in the course of their transmission, and the disclosure of communications data.[154] 'Communications data' includes not only traffic data[155] but also information relating to a person's use of the service or information held by the provider of the service.[156] Although there is no provision for an offence for such obtaining or disclosure, such conduct is lawful if performed in accordance with authorisation granted under that Chapter.[157]

D. The United States

In the United States, the interception of the content of a communication is governed by the Wiretap Act. As content is defined as 'any information concerning the substance, purport, or meaning of that communication',[158] this includes the contents of an email, including any attachments, as well as the 'subject' line of the email.[159]

The interception of traffic data, on the other hand, is governed by the Pen Register Act. Although the terminology of 'pen register' and 'trap and trace' reflects their development in the context of telephone interception, the definitions make clear that both may be a process used to gather information relating to electronic communications.[160] As 'electronic communication' refers to the 'transfer of signals' of 'any nature' by means of virtually any type of transmission, it has been held that the provision applies 'unambiguously' to non-content email interception and is broad enough to encompass other similar signals transmitted over the Internet or any such network used by a provider of electronic communication service to the public.[161] This includes mobile-phone call

---

154 RIPA, s. 21(1).

155 This is defined in RIPA, s. 21(6), but in the same terms as s. 2(9), discussed at p. 160.

156 *Ibid.*, s. 21(4).   157 *Ibid.*, s. 21(2).   158 18 USC § 2510(8).

159 *In re United States for Order Authorizing Use of Pen Register & Trap*, 396 F Supp 2d 45, 48 (D Mass 2005).

160 18 USC § 3127(3)(4).

161 *In re United States*, 416 F Supp 2d 13, 14–16 (2006). Such a conclusion is further supported by the terms of 18 USC § 3123(a)(3)(A) which requires law enforcement agencies to maintain records about pen registers and trap and trace devices used 'on a packet-switched data network of a provider of electronic communication service to the public'.

162 PRINCIPLES OF CYBERCRIME

data,[162] email addresses (including to/from and any person(s) 'cc'd' on the email),[163] and would presumably also apply to addressing information contained in the packet headers associated with the email.[164]

The case of *In re United States for an Order Authorizing Use of Pen Register & Trap*[165] draws a distinction between the IP address and information which is then used to populate forms on the website. For example, the user may type in the URL of their Internet bank or online store and then fill in information such as their name and address or credit card details. This is similar to the situation with telephones where a person dials a telephone number and then, after being connected, is asked to dial a second number such as a personal account number or social security number or any other identifying number in order to receive further information. 'Would anyone doubt . . . [that] the government would be prohibited from obtaining this information on a pen register because it contains the "content" of a communication?'[166]

Consequently, although the IP addresses of the websites visited would fall within the Pen Register Act, the additional information would not:

> While this may be said to be "dialing, routing, addressing and signaling information," it also is "contents" of a communication not subject to disclosure to the government under an order authorizing a pen register or a trap and trace device.[167]

A similar analysis was recently adopted by the Ninth Circuit in *US v Forrester*.[168] In the course of their investigation of the defendant in relation to drug-related offences, the government conducted surveillance of his

---

162 *In re Application of the United States for an Order for Prospective Cell Site Location Information on a Certain Cellular Telephone*, 460 F Supp 2d 448, 455 (SD NY 2006); *In the Matter of the Application of the United States Of America for an Order Authorizing the Installation and Use of a Pen Register and/or Trap and Trace*, 415 F Supp 2d 211, 214 (WD NY 2006); *In the Matter of the Application of the United States of America for an Order: (1) Authorizing the Installation and Use of a Pen Register and Trap and Trace Device, and (2) Authorizing Release of Subscriber and Other Information*, 2007 US Dist LEXIS 77635 at 9 (SD Tex 2007). For a recent review of the authorities in relation to this form of data see *In the Matter of the Application of the United States of America for an Order Directing a Provider of Electronic Communication Service to Disclose Records to the Government*, 534 F Supp 2d 585 (WD Penn 2008).
163 *In re United States for Order Authorizing Use of Pen Register & Trap* 396 F Supp 2d 45, 48 (D Mass 2005).
164 Kerr, 'Big Brother', 646.   165 396 F Supp 2d 45, 48–9 (D Mass 2005).
166 *Ibid.*, 48, citing *United States Telecom Association* v. *FCC*, 227 F 3d 450, 462 (DC Cir 2000).
167 *Ibid.*, 48–9.   168 512 F 3d 500 (9th Cir 2008).

email and Internet activity. This included the to/from addresses of his emails, the IP addresses of the websites that he visited and the volume of information transmitted to or from his Internet account.[169]

The court rejected the defendant's contention that such surveillance violated the Fourth Amendment. First, there is no reasonable expectation of privacy in such data because it is conveyed to third parties for the purposes of directing the routing of information.[170] Secondly, such data does not necessarily reveal anymore about the underlying communication than a phone number. A website, for example, typically has only one IP address although it may consist of hundreds, or thousands of separate pages:[171]

> When the government obtains the to/from addresses of a person's e-mails or the IP addresses of websites visited, it does not find out the contents of the messages or know the particular pages on the websites the person viewed. At best, the government may make educated guesses about what was said in the messages or viewed on the websites based on its knowledge of the e-mail to/from addresses and IP addresses – but this is no different from speculation about the contents of a phone conversation on the basis of the identity of the person or entity that was dialed.[172]

The court did, however, acknowledge that surveillance which captured URLs could be more 'constitutionally problematic', as such data identifies the particular document within a website which is viewed and therefore reveals more about the person's internet activity than the IP address.[173]

Thirdly, although technologically more sophisticated, the surveillance of email is conceptually indistinguishable from surveillance of physical mail:

> E-mail, like physical mail, has an outside address "visible" to the third-party carriers that transmit it to its intended location, and also a package of content that the sender presumes will be read only by the intended recipient. The privacy interests in these two forms of communication are identical. The contents may deserve Fourth Amendment protection, but the address and size of the package do not.[174]

---

169 The defendant did not challenge more intrusive imaging and keystroke monitoring surveillance: *ibid.*, 509.
170 *Ibid.* Although note the recent decision of the Sixth Circuit in *Warshak* v. *United States*, 490 F 3d 455 (6th Cir 2007); vacated and remanded by en banc appeal, *Warshak* v. *United States* 532 F 3d 521 (6th Cir 2008). For a detailed discussion of the third-party doctrine in this context, see O. Kerr, 'The case for the third-party doctrine' (2009) 107 *Michigan Law Review* 561. Also see, P. L Bellia and S. Freiwald, 'Fourth Amendment protection for stored e-mail' (2008) *The University of Chicago Law Forum* 121.
171 *Ibid.*   172 *Ibid.*, at 510.   173 *Ibid.*   174 *Ibid.*, at 511.

Finally, it was held that the data relating to the amount of Internet traffic was no different to pen registers revealing the number of calls made to/from a particular phone number. 'Devices that obtain addressing information also inevitably reveal the amount of information coming and going, and do not thereby breach the line between mere addressing and more content-rich information.'[175]

Therefore this limited authority would seem to suggest that IP addresses are traffic data, while URLs are, at least arguably, content as they reveal something of the user's intentions in seeking a particular website. Data that is entered, such as account numbers and the population of online forms as well as search terms, would seem, on this analysis, clearly to be content. Such data:

> would reveal, in the words of the statute, 'information concerning the substance, purport or meaning of that communication.' . . . The 'substance' and 'meaning' of the communication is that the user is conducting a search for information on a particular topic.[176]

5. 'Interception' (Live vs. Stored communications)

The law relating to telecommunications interception evolved in the context of real-time interception. However, in the 1980s it became apparent that increasing use of voicemail, and subsequently email, was providing opportunities for access to private communications which were not governed by existing intercept laws.[177] Some legislatures responded with laws designed to protect the confidentiality of 'stored communications', reflecting the view that '[j]ust as trespass protects those who rent space from a commercial storage facility to hold sensitive documents . . . the Act protects users whose electronic communications are in electronic storage with an ISP or other electronic communications facility'.[178]

These offences therefore recognise a privacy interest in communications that are held in storage by service providers. Typically, this will include things such as voicemail, emails and SMS – any electronic communication that is stored while being delivered or awaiting delivery. The principal challenge presented in this context is that Internet communications

---

175 *Ibid.*
176 *In re United States for Order Authorizing Use of Pen Register & Trap*, 396 F Supp 2d 45, 49 (D Mass 2005).
177 *US v. Councilman*, 418 F 3d 67, 80–1 (1st Cir 2005).
178 *Theofel v. Farey-Jones*, 359 F 3d 1066, 1072–3 (9th Cir 2003).

may be temporarily stored while en route to their destination. Distinguishing between stored and 'live' communications therefore becomes increasingly difficult.

This issue arises because of the way in which emails and other communications are sent over a packet-switched network, a process commonly known as 'store and forward' delivery.[179] Each service on the Internet has its own protocol for transmitting packets of data from one place to another. For example, the email protocol is known as Simple Mail Transfer Protocol (SMTP). Once an email is composed using an email client program (mail user agent or MUA) a program called a mail transfer agent (MTA) formats the message and sends it to another program that 'packetizes' it. The packets are then sent across the network, with each computer along the route storing the packets in memory, retrieving the destination addresses and determining where to send them next. At various points the packets are reassembled, copied, and then 'repacketized' for the next leg of the journey. Sometimes messages cannot be transferred immediately and must be saved for later delivery. Even when delivery is immediate, intermediate computers often retain backup copies, which they delete later.

Once all the packets reach the recipient's mail server, they are reassembled to form the email message. A mail delivery agent (MDA) accepts the message from the MTA, determines which user should receive the message, and performs the actual delivery by placing the message in that user's mailbox. Once the MDA has deposited a message into the recipient's mailbox, the recipient simply needs to use an MUA to retrieve and read the message.

It can therefore be seen that an email in transit may move from being in transit to being in storage many times during its transmission, with such changes taking place in fractions of seconds. This gives rise to difficulties in determining when a communication ceases to be in transit and is in storage. There are three possible views.[180] The first is when it is read by the intended recipient. This is generally rejected as being untenable as there is no reliable way to determine whether the intended recipient has accessed let alone 'read' a message. The second is when the message reaches the intended recipient's terminal. This would require an interception warrant for every stage of transmission short of the recipient's computer.

179 The following is based on the agreed summary in *US* v. *Councilman*, 418 F 3d 67, 69–71
      (1st Cir 2005).
180 Blunn, *Access to Communications*, [1.5.5]–[1.5.7].

The third view, and that which is generally adopted in the legislation, is when the 'message is "stored" in the sense that it is at rest i.e. it is not being automatically processed by the telecommunications system and has reached the address from which it can be directly accessed by the intended recipient'.[181]

We now turn to consider the meaning of 'interception', with a particular focus on its application to 'stored communications'. Access to stored communications is not addressed by the Cybercrime Convention and the legislative approaches adopted in each jurisdiction vary considerably. There is no specific legislative regime governing access to such communications in Canada, while in the UK stored communications are expressly brought within the interception regime. In contrast, both Australia and the United States have enacted specific provisions governing access to stored communications.

A. Australia

Under s. 6(1) Telecommunications (Interception and Access) Act 1979 (Cth), 'interception' of a communication passing over a telecommunications system consists of 'listening to or recording, by any means, such a communication in its passage over that telecommunications system without the knowledge of the person making the communication'.

In the context of data, which cannot be 'listened' to, the communication must be recorded.[182] It is therefore not sufficient if the person simply views the relevant data; it must be recorded to constitute an interception This is particularly significant given the increasing use of email and SMS,[183] although attempts to broaden the definition of interception to include 'viewing' a communication were rejected by the Senate Committee considering amendments to the Act.[184]

In order to fall under this section, the communication must be 'passing over' the telecommunications system. Consistently with other jurisdictions, it has been held that 'interception' involves 'intrusion into the

---

181 *Ibid.*, [1.5.5].
182 'Record' is defined to mean 'a record or copy, whether in writing or otherwise, of the whole or a part of the communication, being a record or copy made by means of the interception': s. 5(1).
183 Blunn, *Access to Communications*, [1.3.3].
184 NSW Law Reform Commission, *Surveillance*, [2.11], citing Senate Legal and Constitutional Legislation Committee, *Provisions of the Telecommunications Amendment Bill 2004* (Canberra, 2004), [3.66].

frequency'.[185] Therefore the secret recording of a non-telephonic conversation, which is then transmitted by the telephone system, does not constitute an interception. Similarly, participant monitoring where the person receiving the call records it does not fall within the meaning of intercept.[186]

Under s. 5F(2) a communication:

(a) is taken to start passing over a telecommunications system when it is sent or transmitted by the person sending the communication
(b) is taken to continue to pass over the system until it becomes accessible to the intended recipient of the communication.

'Passing over' also includes being 'carried' which is further defined to include 'transmit, switch and receive'.[187]

This section therefore avoids the extensive debates in the United States as to whether a communication which is in temporary storage while en route to the ultimate recipient can be intercepted, or whether it is more appropriately classified as a stored communication.[188] Under the Australian provisions interception may occur at any time between sending and when the communication becomes accessible to the recipient, irrespective of whether it is in transit or in temporary storage. The circumstances in which a communication is accessible to its intended recipient *include*[189] where it:

(a) has been received by the telecommunications service provided to the intended recipient; or
(b) is under the control of the intended recipient; or
(c) has been delivered to the telecommunications service provided to the intended recipient.[190]

The intended recipient of a communication is:

(a) if the communication is addressed to an individual (either in the individual's own capacity or in the capacity of an employee or agent of another person) – the individual; or

---

185 *DPP* v. *Selway (No. 2)* (2007) 16 VR 508 at 517 per Cummins J.
186 *T* v. *Medical Board* (SA) (1992) 58 SASR 382 at 398–9 per Matheson J.
187 Telecommunications (Interception and Access) Act 1979 (Cth), ss. 5(1) and 5F(1).
188 This issue is discussed at p. 173.
189 This subsection does not limit the circumstances in which a communication may be taken to be accessible to its intended recipient for the purposes of the Act: s. 5H(2).
190 S. 5H(1).

(b) if the communication is addressed to a person who is not an
    individual – the person; or
(c) if the communication is not addressed to a person – the person who
    has, or whose employee or agent has, control over the telecommuni-
    cations service to which the communication is sent.[191]

Once the communication becomes accessible to the recipient, it is no
longer subject to the interception provisions. It is then that it may be
regarded as a stored communication, access to which is governed by
Chapter 3 Telecommunications (Interception and Access) Act 1979 (Cth).
Under s. 108(1), a person commits an offence if:

(a) the person:
    (i) accesses a stored communication; or
    (ii) authorises, suffers or permits another person to access a stored
         communication; or
    (iii) does any act or thing that will enable the person or another
          person to access a stored communication; and
(b) the person does so with the knowledge of neither of the following:
    (i) the intended recipient of the stored communication;
    (ii) the person who sent the stored communication.[192]

'Stored communication' is defined to mean a communication that:

(a) is not passing over a telecommunications system; and
(b) is held on equipment that is operated by, and is in the possession of, a
    carrier; and
(c) cannot be accessed on that equipment, by a person who is not a party
    to the communication, without the assistance of an employee of the
    carrier.[193]

'Access' to a stored communication consists of 'listening to, reading
or recording such a communication, by means of equipment operated
by a carrier, without the knowledge of the intended recipient of the
communication'.[194]

    It should be noted that the protection applies only to the communica-
tion stored on equipment operated by the carrier.[195] For example, if an

191 S. 5G.
192 Without limiting paragraph (1)(b), a person is taken to have knowledge of an act referred
    to in paragraph (1)(a) if written notice of an intention to do the act is given to the person:
    s. 108(1A).
193 S. 5.   194 S. 6AA.
195 Cf the recommendation of the Blunn Report that the same regime should apply to
    communications stored on the computer of the intended recipient: Blunn, *Access to
    Communications*, [1.6.3].

email is downloaded onto a person's computer, these provisions do not apply to the copy stored on the computer.[196] Further, the use of peer-to-peer networks, where information is not stored on a central server, would fall outside this regime.[197] Access to such information would be subject to computer access offences, although Chapter 3 would continue to apply to the copy stored by the carrier.

These provisions also help to clarify the demarcation between federal interception laws and state surveillance laws.[198] Previously, there was some confusion as to when an email had passed across a telecommunications system and therefore ceased to be in the course of transmission.[199] State surveillance or search laws may therefore apply to communications prior to or after transmission, other than those which are 'stored communications', access to which is governed by Chapter 3.

B. Canada

Although distinct provisions, the definition of 'intercept' is the same for ss. 184 and 342.1 Criminal Code (Can). It includes 'listening to, recording or acquiring a [communication/function of a computer system] or acquiring the substance, meaning or purport thereof'.[200] In both cases, this must be done by means of an 'electro-magnetic, acoustic, mechanical or other device', defined to mean:

> any device or apparatus that is used or is capable of being used to intercept any private communication/function of a computer system, but does not include a hearing aid used to correct subnormal hearing of the user to not better than normal hearing.[201]

These definitions would seem to apply to a broad range of interceptions, having been 'drafted to cover all possible methods of intercepting private communications with the exception of normal human hearing',[202] including 'sniffer' programs as well as intercepting electromagnetic transmissions such as Bluetooth. Note that it is not necessary for the person to

---

196 This seems to be confirmed in the note which accompanies the section which states that '[t]his section does not prohibit accessing of communications, that are no longer passing over a telecommunications system, from the intended recipient or from a telecommunications device in the possession of the intended recipient'.

197 The Senate Legal and Constitutional Legislation Committee, *Provisions of the Telecommunications (Interception) Amendment Bill 2006* (Canberra, 2006), [3.111]–[3.114].

198 These provisions are discussed further at p. 145.

199 NSW Law Reform Commission, *Surveillance*, [2.11].

200 Criminal Code (Can), ss. 183 and 342.1(2).   201 *Ibid*.

202 Hubbard, Brauti and Fenton, *Wiretapping and Other Electronic Surveillance*, pp. 1–5.

obtain the full meaning of the communication; it is sufficient if he or she acquires the 'substance, meaning or purport thereof'.[203] No distinction appears to be drawn between public or private networks, and no separate provision is made in relation to access to stored communications. Although there is limited authority suggesting that the word 'intercept' implies contemporaneity,[204] the treatment of communications in *temporary* storage is unresolved in Canada. The better view would seem to be that access to stored communications falls outside Part VI.[205]

C. The United Kingdom

Under s. 2(2) RIPA a person intercepts a communication in the course of its transmission by means of a telecommunication system if, and only if, he or she so:

(a) modifies[206] or interferes with the system, or its operation
(b) monitors transmissions made by means of the system
(c) monitors transmissions made by wireless telegraphy to or from apparatus comprised in the system

as to make some or all of the contents of the communication available, while being transmitted, to a person other than the sender or intended recipient of the communication.[207]

It has been held that the natural meaning of the word 'interception' 'denotes some interference or abstraction of the signal, whether it is passing along wires or by wireless telegraphy'.[208] Hence, it is not an interception to record a person while they are talking on a mobile phone[209] nor to record a conversation, which is then transmitted by telephone connection as part of the listening device.[210]

It has also been held that the requirement that the contents be made available, while being transmitted to a person other than the sender or

203 *Ibid.*   204 *R* v. *McQueen* (1975) 25 CCC (2d) 262.
205 Hubbard, Brauti and Fenton, *Wiretapping and Other Electronic Surveillance*, pp. 15–18.5–15–8.7. This issue is discussed in the US context at p. 173.
206 'Modification of a telecommunication system' includes references to 'the attachment of any apparatus to, or other modification of or interference with-(a) any part of the system; or (b) any wireless telegraphy apparatus used for making transmissions to or from apparatus comprised in the system': RIPA, s. 2(6).
207 Note that this provision is concerned with the contents of the communication as opposed to 'traffic data', which is discussed at pp. 159–60.
208 *R* v. *E* [2004] EWCA Crim 1243 at [20] per Hughes J.
209 *Ibid.*, at [20].   210 *R* v. *Allsopp* [2005] EWCA Crim 703.

intended recipient, excludes those situations where the communication is recorded by the person receiving it or with their consent – so called 'participant monitoring'.[211] However, this seems to be implicitly contradicted by s. 3(2), which provides that an interception is authorised if the communication is one sent by, or intended for, a person who has consented to the interception, and surveillance by means of that interception has been authorised under Part II.[212] In understanding these provisions, it is important to distinguish true participant monitoring from interception with the consent of the sender or recipient.

The decision in *R v. Hardy* applied to true participant monitoring. In that case, undercover police officers used tape recorders to record telephone conversations with the defendants. The court held that such recordings did not fall within the definition of 'interception' as the recording did not occur while the communication was being transmitted:

> What happened here was that one party to the telephone calls (the undercover officer) taped the calls... This is not a case of telephone tapping. It is exactly the same as the undercover officer secreting a tape recorder in his pocket or briefcase whilst meeting the suspect face-to-face, something which he also did in this case. It is surveillance. It requires authorisation. The Act provides for it. But it is not interception.[213]

Applying this interpretation, ss. 3(2) and 48(4) may be understood as applying only to interceptions in the true sense where the communication is intercepted in the course of its transmission, but with the consent of the sender/recipient. Such an interception is lawful without an intercept warrant (s. 3(2)) so long as it is authorised by a surveillance warrant (s. 48(4)).

Consequently, the example given in the Explanatory Notes to the Act requires clarification. The example given is of police recording, with consent, a telephone call by kidnappers to relatives of the victim. The notes explain that such a recording would be authorised as surveillance and not an interception. This is correct, but with the qualifier that where the police are with the family and recording the call there is no interception at all.[214] It is only where the recording is made of the call, while being transmitted,

---

211 *R v. Hardy* [2002] EWCA Crim 3012.
212 Walden, *Computer Crimes*, p. 188. Also see RIPA, s. 48(4).
213 *R v. Hardy* [2002] EWCA Crim 3012 at [32] per Hughes J, also citing *R v. Hammond, McIntosh & Gray* [2002] EWCA Crim 1243, where the court reached the same conclusion in relation to the Interception of Telecommunications Act 1985.
214 Explanatory Notes, Regulation of Investigatory Powers Act (2000) (UK), [39].

that there is an interception. Where this occurs with the consent of the recipients, it requires a surveillance rather than an intercept warrant.

In the context of email communications, this analysis would suggest that an email which is accessed on the defendant's computer is not an interception as it is no longer 'being transmitted'. However, interception before that point may fall within the meaning of interception, particularly as a result of s. 2(7)–(8). Under s. 2(7), the times while a communication is being transmitted include those times when the system by means of which the communication is being, or has been, transmitted is used for storing it in a manner that enables the intended recipient to collect it or otherwise to have access to it. Further, the cases in which any contents of a communication are to be taken to be made available to a person while being transmitted include any case in which any of the contents of the communication, while being transmitted, are diverted or recorded so as to be available to a person subsequently.[215] The effect of these provisions is to bring within the ambit of 'interception' what would be regarded as 'stored communications' in other jurisdictions.[216]

The impact of these provisions is illustrated by the decision in *Regina (NTL Group Ltd) v. Crown Court at Ipswich*.[217] The claimant was a telecommunications company which provided an email service to its customers. Emails received by the company were automatically stored and deleted within one hour of being read. Unread emails were stored for a longer period. The company received notice of an application under s. 9 and Sch. 1 Police and Criminal Evidence Act 1984 (UK) for an order that they produce material in relation to a particular customer's email address. Because of the way in which the company's system was configured, it was not possible to prevent emails of only one customer from being automatically deleted. So, in order to comply, it was necessary to transfer a copy of each email to an address different to that of the intended recipient. The question for the court was whether such a diversion would be a breach of RIPA.

The interception in this case was the automatic routing of the emails to a second address. The court expressed the view that this would not, in the ordinary use of language, be described as 'in the course of its transmission'.[218] Nor was it intended to disclose the contents to a third

---

215 RIPA, s. 2(8).
216 See, in particular, the discussion of the Australian and US provisions at pp. 166 and 173 respectively.
217 [2003] 1 QB 131.   218 *Ibid.*, at 135.

party as they were merely to be preserved in accordance with the order. However, the combined effect of subss. (7) and (8) is to extend the time of communication until the intended recipient has collected it, and to extend the meaning of 'made available' to a case such as this where the contents are diverted for subsequent viewing.[219]

Although having 'considerable doubts' as to whether parliament intended to criminalise the conduct under consideration, the terms of the statute are clear. Consequently, the transfer of the contents of an email to another address so that they can subsequently be made available is an offence under the Act, although in this case the notice under the Police and Criminal Evidence Act 1984 (UK) provided sufficient lawful authority.[220]

D. The United States

Interception under the Wiretap Act

Under 18 USC § 2510(4) 'intercept' is defined as 'the aural or other acquisition of the contents of any . . . electronic . . . communication through the use of any electronic, mechanical, or other device'.[221] As defined, it would appear that a person 'intercepts' an electronic communication merely by 'acquiring' its contents, 'regardless of when or under what circumstances the acquisition occurs'.[222] It has, however, been given a narrower interpretation so that 'intercept' with regard to electronic communications means the acquisition of a communication contemporaneous with transmission.[223]

This interpretation is consistent with the ordinary meaning of 'intercept', which is 'to stop, seize, or interrupt in progress or course before arrival'.[224] It is also arguably consistent with Congressional intention, the

---

219 *Ibid.*   220 *Ibid.*, at 136.
221 Clearly the word 'aural' does not apply to electronic communications, as 'aural acquisition' is 'to come into possession through the sense of hearing': *US* v. *Seidlitz*, 589 F 2d 152, 158 (4th Cir 1978), citing *Webster's Third New International Dictionary*, 1967 Ed.
222 *Konop* v. *Hawaiian Airlines, Inc.*, 302 F 3d 868, 876, (9th Cir 2002).
223 *Steve Jackson Games, Inc.* v. *United States Secret Service*, 36 F 3d 457, 460 (5th Cir 1994); *US* v. *Smith*, 155 F 3d 1051, 1057 (9th Cir 1998); *Konop* v. *Hawaiian Airlines, Inc.*, 302 F 3d 868, 878 (9th Cir 2002); *US* v. *Steiger*, 318 F 3d 1039, 1048–9 (11th Cir 2003); *Fraser* v. *Nationwide Mutual Insurance Co.*, 135 F Supp 2d 623, 634 (ED Pa 2001); *Theofel* v. *Farey-Jones*, 359 F 3d 1066, 1077 (9th Cir 2003).
224 *Konop* v. *Hawaiian Airlines, Inc.*, 302 F 3d 868, 878 (9th Cir 2002) citing *Webster's Ninth New Collegiate Dictionary* (1985). Also see *Fraser* v. *Nationwide Mutual Insurance Co.*, 135 F Supp 2d 623, 634 (ED Pa 2001).

SCA being enacted to ensure that stored communications were not subject to the same very high level of protection provided for by the Wiretap Act.[225] Therefore, in order to constitute an interception, the contents of the communication must be acquired after it has been sent by the sender, but before it is received by the recipient.[226] Retrieval of a message after transmission is complete, such as reading emails stored on a server[227] or accessing a website,[228] is not an interception although it may fall within the SCA.

Access under the SCA

The provisions of the SCA apply to a wire or electronic communication which is in 'electronic storage'.[229] There are, in turn, two limbs to the definition: temporary and backup storage.

Temporary storage The first limb of the definition of 'electronic storage' is 'any temporary, intermediate storage of a wire or electronic communication incidental to the electronic transmission thereof'.[230] Prior to *US v Councilman*,[231] there was a generally held view that the Wiretap Act applied to communications which were being transmitted from the sender to the recipient, whereas if the communication was stored electronically then the SCA applied.[232] For example, in *Steve Jackson Games, Inc.* v. *United States Secret Service*[233] the Secret Service seized a computer which was used to operate a BBS. On that computer were numerous unread emails. It was held that the Wiretap Act did not apply as an interception must be contemporaneous with transmission and the messages were already in electronic storage when they were seized.[234]

---

225 *Ibid.*, 879.
226 *Fraser* v. *Nationwide Mutual Insurance Co.*, 135 F Supp 2d 623, 634 (ED Pa 2001).
227 *Ibid.*, 635.
228 *Konop* v. *Hawaiian Airlines, Inc.*, 302 F 3d 868, 878 (9th Cir 2002), cited with approval in *US* v. *Steiger*, 318 F 3d 1039, 1047 (11th Cir 2003).
229 In the majority of cases there is overlap with provisions of the CFAA which are arguably more appropriate for this purpose. On this basis, some have argued that 18 USC § 2701 should be repealed: Kerr, 'Stored Communications Act', 1737–9.
230 18 USC § 2510(17)(A).   231 373 F 3d 197 (1st Cir 2004).
232 Oyama, 'E-mail privacy', 503. Also see, D. J. Solove, 'The future of the Internet surveillance law: A symposium to discuss Internet surveillance, privacy and the USA PATRIOT Act: Surveillance law: Reshaping framework: Electronic surveillance law' (2004) 72 *The George Washington Law Review* 1264, 1283.
233 36 F 3d 457, 460 (5th Cir 1994).   234 *Ibid.*, 462.

This storage/transit approach was followed in numerous decisions in other circuits,[235] and was held to apply even where the communication was only in temporary intermediate storage in the course of transmission.[236] This approach was also adopted by the First Circuit in *US v Councilman*.[237]

The defendant was vice-president of Interloc, Inc., which ran an online rare and out-of-print book listing service. As part of its service, Interloc gave book-dealer customers an email address at the domain 'interloc.com' and acted as the email provider. It was alleged that Councilman directed Interloc employees to intercept and copy all incoming communications to subscriber dealers from the competitor website, Amazon.com. Therefore, before an email from Amazon.com was delivered to the recipient's mailbox, it would be automatically copied to a separate mailbox which Councilman could access. In this way thousands of messages were diverted and read by Councilman and other employees in the hope of gaining a commercial advantage. For the purposes of these proceedings, it was accepted that the software diverting the emails operated only within the confines of Interloc's computer.

The defendant was indicted for conspiracy to violate the Wiretap Act. The defendant's motion to dismiss was granted by the District Court[238] and affirmed by a divided panel of the First Circuit.[239] The majority's decision was based on the fact that the definition of 'wire communication' includes 'electronic storage', but the definition of 'electronic communication' does not. Consequently, the Wiretap Act's prohibition on 'interception' does not apply to messages that are, even briefly, in 'electronic storage'.[240] The Court of Appeals affirmed the finding of the trial court that even though the emails were in the process of being transmitted from sender to the addressee, they were, at the moment when they were acquired by the defendants, in storage.[241] Therefore, the use of a program

235 M. D. Roundy, 'The Wiretap Act – reconcilable differences: A framework for determining the "interception" of electronic communications following United States v. Councilman's rejection of the storage/transit dichotomy' (2006) 28 *Western New England Law Review* 403, 420.

236 *Fraser* v. *Nationwide Mutual Insurance Co.*, 135 F Supp 2d 623, 635 (ED Pa 2001); *In re Doubleclick, Inc. Privacy Litigation*, 154 F Supp 2d 497, 511–12 (SD NY 2001); Cf *Steve Jackson Games, Inc.* v. *United States Secret Service*, 36 F 3d 457, 461–2 (5th Cir 1994) and *Theofel* v. *Farey-Jones*, 359 F 3d 1066, 1075 (9th Cir 2003).

237 *US* v. *Councilman*, 373 F 3d 197 (1st Cir 2004).

238 *US* v. *Councilman*, 245 F Supp 2d 319 (D Mass 2003).

239 *US* v. *Councilman*, 373 F 3d 197 (1st Cir 2004).   240 *Ibid.*, 200–4.   241 *Ibid.*, 203.

within the defendant's own computer to obtain data temporarily resident at that location was held not to violate the Wiretap Act.[242]

The full court granted the government's petition for rehearing en banc[243] and reversed the decision.[244] The court rejected the defendant's argument that Congress intended to exclude any communication that is in (even momentary) electronic storage from the scope of the Wiretap Act. After reviewing the plain text and legislative history of the provisions, the court concluded that such an interpretation would give rise to the 'existential oddity' that electronic communications cease to be electronic communications for very short intervals, and then become electronic communications again.[245]

> [T]he legislative history of the ECPA indicates that Congress intended the term [electronic communication] to be defined broadly. Furthermore, that history confirms that Congress did *not* intend, by including electronic storage within the definition of wire communications, to thereby exclude electronic storage from the definition of electronic communications. We therefore conclude that the term 'electronic communication' includes transient electronic storage that is intrinsic to the communication process, and hence that interception of an e-mail message in such storage is an offense under the Wiretap Act.[246]

It may be argued that the decision in *Councilman* is to be welcomed as providing the higher level of protection under the Wiretap Act to emails in temporary storage.[247] In particular, the exceptions under the SCA do not apply under the Wiretap Act, and such restrictions as do apply under the Wiretap Act are far more restrictive.[248] It also allows for some consistency for protection while in transit, rather than the protection varying according to whether the email was in transmission or storage.[249] However, the decision has created a split with other circuits and is likely to be resolved only by the Supreme Court. A legislative attempt to ensure consistency, the Email Privacy Protection Act of 2005, has not been enacted.[250]

242 *Ibid.*   243 *US* v. *Councilman*, 385 F 3d 793 (1st Cir 2004).
244 *US* v. *Councilman*, 418 F 3d 67 (1st Cir 2005). For a detailed discussion see Oyama, 'E-mail privacy', 499. See also, T. J. Miano, 'Formalist statutory construction and the doctrine of fair warning: An examination of United States v. Councilman' (2007) 14 *George Mason Law Review* 513.
245 *Ibid.*, 78.   246 *Ibid.*, 85.   247 Oyama, 'E-mail privacy', 516.
248 *US* v. *Councilman*, 418 F 3d 67, 75–7 (1st Cir 2005).
249 Oyama, 'E-mail privacy', 516.   250 *Ibid.*, at 519.

Backup storage The second limb of the definition of 'electronic storage' is 'any storage of such communication by an electronic communication service for purposes of backup protection of such communication'.[251] The traditional understanding of 'backup protection' was that it ceased to apply once the email had been accessed by the recipient.[252] For example, in *Fraser* v. *Nationwide Mutual Insurance Co.*[253] it was held that the purpose of the backup referred to in the legislation is to protect the communication in the event the system crashes before transmission is complete. Consequently, communications which are in storage after transmission is complete are not covered by the SCA, which only protects messages which are stored in the course of transmission.[254]

However, this reasoning was rejected by the Ninth Circuit in *Theofel* v. *Farey Jones*.[255] The defendants in this case gained access to emails belonging to the plaintiffs through use of a subpoena which was subsequently described as 'massively overbroad' and 'patently unlawful'.[256] One issue for determination was whether emails which remain on the ISP's server after delivery still fall within the Act. There was no dispute that the messages were stored by an 'electronic communications service', but were they stored for the purposes of backup protection? It was held that they were:

> An obvious purpose for storing a message on an ISP's server after delivery is to provide a second copy of the message in the event that the user needs to download it again – if, for example, the message is accidentally erased from the user's own computer. The ISP copy of the message functions as a 'backup' for the user. Notably, nothing in the Act requires that the backup protection be for the benefit of the ISP rather than the user. Storage under these circumstances thus literally falls within the statutory definition.[257]

The interpretation in *Fraser* was rejected as being contrary to the plain language of the Act. In contrast to subs. (Λ), subs. (B) does not distinguish between intermediate and post-transmission storage. Further, the interpretation in *Fraser* would essentially render (B) superfluous as temporary backup storage pending transmission would already fall within the phrase 'temporary, intermediate storage' in (A). The plain meaning of (B) is that

251 18 USC § 2510(17)(B).   252 Kerr, 'Stored Communications Act', 1710.
253 135 F Supp 2d 623 (ED Pa 2001).   254 *Ibid.*, 636.
255 341 F 3d 978 (9th Cir 2003); cert. denied, *Farey-Jones* v. *Theofel*, 543 US 813 (2004).
256 *Ibid.*, 1072.   257 *Ibid.*, 1075.

it applies to backup storage regardless of whether it is intermediate or post-transmission.[258]

The Act therefore applies even if an email has been opened, so long as it is stored for backup protection. In contrast, if a remote server was the only place where a person stored their emails, then it would not be a 'backup' and the Act would not apply.[259] Precisely for how long the message will fall within the SCA is unclear, the court stating that the protection would apply until 'the underlying message has expired in the normal course'.[260]

It is not clear how this approach would apply to websites. In *Konop* v. *Hawaiian Airlines, Inc.*[261] it was agreed by the parties that the website was the relevant 'electronic communications service', and that it was in 'electronic storage'.[262] The issue was therefore not fully argued. However, the definition of 'electronic storage' would seem to present some difficulties. The electronic communication which can be intercepted is the transfer of data from the website at the request of the recipient. The storage of the data on the server awaiting those requests would not ordinarily be described as a 'backup' of that communication and hence would not fall within (B).

Nor would it seem to be temporary, intermediate storage incidental to the transmission. On the contrary, the data on the server may be stored for long periods of time and its storage is not incidental to the transmission. It may be that this concession in *Konop* would benefit from further judicial analysis.[263]

A fascinating illustration of how issues of interception and access may overlap is found in *US* v. *Steiger*.[264] The defendant was convicted of various offences relating to child pornography. The authorities were alerted to his activities by an anonymous source in Turkey. The source had captured the defendant's IP address, and used a Trojan program attached to a fake image of child pornography which was then posted to a child pornography usergroup. Once the defendant had downloaded the image

---

258 *Ibid.* Also see *Quon* v. *Arch Wireless Operating Co.*, 309 F Supp 2d 1204, 1208 (CD Cal 2004).

259 *Ibid.*, 1077.

260 *Ibid.*, 1076. For a critical discussion of this decision, see Kerr, 'Stored Communications Act', 1711–13.

261 302 F 3d 868 (9th Cir 2002).   262 *Ibid.*, 879–80.

263 It has been argued that the parties wrongly conceded that the SCA applied in this context: Kerr, 'Lifting the "fog"', 833–6.

264 318 F 3d 1039 (11th Cir 2003); cert. denied, *Steiger* v. *US*, 538 US 1051 (2003).

and his computer was infected with the Trojan, the source was able to gain access to the defendant's computer and locate images and identifying information which were then sent to police.

It was held that the access to the defendant's computer was not in violation of the SCA as his computer was not an electronic communication service. It would, of course, be otherwise if the source was accessing the information on the defendant's ISP.[265] Certainly there was no contemporaneous acquisition of an electronic communication in transit. In fact, it would be very difficult to intercept an email on the recipient's computer, unless by using automatic routing software which sends a copy of the mail to the person intercepting.[266] Although not considered in the case, the more likely offence in such cases would be those relating to unauthorised access to a computer.

Although there is some civil authority supporting the view that the placing of cookies on a user's computer allows access to communications in breach of both the SCA and the Wiretrap Act,[267] such claims have been described, at least in a criminal context, as 'ridiculous' and unlikely to be followed by a criminal court.[268] Interestingly, the Explanatory Report to the Cybercrime Convention states that it was 'understood' that the 'use of common commercial practices, such as employing 'cookies', is not intended to be criminalised as such, as not being an interception 'without right'.[269] However, no analysis is provided to support the contention that commercial cookies invariably have the consent of the recipient.[270]

265 *Ibid.*, 1049.
266 *Ibid.*, 1050. For an analysis of such a situation under the English provisions, see pp. 172–3.
267 *In re DoubleClick Inc., Privacy Litigation*, 154 F Supp 2d 497, 519 (SD NY 2001).
268 Kerr, 'Lifting the "fog"', 830–3. Also see P. L. Bellia, 'Spyware and the limits of surveillance law' (2005) 20 *Berkeley Technology Law Journal* 1283.
269 Cybercrime Convention, Explanatory Report, [58].
270 In the United States, the Computer Software Privacy and Control Act, HR 4255, 108th Congress (2004), which was intended to address issues relating to spyware was never enacted.

PART III

Fraud and related offences

7

Fraud

1. Fraud online

Request for urgent assistance

I got to know of you in my search for a reputable person/Company to assist in an urgent business deal requiring utmost trust and confidentiality. I am BARR.(HON.) AZUBUIKE, an Attorney and close confidant of MRS. MARYAM ABACHA, the former first lady and wife of the late GEN. SANI ABACHA, the former head of state and commander in chief of the armed forces of the Federal Republic of Nigeria.[1]

No scam is more emblematic of online fraud than the so-called Nigerian mail frauds.[2] There can hardly be a person with an email account who has not received one of these messages or its many variants. A form of what is known as an 'advance fee' fraud, the unsolicited message typically asks the recipient to help the sender to arrange for a large amount of currency to be illegally moved out of the country. For this, they need the recipient's bank account details and in return will pay a hefty commission. Once the recipient indicates interest in the proposal, they find that payment of upfront funds is required, ostensibly to deal with bribes or red tape, before the money can be released. Of course, the promised commission never eventuates and the victim's money is lost. In some cases, persuasion is replaced with intimidation and there are reports of victims being threatened, kidnapped and even killed while seeking to recover their funds.[3]

The Internet is a paradise for those who prey upon the gullible, the greedy or the vulnerable. First, it provides unprecedented access to

1 Extract from a Nigerian advance-fee email. Original on file with the author.
2 Also known as a '419 fraud' after the provision of the Nigerian Criminal Code which penalises such schemes; R. G. Smith, M. N. Holmes and P. Kaufmann, 'Nigerian advance fee fraud', Trends and Issues in Criminal Justice no. 121 (AIC, 1996), pp. 4–5.
3 *Ibid.*, p. 3–4.

victims. The Nigerian mail fraud, for example, was originally perpetrated by conventional mail. The advent of the Internet has allowed offenders to reach millions of potential victims at virtually no cost. The more people who can be contacted, the greater the chance someone will be taken in by the scam.

Secondly, the Internet is a large marketplace. In 2003, 17.6% of adults in the United States conducted banking online and 32.3% purchased a product or service online.[4] In Canada, 44% of adults had purchased goods or services over the Internet in 2003,[5] while in the UK the figure in 2009 was 80%, with 55% banking online.[6] In excess of 3.8 billion transactions were made on Australian issued cards in the twelve months to 30 June 2008.[7] This activity translates to a lot of 'virtual' money being transferred online. In 2003, Canadians spent an estimated CDN$3,034,000,000 in electronic commerce,[8] while in the UK, the estimated value of Internet sales by business in 2005 was £103.3 billion.[9] According to the US Census Bureau, the seasonally adjusted estimated value of US retail e-commerce sales for the fourth quarter of 2007 was US$36.2 billion.[10]

This increase in commercial and financial transactions conducted online provides an environment where people are less wary of responding to emails or providing information via websites. It also provides opportunities for fraudsters to mimic legitimate organisations. In the online environment, we are divorced from many of the cues that we would ordinarily look for in determining veracity and trustworthiness, and there is an immediacy about online transactions which is also conducive to fraud. Paradoxically, it seems that far from making us more wary, this

4 US Census Bureau, *Computer and Internet Use in the United States 2003* (US Department of Commerce, October 2005), p. 13.
5 Statistics Canada, *Electronic Commerce Households Spending in Canada and in Other Countries, by Region* (Government of Canada, 2005), www40.statcan.ca/l01/cst01/comm07a.htm.
6 W. H. Dutton, E. J. Helsper and M. M. Gerber, *The Oxford Internet Survey: The Internet in Britain 2009* (Oxford Internet Institute, 2009), p. 25.
7 Australian Payments Clearing Association, *Media Release: Payment fraud in Australia*, (Australian Payments Clearing Association, 15 December 2008), www.apca.com.au/Public/apca01_live.nsf/ResourceLookup/Press_Release_Payments_Fraud_Statistics_5.pdf/$File/Press_Release_Payments_Fraud_Statistics_5.pdf.
8 Statistics Canada, *Electronic Commerce*.
9 National Statistics, 'Value of Internet sales rises 56 per cent in 2005', News Release (National Statistics UK, 2006) p. 1, www.statistics.gov.uk/pdfdir/ecom1006.pdf.
10 US Census Bureau News, 'Quarterly retail e-commerce sales 4th Quarter 2007' (US Department of Commerce, 2007), www.census.gov/mrts/www/data/pdf/07Q4.pdf.

lack of traditional authentication tools encourages an attitude of trust rather than suspicion.[11]

Thirdly, it provides anonymity. Offenders are not only able to conceal their real identities, they are able to assume realistic looking alternative identities. Although the Nigerian email scams are a crude example, the phishing emails and websites discussed below illustrate the more sophisticated end of the spectrum. Finally, the multi-jurisdictional nature of online fraud makes investigation and prosecution more difficult, particularly if relatively small amounts are involved.

The types of fraud which may be committed online are too numerous to do more than summarise here.[12] By way of background to the legal challenges which arise, the following is a brief summary of some of the most common online frauds.

A. Fraudulent sales online

While wonderfully convenient, online purchases present a risk for both merchant and customer: the merchant who does not wish to release goods until funds are secured, the purchaser who does not want to pay before delivery. Although still present, such concerns are more easily addressed in offline transactions by making payment at the time of delivery, or at least being able to inspect goods prior to sale. In online sales, there is a greater level of trust required: that the goods will in fact be delivered as ordered, and that payment will be made. According to the Internet Crime Complaint Center, in 2006 auction fraud was by far the most reported form of internet crime (35.7 per cent), followed by non-delivery of merchandise and/or payment (24.9 per cent).[13] An Australian survey of small businesses found that one-third of online retailers had at some stage been the victim of online fraud.[14]

From the purchaser's point of view the risk is that payment is made in advance, only for the goods not to be delivered, or to be different/ inferior

---

11 E. Finch, 'The problem of stolen identity and the Internet' in Y. Jewkes (ed.), *Crime Online* (United Kingdom: Willan Publishing, 2007), p. 38.

12 For a detailed discussion see P. Grabosky, R. G. Smith and G. Dempsey, *Electronic Theft: Unlawful acquisition in cyberspace* (Cambridge: Cambridge University Press, 2001); and Drugs and Crime Prevention Committee, *Inquiry Into Fraud and Electronic Commerce*, Final Report, Parliament of Victoria (2004).

13 Internet Crime Complaint Center, *Internet Crime Report 2007* (2007), p. 5.

14 K. Charlton and N. Taylor, *Online Credit Card Fraud against Small Businesses*, Research and Public Policy Series no. 60 (AIC, 2004), p. 22.

to that which were advertised.[15] There is also the risk that the goods may be stolen.[16] From the merchant's point of view, there is the same danger as in the offline world of sending goods before cheques are cleared or banking details verified.

Older forms of card verification meant that there could be delays between presentation and verification, so that false numbers could be provided and the fraud would not be detected until after the purchase was completed. As the increase in instantaneous online verification systems has reduced the capacity for offenders to provide false information, they have turned to identity theft as a way of acquiring valid account details.

Because online sales are 'card-not-present' transactions, some of the security features which help to protect offline transactions, such as signatures and chip technology, are not present. All that is verified is that the account is valid, not that the purchaser is authorised to use it. For example, in *R* v. *Lukian*[17] the Canadian defendant was able to obtain US credit card numbers off the Internet, which he then used to purchase computers and other items which were then delivered to an accomplice's address in North Dakota, for shipment back to Canada.

Surveys in Australia, Canada and the United States indicate that misuse of credit cards or existing bank accounts is the most common form of identity crime,[18] while misuse of payment cards also represented the highest amount of loss in the UK, with estimated losses of £504.8 million.[19] In Australia, card-not-present transactions are the most common type of payment card fraud (48%) followed by counterfeiting/skimming (32%).[20] Losses from card-not-present fraud in the UK has increased 350% since 2000, largely due to the increase in the value of online sales over that period of 108%.[21]

---

15 See, e.g., *US* v. *Calvin*, 191 Fed Appx 453 (7th Cir 2006).
16 See, e.g., *US* v. *Wasz*, 450 F 3d 720 (7th Cir 2006).   17 [2003] AJ no 1495.
18 Australian Bureau of Statistics, *Personal Fraud*, Cat. no. 4528.0 (Canberra: ABS, 2007), p. 11; *Federal Trade Commission, 2006 Identity Theft Survey Report* (Federal Trade Commission, 2007), p. 4; and Canadian Internet Policy and Public Interest Clinic, *Techniques of Identity Theft*, CIPPIC Working Paper no. 2, ID Theft Series (2007), p. 23.
19 Fraud Prevention Expert Group, *Report on Identity Theft/Fraud* (European Commission, 2007), p. 9.
20 Australian Payments Clearing Association, *Media Release: Payment fraud in Australia* (Australian Payments Clearing Association, 15 December 2008), www.apca.com.au/ Public/apca01_live.nsf/ResourceLookup/Press_Release_Payments_Fraud_Statistics_5.pdf/ $File/Press_Release_Payments_Fraud_Statistics_5.pdf.
21 APACS – the UK Payments Association, *Key Facts and Figures: Card fraud facts and figures* (2008), www.apacs.org.uk/resources_publications/card_fraud_facts_and_figures.html.

Internet users may also find themselves billed for services they didn't realise they had used or which they did not really need. In an early example, users who downloaded software ostensibly in order to view pornography for free would find they had been charged exorbitant long-distance phone call charges. The software had in fact disconnected their modem connection and reconnected via international long-distance number.[22] A more recent example is so-called 'scareware'. The customer receives messages suggesting their computer may be infected with viruses and offering a free security scan. Sure enough the 'free' scan reveals that the computer is infected and the customer is then invited to purchase software in order to fix it. In fact, the software does nothing as there was nothing to fix in the first place.[23]

B. Advance-fee schemes

An advance-fee scheme is where the victim is persuaded to pay fees in anticipation of receiving some service or benefit which turns out to be non-existent. While the Nigerian mail scam is probably the most infamous example, others include pyramid and other 'get rich quick' schemes, business opportunities, educational qualifications and pharmaceuticals.

Despite their infamy and implausibility a significant number of people are still taken in by these scams. According to a recent Australian survey, of those who received a fraudulent request or invitation, 5.7% responded by supplying personal information, money, or both, representing a victimisation rate of 2%.[24] The most successful scams were lotteries, followed by pyramid schemes, followed by phishing-type requests.[25] According to a recent US survey, the top four countries in terms of perpetrators were the US (63.2%), the UK (15.3%), Nigeria (5.7%) and Canada (5.6%).[26] The most common contact method was email (73.6%) or a webpage (32.7%), although conventional phone contact was still significant (18.0%). Online forums such as instant messenger (11.5%), bulletin boards (3.9%) and chat rooms (2.3%) were other ways in which contact was made.[27]

Although in most cases the victims of these schemes receive nothing for their investment, email may also be used to recruit 'money mules' to assist in the laundering of illegal moneys. A typical example would be an

---

22 Federal Trade Commission, *Facts for Consumers: Dot cons* (2000), www.ftc.gov/bcp/edu/pubs/consumer/tech/tec09.shtm.
23 Federal Trade Commission, *FTC Consumer Alert: 'Free Security Scan' could cost time and money* (Federal Trade Commission Bureau of Consumer Protection, 2008), p. 1.
24 Australian Bureau of Statistics, *Personal Fraud*, p. 8.   25 *Ibid.*
26 Internet Crime Complaint Center, *Internet Crime Report*, p. 12.   27 *Ibid.*, p. 13.

email which advertised the opportunity to 'work from home'. The person is then required to open or provide access to a bank account which is then used to transfer the money as part of the laundering process. Although the mule may receive a commission, they are liable to prosecution under anti-money-laundering laws.[28]

C. Electronic funds transfer crime

The days when stealing money meant running from the bank with bags of loot are long gone. While theft of physical cash will always exist, most money in the world now exists in intangible form, providing a tempting target for unauthorised transfers. Unlike hard currency, virtual cash may be moved in large volumes, between jurisdictions and with less chance of immediate detection. This may be achieved by hackers gaining unauthorised access from outside, or by insiders exceeding their level of authorisation. For example, in *R. v. Muir*[29] the defendant, a financial consultant to the Australian Department of Finance and Administration, used another person's name and password to transfer in excess of A\$8 million to company accounts. He also used the log-on codes and passwords of other employees to obscure the audit trial.

The increasing availability of online banking also provides a tempting target, with only a username and password standing between the thief and the funds. In a recent case, four men have been charged in the United States in relation to a conspiracy to defraud victims of Home Loan Equity Accounts by false wire transfer or by gaining access to the victims' online accounts. They had initially gained access to confidential customer and account information of various financial institutions, and are alleged to have withdrawn US\$2.5 million and attempted to withdraw a further US\$4 million.[30]

D. Fraudulent investments

The Internet also provides an excellent opportunity to peddle fraudulent investment schemes. With little sophistication it is possible to generate

---

28 Australian Institute of Criminology and Australian High Tech Crime Centre, *Money Mules*, High Tech Crime Brief no. 16 (AIC, 2007), p. 2.

29 *R v Muir*, Unreported, ACTSC, Gray J, 25 September 2001.

30 US Attorney, District of New Jersey, 'Multi-million dollar home equity line of credit, identity theft and computer intrusion ring busted', Press Release (US Department of Justice, 2008), p. 2, www.usdoj.gov/criminal/cybercrime/polkCharge.pdf.

an authentic-looking website promising high returns and soliciting investment. Further, because many people look to online forums to discover investment opportunities, information about the fraudulent investment can be disseminated very rapidly. For example, the Securities Exchange Commission has in the past created a fake website as a way of warning consumers who were tempted to invest in the non-existent company. The fake news release advertising the investment opportunity was distributed to hundreds of websites resulting in more than 150,000 'hits' in just three days.[31]

Another form of investment fraud is the use of the Internet to disseminate information for the purposes of influencing share prices – so-called 'pump and dump' (or 'trash and cash') schemes. This may involve merely talking up the shares in online forums to placing fake media releases.[32] In a recent example, eleven defendants allegedly ran a 'pump and dump' scheme which involved sending spam emails promoting Chinese 'penny stocks'. Once the price of the stock was driven up, the defendants would then profit by selling at these artificially inflated prices. In the summer of 2005 alone they are alleged to have earned approximately US$3 million.[33]

E. Identity Crime

There are numerous occasions, on a daily basis, where we are required to identify ourselves; to provide evidence that we are who we claim to be. It may be presenting our driver's licence to a police officer, using a credit card to purchase goods or wearing an identity card at work. It is through our ability to identify ourselves that we are able to fully participate in the community.

> At a basic level, the possession of an identity is inseparable from an individual's sense of self and individuality . . . More generally, the recognition and differentiation of individuals and organisations is predicated on some form of identification. Indeed, it can be argued that the participation of any entity in society, be it an individual, organisation or social group, requires the possession of an identity.[34]

---

31 US Securities Exchange Commission, *Regulators Launch Fake Scam Websites to Warn Investors about Fraud*, News Release (2002), www.sec.gov/news/headlines/scamsites.htm.
32 S. Morris, *The Future of Netcrime Now: Part 1 – threats and challenges*, Home Office Online Report 62/04 (2004), p. 17.
33 US Department of Justice, 'Alan Ralsky, ten others, indicted in international spamming and stock-fraud scheme' (2008), www.usdoj.gov/opa/pr/2008/January/08_crm_003.html.
34 S. Cuganesan and D. Lacey, *Identity Fraud in Australia: An evaluation of its nature, cost and extent* (New South Wales: SIRCA, 2003), p. 1.

Consequently, if unable to identify ourselves we may be denied access to our entitlements. Equally, if someone is able to impersonate us, they may be able to gain access to that to which they are not entitled. The use of a false identity in the commission of crime may broadly be described as 'identity crime'.

There is no single definition of identity crime, with the terms 'identity crime', 'identity fraud' and 'identity theft' often being used interchangeably. The Australasian Centre for Policing Research has produced the following taxonomy.[35]

1. *Identity Crime* is a generic term used to refer to offences where the defendant uses a false identity to perpetrate the crime. This may include such offences as money laundering, drug trafficking, tax evasion, illegal immigration or terrorism. It may also include lesser offences such as minors using false identification to purchase alcohol.
2. *Identity Fraud* is a more specific form of identity crime where a false identity is used to gain money, goods, benefits or services.
3. *Identity Theft* is the assumption of a pre-existing identity.

Both 'identity crime' and 'identity fraud' are examples of existing offences which are facilitated by the use of false identities. Typically, law enforcement has focused on the prosecution of the principal offence rather than the unauthorised use of a person's identity. While digital technology has undoubtedly assisted in the use of false identities to commit crimes, the lacuna in the law is offences that punish 'the preliminary steps of collecting, possessing and trafficking identity information'.[36] It is this conduct which may usefully be identified by the term 'identity theft'.

The use of false identities to facilitate the commission of crime is hardly new, and many of the techniques of the past are still used today.[37] In one recent survey, only 8 per cent of information breaches were as a result of online activity.[38] Nonetheless, digital technology has undoubtedly expanded opportunities for offenders to acquire identity information.

---

35 Australasian Centre for Policing Research and the Australian Transaction Reports and Analysis Centre, *Standardisation of Definitions of Identity Crime Terms: A step towards consistency*, Report Series no. 145.3 (2006), pp. 9–10.
36 Model Criminal Code Officers Committee of the Standing Committee of Attorneys-General, *Identity Crime*, Final Report (2008), p. 12.
37 For a detailed discussion, see CIPPIC, *Techniques of Identity Theft*.
38 R. Johannes, *2006 Identity Fraud Survey Report* (Javelin Strategy and Research, 2006), p. 7. It should be emphasised that these figures relate to cases where the person was aware of how the information breach occurred. It may be that this is less likely in the case of online identity theft, in which case the actual rate of online identity theft may be higher.

In some cases, technology has simply amplified opportunities which have always existed. The portability and storage capacity of digital technology is such that loss or theft of a computer, PDA or storage device may have disastrous consequences. In one example, disks lost by HM Revenue and Customs contained the entire child benefits database including the personal details of 25 million people.[39]

A traditional method of identity theft was to search through rubbish, so-called 'dumpster diving', looking for discarded financial statements and other identifying information. Where that rubbish is a discarded computer, it may contain a wealth of private information. In one study, researchers purchased 158 second-hand hard drives from stores and online auctions. Only a minority of these drives had been properly sanitised, with researchers able to retrieve from the others a range of personal information including personal correspondence, medical information and credit card numbers.[40] Rather than searching through rubbish, a basic online search can be a fertile source of personal information.

Another traditional way of obtaining personal information is through social-engineering techniques. Many of the techniques used in advance-fee schemes discussed above may also be used to tempt recipients to submit personal information. For example, the victim is offered the promise of an employment opportunity, asked to participate in a survey or told that they have won a contest. As with 'mail' frauds, this may now be done *en masse* by utilising email or SMS.

Even the staple of identity crime, forgery, has been transformed by digital technology. With the advent of desktop publishing and imaging software, colour scanners and the like, the 'art' of forgery has gone mainstream, with offenders able to produce false identification documents with relative ease. Signatures can also be scanned and reproduced from other documents.

For example, in *R* v. *Zehir*[41] the defendant used his computer to produce forty-one false birth certificates and forty-one false student identification cards. Using these false documents he was able to open bank accounts, register a business name and apply for a driver's licence. In an

39 BBC News, 'Q&A: Child Benefit Records Lost: How worried should people be by the loss of discs containing child benefit recipients' personal details?' BBC News, 22 November 2007, http://news.bbc.co.uk/2/hi/uk_news/politics/7103828.stm.
40 S. L. Garfinkel and A. Shelat, 'Remembrance of data passed: A study of disk sanitization practices' (2003) 1 *IEEE Security & Privacy* 17, 24–6.
41 (1998) 104 A Crim R 109.

example of 'identity breeding'[42] once he had opened bank accounts using the false identification, he was able to use the cards issued by the bank as proof of identity for subsequent transactions.

In addition to these variants of traditional methods of identity theft, there are a number of techniques which are a direct product of digital technology.

Phishing

'Phishing'[43] is a combination of technological development and social engineering, which may broadly be defined as 'the creation and use by criminals of e-mails and websites... in an attempt to gather personal, financial and sensitive information'.[44] A typical phishing email will appear to come from a legitimate organisation, such as a bank, and will state that the organisation requires the recipient to verify their account information. For example, it may state that the person's account may have been compromised and the bank needs to check their security details. The email will usually have a spoofed header and will be designed to resemble that of the real organisation. The recipient is thereby tricked into providing the information, which is then on-sold and/or used in committing identity crime. SMiShing refers to the practice of sending phishing messages via SMS,[45] while 'spear phishing' describes a phishing attack which is targeted to a particular person or group of people.[46]

Although typically used to gain financial information, phishing may be used to gain access to any account information which may be useful for the offender. In one particularly sinister example, the defendant used phishing emails to obtain minors' passwords to a social networking site and then used the passwords to secretly gain access to the minors' webcam sessions.[47]

---

42 Once a person has acquired some personal information, this may then be used to gather more personal information: CIPPIC, *Techniques of Identity Theft*, p. 13.
43 The word 'phishing' is a variant on 'phreaking', which was a term used to describe one of the early forms of hacking whereby hackers would obtain free long distance phone calls: Anti-Phishing Working Group: *Origins of the Word 'Phishing'* (2008), www.antiphishing.org/word_phish.html.
44 Binational Working Group on Cross-Border Mass Marketing Fraud, *Report on Phishing: A report to the Minister of Public Safety and Emergency Preparedness Canada and the Attorney General of the United States* (2006), p. 4.
45 Organisation for Economic Co-operation and Development, *Scoping Paper on Online Identity Theft*, Ministerial Background Report (2007), p. 4.
46 Binational Working Group, *Report on Phishing*, pp. 8–9.
47 *US v. Miller* (SD Ohio 2006) US Department of Justice Press Release, 19 January 2006, www.cybercrime.gov/millerPlea.htm.

There are a number of ways in which phishing emails may capture personal information. The least sophisticated is simply to ask the recipient to respond via email or fax. For example, an email may contain a document which appears to be from the tax department asking the person to complete their details and return by fax within seven days, otherwise the recipient will not gain certain tax benefits.[48] Fraudulent online sales may itself be a way of securing financial account details. That is, the online sale is itself just a ruse to encourage the purchaser to provide their account details.

A more sophisticated version is to incorporate a link or an attachment in the message which, when clicked, leads to the downloading of malware such as keyloggers or Trojans. Yet another version involves providing a link to a fake website which replicates that of a legitimate organisation, often using forged domain names, and captures the personal information of the unsuspecting user. Once the information is entered, further steps may be taken to delay the victim being aware that they have been tricked, such as indicating that the service is temporarily unavailable or redirecting the user to the legitimate website. Because phishing websites are only online for a very short period of time (typically no more than thirty-one days)[49] they will usually be gone by the time law enforcement is notified. False websites may also be used to host malware which is then downloaded on to the victim's computer. Most recently, malware has been identified which uses the processing power of a botnet to crack the password of the target computer.[50]

According to a report by the Anti-Phishing Working Group, there were 18,509 unique phishing sites detected in the second quarter of 2008. Over the same period, 227 unique brands were victimised, with financial services the most targeted industry sector (52 per cent). The number of malware-spreading URLs was a record 9,529, representing an increase of 258 per cent from the end of the second quarter 2007. In June 2008, the top three countries hosting phishing sites were the United States, Turkey and Poland.[51]

'Voice phishing' or 'vishing' typically involves a phishing email, but the victim is then requested to call a number and prompted to log in

---

48 F. Paget, *Identity Theft*, White Paper (McAfee, 2007), p. 8.
49 Anti-Phishing Working Group, *Phishing Activity Trends Report: Q2/2008* (Anti-Phishing Working Group, 2008), p. 3.
50 Agence France Presse, 'Conficker worm wiggles into millions of computers', *The Age*, 21 January 2009.
51 Anti-Phishing Working Group, *Phishing Activity Trends Report*, pp. 3–7.

using username and passwords. VoIP technology provides a cheap way for criminals to establish authentic sounding automated customer service lines. It also mimics banking practice which is to ask customers not to respond to emails, but rather to call a customer service number.[52]

Although email is a common way of directing users to phishing websites, other methods are utilised as well. For example, the domain name for the website may be a common misspelling of the legitimate website (for example, gooogle.com) or a different domain ('com' instead of 'org') making it easy for users to stumble onto the fake website.[53] More sophisticated is the practice known as 'pharming'.

Pharming

'Pharming' is a technique which utilises the way in which internet domain names are resolved to direct unsuspecting users to the false website. Such attacks are particularly pernicious in that a person who knows not to click suspicious links in emails, will still type legitimate emails into their browser, not suspecting it may be lead to a phishing site.

When a text web address is entered into an Internet browser, it must be converted to a numeric IP address. This is achieved by a system of Domain Name Servers (DNS), which process such requests. In a process known as DNS-poisoning, the DNS may be modified so that when a particular IP address is entered, such as a financial institution, the request is automatically directed to the phishing website mimicking that financial institution.[54]

A more limited effect can be achieved by poisoning the DNS cache on the user's computer by modifying the local host file. When a web address is entered into the browser, the computer will look for the numeric address locally in the host file. The host file may therefore be modified to the false website address, to which the user will be directed. This will usually be achieved by a Trojan which places a valid address for the false website in the user's host file.[55] Even more insidious, Trojans may wait until the user visits a legitimate website before creating a false pop-up asking for identifying information, which is then transmitted to a remote server. Such a Trojan was used in relation to American Express websites in 2006.[56]

---

52 Binational Working Group, *Report on Phishing*, p. 10.
53 BC Freedom of Information and Privacy Association, *PIPEDA and Identity Theft: Solutions for protecting Canadians* (FIPA, 2006), p. 13.
54 CIPPIC, *Techniques of Identity Theft*, p. 15.   55 *Ibid.*
56 R. Naraine, 'Computer virus "hijacks" American Express web site', Fox News, 1 May 2006, www.foxnews.com/story/0,2933,193784,00.html.

Hacking and use of malware

The ability for organisations to store large amounts of personal information, which is also easily searched and copied, provides a tempting target for unauthorised access. A review of media reports of data breaches in the United States between January 2005 and December 2006 indicated at least 572 breaches, affecting more than 80 million personal records.[57] These affected a range of organisations, including all levels of government, financial institutions, educational institutions and medical facilities. Another survey found that 6 per cent of fraud cases were due to unauthorised access to company data.[58] Of the twenty-four largest publicly reported data breaches in the United States between January 2000 and June 2005, eleven were a result of hacking.[59]

For example, Philip Cummings was sentenced to fourteen years in prison for his part in what was at the time reported to be one of the largest cases of identity theft in US history. Cummings abused his position working at the help-desk of a company which provided customers with computerised access to credit-history bureaux. By unauthorised use of access codes and confidential passwords he downloaded more than 30,000 consumer credit histories. These would then be passed on to others who would use them, inter alia, to obtain credit cards in the names of those people which would then be used to purchase items which were then on-sold.[60]

Although not involving cybercrime, the case of ChoicePoint illustrates the potential scale of the problem. ChoicePoint is a data-aggregation company, which provides 'comprehensive credentialing, background screening, authentication, direct marketing and public records services to businesses and non-profit organizations'.[61] In 2004, when the company had over 19 billion data files, one of its customers was selling information obtained from the company to criminals. The customer had obtained access to ChoicePoint's database by presenting a false application and

---

57 US Government Accountability Office, *Personal Information: Data breaches are frequent, but evidence of resulting identity theft is limited; however, the full extent is unknown*, Report to Congressional Requesters (Government Accountability Office, 2007), pp. 11–12.

58 Johannes, *Identity Fraud Survey*, p. 3.

59 US Government Accountability Office, *Personal Information*, p. 26.

60 US Attorney Southern District of New York, 'U.S. announces sentencing of man in largest identity theft case in nation's history', Press Release (US Department of Justice, 2005), www.usdoj.gov/usao/nys/pressreleases/January05/cummingssentencingpr.pdf.

61 www.choicepoint.com.

forged business licence, which ChoicePoint failed to verify.[62] Approximately 110,000 Americans were notified that they were possibly the victims of identity theft.[63]

Recent years have seen an increased prevalence in the use of Trojan attacks that seek to acquire passwords as well as other personal information. Unlike indiscriminate virus and worm infections, Trojan attacks may be directed at specific organisations or regions.[64] One Trojan family known as 'Haxdoor', 'A311 Dea†h', or 'Backdoor-BAC', captures network information and logins and waits for the user to browse a website (usually financial) that requires authentication. The keylogger collects transaction data, such as username and password, and then sends the stolen data to a dedicated host, which enters the stolen data into incremental log files. A creation toolkit may be purchased online for between $200 to $500.[65]

In another example, Brian Salcedo was sentenced to nine years' imprisonment for his part in a conspiracy to compromise the computer system of Lowe's stores in the United States. Having first compromised the wireless network of Lowe's store in Michigan, allowing access to the central computer system, the defendants were able to install on store computers malware designed to capture credit card transaction information.[66]

Credit card skimming

Credit card skimming is 'the process by which legitimate credit card data is illicitly captured or copied, usually by electronic means'.[67] This technique exploits the vulnerabilities of magnetic-strip technology, present on many credit, debit and other transaction cards. While allowing cards to be programmed with data quickly and easily, it also means that the data can easily be copied. Although commonly referred to as 'credit card skimming', the practice can be applied to any card which carries data on a magnetic strip.

---

62 *In re ChoicePoint, Inc., Securities Litigation*, 2006 US Dist LEXIS 97903, at 9.
63 *Ibid.*
64 AusCERT, *Australian Computer Crime and Security Survey* (2006), p. 23, www.auscert. org.au/crimesurvey.
65 Paget, *Identity Theft*, p. 8.
66 US Department of Justice, Western District of North Carolina, 'Hacker sentenced to prison for breaking into Lowe's companies' computers with intent to steal credit card information', Press Release (US Department of Justice, 2004), www.usdoj.gov/ criminal/cybercrime/salcedoSent.htm.
67 Model Criminal Code Officers Committee of the Standing Committee of Attorneys-General, *Model Criminal Code: Chapter 3, Credit Card Skimming Offences*, Final Report (2006), p. 1.

The technology required to engage in this practice, known as a 'credit card skimmer,' may be a modified version of commercially available card readers or a purpose-built device.[68] Such devices are becoming increasingly small and easy to conceal. Typically, when the card is out of sight of the owner for a period of time, for example a restaurant or convenience store,[69] an employee will place the card through the skimmer as well as processing the legitimate transaction.

An alternative technique is to conceal the skimming device in the card-slot of an ATM, thereby recording the data of all cards used in that particular ATM until the defendants remove the skimmer and extract the data.[70] If accompanied by a concealed camera, or simply 'shoulder surfing' (covertly observing a person entering their PIN), the PIN attached to the account can also be obtained. Taking this practice a step further, Canadian offenders purchased and modified stand-alone ATMs which would then capture the account and PIN of unsuspecting users. Approximately 4,000 people were victims of the scam which netted approximately CDN$1.2 million.[71]

Skimmers may also be placed inside point-of-sale terminals, which appear to be legitimate, even in some cases producing bogus receipts.[72] PINs may be obtained by hot-wiring PIN key pads or using pinhole cameras. At a more sophisticated level, the data transfer from merchants may be intercepted[73] or malware placed in ATM and EFTPOS (Aus/NZ) or Switch (UK) terminals.[74]

Although the data is commonly written to a replica card, it can be downloaded onto any media with a magnetic strip, for example a library card.[75] While these would not be used for over-the-counter transactions, they may, for example, be inserted in ATM's. The increasing number of 'card not present' transactions means that the information gleaned from the card can be used to make online transactions without the need to create

---

68 Model Criminal Code Officers Committee, *Credit Card Skimming*, p. 5.
69 See, e.g., *R.* v. *Naqvi*, 2005 ABPC 339.
70 Model Criminal Code Officers Committee, *Credit Card Skimming*, p. 5.
71 Nathanson Centre on Transnational Human Rights, Crime and Security, *Organized Crime in Canada: A quarterly summary*, July to September 2003, www.yorku.ca/nathanson/CurrentEvents/2003_Q3.htm.
72 Nathanson Centre on Transnational Human Rights, Crime and Security, *Organized Crime in Canada: a quarterly summary*, January to March 2006, www.yorku.ca/nathanson/CurrentEvents/2006_Q1_.htm.
73 *Ibid.*   74 Model Criminal Code Officers Committee, *Credit Card Skimming*, p. 3.
75 *Ibid.*, p. 4.

a replica card.[76] In 2007, the Interac Association of Canada reported that CDN$106.8 million was reimbursed to victims of debit card fraud as a result of skimming.[77]

Skimmed data may also be sent overseas and forged cards produced. Therefore even in jurisdictions where PIN-and-chip technology has been introduced to improve card security, duplicate cards may be produced in countries without these technologies. The use of the cards overseas may also delay detection and reporting of the fraud, making investigation more difficult.[78]

Carding

Although initially used to refer to the unauthorised use of credit and debit card account information, 'carding' has come to be used more broadly to describe the acquisition, distribution and use of such information.[79] So-called 'carding' websites facilitate the trade in identity information by providing an online marketplace. This market goes beyond identity information to encompass the whole range of services that may be required to commit identity crime:

> Items sold include credit card data, bank account credentials, email accounts, and just about any other information that can be exploited for profit. Services can include cashiers who can transfer funds from stolen accounts into true currency, phishing and scam page hosting, and job advertisements for roles such as scam developers or phishing partners.[80]

Prior to being shut down by the US Secret Service in 2004, the 'Shadowcrew' website allegedly trafficked in at least 1.5 million stolen credit and debit card numbers, resulting in losses of over US$4 million.[81] Operators of the website were able to illegally acquire 18 million email accounts with associated usernames, passwords, dates of birth and other personally

---

76 See, e.g., *US* v. *Drummond*, 255 Fed Appx 60 (6th Cir 2007); and *R* v. *Farkas*, 2006 ONCJ 121.

77 Interac, *Consumers – Security: Fraud* (2008), www.interac.ca/consumers/security_fraud.php.

78 Model Criminal Code Officers Committee, *Credit Card Skimming*, p. 5.

79 K. Peretti, 'Data breaches: What the underground world of "carding" reveals' (2008) 25 *Santa Clara Computer and High Technology Journal* 375, 377.

80 M. Foss and E. Johnson, *Symantec Report on the Underground Economy July 07–June 08* (Symantec, 2008), p. 4. Also see US Senate, *Phony Identification and Credentials Via the Internet* (Permanent Subcommittee on Investigations of the Committee on Governmental Affairs, 2002).

81 US Department of Justice, '"Shadowcrew" Internet identity and credit card thieves plead guilty', Press Release (2005), www.usdoj.gov/usao/nj/press/files/shad1117_r.htm.

identifying information. The website was also a marketplace for false identification documents and duplicate credit and debit cards.[82]

The price of information which is available online varies depending upon its quality and level of authentication, but is surprisingly inexpensive. The data taken from the magnetic strip on a credit or debit card (known as a 'dump')[83] may cost between US$0.10 and US$25 (those which include PIN or the security identification number of the card being more expensive) while bank account details range from US$10–1,000.[84] Packages of personal identifying information about a victim, known as 'Full Info' or 'Fulls',[85] are available for between $0.90 and $25.[86]

2. The scale of the problem

Although widely agreed to be prevalent and increasing, the precise extent of identity crime is difficult to assess for a number of reasons. First, 'identity crime' is ill-defined, making accurate recording problematic. For example, there is some debate as to whether payment card fraud should be regarded as a form of identity theft or should be recorded more generally as 'fraud'.[87] Secondly, crime statistics generally record the commission of frauds, without differentiating the method of commission. Thirdly, there is a range of public and private agencies which may respond to consumer complaints of fraud, thus making statistical collation difficult. A recent Australian survey found that 57 per cent of identity-theft victims reported the incident, but only 22 per cent to police.[88] Finally, its true extent is likely to be under-reported, with some 'victims' unaware of their status as such, while others may write it off as a bad experience/debt. Commercial organisations, in particular, may be reluctant to report for fear of undermining consumer confidence.

Nonetheless, such statistics as there are indicate that identity crime is a significant problem. Recent Australian and US surveys estimated

---

82 US Attorney's Office, District of New Jersey, '"Shadowcrew" identity theft ringleader gets 32 months in prison', News Release (2006), www.usdoj.gov/usao/nj/press/files/mant0629_r.htm.
83 Peretti, 'Data breaches', 387.   84 Foss and Johnson, *Underground Economy*, p. 20.
85 Peretti, 'Data breaches', 388.   86 Foss and Johnson, *Underground Economy*, p. 20.
87 Canadian Internet Policy and Public Interest Clinic, *Identity Theft: Introduction and background*, CIPPIC Working Paper no. 1, ID Theft Series (2007), p. 1.
88 Australian Bureau of Statistics, *Personal Fraud*, p. 11. Similar figures were found in the US, with 26% of victims having contacted police, and 21% contacting one or more credit reporting agencies; Synovate, *Identity Theft Survey*, p. 45.

victimisation rates for identity crime of 3.1 and 3.7 per cent respectively.[89] If applied to the US population as a whole, this equates to approximately 8.3 million victims.[90] In 2007, the UK's fraud prevention service, CIFAS, recorded 77,500 cases of identity and impersonation fraud,[91] while the Canadian equivalent received just over 10,000 complaints of identity theft in the same period.[92] Estimated losses are measured in the billions: A\$1.1 billion in Australia (2001–2),[93] CDN\$2.5 billion in Canada (2002),[94] £1.7 billion in the UK (2003–5)[95] and US\$15.6 billion in the United States (2005).[96]

While the most obvious impact of identity crime is financial, most of the cost is in fact borne by institutions rather than individuals. For example, one survey found that although the average cost per *victim* was US\$6,383, the average *consumer* cost was US\$422.[97] In addition to direct financial losses, there are costs associated with reporting, investigating and rectifying instances of identity crime. Governments must expend money and resources in prevention and law enforcement.[98] Identity crime may also harm the digital economy, with consumers reluctant to shop online.[99]

Individuals and organisations may suffer reputational damage, including impacts on their credit ratings, which may take considerable time, effort and money to rectify. One victim was wrongly identified as a terrorist threat on a 'no-fly' list, leading to the flight on which he was travelling being diverted to a military base and several hours of questioning before the mistake was realised.[100] There may also be psychological distress, such as where the offender assumes the identity of a deceased

---

89 Australian Bureau of Statistics, *Personal Fraud*, p. 11; and Synovate, *Identity Theft Survey*, p. 4. Also see K. Baum, *Identity Theft 2004*, Bureau of Justice Statistics Bulletin (US Department of Justice, 2006).
90 Synovate, *Identity Theft Survey*, p. 4.
91 CIFAS, *Identity Fraud and Identity Theft* (2009), www.cifas.org.uk/default.asp? edit_id=561–56?.
92 The Canadian Anti-fraud Call Centre, *Phonebusters: Monthly summary report* (Competition Bureau Canada, 2008), p. 1.
93 Cuganesan and Lacey, *Identity Fraud in Australia*, p. 55.
94 BC Freedom of Information and Privacy Association, *PIPEDA and Identity Theft*, p. 3.
95 Economic and Domestic Secretariat, *Identity Fraud: A study* (Cabinet Office, 2002), p. 73.
96 Synovate, *Identity Theft Survey*, p. 9.   97 Johannes, *Identity Fraud Survey*, p. 1.
98 Fraud Prevention Expert Group, *Report on Identity Theft/Fraud*, p. 9.
99 The President's Identity Theft Task Force, *Combating Identity Theft: A strategic plan* (2007), pp. 11–12.
100 Paget, *Identity Theft*, p. 11.

child.[101] Identity crime is also seen as intimately connected with organised crime and terrorism. In one infamous example, the 9/11 hijackers utilised fictitious social security numbers, false identities and fraudulent identification documents.[102]

3. Legal responses

Prevention of identity crime is a complex issue, involving a number of different entities and requiring a range of responses, including consumer and business education, privacy legislation, reporting obligations and technical measures.[103] In respect of legal responses, Art. 8 of the Cybercrime Convention provides that:

> each Party shall adopt such legislative and other measures as may be necessary to establish as criminal offences under its domestic law, when committed intentionally and without right, the causing of a loss of property to another person by:
>
> (a) any input, alteration, deletion or suppression of computer data;
> (b) any interference with the functioning of a computer system,
>
> with fraudulent or dishonest intent of procuring, without right, an economic benefit for oneself or for another person.

This provision is aimed at frauds which are committed through the input or alteration of data, and aims to 'criminalise any undue manipulation in the course of data processing with the intention to effect an illegal transfer of property'.[104] The first limb is concerned with any 'input, alteration, deletion or suppression' of data, terms which have already been discussed in Chapter 4. However, the provision is intended to extend to a broad range of conduct, and includes any 'interference with the functioning of a computer programme or system'. This is intended to include 'hardware manipulations, acts suppressing printouts and acts affecting recording or flow of data, or the sequence in which programs are run'.[105]

---

101 Economic and Domestic Secretariat, *Identity Fraud*, p. 7.
102 US Senate, *Phony Identification*, pp. 38–9.
103 See generally Economic and Domestic Secretariat, *Identity Fraud*; The President's Identity Theft Task Force, *Combating Identity Theft*; Canadian Internet Policy and Public Interest Clinic, *Policy Approaches to Identity Theft*, CIPPIC Working Paper no. 6, ID Theft Series (2007); and the OECD, *Scoping Paper on Online Identity Theft*.
104 Cybercrime Convention, Explanatory Report, [86].   105 *Ibid.*, [87].

'Loss of property' is intended to operate broadly, and includes loss of tangible and intangible property.[106] The inclusion of both an intent to engage in the relevant conduct as well as a specific intent to defraud is intended to allow for situations such as the unauthorised use of web crawling software to obtain information about a competitor, conduct which, although it may cause financial harm, is not carried out with dishonest intent.[107]

Such offences are typically found in computer misuse provisions, many of which punish access/modification of data which is carried out with fraudulent intent. More typically, online fraud is prosecuted under general fraud offences[108] as well as any one of a range of specific offences including forgery, personation, false declarations and trading in specified information such as passports and credit card numbers[109] In the United States, for example, it has been estimated that the Identity Theft and Assumption Deterrence Act covers conduct that could also be prosecuted under approximately 180 other federal criminal statutes.[110]

Rather than review the myriad offences which may apply in this context, the focus of this chapter is on specific 'identity theft' offences: those which punish the unauthorised acquisition and distribution of identity information. However, before turning to consider those offences, it is useful to consider some of the specific challenges that have arisen in applying traditional fraud provisions to the online environment.

A. Electronic funds transfer

The movement of money in digital form may present challenges to offences which were originally conceived in the context of tangible goods.

---

106 *Ibid.*, [88].   107 *Ibid* [90]. For examples of such cases, see pp. 82–3.
108 See, in general, Criminal Code (Cth), Part 7.3; Criminal Code (Can), Part X; Fraud Act 2006 (UK); and 18 USC 1343 (the Wire Fraud Statute).
109 For a summary of relevant offences see Model Criminal Law Officers Committee of the Standing Committee of Attorneys-General, *Identity Crime: Discussion paper* (2007), pp. 18–24; Canadian Internet Policy and Public Interest Clinic, *Canadian Legislation Relevant to Identity Theft: An annotated review*, CIPPIC Working Paper no. 3A, ID Theft Series (2007); Canadian Internet Policy and Public Interest Clinic, *United States Legislation Relevant to Identity Theft: An annotated review*, CIPPIC Working Paper no. 3B, ID Theft Series (2007); and Canadian Internet Policy and Public Interest Clinic, *Australian, French and UK Legislation Relevant to Identity Theft: An annotated review*, CIPPIC Working Paper no. 3C, ID Theft Series.
110 J. Lynch, 'Identity theft in cyberspace: Crime control methods and their effectiveness in combating phishing attacks' (2005) 20 *Berkley Technology Law Journal* 259, 294.

Although such offences typically apply to intangible property such as choses in action, other elements of the offence must also be considered. For example, it has been held that the receipt of electronic funds may constitute an 'obtaining' of those funds for the purposes of the offence of theft.[111] Similarly, in the United States it has been held that the electronic transfer of funds constitutes 'transportation' for the purpose of the Wire Fraud statute.[112]

> Electronic signals in this context are the means by which funds are transported. The beginning of the transaction is money in one account and the ending is money in another. The manner in which the funds were moved does not affect the ability to obtain tangible paper dollars or a bank check from the receiving account.[113]

One situation which has caused difficulties is the requirement that property 'belong to another', commonly found in the offence of theft and obtaining property by deception.[114] The application of this requirement in the context of electronic funds transfers was considered by the House of Lords in *R* v. *Preddy*.[115]

The defendant was able to obtain mortgage advances as a result of fraudulent applications. These advances were made either by cheque or by electronic transfer of the moneys from the lender's bank account to the defendant's bank account. It was held that the defendant's convictions for obtaining property by deception must be quashed as he had not received property 'belonging to another'.

In the case of the electronic transfer of funds the money was not physically transferred from one bank to another. The lender had a positive balance in its bank account, which represented a chose in action between the lender and the bank, and was clearly property. The lender instructed its bank to transfer funds to the defendant's bank. The lender's balance was reduced by that amount and the defendant's balance increased by

---

111 *R* v. *Thompson* [1984] 3 All ER 565 at 570 per May LJ.
112 18 USC § 2314. It has been held that computer time is a 'thing of value' for the purposes of this act: *US* v. *Seidlitz*, 589 F 2d 152, 160 (4th Cir 1978).
113 *US* v *Gilboe*, 684 F 2d 235, 238 (2nd Cir 1982). The same view has been adopted in relation to the transportation of obscene materials: see p. 294.
114 Criminal Code (Cth), ss. 131.1 and 134.1; Model Penal Code, §§ 26.01 and 223.3; Theft Act 1968 (UK), ss. 1 and 15 (now repealed and replaced by general fraud offences under the Fraud Act 2006 (UK)). Under the Criminal Code (Can) the defendant must 'deprive . . . the owner of it, or a person who has a special property or interest in it, of the thing or of his property or interest in it' (s. 322) or defraud 'the public or any person, whether ascertained or not, of any property' (s. 380).
115 [1996] AC 815.

the same amount. However, that increase did not represent the same chose in action. A new chose in action had come into existence between the defendant's bank and the defendant, on the basis of the agreement between the two banks. The fact that it was to the same value as the decrease in the chose in action between the lender and its bank did not mean that it was the same property. They were in fact distinct choses in action.[116]

This decision presents a significant obstacle to the charging of obtaining property by deception in such cases, particularly as the same principle may extend to other electronic transfers such as shares or bonds.[117] There are, however, a number of ways in which it may be addressed.[118] One is to amend the offence provisions to encompass the fraudulent transfer of choses in action. Another is to enact a specific offence of obtaining a money transfer by deception,[119] although this does not address other forms of intangible property. The third, and simplest, is to utilise a general obtaining offence which avoids the concept of obtaining property 'belonging to another' and focuses instead on the obtaining of a financial advantage by deception.[120]

B. Deceiving a machine

In many cases of electronic fraud, the defendant will input data which he or she is unauthorised to use, in an effort to obtain funds to which he or she is not entitled. For example, the use of a stolen PIN at an ATM, or a stolen credit card number used for an online purchase. In such cases, the transaction is not with a person; it is the computer that processes the number, checks its validity and approves the request. Given that deception is at the heart of fraud charges, has the machine been deceived?

The essence of a deception is inducing the victim 'to believe that a thing is true which is false, and which the person practising the deceit knows or believes to be false'.[121] Therefore, a deception cannot be practised on a

---

116 *Ibid.*, at 822–4 per Lord Goff. The issue in respect of electronic transfers was left open by the High Court of Australia in *Parsons* v. *R* (1999) 195 CLR 619. Also see *R* v. *Parsons* [1998] 2 VR 478 at 485 per Winneke ACJ.

117 Law Commission, *Fraud*, Final Report, Law Com no. 276 (2002), p. 25.

118 See, e.g., Law Commission, *Offences of Dishonesty: Money transfers*, Item 11 of the Sixth Programme of Law Reform: Criminal Law (1996).

119 Theft Act 1968 (UK), s. 15A (repealed by the Fraud Act 2006 (UK)). Also see Criminal Code (Cth), ss. 134.1(9)–(12).

120 E.g., Criminal Code (Cth), ss. 134.1(9)–(12) and Fraud Act 2006 (UK), s. 5.

121 *Re London and Globe Finance Corporation Ltd* [1903] 1 Ch 728 at 732 per Buckley J.

machine as they do not have beliefs; they simply respond to the information which is provided to them.[122] Accordingly, some jurisdictions have amended their fraud provisions to allow for this situation. For example, s. 480.1(1) Criminal Code (Cth) defines deception to include 'conduct by a person that causes a computer, a machine or an electronic device to make a response that the person is not authorised to cause it to do'.[123] This situation may be contrasted with those where the offence is complete upon the making of an untrue representation, irrespective of whether there was a deception. In such cases, the offence may be made out where the untrue representation was made to a machine.[124]

C. Can a machine consent?

In some circumstances the defendant will be allowed to access funds, despite being unauthorised to do so, because of the way in which the computer is programmed to respond. Can it be said, in such cases, that consent has been given via the machine and therefore there is no fraud?

This issue was considered by the High Court of Australia in *Kennison* v. *Daire*.[125] The accused was charged with larceny after using his ATM card to withdraw funds even though he knew he had insufficient funds in his account. He was able to do this because the machine was offline at the time and unable to determine whether sufficient funds were available. It was programmed, in such circumstances, to allow withdrawals up to a maximum of $200 so long as a card and corresponding PIN were entered.

The defendant argued that by programming the computer in this way, the bank had consented to the taking of the money, in which case there could be no larceny. An analogy was drawn with the bank teller, invested with the general authority of the bank, who pays money on an overdrawn account or on a forged order. In such cases, the bank would be taken to intend the money to pass. It was therefore argued that the ATM is invested with similar authority such that if money is paid out in accordance with the instructions with which it is programmed, that payment should be taken to be with the consent of the bank.[126]

This argument was rejected. 'The fact that the Bank programmed the machine in a way that facilitated the commission of a fraud by a person holding a card did not mean that the Bank consented to the withdrawal of

122 Law Commission, *Fraud*, p. 21.   123 Also see Fraud Act 2006 (UK), s. 2(5).
124 *R* v. *Baxter* [1988] 1 Qd R 537.   125 (1986) 160 CLR 129.
126 *Ibid.*, at 132 per Gibbs CJ, Mason, Wilson, Deane and Dawson JJ.

money by a person who had no account with the Bank.'[127] The machine could not give the bank's consent and it was clear that the bank had not personally consented to the withdrawal. The fact that such a withdrawal was in breach of the card's conditions of use further supported such a conclusion. The only proper inference to be drawn was that 'the Bank consented to the withdrawal of up to $200 by a card-holder who presented his card and supplied his personal identification number, only if the card holder had an account which was current'.[128]

D. Computer-related forgery

It has already been noted that the creation of false documents has long been a staple of identity crime. However, the traditional conception of forgery is of the creation of false documents in tangible form; it does not allow for the falsification of electronic data or the creation of false electronic documents such as a website.[129]

This issue is addressed in Art. 7 of the Cybercrime Convention, which provides that:

> each Party shall adopt such legislative and other measures as may be necessary to establish as criminal offences under its domestic law, when committed intentionally and without right, the input, alteration, deletion, or suppression of computer data, resulting in inauthentic data with the intent that it be considered or acted upon for legal purposes as if it were authentic, regardless whether or not the data is directly readable and intelligible.

A party may require an intent to defraud, or similar dishonest intent, before criminal liability attaches.

This provision is intended to create a parallel offence to the forgery of tangible documents by focusing on the creation or alteration of stored data which may be relied upon in the course of legal transactions.[130] It is intended to apply to data which is the equivalent of a public or private document and which has legal effects:[131]

---

127 *Ibid.*
128 *Ibid.* Applied in *R* v. *Evenett, ex parte Attorney-General* [1987] 2 Qd R 753; *Gilmour* v. *DPP (Cth)* (1995) 43 NSWLR 243; and *Shields* v. *New South Wales Crime Commission* [2007] NSWCA 309. This issue is further discussed in the context of unauthorized access to data: see p. 70.
129 Model Criminal Law Officers Committee, *Identity Crime* (2008), p. 15.
130 Cybercrime Convention, Explanatory Report, [83].   131 *Ibid.*

> The unauthorised 'input' of correct or incorrect data brings about a situation that corresponds to the making of a false document. Subsequent alterations (modifications, variations, partial changes), deletions (removal of data from a data medium) and suppression (holding back, concealment of data) correspond in general to the falsification of a genuine document.[132]

As in the case of computer-related fraud, such conduct may be encompassed by computer misuse offences, which punish access/modification of data carried out with an intention to commit a further offence.[133] In addition, in each jurisdiction the definition of document is sufficiently broad to incorporate false documents that are electronic in form. For example, for the purposes of the forgery provisions under Australian federal law, 'document' is defined to include 'any article or material (for example, a disk or a tape) from which information is capable of being reproduced with or without the aid of any other article or device'.[134]

4. Identity theft

The concept of online identity is notoriously malleable. The famous New Yorker cartoon, with one dog informing another that '[o]n the Internet, nobody knows you're a dog',[135] is as apposite today as when it was first published in 1993. For some, the anonymity of the Internet is a large part of its appeal. Yet as online transactions have become more central to the way in which we interact with each other, valid identification assumes a greater importance.

For example, many of us enjoy the convenience of online banking. While it is wonderful to be able to go online and access our funds, all that is between us and someone else using those funds is a password. If another person has access to those numbers, they are effectively 'you' for the purpose of online transactions. The computer receiving that information does not know who 'you' are; it simply responds as it has been programmed to. There is no need to engage in face-to-face transactions. No chance of being caught on CCTV. That person can access your funds, as if they are you, from anywhere in the world.

The need for a specific offence of 'identity theft' arises from the difficulty of punishing misuse of identity information under the general

---

132 *Ibid.*   133 See chs. 3 and 4 respectively.
134 Criminal Code (Cth), s. 143.1(1). Also see Criminal Code (Can), s. 321; Forgery and Counterfeiting Act 1981 (UK), s. 8(1)(d); and Model Penal Code § 224.1.
135 P. Steiner, 'On the Internet, nobody knows you're a dog', *The New Yorker* (New York), 5 July 1993, p. 61.

criminal law. While there is a plethora of offences which may be applied
to the fraudulent use of identification information, these typically punish
the use which is made of that information, rather than dealing in the
information itself.[136]

Accordingly each jurisdiction has, or is considering, offences which
specifically target identity theft. The United States has led the way in
this regard, with Arizona the first state to enact specific identity-theft
laws in 1996.[137] The principal US federal provisions were enacted as the
Identity Theft and Assumption Deterrence Act of 1998. In particular,
18 USC § 1028 relates to 'fraud and related activity in connection with
identification documents, authentication features, and information'.[138]
There is also an offence of aggravated identity theft where the defendant
knowingly transfers, possesses, or uses, without lawful authority, a means
of identification of another person in connection with specified offences,
including terrorism offences.[139]

In Australia, although two states already have identity-theft provisions,[140] there is currently no federal equivalent. However, following the
recommendations of the Model Criminal Law Officers Committee[141] a
new Part 9.5 'Identity Crime' is to be inserted into the Criminal Code
(Cth).[142]

Canada has also recently introduced Bill S-4, 'An Act to Amend the
Criminal Code (Identity Theft and Related Misconduct)', which introduces a range of offences relating to identity crime.[143] Having passed the

---

136 Model Criminal Law Officers Committee, *Identity Crime* (2008), p. 14.
137 While all states have followed suit, there is a lack of uniformity: G. R Newman and M. M.
    McNally, *Identity Theft Literature Review* (Office of Justice Programs, US Department of
    Justice, 2005), pp. 63–4. Also see C. Pastrikos, 'Identity theft statutes: Which will protect
    Americans the most?' (2004) 67 *Albany Law Review* 1137.
138 The penalties for these offences are found at 18 USC §1028(b).
139 18 USC § 1028A.
140 Criminal Law Consolidation Act 1935 (SA), Part 5A; and Criminal Code 1899 (Qld),
    s. 408D.
141 Model Criminal Law Officers Committee, *Identity Crime* (2008).
142 At the time of writing, the Law and Justice Legislation Amendment (Identity Crimes
    and Other Measures) Bill 2008 (Cth) was recently introduced in the Senate, and was yet
    to be enacted. However, for convenience the proposed sections will be discussed as if in
    force. The Victorian Parliament has also introduced offences based in large part on the
    Commonwealth recommendations: see Crimes Amendment (Identity Crime) Act 2009
    (Vic). Also see Department of Justice, *Crimes Amendment (Identity Crime) Bill Exposure
    Draft: Discussion paper* (2008).
143 For a complete summary, see N. Holmes and D. Valiquet, *Bill S-4: An Act to Amend the
    Criminal Code (Identity Theft and Related Misconduct)*, Legislative Summary LS-637E
    (Legal and Legislative Affairs Division, 2009).

Second Reading stage in the Senate, the bill was referred to the Legal and Constitutional Committee, and at the time of writing, was awaiting further debate in the House of Commons and the Senate.[144]

Finally, the relevant UK offences were enacted as part of broader reforms relating to the introduction of compulsory identity cards.[145] In addition to criminal offences relating to identity cards, the Act also contains provisions punishing the misuse of identity documents more broadly.

Although a convenient and popular term, 'identity theft' is problematic for a number of reasons. First, the term 'theft' is of course not used in its literal sense. The person's identity is not 'stolen'. Rather, aspects of that identity are appropriated by the offender, usually for the purpose of committing a further offence.

Secondly, 'identity theft' is generally used to refer to those situations where an existing identity is appropriated. However, the use of a 'false identity' may also include the creation of a false identity ('identity fabrication') or alteration of an existing identity ('identity manipulation').[146]

Thirdly, there is some debate in the literature about what is, or is not, 'true' identity theft. For example, some view the use of credit card information to make purchases as not 'true' identity theft, but rather as simply fraud. True identity theft is reserved for those situations where there is a more 'concerted' effort to appropriate the person's identity, for example, by using identity information to take over an existing account.[147]

While acknowledging these deficiencies, the term 'identity theft' will be adopted in this chapter to refer to those specific offences which address the unauthorised acquisition and distribution of identity information. These are preparatory offences, which seek to punish the misuse of identity information irrespective of whether that information is ultimately used in the commission of an offence. Each jurisdiction bases its offences around a central concept of 'identity document' or 'identity information'. Certain conduct in relation to that information is then proscribed. Typically, this includes:

---

144 For the purpose of this chapter, the proposed provisions in Bill S-4 will be discussed as if in force.
145 Identity Cards Act 2006 (UK).
146 Australasian Centre for Policing Research, *Identity Crime Terms*, p. 7.
147 BC Freedom of Information and Privacy Association, *PIPEDA and Identity Theft*, p. 3. See also, Canadian Internet Policy and Public Interest Clinic, *Identity Theft: Introduction and background*, p. 2.

1. possessing identification information
2. dealing in identification information
3. possession of equipment used to create identification information.

In addition, both Australia and Canada have specific offences dealing with credit card skimming which pre-date the proposed identity theft laws.[148] In the United States, such conduct is regarded as a form of identity theft[149] and may be prosecuted under a number of federal provisions.[150]

A. Defining identification information

In imposing liability for identity theft, it is first necessary to define what is meant by 'identity'. We are not here concerned with abstract notions of identity:

> Legal identity is concerned not so much with the internalised view of the identity that relates to a person's sense of self or the externalised view that concerns the way that a person is viewed by others but with the way in which an accumulation of information distinguishes one individual from all others.[151]

The process of identification has been described as 'the association of data with a particular human being.'[152] This is typically done by a person demonstrating something they know, such as a PIN; presenting something they have, such as a driver's licence; or by displaying physical characteristics, such as a fingerprint.[153] Although there are myriad ways in which our identification may be verified, the information which may be used for this purpose essentially falls into one of three categories:[154]

1. *biometric identity*: physical features that are unique to the individual such as fingerprints, voice, DNA profile, retina, etc.
2. *attributed identity*: those aspects of identity which we acquire at birth such as name, date and place of birth, parent's names and address

---

148 Criminal Code (Cth), Part 10.8 and Criminal Code (Can), s. 342 and 342.01.
149 Solicitor General, Canada and US Department of Justice, *Public Advisory: Special report for consumers on identity theft* (2003), pp. 2–3 and Model Criminal Code Officers Committee, *Credit Card Skimming Offences*, pp. 12–14.
150 18 USC § 1028 (see p. 208), 18 USC § 1029 (see p. 130), and 18 USC § 1030(a)(2).
151 Finch, 'The problem of stolen identity', p. 30.
152 R. Clarke, 'Human identification in information systems: Management challenges and public policy issues' (1994) *Information Technology and People* 6, 8.
153 *Ibid.*, 17–18.   154 Economic and Domestic Secretariat, *Identity Fraud*, p. 9.

3. *biographical identity*: those aspects of our identity which we acquire over time; qualifications, employment history, licence, passport, bank accounts, etc.

In order to commit identity theft, an offender needs to acquire or fabricate identifying information. This is most easily achieved in relation to attributed and biographical identity which are based on documents and information which may be stolen, bought illegally or forged.[155] Accordingly, in each jurisdiction, identity theft is based around the concept of an 'identity document' and/or 'identity information'.

Before considering the specific definition in each jurisdiction, some general observations should be made. First, as identity crimes may be committed using real or false identities, any definition should allow for fictitious identities. Secondly, because identification information of legal persons such as corporations may also be used to commit identity crime, it is desirable that the definitions incorporate such information.[156] Thirdly, any definition should be technologically neutral.

The narrowest definition of 'identity document' is found in the UK where it is defined by reference to a list of documents, including an ID card,[157] designated documents, immigration documents,[158] passports and licences.[159] In contrast to other jurisdictions, the definition is limited to specific types of identifying information. It does not, for example, incorporate identification information relating to corporations. Although the list may be modified, this requires the approval of both Houses of Parliament.[160]

The Canadian provision also contains an exhaustive definition of 'identity document', which includes documents such as social insurance number card, driver's licence, health insurance card, birth certificate or passport. However, it also extends to 'identity information', defined to mean 'any information – including biological or physiological information – of a type that is commonly used alone or in combination with other information to identify or purport to identify an individual'.[161] An inclusive list is then provided, which includes biometric information, name, address, date of birth, written, electronic or digital signature, financial, passport, insurance or driver's licence number.

---

155 *Ibid.*, p. 17.
156 Model Criminal Law Officers Committee, *Identity Crime* (2008), p. 31.
157 Identity Cards Act 2006 (UK), s. 26(1).
158 'Immigration document' is defined in s. 26(2).   159 S. 26(1).   160 S. 26(4)–(5).
161 Bill S-4: An Act to Amend the Criminal Code (Identity Theft and Related Misconduct) (2009), cl. 10 (Criminal Code (Can), proposed s. 402.1).

This has the advantage of providing an expansive and flexible definition which applies to information in any form. By applying to information that is commonly used to identify 'or purport' to identify, it also includes fictitious information. It is, however, limited to identification of 'individuals' and arguably does not apply to identification of legal persons such as corporations. However, as 'every one', 'person' and 'similar expressions' are defined to include organisations,[162] if 'individual' is found to be a 'similar expression' to 'person', then the provision would apply equally to corporate identity.

A similar approach is taken in Australia where 'identification documentation' is defined as 'any document or other thing that contains or incorporates identification information and is capable of being used by a person for the purpose of pretending to be, or passing the person off as, another person (whether living or dead, real or fictitious)'.[163] 'Identification information' is then defined to mean 'information, or a document, relating to a person (whether living, dead, real or fictitious) that is capable of being used (whether alone or in conjunction with other information or documents) to identify, or purportedly identify, the person.'[164] The Act then provides a list of examples of identification information which includes such things as name and address, date and place of birth, relationship status, driver's licence, passport, financial account information including passwords or personal identification information and biometric data.

As well as clearly extending to fictitious identity information, this provision also applies to the identification of legal persons which come within the meaning of 'person'.[165] The references to 'document or any other thing' and 'information, or other document' facilitates technological neutrality.[166]

The US provision defines four categories of identification information:

1. An *identification document* is a document made or issued by or under the authority of specified US or foreign governmental or quasi-governmental organisations which, 'when completed with information

---

162 Pursuant to s. 2 Criminal Code (Can) the term 'organization' includes a body corporate.
163 Law and Justice Legislation Amendment (Identity Crimes and Other Measures) Bill 2008 (Cth), Sch. 1 (Criminal Code (Cth), proposed s. 370.1).
164 Criminal Code (Cth), proposed s. 370.1.
165 Acts Interpretation Act 1901 (Cth), s. 22(1)(a).
166 Further, 'document' is defined to include 'any article or material from which sounds, images or writings are capable of being reproduced with or without the aid of any other article or device'; *ibid.*, s. 25.

concerning a particular individual, is of a type intended or commonly accepted for the purpose of identification of individuals'.[167]

2. An *authentication feature* is 'any hologram, watermark, certification, symbol, code, image, sequence of numbers or letters, or other feature that either individually or in combination with another feature is used by the issuing authority on an identification document, document-making implement, or means of identification to determine if the document is counterfeit, altered, or otherwise falsified'.[168]

3. A *false identification document* is a document 'of a type intended or commonly accepted for the purposes of identification of individuals' that was not issued by or under the authority of a governmental entity or was so issued but was subsequently altered for purposes of deceit *and* appears to be issued by or under the authority of a specified US or foreign governmental or quasi-governmental organisation.[169]

4. *Means of identification* is 'any name or number that may be used, alone or in conjunction with any other information, to identify a specific individual'.[170] A non-exhaustive list of examples is then provided, and includes name, social security number, date of birth, driver's licence, passport number, taxpayer identification number, unique biometric data or telecommunication identifying information or access device.[171]

Although 'means of identification', in particular, provides a broad definition, it appears to be limited to actual as opposed to fictitious information – that is, information which may actually be used to identify an individual. Further, it has been recommended that these provisions be amended to apply to information used to identify corporations.[172]

B. Possessing identity information

In each jurisdiction it is an offence to possess a person's identity documents/information. The particular challenges that apply to the 'possession' of digital information are discussed in Chapter 10. The additional challenge in relation to identity information is the dual-use nature of such information, and the danger of over criminalising if what is punished is simply possessing another person's identity information. This is typically addressed by requiring proof of a further mental state in respect of that information.

167 18 USC § 1028(d)(3).   168 18 USC § 1028(d)(1).   169 18 USC § 1028(d)(4).
170 18 USC § 1028(d)(7).   171 The latter is defined in 18 USC § 1029(e), see p. 130.
172 The President's Identity Theft Task Force, *Combating Identity Theft*, p. 67.

_or example, under the Australian provision the defendant must possess the identification information intending that any person (including the defendant) will use the information to commit an offence of dealing in identification information.[173] This offence applies even where the person to whom the identification information relates consents, but does not apply to a person possessing their own identification information.[174] As this is a preparatory offence, it is not an offence to attempt to possess identification information.[175]

In Canada, the relevant fault element differs according to whether what is possessed is an identity document or identification information. In relation to an identity document 'that relates or purports to relate, in whole or in part, to another person', the offence is made out if the person is shown to be in possession 'without lawful excuse'; there is no additional fault element to be proved.[176] In contrast, possession of identification information must be 'in circumstances giving rise to a reasonable inference that the information is intended to be used to commit an indictable offence that includes fraud, deceit or falsehood as an element of the offence'.[177]

In the UK, the identity document must either be false, improperly obtained or relate to someone else. An identity document is 'false' for these purposes where it is false within the terms of s. 9(1) Forgery and Counterfeiting Act 1981.[178] This provides an exhaustive list of circumstances in which an instrument is false, for example if it purports to have been made by a particular person and it was not in fact made by that person. An identity document was 'improperly obtained' if false information was provided in, or in connection with, the application for its issue or modification.[179] For an offence to be made out, it must be proved that the defendant knew it was false or improperly obtained, except where the information relates to another person.[180]

There are then two distinct levels of offence depending on whether a further fault element is proved. The less serious offence is possession

173 Criminal Code (Cth), proposed s. 372.2. Maximum penalty 3 years' imprisonment. The offence of dealing in identification information under proposed s. 372.1 is discussed at p. 216 below.
174 Criminal Code (Cth), proposed s. 372.2(3)–(4). This offence may also be an alternative verdict on a charge under proposed s. 372.1 and 372.5.
175 Criminal Code (Cth), proposed s. 372.6.
176 Criminal Code (Can), proposed s. 56.1(1). For further discussion of this section, see p. 217.
177 Criminal Code (Can), proposed s. 402.2(1)). An inclusive list of offences is provided in proposed s. 402.2(3). Maximum penalty 5 years' imprisonment: proposed s. 402.2(5).
178 Identity Cards Act 2006 (UK), s. 25(8)(a).   179 S. 25(8)(b).   180 S. 25(1).

or control of such a document 'without reasonable excuse'.[181] The more serious offence is where the defendant was in possession or control of the document with the intention of using it to establish registrable facts about the defendant, or with the intention of allowing or inducing another to use it for establishing, ascertaining or verifying registrable facts about the defendant or about any other person.[182] 'Registrable facts' are those recorded about an individual on the National Identity Register pursuant to s. 1(1), and are defined to include name, address, gender, date of birth and physical characteristics.[183]

The US provisions contain a range of mental states in relation to possession. The broadest provides that it is an offence to knowingly possess, without lawful authority, a means of identification of another person 'with the intent to commit, or to aid or abet, or in connection with, any unlawful activity that constitutes a violation of Federal law, or that constitutes a felony under any applicable State or local law'.[184]

Further, it is an offence to knowingly possess:

(a) five or more identification documents (other than those issued lawfully for the use of the possessor), authentication features, or false identification documents with intent to use unlawfully or transfer unlawfully[185]

(b) an 'identification document (other than one issued lawfully for the use of the possessor), authentication feature, or a false identification document, with the intent such document or feature be used to defraud the United States'[186]

(c) an 'identification document or authentication feature that is or appears to be an identification document or authentication feature of the United States or a sponsoring entity of an event designated as a special event of national significance which is stolen or produced without lawful authority knowing that such document or feature was stolen or produced without such authority'.[187]

C. Trafficking identity information

As one of the major impacts of digital technology has been to facilitate the trade in identity information, each jurisdiction (other than the UK) makes provision for what may broadly be described as 'trafficking' offences.

181 Maximum penalty 2 years' imprisonment: s. 25(7).
182 S. 25(2). Maximum penalty ten years' imprisonment: s. 25(6).   183 S. 1(5)–(7).
184 18 USC § 1028(a)(7).   185 18 USC § 1028(a)(3).
186 18 USC § 1028(a)(4).   187 18 USC § 1028(a)(6).

Similar to drug and other trafficking offences, this typically encompasses a broad range of conduct, targeting all stages in the chain of supply. As with the concept of 'possession', such concepts may prove challenging in the digital context, as discussed in Chapter 10.

In Australia, the relevant conduct is to 'deal' in identification information, defined broadly to include 'make, supply or use' such information.[188] This offence further requires proof of an intention that 'the user' of the information (which may include the defendant) will use the information to pretend to be, or to pass the user off as, another person (whether living, dead, real or fictitious) for the purpose of committing or facilitating the commission of a specified offence.[189]

This provision is narrower than that recommended by the Model Criminal Law Officers Committee in that it requires the defendant to intend that the user will pretend to be/pass themselves off as another person, as opposed to merely using the identification information with the intention of committing or facilitating the commission of the other offence. This additional requirement is intended to make clear that the offence is one of identity crime, rather than simply using identification information in connection with an indictable offence.[190]

However, what constitutes 'pretend to be' or 'passing off' is unclear. For example, if a person uses unauthorised credit card data for the purpose of making an online transaction, is that person passing themselves off as the owner of the card? Unless given a narrow interpretation, it would seem that merely using identification information would generally involve pretending to be/passing off as another person.

As with possession, because this is a preparatory offence it is not an offence to attempt to commit this offence.[191] It is, however, an offence, even though it is impossible to commit the other offence or that offence is to be committed at a later date.[192] For example, if the identification information is to be used to facilitate the importation of drugs, and the drugs have in fact been seized by customs.[193]

Further, it is an offence even though the person to whom the identification information relates consented to the dealing.[194] In the Committee's

---

188 Criminal Code (Cth), proposed s. 372.1(1).
189 Maximum penalty 5 years' imprisonment: proposed s. 372.1(1).
190 Explanatory Memorandum, Commonwealth Parliament, Law and Justice Amendment (Identity Crimes and Other Measures) Bill 2008 (Cth), pp. 4–5.
191 Criminal Code (Cth), proposed s. 372.6.   192 Proposed s. 372.1(2)(a).
193 Explanatory Memorandum, Law and Justice Amendment (Identity Crimes and Other Measures) Bill 2008 (Cth), p. 4.
194 Criminal Code, proposed s. 372.1(3)(b).

view, innocent use with consent would be addressed by the requirement that the defendant must have intended the commission or facilitation of another offence. If this element was not present, the use with consent would not be an offence. If, however, it were present, it should not matter that the use was with the consent of the person concerned.[195]

It is not, however, an offence for a person to deal in their own identification information.[196] This makes sense, for example, where a person uses their own identification information to purchase and import prohibited drugs.[197] The essence of identity theft is to use another person's identity to commit an offence. Similarly, offences such as forgery may be utilised where a person manufactures their own identification information.[198] However, the term 'deals' is defined to include supplying identification information. It is not clear why it should not be identity theft for a person to supply their own information to another in order for that person to commit an offence. As the provision stands, such conduct would be charged as an accessory to the principal offence (assuming it were committed) rather than identity crime.

In Canada, the relevant conduct varies according to whether it relates to an identity document or identification information. In relation to the former, it is an offence to, without lawful excuse, 'procure to be made, transfer, sell or offer for sale' an identity document that relates or purports to relate, in whole or in part, to another person.[199] The potential breadth of this provision is addressed by a number of defences where the person was acting:

(1) 'in good faith, in the ordinary course of the person's business or employment or in the exercise of the duties of their office'
(2) 'for genealogical purposes'
(3) 'with the consent of the person to whom the identity document relates or of a person authorized to consent on behalf of the person to whom the document relates, or of the entity that issued the identity document'
(4) 'for a legitimate purpose related to the administration of justice'.[200]

---

195 Model Criminal Law Officers Committee, *Identity Crime* (2008), p. 33.
196 Criminal Code (Cth), proposed s. 372.1(4).
197 Explanatory Memorandum, Commonwealth Parliament, Law and Justice Amendment (Identity Crimes and Other Measures) Bill 2008 (Cth), p. 4.
198 *Ibid.*
199 Criminal Code (Can), proposed s. 56.1. Maximum penalty 5 years' imprisonment: proposed s. 56.1(1).
200 Proposed s. 56.1 (2).

In contrast, the offence of identity theft makes it an offence to 'transmit, make available, distribute, sell or offer for sale' another person's identity information, or to possess such information for any of those purposes. This offence also requires proof that the defendant knew, believed, or was reckless as to whether the information would be used to commit an indictable offence that includes fraud, deceit or falsehood as an element of the offence.[201]

In the United States, there are a number of offences which cover what may broadly be described as 'dealing' in identification information. It is an offence to:

(1) knowingly and without lawful authority produce[202] an identification document, authentication feature, or a false identification document[203]
(2) knowingly transfer an identification document, authentication feature, or a false identification document knowing that such document or feature was stolen or produced without lawful authority[204]
(3) knowingly transfer or use, without lawful authority, a means of identification of another person[205] with the intent to commit, or to aid or abet, or in connection with, any unlawful activity that constitutes a violation of Federal law, or that constitutes a felony under any applicable State or local law[206]
(4) knowingly traffic[207] in false or actual authentication features for use in false identification documents, document-making implements, or means of identification.[208]

'Transfer' is defined to include 'selecting an identification document, false identification document, or document-making implement', and includes 'placing or directing the placement of such identification document, false identification document, or document-making implement on an online location where it is available to others'.[209] This provision, amongst others, was inserted by the Internet False Identification Act of 2000 specifically

---

201 Proposed s. 402.2(2). An inclusive list of such offences is specified in proposed s. 402.2(3).
202 Defined to include 'alter, authenticate, or assemble': 18 USC § 1028(d)(9).
203 18 USC § 1028(a)(1).   204 18 USC § 1028(a)(2).
205 This limitation restricts the application of the offence. That is, it does not apply to means of identification of the defendant.
206 18 USC § 1028(a)(7).
207 Defined to mean 'to transport, transfer, or otherwise dispose of, to another, as consideration for anything of value' or 'to make or obtain control of with intent to so transport, transfer, or otherwise dispose of': 18 USC § 1028(d)(12).
208 18 USC § 1028(a)(8).   209 18 USC § 1028(10).

to address concerns about false identification information being available on the Internet.[210]

It has been held in the context of aggravated identity theft[211] that the word 'knowingly' only modifies the verbs 'transfers, possesses, or uses' and not the phrase 'of another person'. Consequently, the prosecution need not prove that the defendant knew that the means of identification belonged to another person.[212]

D. Manufacturing identity information

As with other contexts in which supply and distribution are criminalised, there are also offences which criminalise the possession and distribution of items used in the manufacture of identity documents and information. While items such as card skimmers may readily be identified as having been made or modified for the purpose, there are of course a wide range of items which could potentially be used to create identification information, such as publishing software, laminators and scanners. Accordingly, the fault element associated with such offences is crucial in ensuring they are not over-broad.

For example, the Australian provision uses the term 'equipment', which was deliberately left undefined to avoid the provision becoming outdated as a result of advances in technology.[213] However, in order for a person to be guilty of an offence, they must possess the equipment intending that any person (including the defendant) will use it to make identification documentation *and* that any person will use that identification to commit the offence of dealing in identification information under proposed s. 372.1.[214]

In contrast, the UK provisions refer to any apparatus, article or material which, to the defendant's knowledge, is or has been 'specially designed or adapted' for the making of false identity documents.[215] As with the US

210 Also see US Senate, *Phony Identification.*   211 18 USC § 1028A.
212 *US* v. *Flores-Figueroa*, 274 Fed Appx 501 (8th Cir 2008); cert. granted, *Flores-Figueroa* v. *US*, 2008 US LEXIS 7827. Also see *US* v. *Mendoza-Gonzalez*, 520 F 3d 912 (8th Cir 2008).
213 Explanatory Memorandum, Law and Justice Amendment (Identity Crimes and Other Measures) Bill 2008 (Cth), p. 7.
214 Criminal Code (Cth), proposed s. 372.3. Maximum penalty 3 years' imprisonment: proposed s. 372.3(1). It is not an offence to attempt to commit this offence: proposed s. 372.6.
215 Identity Cards Act 2006 (UK), s. 25(3). This includes the modification of an identity document so that it becomes false: s. 25(8)(b).

provisions discussed below, this wording may be unduly limiting as many items which may be used in creating false identity documents could not be said to be 'specially designed or adapted' for that purpose.

There are two levels of offence depending upon the level of *mens rea*. The first level is where the defendant is in possession or control of such items, without reasonable excuse.[216] The more serious offence applies where it can be shown that the defendant was in possession of the items with intention that it would be used to make a false identity document and that the document would be used by somebody for establishing, ascertaining or verifying registrable facts about a person.[217]

In the United States, it is an offence to knowingly produce, transfer, or possess a document-making implement with the intent it will be used in the production of a false identification document or another document-making implement or authentication feature which will be so used.[218] 'Document-making implement' means:

> any implement, impression, template, computer file, computer disk, electronic device, or computer hardware or software, that is specifically configured or primarily used for making an identification document, a false identification document, or another document-making implement.[219]

The meaning of 'specially configured' or 'primarily used' was considered in *US* v. *Cabrera*.[220] At the time, the definition referred to an implement which was 'specially *designed* or primarily used' for making an identification document, a false identification document, or another document-making implement.[221] In this case, the defendant used a computer, document scanner, printer and commercial software to scan genuine documents, save the images, remove or alter the identifying information and then print them. New identifying information was then entered onto the documents before they were laminated.[222] It was held that the terms 'specially designed' and 'primarily used' referred to their use in the hands of the defendant, rather than an item's general usage.[223] Although the items of equipment in this case all had other legitimate uses, it was open to the jury to find that in the hands of the defendant they were 'specially designed' and 'primarily used' for the prohibited purposes.

---

216 S. 25(5). Maximum penalty 2 years' imprisonment: s. 25(7).
217 S. 25(4). Maximum penalty 10 years' imprisonment: s 25(6).
218 18 USC §1028(a)(5).　　　219 18 USC § 1028(d)(2).
220 208 F 3d 309 (1st Cir 2000).　　　221 *Ibid.*, 310 (emphasis added).
222 *Ibid.*, 311.　　　223 *Ibid.*, 314.

8

Criminal copyright infringement

1. Copyright infringement is (not) theft

Although not fraud in the true sense, criminal copyright infringement may be seen as a related offence, involving as it does unauthorised interference with the property rights of another. Copyright is just one example of an intellectual property right; other examples include trademarks, patents and designs.[1] Contrary to what the copyright industry would have us believe, copyright infringement is neither theft[2] nor 'piracy'. Copyright is a limited monopoly granted to producers of original creative works. It protects the expression of ideas by conferring certain exclusive rights on the creator for a period of time.[3] Copyright is infringed if a person exercises one of the exclusive rights of the copyright holder without authorisation. In the context of criminal copyright infringement, the most significant rights are those of reproduction and distribution.[4]

The increasing availability of copyrighted materials in digital form presents a dilemma. On the one hand, it provides a worldwide market for the distribution and sale of copyrighted goods. For exporters of copyright, such as the United States, this can be a significant component of the economy. In 2002, it was estimated that the 'value added' by the core

1 As to criminal enforcement of intellectual property laws more generally, see Australian Institute of Criminology, *Intellectual Property Crime and Enforcement in Australia*, Research and Public Policy Series no. 94 (2008); M. A. Yu, R. Lehrer and W. Roland, 'Intellectual property crimes' (2008) 45 *American Criminal Law Review* 665, and US Department of Justice, *Prosecuting Intellectual Property Crimes*, 3rd edn (Office of Legal Education, 2006).
2 Although the penalty provisions for criminal copyright infringement in the US are found in 18 USC Part I Chapter 113, 'Stolen Property'.
3 Australian Institute of Criminology, *Intellectual Property Crime*, pp. 42–4. This period varies between jurisdictions but is typically the life of the author plus either 50 or 70 years: Copyright Act 1968 (Cth), s. 33(2); Copyright Act 1985 (Can), s. 6; Copyright, Designs and Patents Act 1988 (UK), Part 1; and 17 USC § 302(a).
4 US Department of Justice, *Prosecuting Intellectual Property Crimes*, p. 3.

copyright industries[5] to US GDP was US$626.2 billion or just under 6 per cent.[6] On the other hand, that ease of distribution and market access equally translates into ease of copyright infringement. Industry estimates put the ratio of infringing copies of music at twenty infringing downloads for every track sold,[7] while in China the digital-piracy rate is estimated to be around 99 per cent.[8] A 2004 British survey found that approximately one-quarter (26 per cent) of 10 to 25-year-old Internet users reported that they had illegally downloaded software, music or films in the last twelve months.[9] Seventy per cent of Internet users surveyed in the UK thought it was appropriate to download music without paying for it.[10]

We have seen the ease with which digital media may be reproduced and copied, and this is clearly the most significant factor in the increase in copyright infringement. Particularly significant in this context are peer-to-peer (p2p) networks. Under the traditional host model, those wishing to access materials for download must access a central website from which material is requested. In contrast, p2p software allows individual computer users to communicate directly with one another. Once the software is downloaded, users wishing to share files simply place them in a 'My Shared Folder' or equivalent.[11] Users can then search the folders of other users in order to locate files they wish to copy. In this way, each user is potentially both a requester and provider of material.

By spreading the transfer of data across users rather than a centralised host, individuals may easily transfer volumes of infringing copies that may be described as 'commercial' in size. Industry estimates claim that 80 per cent of ISP broadband capacity is consumed by p2p file sharing,[12] while on one p2p network it was estimated that almost 90 per cent of

---

5 'Core' copyright industries are those whose primary purpose is to produce or distribute copyrighted materials.
6 S. E. Siwek, *Copyright Industries in the US Economy: The 2004 report*, (International Intellectual Property Alliance, 2004), p. 5.
7 International Federation of the Phonographic Industry, *IFPI Digital Music Report 2008* (IFPI, 2008), p. 18.
8 *Ibid.*
9 D. Wilson et al., *Fraud and Technology Crimes: Findings from the 2003/04 British Crime Survey, the 2004 Offending, Crime and Justice Survey and administrative* sources (Home Office, 2006), p. 8.
10 W. H. Dutton, C. di Gennaro and A. M. Hargrave, *The Internet in Britain: The Oxford Internet survey* (Oxford Internet Institute, 2005), p. 5.
11 For a detailed description of the software, see *Universal Music Australia Pty Ltd* v. *Sharman License Holdings Ltd* (2005) 220 ALR 1 at 3–9 per Wilcox J.
12 IFPI, *Digital Music Report 2008*, p. 19.

available files were copyrighted works.[13] With millions of copies of p2p software downloaded, and billions of files shared, 'the probable scope of copyright infringement is staggering'.[14]

The decentralised nature of p2p networks also frustrates attempts at enforcement. Initial versions, such as Napster, still maintained a centralised presence, which provided an index capacity. Requests would go to the host, which would then search the files of users, although the transfer of data would occur between the two users.[15] More recent versions, such as Morpheus and Kazaa, are true p2p in that they do not require a centralised host at all. While some designate certain computers to perform a temporary indexing function, others dispense with this requirement entirely, allowing computers on the network to communicate with each other directly.[16]

Although criminal copyright infringement has been recognised for some time,[17] the enforcement of copyright laws has traditionally been, and remains, a matter of civil law.[18] Criminal copyright infringement is typically limited to those circumstances where 'infringement is particularly serious, the infringer knows the infringement is wrong, or the type of case renders civil enforcement by individual copyright owners especially difficult'.[19] The perceived need for an increasingly criminal law response has typically followed changes in technology which have threatened copyright and made enforcement more difficult; for example, audio cassettes, then video cassettes and now file sharing. Over the decades, and particularly with the growth of the recording, motion picture and now software industries, there have been repeated revisions to try to strengthen criminal copyright protection, by diluting the *mens rea* requirement, broadening the concept of 'commercial gain' and increasing penalties.[20] More recently, the increasingly transnational and organised nature of

---

13 *Metro-Goldwyn-Mayer Studios Inc. v. Grokster Ltd.*, 545 US 913, 922 (2005).

14 *Ibid.*, 923.   15 *In re Napster, Inc.*, 377 F Supp 2d 796 (ND Cal 2005).

16 *Metro-Goldwyn-Mayer Studios Inc. v. Grokster Ltd.*, 545 US 913, 923–30 (2005).

17 It was first made an offence in the US in 1897: *US* v. *LaMacchia*, 871 F Supp 535, 539 (D Mass 1994).

18 As to the broader question of whether the use of criminal law is appropriate in this context, see S. Penney, 'Crime, copyright, and the digital age' in Law Commission of Canada, *What is a Crime? Defining criminal conduct in contemporary society* (Vancouver: UBC Press, 2004) and G. S. Moohr, 'The crime of copyright infringement: An inquiry based on morality, harm and criminal theory' (2003) 83 *Boston University Law Review* 731.

19 US Department of Justice, *Prosecuting Intellectual Property Crimes*, p. 16.

20 *US* v. *LaMacchia*, 871 F Supp. 535, 539 (D Mass 1994).

intellectual property crimes has also made it increasingly the focus of law enforcement.[21]

In the United States in particular, where intellectual property laws are a significant economic issue, there has been increasingly aggressive enforcement.[22] In the financial year 2008, the US Department of Justice filed 179 cases of intellectual property crimes[23] of which 76 were for wilful copyright infringement.[24] This was up from a total of 101 intellectual property cases filed in 2004.[25] In Australia, the Commonwealth Director of Public Prosecutions brought thirty-eight copyright related prosecutions in the year 2006–7.[26] However, many of these prosecutions are not concerned with infringement involving the use of computers or the Internet, despite the undoubtedly widespread practice of downloading infringing copies.[27]

Because of the global reach of the technology, enforcement has assumed international dimensions. One well-known example, 'Operation Buccaneer', was an undercover investigation undertaken by the US Customs Service in conjunction with authorities in Australia, the UK, Finland, Sweden and Norway.[28] The investigation targeted organised 'warez' groups[29] as well as others involved in the illegal distribution of copyrighted material. It involved the execution of approximately seventy warrants across these countries, and led to the conviction of a number of defendants, some of whom received significant terms of imprisonment. For example, 28-year-old John Sankus Jr was sentenced to forty-six months in federal prison,[30] while two UK defendants received terms of imprisonment of two and two

---

21 Australian Institute of Criminology, *Intellectual Property Crime*, pp. 4–5.
22 See generally, Task Force on Intellectual Property, *Progress Report of the Department of Justice's Task Force on Intellectual Property* (US Department of Justice, 2006).
23 18 USC §§ 2318, 2319, 2319A, 2320 or 17 USC § 506.
24 US Department of Justice, *FY 2008 Performance and Accountability Report* (2008), Appendix F: Intellectual Property Report – FY 2008, pp. F-3 and F-6.
25 *Ibid.*, p. F-6.
26 Australian Institute of Criminology, *Intellectual Property Crime and Enforcement in Australia*, p. 57.
27 G. Urbas and K. R. Choo, *Resource Materials on Technology-Enabled Crime*, Technical and Background Paper (AIC, 2008), p. 28.
28 Computer Crime and Intellectual Property Section, US Department of Justice, *Operation Buccaneer: The investigation*, www.usdoj.gov/criminal/cybercrime/ob/OBinvest.htm.
29 'Warez' refers to copies of infringed copyrighted works with copy protections removed; E. Goldman, 'A road to no warez: The No Electronic Theft Act and criminal copyright infringement' (2003) *Oregon Law Review* 369.
30 US Department of Justice, 'Warez leader sentenced to 46 months' (2002), www.cybercrime.gov/sankusSent.htm.

and a half years.[31] More recently, a British national, resident in Australia, was extradited to the United States as a result of this investigation[32] and ultimately pleaded guilty.[33]

2. Legislative provisions

Under the Cybercrime Convention, the protection of copyright and related rights is governed by Art. 10. It provides that each party 'shall adopt such legislative and other measures as may be necessary to establish as criminal offences under its domestic law':

1. 'the infringement of copyright, as defined under the law of that Party, pursuant to the obligations it has undertaken under the Paris Act of 24 July 1971 revising the Bern Convention for the Protection of Literary and Artistic Works, the Agreement on Trade-Related Aspects of Intellectual Property Rights and the WIPO Copyright Treaty' and
2. 'related rights, as defined under the law of that Party, pursuant to the obligations it has undertaken under the International Convention for the Protection of Performers, Producers of Phonograms and Broadcasting Organisations (Rome Convention), the Agreement on Trade-Related Aspects of Intellectual Property Rights and the WIPO Performances and Phonograms Treaty . . . where such acts are committed wilfully, on a commercial scale and by means of a computer system'.

A limited right is provided not to impose criminal liability. However, this arises in 'limited circumstances' where other effective remedies are available and the party still complies with its international obligations. This is intended to apply to such things as parallel imports and rental rights, and not to the core requirements under Art. 61 of the TRIPS agreement 'which is the minimum pre-existing criminalisation

---

31 BBC News, 'Internet piracy trio sent to jail', 6 May 2005, http://news.bbc.co.uk/1/hi/technology/4518771.stm.
32 *Griffiths* v. *United States of America* [2005] FCAFC 34; special leave to the High Court refused *Griffiths* v. *United States of America and anor* [2005] HCA Trans 666 (2 September 2005).
33 US Department of Justice, 'Extradited software piracy ringleader pleads guilty' Press Release, 20 April 2007, www.usdoj.gov/criminal/pr/press_releases/2007/04/2007_5117_04–20–07rgriffiths-plea.pdf; and Agence France-Presse, 'Briton sentenced to 51 months prison in US for Internet piracy', *The Sydney Morning Herald*, 23 June 2007, www.smh.com.au/news/Technology/Briton-sentenced-to-51-months-prison-in-US-for-Internet-piracy/2007/06/23/1182019396798.html.

requirement'.[34] Although some jurisdictions protect other forms of intellectual property such as patents and trademarks with criminal provisions, the obligations under the Convention do not extend to these.[35]

A related form of protection, but one which is beyond the scope of this book, is digital rights management (DRM) protection.[36] 'Digital rights management' is a 'generic term for a set of technologies for the identification and protection of intellectual property in digital form'.[37] These may be further classified as 'technological protection measures', (TPMs) which are technical measures used to prevent certain activities such as copying, and 'rights management information' (RMI), which identify digital works and are used to manage how that work is provided to consumers.[38] So, for example, DRM may be used to limit the number of copies which may be made of a digital work, whether it can be played on certain devices or whether it can be copied at all. Some jurisdictions provide for criminal offences in respect of removal of such protections. For example, in the United States the Digital Millenium Copyright Act[39] provides for offences relating to the circumvention of copyright protection mechanisms, trafficking in circumvention technology and compromising the integrity of copyright management information.[40] In the UK, the remedies provided are civil in nature.[41]

While each jurisdiction makes provision for criminal liability with respect to copyright infringement,[42] it is not possible within the confines of this book to do more than provide a brief overview of the key copyright offences. Our focus is on those aspects which differentiate civil from criminal copyright infringement and, in particular, those aspects which are especially significant in the digital context. These are:

---

34 Cybercrime Convention, Explanatory Report, [116]. 'TRIPS' is the World Trade Organisation's 'Agreement on Trade-Related Aspects of Intellectual Property Rights'.
35 *Ibid.*, [109].
36 See generally I. Brown, 'The evolution of anti-circumvention law' (2006) 20 *International Review of Law, Computers and Technology* 271.
37 All Party Parliamentary Internet Group, *'Digital Rights Management': Report of an Inquiry by the All Party Internet Group* (2006), p. 5.
38 *Ibid.*   39 Pub. I. no. 105–304, 112 Stat. 2860 (codified at 17 USC §512).
40 17 USC §§ 1201 and 1202. Penalties for these offences are found at 17 USC §1204. Also see, US Department of Justice, *Prosecuting Intellectual Property Crimes*, Part VIII; Copyright Act 1968 (Cth), Part V, Division 5, Subdivisions E and F.
41 Copyright, Designs and Patents Act 1988 (UK), ss. 296–296ZG. See generally All Party Parliamentary Internet Group, *Digital Rights Management*.
42 See, in particular, Copyright Act 1968 (Cth), Part V; Copyright Act 1985 (Can), Part IV; Copyright, Patents and Designs Act 1988 (UK), ss. 107–10; and 17 USC § 506.

1. the requirement that infringement be 'commercial' in nature
2. the meaning of 'distribution'
3. the requirement of *mens rea*
4. the imposition of significant penalties.

A. *Commercial infringement*

Article 61 of the TRIPS agreement provides for copyright infringement on a 'commercial scale' as a trigger for criminal liability,[43] and this requirement is reflected in each jurisdiction. Typically, this involves conduct such as selling or hiring infringing copies or exhibiting, importing or possessing for a commercial purpose.[44] The key US provision simply states that it is an offence to engage in wilful infringement for the purpose 'of commercial advantage or private financial gain'.[45]

However, one of the challenges of digital infringement, particularly p2p transfers, is that the person does not necessarily act for a commercial motive. The ease and low cost of reproduction and distribution is such that many people will distribute in the hope of accessing other materials in return, or simply because they can.[46] Accordingly, some jurisdictions incorporate trading of infringing materials within the definition of 'commercial'. For example, 17 USC § 101 defines 'financial gain' to include the 'receipt, or expectation of receipt, of anything of value, including the receipt of copyrighted works'. More broadly, each jurisdiction has provisions which criminalise distribution to such an extent that it substantially impacts on the interests of the copyright owner.[47]

The United States has two provisions specifically aimed at electronic distribution. Under the first, it is an offence to engage in wilful infringement by reproduction or distribution, including by electronic means, 'during any 180-day period, of 1 or more copies or "phonorecords" of 1 or more copyrighted works, which have a total retail value of more

---

43 Although parties may wish to set a lower threshold: Cybercrime Convention, Explanatory Report, [114].
44 Copyright Act 1968 (Cth), Part V, Division 5, Subdivision C; Copyright Act 1985 (Can), s. 42(1); and Copyright, Patents and Designs Act 1988 (UK), s. 107.
45 17 USC § 506(a)(1)(A).
46 *US* v. *LaMacchia*, 871 F Supp 535, 539–540 (D Mass 1994) where the defendant could not be charged with criminal copyright infringement at that time because he had placed pirated works on his website without a profit motive.
47 See, e.g., Copyright Act 1968 (Cth), s. 132AC(1); Copyright Act 1985 (Can), s. 42(1)(c); and Copyright, Designs and Patents Act 1988 (UK), s. 107(1)(e).

than $ 1,000'.[48] It is also an offence to engage in wilful infringement by the distribution of a work being prepared for commercial distribution by making it available on a computer network accessible to members of the public, if such person knew or should have known that the work was intended for commercial distribution.[49]

A 'computer network accessible to the public' clearly applies to the internet, particularly p2p networks.[50] However, it should arguably also extend to any large network available to a significant number of people, even if not available to all members of the public, for example a LAN in a large organisation such as a university, members-only networks or even password-protected sites.[51] This is consistent with the definition of 'publicly' in the Act which refers to 'any place where a substantial number of persons outside of a normal circle of a family and its social acquaintances is gathered'.[52]

B. Distribution

It seems that the act of uploading and downloading files may clearly infringe the copyright owner's exclusive right of reproduction and distribution.[53] The more difficult question is whether merely making goods available online constitutes 'distribution'. For example, on a p2p network the defendant may have files available in the shared files folder

---

48 17 USC § 506(a)(1)(B). 'Phonorecords' are defined as 'material objects in which sounds, other than those accompanying a motion picture or other audiovisual work, are fixed by any method now known or later developed, and from which the sounds can be perceived, reproduced, or otherwise communicated, either directly or with the aid of a machine or device': 17 USC § 101. In addition to CD's or audio tapes this would include an MP3 or other computer audio file: US Department of Justice, *Prosecuting Intellectual Property Crimes*, p. 37.

49 17 USC § 506(a)(1)(C). A 'work being prepared for commercial distribution' is defined to mean 'a computer program, musical work, motion picture or other audiovisual work or sound recording where, at the time of unauthorized distribution, the copyright owner had a reasonable expectation of commercial distribution and the items had not been commercially distributed, or a motion picture which was available for viewing in a motion picture exhibition facility but not yet for other forms of viewing': 17 USC § 506(a)(3).

50 US Department of Justice, *Prosecuting Intellectual Property Crimes*, pp. 50–1.

51 *Ibid.*, p. 51.

52 17 USC § 101. See, e.g., *Playboy Enterprises, Inc.* v. *Frena*, 839 F Supp 1552, 1557 (MD Fla 1993) holding that display of infringing photographs on a website which was restricted to subscribers was still a 'public display'.

53 *A&M Records* v. *Napster*, 239 F 3d 1004, 1014; 1027 (9th Cir 2001).

of their computer, but there may not be evidence of actual transfer to another computer. Has that person 'distributed' the files?

In the US context, although 'distribution' is not defined it has been held to be 'for all practical purposes synonymous' with publication.[54] The meaning of 'distribute' was recently considered in the context of p2p networks in the civil case of *In re Napster, Inc.*[55] In that case, the plaintiffs alleged that the defendants had engaged in direct infringement of the plaintiffs' distribution rights 'by maintaining a centralized indexing system listing the file names of all MP3-formatted music files available on the Napster network'.[56] The question for determination was whether 'distribution' for these purposes requires the actual dissemination of the copyrighted works, or whether it is sufficient if the works are 'made available' to the public. The court held that, based on earlier authority and the legislative history and text of the statute, distribution requires actual dissemination of the copyrighted work.[57] This is also the view taken by the US Department of Justice.[58] An alternative is to charge the defendants with conspiracy to violate the copyright laws. Being an inchoate crime, conspiracy does not require proof of actual distribution.[59]

One of the major issues litigated in US civil courts has been contributory infringement – that is, where a person is liable not for the actual infringement, but for intentionally facilitating or inducing infringement by others. This has been particularly significant in relation to those who provide peer-to-peer networks.[60] Parallels have been drawn with criminal law

---

54 US Department of Justice, *Prosecuting Intellectual Property Crimes*, p. 41, citing *Ford Motor Co* v. *Summit Motor Products, Inc.*, 930 F 2d 277, 299–300 (3rd Cir 1991). Under 17 USC § 101, 'publication' is defined to mean the 'distribution of copies or phonorecords of a work to the public by sale or other transfer of ownership, or by rental, lease, or lending. The offering to distribute copies or phonorecords to a group of persons for purposes of further distribution, public performance, or public display, constitutes publication.'

55 377 F Supp 2d 796 (ND Cal 2005).   56 *Ibid.*, 802.

57 *Ibid.*, 803–5. To the extent that it expresses a different view, the court considered that *Hotaling* v. *Church of Jesus Christ of Latter-Day Saints*, 118 F 3d 199, 203 (4th Cir 1997) was contrary to the weight of authority.

58 US Department of Justice, *Prosecuting Intellectual Property Crimes*, p. 45. In the US the issue was not resolved by the offence of distribution by making available. Although the offence refers to distribution by making available, it does not define making available to be a form of distribution. It therefore leaves open the question of whether distribution requires the actual dissemination of copies: *ibid.*, pp. 49–50, and *In re Napster, Inc.*, 377 F Supp 2d 796, 805 (ND Cal 2005).

59 *Ibid.*, p. 45.

60 *In re Napster, Inc.*, 377 F Supp 2d 796 (ND Cal 2005); and *Metro-Goldwyn-Mayer Studios Inc.*, v. *Grokster Ltd.*, 545 US 913 (2005). Similar issues may arise, for example in the context of 'authorising' copyright infringement: Copyright Act 1988 (Cth), ss. 36(1) and 101(1).

principles of accessorial liability,[61] and if such cases were to be prosecuted it would be as aiding and abetting or inducing the principal offence.[62]

C. Mens rea

The requirement of proof of *mens rea* not only reflects a level of culpability which may justify criminal sanctions; it is also important in limiting the liability of third parties such as ISPs who may unknowingly contribute to the commission of copyright infringement.[63] In contrast to other Articles of the Convention, the term 'wilfully' is used rather than 'intentionally' as that is the term used in Art. 61 of the TRIPS agreement, which governs the obligation to criminalise copyright violations.[64] The term 'without right' is not included because the fact that there is an infringement presumes that it was 'without right'. Parties may, of course, provide for defences and justifications.[65]

However, only in the United States is the term 'wilfully' used to describe the *mens rea* for criminal copyright infringement.[66] In Canada, the fault element is 'knowingly'[67] while in the UK the requirement is that the defendant 'knows or has reason to believe' that the copy is an infringing work.[68] Although a number of the Australian provisions contain no fault element, it must be remembered that the Criminal Code (Cth) provides for default fault elements for Commonwealth offences where no fault element is specified.[69]

In the United States mere evidence of reproduction or distribution of a copyrighted work is not of itself sufficient to establish wilful infringement.[70] The term 'willful' is not defined in the statute, but is

See generally S. Ricketson and J. C. Ginsburg, *Inducers and Authorisers: A comparison of the US Supreme Court's Grokster decision and the Australian Federal Court's KaZaa ruling* Columbia Public Law and Legal Theory Working Papers, Paper no. 0698 (2006), pp. 9–14. Factors relevant to 'authorisation' are set out in s. 36(1A) of the Copyright Act 1968 (Cth). Also see, *Universal Music Australia Pty Ltd* v. *Sharman License Holdings Ltd* (2005) 220 ALR 1.

61 See generally M. Bartholomew, *Cops, Robbers, and Search Engines: The role of criminal law in contributory infringement doctrine* Buffalo Legal Studies Research Paper Series, Paper no. 2008–19 (2008).
62 Australian Institute of Criminology, *Intellectual Property Crime*, p. 73.
63 Yu, Lehrer and Roland, 'Intellectual property crimes', 704. 'Safe harbor' provisions are found in 17 USC § 512.
64 Cybercrime Convention, Explanatory Report, [113].   65 *Ibid.*, [115].
66 17 USC § 506.   67 *Copyright Act* 1985 (Can), s. 42(1).
68 Copyright, Designs and Patents Act 1988 (UK), s. 107.
69 Criminal Code (Cth), s. 5.6.   70 17 USC § 506(a)(2).

generally taken to require proof that the defendant intended to infringe copyright.[71] For example, a number of courts have found wilfulness to be established where the defendant was aware that the items were copyright but nonetheless chose to offer or sell reproductions.[72]

D. Penalties

Article 61 of the TRIPS agreement provides, in part, that members must provide for criminal procedures and penalties to be applied at least in cases of wilful infringement, with remedies to include imprisonment and/or monetary fines 'consistently with the level of penalties applied for crimes of a corresponding gravity'. This is the case in each jurisdiction, with significant penalties attached to criminal copyright infringement. Each includes significant terms of imprisonment as a possible maximum penalty for serious infringement.[73] In Australia, it is also an aggravating factor in respect of a number of offences if the infringing copy was made 'by converting a work or other subject-matter from a hard copy or analog form into a digital or other electronic machine-readable form'.[74]

---

71 US Department of Justice, *Prosecuting Intellectual Property Crimes*, pp. 30–2. For a general discussion of the wilfulness requirement, see L. Loren, 'Digitization, commodification, criminalization: The evolution of criminal copyright infringement and the importance of the willfulness requirement' (1999) 77 *Washington University Law Quarterly* 835.

72 *US* v. *Draper*, 2005 US Dist LEXIS 24717 (WD Va 2005).

73 Copyright Act 1968 (Cth), Part V, Division 5, Subdivision C; Copyright Act 1985 (Can), s. 42(4)(4A)(5); Copyright, Designs and Patents Act 1988 (UK), s. 107(4)(5); 18 USC § 2319.

74 Copyright Act 1968 (Cth), s. 132AK.

9

'Spam'

1. Electronic junk mail

> It is the sense of Congress that . . . Spam has become the method of choice for those who distribute pornography, perpetrate fraudulent schemes, and introduce viruses, worms, and Trojan horses into personal and business computer systems.[1]

No one with an email account could fail to be aware of the problem of unsolicited emails, more commonly known as 'spam'.[2] While it may be thought to be more annoyance than crime, the volume and sophistication of spam is such that it has gone from 'being a minor nuisance to becoming a significant social and economic issue'.[3] Modern communication networks provide spammers with a potential global audience of millions at negligible cost, giving rise to a number of significant concerns.

First, spam undermines the convenience and efficiency of email for legitimate users. Filtering software is imperfect and may return false-positives. A full inbox may refuse further emails. Wanted emails may therefore be blocked or 'lost, overlooked, or discarded' amidst the larger volume of spam.[4] The numbing barrage of internet advertising and fear of Internet scams may create a general sense of distrust of electronic commerce.[5] The use of forged email addresses may lead to legitimate

---

1 15 USC § 7703(c)(1).
2 The term, as it applies to unsolicited email, has even found its way into the Oxford English Dictionary. There are a number of versions of how the term 'spam' came to be associated with unsolicited email, most referring to a Monty Python sketch set in a café in which every item on the menu contains spam, resulting in the word being repeated with increasingly annoying frequency. For a more detailed discussion, see J. Magee, 'The law regulating unsolicited commercial e-mail: An international perspective' (2003) 19 *Santa Clara Computer and High Technology Law Journal* 333, 336–8.
3 Industry Canada, *Stopping Spam: Creating a stronger, safer Internet*, Report of the Task Force on Spam (2005), p. 7.
4 Congressional findings in relation to the *Controlling the Assault of Non-solicited Pornography and Marketing ('CAN-SPAM') Act*: 15 USC § 7701(a)(4).
5 D. Wall, 'Surveillant Internet technologies and the growth in information capitalism: Spams and public trust in the information society' in K. Haggerty and R. Ericson (eds.),

server operations being blacklisted by anti-spam services,[6] or the unwitting owner of the spoofed address being bombarded by thousands of bounced messages.[7] Although primarily associated with email, spam is becoming increasingly prevalent in other networks, for example the sending of spam SMS/MMS over wireless networks.[8]

These concerns are, to some extent, borne out by surveys of email users. A 2005 survey in the UK found that 46 per cent of users said they received too much spam, and 60 per cent expressed concern about unpleasant email experiences.[9] In the United States, although it appears that spam has not had a significant impact on the use of email, as was once feared, 55 per cent of email users reported losing trust in email because of spam.[10]

Secondly, although improved filtering software has reduced the amount of spam that actually finds its way into inboxes, managing that level of spam is a considerable imposition on ISPs and network administrators, the cost of which is ultimately passed on to consumers. Even with effective filtering software, some spam does get through, requiring users to spend time reviewing and discarding them. Apart from the waste of time and, in a commercial context, lost productivity, there may be direct financial costs where the cost of Internet access is based upon time, or the amount of data downloaded. This is a particular problem in developing countries, which often rely on expensive satellite connections.[11]

While the cost of sending an individual email may be measured in fractions of one cent, the sheer volume of spam imposes a significant cost burden on recipients, ISPs and employers. Although obviously fluctuating, the volume of spam as a percentage of overall email traffic has been steadily increasing, from approximately 10% in 2000 to over 80% by the end of 2004.[12] In 2002, when a number of countries were considering

---

The New Politics of Surveillance and Visibility (Toronto: University of Toronto Press, 2005).

6 *US* v. *Twombly*, 475 F Supp 2d 1019, 1020 (SD Cal 2007).

7 Magee, 'Unsolicited commercial e-mail', 341.

8 Task Force on Spam, *Report of the OECD Task Force on Spam: Anti-Spam toolkit of recommended policies and measures* (Organisation for Economic Co-operation and Development, 2006), pp. 20–1. Also see 15 USC § 7712.

9 W. H. Dutton, C. di Gennaro and A. M. Hargrave, *The Internet in Britain: The Oxford Internet survey* (Oxford Internet Institute, 2005), p. 7.

10 D. Fallows, *Data Memo* (PEW Internet and American Life Project, 2007), p. 1.

11 M. Potashman, 'International spam regulation and enforcement: Recommendations following the World Summit on the Information Society' (2006) 29 *Boston College International & Comparative Law Review* 323, 326.

12 Industry Canada, *Stopping Spam*, p. 1.

enacting anti-spam legislation, it was generally accepted that spam accounted for approximately 50% of email traffic.[13] Although one internet security company reported a peak of nearly 94% in 2006,[14] today, figures typically suggest that approximately 80–90% of email is spam.[15]

Thirdly, although a problem in its own right, spam is ultimately a vehicle for content which may be offensive, fraudulent or malicious. A brief perusal of a typical junk-mail folder reveals promises of sexual enhancement, prizes, job offers, hair replacement, prescription medicines, etc. Although some spam represents a genuine attempt to advertise authentic products, the percentage is relatively small, possibly around 10 per cent.[16] The rest are frauds, with Phishing emails, in particular, becoming more prevalent and sophisticated.[17]

Of particular relevance in the cybercrime context, spam has become increasingly associated with the distribution of malware such as viruses and Trojans. This has led to the phenomenon of 'convergence', whereby spam is used to distribute malware which is then used to install open proxies on the recipient's computer, which are then used to relay spam without the recipient's knowledge.[18]

One of the most significant and concerning trends in this area is the use of botnets as the principal means of distributing spam.[19] Initially, spammers used accounts which could readily be disposed of when blocked. They then moved to using open relay servers which would relay emails for anyone that asked. As these were secured, they took to co-opting innocent computers utilising malware to allow these computers to relay emails, particularly through the use of botnets.[20] According to one organisation,

13 Congressional findings: 15 USC § 7701(2).

14 Postini Inc., *2007 Postini Communications Intelligence Report*, p. 13.

15 Department of Communications, Information Technology and the Arts, *Report on the Spam Act 2003 Review* (Australian Government, 2006), p. 15. See, e.g., Symantec, *Spam Monthly Report January 2009*, http://eval.symantec.com/mktginfo/enterprise/other_ resources/b-state_of_spam_report_01–2009.en-us.pdf and MessageLabs, *MessageLabs Intelligence Report June 2009*, www.messagelabs.com.au/resources/mlireports.

16 D. Wall, 'Digital realism and the governance of spam as cybercrime' (2005) 10 *European Journal of Criminal Policy and Research* 309, 312.

17 Federal Trade Commission, *Spam Summit: The next generation of threats and solutions* (2007), pp. 2–3.

18 R. McCusker, 'Spam: Nuisance or menace, prevention or cure?' Trends and Issues in Criminal Justice no. 294 (AIC, 2005), p. 3. For a description of evolving trends in spam see, S. Hedley, 'A brief history of spam' (2006) 15 *Information and Communications Technology Law* 223.

19 Federal Trade Commission, *Spam Summit*, pp. 2–3.

20 All Party Parliamentary Internet Group, *'Spam': Report of an Inquiry by the All Party Internet Group* (2003), pp. 13–14.

in June 2009 approximately 83.2 per cent of spam was sent from botnets.[21] Recently, the 'Storm' botnet was estimated to consist of 2 million compromised computers, responsible for 96 per cent of all email-borne malware containing a link to websites hosting malicious content.[22] Because many people are now connected by broadband, the number of emails which can be sent from a compromised machine is significant; in one example, 750,000 in one 24-hour period.[23] Although personal computers with inadequate anti-malware protection are a common target, the FBI recently found that over 200 government sites were compromised and being used to send spam.[24]

The distribution of spam also involves associated conduct which may itself be the subject of legal regulation. For example, spammers may attempt to circumvent filtering software by 'spoofing' legitimate domain names or hijacking legitimate servers in order to conceal the true origin of the messages. The large number of valid email addressees required to make spam viable may be obtained by unauthorised access to data sets from organisations[25] or 'directory harvest attacks' where emails are sent to valid corporate domain names using thousands of possible name combinations.[26] Email harvesting software may also be used to compile lists of email addresses available in the public domain, typically from message boards, blogs, chat rooms, social networking sites and video-sharing sites.[27] Some readers may feel a sense of *schadenfreude* knowing that spammers may themselves be the victims of fraudulent email lists.[28]

2. Regulating spam

Given its sophistication and scale, it is widely recognised that any response to spam must be multifaceted.[29] To date, technical solutions have provided the greatest protection against spam, or at least carry the lion's share of the burden.[30] In a study conducted by the US Federal Trade Commission (FTC), it was reported that one ISP blocked 93 per cent of spam, while

---

21 MessageLabs, *MessageLabs Intelligence Report June 2009*, p. 2.
22 MessageLabs, *MessageLabs Intelligence Report April 2008*, p. 1.
23 All Party Internet Group, '*Spam*', p. 14.
24 Federal Trade Commission, *Spam Summit*, p. 15.
25 *Jaynes* v. *Commonwealth of Virginia*, 275 Va 341 (2008). 26 McCusker, 'Spam', 2.
27 Federal Trade Commission, *Spam Summit*, p. A-2. 28 Wall, 'Digital realism', 311.
29 For a more detailed discussion see, Task Force on Spam, *Anti-Spam Regulation* (Organisation for Economic Co-operation and Development, 2005) and Department of Communications, Information Technology and the Arts, *Spam Act 2003 Review*, Part 2.
30 For a summary of technical mechanisms for blocking spam, see Potashman, 'International spam regulation', 328–331.

another blocked 78 per cent.[31] At its peak, one internet security company estimated that it blocked 25 billion spam emails in one month.[32]

Education of email users is also important. This may be as to the nature of spam and the need to exercise caution in opening/responding to unsolicited emails, as well as the importance of using filters and up-to-date malware protection.[33] There is also a need to educate users to exercise caution when placing email addresses in the public domain where they are most likely to be harvested, and to be wary of false 'unsubscribe' options, which are in fact used to confirm the validity of an email address. There is some suggestion that email users are becoming more accustomed to dealing with spam. Although they continue to report increasing levels of spam, it seems to bother them less, with 18 per cent saying spam is a big problem for them, down from 25 per cent three and a half years earlier.[34] One suggested reason for this is an increased awareness of spam and an ability to deal with it effectively.[35]

There is also a role for industry self-regulation, such as codes of conduct for the direct marketing industry and appropriate use policies put in place by ISPs.[36] However, our focus is on formal legal regulation which is of relatively recent origin. Prior to the enactment of specific anti-spam legislation, a variety of legal measures were adopted, some of which continue to be utilised in tandem with more specific measures. For example, privacy and competition laws have been used, with some limited success, against distributors of spam.[37] In the United States in particular, there have been a number of civil actions against spammers, typically involving claims of trespass to chattels or breach of contract,[38] as well as under cybercrime legislation.[39]

However, it is generally acknowledged that existing laws are insufficient to address the problem of spam. First, their application may be too narrow

---

31 Federal Trade Commission, *Spam Summit*, p. 9.
32 Postini Inc., *Postini Report*, p. 13.
33 A recent US survey found that 71% of email users use filters provided by their email provider or employer to block spam: Fallows, *Data memo*, p. 1.
34 *Ibid.*, p. 2.   35 *Ibid.*, p. 3.
36 D. Sorkin, 'Technical and legal approaches to unsolicited electronic mail' (2001) 35 *University of San Francisco Law Review* 325, 341–4.
37 All Party Internet Group, 'Spam', p. 9.
38 *Compuserve Inc.* v. *Cyber Promotions Inc.*, 962 F Supp 1015 (SD Ohio 1997); *Register.com Inc.* v. *Verio Inc.*, 126 F Supp 2d 238, 249 (SD NY 2000); *eBay, Inc.* v. *Bidder's Edge, Inc.*, 100 F Supp 2d 1058 (ND Cal 2000); *Intel Corp.* v. *Hamidi*, 30 Cal 4th 1342 (SC Cal 2003). For a useful summary of actions against spammers in the United States, see Sorkin 'Technical and legal approaches', 357–67 and Magee, 'Unsolicited commercial e-mail', 345–56.
39 See p. 81.

to address the many varieties of techniques used by spammers, particularly the emerging threats. Secondly, agencies charged with enforcing privacy and competition law have limited powers, both in terms of scope and purpose. Thirdly, it may be difficult for individuals to prove damages and, even if successful, the global nature of spam makes enforcement of civil judgments difficult, if not impossible.

There is therefore an arguable need for the enactment of targeted anti-spam legislation. Of course, such legislation is not a panacea. Spam has continued to increase since their enactment, with technological changes in filtering likely to have had a greater impact than law enforcement.[40] In addition, because spam is 'small impact bulk victimisation',[41] it presents considerable enforcement challenges. The individual harm may be too small to worry about, while the impact *en masse* may be too complex to prosecute successfully.

Perhaps the greatest challenge to enforcement is the global nature of spam. The Spamhaus Project lists the 'Top 5 Countries' for spam originating on their networks as the United States, China, Russian Federation, South Korea and the United Kingdom.[42] On the other hand, spamming has become a much more organised business, centralised in the hands of a relatively small number of spammers. It has been estimated that approximately 80 per cent of spam targeting North America is generated by ten known spammers.[43] As with other areas of cybercrime, harmonisation of laws and co-operation between international enforcement agencies is vital. While there have been steps in this regard,[44] we will see that there are significant differences between anti-spam laws in each jurisdiction.[45]

In a work on cybercrime, anti-spam legislation occupies something of a hybrid status. Although undoubtedly sharing many of the features of cybercrime, each jurisdiction primarily adopts a civil enforcement model. Administrative penalties are the more common regulatory response, with criminal sanctions reserved for illegal content or where administrative

---

40 Wall, 'Digital realism', 316, 319–20.   41 *Ibid.*, at 309–10.
42 www.spamhaus.org/statistics/countries.lasso.   43 *Ibid.*
44 E.g., the Undertaking Spam, Spyware and Fraud Enforcement With Enforcers Beyond Borders Act of 2006 (US SAFE WEB Act) provides for increased international co-operation in relation to spam, spyware, internet fraud and the like. See generally, Task Force on Spam, *Anti-Spam Toolkit*; and Task Force on Spam, *Anti-Spam Law Enforcement* (Organisation for Economic Co-operation and Development, 2005).
45 See, more broadly, G. Schryen, 'Anti-spam legislation: An analysis of laws and their effectiveness' (2007) 16 *Information and Communications Technology Law* 17.

orders are not complied with.[46] While these may result in significant
penalties,[47] it strictly falls outside the definition of cybercrime. Nonetheless, some discussion of anti-spam legislation is important for a number
of reasons.

First, spam is commonly a vehicle for other forms of cybercrime.
Secondly, not all jurisdictions adopt an exclusively civil enforcement
approach. The United States, in particular, makes provision for criminal sanctions in respect of certain spam-related conduct. Thirdly, even
if not the subject of specific provisions, much of the conduct associated
with spam may be prosecuted under existing criminal laws. For example,
the use of third-party servers, email harvesting, the use of botnets and
the distribution of malware may be prosecuted under existing cybercrime
statutes. Offensive content may be prosecuted under provisions dealing
with offensive or harassing communications, while fraudulent communications may be dealt with under the general criminal law.[48]

3. Anti-spam legislation

Each jurisdiction has either passed or has proposed legislation specifically
aimed at addressing the problem of spam. In Australia, s. 16 Spam Act 2003
(Cth) precludes the sending of a commercial electronic message that has
an Australian link[49] and which is not a 'designated commercial message'.[50]
As at the time of writing, the Electronic Commerce Protection Bill had
just been introduced into the Canadian Parliament,[51] which prohibits the
sending of commercial electronic messages without consent.[52]

---

46 Task Force on Spam, *Anti-Spam Law Enforcement*, p. 18.
47 In the first enforcement action under the Australian legislation the defendant company
   was required to pay A$4.5 million: *Australian Communications and Media Authority v.
   Clarity1 Pty Ltd* [2006] FCA 1399.
48 See *R v Hamilton* [2005] 2 SCR 432 for an unsuccessful attempt to prosecute spam as
   inciting or counselling the commission of an offence.
49 Defined to include where the sender or intended recipient is in Australia, or the computer,
   service or device used to access the message is located in Australia: s. 7.
50 The attributes of a 'designated commercial message' are set out in Sch. 1 to the Act.
   For a detailed review of the Australian legislation, see Department of Communications,
   Information Technology and the Arts, *Spam Act 2003 Review*.
51 Bill C-27. As to the reform process in Canada, see K. Ng, 'Spam legislation in Canada:
   Federalism, freedom of expression and the regulation of the Internet' (2005) 2 *University
   of Ottawa Law and Technology Journal* 447.
52 Cl. 6.

In the UK, the EC Directive on Privacy and Electronic Com-munications[53] is enforced via The Privacy and Electronic Communi-cations (EC Directive) Regulations 2003 ('Privacy Regulations').[54] Regu-lation 22 provides that a person:

> shall neither transmit, nor instigate the transmission of, unsolicited com-munications for the purposes of direct marketing by means of electronic mail unless the recipient of the electronic mail has previously notified the sender that he consents for the time being to such communications being sent by, or at the instigation of, the sender.

In the United States, § 7704(4) Controlling the Assault of Non-solicited Pornography and Marketing (CAN-SPAM) Act[55] prohibits the trans-mission of a commercial electronic mail message where the sender has received a valid request from the recipient not to receive such messages.[56]

The key features of these laws which will be discussed are:

1. civil or criminal enforcement
2. commercial and/or bulk email
3. consent
4. spam-related conduct
5. criminal provisions.

A. Civil or criminal enforcement

Each jurisdiction primarily adopts a civil enforcement regime in the reg-ulation of spam. The Australian Act is administered by the Australian Communications and Media Authority, and is enforced by civil penal-ties, as well as other remedies including injunctions and enforceable

---

53 Directive 2002/58/EC of the European Parliament and of the Council of the European Union, 12 July 2002.
54 For a more detailed discussion see K. Rogers, 'Viagra, viruses and Virgins: A pan-Atlantic comparative analysis on the vanquishing of spam' (2006) 22 *Computer Law and Security Report* 228, 230–3.
55 Codified at 15 USC §7701 *et seq.* For a summary of state anti-spam legislation, see Magee, 'Unsolicited commercial e-mail', 356–7.
56 For a more detailed analysis of the US provisions see V. Arora, 'The CAN-SPAM Act: An inadequate attempt to deal with a growing problem' (2006) 39 *Columbia Journal of Law and Social Problems* 299; and J. Soma, P. Singer and J. Hurdd, 'Spam still pays: The failure of the CAN-SPAM Act of 2003 and proposed legal solutions' (2008) 45 *Harvard Journal on Legislation* 165.

undertakings.[57] The proposed Canadian provisions are to be enforced by
the Canadian Radio-television and Telecommunications Commission,
through the imposition of administrative monetary penalties, undertakings and notices of violation.[58] In the UK, enforcement is by a
modified version of Part V of the Data Protection Act 1998 (UK).[59]
Under this system, enforcement or information notices can be issued
by the regulator, failure to comply with which may be a criminal
offence.[60]

In the United States, enforcement is primarily by the FTC as if the
conduct were an unfair or deceptive act or practice under the Federal
Trade Commission Act.[61] Civil enforcement is also provided for by state
attorneys-general[62] and internet access providers.[63] In contrast to the
other jurisdictions, these civil provisions are supplemented by a number
of specific criminal offences which are discussed below.

B. Commercial and/or bulk email

There are differing views on whether spam must be commercial in nature,
or whether it is the volume of mail, rather than its content, that is the
primary concern. A distinction is sometimes drawn between unsolicited
commercial email (UCE) and unsolicited bulk email (UBE), it being
argued that the concerns raised by spam apply equally to UBE.[64] Although
most spam statistics define spam as UBE,[65] this is not reflected in the legislation, with each jurisdiction focusing on UCE. For example, the US
legislation defines a 'commercial electronic mail message' as 'any electronic mail message the primary purpose of which is the commercial
advertisement or promotion of a commercial product or service (including content on an Internet website operated for a commercial purpose)'.[66]
In addition, none require a certain volume of emails to be sent, and in

57 Spam Act 2003 (Cth), Parts 4–6. That breach of a civil penalty provision is not of itself a
    criminal offence is expressly stated in s. 27 of the Act. A system of infringement notices
    for contravention of civil penalty provisions is provided for in Sch. 3.
58 Electronic Commerce Protection Bill 2009 (Can), cll. 20–2.
59 Privacy Regulations, reg. 31 and Sch. 1.
60 Data Protection Act 1998 (UK), ss. 47 and 60.   61 15 USC § 7706(a).
62 15 USC § 7706(f).   63 15 USC § 7706(g).
64 Sorkin, 'Technical and legal approaches', 333–6.
65 See, e.g., www.spamhaus.org/definition.html.
66 15 USC § 7702(2)(A). Also see Spam Act 2003 (Cth), s. 6 and Electronic Commerce
    Protection Bill 2009 (Can), cl. 6. The UK legislation applies to 'direct marketing': Privacy
    Regulations, reg. 22.

theory only one email may constitute spam.[67] Consequently, those spam emails which have no commercial purpose but which are used to disseminate malware, fraudulent schemes and the like must be addressed, if at all, by other offences.

C. Consent

A central feature of all spam is that it is unsolicited, it being broadly accepted that there is a legitimate place for email marketing where there is prior and ongoing consent by the recipient.[68] Accordingly, each jurisdiction allows for the sending of such emails with consent. In Australia, Canada and the UK, this involves an 'opt-in' approach. That is, the person sending the emails must first obtain the consent of the recipient, although in limited circumstances this may be implied, for example from an existing business relationship.[69]

In contrast, the United States has adopted an 'opt-out' approach whereby the sending of unsolicited commercial email is lawful unless the person elects not to receive them.[70] This is primarily because commercial speech which is otherwise lawful and not misleading is protected speech under the First Amendment. Any restriction must therefore be based upon advancing a substantial government interest, and be not more extensive than necessary to meet that objective.[71] Although it may be argued that the government has a substantial interest in ensuring email as a viable means of communication, an opt-in approach would likely be seen as more extensive than necessary as it would block a considerable amount of protected speech.[72] In addition, it has been held that the overbreadth doctrine does not apply to the CAN-SPAM Act as the provisions are limited to commercial speech which is 'more hardy, less likely to be "chilled," and not in need of surrogate litigators'.[73]

---

67 In contrast, the Virginia Computer Crime Act refers to 'unsolicited bulk email': Code of Virginia § 18.2–152.3:1. This is also the case under the federal criminal provisions discussed at pp. 242–3 below.

68 All Party Internet Group, 'Spam', p. 5.

69 Spam Act 2003 (Cth), s. 16(2); Electronic Commerce Protection Bill 2009 (Can), cl. 6; and Privacy Regulations, reg. 22(3) and Sch. 2.

70 15 USC § 7704(4).

71 *Central Hudson Gas & Electric Corp.* v. *Public Service Commission of New York*, 447 US 557, 566 (1980). Also see, in the context of spam, *White Buffalo Ventures LLC* v. *University of Texas at Austin*, 420 F 3d 366, 374 (5th Cir 2005).

72 Potashman, 'International spam regulation', 339–40.

73 *US* v. *Twombly*, 475 F Supp 2d 1019, 1024 (SD Cal 2007), citing *Board of Trustees of State University of New York* v. *Fox*, 492 US 469, 481 (1989).

Whether an opt-in or opt-out approach is adopted, it is necessary to have an effective mechanism whereby recipients can request not to receive further communications. Accordingly, each jurisdiction makes provision for commercial emails to contain a functional unsubscribe facility.[74]

D. Spam-related conduct

In addition to the actual sending of unsolicited commercial emails, there is a range of conduct associated with this practice which may also be the subject of regulation. Some examples include prohibitions on the use of misleading, forged or incomplete addressing information or subject lines;[75] address-harvesting;[76] automatic generation of multiple email accounts;[77] unauthorised relaying or retransmitting of messages;[78] or the sending of commercial emails to non-existent addresses.[79] In the United States it is unlawful for a business to knowingly allow itself or goods, services etc. to be promoted by spam,[80] while in the UK it is unlawful for a subscriber to permit his or her line to be used for the sending of spam.[81]

E. Criminal offences

We have seen that each jurisdiction primarily adopts civil enforcement mechanisms in regulating spam. This is not uniformly the case, with US federal law providing for a number of more specific criminal offences related to spam. For example, it is an offence to fail to appropriately label messages containing sexually oriented material.[82] Of most significance is 18 USC §1037(a): 'fraud and related activity in connection with electronic mail'.[83] This provision contains a number of criminal offences which, unlike the civil provisions, apply to 'multiple commercial electronic mail messages'. For these purposes, 'multiple' is defined to mean more than

---

74 Spam Act (Cth), ss. 17 and 18(1); Electronic Commerce Protection Bill 2009 (Can), cl. 11; Privacy Regulations, reg. 22(3) and 23(b); and 15 USC §§ 7704(3)(5).
75 Spam Act 2003 (Cth), s. 17(1); Electronic Commerce Protection Bill 2009 (Can), cl. 7; Privacy Regulations, reg. 23(a); and 15 USC §7704(1)(2).
76 Spam Act (Cth), ss. 21–3; Electronic Commerce Protection Bill 2009 (Can), cl. 8; 15 USC § 7704(b)(1).
77 15 USC § 7704(b)(2).   78 15 USC § 7704(b)(3).
79 Spam Act 2003 (Cth), s. 16(6).   80 15 USC § 7705.
81 Privacy Regulations, reg. 22(4).   82 15 USC § 7704(d).
83 The penalties for these offences are set out in 18 USC § 1037(b), while forfeiture is provided for in 18 USC § 1037(c).

100 messages during a 24-hour period, more than 1,000 during a 30-day period, or more than 10,000 during a 1-year period.[84]

The offences may usefully be considered in two parts. The first relates to unauthorised access to, or use of, protected computers for the purposes of spam,[85] while the second concerns falsifying of addressing or other identifying information.[86]

An example of a prosecution under § 1037 is found in *US* v. *Twombly*.[87] The defendants were indicted under §§ 1037(a)(3)(4) having allegedly used an alias to lease twenty servers, which were then used to send millions of spam emails. These advertised computer software via the website of a software company with an address in Canada. It was further alleged that the website was falsely registered under the name of a non-existent business, and that the messages' routing information and 'From' lines were falsified. Challenges for vagueness and over-breadth were dismissed,[88] although the court made some useful observations on the issue of *mens rea*, it being held that subs. (3) requires a higher *mens rea* than general criminal intent – that is, a defendant must 'knowingly' falsify header information and 'intentionally' transmit it.[89]

The court did, however, acknowledge a possible ambiguity in subs. (4), which may punish innocent behaviour. This depends on whether 'knowingly' modifies only the word 'registers', or whether it also modifies 'using information that materially falsifies the registrant's identity'.[90] Although the issue did not arise on these facts, and therefore the court did not offer a resolution, it would seem that in a penal statute the ambiguity should be resolved in favour of the defendant. This would require the defendant to know that the registration involved the use of false information.

Another notable prosecution was the first anti-spam felony conviction which was recently recorded in the State of Virginia, home to the servers of America Online. Under the Virginia Code,[91] it is an offence to use a computer or computer network with the intent to falsify or forge electronic mail transmission information or other routing information in any manner in connection with the transmission of unsolicited bulk electronic mail through or into the computer network of an electronic mail service provider or its subscribers. This offence becomes a class 6 felony if the amount of unsolicited bulk email exceeds 10,000 attempted recipients

---

84 18 USC § 1037(d)(3).
85 18 USC § 1037(a)(1)(2). For a discussion of these concepts, see Ch. 3.
86 18 USC § 1037(a)(3)–(5).   87 475 F Supp 2d 1019 (SD Cal 2007).
88 *Ibid.*, 1023–4.   89 *Ibid.*, 1025.   90 *Ibid.*   91 § 18.2–152.3:1.

in any 24-hour period, 100,000 attempted recipients in any 30-day time period or one million attempted recipients in any 1-year time period.

Jeremy Jaynes was convicted under this provision and sentenced to a total of nine years in prison.[92] From his home in North Carolina, and using several computers, routers and servers, Jaynes sent over 10,000 emails within a 24-hour period to AOL subscribers on three separate occasions. He was also able to convey false information about his idenity by falsifying the header information and sender domain names. These emails contained advertisements for various products, the sale of which was administered by various companies operated by Jaynes. Evidence was introduced that the defendant received business income from all of his businesses in excess of US$1,000,000 for each of the years 2001–3.[93] A search of his home revealed compact disks containing over 176 million full email addresses and 1.3 billion email user names, as well as a storage disk which contained AOL email address information and other personal and private account information for millions of AOL subscribers. These items had been stolen by a former employee of AOL.[94]

92 *Jaynes* v. *Commonwealth of Virginia*, 275 Va. 341 (CA Va 2008).
93 *Ibid.*, 347–8.   94 *Ibid.*, 348.

PART IV

Content-related offences

10

Child pornography

1. Child abuse online[1]

In pre-Internet days, individuals who wished to view this kind of material would need to seek it out, bring it into their home or have it delivered in physical form as magazines, videos, photographs etc, risking discovery and embarrassment at every stage. Now they are able to access it from their computers at home (or from their place of work) with relative ease.[2]

Perhaps the most tragic aspect of the Internet and the proliferation of digital technology has been their ability to facilitate the production and distribution of child pornography and other forms of child sexual abuse. Prior to the advent of these technologies, such material was difficult to transport without detection, production was hampered by the need to have film processed, and equipment was costly and relatively difficult to use. As digital technology has become more widely available, and the Internet more pervasive, there has been a corresponding rise in the number of child-pornography prosecutions. While this is explained in part by changing priorities of law enforcement agencies, this is itself undoubtedly a response to the proliferation of child pornography on the Internet.

Paedophiles[3] have long seen the potential for new technologies to be used in the production and distribution of child pornography. As early as 1986, the US Attorney General's 'Commission on Pornography' noted

---

1 Sections of this chapter were previously published in J. Clough, 'Now you see it, now you don't: Digital images and the meaning of "possession"' (2008) 19 *Criminal Law Forum* 209.
2 National Offender Management Service and Scottish Executive, *Consultation: On the possession of extreme pornographic material* (Home Office, 2005), p. 6.
3 For convenience, the term 'paedophile' will be used to refer to those involved in sexual offences against minors. It is acknowledged that because of the broad definition of 'minor' this use is not always technically accurate, as in the strict sense paedophilia relates to prepubescent children; American Psychiatric Association, *Diagnostic and Statistical Manual of Mental Disorders IV-TR* (Washington DC: APA, 2000) pp. 571–2.

that computer networks were being used by paedophiles for establishing contacts and exchanging information, and recommended that specific legislation be enacted to prohibit such activity.[4] In 1995, an Australian Parliamentary Committee noted the potential for computers to replace postal services and personal contacts as the main means of distribution for child pornography, but found that '[s]o far, there appears to be no firm evidence that computers are being used to this extent'.[5]

In contrast, between 1996 and 2005 there was a 2,026 per cent increase in the number of cases opened throughout the FBI as part of the 'Innocent Images National Initiative'.[6] The UK experience has been similar. In 1995, the Greater Manchester Police Abusive Images Unit seized twelve indecent images of children, all in hard-copy. In 1999, the figure was 41,000, all but three of which were from the Internet.[7] The number of prosecutions in the UK involving indecent photographs of children increased from 93 in 1994 to 1,890 in 2003.[8]

The connection between digital technology and this type of offending is easily understood. The technology is relatively cheap, easy to access, and portable. It allows for storage of large amounts of material which would be conspicuous if stored in hard copy. For example, in R v. Jones[9] the defendant was found to be in possession of more than 162,600 images of child pornography, although this is by no means the greatest number.[10] More typically, one US study found that 48 per cent of offenders had more than 100 images, with 14 per cent having more than 1,000.[11] The increasing availability of broadband further enables the downloading of large amounts of material, including data-intensive video files.

4 US Department of Justice, *Attorney General's Commission on Pornography: Final report* (1986), Recommendation 39.
5 Parliamentary Joint Committee on the National Crime Authority, *Organised Criminal Paedophile Activity* (Commonwealth of Australia, 1995), [3.69]. Also see Justice J. R. T. Wood, *Royal Commission into the New South Wales Police Service: Final report*, v: *The paedophile inquiry* (New South Wales Government, 1997), [16.11].
6 Federal Bureau of Investigation, *Innocent Images National Initiative*, US Department of Justice, www.fbi.gov/page2/feb06/innocent_images_statistics.htm.
7 J. Carr, *Child Abuse, Child Pornography and the Internet* (NCH, 2005), p. 11.
8 National Offender Management Service, *Extreme Pornographic Material*, p. 6.
9 (1999) 108 A Crim R 50.
10 A UK man was found to be in possession of 450,000 images, while a raid on one New York address recovered approximately 1 million images: Carr, *Child Abuse*, p. 11.
11 J. Wolak, D. Finkelhor and K. J. Mitchell, *Child-Pornography Possessors Arrested in Internet-Related Crimes: Findings from the national juvenile online victimization study* (National Center for Missing & Exploited Children, 2005), p. 7.

The ability to produce child pornography is greatly enhanced by the fact that digital images may be produced cheaply without the need for external processing, and reproduced with no diminution of quality. Images of child abuse may also be transmitted in real time through the use of webcams or instant messaging, sometimes at the request and direction of paying customers.[12] There is also the potential to create 'virtual' child pornography – that is, where imaging software is used to create an image which appears to be of child pornography, but which does not involve any actual children. For example, a UK man was convicted over images of naked women which he manipulated using imaging software to reduce the apparent size of the breasts, made them appear to be partially dressed in school uniforms and apparently under the age of eighteen.[13]

The Internet allows material to be distributed easily, in large volumes, with minimal cost and relative anonymity. Distribution is facilitated by the use of newsgroups, bulletin boards,[14] websites and social networking sites.[15] For example, the 'Candyman' website allowed subscribers free access to child pornography and chat rooms. Before it was closed down it was estimated to have 3,400 members, and as many as 6,300 subscribers.[16] Paedophiles are keeping pace with technology by using peer-to-peer technology[17] and mobile phones.[18] Communication technologies also facilitate the exchange of information on how to access child pornography, techniques for avoiding detection and strategies for

12 D. Muir, *Violence against Children in Cyberspace: A contribution to the United Nations study on violence against children* (Bangkok: ECPAT International, 2005), p. 35. Such conduct could conceivably be charged as complicity in the sexual abuse itself, subject to problems of extraterritoriality: G. Urbas and K. R. Choo, *Resource Materials on Technology-Enabled Crime*, Technical and Background Paper (AIC, 2008), pp. 41–2.
13 A. Norfolk, 'Computer expert faces jail over "made-up" child porn image', *Times Online*, 10 August 2006, http://technology.timesonline.co.uk/article/0,,20411–2306067.html. This issue is discussed further at p. 271.
14 The presence of child pornography on bulletin boards was recognised as long ago as 1995, although at that time the problem was thought to be small: Computer Bulletin Board Systems Task Force, *Regulation of Computer Bulletin Board Systems* (Canberra: AGPS, 1995), pp. 13–14.
15 For a detailed discussion of paedophile activity on the Internet, see P. Jenkins, *Beyond Tolerance: Child pornography on the Internet* (New York: New York University Press, 2001).
16 *US* v. *Perez*, 247 F Supp 2d 459, 465 (SD NY 2003). For a discussion of other child pornography rings, see T. Krone, *International Police Operations against Online Child Pornography*, Trends and Issues in Crime and Criminal Justice (Australian Institute of Criminology, 2005).
17 *R* v. *Dooley* [2005] EWCA Crim 3093.
18 D. M. Hughes, 'The use of new communications and information technologies for sexual exploitation of women and children' (2002) 13 *Hastings Women's Law Journal* 127.

encouraging children to engage in sexual activity.[19] On this latter point, new technologies provide unprecedented opportunities for contacting children for sexual purposes, leading to the enactment of new offences associated with 'grooming'.[20]

Although detection may be made more difficult by the use of proxy servers, passwords, encryption and/or steganography, one study found that relatively few offenders (20%) took such steps. The most popular method used was password protection (12%), with very few using more sophisticated methods such as encryption (6%), file servers (4%), evidence eliminators (3%), remote storage (2%), partitioned hard drives (2%) or anonymous remailers (<1%).[21] However, this study was limited to those who had been arrested by law enforcement agencies and it may be that those with greater technical skills are more able to avoid detection.[22] Some paedophile groups require not only a password, but also child pornography material in order to obtain access to the group. For example, the 'W0nderland Club' [sic] was an international child pornography ring which required members to provide 10,000 images of child pornography in order to join.[23]

The worldwide trade in child pornography can also be very lucrative, leading to the involvement of organised crime groups in both production and distribution. In 2006, it was estimated that there were more than 100,000 websites offering child pornography.[24] Estimates of the worldwide value of the trade vary widely from $US3 billion to $US20 billion.[25] One website offering child pornography was reported to have 35,000 individual subscribers in the United States and grossed $1.4 million in one month, before it was closed down by the FBI.[26]

The criminalisation of child pornography and other offences involving the sexual exploitation of children is of international concern.[27] It is

---

19 M. Taylor and E. Quayle, *Child Pornography: An internet crime* (East Sussex: Brunner-Routledge, 2003) p. 14. Also see *R. v. Larocque* [2004] ABPC 114.

20 These offences are discussed in Ch. 11.

21 Wolak, Finkelhor and Mitchell, *Child-Pornography Possessors*, pp. 9–10.

22 For a useful summary of an online child pornography investigation, see *US v. Polizzi*, 2008 US Dist LEXIS 26223 (ED NY 2008) at 24–31.

23 T. Krone, *A Typology of Online Child Pornography Offending*, Trends and Issues in Crime and Criminal Justice (AIC, 2004), p. 4.

24 Staff Report Prepared for the Use of the Committee on Energy and Commerce, *Sexual Exploitation of Children over the Internet*, US House of Representatives, 109th Congress, January 2007, p. 10.

25 Muir, *Violence against Children*, p. 31.

26 Taylor and Quayle, *Child Pornography*, p. 5.

27 See, for example, the Optional Protocol to the Convention on the Rights of the Child on the Sale of Children, Child Prostitution and Child Pornography, opened for signature

estimated that 55 per cent of child pornography on the Internet originates from the United States, while most 'free to view' sites have been traced to Internet service providers in Russia, the United States, Spain, Thailand, Japan and the Republic of Korea.[28] In stark contrast, the Internet Watch Foundation received no reports of United Kingdom-hosted material in 2003 or 2004.[29] The multi-jurisdictional nature of the offending is graphically illustrated by a recent case where, during a 76-hour period, a website hosting child pornography received 12,000,000 hits from 170 countries.[30] This presents a considerable challenge to law enforcement and reinforces the importance of international co-operation. Although most jurisdictions criminalise conduct relating to child pornography, the Cybercrime Convention identifies the need to modernise such laws in order to address the use of computer systems in the commission of such offences.[31]

2. The criminalisation of child pornography

Traditionally, the possession of obscene materials was not an offence, although production and distribution was.[32] In a number of jurisdictions this was also reflected in child pornography laws that did not extend to possession per se. For example, simple possession of child pornography was not an offence in the UK until the enactment of s. 160 Criminal Justice Act 1988 (UK).[33] As we have seen, the advent of digital technology has transformed the way in which child pornography is produced and distributed, and most jurisdictions have responded with a range of prohibitions against all dealings in child pornography. Although concerned with domestic offending, such broad prohibitions also attempt to stem the international trade in such material.

25 May 2000, A/RES/54/263 (entered into force on 18 January 2002) and the Vienna International Conference on Combating Child Pornography on the Internet (Vienna, 1999).

28 Muir, *Violence against Children*, p. 31.

29 National Offender Management Service, *Extreme Pornographic Material*, p. 8. The Internet Watch Foundation can be accessed at www.iwf.org.uk.

30 G. Griffith and K. Simon, *Child Pornography Law*, Briefing Paper no. 9/08 (NSW Parliamentary Library Research Service, 2008), p. 7.

31 Cybercrime Convention, Explanatory Report, [91].

32 Australian Law Reform Commission, *Film and Literature Censorship Procedure*, Report no. 55 (1991), [5.16].

33 The earlier offence of possession under s. 1(1)(c) Protection of Children Act 1978 (UK) applied only to possession with intent to distribute.

> Production of child pornography is fueled by the market for it, and the
> market in turn is fueled by those who seek to possess it. Criminalizing
> possession may reduce the market for child pornography and the abuse of
> children it often involves.[34]

The rationales underlying the broad criminalisation of child pornography
were summarised by the Supreme Court of Canada in *R v. Sharpe*.[35] This
case considered a challenge to the constitutionality of s. 163.1(4) Criminal
Code (Can) on the basis that it violated the fundamental freedom of
thought, belief, opinion and expression.[36] Subject to two exceptions, the
court upheld the provision as striking a constitutional balance between
freedom of expression and prevention of harm to children.[37] The court
accepted the prosecution's submission that prohibiting the possession of
child pornography is linked to reducing sexual abuse of children in five
ways:[38]

1. Child pornography promotes cognitive distortions such that it may
   normalise sexual activity with children in the mind of the possessor, weakening inhibitions and potentially leading to actual abuse.
   While acknowledging that the evidence is 'not strong', the court
   held that evidence does support a link between child pornography
   reducing paedophile's defences and inhibitions against sexual abuse of
   children.[39]
2. Child pornography fuels fantasies that incite offenders. While not all
   offenders involved with child pornography are necessarily involved in
   direct sexual assaults on children, the court accepted that there are
   some studies which suggest that child pornography may fuel fantasies
   and incite certain people to offend, and that this is a sufficient rational
   connection to justify criminalisation as there is no need for unanimity
   of scientific opinion.

---

34 *R v. Sharpe* [2001] 1 SCR 45 at [99] per McLachlin CJ.   35 *Ibid.*
36 Canadian Charter of Rights and Freedoms, Part 1 Constitution Act 1982, s. 2(b). S. 1 of
    the Charter guarantees the rights and freedoms set out in the Charter 'subject only to
    such reasonable limits prescribed by law as can be demonstrably justified in a free and
    democratic society'.
37 The exceptions apply to auto-depictions made by a person who is under 18, held privately
    and intended only for personal use: *R v. Sharpe* [2001] 1 SCR 45 at [108]. L'Heureux-
    Dube, Gonthier and Bastarache JJ delivered a separate judgment, also allowing the appeal,
    but not accepting the exceptions created by the majority.
38 *R v. Sharpe* [2001] 1 SCR 45 at [96]–[99] per McLachlin J. Also see Taylor and Quayle,
    Child Pornography, pp. 24–6.
39 Cf K. S. Williams, 'Child pornography law: Does it protect children?' (2004) 26 *Journal
    of Social Welfare and Family Law* 245, 253–4.

3. Prohibiting the possession of child pornography assists law enforcement efforts to reduce the production, distribution and use of child pornography that result in direct harm to children. Although this rationale could not be the sole justification for abridging a Charter right, the court held that it was nonetheless a positive side-effect of the law.

4. The court regarded the evidence as 'clear and uncontradicted' that child pornography is used for grooming and seducing victims.[40] For example, in *R v. VH*[41] the defendant used child pornography downloaded from the Internet in an attempt to persuade his twelve-year-old daughter that incest was normal.

5. Some child pornography is produced using real children. The viewer is therefore in a sense an accessory after the fact to an act of child abuse by providing a market for it.[42]

In an effort to address these concerns, each jurisdiction attaches criminal consequences to the conduct of each participant in the chain from production to possession of child pornography. In Australia, the federal offences are found in ss. 474.19 and 474.20 Criminal Code (Cth).[43] In Canada, the relevant provision is s. 163.1 Criminal Code (Can),[44] while in the UK the principal offences are found in s. 1 Protection of Children Act 1978 (UK) and s. 160 Criminal Justice Act 1988 (UK).[45] The former is concerned with offences relating to supply, while the latter criminalises simple possession.

Beginning with the Protection of Children against Sexual Exploitation Act of 1977, which first criminalised child pornography, US federal

---

40 Also see Taylor and Quayle, *Child Pornography*, p. 25. The extent to which research supports this assertion has been questioned; G. Griffith and L. Roth, *Protecting Children from Online Sexual Predators*, Briefing Paper no. 10/107, (NSW Parliamentary Library Research Service, 2007) pp. 13–14.

41 (2001) 10 VR 234.

42 Similar justifications have been accepted in other jurisdictions; *R v. Land* [1999] QB 65 at 69–70 per Judge LJ; *R v. Jones* (1999) 108 A Crim R 50 at 52 per Kennedy J; *R v. Curtain* [2001] VSCA 156 at [25] per Vincent JA; *Badcock* v. *White* [2004] TASSC 59 at [18] per Crawford J. As to the US Supreme Court's consideration of this issue see pp. 274–5.

43 Maximum penalty 10 years' imprisonment: ss. 474.19–474.20. Ss. 474.22 and 474.23 contain mirror provisions dealing with 'child abuse material'. Each state and territory also has provisions dealing with child pornography: see Griffith and Simon, *Child Pornography Law*, pp. 35–6.

44 Maximum penalty 10 years' imprisonment, except possession and accessing where the maximum is 5 years.

45 Maximum penalty 10 years' imprisonment: Protection of Children Act 1978 (UK), s. 6, or 5 years for simple possession: Criminal Justice Act 1988 (UK), s. 160.

law has gone through a number of revisions as a consequence of evolving First Amendment jurisprudence.[46] The Child Protection Act of 1984
first removed obscenity requirements following *New York* v. *Ferber*,[47]
while the Child Protection Restoration and Penalties Enhancement Act of
1990 penalised simple possession following *Osborne* v. *Ohio*.[48] The Child
Pornography Prevention Act of 1996 sought to address the issue of 'virtual'
child pornography and was followed by the Prosecutorial Remedies and
Other Tools to End the Exploitation of Children Today (PROTECT) Act
of 2003 as a response to *Ashcroft* v. *The Free Speech Coalition*.[49] Although
there are a number of relevant provisions, the key US federal provisions
are found in 18 USC §§ 2252 and 2252A.[50]

Given the abuse of children which underpins the trade in child pornography, it is not surprising that '[l]aw enforcement resources . . . have been
focused nearly exclusively on child pornography and child stalking'.[51] In
the UK, as prosecutions in relation to child pornography have increased,
prosecutions in relation to obscene publications have fallen, from 309 in
1994, to 39 in 2003.[52] However, the use of the Internet continues to challenge the boundaries of what is permissible in a liberal society and there
are arguments in favour of a more aggressive approach to other forms
of offensive content on the Internet. For example, most jurisdictions
have offences relating to obscene material[53] and although apparently
less common, prosecutions have been brought in relation to offensive
images including bestiality,[54] coprophilia,[55] and violent sexual imagery.[56]
While the focus of this chapter is on offences relating to child pornography, the issues raised are of general application to offences dealing with
prohibited content in a digital context.[57]

---

46 *US* v. *Polizzi*, 2008 US Dist LEXIS 26223 (ED NY 2008) at 176–200.
47 458 US 747 (1982).   48 495 US 103, 111 (1990).   49 535 US 234 (2002).
50 The penalties for these offences are set out in 18 USC §§ 2252(b) and 2252A(b) respec-
    tively.
51 Commission on Online Child Protection, *Commission on Child Online Protection: Report
    to Congress* (2000), p. 39.
52 National Offender Management Service, *Extreme Pornographic Material*, p. 6.
53 Criminal Code (Cth), s. 474.17; Criminal Code (Can), s. 163; Telecommunications Act
    1984 (UK), s. 43; Obscene Publications Act 1959 (UK); and 18 USC Ch. 71. In *US* v.
    Extreme Associates Inc., 431 F 3d 150, (3rd Cir 2005) it was held that the mere fact that
    the case involved the Internet did not render inapplicable Supreme Court authorities
    concerned with obscenity laws.
54 *Bounds* v. *R* [2005] WASCA 1.   55 *R* v. *Perrin* [2002] EWCA Crim 747.
56 *Haynes* v. *Hughes* [2001] WASCA 397.
57 For a discussion in the English context, see I. Walden, *Computer Crimes and Digital
    Investigations* (New York: Oxford University Press, 2007), pp. 131–7.

3. Defining child pornography

Trials of offences of possessing child pornography are sensitive and difficult because they occur in a society concerned about child abuse but flooded with erotic images.[58]

Although the term 'child pornography' is well known and adopted in most jurisdictions, there is some concern about comparisons it might invite with adult pornography, and the implication that child pornography is anything other than the recording of child abuse.[59] Some jurisdictions adopt more accurate descriptions such as 'child exploitation'[60] or 'child abuse' material.[61] At the other end of the spectrum is the euphemistic 'indecent photograph of a child'.[62] While acknowledging its inappropriateness in describing images of child sexual abuse, 'child pornography' remains the most commonly used term and for convenience will be adopted in this chapter.

The essence of child pornography is the sexual depiction of a child under a certain age, although precisely what constitutes child pornography varies considerably between jurisdictions. Given the international nature of the trade in child pornography, this presents considerable challenges for law enforcement as material which is unlawful in one jurisdiction may be lawful in another. While it is clearly legitimate for countries to determine what may be possessed within their territorial jurisdiction, the global nature of the Internet provides an argument in favour of greater international consistency, at least in respect of offences relating to the distribution of child pornography.

The Cybercrime Convention defines 'child pornography' to include 'pornographic material' that visually depicts:

(a) a minor engaged in sexually explicit conduct;
(b) a person appearing to be a minor engaged in sexually explicit conduct; or

---

58 *Bounds* v. *R* [2006] HCA 39 at [97] per Kirby J.
59 Taylor and Quayle, *Child Pornography*, p. 7.
60 Criminal Code 1899 (Qld), s. 207A; and Classification (Publications, Films and Computer Games) Enforcement Act 1995 (Tas), Part 8.
61 Criminal Code (Cth), ss. 474.22 and 474.23; and Criminal Code (NT), s. 125A(1). In the Australian federal provisions, while 'child pornography' describes material which depicts minors engaged in sexual activity, 'child abuse' material describes images of minors subject to non-sexual physical abuse: s. 473.1. The fact that there may be overlap between these provisions does not suggest that one was intended to be exclusive of the other: *Leonard* v. *R* [2007] NSWCCA 197 at [24] per Spigelman CJ.
62 Protection of Children Act 1978 (UK), s. 1.

(c) realistic images representing a minor engaged in sexually explicit conduct.[63]

Although the precise terminology varies, the definition of child pornography in each jurisdiction is broadly consistent with this provision.[64] Our focus is on four specific issues:

1. the definition of 'minor'
2. what constitutes 'sexually explicit conduct'
3. the application of the definition to data
4. 'virtual' child pornography.

A. The definition of 'minor'

Under the Cybercrime Convention a 'minor' is defined as a person under the age of eighteen years.[65] It is, however, accepted that in some jurisdictions the age of consent is less than eighteen years, and that those parties may adopt a lower age limit in defining child pornography, so long as it is no less than sixteen years.[66] Although in each jurisdiction the age of consent is generally at least sixteen,[67] all define a minor for these purposes to be a person under the age of eighteen.[68] This leads to the potential anomaly that while young people may lawfully engage in consensual sexual activity, recording of that activity may be unlawful.

63 Cybercrime Convention, Art. 9(2).
64 Criminal Code (Cth), s. 473.1; Criminal Code (Can), s. 163.1; Protection of Children Act 1978 (UK), ss. 1 and 7(3); and 18 USC § 2256(8).
65 Cybercrime Convention, Art. 9(3). This is also consistent with the definition of 'child' in Art. 1 UN Convention on the Rights of the Child.
66 Cybercrime Convention, Explanatory Report, [104]. A summary of age of consent around the world may be found at www.avert.org/aofconsent.htm.
67 In the US, 48 states permit 16 year olds to marry with parental consent and in 39 states and the District of Columbia the age of consent is 16 or younger; *Ashcroft* v. *The Free Speech Coalition* 535 US 234, 247 (2002). Also see Sexual Offences Act 2003 (UK), s. 45. The age of consent in Australia varies between jurisdictions but is never less than 16: Model Criminal Code Officers Committee, *Chapter 5: Sexual offences against the person*, Report (1999), pp. 119–21. In Canada, the age of consent is 14, except in cases of sexual exploitation, for example where there is a relationship of trust, authority or dependency, where the age of consent is 18: Criminal Code (Can), Part V.
68 Criminal Code (Cth), s. 473.1; Criminal Code (Can), s. 163.1; Protection of Children Act 1978 (UK), s. 7(6); and 18 USC § 2256(1). In Australia and the US, the definition of 'child' for these purposes varies between the states and territories: see Griffith and Simon, *Child Pornography Law*, p. 10 and Wolak, Finkelhor and Mitchell, *Child-Pornography Possessors*, p. x.

For example, in *State v. Senters*[69] a 28-year-old teacher had a consensual sexual relationship with a 17-year-old student, during which the two agreed to videotape themselves having sex. However, the tape was discovered and police where notified. Although the age of consent in Nebraska is sixteen, the defendant was charged and convicted of manufacturing child pornography.

This apparent discrepancy is not unintentional, the rationale being the distinction between the age at which young people should be able to engage in consensual sexual relations and the age at which they should be regarded as sexual objects.[70] The fact that a community finds it acceptable for young people of a certain age to participate in consensual sexual activity does not necessarily mean that it is appropriate for images or descriptions of such activity to be distributed more widely. Such material may contribute to the global market in child pornography notwithstanding its lawful origins. Any anomalies may be addressed by allowing for appropriate defences, for example where the activity is consensual and only for the private use of the participants.[71] Alternatively, in those jurisdictions where the depiction must be obscene or indecent according to community standards, it may be argued that such depictions do not satisfy that test.[72]

The discrepancy between the age of consent and the definition of minor for the purposes of child pornography may also be justified on the basis that it facilitates the prosecution of child pornography laws. There is some evidence that when child pornography was defined in terms of a person under sixteen, there was sometimes confusion about whether a subject was a minor since children enter puberty at differing ages. It has therefore been held that 'the congressional choice to regulate child pornography by defining minor as an individual under eighteen is rationally related to the government's legitimate interest in enforcing child pornography laws'.[73] By expanding the definition of minor to eighteen years of age, it may allow prosecutors to pursue images which may in the past have been considered as borderline, although whether limited police resources will,

69 699 NW2d 810 (SC Neb 2005).
70 Cybercrime Convention, Explanatory Report, [104].
71 *R v. Sharpe* [2001] 1 SCR 45 at [108] per McLachlin J. Also see Protection of Children Act 1978 (UK), s. 1A and Criminal Justice Act 1988 (UK), s. 160A.
72 T. Krone, '*Does Thinking Make It So? Defining online child pornography possession offences*, Trends and Issues in Crime and Criminal Justice, (Australian Institute of Criminology, 2005), p. 3.
73 *US v. Bach*, 400 F 3d 622, 629 (8th Cir 2005).

or should, be allocated to such marginal images may be questioned.[74] One US study suggests that where arrests were made the nature of the child pornography overwhelmingly related to much younger children, with 83% of offenders possessing at least some images depicting children between six and twelve.[75]

Difficulties may arise in determining whether the person depicted is or 'appears to be' under the relevant age.[76] In the UK, it has been held that whether the person is under the relevant age is a question of fact based on inference without any need for formal proof, and that expert evidence tendered by either side to establish the age of the person depicted would be inadmissible. In *R* v. *Land*[77] the Court of Appeal held that the purpose of expert evidence is to assist the court with information which is outside the normal experience and knowledge of the judge or jury. In such cases, the jury is as well placed as an expert to determine whether the person depicted is under sixteen.[78]

This decision was made at a time when the relevant age in the UK was under sixteen.[79] Even in that context, the proposition seems debatable. Where the relevant age is eighteen it would seem to place too much faith in the trier of fact to determine, in borderline cases, whether a person appears to be under eighteen without even the possibility of expert assistance. Other courts have held that while expert evidence as to the ultimate issue is of course inadmissible, it may nonetheless assist the jury, for example in stating whether certain features are consistent or inconsistent with a person under the relevant age.[80]

However, in order to answer this question fully it is necessary to be precise as to the issue which has to be proved. If it is alleged that the person depicted is actually under eighteen, and that is the issue to be

---

74 A. A. Gillespie, 'The Sexual Offences Act 2003: (3) Tinkering with "child pornography"' (2004) *Criminal Law Review* 361, 363.

75 J. Wolak, K. Mitchell and D. Finkelhor, *Internet Sex Crimes against Minors: The response of law enforcement* (Crimes against Children Research Center, 2003) p. 9.

76 Of course, the relevant time at which the age is determined is the time at which the photographs were taken as opposed to the time at which they were viewed; *US* v. *Marcus*, 193 F Supp 2d 552, 557 (ED NY 2001).

77 [1999] QB 65.

78 *Ibid.* at 70–1 per Judge LJ, cited with approval in *Police* v. *Kennedy* (1998) 71 SASR 175 at 191 per Bleby J, although his Honour did not go so far as to say such evidence would be inadmissible, only that it would be 'seldom helpful'.

79 The relevant age was raised to 18 by the Sexual Offences Act 2003, s. 45(2).

80 *Arnott* v. *McFadyen* (2002) SCCR 96 and *US* v. *Hamilton*, 413 F 3d 1138 (10th Cir 2005). The relevance of expert evidence is discussed further in the context of virtual child pornography at pp. 280–1.

proved, then it would seem that expert evidence would be appropriately admitted. If, on the other hand, it is alleged that the person 'appears to be' or is 'depicted' to be under the age of eighteen, then this would seem to be an issue that the jury is eminently qualified to determine without expert assistance. In such cases, the conduct which the legislature seeks to prohibit is the creation of material which has the appearance of involving a minor. If it appears to a jury or magistrate that the person is under the relevant age, then the offence is made out irrespective of the actual age of the person depicted.

B. The meaning of sexually explicit conduct

Under the Cybercrime Convention, what constitutes 'pornographic material' is to be determined according to national standards. However, 'sexually explicit conduct' is intended at least to encompass, whether real or simulated:

(a) sexual intercourse (including genital–genital, oral–genital, anal–genital or oral–anal) between minors, or between an adult and a minor, of the same or opposite sex;
(b) bestiality;
(c) masturbation;
(d) sadistic or masochistic abuse in a sexual context; or
(e) lascivious exhibition of the genitals or the pubic area of a minor.[81]

This definition replicates that found in 18 USC § 2256(2) and is broadly reflected in the other jurisdictions. The conduct described in paragraphs (a)–(d) are clearly at the most serious end of the spectrum and falls within levels 7–10 of the influential COPINE typology.[82] This ranges from sexual activity by and between children but without the involvement of adults (level 7), assaults involving touching (level 8), sexual assaults involving penetration (level 9) to sadism and bestiality (level 10). Such activity clearly falls within the definition of 'child pornography' in each

---

81 Cybercrime Convention, Explanatory Report, [100].
82 'Combating Paedophile Information Networks in Europe' (COPINE) is a project based at the University College Cork, Ireland and is focused on researching the problem of child sexual abuse on the Internet. See www.ucc.ie/en/equayle/. See also, Taylor and Quayle, *Child Pornography*, p. 32. A modified form of the COPINE categories has been adopted by the UK Sentencing Advisory Panel, *The Panel's Advice to the Court of Appeal on Offences Involving Child Pornography* (2002), [19]–[21]. Also see *R v. Oliver* (2003) *Criminal Law Review* 127.

jurisdiction.[83] In Canada, it has been held that the term 'explicit sexual activity' in s. 163.1 Criminal Code (Can) refers to 'acts which viewed objectively fall at the extreme end of the spectrum of sexual activity – acts involving nudity or intimate sexual activity, represented in a graphic and unambiguous fashion, with persons under or depicted as under 18 years of age'.[84]

In addition to sexual activity, each definition encompasses images of children posing in a sexual context, in particular images which emphasise the child's genitals, anal region or breasts. In general, these images fall within levels 5 and 6 of the COPINE typology – that is, deliberately posed pictures of children in sexualised or provocative poses to images which emphasise the child's genitals, in either case whether they are clothed, partially clothed or naked. Such images may constitute child pornography in each jurisdiction, although subject to a requirement that they be 'indecent',[85] 'lascivious'[86] or the 'dominant characteristic' of the depiction is for a 'sexual purpose'.[87]

In *R v. I (J.E.)*[88] the defendant had secreted a camera which filmed the bathroom of his home. In addition to extensive recordings of an adult woman, there were briefer recordings of four girls under the age of eighteen who could be observed naked with, at various times, their breasts, genital area and buttocks exposed. In determining whether the dominant characteristic of the depictions was for a sexual purpose, the court applied the objective approach stated in *R v. Sharpe*:

> The question is whether a reasonable viewer, looking at the depiction objectively and in context, would see its 'dominant characteristic' as the depiction of the child's sexual organ or anal region. The same applies to the phrase 'for a sexual purpose', which I would interpret in the sense of reasonably perceived as intended to cause sexual stimulation in some viewers.[89]

This test therefore allows for differentiation between innocent photographs, for example those taken by family members, and those taken for

---

83 Criminal Code (Cth), s. 473.1; Protection of Children Act 1978 (UK), s. 1; Criminal Justice Act 1988 (UK), s. 160; and 18 USC § 2256(8).

84 *R v. Sharpe* [2001] 1 SCR 45 at [81] per McLachlin J.

85 Protection of Children Act 1978 (UK), s. 1 and Criminal Justice Act 1988 (UK), s. 160. 'Indecent' is determined objectively, according to 'recognised standards of propriety': *R v. Stamford* [1972] 2 QB 391 at 393 per Ashworth J, and *R v. Smethurst* [2002] 1 Cr App R 6.

86 18 USC § 2256(2).

87 Criminal Code (Cth), s. 473.1 and Criminal Code (Can), s. 163.1(1)(a)(ii).

88 2003 WCBJ Lexis 2628.   89 *R v. Sharpe* [2001] 1 SCR 45 at [82] per McLachlin J.

a sexual purpose. 'Family photos of naked children, viewed objectively, generally do not have as their "dominant characteristic" the depiction of a sexual organ or anal region "for a sexual purpose".[90] In this case, the images were of the girls bathing and grooming in circumstances in which they would expect complete privacy. It was held that as the images clearly had no artistic, educational, scientific or medical purpose it could be inferred that the depictions were for the dominant purpose of sexual stimulation and were, therefore, child pornography within the meaning of the section.[91]

This type of depiction causes most difficulty in the United States where it sits at the margin of protected and unprotected speech. In determining whether an image constitutes a 'lascivious' exhibition, courts have regard to such factors as whether the focal point of the visual depiction is on the child's genitalia or pubic area, whether the setting is sexually suggestive, whether the child is depicted in an unnatural pose or inappropriate attire, whether the child is fully or partially clothed, or nude, whether the visual depiction suggests 'sexual coyness' or a willingness to engage in sexual activity, and whether it is intended or designed to elicit a sexual response in the viewer.[92] In US v. Knox[93] it was held that a lascivious exhibition of the genitals or pubic area may constitute child pornography notwith-standing that those areas are covered by clothing such as underwear or bathers.

It is here that we reach the, albeit blurred, boundary of child pornog-raphy: so-called 'child erotica' – that is, 'any material, relating to chil-dren, that serves a sexual purpose for a given individual'.[94] The COPINE typology identifies a range of images which fall within this category, including images of children in their underwear in family photo albums or catalogues where the context or organisation of the images suggests inappropriateness (level 1); pictures of nude or semi-naked children in appropriate settings and from legitimate sources (level 2); surreptitious photographs of children in appropriate settings in either their underwear or naked or partially naked (level 3); and deliberately posed pictures of children, whether clothed, partially clothed or naked, which fall outside

---

90 *Ibid.*   91 *R* v. *I (J.E.)*, 2003 WCBJ LEXIS 2628 at [50].

92 *US* v. *Dost*, 636 F Supp 828, 832 (SD Cal 1986), aff'd *US* v. *Wiegand*, 812 F 2d 1239 (9th Cir 1987); cert. denied, *Wiegand* v. *US*, 484 US 856 (1987). Also see the cases cited in A. Adler, 'The perverse law of child pornography' (2001) 101 *The Columbia Law Review* 209, 261–4.

93 32 F 3d 733 (3rd Cir 1994); cert. denied, 513 US 1109 (1995).

94 K. Lanning, *Child Molesters: A behavioural analysis* (Washington DC: National Center for Missing and Exploited Children, 1992), p. 52.

the definition of child pornography but where the amount, context and organisation suggests sexual interest (level 4).

Some studies have found that a significant number of offenders found to be in possession of child pornography were also in possession of 'innocent' images of children which were not objectionable, but suspicious in context.[95] While this is not a new phenomenon, once again digital technology has challenged our existing conceptions of these practices both in terms of capacity and scale. All of the factors which facilitate the possession, production and distribution of child pornography apply equally to these ancillary images. In particular, the taking of 'innocent' images of children and posting them on sexual websites has, understandably, caused significant community concern. In Australia, for example, a website was found to contain hundreds of images of children taken at a popular Queensland park.[96] Although the child and his or her carers may be unaware of the photography, and in that sense the child is not harmed, the use of such images may be regarded as 'particularly corrosive and offensive, because they sexualise situations that should be safe and secure environments in which children can play'.[97]

In many cases such images will fall outside existing laws, and it has been suggested that some websites are deliberately tailored to fall outside the definition of 'child pornography'.[98] For example, so-called 'child modelling sites' contain images of young girls in outfits and poses which may be described as provocative, but which arguably fall outside the definition of child pornography.[99]

In some cases it may be possible to argue that such images constitute child pornography because of the context in which they are displayed. In *R* v. *Sharpe* it was suggested, *obiter dictum*, that placing a photograph in an album of sexual photographs, and adding a sexual caption could change its meaning such that its dominant purpose or characteristic becomes

95 J. Wolak, D. Finkelhor and K.J. Mitchell, 'The varieties of child pornography production' in E. Quayle and M. Taylor (eds.), *Viewing Child Pornography on The Internet: Understanding the offense, managing the offender, helping the victims* (Russell House, 2005), p. 39; and A. Carr, *Internet Traders of Child Pornography and other Censorship Offenders in New Zealand* (Department of Internal Affairs, 2004), p. 54.

96 Standing Committee of Attorneys-General, *Unauthorised Photography on the Internet and Ancillary Privacy Issues*, Discussion Paper (Melbourne Department of Justice 2005), p. 5.

97 Taylor and Quayle, *Child Pornography*, p. 35.   98 *Ibid.*, pp. 6–7.

99 C. Calvert, 'Opening up an academic privilege and shutting down child modeling sites: Revising child pornography laws in the United States' (2002) 107 *Dickinson Law Review* 253, 272–4.

unmistakeably sexual in the view of a reasonable observer.[100] In *R* v. *Carr*[101] the defendant was convicted, inter alia, of taking, having, making and distributing indecent photographs or pseudo-photographs of a child. Some of these images formed part of a collection of 12,000 covert images of women and children taken around London. One image, which had been distributed, was a covert photograph showing the underwear of a girl aged about three or four. The email to which the image was attached contained phrases such as 'time to unzip yourself I think', 'hard to keep your hands off them, isn't it' and 'oh God yes, so tempting'.[102]

The same argument could be made in relation to images placed on sexually orientated websites. For example, in Australia pictures of teenage school boys involved in various sporting activities were posted on a website without permission. The context in which the images were displayed suggested they were for the sexual gratification of the viewer, and the website itself contained links to pornographic websites.[103] The fact that images are arranged in galleries, or there are thousands of them, may also be evidence of possession for sexual gratification.[104]

It is also possible for an image, which would not otherwise be indecent, to be altered so that it becomes indecent through a change in emphasis. For example, in *R* v. *Murray*[105] the defendant was convicted of possessing an indecent video of a child. The video recording was in two parts. The first part was a television programme, which showed a doctor examining the genitalia of a naked boy, with commentary explaining what the doctor was doing. It was not suggested that this part was indecent. However, the second part was an altered version of the first, without commentary and focusing on the manipulation of the penis, including slowing the image down at that point. The court upheld the defendant's conviction on the basis that these images were distinct from the original programme, and the jury had been asked to apply the correct test of indecency to those images.[106]

These are ultimately questions of fact. In *R* v. *O'Carroll*[107] the defendant, an avowed paedophile campaigner, brought into the UK a collection of images, each of which depicted 'a young naked child engaging in normal outdoor activity such as playing on a beach'.[108] His convictions on three

100 *R* v. *Sharpe* [2001] 1 SCR 45 at [82] per McLachlin J.
101 [2003] EWCA Crim 2416.   102 *Ibid.*, at [6].
103 Standing Committee of Attorneys-General, *Unauthorised Photographs*, p. 5.
104 Krone, *Does Thinking Make It So?*, p. 4.   105 [2004] EWCA Crim 2211.
106 *Ibid.*, at [6] per Latham J.   107 [2003] EWCA Crim 2338.   108 *Ibid.*, at [2].

counts of being knowingly concerned in evading the prohibition on the importation of indecent material were upheld. On the question of whether these images were indecent, the defendant referred to an earlier dictum of Rose LJ in *R* v. *Oliver* that 'neither nakedness in a legitimate setting, nor the surreptitious procuring of an image, gives rise, of itself, to a pornographic image'.[109] In this case, the court confirmed that the question is ultimately one for the jury, and that '[a] dictum of a judge in one case in this court as to what constitutes a "pornographic image" cannot bind a jury as to what in another case is indecent material, however distinguished that judge may be'.[110] The jury in this case had been properly directed on the question of indecency and found it to be made out. The nature of at least some of the photographs may be inferred from the fact that the court found to be 'perfectly proper' the trial judge's comment that the extent of display of genitalia was a factor which may be considered by the jury.[111]

Where these images fall outside existing offences[112] it may be argued that new provisions should be enacted. For example, a new offence could be created which would criminalise unauthorised use of photographs of children where a reasonable observer would consider the context in which they appear to be exploitative, offensive or for sexual gratification.[113] An alternative formulation was proposed in the, as yet unenacted, Child Modeling Exploitation Prevention Act of 2002.[114] This bill would have made it an offence to display or offer to provide the image of a child under seventeen, with intent to make a financial gain but without a purpose of marketing a product or service other than an image of a child model.

While such offences rightly focus on the use to which images of children are put irrespective of whether they contain sexual activity, they are likely to face a number of challenges. First, such offences are unlikely to gain international agreement, especially in the United States where such laws would undoubtedly be subject to First Amendment challenge.[115] Secondly, even if dual criminality could be achieved, the focus of law enforcement, understandably, appears to be on images which are at the more serious end of the scale. For example, in one study 92% of offenders

---

109 *R* v. *Oliver* [2002] EWCA Crim 2766 at [10] per Rose LJ.
110 *R* v. *O'Carroll* [2003] EWCA Crim 2338 at [17].   111 *Ibid.*, at [12].
112 Other alternative offences include stalking, voyeurism or the use of classification laws to have the material removed: Standing Committee of Attorneys-General, *Unauthorised Photographs*, pp. 21–3.
113 *Ibid.*, p. 33.
114 107th Congress, 2d Session, HR 4667. Referred to House Subcommittee on Workforce Protections on 13 September 2002.
115 Calvert, 'Child modeling', 279–86.

possessed child pornography depicting genitals or explicit sexual activity, 80% penetration of a minor, 71% sexual contact between an adult and a minor and 21% depicting violence:[116]

> This suggests that offenders are not being arrested for possessing marginal or ambiguous sexual images of minors such as images where it is hard to ascertain whether the subject is a minor or where the context was casual nudity without sexual abuse to the child.[117]

Thirdly, apart from the practical difficulties of drafting such a law, we are moving into the realm of punishing thought. 'It is the link between child pornography and sexual abuse that makes child pornography inappropriate and illegal; it is not the fact that people might generate obscene, deviant or inappropriate fantasies around some photographs.'[118] The prohibition of child pornography is based on the link between such material and child abuse. Obscene images may be prohibited because they offend community standards. Here, we are trying to prohibit images based on what the offender thinks about them. Given the range of materials which may be used in this way, such an attempt may ultimately be futile.

C. The medium of depiction

The challenge presented by digital technology is that in many cases the material exists only as data. It is therefore essential to ensure that definitions of child pornography are as technologically neutral as possible. For example, the Australian federal provisions simply refer to 'material', which is defined to include 'material in any form, or combination of forms, capable of constituting a communication'.[119] 'Communication' is in turn defined to include any communication (whether between persons, things or persons and things) in the form of text, speech, sound, visual images (still or moving), signals, data 'or any other form' or in any 'combination of forms'.

In contrast, other jurisdictions define child pornography in conventional terms such as 'photograph',[120] visual 'representation'[121] or 'depiction'.[122] Such terminology is not necessarily appropriate in the

---

116 Wolak, Mitchell and Finklehor, *Internet Sex Crimes against Minors*, p. 10.
117 *Ibid.* Also see Standing Committee of Attorneys-General, *Unauthorised Photographs*, p. 31.
118 Taylor and Quayle, *Child Pornography*, p. 8.   119 Criminal Code (Cth), s. 473.1.
120 Protection of Children Act 1978 (UK), s. 1.   121 Criminal Code (Can), s. 163.1(1).
122 18 USC 2256(8).

digital context, where a distinction must be drawn between the image which is viewed, and the data which produces it.

The potential difficulty is illustrated by the Canadian provision which defines 'child pornography' to mean 'a photographic, film, video or other *visual representation*, whether or not it was made by electronic or mechanical means'.[123] In *R* v. *Weir*[124] the defendant was convicted of possession after images containing child pornography were discovered by the defendant's ISP during maintenance of his electronic mailbox. The trial judge ruled that for the purposes of the Canadian provision, possession of the data in the computer is not sufficient; there must be proof of possession of the visual representation itself. Nonetheless, her Honour concluded that there was sufficient evidence that the appellant had viewed the images on the computer, and that this was sufficient to sustain the conviction. The Alberta Court of Appeal, although declining to rule on the trial judge's narrow interpretation of possession, agreed with her Honour's conclusion as to the sufficiency of the evidence.[125]

On first reading, it would appear that the trial judge was correct in concluding that it is the 'visual representation' which must be possessed by the defendant in such cases. As a digital image is clearly not one of the three enumerated examples in the definition (photograph, film or video) it must be another form of 'visual representation' if it is to fall within the section. The term 'visual' connotes something which can be seen: 'an object of vision or sight; capable of being seen; perceptible, visible'.[126] Applying this interpretation, her Honour was correct in stating that the computer file which produces the image is not a visual representation, a view shared by a US District Court: 'It is true that the GIF, JPG, and ZIP files are not visual depictions themselves – they are computer data stored on diskettes or other media, requiring software and a computer to view the images within.'[127] On this interpretation, the 'visual representation' must therefore be the image on the computer screen.

The question then arises as to how the defendant may be in possession of that image. As discussed below, possession requires custody or control. If the image itself is to be possessed, it must be on the basis that the defendant has control over that image. It was presumably on this basis that the court in *R* v. *Weir* concluded that the defendant was in possession, by *viewing* the image. However, the basis of possession cannot be the act

---

123 Criminal Code (Can), s. 163.1(1) (emphasis added).   124 (2001) 156 CCC (3d) 188.
125 *Ibid.*, at 196–7 per the Court.   126 *Oxford English Dictionary*.
127 *US* v. *Lamb*, 945 F Supp 441, 451 (NDNY 1996).

of viewing as to view something is not to exercise custody or control over it. If it were, any person who intentionally looked at a computer screen displaying child pornography would be in possession of that image. More correctly, it is the act of controlling the data in order to produce the image which must constitute the act of possession.

Such an interpretation presents significant forensic difficulties. If what is possessed must be a visual representation, then the prosecution must prove that the file was in fact displayed. If the image is not displayed, there can be no visual representation. This would render the provisions unenforceable in many cases, for example where the files were found on a memory stick or other storage device with no facility for display.

An alternative view is that the term 'visual representation' includes data files irrespective of whether they are displayed, a view adopted by the Ninth Circuit Court of Appeals in *US* v. *Hockings*.[128] The defendant was convicted of various offences including possession of child pornography after images in the form of GIF files were found on his computer.[129] At the time of the offences, 'visual depiction' was defined to include 'undeveloped film and videotape', but did not include a reference to data. The court rejected the defendant's argument that the GIF files were therefore not 'visual depictions' within the meaning of the statute.

As a matter of statutory interpretation, it was clear that Congress intended such files to constitute 'visual depictions'. First, the provisions were concerned with the transportation of such material by any means 'including computer', and it would lead to an absurdity to find that Congress intended to prohibit the transportation of child pornography by computer, yet not include GIF files within the definition of visual depiction.[130] Secondly, the definition of 'visual depiction' is inclusive and does not state exhaustively all items which constitute a 'visual depiction'. Although software is required to view the images, the 'visual image transported in binary form starts and ends pornographically and that is what Congress seeks to prohibit'.[131] Accordingly, it was held that the files were 'visual depictions' within the meaning of the provision.

Consistent with this interpretation, it has been held that the item need only be *capable* of conversion into a viewable form. It is not necessary to show that they are immediately viewable without further intervention.

128 129 F 3d 1069 (9th Cir 1997). Also see *US* v. *Whiting*, 165 F 3d 631, 633–4 (8th Cir 1999).
129 18 USC §§ 2252(a)(1) and (4)(B).
130 *US* v. *Hockings*, 129 F 3d 1069, 1071 (9th Cir 1997).   131 *Ibid.*, at 1072.

So, for example, files in cache are not viewable until a system command is executed and they are converted to ordinary files. They are nonetheless visual depictions because they are capable of conversion.[132]

Similar arguments may be made in relation to the Canadian provision. The definition is clearly intended to apply to images generated 'by electronic means', and to exclude data files from the ambit of the provision would be to severely limit its application in that context. The inclusion of 'video' in the definition is also a clear indication that parliament intended the term 'visual representation' to apply to images which require additional processing to render them viewable:

> In this regard, an image stored as data which can be read by a computer is directly analogous to an image on video tape. They are both images stored as magnetic signals that require processing by the use of a machine in order to view them. The fact that they cannot be viewed as pornographic images until processed through the appropriate equipment does not place them outside the definition of 'visual depiction' for purposes of the statute.[133]

Such semantic arguments clearly illustrate the importance of crafting definitions to reflect the digital environment, rather than simply importing traditional terms. For example, in the US 'child pornography' is defined in similar terms to the Canadian provision as 'any visual depiction, including any photograph, film, video, picture or computer or computer generated image or picture, whether made or produced by electronic, mechanical or other means'.[134] However, 'visual depiction' is further defined to include 'undeveloped film and videotape, and data stored on computer disk or by electronic means which is capable of conversion into a visual image'.[135]

A similar issue arose in the UK where the term used is 'indecent photograph or pseudo-photograph' of a child.[136] 'Indecent photograph' is defined to include an indecent film,[137] a copy of an indecent photograph or film, and an indecent photograph comprised in a film.[138] 'Pseudo-photograph' is defined to mean an image, whether made by computer-graphics or otherwise howsoever, which appears to be a photograph.[139]

---

132 *US* v. *Romm*, 455 F 3d 990, 998–9 (9th Cir 2006).
133 *US* v. *Whiting*, 165 F 3d 631, 633–4 (8th Cir 1999).   134 18 USC § 2256(8).
135 18 USC § 2256(5).   136 Criminal Justice Act 1988 (UK), s. 160(1).
137 'Film' includes any form of video-recording: Protection of Children Act 1978 (UK), s. 7(5).
138 S. 7(2).   139 S. 7(7).

Prior to this provision being amended, it was held that images on a computer disk did not constitute photographs as a photograph is 'a picture or other image obtained by the chemical action of light or other radiation on specially sensitised materials such as film or glass'.[140] Although images scanned from conventional photographs would constitute a copy of an indecent photograph,[141] this would not be the case for images created wholly in digital format.

The issue has now been addressed with 'photograph' defined to include 'data stored on a computer disk or by other electronic means which is capable of conversion into a photograph'.[142] While this is an improvement, it would have been preferable to use a more neutral term such as 'visual representation' rather than the more traditional term 'photograph'. The difficulties associated with retaining the term 'photograph' are well illustrated by the need for recent amendments which define 'photograph' to include:

> (a) a tracing or other images, whether mady by electronic or other means of whatever nature –
>   (i) which is not itself a photograph or pseudo-photograph, but
>   (ii) which is derived from the whole or a part of a photograph or pseudo-photograph (or a combination of both); and
> (b) data stored on a computer disc or by other means which is capable of conversion into an image within paragraph (a).[143]

Although both the UK and United States provisions refer to 'data stored on a computer disk', this does not connote a requirement that the data must be retained for future use and subsequent retrieval. Both are inclusive definitions and it has been held that it is not necessary that the data be deliberately stored in order to fall within the provision.[144] Data which is downloaded, or even streamed, is nonetheless 'stored' in the computer for the purposes of processing, even if that storage is temporary. In any event, a viewed image will often be contemporaneously stored on the computer hard drive, for example in the cache folder of the Internet browser.

---

140 R v. *Fellows and Arnold* [1997] 2 All ER 548 at 556 per Evans LJ.   141 *Ibid.*
142 Protection of Children Act 1978 (UK), s. 7(4). The equivalent provision as regards pseudo-photographs is found in s. 7(9).
143 Protection of Children Act 1978 (UK), s. 7(4A), as inserted by Criminal Justice and Immigration Act 2008 (UK), s. 69.
144 R v. *Smith*, R v. *Jayson* [2002] EWCA Crim 683. Also see *Atkins* v. DPP, *Goodland* v. DPP [2000] 2 All ER 425 at 436 per Simon Brown LJ, and *US* v. *Tucker*, 305 F 3d 1193, 1204 (10th Cir 2002).

A related issue that arises in a number of US provisions concerns the term 'matter which contains any visual depiction'.[145] The question arises as to whether the 'matter' is the file which contains the visual depiction, or the storage medium which contains the file. This distinction may be particularly relevant in the context of the defendant's knowledge of what is in his or her possession. For example, in *US* v. *Lacy*[146] the defendant maintained that when he opened the files which he had downloaded, and saw that they were images of child pornography, he deleted them. 'If his claim were true, he knew the depictions he downloaded onto his disks and drive were of minors engaged in sexually explicit conduct, but he did not know the depictions were still on his disks and drive.'[147]

It was held that the 'matter' which must contain the visual depiction is the computer hard drive or disk – that is, the physical medium which contains the depiction. The phrase follows the words 'book, magazines, periodicals, films, video tapes' and, applying the principle of *ejusdem generis*, should be interpreted consistently with these terms.[148] The court saw the hard drive as analogous to a book or magazine that contains a picture. It was therefore necessary to instruct the jury that it was not enough that the defendant knew the nature of the images, he must also have known that those images were on his hard drive.

An alternative argument, although one not mentioned in the judgment, is that 'visual depiction' is defined to include 'data stored on a computer disk'.[149] When this is read alongside 'matter which contains any visual depiction', it can be seen that it only makes sense to say that the storage medium contains the data. It would be nonsensical to say that the file contains the data, given that the file *is* the data.

Although our focus is on child pornography in the form of digital images, the definition of child pornography in some jurisdictions includes written depictions.[150] In addition to written fantasies and other descriptions of child pornographic material, this may include information on bulletin boards providing information as to the location of child pornography on the Internet.[151] If not within the meaning of child pornography, such material must be prosecuted, if at all, under general obscenity laws or offences such as incitement or conspiracy.

145 18 USC §§ 2252(a)(4), 2252A(a)(2)(b) and 2252A(5).
146 119 F 3d 742 (1997); cert. denied, *Lacy* v. *US*, 523 US 1101 (1998).   147 *Ibid.*, 748.
148 *Ibid.*   149 18 USC § 2256(5).
150 Criminal Code (Cth), s. 473.1 and Criminal Code (Can), s. 163.1(1).
151 Jenkins, *Beyond Tolerance*, pp. 65–6.

In Canada, the definition of 'child pornography' also includes any written material or visual representation that advocates or counsels sexual activity with a person under the age of eighteen years that would be an offence under the Criminal Code (Can).[152] The question to be determined is not whether the maker or possessor intended to advocate or counsel the crime, but whether the material, viewed objectively, actively induces or encourages the described offences.[153] Although the mere description of the criminal act is not sufficient, the advocating or counselling need not be express. It is enough if the material implicitly suggests that sex with children can and should be pursued.[154]

D. 'Virtual' child pornography

Digital technology has provided offenders with increasingly sophisticated means to create 'virtual' child pornography. At its simplest, this may involve manipulating an image of an adult to appear more childlike, or a composite image where part of one image is transferred on to another image, most commonly the head from one image being placed on the body in another. For example, a UK man was convicted of making an indecent pseudo-photograph of a child after taking photographs of local children and superimposing their faces on to explicit photographs of adults.[155] Alternatively, it may involve so-called 'morphing' where an intermediate image is produced from two other images.

Although much has been made of the potential to create realistic-looking child pornography without the use of actual children, at present even the best examples of computer-generated imagery are readily distinguishable from images of actual children. For example, in *US* v. *Marchand*[156] the defence adduced evidence that software exists, such as 'POSER', which can be used to create virtual images. They were, however, unable to produce any images which were virtually indistinguishable from an image of an actual person:[157]

---

152 Criminal Code (Can) s 163.1(1)(b).
153 *R* v. *Sharpe* [2001] 1 SCR 45 at [65] per McLachlin CJ.
154 *R* v. *Beattie* [2005] OJ no 1302, cited with approval in *R* v. *Missions* [2005] NSJ no 177 at [29] per Roscoe JA. Also see *R* v. *Kuneman* [2003] OJ no 2459.
155 A. Norfolk, 'Computer expert faces jail over "made-up" child porn image', Times Online, 10 August 2006, http://technology.timesonline.co.uk/tol/news/tech_and_web/article604825.ece.
156 308 F Supp 2d 498 (D NJ 2004).   157 *Ibid.*, 509.

> While advances in digital imaging technology have arguably made it pos-
> sible to 'fake' human images by creating convincing digital simulations,
> jurors could draw on their own common sense and experience to recall
> that the most expensive digital special effects Hollywood can command
> only rarely generate images that can be confused with live human actors.[158]

Although technology is rapidly developing, it appears that for the foreseeable future child pornography is likely to be created using real children.[159]
This is particularly the case with moving images, which are prohibitively
expensive to produce.[160] As recently as 2003, Congress reported that
'[t]here is no substantial evidence that any of the child pornography
images being trafficked today were made other than by the abuse of real
children'.[161] This is supported by research which found that only 3 per
cent of a sample of persons arrested for possession of child pornography
were in possession of 'morphed' images:[162]

> The time, expertise, and resources needed to even attempt to create a
> virtual image are overwhelming and completely unwarranted when similar
> images that are real are readily available and infinitely less expensive, or
> free. Unfortunately, in the area of child pornography, those images and the
> children who are sacrificed to make them, are present in abundance.[163]

Although a relatively small proportion of child pornography is apparently
'virtual', it may be argued that it can produce many of the same types of
harm as actual child pornography:

> the harms of child pornography extend far beyond direct, physical exploita-
> tion. It is harmful whether it involves real children in its production or
> whether it is a product of the imagination. In either case, child pornog-
> raphy fosters and communicates the same harmful, dehumanizing and
> degrading message.[164]

---

158 *US* v. *Pabon-Cruz*, 255 F Supp 2d 200, 207 (SDNY 2003).
159 Congressional Findings, Pub.L 108–21, title V, § 501, Apr 30, 2003, 117 Stat. 676, (5).
160 S. S. Kreston, 'Defeating the virtual defense in child pornography prosecutions' (2004)
     Journal of High Technology Law 49, 53.
161 Congressional Findings, Pub.L 108–21, title V, § 501, Apr.30, 2003, 117 Stat. 676, (7).
162 Wolak, Finkelhor and Mitchell, *Child-Pornography Possessors*, p. 7.
163 Kreston, 'Defeating the virtual defense', 54. Also see *US* v. *Rearden*, 349 F 3d 608, 613
     (9th Cir 2003) in which an expert witness stated that 'it was beyond the limits of modern
     computer graphics to create a completely artificial picture of a believable photo-realistic
     human being'.
164 *R* v. *Sharpe* [2001] 1 SCR 45 at [136] per Heureux-Dube, Gonthier and Bastarache JJ.
     Also see *R* v. *Stroempl* (1995) 105 CCC (3d) 187 at 191 per Morden ACJO; *R* v. *Quick*
     (2004) 148 A Crim R 51 at 55 per Redlich J; UK Sentencing Advisory Panel, *Offences
     Involving Child Pornography*, p. 9; and Cybercrime Convention, Explanatory Report,
     [102].

Accordingly, in each jurisdiction the definition of 'child pornography' is sufficiently broad to encompass the various forms of 'virtual' child pornography. For example, the definition of 'child pornography' under the Australian federal provisions applies to material that 'depicts a person, or a representation of a person'.[165] In a recent decision of the Supreme Court of New South Wales, it has been held that the ordinary meaning of the phrase 'depicts a . . . representation of a person' is capable of applying to pornographic cartoons of children – in this case, the characters in 'The Simpsons'.[166] In Canada, it has been held that the word 'person' in the definition of 'child pornography' includes visual works of the imagination, as well as depictions of actual people.[167]

Similarly, under s. 7(8) Protection of Children Act 1978 (UK), if the impression conveyed by a pseudo-photograph[168] is that the person shown is a child, the pseudo-photograph shall be treated for all purposes as showing a child. This applies notwithstanding that some of the physical characteristics shown are those of an adult. Because 'pseudo-photograph' is defined as 'an image, whether made by computer graphics or otherwise howsoever, which appears to be a photograph',[169] it would not apply to cartoons or other depictions which do not appear to be a photograph.[170]

Although such depictions are included within the US provisions, in *Ashcroft* v. *The Free Speech Coalition*[171] the Supreme Court held that certain sections of the definition of 'child pornography' in 18 USC § 2256(8) were unconstitutional as infringing the First Amendment.[172] Of particular importance in the digital context, the court struck down 18 USC § 2256(8)(B), which extended the definition of 'child pornography' to include material that 'is, or appears to be, of a minor engaging in

---

165 Criminal Code (Cth) s 473.1.   166 *McEwen v. Simmons* [2008] NSWSC 1292.

167 *R* v. *Sharpe* [2001] 1 SCR 45 at [53] per McLachlin J; cited with approval in *Holland* v. *R* (2005) 30 WAR 231 at [201] per Roberts J.

168 Where the prosecution concerns a photograph, then the person depicted must actually be under 16. Under s. 2(3) a person is to be taken as having been a child if it appears from the evidence as a whole that he or she was then under the age of 16.

169 Protection of Children Act 1978 (UK), s. 7(7).

170 In *Atkins* v. *DPP*, *Goodland* v. *DPP* [2000] 2 All ER 425 it was held that the term 'pseudo-photograph' did not encompass two separate photographs, one of a young girl the other of the abdomen, genitals and upper thighs of a young woman, taped together so that one was superimposed over the other.

171 535 US 234 (2002).

172 Kennedy J, with whom Stevens, Souter, Ginsburg and Breyer JJ agreed, delivered the majority judgment. Thomas J filed a concurring judgment. O'Connor J concurred in part and dissented in part, with Rehnquist CJ and Scalia J joining in part. Rehnquist CJ also filed a dissenting opinion in which Scalia J joined in part.

sexually explicit conduct'.[173] The definition would therefore encompass 'youthful-adult' pornography (pornographic images of adults that look like children) and 'virtual-child pornography' (pornographic images of children created on a computer without using any actual children).[174]

There are, of course, categories of speech which do not enjoy First Amendment protection. Most relevant in this context is material which is 'obscene' (as opposed to merely indecent) – that is, when taken as a whole, the work appeals to the prurient interest, is patently offensive in light of community standards and lacks serious literary, artistic, political or scientific value.[175] Similarly, it is well established that child pornography which involves the use of actual children is not constitutionally protected speech because of the state's interest in protecting children from being exploited in the production of such material.[176] The challenge presented by 18 USC § 2256(8)(B) was that it encompassed material which is neither obscene nor which involves the use of actual children. Because it was not subject to the obscenity standard, nor incorporated adequate defences allowing for the artistic, scientific or other merit of the work, it could apply to images in a medical text, or to any number of literary or artistic works which may depict sexual activity between or with minors, including 'Romeo and Juliet' and 'American Beauty'.[177]

Although such material does not involve the actual abuse of children, Congress provided a number of justifications for its prohibition.[178] We have seen that the Supreme Court of Canada accepted the rationales justifying the criminalisation of child pornography as applying equally to material where no child was involved in its production.[179] In contrast, each was rejected by the US Supreme Court as 'the causal link is contingent and indirect. The harm does not necessarily follow from the speech, but depends upon some unquantified potential for subsequent criminal acts.'[180]

---

173 The Supreme Court also held that 18 USC § 2256(8)(D) which applies to 'pandering' of child pornography was substantially over-broad and in violation of the First Amendment: *Ibid.*, 258.
174 *Ibid.*, 258, 261.
175 *Miller* v. *California*, 413 US 15, 24 (1973). For a discussion of the difficulty of applying the *Miller* standard to the Internet, see C. Calvert, 'Regulating sexual images on the web: Last call for Miller time, but new issues remain untapped' (2001) 23 *Hastings Communications and Entertainment Law Journal* 507.
176 *New York* v. *Ferber*, 458 US 747 (1982).
177 *Ashcroft* v. *The Free Speech Coalition*, 535 US 234, 247–8 (2002).
178 Congressional Findings, Pub.L 108–21, title V, § 501, Apr.30, 2003, 117 Stat. 676.
179 See pp. 252–3.   180 *Ashcroft* v. *The Free Speech Coalition*, 535 US 234, 250 (2002).

For example, the fact that paedophiles might use such material to encourage children to engage in sexual activity[181] is true of many things which are innocent in themselves that one would not expect to be prohibited.[182] Although the government may punish those who provide unsuitable materials to children,[183] it 'cannot ban speech fit for adults simply because it may fall into the hands of children'.[184] Similarly, the fact that such material may 'whet the appetite' of paedophiles and encourage them to engage in offending behaviour[185] is insufficient. The government may only restrict speech if it is 'directed to inciting or producing imminent lawless action and is likely to incite or produce such action'.[186] Here the 'Government has shown no more than a remote connection between speech that might encourage thoughts or impulses and any resulting child abuse'.[187]

The court also rejected the argument that such a prohibition is necessary to eliminate the market for actual child pornography. Without reference to any supporting material, the court opined that '[i]f virtual images were identical to illegal child pornography, the illegal images would be driven from the market by the indistinguishable substitutes'.[188] It was further argued that the existence of virtual child pornography makes it difficult to prosecute pornographers who do use minors because of the need to prove that actual children were involved. However, such an argument turns the First Amendment upside down by effectively arguing that protected speech may be banned as a means to ban unprotected speech.[189]

Although the court did leave open the possibility that an affirmative defence could save a statute from First Amendment challenge it was stated, *obiter dictum*, that the existing affirmative defence was both incomplete and insufficient. It was incomplete because it applied only to a person charged with possession but not distribution. It was insufficient because it applied only where the defendant could show that only adult actors were involved. It would therefore not extend to truly virtual pornography where no actual people were involved at all.[190] The court therefore

181 Congressional Findings, Section 101 (a) [title I, § 121 [1]] of Pub. L. 104–208, (3).
182 *Ashcroft* v. *The Free Speech Coalition*, 535 US 234, 251 (2002).
183 *Ginsberg* v. *New York*, 390 US 629 (1968).
184 *Ashcroft* v. *The Free Speech Coalition*, 535 US 234, 252 (2002).
185 Congressional Findings, Section 101 (a) [title I, § 121[1]] of Pub.L. 104–208, (4).
186 *Brandenburg* v. *Ohio*, 395 US 444, 447 (1969).
187 *Ashcroft* v. *The Free Speech Coalition*, 535 US 234, 253 (2002).
188 *Ibid.*, 254.   189 *Ibid.*
190 *Ibid.*, 256. Also see J. J. Farhangian, 'A problem of "virtual" proportions: The difficulties inherent in tailoring virtual child pornography laws to meet constitutional standards' (2003) 12 *Journal of Law and Policy* 241, 260.

held that the provision was over-broad and unconstitutional as apply-ing to circumstances where no child was harmed in the production of the material. The situation with actual child pornography is quite differ-ent. In such cases, the protection of children from abuse is a compelling interest, and the production of such material was intrinsically related to the sexual abuse of children.[191] 'Given the importance of the State's interest in protecting the victims of child pornography' the state was jus-tified in 'attempting to stamp out this vice at all levels in the distribution chain'.[192]

Congress was quick to respond with the enactment of the Prosecutorial Remedies and Other Tools to end the Exploitation of Children Today ('PROTECT') Act of 2003 which, inter alia, amended 18 USC § 2256(8)(B) so that it applied to a visual depiction which 'is a digital image, computer image or computer generated image that is, or is indistinguishable from, that of a minor engaging in sexually explicit conduct.' 'Indistinguishable' is defined as 'virtually indistinguishable, in that the depiction is such that an ordinary person viewing the depiction would conclude that the depiction is of an actual minor engaged in sexually explicit conduct'.[193] The amendments also introduced a revised affirmative defence which allows the defendant to prove that 'the alleged child pornography was produced using an actual person or persons engaging in sexually explicit conduct and each such person was adult at the time the material was produced' or that 'the alleged child pornography was not produced using any actual minor or minors'.[194]

It is arguable that these amendments are unlikely to survive First Amendment challenge for two principal reasons.[195] First, the use of the term 'virtually indistinguishable from', although derived from Justice O'Connor's judgment,[196] suffers from the same deficiency as the original provision. It would still apply to material that did not involve actual harm

---

191 *Ashcroft* v. *The Free Speech Coalition*, 535 US 234, 249 (2002).

192 *Osborne* v. *Ohio*, 495 US 103, 111 (1990). Issues of freedom of expression were also discussed, albeit briefly, in *R* v. *Bowden* [2001] QB 88, *R* v. *Smethurst* [2002] 1 Cr App R 6, *R* v. *Quick* (2004) 148 A Crim R 51, *Holland* v. *R* (2005) 30 WAR 231 and *Leonard v. R* [2007] NSWCCA 197.

193 18 USC § 2256(11). The definition specifically excludes drawings, cartoons, sculptures or paintings depicting minors or adults.

194 18 USC § 2252A(c)(2).

195 The revised pandering provision was recently held to be constitutionally valid: *US* v. *Williams*, 128 S Ct 1830 (2008).

196 *Ashcroft* v. *The Free Speech Coalition*, 535 US 234, 265 (2002).

to children.[197] It may also be unconstitutionally vague, being defined in terms of the 'ordinary' person with no clear guidance on who the 'ordinary' person is.[198] Secondly, the affirmative defence imposes too heavy a burden on defendants. As the Supreme Court itself said in *Ashcroft*, 'if the evidentiary issue is a serious problem for the Government . . . it will be at least as difficult for the innocent possessor'.[199]

We therefore have a situation where virtual child pornography is criminalised in each jurisdiction other than the United States. As well as providing the potential for virtual images to be produced lawfully in the United States, the greatest impact of this decision is the hampering of child pornography prosecutions; an impact which is not confined to that country. Given the global nature of the Internet, and the fact that the majority of child pornography apparently comes from the United States, the ability of law enforcement to successfully prosecute child pornography cases has significant implications for other jurisdictions. The impact of *Ashcroft*, while no doubt significant, must nonetheless be kept in perspective.

First, *Ashcroft* only invalidated those provisions relating to virtual child pornography. The prohibition on actual child pornography remains intact.[200] Further, there is some authority that the ruling in *Ashcroft* may not apply to 'morphed' images – that is, where an innocent picture of a child is altered so that it appears to involve sexual activity.[201] The definition of 'child pornography' in 18 USC § 2256(8)(C) covers any visual depiction that 'has been created, adapted, or modified to appear that an identifiable minor is engaging in sexually explicit conduct'. This aspect of the provision was not challenged in *Ashcroft*, and Justice Kennedy commented, *obiter dictum*, that although such images may fall within the definition of virtual child pornography, 'they implicate the interests of real children and are in that sense closer to the images in *Ferber*'.[202]

---

197 Farhangian, 'Virtual proportions', 273. Also see J. P. Feldmeier, 'Close enough for government work: An examination of congressional efforts to reduce the government's burden of proof in child pornography cases' (2003) 30 *Northern Kentucky Law Review* 205, 218–19.

198 A. Rogers, 'Playing hide and seek: How to protect virtual pornographers and actual children on the Internet' (2005) *Villanova Law Review* 87, 101.

199 *Ashcroft* v. *The Free Speech Coalition*, 535 US 234, 255 (2002).

200 *US* v. *Payne*, 519 F Supp 2d 466 (D NJ 2007); *US* v. *Rodriguez-Pacheco*, 475 F 3d 434, 440 (1st Cir 2007); *US* v. *Wyatt*, 64 Fed Appx 350, 351 (4th Cir 2003); *US* v. *Kelly*, 312 F 3d 328 (7th Cir 2002); and *US* v. *Hersh*, 297 F 3d 1233, 1254 (11th Cir 2002).

201 18 USC § 2256(8)(C).

202 *Ashcroft* v. *The Free Speech Coalition*, 535 US 234, 242 (2002). Also see *US* v. *Farrelly*, 389 F 3d 649 (6th Cir 2004) and *US* v. *Rearden*, 349 F 3d 608, 613 (9th Cir 2003).

This issue was considered in *US* v. *Bach*.[203] The defendant was convicted of various offences relating to child pornography. One image which was found in his possession was of a young boy who was depicted naked and with an erection. An image of the face of a well-known child entertainer had been skilfully inserted into the original photograph so that it appeared to be a nude photograph of the child entertainer. On appeal, it was argued that the definition of child pornography in 18 USC § 2256(8)(C) violates the First Amendment as it includes images that only appear to depict an identifiable minor, similar language having been found unconstitutional in *Ashcroft*. This argument was rejected.

The definition in 18 USC § 2256(8)(C) was intended by Congress to prevent harm to minors resulting from the use of 'identifiable images . . . in pornographic depictions, even where the identifiable minor is not directly involved in sexually explicit activities'.[204] The constitutionality of this provision was specifically left open in *Ashcroft*. In contrast to the definitions considered in that case, this section may relate to harm to an identifiable minor in two respects. The first is the boy depicted naked in the picture.[205] The second is the child entertainer whose face was superimposed on the other image.

> Although there is no contention that the nude body actually is that of AC or that he was involved in the production of the image, a lasting record has been created of AC, an identifiable minor child, seemingly engaged in sexually explicit activity. He is thus victimized every time the picture is displayed.[206]

While the court acknowledged that there may be cases in which the application of § 2256(8)(C) violates the First Amendment, this was not such a case. The image in this case created identifiable child victims of sexual exploitation, and these are interests which may constitutionally be prosecuted under *Ashcroft* and *Ferber*.

Secondly, the impact of *Ashcroft* on the prosecution of child pornography trials may not be as great as first expected. The major impact of the decision is not due to a proliferation of virtual child pornography. As outlined above, technology is not yet at the stage where truly realistic images may be created. Nonetheless, the possibility that such technology

---

203 *US* v. *Bach*, 400 F 3d 622 (8th Cir 2005).   204 *Ibid.*, 631.
205 In this respect, this was not a typical 'morphing' case, the provision being aimed at those situations where an innocent picture of a child has been altered to appear that the child is engaging in sexually explicit conduct: *ibid.*, 632.
206 *Ibid.*

exists may be sufficient to satisfy the evidential burden, thereby placing the onus on the prosecution to prove that the image is of an actual child. Technology may further hamper the prosecution by easily disguising depictions of real children to make them unidentifiable or to appear computer generated.[207]

At the time of *Ashcroft*, although the government asserted that defendants had raised such a defence, they could point to no case in which this had been done successfully.[208] Since that time, 'defendants in child pornography cases have almost universally raised the contention that the images in question could be virtual, thereby requiring the government, in nearly every child pornography prosecution, to find proof that the child is real. Some of these defense efforts have already been successful.'[209] This has impacted on both the number of cases brought, and the resources required for those which are pursued.[210] For example, prosecutors may focus on cases where the victim is identifiable, although such cases are the exception. Often images were taken some time ago and the children depicted are now adults, and/or the images are produced in other countries.[211] Of thousands of images in the Interpol database, in 2005 it was reported that only 320 children had been located.[212] Alternatively, expert evidence may need to be procured in order to rebut the suggestion that the material is virtual. While this situation may undoubtedly create difficulties for prosecutors, two points should be emphasised.

First, as already noted, *Ashcroft* is limited to those situations where it is alleged that the image was created entirely without the involvement of a child. It does not apply to those situations where an image of a child has been manipulated in some way. Secondly, the overwhelming majority of US courts have adopted the view that irrespective of whether the defence offers evidence that the images may be virtual or not, it is ultimately a question of fact for the jury.[213]

---

207 Congressional Findings, Pub. L. 108–21, title V, § 501, Apr. 30, 2003, 117 Stat. 676, (11).
208 *Ashcroft* v. *The Free Speech Coalition*, 535 US 234, 259 (2002).
209 Congressional Findings, Pub.L. 108–21, title V, § 501, Apr. 30, 2003, 117 Stat. 676, (10).
210 See generally D. S. Armagh, 'The fate of the Child Pornography Act of 1996: Virtual child pornography: Criminal conduct or protected speech?' (2002) 23 *Cardozo Law Review* 1993.
211 UK Sentencing Advisory Panel, *Offences Involving Child Pornography*, p. 4.
212 Muir, *Violence against children*, p. 31.
213 Kreston, 'Defeating the virtual defense', 54–6. Although there are cases where defendants have had convictions overturned, these related to pre-*Ashcroft* jury instructions; see the cases cited in Rogers, 'Hide and seek', 92–7.

For example, in *US* v. *Farrelly*[214] the defendant was convicted on one count of receiving child pornography. It was held by the Sixth Circuit that *Ashcroft* did not impose a special or heightened evidentiary burden on the prosecution, and no circuit has required expert evidence to be introduced to prove the children depicted are real. The prosecution is required to do no more than present the images to the jury for a determination that the depictions were of actual children, the question of whether the images are virtual or real being one of fact.[215] In this case, the prosecution led evidence from an expert witness as to the apparent age of the children depicted in the images. Although this witness was not qualified to give evidence as to whether they were actual children, this did not preclude the jury making such a finding. The jury had access to the photographs, the defence never challenged the reality of those images and the jury were specifically instructed that in order to convict they must find that they were images of real children. This creates a real forensic risk for the defendant claiming that he did not know that the images were of actual children. Such a tactic places the images in the hands of the jury and it is rare for a jury to acquit on the basis that the defendant did not know that the images were of actual children.[216]

Of course, in some cases, the prosecution may lead expert evidence to assist the jury in this regard. In *US* v. *Rearden*[217] the Ninth Circuit accepted expert evidence from an employee of a visual effects studio whose expertise in the creation of visual effects was based on his training and experience in the film industry.[218] Other forms of expertise which may be relevant include child pornography historians who can testify that the images were created before the advent of suitable technology, paediatricians who may testify as to the apparent age of the child depicted based on physical appearance, and law enforcement agents who may testify as to the identity of known victims of sexual abuse.[219] Further, the

214 389 F 3d 649 (2004).
215 *Ibid.*, 652, 654–5 citing *US* v. *Kimler*, 335 F 3d 1132, 1140–2 (10th Cir 2003). Also see
      US v. *Deaton*, 328 F 3d 454, 455 (8th Cir 2003); *US* v. *Hall*, 312 F 3d 1250, 1260 (11th
      Cir 2002); cert. denied, 538 US 954 (2002); *US* v. *Rearden*, 349 F 3d 608, 614 (9th Cir
      2003); *US* v. *Fuller*, 77 Fed Appx 371 (6th Cir 2003); *US* v. *Slanina*, 359 F 3d 356, 357
      (5th Cir 2004); and *US* v. *Irving*, 452 F 3d 110, 122 (2nd Cir 2006).
216 Rogers, 'Hide and seek', 96–7.
217 *US* v. *Rearden*, 349 F 3d 608 (2003); cert. denied, *Rearden* v. *US*, 2004 US LEXIS 5696.
218 *Ibid.*, 613.
219 *US* v. *Marchand*, 308 F Supp 3d 498, 504–5 (D NJ 2004). See generally Kreston, 'Defeating
      the virtual defense', 52–60.

number of images viewed, and websites visited, will often undermine the defendant's claim that he or she believed that the images were virtual. 'Could the Defendant have thought that each of the 35 images, downloaded from many unrelated websites, was each digitally created by an artist who was skilful enough to complete the task so extraordinarily realistically?'[220]

Consequently, although *Ashcroft* has undoubtedly had an impact on the prosecution of child pornography cases, it may not have been as significant as initially thought. In one survey of state and local prosecutors, only 4 per cent said their offices were pursuing fewer cases as a result of *Ashcroft*. Although a significant number had seen the 'virtual image' defence raised, only 5 per cent had seen these cases go to trial with many defendants electing to plead guilty. When at trial, the defence was addressed either by an agent testifying as to the origins of the image or expert evidence that the images were not virtual. Another alternative is to prosecute under obscenity laws.[221]

We now turn to consider the specific offences relating to child pornography. Such offences are addressed in Title 3, Art. 9 of the Cybercrime Convention, which provides that the following conduct should be criminalised where committed intentionally and without right:

1. *producing* child pornography for the purpose of its distribution through a computer system
2. *offering or making available* child pornography through a computer system
3. *distributing or transmitting* child pornography through a computer system
4. *procuring* child pornography through a computer system for oneself or for another person
5. *possessing* child pornography in a computer system or on a computer-data storage medium.

Of these, the Convention provides that parties may reserve the right not to apply numbers 4 and 5.[222]

---

220 *Ibid.*, 508.
221 Wolak, Finkelhor and Mitchell, *Child-Pornography Possessors*, pp. 22–4. See, e.g., *US* v. *Whorley*, 386 F Supp 2d 693 (ED Va 2005), which concerned a prosecution related to Japanese anime cartoons.
222 Cybercrime Convention, Art. 9(4).

4. Producing child pornography

In Australia, Canada and the UK it is an offence to 'produce'[223] or 'make'[224] child pornography. Although not a specific offence under US federal provisions, the meaning of 'produce' is nonetheless relevant in the interpretation of other offences. In particular, a possible jurisdictional nexus for a number of offences is that the child pornography was 'produced using materials that have been mailed, or shipped or transported in interstate or foreign commerce by any means, including by computer'.[225] 'Producing' for these purposes means 'producing, directing, manufacturing, issuing, publishing, or advertising'.[226]

The concepts of 'production' and 'making' in their ordinary usage clearly encompass such things as taking photographs or video images. They may also include making reproductions of existing images, for example by digital scanning or other forms of copying, using imaging software to create 'virtual' child pornography or copying images of child pornography downloaded from the Internet onto a CD.[227]

The potential scope of these provisions has been increased considerably by their application to the downloading or copying of data. In *R v. Bowden*[228] the English Court of Appeal considered whether downloading and/or printing of computer data could amount to the offence of making an indecent photograph of a child contrary to s. 1(1)(a) Protection of Children Act 1978 (UK). The court considered two different situations:

1. where the defendant viewed the images on screen via the Internet and then printed them out
2. where the defendant downloaded photographs and a pseudo-photograph and stored the image in a computer file on a disk.

---

223 Criminal Code (Cth), ss. 474.20 and 474.23. These offences require proof that the material was produced for the purpose of using a carriage service for child pornography/ child abuse material.

224 Criminal Code (Can), s. 163.1(2) and Protection of Children Act 1978 (UK), s. 1(1)(a). Under the Canadian provision the requirement that the conduct be for the purpose of publication applies only to the word 'possess': *R v. Burrows*, 1995 WCBJ LEXIS 9264; *R v. Horvat*, 2006 W OJ no 1673 at [4]–[5] per Sykes J.

225 18 USC § 2252(a)(3)(B). See also 18 USC §§ 2252(a)(4)(B), 2252A(a)(5)(B) and 2252A(a)(6)(B).

226 18 USC § 2256(3).

227 *People v. Hill*, 715 NW 2d 301 (Mich Ct App 2006). Also see *R v. Horvat*, 2006 W OJ no 1673 at [7] per Sykes J.

228 [2001] QB 88.

It was argued on behalf of the appellant that although he was in possession of the images, he was not guilty of 'making' the images. The argument was that the offence of 'making' applied only to pseudo-photographs and, in any event, the verb 'make' is used in the sense of 'to create' and does not apply to the mere downloading or printing out of computer data.

The court rejected these arguments and held that the section was clear and unambiguous in its terms. It renders unlawful the making of a photograph or pseudo-photograph and, in the absence of a statutory definition, 'make' must be given its ordinary meaning which is 'to cause to exist; to produce by action, to bring about'.[229] Consequently, a person who downloads or prints an image is 'making' an image and has therefore committed an offence under the section.[230]

This decision was cited with approval by the Scottish High Court of Justiciary in *Longmuir* v. *Her Majesty's Advocate*.[231] The court held that a person using a computer to bring into existence an image stored on a computer disk is aptly described by the word 'make', but would not be encompassed by the word 'take'.[232] It was further noted that the definition of 'make' in the New Shorter Oxford English Dictionary includes 'produced by . . . extraction'.

> That is an apt description of the way in which data stored on disk is produced, namely by use of a computer extracting electronic signals from the Internet and converting them into that data for storage. That activity, just as the taking of an indecent photograph of a child does, enables child pornography to proliferate and is thus within the mischief which the [provisions] were clearly intended to extend to and to strike at.[233]

Arguably, the same principles would apply to the verb 'produce' which is defined to mean to 'bring forth, bring into being or existence.'[234] In *US* v. *Lacy*[235] the court rejected the defendant's argument that in downloading the images he was 'reproducing' but not 'producing' visual depictions.[236] 'The statute requires only that *visual depictions* be produced; it does not matter that the depictions . . . were copies rather than

229 *Ibid.*, at 95 per Otton CJ, citing the *Oxford English Dictionary*.
230 Applied in *Atkins* v. *DPP*, *Goodland* v. *DPP* [2000] 2 All ER 425 at 435 per Simon Brown LJ, and cited without apparent disapproval in *R* v. *Quick* (2004) 148 A Crim R 51 at 60 per Redlich J.
231 (2000) SC (JC) 378.   232 *Ibid.*, at [14] per Lord Cameron of Lochbroom.
233 *Ibid.*   234 *Oxford English Dictionary*.   235 119 F 3d 742 (9th Cir 1997).
236 The offence of knowingly *reproducing* child pornography requires proof that it was done for the purposes of distribution in interstate or foreign commerce; 18 USC §§ 2252(a)(2) and 2252A(a)(3)(B).

originals.'[237] Accordingly, the images were 'produced' when the defendant downloaded the data onto his computer.

Where a defendant views images without saving them, he or she may be in possession of the images automatically stored in the cache folder.[238] However, it has been held that such *unintentional* copying does not constitute the offence of 'making'. In *R* v. *Smith, R* v. *Jayson*[239] both defendants were convicted of making an indecent photograph of a child contrary to s. 1(1) Protection of Children Act 1978 (UK). In Smith's case, the images had been sent as an email attachment. The associated email correspondence indicated that the defendant had deliberately sought such images in a newsgroup. He did not save the images to his hard drive, but nor did he delete the emails which remained in his inbox. It was argued that simply opening an attachment to view it could not, without more, constitute the offence of 'making'. It was further argued that the provision should be interpreted as narrowly as possible as the Crown's interpretation would expand the reach of the provision too far, and would produce an overlap between the offences of making and possession.

It was held that a person neither makes nor is in possession of an image contained in an email attachment if, prior to opening it, he or she is unaware that it contains or is likely to contain an indecent image.[240] Accordingly, the defendant would be guilty of the offence of making only if he knew that the attachment contained, or was likely to contain, the indecent photograph or pseudo-photograph. Similarly, the automatic storing of those images on cache would not constitute the offence of making if he was unaware of the existence of the cache.[241]

It therefore appears that the offence of making may be committed intentionally, where the accused knows that the attachment contains an indecent photograph or pseudo-photograph, or recklessly where he or she was aware it was likely to contain such an image. Although the offence cannot be committed inadvertently or negligently, this was not a case of an innocent person who unsuspectingly opens an email attachment containing child pornography. The evidence in this case supported the inference that the defendant was aware of the contents of the image, or

---

237 *US* v. *Lacy*, 119 F 3d 742, 750 (9th Cir 1997), emphasis in original.
238 See pp. 303–4.
239 [2002] EWCA Crim 683. Also see *Atkins* v. *DPP*, *Goodland* v. *DPP* [2000] 2 All ER 425 at 436 per Simon Brown LJ.
240 *Ibid.*, at [19] per Dyson LJ. This is consistent with the offences of obtaining and receiving discussed at p. 295.
241 *Ibid.*

was at least aware of their likely contents, and opened the attachment in that knowledge.

In *Jayson*, the defendant had viewed the images on the Internet. It was accepted that the images had not been deliberately saved to the hard drive, but had been automatically stored in the temporary cache. The accused admitted to being aware of how the cache operated. The court upheld the trial judge's ruling that a person may be guilty of making a prohibited image by browsing on the Internet if either:

(a) an image was displayed on the computer screen or
(b) the image was automatically stored to a temporary Internet cache.[242]

By viewing an image the operator of the computer creates or causes the image to exist on the computer screen. This accords with the ordinary meaning of the word 'make'.[243] The relevant *mens rea* is that 'the act of making should be a deliberate and intentional act with knowledge that the image made is, or is likely to be an indecent photograph or pseudo-photograph of a child'.[244] Although the data may only remain in the computer's memory for as long as it is viewed, '[w]hether its creation amounts to an act of making cannot be determined by the length of time that the image remains on the screen'.[245] This also applies where the image is automatically placed in cache. This may constitute the act of making, so long as the accused was aware of the process and intentionally opened the image knowing, or aware it was likely, to be child pornography.[246]

While the reasoning of the courts seems sound in a technical sense, it undermines the distinction between possession and making which is clearly reflected in the legislation. In general terms, making is regarded as a more serious offence than simple possession. This is reflected in two ways. First, those who make child pornography are often subject to greater penalties than those convicted of possession.[247]

Secondly, because making is generally regarded as more serious, it may not be subject to defences that are available to a person charged with possession. For example, under the UK provisions, the statutory defences

---

242 *Ibid.*, at [23].   243 *Ibid.*, at [33].   244 *Ibid.*, at [34].
245 *Ibid.*, at [33].   246 *Ibid.*, at [37].
247 E.g., in the UK, a person found guilty of possessing an indecent photograph/pseudo photograph of a child is liable, on indictment, to a maximum of 5 years' imprisonment while a person found guilty of making indecent photographs/pseudo photographs of children is liable to a maximum of 10 years' imprisonment: Protection of Children Act 1978 (UK), s. 6. Also see *R* v. *Hewlett* 2002 WCBJ LEXIS 1257 at [27] per Fraser CJA.

are not available on a charge of making, but are available in relation
to other offences under s. 1(1)(b)(c) Protection of Children Act 1978
(UK).[248] The prosecution may therefore elect to charge what would otherwise be 'possession' as the more serious offence of 'making', with the
defendant not having the protection of a statutory defence.

This situation arises not from the clear intention of Parliament, but
the peculiarities of digital technology, which challenge our traditional
conceptions of what it is to 'make' an image. It is most likely that the
statutory offences were not applied to offences of taking or making on
the assumption that a person taking or making such an image in a conventional sense would know, or have reason to suspect, that the subject
was a child. Such an assumption is no longer warranted given the broad
application of these concepts in a digital context.[249]

The issue is, to some extent, addressed by the differential *mens rea*
applied to these offences. In the context of possession, where statutory
defences are available, it has been held that a charge of possession does
not require proof that the defendant was aware that the image was of a
child.[250] However, the offence of 'making', for which no statutory defence
is available, requires proof that the defendant knew, or was aware that
it was likely, that the image was child pornography. 'It follows (very
ironically) that the prosecution have a heavier burden in the absence of
the statutory defence.'[251]

In addition, the issue has been addressed by the UK Sentencing Advisory Panel which has recommended that where the offence of making is
based on the downloading of images for personal use, it should be treated
for sentencing purposes as equivalent to possession.[252] This is, however,
a stop-gap measure which should ideally be addressed by amendments to
the legislation itself.

5. Offering or making available

Title 3, Art. 9(1)(b) of the Cybercrime Convention refers to 'offering or
making available' child pornography through a computer system. 'Offering' is intended to cover soliciting others to obtain child pornography, and

248 A. A. Gillespie, 'Child pornography: Balancing substantive and evidential law to safe-
      guard children effectively from abuse' (2005) 9 *The International Journal of Evidence and
      Proof* 29, 44.
249 *Ibid.*, 39.   250 See pp. 318–19.
251 *R* v. *C* [2004] All ER 82 at [30] per Hooper LJ.
252 UK Sentencing Advisory Panel, *Offences Involving Child Pornography*, p. 7.

implies that the person offering the material can actually provide it.[253] 'Making available' is 'intended to cover the placing of child pornography on line for the use of others' – for example, via websites, and includes the creation or compilation of hyperlinks to child pornography sites.[254]

These offences do not necessarily involve the active dissemination of child pornography; it is enough to simply offer such material to others:

> The fact that a web site is a somewhat passive medium, requiring the reader to take positive steps in order to access the posted material does not detract from the fact that, in up-loading the material to the web site, [the respondent] communicated the material in issue.[255]

The Convention and each jurisdiction, other than the United States, focus on those who are offering rather than seeking such material. In the United States it is also an offence to seek child pornography. This is distinct from offences relating to procuring as it does not require material to in fact be downloaded. Although this relates to conduct which indicates a willingness to deal in child pornography rather than dealing in specific items of child pornography, it is prohibited because it directly encourages the production and distribution of material created by abusing children.[256]

The following offences fall within the category of 'offering or making available':

1. publish
2. make available
3. show
4. advertise.

A. Publish

In Australia and Canada it is an offence to publish child pornography.[257] The ordinary meaning of 'publish' is 'to make publicly or generally known', and would seem readily applicable to material posted on a website, bulletin board, or other public forum. In R v. *Fellows and Arnold*[258] it was held that placing material on the Internet for downloading, even if subject to

253 Cybercrime Convention, Explanatory Report, [95].   254 *Ibid.*
255 *Warman* v. *Kyburz*, 2003 CHRT 18 at [9].
256 *US* v. *Pabon-Cruz*, 255 F Supp 2d 200, 210 (SD NY 2003).
257 Criminal Code (Cth), s. 474.19(1)(a)(v) and Criminal Code (Can), s. 163.1(2).
258 *R* v. *Fellows and Arnold* [1997] 2 All ER 548 at 558–9 per Evans LJ. Also see *Dow Jones & Company Inc.* v. *Gutnick* (2002) 210 CLR 575.

a password, was to 'publish' within the terms of the Obscene Publications Act 1959 (UK).

By definition, 'publish' implies that the material is made available to the public or a section of the public. It is therefore not apt to describe the transmission of material between two people or to the creation of material purely for personal use.[259] Such conduct would have to be charged as distribution or possession.

B. Make available

In Australia and Canada, it is an offence to 'make available' child pornography.[260] As noted above, this term is included within the Convention and is intended to cover the placing of pornography on websites,[261] and the use of hyperlinks to facilitate access to child pornography.[262]

Hyperlinks facilitate movement from one webpage to another and are generally one of three types.[263] The first is where the user is transferred to another page which itself contains a number of links but not the infringing material. It is then for the user to further navigate to find the infringing material. The second type takes the user to another page which contains the infringing material, but the user must click on the relevant link to commence the download. The third type directly transfers the user to a file on the linked-to website such that the download commences automatically.

The question of whether hyperlinking material falls within the meaning of 'make available' was considered in the context of copyright infringement in *Universal City Studios* v. *Reimerdes*.[264] The defendant had devised a computer program which would circumvent encryption on DVDs so that the contents could be copied. It was alleged that this was in breach of the Digital Millennium Copyright Act, in particular 17 USC § 1201(a)(2) prohibits offering to the public, providing or otherwise trafficking in circumvention technology. There was no doubt that the defendants' website had offered the technology. However, when they removed the material in response to an injunction, they provided links to as many mirror sites as possible in order to make an effective remedy difficult if not impossible.

259 *R* v. *Quick* (2004) 148 A Crim R 51 at [65]–[66] per Redlich J.
260 Criminal Code (Cth), s. 474.19(1)(a)(iv) and Criminal Code (Can), s. 163.1(2).
261 *Leonard* v. *R* [2007] NSWCCA 197.
262 Cybercrime Convention, Explanatory Report, [95].
263 *Universal City Studios* v. *Reimerdes*, 111 F Supp 2d 294, 325 (SD NY 2000).
264 *Ibid.*

It was held that this constituted 'offering to the public' or 'providing or otherwise trafficking in' the circumvention technology.

To 'traffic' in something is to engage in dealings in it. 'To provide' is to make available or furnish and 'to offer' is to present or hold out for consideration.[265] The court held that all three forms of hyperlink discussed above may fall within this definition.[266] Where the link creates an automatic download, it was held that they are engaged in the functional equivalent of transferring the material themselves. The same is true where the link was to a site with only the code on it, but the requester had the option of commencing the download. 'The only distinction is that the entity extending to the user the option of downloading the program is the transferee site rather than defendants, a distinction without a difference.'[267]

More difficult is the situation where there is other material on the site, including the offending software. A person who links to another site does not necessarily offer, traffic or provide everything that is on that site. The example given was that if the offending software were on the website of the *Los Angeles Times*, every person who linked to that site would not be guilty of offering or trafficking in the software. The difference here was that the defendants urged others to link to these sites in order to download the offending material.[268]

It is arguable that this decision is of limited authority in this context, given that the meaning of 'make available' was considered within the much more expansive phrase 'offering to the public' or 'providing or otherwise trafficking in' the infringing material. However, the phrase was specifically considered, and a contrary view reached, by the Federal Court of Australia in *Universal Music Australia Pty Ltd* v. *Cooper*.[269]

This case also concerned an action for copyright infringement, this time against a website which allowed users to download files of copyrighted works in mp3 format. To the extent that the site was itself hosting material for download, it was clearly infringing copyright. However, the site also provided hyperlinks to other websites which would allow copyrighted material to be downloaded directly from that other site. A specific question which the court considered was whether this fell within the definition of 'communicate', which includes 'to make available online or electronically transmit'.[270]

---

265 *Ibid.*, 325 citing the Compact Edition of the *Oxford English Dictionary* (1971).
266 *Ibid.*, 325.   267 *Ibid.*   268 *Ibid.*   269 (2005) 150 FCR 1.
270 Copyright Act 1968 (Cth), s. 10(1).

It was held that in the absence of a definition, the words 'make available on-line' must be given their ordinary meaning. Although citing *Universal City Studios* v. *Reimerdes* without apparent disapproval, Justice Tamberlin held that in providing hyperlinks to other sites hosting the infringing material the defendant had not 'made available' the recordings. He had merely facilitated access to other websites which made such material available. The file did not pass through or via the website, but was downloaded directly between the remote website and the requester.[271] 'While the request that triggers the downloads is made from the [defendant's] website, it is the remote website which makes the music available.'[272] For the same reason it could not be said that the defendant electronically transmitted the work.[273]

C. Show

Under s. 1(1)(b) Protection of Children Act 1978 (UK) it is an offence to 'show' child pornography. Although the commission of the offence may be as simple as showing an image to another person,[274] 'to show' in this context requires a showing to a third party. It is not satisfied by a showing by and to the person in possession.[275]

This provision was considered by the Court of Appeal in *R* v. *Fellows and Arnold*.[276] The defendant made images of child pornography available for download on the Internet, subject to users providing a password. Although the court accepted for the purposes of the proceedings that 'to show' is active, rather than passive, it rejected the suggestion that the defendant had been passive in simply allowing others access to his archive of images. Far from passively storing the images:

> [h]e took whatever steps were necessary not merely to store the data on his computer but also to make it available worldwide to other computers via the internet. He corresponded by e-mail with those who sought to have access to it and he imposed certain conditions before they were permitted to do so. He gave permission by giving them the password. He did all of this with the sole object of allowing others, as well as himself, to view exact reproductions of the photographs stored in his archive.[277]

271 *Universal Music Australia Pty Ltd* v. *Cooper* (2005) 150 FCR 1 at [16] per Tamberlin J.
272 *Ibid.*, at [17].   273 See p. 294.
274 *Lee* v. *R* (2000) 112 A Crim R 168 in the context of the offence of 'displaying' under the Western Australian legislation.
275 *R* v. *ET* (1999) *Criminal Law Review* 749.   276 [1997] 2 All ER 548.
277 *Ibid.*, at 558 per Evans LJ.

Giving others the password was akin to giving them the key to a library where the picture was exposed, and would amount to 'showing' the picture to those persons.[278] Equally, the data was 'shown, played or projected' to those who gained access within the meaning of the Obscene Publications Act 1959. Although these particular means were not available in 1959, they could nevertheless be regarded as within the ordinary meaning of those words.[279]

D. Advertise

In some jurisdictions it is an offence to advertise child pornography. For example, under s. 1(1)(d) Protection of Children Act 1978 (UK) it is an offence for a person to publish or cause to be published any advertisement likely to be understood as conveying that the advertiser distributes or shows such indecent photographs or pseudo-photographs of children, or intends to do so.[280] Consistent with the Cybercrime Convention, these provisions apply only to advertisements which offer child pornography to others. In contrast, 18 USC § 2251(d) makes it an offence to knowingly make, print, publish, or cause to be made, printed, or published, any notice or advertisement *seeking or offering* visual depictions of minors engaging in sexually explicit conduct, or participation in such conduct for the purpose of producing such depictions.[281]

In *US* v. *Rowe*[282] the defendant appealed his conviction under what was then 18 USC § 2251(c) (now § 2251(d)) in respect of a posting he made to an Internet chat room known as 'preteen00'. The posting read '[v2.3b] Fserve Trigger: !*tun* Ratio 1:1 Offering: *Pre boys/girl pics.* Read the rules. [1 of 2 slots in use].' Evidence was tendered by the prosecution which explained that this posting indicated the software program used by the defendant, the password needed to access the file server, that the pictures were of pre-teen boys and girls and that a person wishing to access the images would have to read the rules of use and upload an equivalent number of images to his computer.[283] When a detective attempted to access the material without uploading equivalent images he

---

278 *Ibid.*   279 *Ibid.*, at 559. Also see *US* v. *Pabon-Cruz*, 255 F Supp 2d 200 (SD NY 2003).
280 Also see Criminal Code (Can), s. 163.1(3).
281 Emphasis added. Also see 18 USC 2252A(a)(3)(B). In contrast to other provisions concerned with child pornography, this offence does not require proof that the defendant knew that the visual depictions advertised were of actual children: *US* v. *Pabon-Cruz*, 255 F Supp 2d 200, 209–11 (SD NY 2003).
282 414 F 3d 271 (2nd Cir 2005).   283 *Ibid.*, 273.

was disconnected. A search warrant was subsequently executed and 12,000 child pornographic images and videos were found on the defendant's computer.

The court rejected the defendant's argument that the posting did not constitute an advertisement as it did not specifically refer to pornography, but rather only referred to pictures of prepubescent boys and girls. '[T]here is no requirement that an advertisement must specifically state that it offers or seeks a visual depiction to violate 18 USC § 2251(c)(1)(A)... "No particular magic words or phrases need to be included."'[284] Viewed in the context of a chat room with postings such as 'anybody with baby sex pics for trade?', there was no doubt that the defendant's posting knowingly offered or sought images depicting minors engaged in sexually explicit conduct.[285]

6. Distributing or transmitting

We have seen that digital technology has contributed to the worldwide distribution of child pornography, and that combating this illicit trade is a major focus of law enforcement. Accordingly, the Cybercrime Convention requires parties to criminalise the distribution or transmission of child pornography through a computer system.[286]

Although most jurisdictions already criminalise the physical distribution of child pornography, it was considered that the increasing use of the Internet as the primary instrument for trading such material required specific provisions to be made in the Convention.[287] In most jurisdictions this is encompassed by offences of distributing and/or transmitting child pornography which are readily applicable to the online environment. More challenging are offences such as 'transporting' or 'importing' which more strongly connote the physical movement of goods. Their application in a digital context requires an internal perspective, whereby transfer of data is seen as equivalent to moving an image from one place to another. While an external perspective may suggest that there is no physical movement of the image and therefore no offence, in practice courts have had no difficulty in applying the ordinary meaning of these words to the transmission of digital images.

---

284 Ibid., 277, citing US v. Pabon-Cruz, 255 F Supp 2d 200, 218 (SD NY 2003).
285 Ibid., 276.   286 Art. 9(1)(c).
287 Cybercrime Convention, Explanatory Report, [93].

There are four categories of offence which broadly fall within the notion of distributing or transmitting. They are:

1. distribution
2. transmitting
3. transporting
4. importing/exporting.

A. Distribution

Each jurisdiction prohibits the distribution of child pornography,[288] and in all but the UK the term is undefined. In the UK, 'distribution' is defined to include parting 'with possession of it to, or expose(ing) or offer(ing) it for acquisition by, another person'.[289] In other jurisdictions, the word is given its ordinary meaning which is to 'deal out, give share of to each of a number; spread about, scatter, put at different points, divide into parts, arrange, classify'.[290]

'Distribution' involves the active dissemination of child pornography,[291] and is arguably inapplicable to the process of downloading images where the recipient is the end-user. It is, however, clearly applicable to the process of sending images over computer or other networks by email[292] or in chat rooms,[293] and has been held to apply to the uploading of files onto bulletin boards, including those requiring a password to access.[294] Although it has been applied in the context of peer-to-peer networks,[295] this would seem more accurately to be described as 'making available'.[296]

---

288 Criminal Code (Cth), s. 474.19(1)(a)(v), Criminal Code (Can), s. 163.1(3), Protection of Children Act 1978 (UK), s. 1(1)(b), and 18 USC § 2252A(a)(2). In relation to the US provision, it has been held that, consistent with other provisions, the word 'knowingly' modifies the whole phrase so that the prosecution must prove that the defendant was aware that the material he was distributing was child pornography: *US* v. *Pabon-Cruz*, 255 F Supp 2d 200, 205–6 (SD NY 2003).
289 Protection of Children Act 1978 (UK), s. 1(2).
290 *R* v. *Hurtubise*, 1997 BCTC LEXIS 4227 at [11] per Smith J, citing the *Concise Oxford Dictionary* (1982).
291 Cybercrime Convention, Explanatory Report, [96].
292 *R* v. *Elder*, 2002 MB C LEXIS 533.
293 *R* v. *Dunphy*, 2003 NBQB 277; *R.* v. *Larocque* 2004 ABPC 114.
294 *R* v. *Pecciarich* (1995) 22 OR (3d) 748 at 765 per Sparrow Prov Div J. Also see *R* v. *Hurtubise*, 1997 BCTC LEXIS 4227.
295 *R* v. *Walsh*, 75 OR (3d) 38 (2005).   296 See p. 288.

B. Transmit

In Australia it is an offence to 'transmit' child pornography.[297] While the term is undefined, its ordinary meaning is 'to cause (a thing) to pass, go, or be conveyed to another person, place, or thing; to send across an intervening space; to convey, transfer'.[298] It is therefore well suited to the sending of child pornography via a computer system,[299] whether by uploading, email, peer-to-peer or any other form of electronic communication. However, it has been held in the context of copyright infringement that because the files do not pass through or via the website, but are downloaded directly between the remote website and the requester, the use of hyperlinks does not constitute electronically transmitting the work.[300]

C. Transport

In the United States it is an offence to transport or ship child pornography, including by means of a computer system.[301] We will see that an individual who downloads material takes possession or accepts delivery of the visual image has 'received' that image.[302] Equally, such conduct may be encompassed by the dictionary definitions of 'transport' and 'ship', where 'transport' is defined as 'to carry, convey, or remove from one place or person to another; to convey across,' and 'shipping' is one manner of transporting.[303] Consequently, while downloading undoubtedly constitutes receiving, it could also be argued that the defendant has moved that image from one place to another and thereby transported it.[304]

The fact that Congress made separate provision for transporting/shipping and receiving suggests that they are meant to regulate different types of behaviour. What, then, is the difference between receiving, shipping and transporting? Looking to the purpose of the statute is unhelpful as the penalties and sentencing guideline ranges for both provisions are identical.[305] It has been held that that the act of downloading images 'is more analogous to ordering materials over the phone and receiving

---

297 Criminal Code (Cth), ss. 474.19(1)(a)(iii) and 474.22(1)(a)(iii).
298 *Oxford English Dictionary.*   299 Cybercrime Convention, Explanatory Report, [96].
300 *Universal Music Australia Pty Ltd* v. *Cooper* (2005) 150 FCR 1 at 17 per Tamberlin J.
301 18 USC §§ 2252A(a)(1)(2).   302 See p. 298.
303 *US* v. *Mohrbacher*, 182 F 3d 1041, 1048–9 (9th Cir 1999), citing the *Oxford English Dictionary* and *Webster's Third New International Dictionary* (1986). Also see *US* v. *Thomas*, 74 F 3d 701 (6th Cir 1996).
304 *Ibid.*, 1049.   305 *Ibid.*

materials through the mail than to sending or shipping such materials'.[306] Consequently, the person who is responsible for making the images available on a bulletin board or similar mechanism such as a webpage is properly charged with shipping or transporting images, while the person who downloads an image is guilty of receiving or possessing but not of shipping or transporting them.[307]

It has been pointed out that 18 USC § 2252(a)(2) prohibits 'receiving or *distributing*' images rather than 'receiving or possessing' images as stated in *US* v. *Mohrbacher*.[308] This then raises the question of why Congress would prohibit shipping and transporting in § 2252(a)(1) and also distributing in § 2252(a)(2). Professor Kerr suggests that the answer lies in the jurisdictional differences between the provisions, with § 2252(a)(1) prohibiting the movement of images across state lines, while § 2252(a)(2) is concerned with images that have been shipped in interstate or foreign commerce.[309] Although there will still be overlap, this does carve out a distinct role for each provision.

D. Importation/exportation

Ordinarily, the importation of child pornography will fall within customs legislation. However, both Canada[310] and the United States[311] have provisions which deal expressly with the importation/exportation of child pornography. Because child pornography will be downloaded commonly from another jurisdiction, evidence of possession may also be evidence of importation. For example, in *R* v. *Daniels*[312] where the defendant downloaded material from outside Canada it was conceded by defence counsel that if the defendant was found to be in possession of the material, then he must necessarily have imported it.

7. Procuring child pornography

We will see that traditional notions of possession may prove problematic in the digital environment, principally due to notions of physical custody and control which evolved in the context of tangible items. While actual

---

306 *Ibid.*, 1050.   307 *Ibid.* Also see *US* v. *Hamilton*, 413 F 3d 1138 (10th Cir, 2005).
308 Kerr, *Computer Crime Law*, p. 220.   309 *Ibid.*, p. 221.
310 Criminal Code (Can), s. 163.1(3).
311 18 USC § 2260 (b). In contrast to 18 USC § 2252A(a)(2), this offence is clearly targeted at extraterritorial conduct: *US* v. *Reeves*, 62 MJ 88, 93 (2005).
312 *R* v. *Daniels*, 2004 NLSCTD 27 at [22] per Fowler J.

possession may be difficult to prove, in many cases it is clearly established, often on their own admission, that the defendant did in fact view child pornography. In addition, Internet records, both on the defendant's computer and in the records of ISPs, may provide evidence that the defendant in fact downloaded child pornography, irrespective of whether it was viewed, saved to disk or otherwise dealt with. It may therefore be argued that rather than prosecuted for possession, they should be prosected for 'accessing' child pornography.[313]

Within the framework of the Cybercrime Convention, such conduct falls under the heading of 'procuring', which is intended to encompass a person who actively obtains child pornography; for example, by downloading it, whether for himself or another.[314] As with other offences, the rationale for punishing the act of procuring is that it increases market demand for child pornography.[315] Relevant offences are found in Australia,[316] Canada[317] and the United States,[318] with the relevant conduct falling within four categories:

1. accessing
2. causing to transmit
3. receiving
4. requesting.[319]

Each jurisdiction requires a high level of culpability in relation to such conduct, with each requiring proof of intention and knowledge or, at the very least, recklessness.[320] This is an important limitation in ensuring such offences do not capture access which is truly inadvertent. Spam emails, the use of pop-ups, or mislabelled hyperlinks all provide plausible scenarios where a person may inadvertently find they have accessed child pornography.[321] The Internet Watch Foundation in the United Kingdom

---

313 State v. Jensen, 173 P 3d 1046, 1051–2 (Ariz Ct App 2008).
314 Cybercrime Convention, Art. 9(1)(d); Cybercrime Convention, Explanatory Report, [97].
315 US v. Barevich, 445 F 3d 956, 959 (7th Cir 2006).
316 Criminal Code (Cth), ss. 474.19(1)(a)(i)(ii) and 474.22(1)(a)(i)(ii).
317 Criminal Code (Can), s. 163.1(4.1).   318 18 USC §§ 2252(a)(2) and 2252A(a)(2).
319 It may also be possible to charge a defendant with inciting another to distribute child pornography; R v. O'Shea [2004] Criminal Law Review 894.
320 Criminal Code (Cth), ss. 474.19(2) and 474.22(2), Criminal Code (Can), s. 163.1(4.1) and 18 USC §§ 2252(a)(2) and 2252A(a)(2).
321 For a detailed discussion of the various ways in which material may inadvertently be accessed, see M. J. Zappen, 'How well do you know your computer? The level of scienter in 18 U.S.C. §1462' (2003) 66 Albany Law Review 1161.

reported that in one week in June 2003 they received 435 reports of child pornography-related spam, with 5 per cent of those being found to relate to child-abuse websites.[322]

Courts in the United States have clearly rejected any suggestion that procuring offences should not apply where the material is received only for 'personal use'.[323] Ordinarily, procuring-type offences would be punished more severely than simple possession on the basis that procuring increases the market for child pornography whereas possession for personal use does not.[324] However, in many cases procuring is simply an alternative to a charge of possession, punishing essentially the same conduct.[325] On the other hand, it is increasingly accepted that the possessor must at some point have received or created the material, and as such is not entitled to particular leniency. Traditional sentencing distinctions may therefore no longer be appropriate in the online environment.

A. Accessing

In Australia it is an offence for a person to intentionally use a carriage service to access material, being reckless as to whether that material is child pornography or child abuse material respectively.[326] 'Access' is defined to include:

(a) the display of the material by a computer or any other output of the material from a computer; or
(b) the copying or moving of the material to any place in a computer or to a data storage device; or
(c) in the case of material that is a program – the execution of the program.[327]

Similarly, under s. 163.1(4.1) Criminal Code (Can) it is an offence to 'access' child pornography, where 'accesses' means 'knowingly causes child pornography to be viewed by . . . himself or herself'.[328]

---

322 All Party Parliamentary Internet Group, 'Spam': Report of an Inquiry by the All Party Internet Group (2003), p. 6.
323 US v. Ellison, 113 F 3d 77, 81 (7th Cir 1997). Also see US v. Moore, 916 F 2d 1131, 1137 (6th Cir 1990) and US v. Watzman, 486 F 3d 1004 (7th Cir 2007).
324 US v. Richardson, 238 F 3d 837, 839 (7th Cir 2001).
325 Kerr, Computer Crime Law, p. 222.
326 Criminal Code (Cth), ss. 474.19(1)(a)(i)(ii), 474.19(2)(b), 474.22(1)(a)(i)(ii) and 474.22(2)(b).
327 S. 473.1.
328 Criminal Code (Can), s. 163.1(4.2). It is an aggravating factor if the person committed the offence with intent to make a profit: s. 163.1(4.3).

The words 'displaying' or 'viewing' of child pornography may apply to those situations where it is difficult to prove that the defendant knowingly had custody or control of such images, but there is evidence that the defendant did in fact view or display the material. Insofar as the Australian provisions apply to 'copying or moving' of material or 'execution' of a program, these are likely to encounter many of the same difficulties as proof of possession, discussed below.

These provisions avoid problems of over-breadth by requiring that the defendant *caused* the access. They do not apply to a person who simply views child pornography which is not in his or her possession and which has been procured by another. Unlike the Australian provision, the Canadian offence is not limited to access which is via a computer.

B. Causing to transmit

In Australia and Canada it is an offence for a person to cause child pornography to be transmitted to himself or herself.[329] Such offences obviously apply only where there is evidence that the material has been received from an external source. They do, however, have the advantage over offences of possession and displaying/viewing in that they do not require proof that the defendant interacted with the material beyond the act of causing it to be transmitted.

It is unclear whether such provisions encompass situations such as that in *R* v. *Daniels* where the defendant sought to access child pornography but the download was only partial.[330] On a strict reading, it would appear that there is no need to prove that the material was actually received by the defendant, so long as it was transmitted. While the ordinary meaning of 'transmit' would suggest that the item transmitted must be conveyed to another person or place, that person does not have to be the defendant. Data which is requested and then terminated is still transmitted, even if it does not reach its intended destination.

C. Receiving

In the United States it is an offence to knowingly receive visual depictions of minors engaging in sexually explicit conduct and child pornography

---

329 Criminal Code (Cth), ss. 474.19(1)(a)(i)(ii) and 474.22(1)(a)(i)(ii), and Criminal Code (Can), s. 163(4.2).

330 See p. 308.

respectively.[331] The meaning of 'receiving' in this context was considered by the Ninth Circuit in *US v. Mohrbacher*.[332] In this case, the defendant was convicted of transporting, receiving and possessing child pornography having downloaded images from an electronic bulletin board based in Denmark.[333] The court looked to the ordinary meaning of 'receive', which is 'to take into one's hand, or into one's possession (something held out or offered by another); to take delivery of (a thing) from another, either for oneself or for a third party'.[334] It was held that as an individual who downloads material takes possession or accepts delivery of the visual image he or she has therefore certainly received it.

It seems clear that these provisions require proof that the defendant in fact received the material. It would not be enough to prove that he had caused it to be transmitted, but that it had not arrived at its destination, either through the actions of the defendant or some other cause. For this reason, it has been held that the act of downloading child pornography may constitute both the offence of possession and receiving.[335]

It is also possible to possess an image, without having received it. For example, a person who requests adult pornography but unknowingly receives child pornography would not be guilty of receiving. He may, however, be guilty of possession if he decided to retain it.[336] A person who discovers child pornography on another's computer, or who creates an image of child pornography, may be in possession although he has not received that image.[337]

At a more general level, it is arguable that 'receiving' does not require the same level of control by the defendant as possession. One meaning of 'receive' is to ' take... into one's possession'. An analogy may therefore be drawn with the offence of obtaining possession of objectionable material under s. 101(b) Classification (Publications, Films And Computer

---

331 18 USC §§ 2252(a)(2) and 2252A(a)(2).

332 182 F 3d 1041 (9th Cir 1999). See generally, J. Hitt, 'Child pornography and technology: The troubling analysis of United States v Mohrbacher' (2001) 34 *University of California Davis Law Review* 1129.

333 18 USC § 2252(a)(1).

334 *US v. Mohrbacher*, 182 F 3d 1041, 1048 (9th Cir 1999) citing *Oxford English Dictionary* (1989).

335 *US v. Romm*, 455 F 3d 990, 1002 (9th Cir 2006); *US v. Kamen*, 491 F Supp 2d 142, 150 (D Mass 2007); *US v. Watzman*, 486 F 3d 1004 (7th Cir 2007). Cf *US v. Gourde*, 440 F 3d 1065, 1081–2 (9th Cir 2005).

336 *US v. Myers*, 355 F 3d 1040, 1042 (7th Cir 2004); *US v. Watzman*, 486 F 3d 1004, 1009 (7th Cir 2007).

337 *US v. Malik*, 385 F 3d 758, 759 (7th Cir 2004).

Games) Enforcement Act 1996 (WA). The interpretation of this provision was considered by the Supreme Court of Western Australia in *Haynes v. Hughes*.[338] The defendant was charged after an image file was found on his work computer, depicting sexual activity between a man and a woman where the woman was suspended above the man by a large cargo hook. The defendant's explanation as to how the file came to be there was that he had moved a number of unopened emails to his work folder for later perusal. When he eventually opened the file he claimed he was shocked at its content and deleted it immediately.

It was held that on a charge of this nature, 'possession of the offending article was obtained when it was received into the computer's programs, not when it was dealt with internally within the computer system by transferring it to a personal directory or otherwise'.[339] It is therefore arguable that on a charge of receiving it is not necessary to prove that the accused knowingly stored or otherwise dealt with the material as would be the case with possession.

In the context of the US provisions it has been held that although they relate to receiving, not possession, it is still necessary to prove knowing receipt. This requires proof not only that the defendant knew of the explicit nature of the material, but also the age of the performers.[340] This knowledge must exist at the time of receiving. It is not sufficient to show merely that the defendant received the material without knowledge of its content, for example where the material is received by accident or mistake.[341]

D. Requesting

Although the combination of displaying, viewing, transmitting and receiving is likely to cover the majority of circumstances, it would seem that none of the above provisions would apply where the defendant requested data but no data was provided. For example, a broken hyperlink or a so-called 'honey pot' website – that is, a website established by law enforcement which falsely advertises child pornography for

---

338 [2001] WASCA 397.   339 *Ibid.*, at [3] per Murray J and at [21] per Anderson J.
340 *US* v. *X-Citement Video Inc.*, 513 US 64 (1994); *US* v. *Pabon-Cruz*, 255 F Supp 2d 200, 205–6 (SD NY 2003); *US* v. *Irving*, 452 F 3d 110, 122 (2nd Cir 2006).
341 *US* v. *Fabiano*, 169 F 3d 1299, 1304 (10th Cir 1999). Also see *Haynes* v. *Hughes* [2001] WASCA 397 and *US* v. *Myers*, 355 F 3d 1040 (7th Cir 2004). Cf *US* v. *Polizzi*, 2008 US Dist LEXIS 26223 (ED NY 2008).

the purpose of capturing the IP addresses of those who request such content.[342]

In each jurisdiction, such conduct may be charged as an attempt as it is likely that where the defendant clicks on a link clearly designated as providing child pornography, such conduct will be regarded as sufficiently proximate to the completed offence notwithstanding the material was not downloaded. Alternatively, consideration could be given to an offence of 'requesting' child pornography. For example, under s. 101(1)(e) Classification (Publications, Films And Computer Games) Enforcement Act 1996 (WA) it is an offence to use a computer service to request the transmission of objectionable material knowing it to be objectionable material.

8. Possession of child pornography

The possession of child pornography is an offence in each jurisdiction and essentially takes two forms. The first is simple possession, where possession alone is sufficient to constitute an offence. This is an offence in Canada,[343] the UK[344] and the United States.[345] Although there is no federal offence of 'simple possession' in Australia, it is an offence in all states and territories.[346] The second category of offence is possession with an additional intent, such as an intention to sell or supply. Such offences are also found in Australia,[347] Canada,[348] the UK[349] and the United States.[350]

Although there are of course variations, the concept of possession is similar in each jurisdiction and may be divided into four components.[351] Did the defendant:

---

342 Krone, *International Police Operations*, pp. 4–5. Also see, Jenkins, *Beyond Tolerance*, pp. 159–64.
343 Criminal Code (Can), s. 163.1(4).
344 Criminal Justice Act 1988 (UK), ss. 160 and 161.
345 18 USC §§ 2252(a)(4) and 2252A(a)(5).
346 Crimes Act 1900 (ACT), s. 65; Crimes Act 1900 (NSW), s. 91H(3); Criminal Code Act (NT), s. 125B(1); Criminal Law Consolidation Act 1935 (SA), s. 63A(1); Criminal Code Act 1899 (Qld), s. 228D; Classification (Publications, Films and Computer Games) Enforcement Act 1995 (SA), s. 74A; Crimes Act 1958 (Vic), s. 70(1); and Classification (Publications, Films and Computer Games) Enforcement Act 1996 (WA), s. 60(4).
347 Criminal Code (Cth), ss. 474.2 and 474.23.
348 Criminal Code (Can), s. 163.1(2)(3). See, e.g., *R v. Faget*, 2004 BC C LEXIS 264.
349 Protection of Children Act 1978 (UK), s. 1(1)(c).
350 18 USC §§ 2252(a)(3) and 2252A(a)(4).
351 *Moors* v. *Burke* (1919) 26 CLR 265; Criminal Code (Can), s. 4(1); *DPP* v. *Brooks* [1974] AC 862 at 866 per Lord Diplock; *R v. Boyesen* [1982] AC 768 at 773–4 per Lord Scarman;

(a) have physical possession of the item
(b) know that he or she had physical possession of the item
(c) intend to exercise physical possession of the item
(d) know the nature of the thing possessed?

A. *Physical possession*

A defendant may be in possession of an item in one of two ways. The
first is where the item is in the physical custody or control of the defendant. The second is where the item is 'in a place to which he ... may go
without physical bar in order to obtain such manual possession'.[352] These
two forms of possession are referred to as actual and de facto custody
respectively.[353] They were described by the High Court of Australia in
Moors v. *Burke*[354] where it was held that in order to prove possession, it
must be shown that the accused had:

> at the time, in actual fact and without the necessity of taking any further
> step, the complete present personal physical control of the property to the
> exclusion of others not acting in concert with the accused, and whether he
> has that control by having the property in his present manual custody, or
> by having it where he alone has the exclusive right or power to place his
> hands on it, and so have manual custody when he wishes.[355]

Actual custody

The most obvious form of possession is where the accused literally has the
item in his or her 'present manual custody'. For example, if the defendant
was found to be holding the laptop, memory stick or camera[356] containing
the relevant images then, subject to the requirement of knowledge, he
would be in possession of those images. However, in order to prove
possession it is not necessary for the item to be literally in the defendant's

---

US v. *Tucker*, 305 F 3d 1193, 1204 (10th Cir 2002); and *US* v. *Romm*, 455 F 3d 990, 998 (9th Cir 2006).
352 *Dib* v. *R* (1991) 52 A Crim R 64 at 66 per Hunt J.
353 *Williams* v. *Douglas* (1949) 78 CLR 521 at 527 per Latham CJ, Dixon and McTiernan JJ. 'De facto' possession is also referred to as 'constructive possession' in Canada and the US: *R* v. *Daniels* [2004] NLSCTD 27 at [38]–[40] per Fowler J; *US* v. *Tucker*, 305 F 3d 1193, 1204 (10th Cir 2002); and W. R. LaFave, *Criminal Law*, 4th edn (St. Paul, MN: Thomson, 2003), p. 309.
354 (1919) 26 CLR 265.   355 *Ibid.*, at 274 per Isaacs J.
356 For convenience, the various items which may be used to store digital images will be referred to collectively as 'storage devices'.

hands; it is sufficient if it is under his physical control.[357] So, for example, a computer that is in a person's house while that person is present, or in a car which he or she is driving, may still be regarded as being in that person's physical custody or control, the issue being a question of fact for the jury.

In this respect, possession of digital images is no different to possession of other tangible items. The defendant is in possession of a tangible item which he knows to contain the intangible images. However, in the context of data, custody or control may also be proved by the defendant's ability to control that data in some way; whether by displaying an image, copying the file, printing, sending in an email or the like.

For example, in US v. Tucker[358] the defendant, an admitted paedophile, accessed images of child pornography using his computer to visit websites and newsgroups, some of which required payment of a membership fee and a password. Forensic examination recovered some 27,000 images, an estimated 90–95 per cent of which were child pornography. These images were primarily recovered from the 'Internet Explorer' cache file and the temporary internet files in the computer hard drive's 'recycle bin'. Although the defendant routinely viewed child pornography, he did not ordinarily save them to disk. He was also in the habit of deleting files in the cache when he had finished viewing the images. The defendant therefore denied being in possession of the images on the basis that he could not be found to be in possession of something which he didn't 'down load, copy or intentionally store'.[359]

This argument was rejected. The defendant clearly exercised control over the images in a number of ways. He could enlarge or otherwise manipulate them, he could print and he could copy them. In particular, his control over the images automatically stored in the cache was illustrated by his practice of deleting them. This analysis was upheld by the Tenth Circuit. There was expert evidence that the defendant could access the images in the cache file, attach them to emails, rename them, print them; '[a]nything he could do with any other file he could do with these files'.[360]

While Tucker was concerned with the defendant's control over images found in the cache folder subsequent to viewing the images, the same

---

357 R v. Maio [1989] VR 281 at 287–8 per O'Bryan J, citing DPP v. Brooks [1974] AC 862 at 866 per Lord Diplock.
358 150 F Supp 2d 1263 (D Utah 2001).   359 Ibid., 1268.
360 US v. Tucker, 305 F 3d 1193, 1204–5 (10th Cir 2002); cert. denied, Tucker v. US, 537 US 1223 (2003).

analysis may be applied to control which is contemporaneous with viewing. In *US* v. *Romm*[361] the defendant admitted to viewing images of child pornography on the Internet. He would save them to disk, view them for about five minutes, then delete them. The court held that a person 'can receive and possess child pornography without downloading it, if he or she seeks it out and exercises dominion or control over it'.[362] This dominion or control is evidenced by the fact that when viewing the images on the screen, the defendant was able to print them, save them, forward them or delete them. He therefore knowingly exercised custody or control over those images and was consequently in possession.[363]

This raises an important general distinction between merely viewing child pornography and possessing child pornography. Without evidence of custody or control, merely viewing child pornography is not an offence. We therefore see that defendants will sometimes argue that although they admittedly viewed child pornography, they did not actively save the images nor were they aware that the computer automatically did so. It would therefore seem that they are not in possession. Analogies are sometimes drawn with the person walking along a street and seeing a magazine displaying unlawful material. If the person looks, and nothing more, then he or she is not in possession. If, however, he reaches out and takes the magazine then he is in possession.

Such analogies are inapposite in the online environment. Looking at images on the Internet is not analogous to looking at a magazine displayed on a street. Although it may feel like this from an internal perspective, an external perspective tells us that any image displayed on a screen (excepting automatic operations such as pop-ups) results from the voluntary actions of the accused. The link must be clicked in order for the data to be displayed. A person looking over the shoulder of the defendant at an image on screen would not be liable for possession (other than perhaps as an accessory) but the defendant is controlling the image on the screen regardless of whether the image is consciously saved, or whether he is aware it is automatically saved. Subject to satisfying the requisite *mens rea*, the defendant is in possession of the image.

It will commonly be the case that the storage device which contains the prohibited images is shared by a number of people, for example family

---

361 455 F 3d 990 (9th Cir 2006).   362 *Ibid.*, 998.

363 *Ibid.*, 1000. Also see *Atkins* v. *DPP, Goodland* v. *DPP* [2000] 2 All ER 425 at 436 per Simon Brown LJ; leave to appeal to the House of Lords refused: *Atkins* v. *DPP* [2001] 1 WLR 1122.

members or co-workers. In such cases the defendant may plausibly claim that he or she was not in possession of the images; that they were, in fact, in the possession of another person or persons. Where the prosecution cannot exclude the reasonable possibility that another person was in possession of the images then, in the face of the accused's denials, it may not be possible to prove that the accused was in possession.[364] It is therefore necessary either to exclude the possibility of another person being in possession, or prove that the other person was in joint possession.

In this context, the distinction between custody or control of the storage device containing the images, and custody or control of the images themselves, is particularly important. While a number of people may be in possession of the storage device, it is possible that only the defendant is in possession of the relevant files. It is not sufficient to prove that the defendant had custody or control of the storage device which contained the images, it must be proved that he or she had knowing custody or control of the files contained within the device.[365] Relevant factors will include whether the material was hidden, for example in obscure folders. Who else, if anyone, had access to the computer? Could the likelihood that those others were aware of the material be excluded? Were the images password protected and, if so, who knew the passwords?[366]

For example, in *R v. Missions*[367] the accused was charged with possession of child pornography. One image was found on the family computer, to which five other family members had access, while a further sixty-three images were found on three zip disks. The Nova Scotia Court of Appeal upheld the trial judge's finding that the Crown had proved, beyond reasonable doubt, that the accused was in sole possession of those images. Relevant factors included plausible denials of possession by the other residents and evidence that the defendant often downloaded adult pornography, that the zip disks were used by him, that there had been some attempt to organise the files and that in almost all cases the file name gave some indication that the content was child pornography.[368]

Many cases of possession of child pornography are based on images recovered from cache or in the computer's 'recycle bin'. Clearly, where the accused is able to exercise custody or control over those images, he or she

---

364 *US v. Irving*, 452 F 3d 110, 122 (2nd Cir 2006).
365 *R v. Porter* [2006] EWCA Crim 560 at [16] per Dyson LJ.
366 *US v. Kimler*, 335 F 3d 1132, 1140 (10th Cir 2003). Also see *Knight v. McDonald* [2002] TASSC 81 at [11] per Evans J.
367 [2005] NSJ no 177.   368 *Ibid.*, at [10] per Roscoe JA.

may be in possession subject to the requirement of knowledge. However, where an image is deleted and cannot be retrieved by the defendant there is authority that he or she is no longer in possession of that image. In *R* v. *Porter*[369] the defendant was convicted of fifteen counts of making an indecent photograph of a child and two counts of possessing indecent photographs of children.[370] A search of his computer uncovered 3,575 still images and 40 movie files of child pornography. A significant number of the still images, and all of the movie files, had been deleted, including by emptying the computer's 'recycle bin'. A large number of images were also recovered in the form of thumbnails found in a database of a programme called 'ACDSee'. As the larger files associated with the thumbnails had been deleted, they could no longer be viewed. However, a trace of each thumbnail could be recovered using specialist techniques. Other images were also recovered from the cache folder.

It was conceded that the defendant did not have the software to retrieve or view the deleted still or movie files. Further, retrieval of the thumbnail images required specialist forensic techniques and equipment which could only be provided by the US government. The appellant could, however, have acquired software to enable recovery of items emptied from the recycle bin, although there was no evidence he had done this. It was conceded that the thirty-three files in the cache were retrievable and therefore in his possession. The question for the court was whether the defendant could be said to be in possession of those images which were irretrievable, at least by him. Although acknowledging that there are of course differences between possession of illegal drugs and possession of digital images, the court nonetheless could see no reason not to import the concept of having custody or control of the images.[371]

> In the special case of deleted computer images, if a person cannot retrieve or gain access to an image, in our view he no longer has custody or control of the image. He has put it beyond his reach just as does a person who destroys or otherwise gets rid of a hard copy photograph. For this reason, it is not appropriate to say that a person who cannot retrieve an image from the hard disk drive is in possession of the image because he is in possession of the hard disk drive and the computer.[372]

369 *R* v. *Porter* [2006] EWCA Crim 560, cited with approval in *Clark* v. *R* [2008] NSWCCA 122 at [228]–[233] per Bell JA.
370 Protection of Children Act 1978 (UK), s. 1(1)(a)(c) and Criminal Justice Act 1988 (UK), s. 160(1).
371 *R* v. *Porter* [2006] EWCA Crim 560 at [20]–[21] per Dyson LJ, citing *DPP* v. *Brooks* [1974] AC 862 and *R* v. *Boyesen* [1982] AC 768.
372 *Ibid.*, at [22].

It appears that this requirement is independent of knowledge that the image is on the computer drive. The court specifically rejected the suggestion that it would be sufficient to prove possession if the defendant was knowingly in possession of the computer or other device which in turn contained the images, even if the images were in fact irretrievable.[373] Such an interpretation would produce consequences 'so unreasonable that we are not willing to accept it unless we are compelled to do so by the express words of the statute or by necessary implication'.[374] For example, in this case the defendant would remain in possession of deleted images which could only have been retrieved using specialist techniques and equipment supplied with the authorisation of the US government.[375]

The court also considered the example of a person who receives unsolicited images of child pornography by email and deletes them immediately. Suppose that person is aware that the images remain on the hard drive, but are recoverable only by using specialist techniques which he or she does not possess. In the opinion of the court, although the person has knowledge he or she has done all that is reasonably necessary to make them irretrievable and is not guilty of possession. Such evidence may nonetheless prove *prior* possession.[376]

It is a question for the jury whether, at the relevant time, the defendant had custody or control of the image(s). This will in part depend upon the technical skills of the defendant, and will alter over time as the ordinary user becomes progressively more sophisticated. For example, once it may have been difficult to recover images from cache as they are 'system-protected' – that is, access is blocked unless the user executes a 'system command'. However, such commands may now be performed simply by right clicking the mouse and selecting the appropriate command. The images may then be treated in the same way as any other file.[377] Similarly, the defendant who deletes images intending to recover them at a later stage with specialist software may nonetheless be said to remain in possession of those images.[378]

Similar principles could also apply to situations where the defendant has knowledge but cannot exercise custody or control,[379] for example

373 *Ibid.*, at [16].   374 *Ibid.*, at [17].   375 See p. 306.
376 *R* v. *Porter* [2006] EWCA Crim 560 at [18] per Dyson LJ.
377 *US* v. *Romm*, 455 F 3d 990, 995–6, 998 (9th Cir 2006).
378 Y. Akdeniz, 'Possession and dispossession: A critical assessment of defences in cases of possession of indecent photographs of children' (2007) *Criminal Law Review* 274, 284.
379 An analogy may be drawn with drugs cases; see *Davis* v. *R* (1990) 5 WAR 269 at 276 and 279–80 per Malcolm CJ, and *R* v. *Boyce* (1976) 15 SASR 40 at 46 per Bray CJ with whom Zelling J agreed.

where a person is aware that a computer contains child pornography but he or she does not have the password and is therefore unable to gain access. In such cases, it could be argued the accused is not in possession as he or she does not have custody or control.

What of the situation where the defendant begins to download child pornography but for some reason the download is terminated? This issue was considered by the Supreme Court of Newfoundland and Labrador in *R v. Daniels*.[380] In addition to evidence that the accused had in fact downloaded child pornography from a server in Mexico, there was evidence that he had requested that such material be downloaded but terminated the download before it was complete. On the evidence, there was no doubt that the defendant was aware that he was ordering child pornography as he had to read a graphic description before proceeding to download. It was, however, impossible to establish how much of the image appeared on the defendant's screen, and none of the requested images were found on the defendant's computer. It was therefore argued that he was not in possession of the partially downloaded images.

This argument was rejected by the trial judge. Irrespective of whether the image was displayed on the screen, once he requested the image he had complete control over the entire image, or images being sent to him.

> The fact that he chose to 'skip' or 'abort' the transmission after it had begun to appear on his screen establishes the total control he had over the images being sent. It is of no consequence that only a partial image or indeed a random image is being received. The pixels, whether one or a million represent a component and are individually or collectively part of the whole image ... It was his own personal choice as to how much of the image he wished to receive. It is not open to him to say that he did not receive child pornography when he clearly received part of the entire images that he ordered and controlled the amount of the total package he would receive.[381]

This decision was upheld by the Court of Appeal:

> once the downloading had begun, absent some computer malfunction, Daniels had complete control in deciding how much of the image would be displayed on the computer screen. To be in possession of child pornography, it is not necessary for the individual to have viewed the material. For

---

380 *R v. Daniels*, 2004 NLSCTD 27.   381 *Ibid.*, at [34] per Fowler J.

example, a person may obtain pornographic material in an envelope, but without viewing it, either place it in a draw or dispose of it in the garbage. It is the element of control, including deciding what will be done with the material, that is essential to possession.[382]

It is clear that the courts' decision was based on custody or control of the data which was downloaded, and this analysis could equally apply to any situation where the download is terminated, either by the recipient or some other cause. However, it raises a number of issues which were not resolved in the case.

First, as already noted the offence of child pornography in Canada relates to a 'visual representation'. Even if, as is likely, a data file is held to constitute a visual representation, it is unclear whether this could apply to only a part of that file. This would seem to depend on whether the partial file could be converted into an image depicting child pornography. Otherwise, all that could be established on these facts was that part of an image which might ultimately become an image of child pornography, was downloaded. It could not be established that the data was, in fact, a 'visual representation'.

Secondly, the court did not state with precision the location of the data which is in the custody or control of the defendant. There are a number of possible options. It is arguable that the defendant was exercising control of the data in Mexico by sending a request that it be downloaded. If that is correct, then implicit in the judgment is a finding that the offence of possession may be extraterritorial in operation. While that may be correct, it is unfortunate that the issue was not addressed directly. It is more difficult to argue that the defendant has control of data which is actually in transit as the defendant does not at that point have the necessary control: 'It would seem to me that to have the manual handling element . . . necessary to constitute actual possession would require something more than an image in transit . . .'[383] Perhaps the most practical interpretation is that it is only when the data is actually received that there may be some control, or at least the ability to control, such as to demonstrate actual custody. While this would most clearly be satisfied by the defendant printing or saving the images, in this case the defendant 'was directing the computer by his personal input and direction and thereby manually handling the child pornographic material'.[384]

---

382 *Ibid.*, at [12] per Welsh JA.　　383 *Ibid.*, at [33] per Fowler J.　　384 *Ibid.*

De facto custody

The concept of possession also extends to those situations where the defendant does not have physical custody or control of an item, but where 'he alone has the exclusive right or power to place his hands on it, and so have manual custody when he wishes'.[385] Such situations may be described as 'de facto custody', and includes cases where the defendant 'has hidden the thing effectively so that he can take it into his physical custody when he wishes and where others are unlikely to discover it except by accident'.[386] In the context of drug offences this typically applies where the drugs are hidden at another location, such as a locker, to which the defendant has access. The analogous situation in the digital context would be where a storage device is found in premises to which the accused has access, but where he or she is not in actual custody.

However, if applied more broadly it has the potential to greatly expand the notion of possession when applied to digital images. Clearly, it would seem to apply to remote storage of digital files such as where the accused uploads material to a local server or ISP. Where the defendant is able to copy, delete or otherwise manipulate such files remotely, then he or she may be said to be in possession of those files, for example where the images are found on a website maintained by the defendant.[387] Further, the concept could arguably extend to accessing or attempting to access material on a website. Although the defendant would not have the ability to delete such images, it may be argued that he or she is able to exercise control by copying or viewing the file. As discussed above in the context of *Daniels*, this raises significant issues as to the scope of the offence of possession, and in particular whether it is extraterritorial in operation.

There is some authority that, in the context of de facto custody, the prosecution must prove that the defendant has 'the right to exclude any person not acting in concert with him from interference with the property in question.'[388] Such a requirement should not cause difficulties in cases where the defendant has stored material on a network to which only he or she, and possibly a co-offender(s) has access. It would, however, cause considerable, if not insurmountable, obstacles for the prosecution

---

385 *Moors* v. *Burke* (1919) 26 CLR 265 at 274 per Isaacs J, and *US* v. *Taylor*, 13 F 3d 1136, 1144–5 (10th Cir 1997).
386 *Williams* v. *Douglas* (1949) 78 CLR 521 at 527 per Latham CJ, Dixon and McTiernan JJ.
387 *R* v. *W (A Child)* (2000) 27 SR (WA) 148.
388 *Dib* v. *R* (1991) 52 A Crim R 64 at 66 per Hunt J.

in the context of accessing websites, as in such cases the defendant clearly does not have exclusive access. It is, in fact, 'a place where any other person independently of him has an equal right and power of getting it'.[389] Consequently, the defendant would arguably not be in possession of those images.

Such a requirement developed in the context of tangible items which could be reduced to the exclusive possession of either person. For example, in *Moors* v. *Burke* it was held that the defendant was not in possession of the property because it was in a locker to which another person, not acting in concert, had access.[390] It may therefore be argued that this requirement should be reconsidered in its application to intangible digital files which are not necessarily reduced to the exclusive possession of any person who has access to them. Alternatively, such conduct may more appropriately be charged as accessing child pornography.[391]

B. Knowledge

In considering the fault element for possession, it is necessary to distinguish between two types of knowledge. The first is the defendant's knowledge that the item was within his or her custody or control. Secondly, in some jurisdictions, it is also necessary to prove that the defendant knew the nature of the material in his or her possession.

Knowledge of possession

It is well established that the external element of possession also connotes a fault element. That is, it must be proved that the defendant was, at the very least, aware that he or she had custody or control of the particular object. 'You may possess a thing without knowing or comprehending its nature: but you do not possess it unless you know you have it.'[392] A defendant may therefore argue that although child pornography was found in his custody or control, he was unaware of its presence. This most commonly arises in four situations: accident, ignorance, forgetfulness and deletion.

389 *Moors* v. *Burke* (1919) 26 CLR 265 at 274 per Isaacs J.
390 *Ibid.*, at 274–5.   391 See p. 295.
392 *R* v. *Boyesen* [1982] AC 768 at 774 per Lord Scarman. Also see *He Kaw Teh* v. *R* (1985)157 CLR 523 at 539 per Gibbs CJ (with whom Mason J agreed), at 585 per Brennan J and at 599–600 per Dawson J; *R* v. *Beaver* [1957] SCR 531 at 541–2 per Cartwright J; *US* v. *Tucker*, 150 F Supp 2d 1263, 1266 (D Utah 2001); *US* v. *Lacy*, 119 F 3d 742, 747–8 (9th Cir 1997), *US* v. *Romm*, 455 F 3d 990, 1003 (9th Cir 2006).

Accident In some cases, the defendant may allege that material found in his or her custody or control must have been placed there without the defendant's knowledge, for example by another person or by an automatic operation such as a 'pop up'. It is then a question of fact for the prosecution to prove, beyond reasonable doubt, that the defendant was in fact aware of the presence of the material. Failure to do so must result in an acquittal.

As the majority of cases involve considerably more than one or two images of child pornography, this does not generally present a significant obstacle to prosecution. Relevant factors include evidence of downloading,[393] the number of images present, the nature of the file names and evidence of deliberate organisation of the images.[394] For example, in *R v. Liddington*[395] supposed 'accidental' viewing was clearly contradicted by evidence of deliberate downloading and copying even after the accused was aware of the nature of the material. Similarly, in *R v. W (A Child)*[396] the defendant was convicted of possessing child pornography which was found on a website which he maintained. The defendant admitted maintaining the sexually explicit website with a view to making money, but claimed to believe that all of the material on the site related to girls over eighteen. Nonetheless, he conceded that the site was found to contain child pornography, and maintained that someone must have hacked into the site and placed the offending material there without his knowledge. While expert evidence suggested that such a scenario was a theoretical possibility, in the circumstances it was dismissed as 'remote and fanciful'.[397] It is also possible to provide for specific defences to address circumstances of inadvertent possession.[398]

Ignorance The second, and more problematic situation, is where the defendant is shown to have viewed child pornography, but not to have downloaded or otherwise saved the data to a storage device. Although the file may be physically within the custody or control of the defendant, he or she may claim to be unaware of that fact. In such cases, whether

393 *R v. B (DEW)* 2003 WCBJ LEXIS 2477 at [25] per Fradsham Prov Ct J.
394 These factors are discussed in more detail in the context of actual custody (p. 302) and intention to possess (p. 320).
395 *R v. Liddington* (1997) 18 WAR 394 at 402–3 per Ipp J. Also see *Bird v. Peach* [2006] NTCA 7.
396 (2000) 27 SR (WA) 148.
397 *Ibid.*, at 157 per French J. Also see *US v. Stulock*, 308 F 3d 922, 926 (8th Cir 2002).
398 See p. 324.

the defendant is found to be in possession may therefore depend on the extent to which he or she is aware of the way in which computers operate.

In *Atkins v. DPP, Goodland v. DPP*[399] a number of images of child pornography were found on the defendant's computer. While some had been deliberately saved to the hard drive, others had not and were recovered from the cache folder. The Divisional Court held that as knowledge is an essential element of possession under s. 160 Criminal Justice Act 1988 (UK), a defendant cannot be in possession of images if he is unaware that they are stored in the computer, for example images recovered from cache which were viewed by the defendant but not deliberately saved.[400]

A similar approach was adopted in *US v. Bass*,[401] in which the defendant was convicted of knowing possession of over 2,000 images of child pornography. Although the defendant admitted viewing child pornography on the Internet, he denied ever deliberately saving or downloading any of those images. In fact, he claimed that he did not know how to download images, nor that the computer was automatically saving the images he viewed. He did, however, admit using file-deleting software to ensure his mother would not see the images.

It was argued that this case raised the issue specifically left unanswered by the Tenth Circuit in its earlier decision in *US v. Tucker*[402] – that is, can a defendant be guilty of knowing possession of child pornography while viewing those images but ignorant of the fact that they are automatically stored on the computer?[403] The issue remained unresolved as the court considered that the issue did not arise on these facts. Despite the defendant's statement to the contrary, it was open to the jury to be satisfied that he did in fact know that the images were stored automatically. In particular, his use of file-deleting software was evidence that he was well aware that the images had been stored even though he had merely 'viewed' them.[404]

399 [2000] 2 All ER 425; *R v. C* [2004] All ER 82 at [20] per Hooper LJ; *R v. Porter* [2006] EWCA Crim 560 at [14] per Dyson LJ; and *Clark v. R* [2008] NSWCCA 122 at [234]–[237] per Barr J.
400 *Atkins v. DPP, Goodland v. DPP* [2000] 2 All ER 425 at 436–7 per Simon Brown LJ. Also see *Clark v. R* [2008] NSWCCA 122 at [246] per Barr J.
401 411 F 3d 1198 (10th Cir 2005).
402 150 F Supp 2d 1263 (D Utah 2001). See p. 303.
403 *US v. Bass*, 411 F 3d 1198, 1201–2 (10th Cir 2005).   404 *Ibid.*

In a strong dissent, Judge Kelly disagreed with the majority's conclusion as to the sufficiency of the evidence and made clear the requirements of knowing possession:

> Knowing possession of pornography cannot be established merely by demonstrating that Mr. Bass was ignorant, negligent, careless, or foolish not to have known that downloading files is easy, and material is saved in temporary internet files ... the court's leap from viewing child pornography to knowingly possessing it based solely on a computer default operation without any proof the defendant knew about such operation, establishes a precedent that mere negligence suffices for criminal liability ...[405]

Although the issue was not resolved, it is submitted that as a matter of principle the defendant cannot be in possession of images if he or she is unaware of their existence, or unaware that he or she has custody or control of them.

This was the view adopted by the Ninth Circuit in *US* v. *Kuchinski*.[406] In reviewing the defendant's sentence on child pornography charges, it was held that the images stored in cache (somewhere between 13,904 to 17,984 images) were improperly considered and the sentence was vacated and remanded. The court referred to evidence that the operation of images being stored in cache was automatic, and while a sophisticated user might be aware of the process and might access the files 'most sophisticated – or unsophisticated – users don't even know they're on their computer'.[407] The court went on to hold that:

> [w]here a defendant lacks knowledge about the cache files, and concomitantly lacks access to and control over those files, it is not proper to charge him with possession and control of the child pornography images located in those files, without some other indication of dominion and control over the images. To do so turns abysmal ignorance into knowledge and a less than valetudinarian grasp into dominion and control.[408]

This does not mean that the defendant must necessarily escape prosecution. The images in cache are evidence that the defendant had previously viewed those images. We have seen that in viewing the images the defendant may be said to be in possession, notwithstanding that he or she did not knowingly save the files. We have also seen some authority for the fact that the act of accessing and viewing child pornography is sufficient

---

405 *Ibid.*, at 1208.   406 469 F 3d 853 (9th Cir 2006).
407 *Ibid.*, at 862. Also see *Barton* v. *State*, 286 Ga App 49 (2007).   408 *Ibid.*, at 863.

evidence of 'control' for the purposes of possession.[409] Alternatively, the defendant could be prosecuted for 'accessing', rather than 'possessing', child pornography.[410]

Forgetfulness What of the defendant who claims to no longer be in possession because he or she has forgotten that the images are in his or her custody or control? There is considerable UK authority in the context of drug offences that a person remains in possession of something, even though he no longer remembers it being in his or her custody or control:

> Possession does not depend on the alleged possessor's powers of memory. Nor does possession come and go as memory revives or fails. If it were to do so, a man with poor memory would be acquitted, he with the good memory would be convicted.[411]

The UK courts appear to distinguish three different scenarios. The first is where an item is placed on the defendant's person without his or her knowledge. The second is where a person relinquishes control of an item but, unknown to him or her, it is returned. In neither of these scenarios is the person in possession.[412] Where the courts draw the line is in circumstances where the object was once knowingly in the custody or control of the defendant, and remains in the physical custody of the defendant, but he or she is unaware of it:

> one continues to have or possess it until one does something to rid oneself of having or possessing it; that merely to have forgotten that one has possession of it is not sufficient to exclude continuing to have or possess it . . . there is no limbo into which the article can go if recollection dims.[413]

This line of authority was applied by the Supreme Court of South Australia in *Police* v. *Kennedy*.[414] Although dealing with pornographic magazines, it is equally relevant in a digital context. The defendant was convicted of being in possession of child pornography, the items being magazines which the defendant had bought in the 1970s. According to the defendant, he could recall seeing them in the mid 1970s but could not remember seeing them 'for a long time'.[415] The complicating factor was that at

---

409 *US* v. *Romm*, 455 F 3d 990, 998 (9th Cir 2006), discussed at p. 303.
410 See p. 295.   411 *R* v. *Martindale* [1986] 3 All ER 25 at 26 per Lane LCJ.
412 *R* v. *Buswell* [1972] 1 All ER 75 at 78 per Phillimore LJ.
413 *McCalla* v. *R* (1988) 87 Cr App R 372 at 379 per May LJ. Also see *R* v. *Buswell* [1972] 1 All ER 75 at 78 per Philimore LJ.
414 *Police* v. *Kennedy* (1998) 71 SASR 175.   415 *Ibid.*, at 180.

the time that the defendant was, by his own admission, knowingly in possession, simple possession of child pornography was not an offence. By the time it was made an offence in 1992, the defendant claimed to have forgotten the items were in his possession.

Following the UK cases already referred to, the court held that:

> even though the respondent may have forgotten that he had the magazines in his possession, he is taken to have had the required state of knowledge . . . That imputed state of knowledge continued with the change in the law effected in 1992, when, assuming the material to be child pornography, it became an offence to possess it.[416]

On this approach, so long as the defendant was at some point knowingly in possession of the material, he would continue to be in possession until the material was disposed of, even if the defendant had forgotten its existence.

With respect, it is submitted that this approach is incorrect. It is well established that it is the combination of *knowing* custody or control which constitutes possession. A person cannot possess something of which he or she is unaware. This is clearly accepted in circumstances where the item is placed on the defendant's person or returned to the defendant without his or her knowledge. In both cases, until the defendant becomes aware of its presence he or she cannot be in possession.

The distinction which seems to cause concern in the forgetfulness cases is that the item has never left the custody or control of the defendant. It is in this context that judges ask, rhetorically, whether the item goes into some form of limbo. In a sense, the item does go into legal limbo as although the item is still physically there, it is impossible for the defendant to exercise custody or control if he or she is unaware of its existence. If, and it may be a big 'if', the jury accepts that the defendant was no longer aware that it was in his or her custody or control, then the defendant is not in possession *at that time*. To treat the defendant's former knowledge as having somehow continued, despite evidence to the contrary, offends against the fundamental principle that the external and fault elements of an offence must exist at the same time.[417] It also imposes an objective fault element as the defendant's earlier state of mind is effectively deemed to continue until such time as he or she disposes of the item, irrespective of the actual subjective mental state of the defendant.

---

416 *Ibid.*, at 181.   417 *Fagan* v. *Metropolitan Police Commissioner* [1968] 3 All ER 422.

This distortion of principle is particularly unfortunate as in the vast majority of cases it will be unnecessary. The defendant's assertion that he or she had 'forgotten' the item is an implied admission of prior knowledge, as one cannot forget what one did not know. This is in contrast to statements such as 'I've never seen that before' or 'I don't know how that got there' which indicate that the defendant does not, and did not, have knowledge of the item. The defendant's claim of forgetfulness is therefore evidence that on a prior occasion the defendant *was* knowingly in possession. In the digital context, there may be supporting evidence which can show with precision when files were stored, opened, etc. It is only in the unusual circumstances of this case where the law had changed, or perhaps where a limitation period applies, that there would be no prosecution for the earlier possession.

Deletion In many cases, prosecution for possession is based on deleted images which have been recovered by forensic analysis. There is some authority in the context of drug offences that so long as the item remains in the custody or control of the defendant, he or she remains in possession notwithstanding a belief that the item no longer exists. For example, in *R* v. *Buswell*[418] it was stated, *obiter dictum*, that where the defendant mistakenly believed that the tablets were in his jeans and destroyed in the wash, when in fact they were safe in his drawer, the items 'have never left your care and control and accordingly . . . remain in your possession'.[419] This case was cited with apparent approval in *Atkins* v. *DPP, Goodland* v. *DPP*,[420] it being suggested that the same reasoning could apply where a defendant tried but failed to delete images.

It is submitted that where the defendant has deleted an image, and believes it to have been removed from the computer, he or she has not merely forgotten that the image was there, but has an affirmative belief that it is no longer there, thereby negating an essential element of the offence. The fact that the defendant is mistaken, or that other people may be aware that such images may be recovered, is irrelevant to the subjective knowledge of the defendant.

The recovered image is, however, evidence that the image *was* in the possession of the accused in the past. This may be supported by forensic evidence indicating when the file was created, viewed, etc. Further, the deletion of the data is itself evidence of earlier knowing possession, not

418 *R* v. *Buswell* [1972] 1 All ER 75.   419 *Ibid.*, at 78 per Phillimore LJ.
420 *Atkins* v. *DPP, Goodland* v. *DPP* [2000] 2 All ER 425 at 437 per Simon Brown LJ.

to mention consciousness of guilt. For example, in *US* v. *Tucker*[421] it was held that the defendant's habit of deleting the images in cache, far from proving a lack of intent on his part, proves the opposite:

> Just as a possessor of illegal narcotics is not able to escape criminal liability for possession by throwing drugs out a window, a person who possesses contraband such as child pornography cannot escape criminal liability by destroying it. Destruction of contraband does not logically lead to the conclusion that one *never* possessed it; indeed, it leads to the exact opposite.[422]

It is submitted that the correct interpretation in such cases is not that the defendant somehow remains in possession of material which he or she believes to have been destroyed. Rather, evidence of the recovered material, together with the accused's actions in deleting the material is evidence of previous knowing possession for which the defendant may be convicted. There is also support for this proposition in *Atkins* v. *DPP, Goodland* v. *DPP*[423] where it was stated, *obiter dictum*, that it was 'common ground' that there would have been no defence on a charge of possession if the charge was put on the basis of the transient downloading of the image onto the screen, rather than on the basis of its subsequent inadvertent storage in the cache.[424]

Knowledge of the nature of the thing possessed We have seen that, at the very least, the offence of possession requires knowledge that the thing possessed is in the defendant's custody or control. The question then arises as to whether some greater level of knowledge must be proved. In particular, is it necessary for the prosecution to prove that the defendant knew that the material was child pornography? Each jurisdiction adopts a different answer to this question.

The most limited *mens rea* is found in the UK where the fault element of s. 1(1)(c) Protection of Children Act 1978 was considered by the Court of Appeal in *R* v. *Land*.[425] It was argued that despite the absence of express words, there was a requirement on the Crown to prove knowledge on the part of the defendant that the defendant knew that the photographs which were found to be indecent were photographs of a child or children.[426]

---

421 150 F Supp 2d 1263 (D Utah 2001).   422 *Ibid.*, 1268 (emphasis added).
423 [2000] 2 All ER 425.   424 *Ibid.*, at 436 per Simon Brown LJ.
425 [1999] QB 65; applied in *Police* v. *Kennedy* (1998) 71 SASR 175 at 186–8 per Bleby J.
426 It seems that the defendant must be aware of the indecent nature of the images; see *R* v. *Porter* [2006] EWCA Crim 560 at [8] per Dyson LJ.

The court rejected this argument and held that the terms of the section were unambiguous. The purpose of the Act is to, as far as possible, eliminate trade in, or possession of such material. 'At the same time statutory defences provide a framework protecting from conviction for those whose possession of such material is not prurient.'[427] These defences apply in limited situations and if Parliament had wished to include such a defence, it could very easily have done so.[428] This is in contrast to the offence of 'making' where the defendant must know, or be aware it is likely, that the indecent image was of a child.[429]

Under s. 163.1(5) Criminal Code (Can), on a charge of making, printing, publishing or possessing child pornography it is not a defence that the accused believed that a person shown in the representation was or was depicted as being eighteen years of age, unless he or she took all reasonable steps to ascertain the age of that person and to ensure that, where the person was eighteen years of age or more, the representation did not depict that person as being under the age of eighteen years. Factors relevant to the defendant's state of mind include the number and length of downloading sessions, the actual content of the files and the titles of the files.[430]

At the next level are the Australian federal provisions. Where no fault element is specified, the Criminal Code (Cth) specifies default fault elements. It has been said that '[h]aving something in possession is not easily seen as an act or omission; it is more easily seen as a state of affairs . . . but it is a state of affairs that exists because of what the person who has possession does in relation to the thing possessed'.[431] If seen as a 'state of affairs' or 'circumstance',[432] then the relevant fault element is recklessness.[433] That is, it must be proved that the defendant was at least aware of a substantial risk that the circumstance existed or would exist and, having regard to the circumstances known to him or her, it was unjustifiable to take the risk.[434] If possession is seen as conduct, then the relevant fault element is intention.[435] In either case, the fact that the images depict a child would appear to be a 'circumstance', in which case the default fault element in respect of that element is recklessness.

In the United States it has been held that the fault element for possession requires that the accused knew both the sexually explicit nature of

427 *Ibid.*, at 70 per Judge LJ.   428 *Ibid.*   429 See p. 285.
430 *R* v. *Dixon* [2005] 64 WCB (2d) 50 at [8] per Letorneau JA.
431 *He Kaw Teh* v. *R* (1985) 157 CLR 523 at 564 per Brennan J.
432 Criminal Code (Cth), s. 4.1(1)(c).   433 S. 5.6.(2).   434 S. 5.4(1).
435 S. 5.6.(1). The fault element of the South Australian legislation is discussed in *R* v. *Clarke* [2008] SASC 100.

the material and that the images were of minors.[436] Relevant factors in determining the defendant's state of mind include the appearance of the images, the number of images, the number and identity of websites the defendant accessed, the language used in the websites and the mode and manner by which the defendant viewed and stored the images.[437]

Although possession of a relevant document may be some evidence from which knowledge of its contents may be inferred, or otherwise to demonstrate the accused's connection with the document,[438] the mere fact of downloading is not, of itself, proof of knowledge. It is merely some evidence from which knowledge may be inferred, and it is possible to download images without being aware of their contents.[439] For example, simply right-clicking on the file and saving will only give information as to the filename. If there is no associated description, or that description is incorrect, then the person will not know the contents of the file being downloaded. Downloading is an act of faith, not actual knowledge.[440] However, the surrounding circumstances will often provide a clear inference that the defendant was aware of the nature of the material downloaded.

Similarly, where an accused is found to be in possession of the material, it is not necessary to prove that he or she downloaded the material or otherwise placed it on the computer. Some other person may have done so but as long as the accused knew that the material was on the computer in his or her possession, the offence is made out. Evidence of downloading is merely some evidence from which possession may be inferred.[441]

C. Intention to possess

According to the 2003–4 British Crime Survey, one-quarter of people who used the Internet at home 'had unwittingly accessed or received offensive or upsetting unsolicited material via the Internet' in the previous twelve

---

436 *US* v. *Tucker*, 150 F Supp 2d 1263 (D Utah 2001), applying *US* v. *X-Citement Video, Inc.*, 513 US 64 (1994). Also see *US* v. *Lacy*, 119 F 3d 742, 747–8 (9th Cir 1997) and *US* v. *Romm*, 455 F 3d 990, 1003 (9th Cir 2006).

437 *US* v. *Marchand*, 308 F Supp 2d 498, 505–6 (D NJ 2004).

438 *R* v. *Pecciarich* (1995) 22 OR (3d) 748 at 757 per Sparrow Prov Div J.

439 *Bounds* v. *R* [2005] WASCA 1 at [22] per Steytler J.

440 That it is possible that in seeking to download a particular file, another file may be received by mistake was accepted in *R* v. *Missions* [2005] NSJ no 177 at [18] per Roscoe JA.

441 *R* v. *B (DEW)* 2003 WCBJ LEXIS 2477 at [25] per Fradsham Prov Ct J.

months.[442] The digital environment provides a number of plausible situations in which a person could unwittingly find themselves in possession of child pornography. For example, a person who receives and opens an email attachment which is not labelled in any way as to suggest it contains child pornography; or a person who is viewing adult pornography on the Internet and clicks on a hyperlink which does not suggest in any way that the associated image is in fact child pornography. Imagine that in both cases the recipient deletes the email/exits the webpage immediately. In addition, he or she may take further steps such as deleting the image from the 'recycle bin' or otherwise removing temporary files. Alternatively, the recipient may believe that the images should be preserved and police notified. For the period between awareness and deletion/notification, is the recipient in possession of that image?

On a strict interpretation the answer must be 'yes' as the recipient had custody or control of an image which was known to be child pornography. The ability to delete the image or exit the page is itself evidence of that custody or control. The fact that the recipient may only have been in possession for a short period of time is irrelevant, as it is the fact of control, not the period of control, which forms the basis of possession.[443] Yet it seems clear that in such situations the unwitting recipient is not deserving of punishment. Although some jurisdictions provide specific defences to address such situations,[444] these place the onus on the defendant, albeit on the balance of probabilities, to prove 'innocent' possession. Where no such defence exists the defendant must rely on prosecutorial discretion.

An alternative approach is to recognise that in such cases the defendant is not in possession as he or she does not intend to exercise custody or control over the image. An analogy may be drawn with drug cases, where there is some authority that the notion of possession connotes not only knowledge of the object possessed, but an *intention* to exercise custody and control over that object.[445] For example, in R v. Boyce[446] Chief Justice Bray

442 D. Wilson et al., *Fraud and Technology Crimes: Findings from the 2003/04 British Crime Survey, the 2004 Offending, Crime and Justice Survey and administrative* sources (Home Office, 2006), p. 8.
443 R v. Boyce (1976) 15 SASR 40 at 44 per Bray CJ.   444 See p. 324.
445 He Kaw Teh v. R (1985) 157 CLR 523 at 582 per Brennan J, and at 599 per Dawson J; Pearce v. Director of Public Prosecutions (No. 2) (1992) 59 A Crim R 182 at 183 per King CJ; Davis v. R (1990) 5 WAR 269 at 276 per Malcolm CJ, and at 288 per Wallace J; R v. Beaver [1957] SCR 531 at 541–2 per Cartwright J; R v. Kocsis (2001) 157 CCC (3d) 564 at [22] per MacPherson JA, cited with approval in R v. Daniels 2004 NLSCTD 27 at [9] per Welsh JA.
446 (1976) 15 SASR 40 at 46 per Bray CJ.

stated, *obiter dictum*, that there must be situations where an accused is not in possession despite knowingly having custody or control of the object. For example, a bus driver who is informed that there is a parcel containing drugs on the bus, or a person in charge of a storage deposit. Similarly, in *R v. Christie*[447] the defendant's car was searched after an accident, and marijuana was found in the boot. The defendant claimed that she had found the marijuana in the car, and had been driving around seeking friends to advise her on what to do with it, when the accident occurred. The trial judge acquitted her on the basis that she had not consented to possess the drugs. On appeal, it was held that a person will not be in possession where he or she does not have an intention to exercise custody or control. Examples include the person who finds a package on his or her doorstep and opens it only to discover it contains drugs. This extends to the person who manually handles the object 'for the sole purpose of destroying it or reporting it to the police'.[448]

In addition to those already stated, ready analogies can be found in the digital context; the ISP who becomes aware of child pornography held on the server or the computer repairer, a common source of information to police, who becomes aware of child pornography on a customer's computer. Assuming immediate steps are taken to delete the images, or immediately notify police, it may be argued that there is no intention to possess in such cases.

It could be argued that a distinction should be drawn between the person who takes immediate steps to relinquish custody of the object, and the person who retains it in order to inform police. Arguably it is only the former who has no intention to possess. The person in the latter situation is knowingly in possession and intends to exercise custody or control, albeit for a noble purpose. Although motive is potentially relevant to sentence or the decision to prosecute, '*mens rea* is not excluded because the *actus reus* is done with a good motive or without an evil motive'.[449] Nonetheless, it seems desirable to incorporate within the concept of intention to possess those situations where the accused possesses the material solely for the purpose of notifying law enforcement. In such cases, the defendant is unwillingly in possession and may be said to lack the necessary intention to possess. Such a view obviously facilitates the important public purpose of encouraging reporting of such material, and

447 *R v. Christie* (1978) 21 NBR (2d) 261.
448 *Ibid.*, at [19] per Hughes CJNB. Also see *R v. York* (2005) 193 CCC (3d) 331 at 336–8 per Oppal JA.
449 *He Kaw Teh v. R* (1985) 157 CLR 523 at 588 per Brennan J.

if not accepted, it is vital that jurisdictions incorporate a suitable specific or general defence.

Such a view was adopted by the Ontario Court of Appeal in *R* v. *Chalk*.[450] The defendant was convicted of possessing several videos of child pornography. These had been found on a computer at the home which he shared with his girlfriend and her two children. The videos came to light when the defendant was arrested in relation to unrelated allegations in respect of his girlfriend's daughter. While in custody, the defendant urged his girlfriend to delete his files. On inspecting the files, she realised they contained child pornography and notified police. The defendant acknowledged that he knew the material was child pornography (apparently by its titles) and that he had been aware of its presence for some months. He denied, however, downloading the material nor any knowledge of how it came to be on the computer. There was some evidence which indicated that the videos had been accessed at a time when the defendant did not have access to the computers. However, his conviction for possession was not based on his having downloaded or having accessed the files. Rather, it was based on his direction to his girlfriend to delete the files.

This verdict was upheld by the Court of Appeal. The court reviewed and agreed with the line of authority, including *R* v. *Christie*, which indicates that there are cases of 'innocent possession' which should not be the subject of criminal liability:

> There are cases where an individual has the requisite control and knowledge, but cannot be said to be in possession for the purpose of imposing criminal liability. These cases will include cases in which a person takes control of contraband exclusively for the purpose of immediately destroying the contraband or otherwise placing it permanently beyond that person's ability to exercise any control over the contraband. In such cases, the intention is solely to divest oneself of control rather than to possess. Like the other appellate courts whose discussions are referred to above, I do not think that criminal liability should attach to that kind of brief, 'innocent' possession . . . [451]

The defendant's conduct in this case, however, was not one of 'innocent possession'. He did not have possession solely for the purpose of destroying the child pornography. He had known of its presence for months and during that time had control over it in the sense that he could have

---

450 *R* v. *Chalk* [2007] OJ no 4627.
451 *Ibid.*, at [25] per Doherty JA. Also see *US* v. *Polizzi*, 2008 US Dist LEXIS 26223 (EDNY 2008) at 71 and 82–3.

deleted it at any time. He ultimately sought to delete it for fear of it being discovered. In these circumstances his instruction to delete the child pornography was 'a manifestation of his longstanding power or authority over the material'.[452]

This issue was recently considered by a US District Court in *US v. Polizzi*.[453] The defendant was convicted on twelve counts of receiving and eleven counts of possessing child pornography having been found in possession of over 5,000 images and some videos. The defendant claimed to have first come across child pornography accidentally, and been shocked at what he saw. He further claimed to have believed that such images *should* be illegal, but did not realise that they were in fact illegal, reasoning that if they were illegal they would not be so readily available on the Internet. For approximately five years prior to his arrest, he had downloaded all of the images he could find, ostensibly with a view to handing them over to law enforcement agencies.

Amongst a number of challenges to his conviction and sentence, it was argued that both the receiving and possession provisions were unconstitutional for vagueness and overbreadth. In particular, it was argued that because both offences only require proof that the defendant knowingly, not wilfully, received or possessed child pornography, they had the potential to criminalise innocent conduct. That is, because it is possible to become aware of the nature of a digital image only after it has been received, a person may unwittingly commit the offences of receiving and/or possession.[454] Despite a lengthy analysis sympathetic to the defendant's position, the court was ultimately bound by appellate authority.[455] Nonetheless, it did express the view that:

> [a]ppellate courts should reconsider the constitutional issues of whether 'knowledge' obtained when an image appears on the computer screen constitutes sufficient *mens rea* for section 2252 charges and, if not, whether an intent to acquire and possess child pornography requirement may be properly implied.[456]

9. Defences

The sweeping nature of child pornography offences clearly has the potential to inadvertently capture legitimate expression. In order to address

---

452 *Ibid.*, at [26].   453 2008 US Dist LEXIS 26223 (EDNY 2008).
454 *Ibid.*, at 68.   455 *Ibid.*, at 70 citing *US v. X-Citement Video, Inc.*, 513 US 64 (1994).
456 *Ibid.*, at 71.

such concerns, some jurisdictions provide for a general defence of 'legitimate reason'[457] or 'public good'.[458] Such defences would clearly seem to encompass a police officer possessing or distributing such material in the course of his duty,[459] although a number of jurisdictions provide for specific defences in this regard.[460]

It has been held that what constitutes a 'legitimate reason' for the purposes of the UK provision is a question of fact for the jury.[461] Although each reason that is advanced must be considered on its own facts, the courts are 'plainly entitled to bring a measure of scepticism to bear upon such an enquiry: they should not too readily conclude that the defence has been made out'.[462]

In Canada, 'public good' has been interpreted as 'necessary or advantageous to religion or morality, to the administration of justice, the pursuit of science, literature, or Art, or other objects of general interest'.[463] Examples include 'people in the justice system for purposes associated with prosecution, by researchers studying the effects of exposure to child pornography, and by those in possession of works addressing the political or philosophical aspects of child pornography'.[464] In contrast to the UK position, it is for the trial judge to determine, as a matter of law, whether what was done served the public good and whether there is evidence that the act alleged went beyond what served the public good. However, it is a question of fact whether the acts did or did not extend beyond what served the public good.[465] Further, the motives of the accused are irrelevant.[466]

These defences may also encompass genuine academic research, although such arguments are fraught with difficulty, as famous guitarist Pete Townshend discovered. The former member of 'The Who' used his credit card to access child porngraphy on the Internet, allegedly for the purposes of research into child abuse. Although apparently accepting his explanation, police cautioned him and he was placed on the Sex Offenders Register for five years.[467] 'The central question where the defence is legitimate research will be whether the defendant is essentially

---

457 Protection of Children Act (UK), s. 1(4)(a).
458 Criminal Code (Can), s. 163(3) which applies by virtue of s. 163.1(7).
459 R v. Land [1999] QB 65 at 70 per Judge LJ.
460 Criminal Code (Can), s. 163.1(6)(a) and Protection of Children Act 1978 (UK), s. 1B.
461 Atkins v. DPP, Goodland v. DPP [2000] 2 All ER 425 at 432 per Simon Brown LJ.
462 Ibid., at 433.   463 R v. Sharpe [2001] 1 SCR 45 at [90] per McLachlin CJ.
464 Ibid.   465 Criminal Code (Can), s. 163(3).   466 S. 163(5).
467 'Caution for Who star Townshend', BBC Online, 7 May 2003, http://news.bbc.co.uk/1/hi/uk/3007871.stm.

a person of unhealthy interests in possession of indecent photographs in the pretence of undertaking research, or by contrast a genuine researcher with no alternative but to have this sort of unpleasant material in his possession.'[468]

In *US* v. *Matthews*[469] an award-winning journalist was prosecuted for sending and receiving child pornography. The defendant maintained that he did so only for the purposes of researching the issue of child pornography on the Internet. It was argued that a First Amendment defence should be recognised where child pornography is:

> utilized as part of any 'work of educational, medical or artistic value,' to 'create a work of academic, educational or political significance,' or 'a work of educational, literary, and political value,' and for other 'legitimate uses,' including 'journalistic uses.'[470]

This argument was rejected by the Fourth Circuit. The fundamental distinction between adult and child pornography is that while the former may be regulated where it is obscene, the latter need not be obscene. While the obscenity standard allows for 'serious literary, artistic, political, or scientific value', such a defence was rejected in *Ferber* because the presence of such value does nothing to ameliorate its harm to children.[471] Although the court did not define the parameters of any First Amendment protection which may be available to those who distribute child pornography, it did note that such a defence would only be available if the material did not threaten the enormous harms to children identified in *Ferber*. As noted in that case, it is 'unlikely that visual depictions of children performing sexual acts . . . would often constitute an important and necessary part of a literary performance or scientific or educational work'.[472]

Of course, the definition of child pornography encompasses far more than 'depictions of children performing sexual acts', and has the potential to capture legitimate artistic or scientific work. Such a defence is specifically incorporated in Canada, where the conduct has a legitimate purpose related to science, medicine, education or art and does not pose an undue risk of harm to persons under the age of eighteen years.[473] In the context

---

468 *Atkins* v. *DPP, Goodland* v. *DPP* [2000] 2 All ER 425 at 432–3 per Simon Brown LJ. Also see *R* v. *Wrigley* [2000] EWCA Crim 44.
469 209 F 3d 338 (4th Cir 2000); cert. denied, 531 US 910 (2000). For arguments in favour of such a privilege, see Calvert, 'Child modeling', 272–4.
470 *Ibid.*, 344.   471 *Ibid.*, 345. Also see *Knight* v. *McDonald* [2002] TASSC 81.
472 *New York* v. *Ferber*, 458 US 747, 762–3 (1982).
473 Criminal Code (Can) s 163.1(6). The accused bears only an evidential burden, it is for the Crown to disprove these defences beyond reasonable doubt: *R* v. *Sharpe* [2001] 1 SCR 45 at [112]–[113] per McLachlin CJ.

of this provision it has been held that 'artistic merit' includes any expression that may reasonably be viewed as art. 'Any objectively established artistic value, however small, suffices to support the defence.'[474]

We have also seen that the nature of the Internet is such that it provides opportunities for unwitting receipt and possession of child pornography, and that some jurisdictions provide specific defences to address such instances. For example, in the UK it is a defence to a charge of distributing, showing or possession if the defendant proves that he had not seen the photographs or pseudo-photographs and did not know, nor had any cause to suspect, them to be indecent.[475]

In addition, under s. 160(2) Criminal Justice Act 1988 (UK) it is a defence to a charge of possession for the person to prove that the photograph was sent to the defendant without any prior request and that he or she did not keep it for an unreasonable time. Similarly, in the United States, it is a defence to possession charges for the accused to prove that he or she possessed less than three images of child pornography and 'promptly and in good faith' took reasonable steps to destroy each image or reported the matter to law enforcement.[476]

In a similar vein, under s. 1B Protection of Children Act 1978 (UK) it is a defence to a charge of making an indecent photograph or pseudo-photograph of a child for the defendant to prove that the conduct was necessary for the purposes of the prevention, detection or investigation of crime, or for the purposes of criminal proceedings, in any part of the world.

Of course, ISPs are placed in a difficult position, being the (generally) unwitting conduit for child pornography. Where an ISP is aware that such material is within its custody or control, then it may be subject to prosecution in the same way as an individual. In addition, some jurisdictions impose special obligations on ISPs found to be in possession of child pornography. For example, under s. 474.25 Criminal Code (Cth) a person commits an offence if the person:

(a) is an Internet service provider or an Internet content host; and
(b) is aware that the service provided by the person can be used to access particular material that the person has reasonable grounds to believe is:

---

474 *R* v. *Sharpe* [2001] 1 SCR 45 at [80] per McLachlin J.
475 Protection of Children Act 1978 (UK), s. 1(4)(b) and Criminal Justice Act 1988 (UK), s. 160(2)(b). The legal burden for these defences is on the defendant; *R* v. *C* [2004] All ER 82 at [40] per Hooper LJ.
476 18 USC § 2252A(d).

    (i) child pornography material; or

    (ii) child abuse material; and

(c) does not refer details of the material to the Australian Federal Police within a reasonable time after becoming aware of the existence of the material.[477]

In the United States, providers of electronic communication[478] or remote computing services[479] who become aware of child pornography are under a duty to report as soon as reasonably possible to the National Center for Missing and Exploited Children, which will then forward the report to relevant law enforcement agencies.[480] Knowingly and wilfully failing to make a report is an offence.

---

477 'Internet service provider' and 'Internet content host' have the same meaning as in Sch. 5 to the Broadcasting Services Act 1992 (Cth); Criminal Code (Cth), s. 473.1.

478 An 'electronic communication service' is defined as 'any service which provides to users thereof the ability to send or receive wire or electronic communications': 18 USC § 2510(15).

479 Defined as 'the provision to the public of computer storage or processing services by means of an electronic communications system': 18 USC § 2711(2).

480 42 USC § 13032(b).

PART V

Offences against the person

11

'Grooming'

1. Sexual predators online

caspercock (1:26:46 PM): hello, enjoying yourself?
angelgirl12yo (1:26:53 PM): its ok
angelgirl12yo (1:26:57 PM): kinda quiet
caspercock (1:27:15 PM): what you doing?
angelgirl12yo (1:27:26 PM): just chattin
caspercock (1:27:49 PM): cool,
caspercock (1:28:05 PM): I like your name, got a pic?
angelgirl12yo (1:28:13 PM): no sorry
caspercock (1:28:23 PM): that's ok.
caspercock (1:28:28 PM): u really 12?
angelgirl12yo (1:28:35 PM): ya
caspercock (1:28:50 PM): that's cool
caspercock (1:29:08 PM): I've never chatted with someone 12 on here.
angelgirl12yo (1:29:16 PM): ok, nice meetin u tho
caspercock (1:29:24 PM): nice meeting you too.
caspercock (1:29:30 PM): I'm 21[1]

This transcript records an actual online conversation which, after this point, became increasingly sexual with 'caspercock' trying to persuade 'angelgirl12yo' to send photographs of herself masturbating. 'Angelgir12yo' was in fact a male Special Agent from the Wyoming Division of Criminal Investigation, while 'caspercock' was Timothy Wales, already on probation for an earlier sexual assault. Wales was convicted of one count of attempting to entice a minor to engage in illegal sexual activity (18 USC § 2422(b)) and one count of attempted child sexual exploitation (18 USC § 2251(a)(d)) and sentenced to just over fifteen and a half years in prison.

---

1 Extracted from *US* v. *Wales*, 127 Fed Appx 424, 425–7 (10th Cir 2005).

In its relatively short life, the Internet has introduced us to many new terms and phenomena. One which has received considerable attention is that of online 'grooming'. Although widely used, the term 'grooming' is neither well-defined nor understood.[2] It may be summarised as 'the process by which a child is befriended by a would-be abuser in an attempt to gain the child's confidence and trust, enabling them to get the child to acquiesce to abusive activity'.[3]

While grooming itself is not new, the Internet and other forms of electronic communication have provided offenders with greatly increased opportunities for contact with children. In the past, it was generally only family members or trusted friends, or perhaps clergy or teachers, who had private access to children. Now, 'the Internet enables virtually anyone to communicate privately with children in their homes'.[4] Paradoxically, parents concerned about threats from 'strangers' may erroneously believe that their children are safer inside and on the computer.[5] In fact, a 2006 survey of young Internet users aged 10–17 found that 13 per cent had received an unwanted sexual solicitation or approach in the previous year, of which almost 40 per cent were by adults.[6]

While some online grooming occurs gradually, 'a distinctive aspect of interaction in cyberspace that facilitates the grooming process is the rapid speed with which communications can become intimate'.[7] Electronic communications provide relative anonymity and the ability to adopt different personae. Lack of actual contact may also facilitate the projection of fantasy, both for victim and offender. 'A shy, troubled person may find it easy to share his pain with a faceless "listener." Such effortless and rapid intimacy can be very seductive.'[8] For the offender, the Internet may also provide 'peer support', helping them to rationalise their behaviour.[9]

---

2 See generally S. Craven, S. Brown and E. Gilchrist, 'Sexual grooming of children: Review of literature and theoretical considerations' (2006) 12 *Journal of Sexual Aggression* 287.

3 A. A. Gillespie, 'Child protection on the Internet – challenges for criminal law' (2002) 14 *Child and Family Law Quarterly* 411, 412.

4 M. McGrath and E. Casey, 'Forensic psychiatry and the Internet: Practical perspectives on sexual predators and obsessional harassers in cyberspace' (2002) 30 *Journal of the American Academy of Psychiatry and the Law* 81, 87.

5 Internet Crime Forum, *Chat Wise, Street Wise: Children and Internet chat services* (2001), www.internetcrimeforum.org.uk/chatwise_streetwise.pdf, p. 15.

6 J. Wolak, K. Mitchell and D. Finkelhor, *Online Victimization of Youth: Five years later* (National Center for Missing and Exploited Children, 2006), pp. 1–2, 17.

7 D. Muir, *Violence against Children in Cyberspace: A contribution to the United Nations study on violence against children* (Bangkok: ECPAT International, 2005), p. 48.

8 McGrath and Casey, 'Forensic psychiatry and the Internet', 86.   9 *Ibid.*, 88.

Digital technology may also advantage the prosecution, providing clear evidence of communications between offender and victim. In the past, such communications would have occurred in private, and been denied by the offender if revealed. In contrast, electronic communications may be saved by the victim or retrieved from the victim's or offender's computers or from ISPs. As many cases in this chapter illustrate, the anonymity of online communications also allows law enforcement to engage in undercover operations and obtain compelling evidence of offending.

Although the precise sequence will vary, 'grooming' in fact describes a range of behaviours, of which Professor O'Connell has proposed the following typology:[10]

1. *Friendship-Forming Stage* The offender makes initial contact and establishes rapport, and also determines whether he or she wishes for communication to continue. A US survey of Internet sex offences found that 76 per cent of initial encounters occurred in online chat rooms.[11] Other methods of contact include online interactive games,[12] mobile phones[13] and social networking sites. For example, in *US* v. *Dhingra*[14] the forty-year-old defendant contacted the then fourteen–year-old victim having seen the victim's personal homepage in which she mentioned her age and discussed a sexual experience she had during her freshman year of high school. In 2007, the profiles of 29,000 convicted sex offenders were removed from the popular social networking site 'MySpace'.[15]

2. *Relationship-Forming Stage* The offender then tries to establish a sense of trust and also gather information relevant to the next stage. In general, those children who are particularly vulnerable are those with poor familial relationships, those experiencing loneliness and depression, and boys who are becoming aware of their homosexuality or questioning their sexuality.[16]

---

10 R. O'Connell, *A Typology of Cybersexploitation and On-line Grooming Practices* (Cyberspace Research Unit, University of Central Lancashire, 2003), pp. 6–10.

11 J. Wolak, K. Mitchell and D. Finkelhor, 'Internet-initiated sex crimes against minors: Implications for prevention based on findings from a national study' (2004) 35 *Journal of Adolescent Health* 424e11, 424e15.

12 Muir, *Violence against Children*, pp. 49–50.

13 *R* v. *Shepheard* [2008] ACTSC 116.   14 371 F 3d 557 (9th Cir 2004).

15 G. Griffith and L. Roth, *Protecting Children from Online Sexual Predators*, Briefing Paper no. 10/107, NSW Parliamentary Library Research Service (2007), p. 2.

16 Finkelhor, Mitchell and Wolak, *Online Victimization*, p. 33. Also see J. Wolak, K. Mitchell and D. Finkelhor, 'Escaping or connecting? Characteristics of youth who form close online relationships' (2003) 26 *Journal of Adolescence* 105, 116.

Grooming usually involves a sexual predator's exploiting of a victim's feelings (e.g., loneliness, low self-esteem, sexual curiosity and inexperience) or needs (e.g., money) and taking advantage of this vulnerability to develop a bond. Once a bond is developed, the offender can easily persuade a victim to follow the offender's instruction to keep the relationship secret. Subtle psychological force is a potent weapon for the sexual predator.[17]

Although some offenders pretend to be a peer of the victim, one study suggests that this is relatively rare. Only 5 per cent of offenders pretended to be peers of their victims (and of those some went on to reveal that they were in fact older), while 25 per cent indicated they were younger than they in fact were, but still presented as much older than their victim.[18] Other forms of deception, such as physical appearance, family and work status, were more common, with 52 per cent of offenders engaging in some form of deception in the course of the encounters.[19]

3. *Risk-Assessment Stage* At this stage, the offender will seek information which helps to assess the risk of getting caught such as the location of the computer, others who have access, presence of adults/siblings, etc.

4. *Exclusivity Stage* The offender seeks to create a sense of mutual trust which can then be exploited at the next stage. This may also involve moving to other more private forms of communication such as email, private chat room or telephone. Research in the US found that 64 per cent of defendants communicated with victims for more than one month, and most evolved into multiple forms of contact, including 47 per cent who sent or offered gifts or money.[20] This exclusivity and sense of a relationship may be such that in some cases the minors do not see themselves as victims, and may resist co-operating with authorities.[21] In *R* v. *Jongsma*[22] the 49-year-old accused made contact with a 14-year-old girl via 'Yahoo Chat'. The victim gave the defendant her home address and a 'relationship' developed whereby she would provide sexual favours in exchange for money and/or cigarettes. Also involved were the victim's fourteen-year-old friend and sixteen-year-old sister. The court accepted that 'once snared' the girls were 'willing participants' and not physically forced to participate.

---

17 McGrath and Casey, 'Forensic psychiatry and the Internet', 87.
18 Wolak, Mitchell and Finkelhor, 'Internet-initiated sex crimes against minors', 424e15.
19 *Ibid.*, 424e16–424e17.   20 *Ibid.*   21 *Ibid.*, 424e15.
22 (2004) 150 A Crim R 386.

5. *Sexual Stage* At this point, the offender will typically introduce more intimate topics. These may be relatively innocuous, for example about kissing, or overtly sexual. Contrary to what might be expected, one US survey found that a majority of defendants were open about wanting sex from their victims, with 80 per cent bringing up sexual topics during online communications, 20 per cent engaging in cybersex and 18 per cent transmitting sexual pictures online.[23] In another survey, almost one-quarter of online solicitations of minors involved requests for sexual photographs.[24]

6. *Conclusion* There are a number of ways in which the offender may conclude the encounter. There may be an attempt to continue the relationship, 'damage limitation' to reduce the risk that the child will talk to others, or an abrupt cessation of contact.[25] In some cases, the offender will try to arrange to meet the minor. Of the cases surveyed in the US, 74 per cent involved face to face meetings, with 93 per cent of those involving illegal sexual activity.[26] In the UK, over the period 2000–3, twenty-seven people were convicted of sexual offences against children having made initial contact in chatrooms.[27]

The dangers of online grooming, and the need for legislative action, have been recognised for some time.[28] Because grooming-type behaviour precedes the commission of a sexual offence, it appropriately falls within the realm of inchoate offences. However, the traditional inchoate offences of incitement, conspiracy and attempts are generally unsuited to this context.[29] In some jurisdictions, there can be no conspiracy where the only other party to the agreement is an intended victim of the offence.[30] Although an offender may encourage a minor to engage in a sexual act, incitement requires the defendant to incite another to commit an offence. This will not generally be the case where the person incited is the victim.

23 Wolak, Mitchell and Finkelhor, 'Internet-initiated sex crimes against minors', 424e16.
24 Wolak, Mitchell and Finkelhor, *Online Victimization*, p. 19.
25 O'Connell, *A Typology of Cybersexploitation*, pp. 9–10.
26 Wolak, Mitchell and Finkelhor, 'Internet-initiated sex crimes against minors', 424e17.
27 J. Carr, *Child Abuse, Child Pornography and the Internet* (NCH, 2005), p. 3. For an excellent summary of research into Internet safety see Griffith and Roth, *Protecting Children*, pp. 15–29.
28 Justice J. R. T. Wood, *Royal Commission into the New South Wales Police Service: Final report*, v: *The paedophile inquiry* (1997) [16.27].
29 A. A. Gillespie, 'Children, chatrooms and the law' (2001) *Criminal Law Review* 435, 436–40.
30 Criminal Law Act 1977 (UK), s. 2(2)(c). Cf Criminal Code 1995 (Cth), s. 11.5(3)(c)(ii).

An attempt is also unlikely to be made out as the conduct is not sufficiently 'proximate' to the completed offence.

Legislatures have generally accepted the need for a range of offences to address this gap in the law and have enacted a range of 'grooming' offences. Although their precise scope varies, their common aim is 'to implement society's abhorrence of the practice of inducing children to engage in inappropriate sexual behaviour'.[31]

As with inchoate offences generally, such offences may be justified on both consequentialist and retributivist grounds.[32] The consequentialist argument is that such offences are necessary to prevent harm by allowing police to intervene at an early stage. While it is impossible to quantify the precise risk that a person who solicits children online will go on to commit an offence against children, one US study found that of 143 offenders arrested in undercover investigations, 13 per cent had previously committed offences against minors.[33]

Although the consequentialist argument is sound in this context, some of the offences discussed below go beyond the normal realm of inchoate offences and punish preparatory conduct, for example punishing the facilitation of incitement. Although preparatory offences are nothing new in the criminal law, and in this context may be justified on the basis that the more serious the harm to be averted the greater should be the reach of inchoate offences,[34] it is vital that the harm to be avoided is clearly defined, and that the offender's intention to cause that harm is manifest.

The same is true where a retributivist or 'desert' justification is relied upon. Such a view states that even in the absence of harm the defendant's intention to commit an offence, manifested by some overt act, is culpable and deserving of punishment in its own right. This may be so even if the commission of the planned offence is impossible. As with the consequentialist argument, the validity of this rationale depends upon the defendant's culpability being clearly reflected in the elements of the offence.

---

31 *R (Cth)* v. *Poynder* (2007) 171 A Crim R 544 at 558. The UK offences implemented the recommendations of the Task Force on Child Protection on the Internet, *Protecting the Public*, Cm. 5668 (Home Office, 2002), p. 25.

32 A. Ashworth, *Principles of Criminal Law* (New York: Oxford University Press, 2006), pp. 470–1.

33 K. J. Mitchell, J. Wolak and D. Finkelhor, 'Police posing as juveniles online to catch sex offenders: Is it working?' (2005) 17 *Sexual Abuse: A Journal of Research and Treatment* 241, 254.

34 Ashworth, *Criminal Law*, p. 471.

The need to reflect fault must also take into account two issues which often arise in this context. The first is the use of covert investigations. Officers posing as children on the Internet in order to obtain evidence of offending conduct is a common method of law enforcement, and has the particular advantage of allowing all communications with the defendant to be recorded and used as evidence. The legal challenge this presents is that the provision must be drafted so that an offence is committed notwithstanding that the 'minor' communicated with was in fact an adult. The fault element must also allow for the fact that the defendant cannot have known that the person was a minor, but rather believed them to be so.

Secondly, in some cases the defendant will argue that he did not believe that the person with whom he was communicating was a minor, but rather an adult engaged in role-playing. This so-called 'fantasy defence' is often not a true defence but attempts to provide a plausible reason as to why the defendant did not have the necessary belief. Of course, it is a matter for the trier of fact whether such arguments are believed, and in some jurisdictions the prosecution is assisted by evidentiary provisions which allow prima facie proof of the defendant's belief and/or placing a reverse onus on the defendant.

We have seen that grooming typically reflects a continuum of conduct, and each jurisdiction provides for a range of offences which can be applied at various points on that continuum. These will be considered under the following headings:

1. transmitting indecent or obscene material to minors
2. grooming
3. inducing or procuring
4. travelling with intent.

2. Transmitting indecent or obscene material to minors

Realistically, it is the 'sexual stage' in the above typology where criminal liability may first attach, as it is here that the sexual nature of the communications becomes overt. Such communications may be a precursor to further offending, or may be carried out for sexual gratification in themselves. The communication may be written, commonly expressed in strong sexual language,[35] or indecent images such as pornography or images of the defendant exposing himself.[36]

35 R v. *Campbell* [2004] QCA 342.
36 R v. *Burdon, ex parte Attorney General (Qld)* [2005] QCA 147.

In either case, depending on their content, such communications may be prosecuted under general laws prohibiting indecent or obscene communications.[37] In addition, some jurisdictions have enacted offences which apply specifically to indecent communications with minors. Such offences are really an extension of classification laws which seek to shield minors from objectionable material. The act of sending indecent or obscene material to a minor is therefore regarded as criminal in itself, regardless of the motivation behind it. Where there is an intention to groom the minor for further sexual activity, such offences allow intervention at a very early stage.

A. Australia

In Australia, s. 218A(1)(b) Criminal Code Act 1899 (Qld) provides that it is an offence for an adult to use an electronic communication with intent to 'expose, without legitimate reason, a person under the age of 16 years, or a person the adult believes is under the age of 16 years, to any indecent matter either in Queensland or elsewhere'.[38] 'Indecent matter' is defined to include indecent film, videotape, audiotape, picture, photograph or printed or written matter.[39] Although not specifically mentioned in the definition, the fact that the offence is concerned with 'electronic communications'[40] clearly indicates 'indecent matter' must include material in electronic form.

Where the young person was in fact under the age of sixteen or twelve (depending on the offence), the prosecution must prove that the defendant intended to expose a person under the relevant age to indecent matter. In such cases, the defendant may rely upon the defence that he or she believed, on reasonable grounds, that the person was at least (depending on the offence) sixteen or twelve years of age.[41] In such cases, the burden of proof is on the defendant to prove, on the balance of

---

37 See, e.g., Criminal Code 1995 (Cth), s 474.17; Criminal Code (Can), s. 163; Communications Act 2003 (UK), s. 127; and 18 USC § 1465.

38 Maximum penalty of 5 years' imprisonment. Increased penalties apply if the person was, or the defendant believed them to be, under 12 years: s. 218A(2). In Australia there is no federal offence of this nature, although there are a number of state equivalents; e.g., Criminal Code Act (NT), s. 132(2)(e) and Criminal Code (WA), s. 204B. See, e.g., *Speering* v. *WA* [2008] WASCA 266; *WA* v. *Collier* (2007) 178 A Crim R 310.

39 Criminal Code Act 1899 (Qld), s. 1.

40 Defined to mean 'SMS messages, real time audio/video or other similar communication': s. 218A(10).

41 S. 218A(9). *R* v. *Shetty* [2005] 2 Qd R 540 at 543.

probabilities, not only that he held such a belief, but that it was reasonably held.

As noted above, in many cases prosecutions will arise as a result of covert investigations where the young person is, in fact, an undercover police officer. This section facilitates such investigations in a number of ways. First, it is not necessary for the defendant to have exposed a young person to indecent matter, only that he or she intended to do so. Secondly, the provision specifically states that the offence may be made out even where the young person is a fictitious person represented to the defendant as a real person.[42] In such cases, the prosecution must prove that the defendant believed the person to be under 16/12 years of age. The fact that the person was represented to the defendant as being under the age of 16/12 years is, in the absence of evidence to the contrary, taken to be proof of that fact.[43] This creates a rebuttable presumption whereby if the trier of fact is satisfied that the representation was made, and the defendant does not adduce evidence to the contrary, then the belief element is made out. If the defendant adduces evidence of his belief, it is for the jury to assess its credibility. If the jury accepts that the defendant had no belief one way or the other, then the jury should be directed that he had no belief as an absence of belief is inconsistent with holding a belief.[44]

B. The United Kingdom

Under s. 12 Sexual Offences Act 2003 (UK) it is an offence for a person aged eighteen or over (A) to, for the purpose of obtaining sexual gratification, intentionally cause another person (B) to watch a third person engaging in a sexual activity, or to look at an image of any person engaging in a sexual activity, where B is under sixteen and A does not reasonably believe that B is sixteen or over, or B is under thirteen.[45]

This provision is technologically neutral and therefore could equally apply where B sees the image or activity via a communication device. The section specifically includes images of sexual activity and would therefore apply where A sends pornographic material to B. It might be thought that the section does not apply where A causes B to watch him masturbate online as it applies only where A causes B to watch 'a third person' engaging in a sexual activity. While this might be the case in the offline environment, in the online environment it is arguable that whenever B

---

42 S. 218A(7).   43 S. 218A(8).   44 *R* v. *Shetty* [2005] 2 Qd R 540 at 542.
45 Maximum penalty 10 years' imprisonment: s. 12(2).

is watching via a communication device he or she is necessarily looking at an image of sexual activity, in which case that image may be of 'any person'.

The fault element of the offence is that A must intentionally cause B to watch the activity or look at the image. Where B is under sixteen the defence may argue that A reasonably believed B was sixteen or over. It is for the prosecution to disprove this possibility beyond reasonable doubt. Where B is under thirteen, A's belief as to age is irrelevant.

The most significant limitation on the offence is that A must act 'for the purpose of obtaining sexual gratification'. The term is not defined, and presumably bears its ordinary meaning of obtaining pleasure or satisfaction of a sexual nature. Such a limitation is important as not only reflecting the culpability of A's conduct, but also allowing for legitimate conduct. For example, a parent may show to their child an image of sexual activity for the purposes of sex education, but would not fall within the provision because this was not done for the purpose of obtaining sexual gratification.

It has been argued that this requirement may cause difficulties where the defendant's purpose is to groom the child for future sexual activity but he does not obtain immediate sexual gratification from causing the child to watch the activity/look at the image.[46] This would require the courts to interpret the section as requiring not only a causal nexus between the conduct and the obtaining, but a degree of imminence.[47]

However, the section does not require the defendant to have obtained sexual gratification from the conduct. Rather, the conduct must have been engaged in for the purpose of sexual gratification. This is an important distinction. It allows for the fact that the defendant may not obtain sexual gratification from the conduct itself, but engages in the conduct for the purpose of obtaining sexual gratification in the future. On a natural reading of the section, it is not necessary to imply a time limit in the meaning of 'obtaining'; there being no reason that the obtaining of sexual gratification must be immediate or even imminent.

In a practical sense, such difficulties are unlikely to arise. A defendant who claims not to have obtained sexual gratification is unlikely to admit that his purpose was in fact grooming for future sexual activity. Even if

---

46 S. Ost, 'Getting to grips with sexual grooming? The new offence under the Sexual Offences Act 2003' (2004) 26 *Journal of Social Welfare and Family Law* 147, 154.
47 A. A. Gillespie, 'Indecent images, grooming and the law' (2006) *Criminal Law Review* 412, 414.

he did, a jury is unlikely to accept that a person grooming a child for sexual activity derived no sexual gratification from causing that child to watch or look at an image of sexual activity. Other than circumstances of sexual education and the like, the fact that the defendant engaged in the relevant conduct is likely to give rise to a strong inference that he did so for the purposes of sexual gratification. The plausibility of alternative explanations, for example that it was done to harass or as a joke, are appropriately determined by the trier of fact.

C. The United States

In the United States, such provisions are essentially restricted to material which is obscene according to the *Miller* standard in order to avoid First Amendment challenge.[48] The potential impact of this limitation is clearly demonstrated by the fate of the Child Online Protection Act,[49] an act specifically aimed at protecting minors from accessing sexually explicit material on the Internet. It sought to impose criminal penalties for any communication made for 'commercial purposes' and 'by means of the World Wide Web'[50] that was available to any minor and which contained 'material that is harmful to minors'.[51]

Although the term 'material that is harmful to minors' encompassed material that was obscene, it also covered sexually explicit material which, according to the average person applying contemporary community standards, was patently offensive with respect to minors and which lacked serious literary, artistic, political, or scientific value for minors.[52] In an attempt to avoid problems of over-breadth, the Act exempted telecommunications carriers, Internet service providers and providers of Internet information location tools.[53] For all others, it provided an affirmative defence whereby access to the material was restricted by use of a credit card or similar identification number, digital verification certificate or by any other reasonable measure that was feasible under available technology.[54]

Nonetheless, a number of Internet content providers and free-speech advocates sought, and were granted, a preliminary injunction on the basis that the Act was unconstitutional. The injunction was upheld and remanded by the Supreme Court in *Ashcroft* v. *American Civil Liberties*

---

48 The *Miller* standard is discussed at p. 274.   49 47 USC § 231.
50 Defined at § 231(e)(3).
51 'Minor' is defined as any person under 17 years of age: § 231(e)(7).
52 § 231(e)(6).   53 § 231(b).   54 § 231(c).

Union.[55] Content-based restrictions subject to severe criminal penalties are presumed invalid. The District Court had not abused its discretion as the legislation was not narrowly tailored to serve a compelling government interest, and the government had failed to show that there were no less restrictive alternatives available.[56] Recent decisions have also granted permanent injunctions on the basis that the Act violated both the First and Fifth Amendments.[57]

In the absence of the Child Online Protection Act, the principal US provisions in this context are found in the Communications Decency Act of 1996.[58] Under 47 USC § 223(d)(1) it is an offence to knowingly use an interactive computer service[59] to send to a specific person or persons under eighteen years of age, or to display in a manner available to a person under eighteen years of age, 'any comment, request, suggestion, proposal, image, or other communication that is obscene or child pornography, regardless of whether the user of such service placed the call or initiated the communication'.[60] It is also an offence for a person to knowingly permit any telecommunications facility under his or her control to be used for such activity.[61] The provision excludes from liability a person solely providing access or connection to or from a facility, system, or network not under that person's control.[62] It is also a defence where the person has taken, in good faith, 'reasonable, effective, and appropriate actions' to restrict or prevent access by minors, for example an age-verification device.[63]

Also relevant is 18 USC § 1470 which makes it an offence, using the mail or any facility or means of interstate or foreign commerce, to knowingly transfer obscene matter to a person under the age of sixteen knowing that person to be under sixteen.[64] This offence has been used to prosecute defendants emailing obscene pictures[65] or images of themselves

55 542 US 656 (2004).   56 *Ibid.*, 659–61.
57 *American Civil Liberties Union* v. *Gonzales*, 478 F Supp 2d 775, 821 (ED Pa 2007) and *American Civil Liberties Union* v. *Mukasey*, 534 F 3d 181 (3rd Cir 2008); cert. denied, 2009 US LEXIS 598.
58 These provisions were also subject to challenge, with aspects of the original provision prohibiting 'indecent communications' with minors found to be unconstitutional in *Reno* v. *American Civil Liberties Union*, 521 US 844 (1997).
59 As to the meaning of 'interactive computer service', see p. 375.
60 Maximum penalty is 2 years' imprisonment: 47 USC § 223(a), 47 USC § 223(d). § 223(a)(1)(B) is a similar provision in relation to use of a telecommunications device.
61 § 223(d)(2).   62 § 223(e)(1).   63 § 223(e)(5).
64 Maximum penalty is 10 years' imprisonment: 18 USC § 1470.
65 *US* v. *Schnepper*, 161 Fed Appx 678 (9th Cir 2006).

masturbating.[66] Where the person to whom the material is transferred is in fact an adult, such as a police officer, the defendant may be guilty of an attempt so long as he believed the person to be under sixteen.[67]

3. Grooming

The next category of offences specifically targets sexual grooming by applying to conduct which is intended to facilitate a sexual offence against a minor. These are preparatory offences that aim to 'protect children from persons who use the internet to target them and where the potential for their victimization could become a reality'.[68] Although there may be overlap with procuring offences, in broad terms 'grooming' offences are aimed at offenders who seek to win the trust of a child as a first step towards the future sexual abuse of that child, while procuring offences apply once the child's trust has been secured, and the defendant seeks to arrange a meeting for the purposes of sexual activity with that child.[69] A specific grooming offence is found in each jurisdiction other than the United States where the broad scope of such offences could lead to challenges that they are unconstitutionally 'vague and overbroad'.

A. Australia

Under s. 474.27(1) Criminal Code (Cth)[70] it is an offence for a person who is over eighteen (the 'sender') to use a carriage service[71] to transmit a communication containing indecent material to another person who is, or who the sender believes to be, under sixteen years of age (the 'recipient'), with the intention of making it easier to procure the recipient to engage in, or submit to, sexual activity[72] with the sender.[73] Section 474.27(2)–(3) contains mirror provisions which apply where the sender grooms the recipient to engage in sexual activity with another person who is, or is believed to be, over eighteen, or where the sender intends that the sexual

---

66 *US* v. *Jenkins*, 2007 US Dist LEXIS 25420 (ND Ga 2007).
67 *US* v. *Spurlock*, 495 F 3d 1011, 1013 (8th Cir 2007); *US* v. *Rudzavice* 548 F Supp 2d 332 (ND Tex 2008).
68 *R* v. *Randall* [2006] NSJ no 180 at [14].
69 Commonwealth of Australia, *Parliamentary Debates*, Senate, 30 August 2004, 26620 (Christopher Ellison, Minister for Justice and Customs).
70 Also see Crimes Act 1900 (NSW), s. 66EB(3) and Criminal Code (WA), s. 204A(2).
71 The meaning of 'carriage service' is discussed at p. 48.
72 The terms 'procure' and 'sexual activity' are defined in s. 474.28(11).
73 Maximum penalty is 12 years' imprisonment: s. 474.27(1).

activity with the other person will occur in the presence of the sender or another person who is, or is believed to be, over eighteen.

This offence applies only to the transmission of indecent material, and one communication is sufficient. The fact that it is limited to the use of a carriage service is a product of constitutional limitations on the exercise of federal power, which does not apply to equivalent state offences. Whether the material is indecent is a question of fact,[74] and is determined according to the standards of ordinary people.[75] Given that this provision relates to conduct that is preparatory at most, it is not possible to attempt to commit this offence.[76] In order to facilitate undercover investigations, the offence may be committed even if it is impossible for the sexual activity to take place and/or where the recipient is a fictitious person represented to be a real person.[77]

The age of the recipient, and in appropriate cases the third person, are matters of absolute liability.[78] That is, the prosecution need not prove that the defendant believed that the person was above or below that age respectively. It is, however, a defence to prove that the defendant believed that the person was 'not under 16' or 'not at least 18' respectively.[79] Where the defence is raised, the accused bears only an evidential burden in relation to these matters. Ultimately it is for the prosecution to prove, beyond reasonable doubt, that the accused did not have the necessary belief. However, in determining whether or not the accused held such a belief, the trier of fact is entitled to take into account whether the alleged belief was reasonable in the circumstances.[80] Further, evidence that the recipient or 'other person' was represented to the sender as being under or of a particular age is, in the absence of evidence to the contrary, proof that the sender believed the recipient to be under or of that age.[81]

The central aspect of this provision is that the communication must be sent 'with the intention of making it easier' to procure the recipient to engage in, or submit to, sexual activity. Although 'making it easier' is not defined, its plain meaning is synonymous with 'facilitate', a term used in both the Canadian and UK provisions. Importantly, what the defendant must intend to facilitate is not the sexual activity itself, but the *procuring* of the sexual activity. It is this aspect of the offence which makes it a preparatory offence, allowing intervention by police at an early stage. For example, the defendant may engage in sexually explicit communications

---

74 S. 474.27(4).   75 S. 474.27(5).   76 S. 474.28(10).   77 Ss. 474.28(8)–(9).
78 Ss. 474.28(1)–(2).   79 Ss. 474.29(1)–(2).   80 *Ibid.*
81 Ss. 474.28(3)–(4). A similar Queensland provision is discussed at p. 339.

with a person whom he believes to be a minor. At this point, the defendant has not induced or procured the minor to engage in sexual activity. It may be proved, however, that he intends these communications to make it easier to procure the minor at a later point, thus allowing for an arrest at this early stage.

The broad reach of the offence is offset to some extent by the requirement of proof of intention rather than recklessness. It is not sufficient that the defendant realised it *might* make it easier to procure sexual activity, he must intend for it to do so. The prosecution must therefore exclude alternative explanations such as it being sent purely for sexual gratification (his and/or the minor's) with no intention that sexual activity would occur, that it was sent to harass the minor, or as a joke. Of course, depending on its content, the sending of the communication to a minor, or a person whom the defendant believed to be a minor, may be an offence in its own right.

B. Canada

In Canada, the equivalent offence of 'luring' is found in s. 172.1 Criminal Code (Can). This provides that it is an offence for any person, by means of a computer system,[82] to communicate with a person who is, or who the accused believes is, a minor for the purpose of facilitating the commission of a designated offence.[83] The term 'communication' is not defined and presumably carries its ordinary meaning of 'to impart, transmit, or exchange thought or information'.[84] One communication is sufficient for the offence to be made out. The ordinary meaning of 'facilitate' in the context of the criminal law is to make the commission of a crime easier[85] or even possible.[86]

In *R* v. *Randall*[87] the 31-year-old defendant believed he was communicating with a 13-year-old girl in an Internet chat room when he invited her to meet in order to engage in sexual acts. He was, in fact, communicating

---

82 See p. 54.
83 Maximum penalty 10 years' imprisonment: s. 172.1(2). The designated offences include sexual interference (s. 151), invitation to sexual touching (s. 152) and exposure of genitals (s. 173(2)). The precise nature of the offence varies according to whether the person is, or is believed to be, under the age of 18, 16 or 14: s. 172.1(4).
84 *Oxford English Dictionary*.
85 *R* v. *Randall* [2006] NSJ no 180 at 11, citing *Black's Law Dictionary*, 7th edn (St. Paul, MN: West Group, 1999) and *R* v. *Legare* [2008] ABCA 138 at [58].
86 *R* v. *Smith* [2007] BCSC 1955 at [17].   87 [2006] NSJ no 180.

with an undercover police officer and was arrested when he arrived at the arranged rendezvous. The defendant claimed that he did not intend to carry out the secondary offences and that his intention at all times was to scare her off and to warn her of the dangers of communicating in a sexual way on the Internet.

The court rejected the defendant's submission that in order for the offence to be made out there must be proof that the secondary offence was committed. What is required is for the prosecution to prove that the accused:

> intentionally communicated, by means of a computer . . . with someone whom he believes to be or is in the prohibited class of persons, to urge that person to participate in one of the listed prohibited acts, in language that indicates objectively that he wishes that person to take his intentions seriously.[88]

Although the commission of the secondary offence need not be proved, evidence that the defendant acted in a way which 'reasonably and objectively demonstrates' an intention to commit the offence would add weight to any assertion that the communication was made for the purpose of facilitating the commission of that offence.[89] For example, the defendant arriving at the rendezvous point in possession of condoms, when he and his girlfriend rarely used them, suggested the purpose of the communications was to make it easier to commit a prescribed offence rather than his suggested altruistic motives. In the circumstances, the court found his explanation 'lacked an air of reality and . . . was a smooth-tongued rationalization of his exposed harmful intentions to a child'.[90]

The proposition that the subsequent conduct of the accused is relevant evidence from which the purpose of the communication may be inferred is uncontroversial. However, his Honour then continued, *obiter dictum*, to suggest that some form of overt activity is necessary in order for the offence to be completed.

> The 'purpose' is expressed by the words used and the intention is the deliberate and conscious expressions. Thus, the *mens rea* is the intentional communication by the proscribed means knowingly and consciously expressing the desire to commit the proscribed act. The *actus reus* is partly the communication via the prohibited medium, the computer, completed when he does any overt physical activity that signifies objectively an intention to carry out, if circumstances permitted, the proscribed act . . . Therefore, I think that it is any such sexually pernicious and

88 *Ibid.*, at 16 per Williams Prov. Ct. J.   89 *Ibid.*, at 16–17.   90 *Ibid.*, at 24.

predacious communications directed to a child by means of a computer, accompanied by any directly related behaviour, regardless of the commission of a listed secondary offence, is what Parliament has prohibited.[91]

The clear implication of this statement is that some overt activity on the part of the defendant is necessary in order for the offence to be completed. With respect, it is submitted that such an additional element does not appear from a plain reading of the section. It also militates against the purpose of the legislation which, as his Honour found, 'is intentionally not only proactive and inchoate with respect to the listed secondary offences, but, it also acts as an effective prophylactic against a baneful predacious syndrome that is apparently prevalent on the internet'.[92] To require some overt activity before the offence is complete seems to undermine the effectiveness of the provision, and to be contrary to Parliament's clear intention.

In addition, his Honour indicated that proof of this offence requires the prosecution to prove that the purpose of the communication was 'to urge' the minor to engage in the prohibited activity.[93] With respect, it is submitted that this is too narrow a reading of the provision. The offence punishes communications which are made 'for the purpose of facilitating' the commission of a prescribed offence. While urging the other person to engage in sexual activity is certainly one way of facilitating the commission of an offence, there may be other examples which fall short of 'urging'. For example, pornographic material may be sent in order to facilitate a sexual offence but would not necessarily constitute 'urging'. Nor is there any requirement that the communication be indecent. To limit the provision to communications which 'urge' the minor to engage in the prohibited conduct imposes an unnecessary limitation on the scope of the offence, making it an offence of procuring rather than facilitation.

Similar issues were raised by the decision of the Alberta Court of Appeal in *R* v. *Legare*.[94] In this case, the defendant, a 32-year-old man, posed as a 17-year-old youth in order to meet the 12-year-old complainant in an Internet chat room. They engaged in sexually explicit exchanges and had two telephone conversations, one of which was sexual in nature. According to the 'Agreed Statement of Facts', although the defendant admitted the sexual nature of the communications, he did not intend to commit or facilitate a sexual offence with the complainant, nor did he intend to meet the complainant.[95]

---

91 *Ibid.*, at 17–18.   92 *Ibid.*, at 16.   93 *Ibid.*, at 16.
94 [2008] ABCA 138.   95 *Ibid.*, at [10]–[11].

At trial, the accused was found not guilty on the basis that for an offence to be committed under s. 172.1 the communication must be for the purpose of facilitating the commission of an offence. Although his comments were 'reprehensible in the extreme', there was no evidence that the accused intended the complainant to take his words seriously.[96] He was therefore not acting with the requisite purpose. The defendant's appeal on this count was allowed and a retrial ordered.

The offence under s. 172.1(1) is not limited to those circumstances where the accused attempts to persuade the child the meet.[97] The trial judge was unduly influenced by the term 'luring' which is used in the marginal note to the section but not in the section itself. The notion of luring would unduly limit the scope of the section by 'introducing a notion of enticing a child to move physically from one place to another'.[98]

On the question of *mens rea*, this is commensurate with the preparatory nature of the offence. The purpose of facilitating the commission of an offence need not be likely to eventuate; it may even be 'far off or unlikely'.[99] Even where an accused claims that the communications were for his sexual gratification, it may still be open to the trier of fact to find that he had the purpose of facilitating a sexual offence:

> a *present* intent to *meet* the child communicated with, is not required. Indeed, the accused may merely hope to bring the child around to acquiescence in some form of offence . . . An accused may elect to target many children, cognizant that some contacts may be unavailing.[100]

The court then went on to say that:

> [t]he question for the trial judge was whether the respondent's communication by means of a computer system made it easier for the commission of one of the enumerated offences . . . and whether the respondent's *mens rea* conformed to that situation.[101]

With respect, the court's interpretation imposes an additional element which is not found in the plain language of the section. The section does not require that the communication in fact facilitate the commission of the offence, merely that it was made for that purpose. Although the two will often be closely related, this adds an additional element which is not found in the section and has not been found by other courts.[102]

---

96 *Ibid.*, at [13]–[14].   97 *Ibid.*, at [55].   98 *Ibid.*, at [56].   99 *Ibid.*, at [63].
100 *Ibid.*, at [62] (original emphasis).   101 *Ibid.*, at [65].
102 *R* v. *Dhandhukia* [2007] OJ no 592 at [2]; *R* v. *Smith* [2007] BCSC 1955 at [12].

Where the secondary offence has been committed, the defendant may be charged with both luring and the offence itself.[103] However, it is arguable that the offence of luring must relate to the preparatory communications, the commission of the offence being inconsistent with the facilitation of that offence.[104]

Under s. 172.1(4) it is *not* a defence that the defendant believed that the person communicated with was at least the relevant age, unless the defendant took all reasonable steps to ascertain the person's age. The implication of this provision is that it is in fact a defence to prove such a belief where the defendant had taken all reasonable steps. Where the person communicated with was not, in fact, a minor – as in undercover police operations – evidence that the person communicated with was represented to the defendant as being under the relevant age is, in the absence of evidence to the contrary, proof that the accused believed that the person was under that age.[105]

One notable feature of s. 172.1 is that it is technologically specific in applying only to communications by a computer system. While computers have certainly given rise to a greater need for such provisions, grooming is not exclusively a digital phenomenon. In many cases there will be a mixture of online and offline communications, and it is difficult to see what would justify this departure from the principle of online/offline consistency. In contrast to the equivalent Australian provision, this cannot be explained by limitations on the exercise of federal power.[106]

C. The United Kingdom

The relevant UK offence is that of arranging or facilitating the commission of a child sex offence. Under s. 14(1) Sexual Offences Act 2003 (UK) it is an offence for a person to intentionally arrange or facilitate something that he 'intends to do, intends another person to do, or believes that another person will do' and which will involve the commission of a specified child sex offence.[107]

The offending conduct is 'arranges or facilitates' something which will involve a specified offence – words that, when given their ordinary meaning, may encompass a broad range of conduct.[108] In contrast to the

---

103 *R* v. *Randall* [2006] NSJ no 180 at 14–15.   104 *R* v. *Smith* [2007] BCSC 1955 at [17].
105 Criminal Code (Can), s. 172.1(3). A similar Australian provision is discussed at p. 339.
106 See p. 344.   107 Maximum penalty 14 years' imprisonment: s. 14(4).
108 As to the ordinary meaning of 'facilitating', see p. 345.

Australian provision, the conduct need not be indecent, and in contrast to both the Australian and Canadian provisions, it need not be conducted via a computer or carriage service. The section may therefore apply to a range of conduct which may or may not be online. For example, obscene communications, the purchasing of tickets, the sending of gifts or money, could all be said to facilitate the commission of an offence if accompanied by the necessary intent.

The relevant intent is an intention to arrange or facilitate the prohibited conduct. As that intention relates to conduct which will be done in the future, or which the defendant believes another person will do in the future, it seems unnecessary to prove that the prohibited conduct in fact occurred, only that the defendant arranged or facilitated it to occur. For example, paying money to a website which purports to allow 'customers' to direct live sex acts performed by under-age girls could constitute an offence, without the defendant actually directing such acts. This is also consistent with the need to allow for undercover operations and early intervention by law enforcement. It is, nonetheless, unfortunate that the section is phrased in terms of doing it 'will' rather than 'would' involve the commission of an offence.

The specified offences are found in ss. 9 to 13 of the Act and cover a range of offending. Importantly, they include offences of causing a child to engage in sexual activity or to watch a sexual act and engaging in sexual activity in the presence of a child. They are therefore capable of applying where the defendant arranges or facilitates the minor to perform a sexual act or to watch the defendant perform a sexual act.

There is no provision under s. 14 for defences where, for example, the defendant believed the minor to be over sixteen. Because liability under s. 14 is predicated on conduct which will constitute an offence under one of the other provisions, the relevant defences are found in those predicate offences. For example, imagine that the defendant is charged under s. 14 with facilitating the offence of causing or inciting a child to engage in sexual activity under s. 10. For the defendant to be liable under s. 14 the proposed conduct must be such that it will be an offence under s. 10. However, it is a defence under that section if the defendant reasonably believed the person was over 16. If the defendant could raise a reasonable doubt on that issue, there would be no predicate offence under s. 10 and therefore no liability under s. 14.

One potentially problematic aspect of this provision is that the 'something' which is arranged or facilitated may occur 'in any part of the world'. Given the global nature of modern communications, this seems a desirable expansion of extraterritoriality, bringing within the scope of the offence sexual exploitation of minors wherever they are in the world. Such conduct must, however, constitute an offence under one of the specified provisions. As none of these offences are expressly extraterritorial, if read literally there would be no offence if the minor was located outside the jurisdiction. It would have been preferable for the provision to read 'would involve the commission of an offence under any of sections 9 to 13 if the conduct occurred in England and Wales'.[109]

Because the provision is phrased in broad terms and is not limited to indecent communications, there is a danger that it may restrict appropriate sexual communications with minors.[110] This is addressed by s. 14(2) which provides that it is not an offence if the person 'arranges or facilitates something that he believes another person will do, but that he does not intend to do or intend another person to do, and any [specified offence] would be an offence against a child for whose protection he acts'. A person acts for the protection of a child if he or she acts for the purpose of 'protecting the child from sexually transmitted infection, protecting the physical safety of the child, preventing the child from becoming pregnant, or promoting the child's emotional well-being by the giving of advice'.[111] In addition, the arranging or facilitating must not be for the purpose of obtaining sexual gratification or causing or encouraging the child's participation in the activity constituting the specified offence.[112]

For example, a parent provides contraception to their under-age daughter who they believe is having under-age sex with her older boyfriend. They do so for the purpose of protecting her from pregnancy and sexually transmitted infections. Although this may be said to facilitate the commission of an offence against her, and the parent believes that sex will occur, he or she does not intend for the sex to occur, nor is the parent acting for the purposes of sexual gratification or encouraging the activity.

4. Inducing or procuring

The next category of grooming offences apply where the defendant encourages or induces a minor to engage in sexual activity. Typically, the sexual activity is intended to be with the defendant or a third

---

109 Cf Sexual Offences Act 2003 (UK), s. 15(2)(b).
110 Similar issues are discussed in the US context, see p. 355.
111 Sexual Offences Act 2003 (UK), s. 14(3).   112 *Ibid.*

person, but it is also common for defendants to try to persuade minors to engage in acts of masturbation, or to persuade the minor to observe the defendant masturbating.

Although the defendant has moved from facilitating to actively encouraging such conduct, as noted above the traditional inchoate offences are of limited assistance in this context.[113] Accordingly, a number of jurisdictions have more targeted incitement provisions such as inciting a child to engage in an act of indecency,[114] or causing or inciting a child to take part in child pornography.[115] While most offences of this nature are technologically neutral, and can apply equally in a digital context, some difficulty may arise where the offence requires the conduct to have occurred 'in the presence of' a minor.[116] For example, where the conduct is viewed by the minor via a webcam can it be said to have occurred 'in the presence of' that minor?

This issue was considered in *US* v. *Cochran*[117] where the defendant was charged under 18 USC § 2422(b) with knowingly persuading, inducing, enticing or coercing a minor to engage in sexual activity for which any person can be charged with a criminal offence.[118] The defendant was charged after masturbating via webcam for an undercover police officer whom he believed to be a thirteen-year-old girl. The underlying offence in this case was fondling in the presence of a minor, which was an offence under Indiana law.[119] The court had no difficulty in applying this offence to the facts of this case. 'Nothing in the Indiana statute would indicate that "presence" required physical presence in the same room, rather than presence through visual perception.'[120]

In addition, Australia, the UK and the United States each have specific provisions which punish inducing or procuring a minor to engage in sexual activity.

---

113 See pp. 335–6.
114 Indecency with Children Act 1960 (UK), s. 1; Criminal Code (Can), ss. 152–3; and Criminal Law Consolidation Act 1935 (SA), s. 63B. For an analysis of the Canadian provision in an online context, see *R* v. *Legare* [2008] ABCA 138 at [32]–[51].
115 Crimes Act 1900 (ACT), s. 64; Crimes Act 1900 (NSW), s. 91G; Crimes Act 1958 (Vic), s. 69; Criminal Code Act 1924 (Tas), s. 130; Criminal Code Act 1983 (NT), s. 125E; and Sexual Offences Act 2003 (UK), ss. 48–50.
116 E.g., engaging in a sexual activity in the presence of a child: Sexual Offences Act 2003 (UK), s. 11.
117 510 F Supp 2d 470 (ND Ind 2007).
118 This section is discussed in detail below at p. 355.
119 Indiana Code § 35–42–4–5(c).
120 *US* v. *Cochran*, 510 F Supp 2d 470, 478 (ND Ind 2007).

A. Australia

The Australian federal provision is found in s. 474.26 Criminal Code (Cth).[121] Under this provision it is an offence for a person who is at least eighteen years of age (the 'sender') to use a carriage service to transmit a communication to another person who is, or who the sender believes to be, under sixteen years of age (the 'recipient') with the intention of procuring the recipient to engage in, or submit to, sexual activity with the sender.[122]

This section mirrors the grooming provision discussed earlier, and that discussion should be referred to.[123] The key distinction is that this provision applies at the point of 'procuring', defined to mean:

> (a) encourage, entice or recruit the person to engage in that activity; or
> (b) induce the person (whether by threats, promises or otherwise) to engage in that activity.[124]

The words 'encourage', 'entice', 'recruit' and 'induce' are not defined and are presumably to be given their ordinary meaning.[125] It is sufficient that the defendant intended to procure the sexual activity; there is no requirement that the minor actually engaged in the relevant conduct. This not only facilitates the use of undercover operations, it also allows intervention before any sexual activity has occurred.

For example, in the first prosecution under this provision, a 54-year-old Victorian man pleaded guilty to communicating with a 14-year-old girl through emails, text messages and phone calls. The communications began when the girl accidentally sent an SMS to the man while trying to contact an old schoolteacher. He replied and they continued to communicate, via text messages, email and the Internet. Some of the communications were of a sexual nature, and the girl sent pictures of herself to the defendant. He then travelled interstate to meet her but, after an apparent change of heart, the girl refused to kiss him and he returned

---

121 Maximum penalty 15 years' imprisonment: s. 474.26. See, e.g., *R* v. *Gajjar* [2008] VSCA 268; *Commonwealth Director of Public Prosecutions* v. *Hizhnikov* [2008] VSCA 269; *Tector* v. *R* [2008] NSWCCA 151.

122 A number of state provisions may also apply in this context, Crimes Act 1900 (ACT), s. 66; Crimes Act 1900 (NSW), s. 66EB; Criminal Code Act 1983 (NT), s. 131; Criminal Code Act 1899 (Qld), s. 218A; Criminal Code Act Compilation Act 1913 (WA), s. 204B; Criminal Code Act 1924 (Tas), s. 125D; and Crimes Act 1958 (Vic), s. 58.

123 See p. 343.   124 Criminal Code (Cth), s. 474.28(11).

125 The ordinary meaning of some of these words is discussed in the context of the US provision at p. 356.

to Melbourne. However, a subsequent meeting was arranged before the girl's mother discovered the communications and informed police.[126]

The defendant must procure the recipient to 'engage in, or submit to, sexual activity with the sender'. This may cause difficulties where the sender is procuring the recipient to, for example, masturbate. While the definition of 'sexual activity' is broad enough to encompass such conduct, it may be argued that the conduct is not 'engaged in' with the sender.[127] This is in contrast to the equivalent Queensland provision which applies to a 'sexual act' which need not involve the defendant.[128]

B. The United Kingdom

In the UK, the equivalent offences of intentionally causing or inciting a child to engage in sexual activity are found in ss. 8 and 10 Sexual Offences Act 2003 (UK). The offences are in similar terms with s. 8 applying where the victim is under thirteen and the defendant is of any age. Section 10 applies where the defendant is over eighteen and the victim is either under sixteen and the defendant does not reasonably believe that the victim is sixteen or over, or the victim is under thirteen.[129] The use of the word 'incite' ensures that the section applies in circumstances where the young person does not engage in the activity, including where no minor is in fact involved.

The term 'sexual activity' is not defined and is capable of broad application. It would clearly apply to situations where the defendant causes or incites the young person to have sex with the defendant, or another person, or to masturbate. Where the defendant causes or incites the young person to watch him masturbate, difficulties may arise as it may be argued that the minor has not 'engaged in' that activity.[130] It has also been argued that the provision may encompass a defendant who causes or incites a young person to look at pornography.[131] In such cases, for the offence to apply the act of viewing the conduct or images would have to be interpreted as a 'sexual activity' in itself. Unlike the offence of arranging or facilitating sexual activity by a minor, this offence does not apply to conduct occurring 'in any part of the world'.[132]

---

126 D. Miletic, '"Groomer" guilty of procuring girl, 14, for sex', *The Age*, 26 May 2006. Also see Griffith and Roth, *Protecting Children*, p. 71.
127 Cf the equivalent US provision, see p. 358.   128 *R* v. *Campbell* [2004] QCA 342.
129 Maximum penalty 14 years' imprisonment: ss. 8(3), 10(3).
130 Cf the interpretation of the equivalent US offence at p. 358.
131 Gillespie, 'Indecent images', 415–16.   132 See pp. 350–1.

C. The United States

The principal US federal offence in this context is 18 USC § 2422(b) which makes it an offence to:

> use the mail or any facility or means of interstate or foreign commerce . . . to knowingly persuade, induce, entice, or coerce any individual under 18 to engage in prostitution or any sexual activity for which any person can be charged with a criminal offense, or attempts to do so.[133]

This section has survived numerous constitutional challenges. For example, in *US* v. *Dhingra*[134] the appellant, who was forty years old at the time of the offence, contacted the then fourteen-year-old victim having seen the victim's personal homepage. The defendant represented himself as being twenty-seven. They communicated via the 'America Online' Instant Messenger service and subsequently by email. The exchanges became increasingly sexual, with the defendant repeatedly urging the victim to meet him. When they finally met the defendant fondled the victim beneath her clothing and later placed her hand on his penis. Further sexual activity took place in the defendant's car.

The court rejected the defendant's various constitutional challenges, confirming its earlier decision in *US* v. *Meek*[135] that the section regulates conduct, not speech. 'Simply put, the inducement of minors to engage in illegal sexual activity enjoys no First Amendment protection.'[136] The court rejected the suggestion that the section may chill legitimate speech, such as a parent discussing sexual health issues with their teenage child, or a general informational website about birth control and safe sex. 'The statute's intent provision, coupled with the requirement that the purpose of the conduct must be for criminal sexual activity, sufficiently excludes legitimate activity, including speech, from its scope.'[137]

Courts have generally taken the view that the terms 'persuade', 'induce', 'entice' or 'coerce' are ordinary words that do not need further technical

---

133 Maximum penalty is 30 years' imprisonment: 18 USC § 2422(b). Other relevant provisions include 18 USC §§ 2251, 2252(a)(2) and 2425 (considered in *US* v. *Giordano*, 442 F 3d 30 (2nd Cir 2006)).

134 371 F 3d 557 (9th Cir 2004), amended by *US* v. *Dhingra*, 2004 US App LEXIS 15288, rehearing denied by, corrected by, *US* v. *Dhingra*, 2004 US App LEXIS 15302.

135 366 F 3d 705, 720–2 (9th Cir 2004).

136 *US* v. *Dhingra*, 371 F 3d 557, 563 (9th Cir 2004). Also see *US* v. *Bailey*, 228 F 3d 637, 639 (6th Cir 2000); cert. denied, 532 US 1009 (2001); *US* v. *Thomas* 410 F 3d 1235, 1244 (10th Cir 2005); *US* v. *Tykarsky*, 446 F 3d 458, 473 (3rd Cir 2006); and *US* v. *Gagliardi*, 506 F 3d 140, 147–8 (2nd Cir 2007).

137 *US* v. *Dhingra*, 371 F 3d 557, 562 (9th Cir 2004).

explanation,[138] although some courts have provided guidance on the
ordinary meaning of these words. For example, 'persuade' is synonymous
with 'convince',[139] the dictionary definition being 'to move by argument,
entreaty, or expostulation to a belief, position, or course of action'.[140] To
'entice' is 'to attract artfully or adroitly or by arousing hope or desire:
tempt',[141] and is synonymous with 'lure'.[142] Finally, 'induce' has been held
to mean 'to lead or move by influence or persuasion; to prevail upon' or
'to stimulate the occurrence of; cause'.[143]

The fault element 'knowingly' refers both to the verbs (persuades,
induces, entices, or coerces) as well as to the fact that the person is under
18.[144] The completed offence requires proof only that the defendant had
an intention to persuade or to attempt to persuade, not the performance
of the sexual acts themselves.[145] Although it is not necessary to prove
that the defendant intended to engage in the underlying sexual act, evidence that the defendant did have such an intention is nonetheless relevant evidence from which the jury may infer the necessary intention to
persuade.[146] However, the victim's willingness to engage in sexual activity
is irrelevant.[147]

The onus remains on the prosecution to prove knowledge; leaving open
the possibility that the defendant will raise the 'fantasy defence' discussed
above.[148] For the prosecution to succeed, the defendant's subjective belief
must therefore be determined as a matter of inference in light of the
evidence. For example, in US v. Kaye[149] the defendant was convicted
under 18 USC §§ 2422(b) and 2423(b). The defendant had initiated an
Instant Message conversation with a boy, 'Conrad', whom he believed was

---

138 Ibid.; US v. Panfil, 338 F 3d 1299, 1300–1 (11th Cir 2003).
139 US v. Thomas, 410 F 3d 1235, 1245 (10th Cir 2005).
140 US v. Rashkovski, 301 F 3d 1133, 1136–7 (9th Cir 2002), citing Merriam-Webster's
     Collegiate Dictionary (2002). Also see US v. Goetzke, 494 F 3d 1231, 1235 (9th Cir 2007).
141 Ibid.   142 US v. Thomas, 410 F 3d 1235, 1245 (10th Cir 2005).
143 US v. Murrell, 368 F 3d 1283, 1286–7 (11th Cir 2004). Also see US v. Rashkovsk, 301 F
     3d 1133, 1137 (9th Cir 2002); US v. Thomas, 410 F 3d 1235, 1244–5 (10th Cir 2005);
     and US v. Goetzke, 494 F 3d 1231, 1235 (9th Cir 2007).
144 US v. Meek, 366 F 3d 705, 718 (9th Cir 2004); US v. Cote, 504 F 3d 682, 686 (7th Cir
     2007).
145 US v. Bailey, 228 F 3d 637, 639 (6th Cir 2000). Also see US v. Murrell, 368 F 3d 1283,
     1286 (11th Cir 2004); US v. Brand, 467 F 3d 179, 202 (2nd Cir 2006); US v. Thomas, 410
     F 3d 1235, 1244 (10th Cir 2005); US v. Patten, 397 F 3d 1100, 1103 (8th Cir 2005); and
     US v. Dwinells, 508 F 3d 63, 70 (1st Cir 2007).
146 US v. Thomas, 410 F 3d 1235, 1245 (10th Cir 2005).
147 US v. Dhingra, 371 F 3d 557, 568 (9th Cir 2004).   148 See p. 337.
149 451 F Supp 2d 775 (ED Va 2006).

13 years of age. The 'boy' was in fact a 26-year-old member of 'Perverted Justice', an organisation which exposes adults who use the Internet to seek sexual activity with children.

During the sexually explicit conversation which followed, the defendant expressed his desire to engage in sexual activity with 'Conrad'. Pictures were exchanged; the picture of 'Conrad' being of a young boy taken from an adoption website, while the defendant sent pictures of himself engaging in sexual acts with another man. The defendant even had a telephone conversation with a person he believed was 'Conrad' but who was in fact another, female, member of Perverted Justice. The defendant subsequently travelled from Maryland to Virginia for a sexual rendezvous with the 'boy'. Upon arriving at the address provided by 'Conrad' he entered the house through the garage and was met by an NBC reporter, the event having been staged in a co-operative 'sting' operation between NBC Dateline and Perverted Justice.

The court rejected the defendant's argument that 'he believed he was meeting a young adult (of consenting age) for a homosexual encounter and that the picture and voice of the person purporting to be "Conrad" were that of an eighteen-year-old male'.[150] First, without any reference to age by 'Conrad' the defendant asked during their initial contact 'ok you are only 13?' Secondly, throughout their conversations he repeatedly and unambiguously acknowledged Conrad's age as 13 and 'sooo sooo young'. Thirdly, his reaction to being confronted by the NBC reporter contained incriminating statements such as 'I know I'm in trouble.' Fourthly, the defendant was not a credible witness. Finally, expert evidence was adduced as to the apparent age of the young boy portrayed in the photograph, and whether it was likely the voice of the woman on the telephone could be mistaken for an eighteen-year-old male. In conclusion, the court found beyond reasonable doubt that the defendant believed he was 'enticing, persuading, and inducing' an individual who was thirteen years of age.

The term 'sexual activity' is not defined and applies to *any* sexual activity by *any* person.[151] The only qualification is that it must be conduct 'for which any person can be charged with a criminal offense'.[152] It has been held that the question of whether the sexual activity would constitute

---

150   *Ibid.*, 784–6.
151   *US* v. *Cochran*, 510 F Supp 2d 470, 478 (ND Ind 2007). The facts of this case are set out at p. 352.
152   *Ibid.*

a criminal offence is determined according to the laws of the jurisdiction in which the defendant is prosecuted.[153] In some cases, this may be a jurisdiction other than that in which the defendant resides.[154]

Difficulties may arise where the minor is encouraged to perform a sexual activity by him or herself as this may not be a sexual activity for which a person could be charged with an offence. In such cases, it would be necessary to rely upon specific offences relating to inciting a minor to engage in an indecent act. Circumstances where the defendant encourages a minor to watch him masturbate may also prove problematic as the statute requites that the minor 'engage in' the sexual activity. This issue arose in *US* v. *Cochran*[155] where it was held that an Indiana offence of fondling in the presence of a minor could apply where the defendant masturbated in the 'presence' of a minor via webcam. Although the court acknowledged that it was 'somewhat awkward' to read the offence as inducing or persuading a minor to engage in the sexual activity of the defendant fondling in the presence of a minor, the jury found this to be the case and the court upheld its verdict.[156]

It is well established that an offence under 18 USC § 2422(b) does not require the involvement of an actual minor,[157] an interpretation which is vital in permitting the use of undercover agents. For example, in *US* v. *Murrell*[158] the defendant used the Internet to contact a man who purported to be a father, but who was in fact an undercover officer, and arranged to have sex with the person's daughter. The court rejected the defendant's argument that the offence could not be committed where, as here, the defendant does not communicate with a minor, but only through an adult intermediary. On a plain reading of the section, direct communication with a minor or supposed minor is unnecessary.[159]

153 *US* v. *Dhingra*, 371 F 3d 557, 565 (9th Cir 2004). The question of whether it may be an offence under federal law has been left open: *US* v. *Dwinells*, 508 F 3d 63, 71 (1st Cir 2007).
154 *US* v. *Byrne*, 171 F 3d 1231, 1235 (10th Cir 1999). Because such offences are often committed across borders, difficulties may arise where conduct is criminal in one jurisdiction, but not another; see *US* v. *Patten*, 397 F 3d 1100 (8th Cir 2005).
155 510 F Supp 2d 470, 477 (ND Ind 2007).   156 *Ibid.*, 478.
157 *US* v. *Farner*, 251 F 3d 510, 513 (5th Cir 2001); *US* v. *Root*, 296 F 3d 1222, 1227–9 (11th Cir 2002); *US* v. *Meek*, 366 F 3d 705, 717–20 (9th Cir 2004); *US* v. *Hornaday*, 392 F 3d 1306 (11th Cir 2004); cert. denied, 545 US 1134 (2005); *US* v. *Sims*, 428 F 3d 945, 960 (10th Cir 2005); *US* v. *Helder*, 452 F 3d 751, 756 (8th Cir 2006); *US* v. *Tykarsky*, 446 F 3d 458, 466 (3rd Cir 2006); *US* v. *Hicks*, 457 F 3d 838, 841 (8th Cir 2006); *US* v. *Gagliardi*, 506 F 3d 140, 145 (2nd Cir 2007).
158 368 F 3d 1283 (11th Cir 2004).   159 *Ibid.*, 1287.

Where the defendant was in fact communicating with an undercover police officer the offence must be charged as an attempt. In such cases it must not only be shown that the defendant acted with intent to induce a minor to engage in unlawful sexual activity, but that he also took a substantial step toward that goal.[160] It is important to emphasise that an attempt under 18 USC § 2422(b) is an attempt to persuade, etc., not an attempt to engage in the underlying act.[161] It is 'an attempt to achieve the mental state of assent' rather than the physical act of sex.[162] Consequently the 'substantial step' which is necessary to prove relates to persuading, enticing, etc., not a substantial step towards the commission of the underlying act. Relevant factors which the courts have looked to in determining this issue include sexual dialogue between the defendant and the 'minor', repeated references to what actions would be performed upon meeting the 'minor', sending sexually suggestive images and travel by the defendant to meet the 'minor'.[163] While physical proximity or travel may be probative, it is not necessary to constitute a substantial step.[164]

A good example is found in *US* v. *Brand*.[165] In that case, the defendant initially contacted two girls whom he believed were thirteen years of age. This contact occurred in a chat room entitled 'I Love Older Men', which was notorious for illegal activity, including the enticement of minors. Brand then made repeated sexual advances towards the 'girls', describing in graphic terms the sex acts which he would like to perform and attempting to set up a meeting. Finally, he took a 'substantial step' towards the completion of the crime by going to the meeting place that had been arranged with one of them. In his possession was a sign with the girl's name written on it, and three condoms in the glove compartment of his car. This was held to be 'more than sufficient evidence for the jury to conclude that Brand attempted to entice a minor to engage in sexual activity in violation of 18 USC § 2422(b)'.[166]

---

160 *US* v. *Fuller*, 77 Fed Appx 371, 378 (6th Cir 2003); *US* v. *Farner*, 251 F 3d 510, 512 (5th Cir 2001); *US* v. *Root*, 296 F 3d 1222, 1227 (11th Cir 2002); *US* v. *Meek*, 366 F 3d 705, 717–18 (9th Cir 2004); *US* v. *Sims*, 428 F 3d 945, 959 (10th Cir 2005); *US* v. *Brand*, 467 F 3d 179, 202 (2nd Cir 2006); *US* v. *Helder*, 452 F 3d 751, 756 (8th Cir 2006); *US* v. *Tykarsky*, 446 F 3d 458, 465–9 (3rd Cir 2006); and *US* v. *Cote*, 504 F 3d 682, 687 (7th Cir 2007).
161 *US* v. *Thomas*, 410 F 3d 1235, 1244 (6th Cir 2005).
162 *US* v. *Goetzke*, 494 F 3d 1231, 1236 (9th Cir 2007).
163 *US* v. *Kaye*, 451 F Supp 2d 787 (ED Va 2006); *US* v. *Goetzke*, 494 F 3d 1231 (9th Cir 2007).
164 *US* v. *Goetzke*, 494 F 3d 1231, 1236 (9th Cir 2007).
165 467 F 3d 179, 202–4 (2nd Cir 2006).   166 *Ibid.*, 204.

Similarly, in *US* v. *Murrell*[167] the defendant made several explicit incriminating statements to the undercover officer, travelled two hours to another county and was carrying a teddy bear, US$300 and a box of condoms when he arrived at the meeting site. 'His actions, taken as a whole, demonstrate unequivocally that he intended to influence a young girl into engaging in unlawful sexual activity.'[168]

Courts have also rejected arguments that the defence of legal impossibility may apply in such cases. In *US* v. *Farner*[169] the defendant communicated with 'Cindy' via America Online's Instant Messenger service. The defendant, believing Cindy to be fourteen years old, communicated with her over three months, using instant messaging, email and telephone calls. During this time he sent adult pornographic pictures to her and tried to persuade her to have sex with him. An arrangement was made for the defendant and Cindy to meet for the purposes of sex. He was arrested on arrival, 'Cindy' being an FBI agent.

The defendant argued that it was legally impossible for him to have committed this offence, as the 'victim' was in fact an adult, and therefore he ought to have been acquitted. The court noted the difficulties which have arisen in trying to draw a distinction between factual and legal impossibility, a distinction which has been repudiated, or at least questioned, by most federal courts.[170] In any event, this was a case of factual impossibility because the defendant unquestionably intended to engage in the conduct proscribed by law but failed only because of circumstances unknown to him.[171] It was not a situation where 'the actions which the defendant performs or sets in motion, even if fully carried out *as he desires*, would not constitute a crime'.[172]

A defendant may, in some cases, not be guilty of an attempt where he has abandoned his criminal purpose. In *US* v. *Wales*[173] the defendant had online conversations with an agent posing as a twelve-year-old girl, and tried to persuade the 'girl' to send him photographs of herself masturbating. In order to encourage her he sent her pornographic images and used a webcam to show himself masturbating. He even adopted an alternate persona, a fourteen-year-old girl he named 'sassyangelgoddess', to engage in simultaneous chat with the girl, encouraging her to take the

---

167 368 F 3d 1283 (11th Cir 2004).   168 *Ibid.*, 1287–9.
169 251 F 3d 510 (5th Cir 2001).   170 *Ibid.*, 512.   171 *Ibid.*, 512–13.
172 *Ibid.*, 513, citing *US* v. *Oviedo*, 525 F 2d 881, 883 (5th Cir 1976) (emphasis added by the court). Also see *US* v. *Root*, 296 F 3d 1222, 1227 (11th Cir 2002); *US* v. *Gagliardi*, 506 F 3d 140, 146 (2nd Cir 2007) and *US* v. *Cote* 504 F 3d 682, 687 (7th Cir 2007).
173 127 Fed Appx 424 (2005).

photographs of herself. The online conversations ended with an invitation by the agent to meet so that 'she' could give him photos she had taken. The defendant indicated that he had to work and could not make it, after which point there were no further conversations.

The court rejected the defendant's assertion that he had abandoned or renounced his criminal purpose.[174] Federal courts have rejected such a defence but even if available it was not made out in this case. Although the online conversations ceased, the defendant's last conversation showed a continued interest in the girl and pictures that he believed she had taken. His conduct did not demonstrate complete and voluntary abandonment and could equally indicate a fear of being caught as much as renunciation of his criminal purpose.[175]

5. Travelling with intent

The final stage in the continuum of grooming-type conduct is where the defendant travels to meet a minor for a sexual purpose. Ordinarily, such conduct would fall short of being an attempt as it is not sufficiently proximate to the commission of the completed offence. It does, however, provide what is practically the last opportunity to intercept an offender either before he meets with the minor or, where there is no actual minor, the undercover operation is revealed. Relevant offences are found in both the UK and the United States.

A. The United Kingdom

In the UK, the offence of meeting a child following sexual grooming is found in s. 15 Sexual Offences Act 2003 (UK). This provides that a person aged eighteen or over (A) commits an offence if:

(a) A has met or communicated with another person (B) on at least two occasions and subsequently—
  (i) A intentionally meets B,
  (ii) A travels with the intention of meeting B in any part of the world or arranges to meet B in any part of the world, or
  (iii) B travels with the intention of meeting A in any part of the world,
(b) A intends to do anything to or in respect of B, during or after the meeting mentioned in paragraph (a)(i) to (iii) and in any part of the

---

174 *Ibid.*, 432.   175 *Ibid.*

world, which if done will involve the commission by A of a relevant
offence,

(c) B is under 16, and
(d) A does not reasonably believe that B is 16 or over.[176]

The physical element of this offence first requires that there has been at
least two meetings or instances of communication between A and B prior
to the alleged offence. There is no requirement that these communications
or meetings be sexual in nature. It is presumably intended to ensure that
the provision targets grooming-type behaviour, rather than any arrangement to meet with a minor for a sexual purpose. Bearing in mind that
the section applies equally to the offline environment, it could have very
broad application if not limited in this way. For example, it could apply
where the defendant spoke to an under-age male prostitute and arranged
a subsequent meeting for sex. While an offence may have been committed
in this scenario, it is not an example of the grooming-type behaviour at
which this section is directed.

It is arguable that the offence need not be so limited, and should be
part of a broader attack on so-called 'sex tourism'. That is, regardless
of whether the defendant has previously communicated with a minor,
travelling with the intention of engaging in illegal sex, wherever that sex
occurs, should be an offence. This would complement offences such as
s. 72 Sexual Offences Act 2003 (UK) which apply extraterritorial jurisdiction to sexual offences committed outside the UK. By way of contrast, the
equivalent US provision is not so limited.[177]

The offence requires that the defendant either met with the minor,
was travelling to meet or arranging to meet the minor, or the minor was
travelling to meet the defendant. Obviously, the offence of meeting with
a minor can only occur where 'B' is in fact a minor. For example, Lee
Costi, aged twenty-one, was sentenced to nine years' imprisonment after
pleading guilty to various offences including three counts of meeting
a child following sexual grooming. Costi first communicated with his
thirteen- and fourteen-year-old victims in Internet chat rooms where he
arranged to meet them for sex.[178]

176 As amended by Criminal Justice and Immigration Acct 2008 (UK), s. 73 and Sch. 15 [1].
Maximum penalty 10 years' imprisonment: s. 15(4). For a discussion of the equivalent
Scottish offence, see A. A. Gillespie, 'Enticing children on the Internet: The response of
the criminal law' (2006) 3 Juridical Review 229.
177 See p. 364.
178 Virtual Global Taskforce Press Release, 'Website snares its first online grooming offender',
22 June 2006, www.virtualglobaltaskforce.com/news/article_22062006.html; and BBC

In order to facilitate early intervention, the offence equally applies where the defendant is found to be travelling with the relevant intention or arranging to meet B. This would also apply where the 'minor' is in fact an undercover police officer as in such cases it is not possible to meet 'B.'

Although there may be a potential overlap with the general doctrine of attempts, s. 15 applies at an earlier stage without the need to prove the level of proximity necessary for an attempt. The prosecution need only prove that the defendant intended to engage in conduct during or after the meeting which would involve a specified offence.

The fault element of this offence is in two parts. The first is that the offender intended to engage in conduct which would constitute a relevant offence. Actual intention must be proved and it has been suggested that this may present a considerable obstacle to successful prosecutions.[179] However, the experience in reported US cases suggests that an offender's intention will often be manifest by earlier communications as well as overt conduct.

The second aspect is that 'A does not reasonably believe that B is over 16'. This is unusual in that it is expressed in the negative, and contains an objective requirement. It is not a defence, and so the onus is on the Crown to prove that the defendant did not have such a belief. Consequently, if there is a reasonable doubt that the defendant held such a belief, he must be acquitted. Although it may seem that this would present considerable difficulties in the context of the 'fantasy defence', the fault element contains an objective element. Therefore the Crown need not exclude the possibility that the defendant held a subjective belief, but rather that he did not hold a reasonable belief.

The section is given extended jurisdictional reach. A plain reading of the section would suggest that the meeting or the act of travelling must occur within the territorial jurisdiction of the UK, even though the intended meeting may be 'in any part of the world'.[180] However, the previous meetings or communications may have occurred in, from or to any place in the world.[181] For example, A may have met B overseas and exchanged contact details. He or she may then make contact with B electronically, by phone, SMS, or email, on their return. This would be sufficient to constitute the predicate meetings/communications.

News, 'Web paedophile given nine years', 22 June 2006, http://news.bbc.co.uk/2/hi/uk_news/england/5106612.stm.
179 Ost, 'Sexual grooming', 152–3.   180 Sexual Offences Act 2003 (UK), s. 15(1)(b).
181 S. 15(2)(a).

Alternatively, A may communicate with B via the Internet where B is in another jurisdiction. Where A meets with B, or is en route to meeting B with the relevant intention, then the offence has been made out. In this context, the definition of 'relevant offence' is particularly important. A relevant offence is defined as one of a number of sexual offences under Part 1 and Sch. 3 of the Act. It also extends to conduct occurring outside the jurisdiction which is not an offence in that country, but which would be an offence if done in England and Wales.[182]

B. The United States

The equivalent US offence, and one which has been frequently utilised, is travelling with intent to engage in illicit sexual conduct.[183] Under this provision it is an offence to travel in interstate commerce or into the United States or, in the case of a US citizen or permanent resident, in foreign commerce, for the purpose of engaging in any illicit sexual conduct. 'Illicit sexual conduct' means a sexual act[184] with a person under eighteen years of age that would be in violation of 18 USC Chapter 109A if it occurred in the special maritime and territorial jurisdiction of the United States, or any commercial sex act.[185] Only where the offence consists of a commercial sex act with a person under eighteen is it a defence to prove that the defendant reasonably believed that the other person was at least eighteen years of age.[186]

As with 18 USC § 2422, there is no need to prove an actual minor was involved.[187] Because the offence relates to travel with the relevant purpose, even where an undercover officer is involved the defendant can be charged with the substantive offence rather than attempt.[188] For the same reason, no issue of impossibility arises where the offence itself is travelling with a specific purpose.[189]

---

182 S. 15(2)(b).
183 18 USC § 2423(b). Maximum penalty 30 years' imprisonment: 18 USC § 2423(b).
184 As defined in 18 USC § 2246.   185 As defined in 18 USC § 1591.
186 18 USC § 2423(g).
187 *US* v. *Root*, 296 F 3d 1222, 1231–2 (11th Cir 2002); *US* v. *Vail*, 101 Fed Appx 190, 192 (9th Cir 2004); *US* v. *Sims*, 428 F 3d 945, 959 (10th Cir 2005); *US* v. *Hicks*, 457 F 3d 838, 841 (8th Cir 2006) and *US* v. *Tykarsky*, 446 F 3d 458, 469 (3d Cir 2006).
188 *US* v. *Root*, 296 F 3d 1222, 1231–2 (11th Cir 2002).
189 *US* v. *Sims*, 428 F 3d 945, 959 (10th Cir 2005).

12

Cyberstalking

1. Harassment in cyberspace

The offence of stalking illustrates perfectly how rapidly technology can be adapted to criminal purposes, and even relatively new laws soon overtaken by technological developments. The first anti-stalking law was introduced as recently as 1990 in California, with other jurisdictions soon following. Yet in the intervening years technology has not only facilitated stalking-type behaviour, it has presented considerable challenges to the effectiveness of anti-stalking provisions.

The use of the term 'stalking' in this context is relatively recent,[1] and 'like shoplifting, hooliganism and vandalism, is a description rather than a legal category'.[2] In general terms, 'stalking' may be described as 'a course of conduct in which one individual inflicts on another repeated unwanted intrusions and communications, to such an extent that the victim fears for his or her safety'.[3] It is a complex phenomenon with a range of motivations including jealously, resentment, obsession or the desire to exert control.[4] The stalker may be known to the victim, a former partner, relative, acquaintance or a complete stranger. Although popularly associated with celebrities, stalking-type behaviour commonly occurs in the context of domestic violence.[5] While women

---

1 The *Oxford English Dictionary* cites the first example in 1984.
2 C. Wells, 'Stalking: The criminal law response' (1997) *Criminal Law Review* 463, 463.
3 R. Purcell, M. Pathé and P. E. Mullen, 'Stalking: Defining and prosecuting a new category of offending' (2004) 27 *International Journal of Law and Psychiatry* 157, 157. For a detailed discussion of the nature of stalking see E. Finch, *The Criminalisation of Stalking* (London: Routledge-Cavendish, 2001) and P. E. Mullen, M. Pathé and R. Purcell, *Stalkers and Their Victims* (New York: Cambridge University Press, 2000).
4 E. Ogilvie, *Stalking: Legislative, policing and prosecution patterns in Australia*, AIC Research and Public Policy Series no. 34 (AIC, 2000), pp. 19–20.
5 A. G. Burgess, J. E. Douglas and R. Halloran, 'Stalking behaviours within domestic violence' (1997) 12 *Journal of Family Violence* 389; S. Walby and J. Allen, *Domestic Violence, Sexual Assault and Stalking: Findings from the British Crime Survey*, Home Office Research Study 276 (2004).

are more likely to be the victims of stalking, offenders are predominately male.[6]

Stalking may take a variety of forms including following and/or keeping the victim under surveillance, repeated and harassing phone calls or other communications such as letters or emails, leaving offensive material for the victim and property damage.[7] This conduct may continue for considerable periods of time – often months, sometimes years. Despite a lack of physical violence, stalking can have a significant psychological impact on the victim, including anxiety, sleep disturbances, suicidal thoughts and post-traumatic stress disorder.[8] In some cases, stalking may also be a prelude to actual violence against the victim and/or someone known to the victim.

Although such conduct is not new, in the absence of a specific offence it was difficult to prosecute. While a stalker may engage in conduct which gives rise to a reasonable fear on the part of the victim for his or her safety, in the absence of an actual threat it may be difficult, if not impossible, to prosecute. Prior to the enactment of anti-stalking legislation, victims were forced to rely upon a mixed-bag of possible offences including property offences, offences against the person, offensive or harassing communications and the like.[9] The offence of stalking was therefore a response to this gap in the law. More broadly, it recognises that to focus on the composite elements is to misconstrue and trivialise the totality of the conduct; 'it is not so much the conduct which causes distress as the continuance of the conduct and the ensuing uncertainty and anxiety which this engenders in the victim'.[10]

At the risk of compounding imprecision with imprecision, 'cyberstalking' is simply a descriptive term for the use of new technologies for the purposes of stalking; that is, 'the use of the Internet, e-mail, and other electronic communication devices to stalk another person'.[11] While the

---

6 P. Tjaden and J. Thoennes, *Prevalence, Incidence, and Consequences of Violence Against Women: Findings from the National Violence against Women Survey*, US Department of Justice, Office of Justice Programs (1998), p. 10; I. Grant, N. Bone and K. Grant, 'Canada's criminal harassment provisions: A review of the first ten years' (2003) 29 *Queen's Law Journal* 175, 185–8 and D. Lamplugh and P. Infield, 'Harmonizing anti-stalking laws' (2003) 34 *George Washington International Law Review* 853, 856.

7 Tjaden and Thoennes, *Violence against Women Survey*, p. 13. For a series of case studies see Ogilvie, *Stalking*, pp. 33–52; and Finch, *The Criminalisation of Stalking*, pp. 289–305.

8 Ogilvie, *Stalking*, pp. 21–2.   9 Finch, *The Criminalisation of Stalking*, pp. 119–72.

10 *Ibid.*, p. 171.

11 US Attorney General, *Report to Congress on Stalking and Domestic Violence* (US Department of Justice, Office of Justice Programs, 2001), p. 1. For a general discussion of cyberstalking, see J. M. Deirmenjian, 'Stalking in cyberspace' (1999) 27 *Journal of the*

use of technology in this context is not new, with silent telephone calls being a well-established form of harassment, digital technology has provided a host of new ways in which offenders may stalk their victims. Similar issues have also arisen in the context of online harassment amongst young people: so-called 'cyberbullying'.[12]

Technology not only provides new ways of stalking, it may also help to overcome traditional obstacles to offending, both physical and psychological, and may consequently facilitate, or even encourage, offending behaviour. For example, the relative anonymity of the Internet can cause a loss of social inhibitions and constraints, thereby emboldening offenders to act. It also provides a direct line of communication to the victim which may be more difficult to replicate in the off-line environment.[13] A person who would not contemplate confronting their victim personally may feel no hesitation in sending threatening messages to that person via email. This lack of inhibition may be further encouraged by so-called 'pseudonymity'; the ability to adopt different personae including, in some cases, that of the victim themselves.[14] Lack of personal contact may also encourage the projection of fantasy such that '[t]he victim becomes an easy target for the stalker's projections and narcissistic fantasies that can lead to real-world rejection, humiliation, and rage'.[15]

The ready availability of personal information on the Internet may also facilitate stalking. An offender may search the Internet for information about the victim or may lurk in chat rooms or other online forums frequented by the victim. Stalkers may access mobile phones, computers and PDAs, all of which may contain a wealth of private information such as address books, calendars, call records, SMS/MMS and the like. Simply reading the call register on a mobile phone, for example, tells the stalker when and to whom the victim has been speaking. A more technically sophisticated offender may install malware such as Trojans or key-loggers to gain access to the victim's personal information.

American Academy of Psychiatry and the Law 407; and L. Ellison and Y. Akdeniz, 'Cyberstalking: The regulation of harassment on the Internet' (1998) *Criminal Law Review*, Special Edition: 'Crime, criminal justice and the Internet' 29.

12 A. Gillespie, 'Cyber-bullying and harassment of teenagers: The legal response' (2006) 28 *Journal of Social Welfare & Family Law* 123. Also see www.cyberbullying.org.

13 M. McGrath and E. Casey, 'Forensic psychiatry and the Internet: Practical perspectives on sexual predators and obsessional harassers in cyberspace' (2002) 30 *Journal of the American Academy of Psychiatry and the Law* 81, 85.

14 L. Ellison, 'Cyberstalking: Tackling harassment on the Internet' in D. S. Wall (ed.), *Crime and the Internet* (London: Routledge, 2001), p. 143.

15 McGrath and Casey, 'Forensic psychiatry', 86.

Stalking is often not reported as a separate category in crime statistics, and there is considerable variation as to precisely what constitutes stalking. It is therefore difficult to gain accurate data as to the extent of stalking, let alone cyberstalking. Nonetheless, those statistics which are available indicate that it is an issue of significant concern. A 1998 US survey estimated that 8 per cent of women and 2 per cent of men had been stalked at some time in their lives.[16] In Britain in 2007–8, harassment accounted for 25 per cent of police recorded violence.[17]

Although the picture is less clear with cyberstalking, it seems reasonable to conclude that it is increasing along with the increasing prevalence of digital technology. One study involving female college students found that of a total of 696 stalking incidents, 24.7 per cent involved email.[18] As long ago as 1999, when the technology was in its relative infancy, the Los Angeles District Attorney's Office estimated that email or other electronic communications were a factor in approximately 20 per cent of the roughly 600 cases handled by its Stalking and Threat Assessment Unit.[19] More-recent data indicates that online harassment is a significant issue, with 8 per cent of Canadians indicating they had received threatening or harassing email,[20] while the equivalent figure in Britain was 12 per cent.[21]

2. Legislative responses

Although there are those who argue that cyberstalking is a distinct but related offence,[22] most jurisdictions prosecute cyberstalking as part of a

---

16 Tjaden and Thoennes, *Violence against Women Survey*, p. 2. Similar findings have been made in Australia and Britain: see R. Purcell, M. Pathé and P. Mullen, 'The prevalence and nature of stalking in the Australian community' (2002) 36 *Australian and New Zealand Journal of Psychiatry* 114; and T. Budd and J. Mattinson, *The Extent and Nature of Stalking: Findings from the 1998 British Crime Survey*, Home Office Research Study no. 210 (2000).

17 C. Kershaw, S. Nicholas and A. Walker, *Crime in England and Wales 2007/08*, Home Office Statistical Bulletin (2008), p. 65.

18 B. S. Fisher, F. T. Cullen and M. G. Turner, 'Being pursued: Stalking victimization in a national study of college women' (2002) 1 *Criminology and Public Policy* 257, 282.

19 US Attorney General, *Stalking and Domestic Violence*, p. 4.

20 M. Kowalski, *Cyber-Crime: Issues, data sources, and feasibility of collecting police-reported statistics*, Cat no. 85–558, Canadian Centre for Justice Statistics (2002), p. 15.

21 D. Wilson et al., *Fraud and Technology Crimes: Findings from the 2003/04 British Crime Survey, the 2004 Offending, Crime and Justice Survey and Administrative Sources* (Home Office, 2006), p. 8.

22 P. Bocij, *Cyberstalking: Harassment in the Internet age and how to protect your family* (Westport: Praeger Publishers, 2004), pp. 19–31.

more general 'stalking' offence.[23] Such offences exist in each jurisdiction, with some adopting the term 'harassment'. Others provide for two tiers of offence, with provisions punishing more general harassment as distinct from more serious stalking offences. Some commentators have suggested this is an appropriate framework, reflecting the difference between harassing and stalking-type behaviours.[24]

In Australia there is no specific anti-stalking offence under federal law, although it is an offence to use a carriage service to harass.[25] Specific anti-stalking offences do, however, exist in all states and territories.[26] For the purposes of this discussion, we will focus on s. 21A of the Crimes Act 1958 (Vic),[27] being one of the more modern and comprehensive state provisions. This makes it an offence to stalk another person, where 'stalk' means to engage in a course of conduct 'with the intention of causing physical or mental harm to the victim or of arousing apprehension or fear in the victim for his or her own safety or that of any other person'.

In Canada, the offence of 'criminal harassment' is found in s. 264(1) of the Criminal Code which makes it an offence to engage in specified conduct, without lawful authority, that causes another person reasonably, in all the circumstances, to fear for their safety or the safety of anyone known to them, knowing or reckless as to whether that other person is harassed.[28] In contrast to other jurisdictions, criminal harassment under the Canadian provision does not necessarily require a 'course of conduct'. For example, where the conduct consists of threatening conduct, one instance is sufficient to constitute harassment.[29]

In the UK, s. 1 Protection from Harassment Act 1997 states that a person must not pursue a course of conduct which amounts to harassment of

23 Some US states have enacted specific cyberstalking provisions in addition to traditional anti-stalking provisions; N. H. Goodno, 'Cyberstalking: A new crime: Evaluating the effectiveness of current state and federal laws' (2007) 72 *Missouri Law Review* 125, 144.
24 T. McEwan, P. Mullen and R. MacKenzie, 'Anti-stalking legislation in practice: Are we meeting community needs?' (2007) 14 *Psychiatry, Psychology and Law* 207, 215.
25 See n. 69 below.
26 Queensland was the first Australian state to enact specific anti-stalking laws in 1993; see Criminal Code Act 1899 (Qld), s. 359E. Also see Crimes Act 1900 (ACT), s. 35; Crimes (Domestic and Personal Violence) Act 2007 (NSW), s. 13; Criminal Code 1983 (NT), s. 189; Criminal Law Consolidation Act 1935 (SA), s. 19AA; Criminal Code Act 1924 (Tas), s. 192; and Criminal Code Act 1913 (WA), s. 338E.
27 Maximum penalty 10 years' (level 5) imprisonment: s. 21A(1).
28 The Canadian provision was introduced in 1993, and carries a maximum penalty of 10 years' imprisonment: s. 264(3).
29 Department of Justice Canada, *A Handbook for Police and Crown Prosecutors on Criminal Harassment* (2004) p. 33. Also see *R* v. *Pastore* (2005) [2005] OJ no 2807.

another, and which he or she knows, or ought to know, amounts to harassment of the other.[30] Section 4 provides for a more serious offence where the course of conduct causes another to fear, on at least two occasions, that violence will be used against him or her.

Although a number of US federal provisions may apply in this context,[31] the most relevant is the offence of stalking under 18 USC § 2261A,[32] which was recently amended specifically to address concerns about cyberstalking. Under this provision it is an offence to use the mail, any interactive computer service, or any facility of interstate or foreign commerce to engage in a course of conduct that causes substantial emotional distress to a person, or places that person in reasonable fear of the death of, or serious bodily injury to, that person, a member of their immediate family, their spouse or intimate partner.[33] The course of conduct must be carried out with either an intent to kill, injure, or harass; to place under surveillance with intent to kill, injure, harass or intimidate; to cause substantial emotional distress; or to place a person in reasonable fear of the death of, or serious bodily injury of that person, a member of their immediate family, their spouse or intimate partner.[34]

Stalking offences are also found in all US states and the District of Columbia, with many having been influenced by the Model Anti-Stalking Code developed by the National Institute of Justice.[35] The code provides that stalking consists of a 'course of conduct' which is directed at a particular person, causes the victim to fear some sort of injury or death and would cause a 'reasonable' person the same or similar type of fear. In addition, the defendant must know, or should know, that his or her conduct will place the victim in fear.

Despite unanimity in the need to enact anti-stalking laws, it can be seen even from this small sample that such laws vary considerably both between and within jurisdictions. Even without the involvement of technology,

---

30 Maximum penalty 6 months' imprisonment: s. 2. For a detailed discussion of the English provisions see E. Finch, 'Stalking the perfect stalking law: An evaluation of the efficacy of the Protection from Harassment Act 1997' (2002) *Criminal Law Review* 703.
31 See, in particular, 18 USC § 875(c) (discussed at p. 377) and 47 USC § 223(a)(1) (A)(C)(D)(E) (discussed at pp. 375–6).
32 The penalties for this provision are described in 18 USC § 2261(b).
33 18 USC § 2261A(2). (For convenience, some jurisdictional requirements have been omitted.)
34 *Ibid.*
35 National Institute of Justice, *Project to Develop a Model Anti-Stalking Code for States*, Department of Justice (1993). For a discussion of state stalking offences see Goodno, 'Cyberstalking', 125.

anti-stalking offences are notoriously difficult to draft, reflecting the need to encompass a broad range of conduct without punishing legitimate activities. In general, legislatures have tried to achieve this balance by defining the conduct requirement in broad terms, offset by the fault element and a requirement that the conduct have an impact on the victim. Some jurisdictions also provide for specific defences to ensure the provisions do not interfere with, for example, legitimate journalistic activity.[36] Before considering the impact of technology on stalking, it is useful briefly to consider the three key components of all stalking offences: the conduct element, the fault element and the requirement of some impact on the victim.

A. Conduct element

In defining the conduct element, legislatures have generally taken one of two approaches. The first is that adopted in the US federal provision which is to simply refer to a 'course of conduct' or equivalent term, which is then left undefined.[37] In the UK, 'course of conduct' is defined, but only to the extent that 'conduct' includes speech and a 'course of conduct' must involve conduct on at least two occasions.[38] While this approach has the advantage of flexibility, allowing the courts to respond to novel situations as necessary, it may be criticised as contrary to the general principle that it should be possible to determine, with reasonable precision, what conduct is impermissible under the criminal law.[39] In this respect the remaining elements assume particular significance in more clearly defining the scope of the offence.

At the other extreme, some jurisdictions provide a definitive list of conduct which constitutes stalking. While this approach has the advantage of certainty, its inflexibility makes it difficult to adapt to novel forms of stalking. For example, in Canada the conduct which may constitute criminal harassment is defined exhaustively as:

---

36 See for example, Protection from Harassment Act 1997 (UK), ss. 1(3) and 4(3), and Crimes Act 1958 (Vic), s. 21A(4).
37 18 USC § 2261A(2).
38 Protection from Harassment Act 1997 (UK), s. 7(3)–(4). Even where there are two incidents, the circumstances must be such that they may properly be described as a 'course of conduct': see *Lau* v. *DPP* [2000] EWHC QB 182 at [15].
39 This concept is given constitutional protection under the due process clause of the Fourteenth Amendment to the US Constitution; see generally, A. Packard, 'Does proposed federal cyberstalking legislation meet constitutional requirements?' (2000) 5 *Communication Law and Policy* 505.

(a) repeatedly following from place to place the other person or anyone
known to them;
(b) repeatedly communicating with, either directly or indirectly, the other
person or anyone known to them;
(c) besetting or watching the dwelling-house, or place where the other
person, or anyone known to them, resides, works, carries on business
or happens to be; or
(d) engaging in threatening conduct directed at the other person or any
member of their family.[40]

It is immediately apparent that concepts such as 'besetting or watching' or
'engaging in threatening conduct' may create difficulties when applied in a
digital context. Similarly, the US Model Anti-Stalking Code defines 'course
of conduct' as 'repeatedly maintaining a visual or physical proximity to a
person or repeatedly conveying verbal or written threats or threats implied
by conduct or a combination thereof directed at or toward a person'. In
the discussion below we will see that remote surveillance, in particular,
challenges such conventional conceptions of stalking.

An obvious compromise is to provide for an inclusive definition of
'course of conduct', thereby allowing for both precision and flexibility.
Section 21A(2) Crimes Act 1958 (Vic) provides an extensive, but not
exhaustive, list of conduct which includes the catch-all provision 'acting
in any other way that could reasonably be expected to arouse apprehension
or fear in the victim for his or her own safety or that of any other person'.[41]
The legislation then provides specific examples, some of which are clearly
relevant in the digital context. These include:

(b) contacting the victim or any other person by post, telephone, fax,
text message, e-mail or other electronic communication or by any
other means whatsoever;
(ba) publishing on the Internet or by an e-mail or other electronic communication to any person a statement or other material
(i) relating to the victim or any other person; or
(ii) purporting to relate to, or to originate from, the victim or any
other person;
(bb) causing an unauthorised computer function . . . in a computer owned
or used by the victim or any other person;
(bc) tracing the victim's or any other person's use of the Internet or of
e-mail or other electronic communications;
. . .
(f) keeping the victim or any other person under surveillance.

40 Criminal Code (Can), s. 264(2).   41 Crimes Act 1958 (Vic), s. 21A(2)(g).

B. Fault element

There are two principal considerations in drafting the fault element for the offence of stalking. First, it is an important limitation on an offence which is potentially over-broad. Ordinarily, this would be achieved by imposing a subjective fault element such as intention or recklessness. For example, the US federal provision requires proof of intention,[42] while in Canada the prosecution must prove that the defendant acted knowingly or recklessly as to whether the victim was harassed.[43]

The second consideration is that '[m]any stalkers do not intend to harm or alarm; instead, they may possess the, albeit misguided, intention to establish a relationship with the object of their attention'.[44] It may therefore be difficult to prove a subjective fault element as the defendant may claim to be unaware that his or her conduct was harassing.[45] Further, a significant proportion of stalkers suffer psychiatric conditions such as erotomania or other delusional conditions.[46] Consequently, in addition to subjective fault elements some jurisdictions impose an objective fault element whereby the defendant may be guilty because of what he or she ought reasonably to have known.

For example, the UK provision extends to situations where the defendant 'ought to know' that his or her conduct amounts to harassment. The test is whether a reasonable person in possession of the same information would think the course of conduct amounted to or involved harassment of the other person(s).[47] It has been held that this is a purely objective test, and does not take into account the circumstances as the accused perceived them to be.[48] Similarly, under the US Model Anti-stalking Code the defendant must know, or should know, that his or her conduct will place the victim in fear.[49] Although the Victorian provision requires proof of intention, the defendant is deemed to have the necessary intention if he or she either knew or, in all the circumstances, 'ought to have understood' that engaging in a course of conduct of that kind would be likely to cause harm or arouse apprehension or fear.[50]

---

42 18 USC § 2261A(2).   43 Criminal Code (Can), s. 264(1).
44 Purcell, Pathé and Mullen, 'Stalking', 163.
45 Grant, Bone and Grant, 'Canada's criminal harassment provisions', 216.
46 Purcell, Pathé and Mullen, 'Stalking', 163.
47 Protection from Harassment Act 1997 (UK), s. 1(2).
48 *R* v. *Colohan* [2001] EWCA Crim 1251, discussed in E. Finch, 'The objective standard of reasonableness and the mentally ill stalker' (2001) 65 *The Journal of Criminal Law* 489.
49 National Institute of Justice, *Model Anti-Stalking Code.*
50 Crimes Act 1958 (Vic), s. 21A(3).

C. Impact on the victim

Another important limitation found in many anti-stalking provisions is that the conduct must have had some impact on the victim; usually that he or she was placed in fear. Such provisions recognise that it is the impact of the conduct on the victim, rather than the nature of the conduct per se, that constitutes the harm which the offence seeks to punish. In some jurisdictions, this requirement is determined subjectively. For example, although not expressly stated, the wording of the UK provision suggests that it must be proved that the victim was in fact harassed, where 'harassment' is defined to include causing alarm or distress to another person.[51] As noted above, a more serious offence is committed where the conduct causes the victim to fear that violence will be used against him or her. Similarly, the US Model Anti-Stalking Code requires that the accused's conduct 'causes the victim to fear some sort of injury'.

However, a purely subjective test may be criticised on the basis that the scope of the offence will vary according to the fortitude of individual victims. Consequently, some jurisdictions impose an objective standard. In Canada, for example, the prosecution must prove that the victim was fearful for his or her safety, or the safety of someone known to them, and that the fear was reasonable in all the circumstances.[52] The US federal provision contains both subjective and objective elements, requiring that the course of conduct 'causes substantial emotional distress to that person or places that person in reasonable fear of the death of, or serious bodily injury to' a person.[53] The Victorian provision adopts a compromise whereby proof of harm is only required where the objective fault element is relied upon.[54]

Some other jurisdictions do away with any requirement that the victim feel fear or distress; the focus of the offence being on the conduct of the defendant rather than its impact on the victim. Such provisions greatly expand the offence of stalking to encompass those who are unaware of the stalking conduct, or who are aware but not fearful.[55] As will be discussed below, such an approach may have particular significance in the context of certain forms of cyberstalking.

51 Protection from Harassment Act 1997 (UK), s. 7(2); *DPP* v. *Ramsdale* [2001] EWHC Admin 106.
52 Criminal Code (Can), s. 264(1).   53 18 USC § 2261A(2).
54 Crimes Act 1958 (Vic), s. 21A(3)(b).
55 McEwan, Mullen and MacKenzie, 'Anti-stalking legislation', 210.

3. Forms of cyberstalking

Following this brief summary of anti-stalking provisions, we now turn to consider the challenges that cyberstalking presents, both to our conception of stalking and the applicability of existing anti-stalking laws. Forms of cyberstalking are as varied as stalking itself, and generally mirror more traditional types of stalking. In most cases, the offences are drafted so broadly that they are able to adapt to novel forms of stalking. The main difficulties arise when the relevant conduct is defined exhaustively, as in Canada, or where technology-specific terminology is used.

A good example of this latter problem is 47 USC § 223(a)(1)(C) which prohibits silent telephone calls. Although it might be thought that this provision could apply to other forms of anonymous communication, such as emails, it applies only to the use of a 'telecommunications device', which is defined to exclude an 'interactive computer service'.[56] To further confuse matters, it has been held that a modem is a 'telecommunications device',[57] and therefore it could be argued that an individual who used a modem to connect to the Internet and harass an individual may fall within the provision.[58] Although subsequently amended to include email and other Internet communications,[59] such technical legal arguments clearly illustrate the need for technologically neutral provisions, and many jurisdictions have amended their laws to specifically incorporate cyberstalking.[60]

In general, cyberstalking falls within the following categories, each of which may overlap and will commonly be combined with conventional stalking behaviours:

(a) communicating with the victim
(b) publishing information about the victim
(c) targeting the victim's computer
(d) placing the victim under surveillance.

---

56 47 USC § 223(h)(1)(B). 'Interactive computer service' is defined at 47 USC § 230(f)(2).
57 *American Civil Liberties Union* v. *Reno*, 929 F Supp 824, 829 (ED Pa 1996); affirmed, *Reno* v. *American Civil Liberties Union*, 521 US 844 (1997).
58 US Attorney General, *Stalking and Domestic Violence*, p. 45.
59 47 USC § 223(h)(1)(C).
60 In the US, only 4 states and the District of Columbia make no specific provision for cyberstalking, with the remaining states all having current or pending cyberstalking laws: www.haltabuse.org/resources/laws/index.shtml. Also see S. Jefferson and R. Sharfritz, 'A survey of cyberstalking legislation' (2001) 32 *University of West Los Angeles Law Review* 323. There have also been calls for the Model Anti-stalking Code to be appropriately broadened: M. L. Boland, 'Model code revisited: Taking aim at the high-tech stalker' (2005) 20 *Criminal Justice* 40, 42.

A. Communicating with the victim

The sending of unsolicited communications is a staple of stalking behaviour and a common form of cyberstalking, for example sending threatening or offensive emails.[61] Anonymity may be achieved through anonymous email accounts and/or remailers, as with the Massachusetts man who used anonymous remailers to engage in a systematic pattern of harassment of a co-worker, culminating in an attempt to extort sexual favours from the victim.[62] Ease of communication also means that an offender may bombard the victim with messages. For example, an honours graduate from the University of San Diego terrorised five female university students by sending hundreds of violent and threatening emails.[63] Increasingly, other forms of electronic communication are being adopted including chat rooms,[64] Instant Messenger[65] and SMS/MMS.[66] According to the 2003/2004 British Crime Survey, 5 per cent of mobile phone users reported having received an offensive or harassing text message within the previous twelve months.[67]

In general, such conduct will fall within the conduct requirement of most stalking statutes, which are phrased in broad terms and avoid technologically specific terminology. However, the factual difficulties that the courts have encountered in defining a 'course of conduct' may be exacerbated in the online environment. As electronic communications may be sent in rapid succession, the question may arise as to whether each message is to be treated separately or as one instance of harassment?[68] Alternatively, electronic communications that do not fall within anti-stalking offences may be charged under specific provisions dealing with the use of telecommunication services for harassing or offensive communications.[69]

---

61 See, for example, *Washington v. Davila-Mendez*, 103 Wn App 1044 (Wash App 2000); *People v. Starkes*, 185 Misc 2d 186 (NYC Crim Ct 2000); *DPP v. Sutcliffe* [2001] VSC 43; and *R. v. Debnath* [2005] EWCA Crim 3472.
62 US Attorney General, *Stalking and Domestic Violence*, p. 4.   63 *Ibid.*
64 *US v. Morales*, 272 F 3d 284 (5th Cir 2001).
65 *US v. Kammersell*, 196 F 3d 1137 (10th Cir 1999).
66 *R v. Merrick* [2007] EWCA Crim 1159.
67 D. Wilson et al., *Fraud and Technology Crimes*, p. 8.
68 Gillespie, 'Cyber-bullying', 129.
69 See, for example, Criminal Code (Cth), ss. 474.15–474.17 (*Crowther v. Sala* (2007) 170 A Crim R 389); Criminal Code (Can), s. 372(1); Malicious Communications Act 1988 (UK), s. 1; Communications Act 2003 (UK), s. 127 (*DPP v. Collins* [2006] 4 All ER 602); and 47 USC § 223(a)(1)(A)(C)(D)(E).

One difficulty which arises in a number of US statutes is the requirement of proof of a 'credible threat'. Such limitations are important in ensuring that the provision does not fall foul of the First Amendment, as only true threats are not protected speech.[70] The requirement of a 'true threat' may be problematic in the context of stalking generally, as in many cases the defendant's conduct does not amount to a threat as such. They present particular difficulties in the context of cyberstalking as the defendant may be remote from the victim, raising the question of whether the threat is in fact credible and/or whether the defendant is proximate to the victim.[71] Similar issues may also arise in relation to the Canadian provision, which refers to 'engaging in threatening conduct'.[72]

These difficulties are well illustrated by the decision of the Sixth Circuit in *US* v. *Alkhabaz*.[73] This case concerned 18 USC § 875(c) which makes it an offence to transmit in interstate or foreign commerce 'any communication containing any threat to kidnap any person or any threat to injure the person of another'. The defendant, also known as 'Jake Baker', had posted a number of fictional stories on an electronic bulletin board which described the abduction, rape, torture, mutilation and murder of women and young girls. One particular posting described the torture, rape and murder of a person with the same name as one of Baker's classmates at the University of Michigan. A subsequent search of his computer files and email account revealed a second story involving the classmate, including her home address. Email correspondence between the defendant and another man was also found in which the two men discussed acting out their fantasies by actually abducting, raping and murdering a woman.

Baker's indictment was quashed by the District Court on the basis that the email messages did not constitute 'true threats' and were consequently protected speech under the First Amendment.[74] The Sixth Circuit agreed, citing with approval *US* v. *Bellrichard*[75] where it was held that a threat must be communicated to the threatened individual or to a third party with 'some connection' to the threatened individual.[76] However, the court

70 *Watts* v. *US*, 394 US 705, 708 (1969).
71 A. C. Radosevich, 'Thwarting the stalker: Are anti-stalking measures keeping pace with today's stalker?' (2000) *University of Illinois Law Review* 1371, 1384.
72 Criminal Code (Can), s. 264(2).
73 104 F 3d 1492 (6th Cir 1997); rehearing en banc denied, *US* v. *Alkhabaz*, 1997 US App LEXIS 9060.
74 *US* v. *Baker*, 890 F Supp 1375, 1381 (ED Mich 1995).
75 779 F Supp 454 (D Minn 1991).
76 *Ibid.*, at 459, affirmed *US* v. *Bellrichard*, 994 F 2d 1318 (8th Cir 1993).

in *Alkhabaz* went further; '[a]lthough it may offend our sensibilities, a communication objectively indicating a serious expression of an intention to inflict bodily harm cannot constitute a threat unless the communication also is conveyed for the purpose of furthering some goal through the use of intimidation'.[77] Consequently, on the facts of this case there could be no threat as 'no reasonable person would perceive such communications as being conveyed to effect some change or achieve some goal through intimidation'.[78] In fact, the email exchange was characterised by the court as an attempt to foster a friendship based on shared sexual fantasies.[79]

The merits or otherwise of this decision will not be resolved here.[80] For our purposes, it illustrates two important points. First, the requirement of a 'credible threat' is arguably inconsistent with the offence of stalking in general. According to one survey, less than half of stalking victims were directly threatened,[81] and the elimination of such a requirement from anti-stalking statutes has been suggested.[82] Anti-stalking offences were created precisely to address those situations where the victim is not threatened as such, but where the defendant's actions give rise to a fear of harm. These difficulties are exacerbated in the context of cyberstalking where the defendant may be remote from the victim and the threat, if any, less 'credible'.[83]

Secondly, this case raises the broader issue of communications which are not sent directly to the victim or anyone connected with the victim. In particular, this may arise in situations, such as those discussed below, where the defendant places material on the Internet, or on bulletin boards, encouraging others to harass the victim. Can such conduct constitute a 'true threat'?

In *People* v. *Munn*,[84] the defendant posted a message on an Internet newsgroup saying, 'Please kill Police Lt Steven Biegel, all other NYPD

77　*US* v. *Alkhabaz*, 104 F 3d 1492, 1495 (6th Cir 1997).　　78　*Ibid.*, at 1496.
79　*Ibid.* Also see *US* v. *Scott*, 42 Fed Appx 264, 265 (10th Cir 2002) in relation to an email death threat.
80　As to the constitutional difficulties in defining 'true threats' see K. L. Karst, 'Threats and meanings: How the facts govern first amendment doctrine' (2006) 58 *Stanford Law Review* 1337.
81　Tjaden and Thoennes, *Violence against Women Survey*, pp. 7–8.
82　J. L. Bradfield, 'Anti-stalking laws: Do they adequately protect stalking victims?' (1998) 21 *Harvard Women's Law Journal* 229, 249–53.
83　J. L. Mishler, 'Cyberstalking: Can communication via the Internet constitute a credible threat, and should an Internet service provider be liable if it does?' (2000) 17 *Santa Clara Computer and High Technology Law Journal* 115.
84　179 Misc 2d 903 (NYC Crim Ct 1999).

cops, and all of their adult relatives and friends.' Lieutenant Biegel read the message and was understandably alarmed. The defendant was convicted of aggravated harassment in the second degree under New York law.[85] This makes it an offence for a person, with intent to harass, annoy, threaten or alarm another person, to communicate by mechanical or electronic means in a manner likely to cause annoyance or alarm.

The court upheld the defendant's conviction. It was clearly accepted that the Internet posting was a 'communication' for the purposes of the section.[86] In addition, it was a communication which was directed at the complainant. The inclusion of the complainant's name 'transformed the communication to one not only intended for the general public, but specially generated to be communicated to the complainant'.[87] As discussed below, where the content of the threat is less direct there may be difficulty showing that the communication constitutes a 'true threat'.[88]

Such situations not only present challenges to provisions requiring proof of a credible threat; they may fall outside more general anti-stalking provisions. While the sending of communications, or the posting of a webpage, may constitute a 'course of conduct', in cases where the victim is unaware of them, and/or the defendant intends the victim to be unaware, then the remaining elements of the offence may not be made out. Such cases would have to be prosecuted, if at all, as incitement,[89] conspiracy[90] or offences concerned with the improper use of telecommunications networks.[91] In Canada, it may be difficult to prove that the website amounted to 'repeatedly communicating with, either directly or indirectly, the other person or anyone known to them'.[92]

B. Publishing information about the victim

The ease with which anyone may publish information on the Internet provides fertile ground for stalkers to seek to humiliate their victims. For

---

85 New York Penal Law § 240.30(1).
86 *People* v. *Munn*, 179 Misc 2d 903, 905 (NYC Crim Ct 1999).
87 *Ibid*. Also see *People* v. *Kochanowski*, 186 Misc 2d 441, 443 (NY Sup Ct 2000).
88 See pp. 382–3.
89 Although in the US the test for incitement is equally onerous, requiring that the communication be 'directed to inciting or producing imminent lawless action and is likely to incite or produce such action': see *Brandenburg* v. *Ohio*, 395 US 444, 447 (1969).
90 *US* v. *Alkhabaz*, 104 F 3d 1492, 1507 (6th Cir 1997).
91 See n. 69 above.   92 Criminal Code (Can), s. 264(2)(b).

example, an English woman who believed she had contracted a sexually transmitted disease from her former lover registered the complainant on a website for people with such diseases. She also posted a fake newspaper article on the Internet, which alleged that the complainant engaged in homosexual activity, as a result of which the victim received a large amount of homosexual pornographic material.[93] Similarly, in *R v Perrier*[94] the defendant pleaded guilty to criminal harassment for conduct which involved posting obscene comments on the Internet concerning his ex-girlfriend, together with nude images purportedly of her. The threat of publication may even form part of the stalking itself. A Queensland woman received emails, which became increasingly more threatening until they threatened that she would be 'pack-raped, videotaped and uploaded on the Internet'.[95]

The ability to publish information also provides the means to co-opt third parties to harass or intimidate the victim. Far from being 'buried', the Internet can transform an obscure threat into a publication potentially accessible to millions.[96] In one notorious example, a Los Angeles man was convicted of stalking after using the Internet to solicit the rape of a woman who rejected his romantic advances. The defendant impersonated the victim in various Internet chat rooms and bulletin boards where he provided her name and address and indicated that she had fantasies about being raped. Thankfully the woman was not raped, but at least six men knocked on her door at night saying they wanted to rape her.[97] In another case, the defendant posted pictures of the victim's children, together with their full names, address, and telephone number, on websites which encouraged men to rape the children. The victim's family received numerous phone calls from men from around the country and the world in response to these postings.[98]

Such conduct may clearly fall within stalking offences, other than perhaps those requiring a credible threat. In general, the publishing of information forms part of a broader course of conduct and so satisfies the

93 *R v. Debnath* [2005] EWCA Crim 3472. Also see *Cray v. Hancock* [2005] All ER (D) 66.
94 1999 Nfld & PEIR LEXIS 253.
95 E. Ogilvie, 'The Internet and cyberstalking', Paper presented at the 'Stalking: Criminal Justice Responses Conference', AIC, Sydney, 7–8 December 2000, p. 3.
96 *People v. Neuman*, 2002 Cal App Unpub LEXIS 734 (2002) at 12.
97 J. C. Merschman, 'The dark side of the web: Cyberstalking and the need for contemporary legislation' (2001) 24 *Harvard Women's Law Journal* 255, 256–7. Also see *People v. Kochanowski*, 186 Misc 2d 441 (NY Sup Ct 2000).
98 *US v. Rose*, 315 F 3d 956 (8th Cir 2003).

conduct requirement of the offence. For example, a 28-year-old Victorian man was convicted of stalking a 12-year-old boy and his family. In addition to a number of incidents where the defendant approached the boy and repeatedly attended locations where the boy was present, he maintained a website that contained photographs of the young boy, some of which had been taken surreptitiously by the defendant. These images were accompanied by text describing the defendant's sexual interest in the boy and in paedophilia more generally.[99]

In *Dayton v. Davis*[100] the defendant was convicted on one count of menacing by stalking and one count of aggravated menacing in violation of the Ohio Revised Code. The defendant, a married law student at the University of Dayton, began seeing a first-year law student, Johanna Barba. Their relationship continued for over twelve months until it was ended by Ms Barba. After an unsuccessful suicide attempt, the defendant sent numerous emails to Ms Barba indicating that he had been researching her home town and regularly spending time in a park near her apartment. He also included details of her television viewing and social activities, which clearly suggested he was keeping her under surveillance. 'No explicit threats of harm to Barba were made in any of the e-mails, but Davis' tone in them fluctuated between despair over the break-up, anger, threats to commit suicide, a desire to see Barba in pain, and blaming Barba for ruining Davis' life.'[101] The defendant also included a link to a website he had created, which 'portrayed, among other things, the image of Barba's head transforming into a skull amidst flames, dripping blood, and charging horses ridden by robed skeletons'.[102]

The relevant stalking offence states that no person by engaging in a pattern of conduct shall knowingly cause another to believe that the offender will cause physical harm to the other person or cause mental distress to the other person. 'Pattern of conduct' is defined as two or more actions or incidents closely related in time.[103] The court rejected the defendant's argument that the posting of the website was one act, and therefore insufficient to constitute a course of conduct. The posting had to be seen in context. He had also communicated with the victim, had visited her apartment and kept her under surveillance. Against, this background there was clearly sufficient evidence that he had engaged in a 'pattern of conduct'.

99 *R* v. *Vose* (1999) 109 A Crim R 489.
100 136 Ohio App 3d 26 (2d Dist Montgomery County 1999).   101 *Ibid.*, at 29.
102 *Ibid.*   103 Ohio Revised Code § 2903.211(D)(1).

If it were the case that the posting of a website was not accompanied by other conduct, then it may be difficult to establish that it is a 'course of conduct' for these purposes as arguably the posting of the website is only a single action.[104] In order to address such situations, the Victorian provision specifically provides that 'course of conduct' includes 'publishing on the Internet ... a statement or other material relating to the victim or any other person or purporting to relate to, or to originate from, the victim or any other person'.[105] Further, it has been held that a 'course of conduct' may be conduct which is protracted, as well as conduct which is engaged in on more than one separate occasion.[106] In any event, in the majority of cases the posting of a website will be accompanied by other conduct. Further, the webpage is unlikely to remain static and changes to the website may arguably constitute a course of conduct. It will then be necessary to determine whether that conduct had the requisite impact on the victim, and was accompanied by the necessary fault element.

As discussed above, the publishing of information on websites presents particular difficulties in those jurisdictions which require proof of a 'credible threat'. Similar issues may arise in Canada where the relevant provision refers to 'engaging in threatening conduct directed at the other person or any member of their family'.[107]

In *US* v. *Carmichael*[108] the defendant was charged with conspiracy in relation to drugs and money laundering. Shortly after being charged, he created a website which, after a number of iterations, contained the statement 'Wanted. Information on these Agents and Informants.' The website then listed the names, and in some cases pictures, of witnesses and agents involved in the case. The website was amended to contain a disclaimer stating that it was 'definitely not an attempt to intimidate or harass any informants or agents, but is simply an attempt to seek information'.[109] The website was also reproduced in an advertisement in local newspapers. The government sought a protective order prohibiting the publication of the material on the grounds that it was intimidating of witnesses. The District Court refused to issue the order, inter alia, on the

---

104 Particular difficulties arise in Canada where the reference is to 'repeatedly communicating with, either directly or indirectly, the other person or anyone known to them': Criminal Code (Can), s. 264(2)(b).
105 Crimes Act 1958 (Vic), s. 21A(2)(ba).
106 *Gunes* v. *Pearson*; *Tunc* v. *Pearson* (1996) 89 A Crim R 297. Although 'course of conduct' does require some continuity of purpose: *Berlyn* v. *Brouskos* (2002) 134 A Crim R 111.
107 Criminal Code (Can), s. 264(2)(d).   108 326 F Supp 2d 1267 (MD Ala 2004).
109 *Ibid.*, at 1272.

ground that the website was not a 'true threat' and was therefore protected speech under the First Amendment.

'True threats' encompasses serious expressions of an intent to commit an act of unlawful violence to a particular individual or group of individuals, even if the speaker does not actually intend to carry out the threat.[110] Intimidation may be a form of a 'true threat', and prohibitions on such speech protects people from the fear of violence, as well as the possibility that the threatened violence may eventuate.[111] The test for whether speech is a 'true threat' is objective, requiring the court to determine whether there is sufficient evidence to prove beyond a reasonable doubt 'that the defendant intentionally made the statement under such circumstances that a reasonable person would construe them as a serious expression of an intention to inflict bodily harm'.[112] Relevant to this determination is the language itself, its context and the testimony of recipients.[113]

On the facts, the court held that the website did not constitute a 'true threat'. The website contained no express threats and contained a disclaimer of any intent to threaten. The format of the site was not sufficiently threatening, and did not contain such things as references to killing, disfigured images or threatening epithets as had been present in other images held to be true threats. In terms of context, the court acknowledged that viewed in the light of the general history of informants being killed in drug cases, the website could look more like a threat. Nonetheless, it concluded that these background facts were 'too general' to make the website a true threat.[114]

Although the fact that the information was found on the Internet formed part of the context in which the information was viewed, it was not enough to transform it into a true threat.[115] The court specifically rejected suggestions by some commentators that a new standard for 'true threat' analysis is required as a result of material posted on the Internet.[116]

---

110 *Virginia* v. *Black*, 538 US 343, 359–60 (2003).   111 *Ibid.*, at 360.

112 *US* v. *Carmichael*, 326 F Supp 2d 1267, 1280 (MD Ala 2004), citing *US* v. *Alaboud*, 347 F 3d 1293, 1296–7 (11th Cir 2003).

113 *Ibid.*, at 1281.

114 *Ibid.*, at 1285. For a critical analysis of the decision, see A. E. McCann, 'Comment: Are courts taking Internet threats seriously enough? An analysis of true threats transmitted over the Internet, as interpreted in United States v. Carmichael' (2006) 26 *Pace Law Review* 523.

115 *US* v. *Carmichael*, 326 F Supp 2d 1267, 1288 (MD Ala 2004).

116 *Ibid.* S. Hammack, 'The Internet loophole: Why threatening speech on-line requires a modification of the courts' approach to true threats and incitement' (2002) 36 *Columbia Journal of Law and Social Problems* 65; and J. L. Brenner, 'True threats: A more appropriate

First Amendment analysis is not altered by the fact that the material was posted on the Internet, as 'speech on the internet is subject to no greater or lesser constitutional protection than speech in more traditional media'.[117]

C. *Targeting the victim's computer*

It is also possible for a stalker to interfere with his or her victim's computer, either as a form of intimidation or for the purposes of surveillance. A stalker with sufficient technical ability may gain remote access to the victim's computer in order to gain information, to delete or modify data, or to exercise control over the victim's computer. In one example, a woman received a message saying 'I'm going to get you'. Her CD-Rom drive was then opened remotely as an indication that the stalker had control over her computer.[118] In another example, the defendant altered the victim's email account so that messages were forwarded to an account to which she had exclusive access.[119]

Such conduct may fall within the broad concept of 'course of conduct' except in Canada where it would need to constitute 'threatening conduct'. The Victorian provision specifically refers to 'causing an unauthorised computer function in a computer owned or used by the victim or any other person'.[120] Such conduct may also be charged under specific computer access or modification offences.[121]

D. *Surveillance*

> The crux of a stalker's power is knowledge of the victim. A harasser's ability
> to frighten and control a victim increases with the amount of information
> that the harasser can gather.[122]

Keeping the victim under surveillance is a common feature of stalking, and one which is greatly assisted by digital technology. In general, surveillance in this context takes one of two forms. The first is gaining information about the victim, or people connected with the victim, which is then

---

standard for analyzing First Amendment protection and free speech when violence is perpetrated over the Internet' (2002) 78 *North Dakota Law Review* 753.
117 *US* v. *Carmichael*, 326 F Supp 2d 1267, 1288–9 (MD Ala 2004), citing *Reno* v. *American Civil Liberties Union*, 521 US 844, 851 (1997).
118 E. Ogilvie, 'Cyberstalking', Trends and Issues in Crime and Criminal Justice no. 166 (AIC, 2000) 4.
119 *R* v. *Debnath* [2005] EWCA Crim 3472.   120 Crimes Act (Vic), s. 21A(2)(bb).
121 These offences are discussed in Part II of this book.
122 McGrath and Casey, 'Forensic psychiatry and the Internet', 89.

used as part of the stalking behaviour. For example, the stalker may send messages indicating knowledge of the victim's whereabouts, or that the victim is seeing a particular person. The gathering of information may also be used to assist more direct surveillance, allowing the stalker to know where the victim will be. This is a potent form of intimidation because of the invasion of privacy and the sense that the stalker knows where the victim will be at any time – a sense that nowhere is safe.

The Internet provides ready access to private information with little chance of detection. A great deal of information is placed online voluntarily, in social network sites such as 'Facebook' and 'MySpace'. Search engines such as 'Google Groups', 'NetDetective' or 'AnyWho' are another easily accessible source of personal information. In addition, some online services provide personal information for a fee. In one infamous case, twenty-year-old Amy Boyer was murdered by a former classmate with whom she had no prior acquaintance. He maintained a website outlining her movements for over two years, including statements outlining his murderous intentions. After acquiring Amy's work address from a company on the Internet, he went to her work and shot her before shooting himself.[123]

The second form of surveillance is of the more conventional variety – that is, observing or monitoring the victim's movements. There are a number of ways in which digital technology assists such conduct. Miniaturisation has made surveillance technology easily accessible, relatively inexpensive and difficult to detect. The recording and storing of high-quality images, both still and moving, is greatly enhanced. It is now far easier to conceal a surveillance device in a private space and in household or innocuous objects with little chance of detection. Wireless technology adds yet another dimension, allowing surveillance to be carried out remotely, while GPS technology allows tracking devices to be placed on the victim.

For example, in *Colorado* v. *Sullivan*[124] the defendant was convicted, inter alia, of harassment by stalking. Following divorce proceedings instituted by his wife, the defendant attached a GPS device to his wife's car in order to track her movements. The information in the device was then retrieved by the defendant and uploaded to a computer. Under the relevant statute, stalking could include 'repeatedly keeping a person under surveillance'. The court rejected the defendant's argument that he did not

123 *Remsburg* v. *Docusearch*, 149 NH 148 (SC NH 2003).
124 53 P 3d 1181 (Colo Ct App 2001).

have his wife under surveillance as he did not know her whereabouts until he retrieved the data from the GPS. In contrast to the definition of 'surveillance' in some states, the Colorado statute contained no requirement of physical presence. The ordinary meaning of 'surveillance' is 'to keep a watch over someone or something' or 'the close observation of a person or place in the hope of gathering evidence'.[125] The court could see no significant difference between physically engaging in surveillance as opposed to using a device such as a GPS, which is designed to achieve the same result. Consequently, it was held that the phrase 'under surveillance' includes 'electronic surveillance that records a person's whereabouts as that person moves from one location to another and allows the stalker to access that information either simultaneously or shortly thereafter'.[126]

The court also rejected the defendant's argument that he had not 'repeatedly' placed the victim under surveillance because the device was installed and removed only once. The ordinary meaning of 'repeatedly' is 'on more than one occasion' and although the defendant had installed and removed it only once, he admitted downloading information from the device at least twice.[127] In any event, the device 'repeatedly' stored information about the victim's movements and this was sufficient to satisfy this element of the offence.[128]

Although surveillance may clearly fall within a 'course of conduct' under the US and UK provisions, and is specifically referred to in Victoria,[129] difficulties may arise in Canada where the relevant conduct is 'besetting or watching the dwelling-house, or place where the other person, or anyone known to them, resides, works, carries on business or happens to be'.[130] Similarly, under the US Model Anti-Stalking Code 'course of conduct' includes 'repeatedly maintaining a visual or physical proximity' to the victim. Both provisions suggest that the defendant must have the victim under physical surveillance, whereas he or she may be remote from the victim while still monitoring his or her movements. In addition, such descriptions are not readily applicable to other forms of surveillance such as monitoring emails or other communications.[131]

---

125 *Colorado* v. *Sullivan*, 53 P 3d 1181, 1184 (Colo Ct App 2001), citing *Webster's Third New International Dictionary*, p. 2302 (1968) and *Black's Law Dictionary*, p. 1459, 7th edn (1999) respectively.
126 *Ibid.*   127 *Ibid.*   128 *Ibid.*, at 1185.
129 Crimes Act 1958 (Vic), s. 21A(2)(f). Also see *R* v. *Anders* [2009] VSCA 7.
130 Criminal Code (Can), s. 264(2)(c).
131 Crimes Act 1958 (Vic), s. 21A(2)(bc) specifically includes 'tracing the victim's or any other person's use of the Internet or of e-mail or other electronic communications'.

In all jurisdictions, surveillance is unlikely to constitute stalking unless the defendant is aware of it and/or it is combined with other conduct. Surveillance which is unknown to the victim is unlikely to satisfy the remaining elements, both in terms of impact on the victim and the fault element. For example, in the civil case of *H.E.S. v. J.C.S.*[132] the plaintiff and defendant had been married for eighteen years. Although petitioning for divorce, they continued to live in the same house, but in separate bedrooms. The wife found a small video surveillance device hidden in a picture in her bedroom, with wires leading to the defendant's bedroom where it was connected to a VCR. The Appellate Division had held that the defendant did not engage in harassment. As he did not intend for her to find the camera, he could not have intended to annoy or alarm her.[133] The defendant further argued that the surveillance could not constitute stalking as it could not, in the circumstances, cause a reasonable person to fear bodily injury as required by the relevant statute.

The New Jersey Supreme Court rejected these arguments. The surveillance could not be looked at in isolation, but had to be viewed in the context of the defendant's alleged behaviour. In addition to observing and listening to his wife in the privacy of her bedroom, this included following her while she was working, appearing in places where he otherwise could not have known she would be, stealing items from her bedroom and threatening to kill her unless she dropped the divorce proceedings. Viewed against this backdrop, and in light of the party's history, there was sufficient evidence of conduct which could amount to both harassment and stalking.[134]

It would seem, therefore, that in a situation where the defendant conducts surveillance in isolation and unknown to the victim, it is unlikely to constitute stalking. If the victim is unaware then it can have no impact on him or her, nor on a reasonable person in the same circumstances. Even if the victim does become aware of it, whether the offence is made out will depend on whether the fault element of the offence is satisfied. Such conduct may, however, be in breach of surveillance devices legislation.[135]

---

132 175 NJ 309 (SC NJ 2003).   133 *Ibid.*, at 415.
134 *Ibid.*, at 417.   135 See p. 390.

13

Voyeurism

1. Digital voyeurs

The increased miniaturisation of digital technology, the ready availability of recording devices, coupled with the ease with which digital images can be reproduced and uploaded, has led to an apparent increase in conduct which may broadly be described as 'voyeurism'.[1] Typically, this involves a person surreptitiously observing, and in some cases recording, another person in what would generally be regarded as a private place. For example, the sports centre manager who installed a camera to film women in the shower and using sunbeds,[2] the apartment building superintendent who concealed surveillance equipment in the apartments of two female tenants,[3] or the stepfather who concealed a video camera to secretly record his adult stepdaughter showering.[4]

Of course, such conduct is not new, and specific 'peeping Tom' statutes have existed in some jurisdictions since at least the beginning of the nineteenth century.[5] Such statutes have, however, been the exception, with most jurisdictions relying upon other offences such as nuisance, stalking, offensive behaviour, public disorder or trespass.[6] That situation has changed in recent years with the enactment of specific voyeurism statutes.

Because it is surreptitious by nature, it is difficult to assess how prevalent voyeurism is. The lack of a specific offence also means it has traditionally

---

1 The *Oxford English Dictionary* defines a 'voyeur' as someone 'whose sexual desires are stimulated or satisfied by covert observation of the sex organs or sexual activities of others'.
2 *R* v. *Turner* [2006] EWCA Crim 63.
3 L. E. Rothenberg, 'Re-thinking privacy: Peeping Toms, video voyeurs, and failure of the criminal law to recognize a reasonable expectation of privacy in the public space' (2000) 49 *American University Law Review* 1127, 1150–2.
4 *R* v. *I.P.* [2004] EWCA Crim 2646.
5 C. Calvert and J. Brown, 'Video voyeurism, privacy and the Internet: Exposing Peeping Toms in cyberspace' (2000) 18 *Cardozo Arts & Entertainment Law Journal* 469, 516.
6 *Ibid.*, 518–23.

not been reflected in official crime statistics. Anecdotally, it seems to be increasing, and while digital technology has not created this phenomenon, it has undoubtedly facilitated it in a number of ways.

First, as outlined in the context of stalking,[7] such technology makes it much easier to engage in covert surveillance. Miniature cameras may easily be concealed in everyday items. Mobile phone cameras are particularly insidious, being so ubiquitous that we accept their presence in areas where a camera would otherwise seem suspicious.

One consequence of this, which may surprise many, is the extent to which surveillance technology is used to capture so-called 'up-skirt' and 'down-blouse' images. As their names suggest, these are images taken surreptitiously up a woman's skirt or of her cleavage, and are widely available on the Internet. While once a person may have concealed them- selves underneath a staircase or other vantage point to gain such a view, cameras may now easily be concealed in a bag, or other item, which is then placed at the woman's feet. In one example, a man allegedly used a camera concealed in the toe of his shoe to take pictures up women's skirts while they were on public transport.[8]

Secondly, and perhaps most disturbingly, still or video images may easily be reproduced and distributed via the Internet where they are effectively irretrievable. This may be on a personal website created by the voyeur, on an image-sharing website or any one of numerous 'voyeuristic' adult websites which provide a ready market for such material. Mobile phone cameras allow recording and distribution to be performed with one device.

2. Criminalising voyeurism

'Voyeurism', broadly defined, goes beyond being watched without one's knowledge. It is concerned with the covert observing and recording of others, for a sexual purpose, in situations which may broadly be described as 'private'. Although successful in some cases,[9] existing offences are gen- erally ill-suited to the task. Offences such as stalking or trespass may require the offender to be physically proximate to the victim. The fact

7 See p. 384.
8 C. Evans and K. Nguyen, 'Second man arrested for upskirt pics', *The Age*, 23 January 2007, p. 2.
9 S. Butcher, 'Upskirt student jailed for six months', *The Age*, 25 January 2007. Also see *Vigon v. DPP* [1998] *Criminal Law Review* 289.

that the victim, or anyone else for that matter, is often unaware of the defendant's conduct, may make it difficult to prosecute for indecency or public nuisance offences.[10] Such offences also fail to address the distribution of voyeuristic images, one of the more challenging aspects of modern technology.

Where the images are, for example, obscene or child pornography, then clearly they may fall within existing classification laws.[11] However, not all voyeuristic images will fall within these categories and may give rise to protracted disputes about classification. In the United States for instance, sexual material which is indecent but not obscene, is prima facie protected speech.[12]

Some jurisdictions provide for criminal offences governing the use of surveillance devices.[13] For example, under s. 7(1) of the Surveillance Devices Act 1999 (Vic) it is an offence, without lawful excuse, to knowingly install, use or maintain an optical surveillance device to record visually or observe a private activity to which the person is not a party, without the express or implied consent of each party to the activity. While such provisions may be utilised in many cases of voyeurism,[14] their scope is often limited by the definition of 'private activity'. The Victorian provision, for example, excludes an activity carried on outside a building.[15]

It is therefore clear that modern forms of voyeurism present a challenge to existing laws, arguably creating a need for specific offences to be enacted. The privacy rights of individuals, especially in public places, have traditionally received little attention in the criminal law. Such legislation as there is tends to be concerned with regulating surveillance by law enforcement, focusing on the rights of defendants rather than

---

10 Although see *R* v. *Hamilton* [2007] EWCA Crim 2062 where the court held that the offence of 'outraging public decency' did not require anyone to see the act whilst it was being carried out. Also see A. A. Gillespie, '"Up-skirts" and "down-blouses": Voyeurism and the law' (2008) *Criminal Law Review* 370, 372–5.

11 See, e.g., *R* v. *Carr* [2003] EWCA Crim 2416; *R* v. *Henderson* [2006] EWCA Crim 3264; *R* v. *Hamilton* [2007] EWCA Crim 2062; *R* v. *Drummond* [2008] NSWLC 10; and *Overend* v. *Department of Internal Affairs* (1998) 15 CRNZ 529.

12 *Sable Communications of California Inc.* v. *FCC*, 492 US 115, 126 (1989).

13 Relevant legislation includes Surveillance Devices Act 2004 (Cth) Part 4; Criminal Code (Can) s. 487.01; and Regulation of Investigatory Powers Act 2000 (UK), Part II. In the US, there is no general federal surveillance offence dealing with optical surveillance; *US* v. *Falls*, 34 F 3d 674, 678 (8th Cir 1994).

14 See, e.g., *Brown* v. *Palmer* [2008] VSC 335.

15 Surveillance Devices Act 1999 (Vic), s. 3.

those whose privacy may be violated in other contexts.[16] The arguments in favour of a specific voyeurism offence may be conceptualised in two ways.

The first is as a privacy offence. In broad terms, the privacy interests which may be compromised by voyeuristic conduct may be further divided into two categories. The first is the traditional 'right to be let alone'[17] – that is, the right of an individual to determine by whom, and to what extent, they will be seen by others. This interest applies at the point of the image being captured and is irrespective of it being recorded. The second privacy interest is 'the ability of individuals to control the flow of information about themselves'.[18] Although not limited to circumstances where an image is recorded, it assumes particular significance in such cases. It is in this context that digital technology has had the greatest impact, allowing images to be replicated and distributed rapidly, cheaply and to a potential audience of millions.

The impact of covert surveillance on the person observed will of course vary considerably depending on the person concerned. Other factors include what was observed, where it was observed, who it was observed by and whether it has been distributed more widely.[19] Nonetheless, there is no doubt that it can cause significant harm, with many victims describing feelings of distress, disgust, helplessness, humiliation and a sense of violation.[20]

However, the impact of covert surveillance goes beyond the privacy of the individual observed. The right for a person's privacy to be protected from arbitrary or abusive interference, a right recognised in international law,[21] is 'an essential element in fostering and preserving the dignity, autonomy and freedom of the individual'.[22] One of the most important societal benefits of privacy is that people feel that there is somewhere they can go to as a form of sanctuary, a place where they will not be observed other than by those they allow to observe them. Traditionally, the focus has been on preventing the state from unreasonably entering the

---

16 Rothenberg, 'Re-thinking privacy', 1139.
17 S. D. Warren and L. D. Brandeis, 'The right to privacy' (1890) 4 *Harvard Law Review* 193, 193.
18 Calvert and Brown, 'Video voyeurism', 488.
19 New Zealand Law Commission, *Intimate Covert Filming*, Study Paper, no. 15 (2004), p. 8.
20 *Ibid.*
21 International Covenant on Civil and Political Rights, 999 UNTS 171, Art. 17 (entered into force 23 March 1967).
22 New Zealand Law Commission, *Intimate Covert Filming*, p. 8.

private sphere. Equally, if not more insidious, is the potential for ordinary members of the community to intrude on our private moments for their own motives. 'In an important sense, one person's loss [of privacy] is every person's loss since it tears away at the terms of peaceful co-existence in society.'[23]

Notwithstanding its importance, the individual's interest in privacy must be balanced against countervailing interests, most notably freedom of speech and expression. In particular, there is some concern that voyeurism laws, if drafted too broadly, might restrict legitimate journalistic activity, or the ability of photographers to take pictures in public places as a form of artistic expression.[24] Such laws must also not unduly impinge on the ability of law enforcement agencies to engage in surveillance, nor for individuals to use surveillance devices for appropriate purposes, for example legitimate workplace surveillance.

The individual's interest in privacy must also be balanced against the social reality of living in a community. While it may seem obvious that a person's privacy should be protected in their own home, or an obviously private place such as a bathroom, difficulties arise where the image is captured in a public place, but is of a sexual nature. For example, if we consider an up-skirt photo taken in a shopping mall. If the photo was of a woman in an extremely short skirt sitting down with her underwear in plain view, then arguably she may not have a reasonable expectation of privacy. On the other hand, a woman standing looking at items in a store, or waiting to be served, does not anticipate that a surveillance device may be used to look up her skirt. She should, arguably, have a right to privacy in respect of her otherwise concealed underwear, notwithstanding that she is in a public place. A further distinction must also be drawn between consenting to being looked at and consent to being recorded. While the woman in the short skirt may accept that others are able to see her underwear, she may not consent to having that image recorded and possibly widely distributed for the sexual pleasure of strangers – to becoming 'non-consensual pornography'.[25]

The second conceptualisation of voyeurism is as a sexual offence. Voyeurism is 'at heart a sexually motivated behaviour, and the act of

---

23 Law Reform Commission Ireland, *Report on Privacy: Surveillance and the interception of communications*, no. 57 (1998), p. 3.
24 For example, a Wisconsin voyeurism statute was found to be constitutionally over-broad in respect of the First Amendment: see A. H. Kastens, 'State v Stevenson, The "Peeping Tom" case: Overbreadth or overblown?' (2001) *Wisconsin Law Review* 1371.
25 Rothenberg, 'Re-thinking privacy', 1145.

taking and distributing photographs of people in intimate situations will very often have a sexual motivation'.[26] The policy justification for prohibiting voyeurism in this context is to prevent sexual exploitation of one person by another, irrespective of whether the person viewed is aware of it.[27] In addition, voyeurism may be evidence of a sexual disorder which, in some cases, may be a precursor to more serious disorders.[28] While not all, or even most, voyeurs will go on to commit sex offences, it can form part of a continuum of sexual offending, with many convicted sex offenders having previously engaged in voyeurism or similar behaviour.[29]

It can therefore be seen that 'the state's interest in protecting the privacy of individual citizens and its interest in preventing sexual exploitation of its citizens coalesce where the breach of privacy also involves a breach of the citizen's sexual or physical integrity'.[30] Even in the absence of a sexual motivation, it may be argued that the impact of voyeurism on privacy, both for the victim and for society, supports the case for a criminal offence.[31] Further, as many victims may not even realise that their privacy has been violated, there is an argument that this is an appropriate area for public enforcement.[32]

3. Legislative responses

Specific voyeurism statutes have now been enacted in Canada,[33] the UK[34] and the United States.[35] Although there is no federal voyeurism offence

---

26 New Zealand Law Commission, *Intimate Covert Filming*, p. 12.
27 Department of Justice Canada, *Voyeurism as a Criminal Offence*, Consultation Paper (2002), p. 8.
28 Department of Justice, *Voyeurism*, pp. 3–4. Also see American Psychiatric Association, *Diagnostic and Statistical Manual of Mental Disorders IV-TR* (Washington DC: American Psychiatric Association, 2000) p. 575.
29 Home Office, *Setting the Boundaries: Reforming the law on sex offences* (2000), vol. i, p. 122.
30 Department of Justice Canada, *Voyeurism*, p. 8.
31 New Zealand Law Commission, *Intimate Covert Filming*, p. 25.
32 Rothenberg, 'Re-thinking privacy', 1149.
33 Criminal Code (Can), s. 162(1). Maximum penalty 5 years' imprisonment: s. 162(5).
34 Sexual Offences Act 2003 (UK), s. 67. Maximum penalty 2 years' imprisonment.
35 18 USC § 1801. Maximum penalty 1 year's imprisonment. This provision applies only in the special maritime and territorial jurisdiction, defined in 18 USC § 7. For a discussion of state laws see T. J. Horstmann, 'Protecting traditional privacy rights in a brave new digital world: The threat posed by cellular phone-cameras and what states should do to stop it' (2007) 111 *Pennsylvania State Law Review* 739.

in Australia, the issue is under active consideration.[36] We will therefore consider ss. 227A and 227B of the Criminal Code 1899 (Qld), being one of the first and most comprehensive state provisions addressing this issue.[37]

Although clearly concerned with privacy rights, none of these provisions create a general right of privacy. The offences all focus on the sexual nature of what is observed and/or the sexual motivation of the voyeur. Rather than discussing each provision separately, this discussion will focus on the following issues:

1. To what depictions does it apply?
2. Where does it apply?
3. To what conduct does it apply?
4. What is the fault element?
5. Does it extend to distribution of images?
6. What defences are available?

A. To what depictions does it apply?

Each provision focuses on depictions which may be described as being of an intimate or private nature. None require that the person depicted be identifiable.[38] In some jurisdictions, the offence is limited to images which depict nudity, semi-nudity or sexual activity. For example, in the United States, the defendant must capture an image of a 'private area', defined as the naked or undergarment-clad genitals, pubic area, buttocks, or female breast.[39]

Similarly, the UK provision requires that the person be observed or recorded doing a 'private act'.[40] A 'private act' is one which is done in a place which, in the circumstances, would reasonably be expected to provide privacy, and either the person's genitals, buttocks or breasts are exposed or covered only with underwear, the person is using a lavatory,

---

36 Standing Committee of Attorneys-General, *Unauthorised Photographs on the Internet and Ancillary Privacy Issues*, Discussion Paper (Commonwealth Attorney-General's Department, 2005).

37 Maximum penalty 2 years' imprisonment. Also see Summary Offences Act 1966 (Vic), Part I, Div. 4A and Crimes Act 1900 (NSW), Div. 15B. Crimes Act 1961 (NZ), Part 9A also contains offences relating to 'intimate visual recordings'.

38 Cf the Californian provision cited in *Washington v. Glas*, 147 Wn 2d 410, 418 (SC Wash 2002).

39 18 USC § 1801(b)(3). 'Female breast' means any portion of the female breast below the top of the areola: § 1801 (b)(4).

40 Sexual Offences Act 2003 (UK), s. 67(1)–(3).

or the person is doing a sexual act that is not of a kind ordinarily done in public.[41] This latter requirement may prove problematic in defining sexual acts which are not 'ordinarily' done in public. Obviously it includes sexual intercourse or masturbation, but at what point does passionate kissing, or the fondling of buttocks, for example, become a sexual act not 'ordinarily' done in public?

In contrast the Canadian and Queensland provisions, while equally capturing such images, may extend to images which are simply taken in a 'private place' with no requirement that the image depict nudity or sexual activity.[42] So, for instance, it would be an offence under these sections to record a person in a changing room even while that person is clothed.

B. Where does it apply?

Each jurisdiction makes use of the concept of a 'reasonable expectation of privacy' to broadly define those places where the offence may be committed. This is then further refined by reference to specific instances.

The Canadian and Queensland provisions both specify categories of prohibited conduct, subject to the overarching requirement that the conduct occurred in circumstances that give rise to a reasonable expectation of privacy.[43] The first limb is where a person 'can reasonably be expected to be nude, to expose his or her genital organs or anal region or her breasts, or to be engaged in explicit sexual activity'.[44] Similarly, in Queensland a 'private place' is one where a person might reasonably be expected to be engaging in a 'private act'. This is defined as showering or bathing, using a toilet, or another activity when the person is in a state of undress or intimate sexual activity that is not ordinarily done in public.[45]

Such descriptions clearly apply to places such as bathrooms, bedrooms, changing rooms, tanning salons and the like. In such places, it does not actually matter that the person was not in fact naked, engaging in sexual activity, etc. The observation or recording in that place and for that purpose is sufficient.[46] They may not, however, apply to places such as an

---

41 S. 68.   42 Criminal Code (Can), s. 162(1) and Criminal Code 1899 (Qld), s. 227A(1).
43 *Ibid.*   44 Criminal Code (Can), s. 162(1)(a).
45 Criminal Code 1899 (Qld), s. 207A. 'State of undress' means the person is naked or the person's genital or anal region (or breasts in the case of women) is bare, the person is wearing only underwear or only some outer garments so that some of the person's underwear is not covered by an outer garment: s. 207A.
46 Department of Justice, *Voyeurism*, p. 9.

enclosed office where although a person may reasonably expect a degree of privacy, it may not be possible to say that it could reasonably be expected that he or she would be naked.

Such circumstances are addressed by the second limb which applies where the person is:

> nude, is exposing his or her genital organs or anal region or her breasts, or is engaged in explicit sexual activity, and the observation or recording is done for the purpose of observing or recording a person in such a state or engaged in such an activity.[47]

Therefore, the person need not be in a place where one could reasonably be expected to be engaging in such activity, but he or she was engaging in such conduct and being observed or recorded for that purpose.

The crucial limitation is that the recording or observation was for the purpose of seeing or recording the person in that state. It would therefore presumably not apply to legitimate workplace surveillance, for example, which happened to capture a person changing clothes in their office. Note that the defendant's motivation in observing or recording need not be sexual; it may be for harassment or personal amusement.[48] So long as the purpose was to record the particular activity, the offence is made out.[49]

These provisions could also apply to a person on a nude beach who is deliberately observed or recorded. They are, however, subject to the overarching requirement that this occur in circumstances that give rise to a reasonable expectation of privacy. This may address the distinction between consent to being observed and consent to being recorded. Obviously a person on a nude beach consents to being observed in that state. Therefore he or she does not have a reasonable expectation of privacy, at least in respect of being observed. It may, however, be argued that in the circumstances there is a reasonable expectation of privacy in respect of being deliberately recorded in that state without consent.

Neither of these provisions addresses the issue of 'up-skirting' where the victim is clothed and in a public place. In Canada, such conduct may be captured by the third category which applies to an observation or recording which is 'done for a sexual purpose'.[50] Such conduct is prohibited irrespective of where it occurs, or whether nudity or sexual activity is depicted. It could therefore apply to 'up-skirt' photographs,

---

47 Criminal Code (Can), s. 162(1)(b). A similar provision is found in Criminal Code 1899 (Qld), s. 227A(1)(b)(ii).
48 See, e.g., the unsuccessful argument raised in the UK case of *R v. Sawyer* [2007] EWCA Crim 204.
49 Department of Justice, *Voyeurism*, pp. 9–10.   50 Criminal Code (Can), s. 162(1)(c).

subject to the requirement that the victim must be in circumstances that give rise to a reasonable expectation of privacy.

Such situations are specifically addressed in the Queensland provision which makes it an offence to observe or visually record another person's genital or anal region without consent and in circumstances where a reasonable adult would expect to be afforded privacy in relation to that region. In addition, the observation or visual recording must be made for the purpose of observing or visually recording the other person's genital or anal region.[51]

In contrast, the UK provision refers to 'a *place* which, in the circumstances, would reasonably be expected to provide privacy'.[52] In addition to obvious places such as changing rooms and bathrooms, this might conceivably cover places such as an enclosed office, a living room or a tanning salon. It may even be that a person may engage in a private act in an otherwise open space, for example by urinating behind a shrubbery.[53] However, it arguably does not apply, for example, to up-skirt photos in a public place as in such cases, the 'place' cannot reasonably be expected to provide privacy, even though it might be reasonable to expect privacy in the circumstances.

This issue has arisen in relation to some similarly worded US state laws.[54] For example, in *Washington* v. *Glas*[55] the defendant used a small digital camera to record both still and moving images up the skirts of women and young girls, without their consent, in a shopping centre. He was convicted of voyeurism under the relevant Washington statute[56] but appealed, inter alia, on the basis that the offence had not occurred 'in a place where [the victim] would have a reasonable expectation of privacy'.[57]

This argument was accepted by the Washington Supreme Court. The statute defines a place where a person would have a reasonable expectation of privacy to include a 'place where one may reasonably expect to be safe from casual or hostile intrusion or surveillance'.[58] The section would therefore apply to those situations where a person might not normally disrobe but would expect to have privacy if he or she did. For example, rooms in a house other than the bedroom or bathroom, changing rooms

---

51 Criminal Code 1899 (Qld), s. 227A(2)(b). Also see Summary Offences Act 1966 (Vic), Part I, Div. 4A.
52 Sexual Offences Act 2003 (UK), s. 68(1) (emphasis added).
53 *R* v. *Sawyer* [2007] EWCA Crim 204.
54 Calvert and Brown, 'Video voyeurism', 528–9.
55 147 Wn 2d 410 (SC Wash 2002).   56 RCW 9A.44.115.
57 *Washington* v. *Glas*, 147 Wn 2d 410, 414 (2002).   58 *Ibid.*

where a person may expect to be seen but not to be filmed, or an enclosed office where a person may choose to breast feed or change clothes. However, as casual surveillance frequently occurs in public places, they could not logically be places where a person could reasonably expect to be safe from casual or hostile intrusion or surveillance.[59]

An alternative analysis is that privacy is not an 'all-or-nothing' concept which is forfeited as soon as a person goes out in public.[60] Although we accept that we will be observed by others when in public, most people still take steps to conceal certain intimate parts of their body which they do not wish to be viewed by others. It is arguable that this more limited sphere of privacy should be respected and protected, even in an otherwise public place:

> In the great majority of situations it is common sense that the woman who wears a dress in public does not expect others to view under her dress, except to the degree that may be possible in a fleeting moment, and certainly not as a permanent image that can be endlessly manipulated and enhanced.[61]

This was the view adopted in *Minnesota* v. *Morris*,[62] another case of surreptitious recordings in a shopping mall. The relevant Minnesota statute applied to any 'place where a reasonable person would have an expectation of privacy and has exposed or is likely to expose their intimate parts'.[63] The court rejected the defendant's argument that the statute did not apply to images recorded up a woman's skirt when she is in a public place:

> The area under a skirt (or, for that matter, a Scotsman's kilt . . .) *is* a place or location. It is spatial, not conceptual. By reason of the act of wearing of a covering, the person has defined a spatial location, associated with his or her intimate parts, as a zone of privacy.[64]

This issue is expressly addressed by the US provision which defines circumstances in which a person has a reasonable expectation of privacy as:

> (a) circumstances in which a reasonable person would believe that he or she could disrobe in privacy, without being concerned that an image of a private area of the individual was being captured; or

---

59 *Ibid.*, at 415–16.   60 New Zealand Law Commission, *Intimate Covert Filming*, p. 6.
61 *Ibid.*, pp. 6–7.   62 644 N W 2d 114 (CA Minn 2002).
63 Minn. Stat. § 609.746, subd. (1)(c)(1) (2000).
64 *Minnesota* v. *Morris*, 644 N W 2d 114, 117 (CA Minn 2002) (original emphasis).

(b) circumstances in which a reasonable person would believe that a
    private area of the individual would not be visible to the public,
    regardless of whether that person is in a public or private place.[65]

The first limb of this definition clearly encompasses not only traditional
private spaces, but also offices or rooms in a house other than the bathroom or bedroom.[66] The second limb specifically addresses the viewing
of private areas of the body even in public places.

C. To what conduct does it apply?

Digital technology facilitates both the ability to observe and to record, and
in most jurisdictions both are punishable. For instance, under the Canadian provision it as an offence to surreptitiously observe, including by
mechanical or electronic means, or make a visual recording of a person.[67]
In contrast, the US provision applies only where the defendant 'captures'
the image, defined to mean 'videotape, photograph, film, record by any
means, or broadcast'.[68] Although the provision does not strictly apply to
observing per se, in many cases where remote electronic surveillance is
used this would constitute a 'broadcast' within the terms of the section.[69]

Each jurisdiction expresses the offence in terms which are sufficiently
broad to encompass new technologies. For example, 'observing' under
the Canadian provision includes by 'mechanical or electronic means',[70]
while 'visual recording' is defined to include a photographic, film or
video recording made by any means.[71] The UK provision simply refers to
'observes' or 'records', including by the use of 'equipment'.[72]

In contrast to other jurisdictions, the Canadian provision requires
that the observation or recording occur 'surreptitiously'. Although in
many cases the defendant's conduct will indeed be surreptitious, this
seems an unnecessary limitation. A person may brazenly take an intimate

---

65 18 USC § 1801(b)(5).
66 *Washington* v. *Glas*, 147 Wn 2d 410, 416 (SC Wash 2002) considering a similar state
    provision.
67 Criminal Code (Can), s. 162(1). 'Visual recording' is defined to include a photographic,
    film or video recording made by any means: s. 162(2). Also see Criminal Code 1899
    (Qld), s. 227A and Sexual Offences Act 2003 (UK), s. 67(1)–(3).
68 18 USC § 1801(b)(1).
69 'Broadcast' is defined to mean 'electronically transmit a visual image with the intent that
    it be viewed by a person or persons': § 1801(b)(2).
70 Criminal Code (Can), s. 162(1).
71 S. 162(2). Also see Criminal Code 1899 (Qld), s. 207A and 18 USC § 1801(b).
72 Sexual Offences Act 2003 (UK), s. 67.

photograph in a changing room, or up a woman's skirt, and would consequently fall outside the provision. This requirement may assume that where the conduct is not surreptitious, then the victim may be taken to have consented. Such a presumption is of course false, and the preferable approach would be to require a lack of consent on the part of the victim as occurs in the other jurisdictions.

D. What is the fault element?

The fault element of such offences is an important limitation on their reach. In Canada, no specific fault element is expressed where the person is in a place where he or she can reasonably be expected to be nude or engaged in sexual activity, or where actually nude or engaging in sexual activity. In such cases, it is presumably sufficient that the defendant intentionally observed or recorded the person in such circumstances.[73] Where neither of these situations apply, then the observation or recording may still be penalised if done 'for a sexual purpose'. This presumably encompasses both the sexual pleasure of third parties, as well as the defendant. As discussed in the context of child pornography, the phrase 'for a sexual purpose' has been interpreted objectively as meaning 'reasonably perceived as intended to cause sexual stimulation in some viewers'.[74]

In the UK, the defendant must have engaged in the conduct for the purpose of obtaining sexual gratification for himself or herself knowing that the person does not consent to being observed or recorded for the sexual gratification of the defendant, or a third party.[75] In appropriate cases, this includes the sexual gratification of third parties. This is important as the images may be recorded, not for the sexual pleasure of the photographer, but for the purpose of passing on to others for sexual gratification.

While understandable, proof of a sexual purpose may place a significant obstacle in the path of the prosecution. In some cases there may be non-sexual motivations which nonetheless do not justify the conduct. For example, the image may be recorded for malicious reasons, economic gain or just for amusement. In contrast, the US provision simply requires

---

73 In Queensland, no specific fault element is specified in the provisions. Culpability is therefore governed by the general principles of criminal responsibility set out in Chapter 5 Criminal Code 1899 (Qld).

74 *R v. Sharpe* [2001] SCR 45 at 50 per McLachlin CJ. See p. 260.

75 Sexual Offences Act 2003 (UK), s. 67(1)–(3).

that the defendant acted knowingly and with intent to capture an image of a private area of an individual without his or her consent. [76]

E. Does it extend to distribution of images?

One of the most dramatic impacts of digital technology is the ease with which images may be reproduced and distributed. This has the potential to both magnify and make permanent the victim's humiliation, and is specifically addressed in both the Canadian and Queensland provisions. Under s. 162(4) Criminal Code (Can) it is an offence for a person to print, copy, publish, distribute, circulate, sell, advertise or make available the recording, knowing that it was obtained in breach of the section.[77] Similarly, under s. 227B Criminal Code 1899 (Qld) it is an offence to distribute a prohibited visual recording of another person having reason to believe it to be a prohibited visual recording.[78]

Importantly, these offences are not limited to the person who made the recording as the photographer may well not be the distributor. The relevant knowledge is presumably knowledge of the circumstances in which the image was taken (which happen to constitute an offence) as opposed to knowledge that such conduct is an offence, as otherwise ignorance of the law would constitute a defence. One situation in which the defendant may raise a reasonable doubt as to whether he or she believed the images were obtained consensually is where the defendant believed the image to be an example of pseudo-voyeurism – that is, recorded consensually but given the appearance of a surreptitious recording.[79]

In other jurisdictions, distribution is dealt with obliquely, if at all. The US provision includes the 'broadcast' of an image, which is defined to mean 'electronically transmit a visual image with the intent that it be viewed by a person or persons'.[80] There is no specific offence relating to distribution under the UK legislation. There are, however, offences of enabling another person to observe a third person[81] and installing equipment or constructing or adapting a structure to enable the commission of an offence under subs. (1).[82] These would apply, for example, to a person installing a webcam to allow people on the Internet to observe,

---

76 18 USC § 1801(a).
77 The meaning of some of these phrases is discussed in the context of child pornography in Ch. 10.
78 'Distribute' is defined in s. 227B(2).   79 Calvert and Brown, 'Video voyeurism', 485–7.
80 18 USC § 1801(b)(2).   81 Sexual Offences Act 2003 (UK), s. 67(2).
82 S. 67(4).

without consent, another person engaged in a private act.[83] Depending on the content of the images, their distribution may also be punished under legislation prohibiting indecent or obscene communications.[84]

Simple possession of a prohibited recording is not an offence in any of the jurisdictions, although possession for the purposes of distribution is an offence in Canada.[85] Possession may, in appropriate cases, be an offence under laws concerning prohibited content such as child pornography or obscene material.

F. What defences are available?

As noted above, restrictions on observing or recording may come into conflict with other legitimate interests; particularly those of law enforcement and freedom of expression. Where the prosecution must prove that the observation and/or recording was for sexual gratification, as in the UK, then there is little if any need for specific defences to be provided for.[86] However, where the observation or recording may be for a non-sexual purpose, it is necessary to provide for exceptions for legitimate purposes. In particular, each jurisdiction, other than the UK, makes an exception for legitimate law enforcement-related activities.[87]

More broadly, the Canadian provision also provides for a defence where the alleged act serves the public good and does not extend beyond what serves the public good. This therefore addresses some concerns relating to free speech and freedom of expression, and could, for example, encompass legitimate journalistic activity or artistic expression. Whether or not the acts are for the public good, and whether there is evidence that the acts do not extend beyond what services the public good, are questions of law. Whether those acts did or did not extend beyond what serves the public good is a question of fact, the motives of the accused being irrelevant to this question.[88]

---

83 Explanatory Notes, Sexual Offences Act 2003 (UK), [127].   84 See p. 254.
85 Criminal Code (Can), s. 162(4). Cf New Zealand Law Commission, *Intimate Covert Filming*, p. 30 where an offence of simple possession was recommended.
86 This is also the case in relation to observations or recording made for a 'sexual purpose' under Criminal Code (Can), s. 162(1)(c).
87 Criminal Code (Can), s. 162(3), Criminal Code 1899 (Qld), s. 227C and 18 USC § 1801(c).
88 Criminal Code (Can), s. 162(7).

PART VI

Jurisdiction

14

Jurisdiction

1. Crime in cyberspace

> With the continually expanding global information infrastructure, with numerous instances of international hacking, and with the growing possibility of increased global industrial espionage, it is important that the United States have jurisdiction over international computer crime cases.[1]

It is one thing to enact criminal offences to address online conduct; it is quite another to assert jurisdiction over offenders who may be located anywhere in the world. We saw in Chapter 1 that early scholarship postulated cyberspace as a distinct place, beyond traditional rules based on geographical location.[2] This has not, however, proved to be the case, 'with States now consistently applying traditional territorially based rules to online activity and largely refusing to treat the Internet as beyond their competence'.[3] This is particularly true in the criminal law which is necessarily 'grounded' in notions of territoriality.

This chapter provides an overview of the principles which apply to the exercise of criminal jurisdiction over extraterritorial conduct.[4] In this context, the term 'jurisdiction' in fact conceals three distinct concepts which require separate discussion:

1. Does the state have legislative power over the relevant conduct ('prescriptive jurisdiction')?
2. Do the courts have power to hear the particular dispute ('adjudicative jurisdiction')?

1 Computer Crime and Intellectual Property Section, *The National Information Infrastructure Protection Act of 1996: Legislative Analysis* (US Department of Justice, 2003).
2 See p. 17.
3 U. Kohl, *Jurisdiction and the Internet: Regulatory competence over online activity* (Cambridge: Cambridge University Press, 2007) pp. 11–12.
4 For a detailed discussion across a range of jurisdictions see B. J. Koops and S. W. Brenner (eds.), *Cybercrime and Jurisdiction: A global survey* (The Hague: TMC Asser Press, 2006).

3. Does the state have jurisdiction to enforce the law ('enforcement jurisdiction')?[5]

2. Prescriptive jurisdiction

Prescriptive jurisdiction, also known as subject matter or legislative jurisdiction, is addressed in Art. 22 of the Cybercrime Convention. This sets out a number of bases on which parties are to establish jurisdiction.[6] The first is where the offence is committed within its territory, reflecting the principle of territoriality.[7] This is the most common basis for the exercise of criminal jurisdiction,[8] there being a general presumption that criminal laws are local in operation.[9] Although allowing a country to exercise jurisdiction over conduct which occurs within its sovereign territory, there are a number of ways in which the territorial principle operates to encompass extraterritorial conduct.[10]

First, a country may assert territorial jurisdiction over conduct which occurs on a flagged ship or registered aircraft of that country. This is specifically recognised in the Convention, and expands the scope of territorial jurisdiction to those situations where the ship or aircraft is outside the terrestrial jurisdiction of the relevant country.[11] Such an extension of territorial jurisdiction is important in closing potential gaps in jurisdictional reach. For example, if the ship or aircraft is in international waters or airspace, no other country may be able to assert jurisdiction in respect of that conduct.[12] Alternatively, even where a ship or aircraft is

---

5   Kohl, *Jurisdiction and the Internet*, p. 17.

6   These do not exclude other forms of jurisdiction exercised by a country under its domestic law: Cybercrime Convention, Art. 22(4).

7   *Ibid.*, Art. 22(1)(a) and Cybercrime Convention, Explanatory Report, [233]. For a more detailed discussion of jurisdiction under the Convention see H. W. K. Kaspersen, 'Jurisdiction in the Cybercrime Convention' in Koops and Brenner, *Cybercrime and Jurisdiction*, Ch. 2.

8   Council of Europe: European Committee on Crime Problems, 'Extraterritorial criminal jurisdiction' (1992) 3 *Criminal Law Forum* 441, 446; Restatement (Third) of Foreign Relations Law of the United States § 402, comment c; and D. Lanham, *Cross-Border Criminal Law* (Sydney: FT Law & Tax, 1997), p. 30.

9   *Treacy* v. *DPP* [1971] AC 537 at 561 per Lord Diplock; *Equal Employment Opportunity Commission* v. *Arabian American Oil Co.*, 499 US 244 (1991); and *R* v. *Finta* [1994] 1 SCR 701 at 805–6 per Cory J.

10   Council of Europe, 'Extraterritorial criminal jurisdiction', 447; 462.

11   Cybercrime Convention, Art. 22(1)(b)–(c) and Cybercrime Convention, Explanatory Report, [235].

12   *Ibid.*

within the territorial jurisdiction of another country, its presence may be so transient as to the make the assertion of jurisdiction impractical.[13]

Second, the principle of 'objective territoriality' allows a claim of criminal jurisdiction for conduct occurring outside the jurisdiction but which has a substantial effect in the jurisdiction.[14] This is specifically envisaged in the Convention and is intended to apply where the victim is within the jurisdiction.[15] A narrower principle which may be applied in such cases, the 'Protective Principle', applies where the offence is committed with the intention of damaging the fundamental interests of that state.[16]

The other basis of jurisdiction recognised under the Convention is the 'Nationality Principle'.[17] This requires parties to establish jurisdiction where the offence is committed by one of its nationals, irrespective of where it occurs in the world.[18] For this principle to apply, the conduct must have also been punishable under the laws of the country where the offence was committed, or where the offence was committed outside the territorial jurisdiction of any state.[19] Although parties may opt out of asserting jurisdiction on the basis of nationality or in respect of its ships or aircraft, they must apply territorial jurisdiction.[20]

The assertion of jurisdiction is, in the first instance, a matter of legislative intent. Assuming the legislature is competent to legislate extraterritorially, has it clearly expressed its intention to do so? Ideally, the legislature makes its intention express, as in the Criminal Code (Cth). Jurisdiction under that act is determined by reference to defined jurisdictional categories, identified as Extended Geographical Jurisdiction Categories A–D.

---

13 *Ibid.*
14 E. S. Podgor, 'Extraterritorial criminal jurisdiction: Replacing "objective territoriality" with "defensive territoriality"' in A. Sarat and P. Ewick (eds.), *Studies in Law, Politics, and Society* (2003) 117, 123–5; and US Restatement (Third) § 402, comment d.
15 Cybercrime Convention, Explanatory Report, [233].
16 Council of Europe, 'Extraterritorial criminal jurisdiction', 451. See also US Restatement (Third) § 402, comment f; and Lanham, *Cross-Border Criminal Law*, pp. 35–7.
17 The principle of universal jurisdiction, which recognises the right of any country to exercise jurisdiction over a defendant in respect of 'universal crimes' such as piracy, genocide, and war crimes, is of limited significance in the cybercrime context.
18 Cybercrime Convention, Art. 22(1)(d); Cybercrime Convention, Explanatory Report, [236] and Council of Europe, 'Extraterritorial criminal jurisdiction', 448. This is also known as the 'active personality principle', in contrast to the less common 'passive personality principle' where extraterritorial jurisdiction is based upon the nationality of the victim: Council of Europe, 'Extraterritorial criminal jurisdiction', 448–50; and US Restatement (Third) § 402, comment g.
19 Cybercrime Convention, Art. 22(1)(d).   20 *Convention on Cybercrime*, Art. 22(2).

In the case of the cybercrimes found in Part 10.7 of the code, these are subject to extended geographical jurisdiction Category A.[21] This is further defined in s. 15.1 and reflects the bases of liability describe above.

First, it applies where the conduct occurs wholly or partly in Australia or on board an Australian aircraft or ship. This clearly illustrates the territorial principle in its extended form. Secondly, the legislation also applies 'objective territoriality' by extending jurisdiction to those situations where the conduct occurs wholly *outside* Australia but where a result of the conduct occurs wholly or partly in Australia or on board an Australian aircraft or ship.[22] Thirdly, the nationality principle applies so that an offence is committed where the conduct occurs wholly outside Australia and the person is an Australian citizen or body corporate.[23]

The Australian provisions are also defined in such a way as to take account of the mobility of modern communications. So, if a person sends, or causes to be sent, an electronic communication to/from a point outside Australia to/from a point in Australia, that conduct is taken to have occurred partly in Australia.[24] 'Point', for these purposes, 'includes a mobile or potentially mobile point, whether on land, underground, in the atmosphere, underwater, at sea or anywhere else'.[25] This is consistent with the decision not to incorporate within the Convention a special basis of jurisdiction for satellites registered in a county's name. Because the communication must originate and terminate in a terrestrial jurisdiction, and/or be transmitted by a country's national, the jurisdictional bases outlined in Art. 22(1)(a)–(d) should be sufficient.[26]

In the UK, the offences of unauthorised access or modification of computer material under ss. 1 and 3 of the Computer Misuse Act may be prosecuted in the 'home country',[27] even if no element of the offence occurred in that country and/or the defendant was not present in that country, so

---

21 Criminal Code (Cth), s. 476.3.

22 This further extends to ancillary offences such as attempt, incitement or conspiracy, where the conduct occurs wholly outside Australia but the primary offence occurs, or is intended to occur, wholly or partly in Australia or on board an Australian aircraft or ship: Criminal Code (Cth), s. 15.1(1).

23 A UK example of extraterritorial jurisdiction based on nationality is found in s. 72(1)(2) Sexual Offences Act 2003 (UK).

24 Criminal Code (Cth), s. 16.2(2).   25 *Ibid.*, s. 16.2(3).

26 Cybercrime Convention, Explanatory Report, [234]. In Canada, limited extraterritorial jurisdiction is provided for in Part XIV Criminal Code (Can).

27 Defined as England and Wales, in so far as the Act applies to England and Wales, and similarly for Scotland and Northern Ireland: Computer Misuse Act, s. 4(6).

long as there is at least one 'significant link' with the jurisdiction.[28] In essence, a 'significant link' arises where either the defendant was in the home country when he or she did the relevant act, or the unauthorised access or modification occurred in the home country.[29] British citizenship is immaterial to the question of guilt.[30]

Another example of express extraterritorial jurisdiction is found in the CFAA. A number of provisions apply to a 'protected computer',[31] defined to include a computer 'which is used in interstate or foreign commerce or communication, including a computer located outside the United States that is used in a manner that affects interstate or foreign commerce or communication of the United States'.[32] It has been held that to not be superfluous the word 'foreign' must mean something other than 'interstate' – that is, 'international'.[33] This has the potential to greatly expand federal extraterritorial laws, as any computer which is connected to the Internet can be said to be used in an interstate or foreign communication.[34] Further, the computer need not even be located in the United States; so long as it is connected to the Internet it could be described as being used in a manner which affects interstate or foreign communication or communication of the United States.

In other cases, extraterritorial jurisdiction may be implied. For example, in *DPP* v. *Sutcliffe*[35] it was alleged that the defendant engaged in a course of conduct which amounted to stalking in the Australian state of Victoria.[36] The victim was a woman called Sara Ballingall who had acted in the TV series 'Degrassi Junior High'. What made this case particularly notable was that the victim was at all times in Canada while the accused was from Victoria and had never had personal contact with her. Between 1993 and 1999 the defendant sent letters, presents and emails, some of which demonstrated an interest in guns and with some threatening statements.

On appeal from the magistrate's decision that the offence was not extraterritorial in application, Justice Gillard looked to the presumed

---

28 *Ibid.*, s. 4(1)–(2).
29 *Ibid.*, s. 5. The provision for extraterritorial jurisdiction in respect of a s. 2 offence is found in ss. 4(3) and 8(1). For a more detailed discussion of these provisions, see M. Hirst, *Jurisdiction and the Ambit of the Criminal Law* (Oxford: Oxford University Press, 2003), pp. 195–7.
30 Computer Misuse Act, s. 9(1).   31 18 USC §§ 1030(a)(2)(4)(5)(7).
32 18 USC § 1030(e)(2)(B).   33 *US* v. *Ivanov*, 175 F Supp 2d 367, 374 (D Conn 2001).
34 J. R. Herrera-Flanigan, 'Cybercrime and jurisdiction in the United States' in Koops and Brenner, *Cybercrime and Jurisdiction*, p. 315.
35 [2001] VSC 43.   36 Crimes Act 1958 (Vic), s. 21A.

intention of the legislature. Given the changing nature of crime, it would have been apparent to those drafting the legislation that conduct may have an effect in another jurisdiction. This was particularly true in a federation like Australia where it was quite possible that a person in one state could engage in conduct which amounted to stalking of a person in another state. It was held that for the legislation to be confined to conduct which occurred and had its effect only in Victoria would be to stultify it or make it unworkable in respect to certain conduct which was clearly stalking. It was therefore presumed that Parliament intended the section to be extraterritorial in application.[37]

3. Adjudicative jurisdiction

Once prescriptive jurisdiction has been established, the question remains whether the particular court has adjudicative jurisdiction over the specific case. Recent decades have seen a liberalisation of courts hearing extraterritorial cases, as summarised by the Supreme Court of Canada:

> all that is necessary to make an offence subject to the jurisdiction of our courts is that a significant portion of the activities constituting that offence took place in Canada. As it is put by modern academics, it is sufficient that there be a 'real and substantial link' between an offence and this country, a test that is well-known in public and private international law.[38]

The application of these principles in a cybercrime context arose in *R v. Governor of Brixton Prison and anor, ex parte Levin*.[39] One issue for determination was whether the appropriation in respect of Citibank's accounts occurred in St Petersburg, Russia, where the computer instructions were sent, or in Citibank's computers in 'Parsipenny' [sic], New Jersey. It was held that given the virtually instantaneous nature of electronic transactions, it was 'artificial' to regard the offence as having occurred in one place or the other.[40] However, on the assumption that an offence could not have two loci it was held that the offence occurred in the United States. The act of appropriation in this case was access to Citibank's computers,

---

37 *DPP v. Sutcliffe* [2001] VSC 43 at [36]–[47] per Gillard J. The issue has now been put beyond doubt by legislative amendment: Crimes Act 1958 (Vic), s. 21A(7).

38 *Libam v. R* [1985] 2 SCR 178, 212–13 per La Forest J. Also see *R v. Smith (Wallace Duncan) (No. 4)* [2004] QB 1418, 1435 per Lord Woolf CJ; and *R v. Liphar* (1999) 200 CLR 485, 534–5 per Gaudron, Gummow, and Hayne JJ.

39 [1997] QB 65. The facts of this case are discussed at p. 115.

40 *Ibid.*, 81 per Beldam LJ.

and this occurred in New Jersey as it was there that the instructions were recorded on the disk and the impairment occurred. Prior to that point, there was no appropriation.[41]

In federations such as Australia and the United States, a jurisdictional nexus may also be required as a precondition of federal jurisdiction. For example, many US federal provisions derive their jurisdictional authority from the 'interstate commerce' power.[42] In cybercrime cases, the Internet itself is generally regarded as an 'instrument of interstate commerce'.[43] So, for example, 'transmission of photographs by means of the Internet is tantamount to moving photographs across state lines and thus constitutes transportation in interstate commerce'.[44] Because of the nature of the Internet, even intrastate communications will commonly be routed through servers outside the state of origin, thus forming the basis for federal jurisdiction.[45] The situation would be different, however, for a purely intrastate communication such as infrared transmission or other point-to-point transmissions.

Further, because cybercrimes commonly involve the use of telecommunications networks, there is the potential for a considerable expansion of federal criminal jurisdiction. For example, in Australia, although criminal law is primarily a state matter, the commonwealth may enact criminal laws which relate to commonwealth matters, such as commonwealth computers, or which involve the use of 'postal, telegraphic, telephonic and other like services'.[46] Given the reliance of modern computer networks on the telecommunications system, this has given the commonwealth expansive jurisdiction in this area.

One of the primary concerns in relation to the assertion of extraterritorial criminal jurisdiction, or even the broad application of the Territorial Principle, is that it may give rise to competing jurisdictional claims.[47] In particular, the use of objective territoriality has meant that states will assert jurisdiction because an element of the offence has occurred within their territory, even if the effect on the jurisdiction is minimal. No standard

41 *Ibid.*, 81–2.　42 US Const. Art. I, § 8, cl.3.
43 *US* v. *Runyan*, 290 F 3d 223, 239 (5th Cir 2002); cert. denied, *Runyan* v. *US*, 537 US 888 (2002); *US* v. *Schaffner*, 258 F 3d 675, 679–83 (7th Cir 2001); and *US* v. *Panfill*, 338 F 3d 1299, 1300 (11th Cir 2003).
44 *US* v. *Carroll*, 105 F 3d 740, 742 (1st Cir 1997).
45 *US* v. *Kimler*, 335 F 3d 1132, 1140 (10th Cir 2003) and *US* v. *Dhingra*, 371 F 3d 557, 559 (9th Cir 2004). Also see *US* v. *Murrell*, 368 F 3d 1283, 1286 (11th Cir 2004) and *US* v. *Giordano*, 442 F 3d 30, 37 (2nd Cir 2006).
46 Australian Constitution, s. 51(v).
47 Council of Europe, 'Extraterritorial criminal jurisdiction', 465.

of 'reasonableness' is applied.[48] Because of varying standards associated with criminal law, there is legitimate concern that expansive exercise of extraterritorial jurisdiction will be an unjustifiable interference in the sovereignty of other states.[49]

For example, it is reasonably well-established that publication on the Internet occurs both where the images are uploaded and where they are downloaded.[50] The person who places material on a website may therefore potentially be liable in each jurisdiction in which the Internet is accessible. The challenge this presents for publishers was summarised by the Supreme Court of the United States:

> If a publisher chooses to send its material into a particular community, this Court's jurisprudence teaches that it is the publisher's responsibility to abide by that community's standards. The publisher's burden does not change simply because it decides to distribute its material to every community in the Nation.[51]

Of course, the global nature of modern communications magnifies the problem, as illustrated by the often-cited case of *Yahoo!, Inc. v. La Ligue Contre Le Racisme et L'Antisemitisme.*[52] In that case, Yahoo! sought a declaratory judgment against orders of a French court. The French court required Yahoo! to take all necessary measures to make it impossible for Nazi-related material to be accessible by French users of its services, such material being unlawful in France. The judgment was initially granted on First Amendment grounds, although that decision was subsequently reversed on appeal.[53]

The case clearly illustrates the tension presented by a truly global medium of communication: on the one hand is the freedom of users to disseminate information which is lawful in the country of origin; on the other is the right of the country of destination to not 'tolerate activity that it defines as illegal merely because it affects some who may live in a country where the activity is legal'.[54]

---

48 Kohl, *Jurisdiction and the Internet*, p. 96.
49 See generally, E. S. Podgor, 'International computer fraud: A paradigm for limiting national jurisdiction' (2002) 35 *University of California, Davis Law Review* 267.
50 See, e.g., *Godfrey* v. *Demon Internet Ltd* [2001] QB 201 and *R* v. *Perrin* [2002] EWCA Crim 747. Also see *Dow Jones & Co Inc.* v. *Gutnick* (2002) 210 CLR 575.
51 *Ashcroft* v. *American Civil Liberties Union*, 535 US 564, 583 (2002).
52 169 F Supp 2d 1181 (ND Cal 2001).
53 *Yahoo! Inc.* v. *La Ligue Contre Le Racisme*, 433 F 3d 1199 (9th Cir 2006); cert. denied, *La Ligue Contre Le Racisme et l'Antisemitisme* v. *Yahoo! Inc.*, 547 US 1163 (2006).
54 *US* v. *American Sports Ltd.*, 286 F 3d 641, 660 (3rd Cir 2002).

Under the Convention, parties in such cases are required, 'where appropriate, [to] consult with a view to determining the most appropriate jurisdiction for prosecution'.[55] This reflects the need for international comity – that is, 'mutual respect for the sovereignty of other States and refraining from unjustified interference in the internal affairs of those States'.[56] There is also a general requirement of international law that the exercise of jurisdiction must be 'reasonable'.[57]

A requirement to consult provides little practical guidance as to how such disputes are to be resolved. A range of factors may be relevant, including the location of the offence and offender, the nationality of the offender and victims, the degree of harm caused, the location of evidence and the level of punishment.[58] Resolution is further complicated in the case of cybercrimes where the correlation between factors cannot be assumed. For example, in offline crimes the offence is usually only committed in one place whereas cybercrimes may be committed in multiple jurisdictions.[59] Equally, in offline crimes, victims and offenders will generally be in the same jurisdiction. This is not true of cybercrimes where the location of the offender may have little relation to the location of the offence.[60] 'Given the vast amount of online activity, the number of cases in which States have actually sought to assume jurisdiction over foreign online activity is astoundingly small.'[61] In practical terms, such issues are generally resolved by enforcement jurisdiction, in particular the law of extradition.

4. Enforcement jurisdiction

Even if there is both prescriptive and adjudicative jurisdiction, the ability to enforce presents the most significant limitation on criminal jurisdiction. Unlike civil actions, where principles of *forum non conveniens* may apply, in criminal law the issue is effectively reduced to the question of who has the defendant in custody? This has the practical effect of limiting the number of cases in which states assert jurisdiction.[62]

---

55 Cybercrime Convention, Art. 22(5).
56 Council of Europe, 'Extraterritorial criminal jurisdiction', 459.
57 US Restatement (Third) § 403.
58 S. W. Brenner, 'The next step: Prioritizing jurisdiction' in Koops and Brenner, *Cybercrime and Jurisdiction*, Ch. 17.
59 *Ibid.*, p. 32.   60 *Ibid.*, p. 336.   61 Kohl, *Jurisdiction and the Internet*, p. 102.
62 *Ibid.*, p. 106.

It is a general principle that individuals will not be tried *in absentia* for serious offences. This is based in part on fairness to defendants but also the pragmatic fact that a foreign state will not enforce another state's public law judgments.[63] Criminal courts also invariably apply local law.[64] The effect of this is that 'on those fairly rare occasions when in possession of enforcement power, [states] have not been too concerned about the limits of their legislative/adjudicative jurisdiction under public international law'.[65]

Hence, it is the jurisdiction which has the defendant in custody which has the practical ability to exercise jurisdiction. In this respect, the Convention recognises the principle of *aut dedere aut judicare*: the obligation to extradite or prosecute.[66] That is, a country must assert jurisdiction where one of its nationals has committed an offence within its jurisdiction, and a request for extradition has been refused solely on the basis of nationality.[67]

Extradition is the process whereby one state will formally surrender a person for prosecution in another state. This is a matter of international comity rather than an obligation under international law, and is typically supported by bilateral treaties and domestic legislation in each country.[68] Detailed discussion of extradition and related matters is beyond the scope of this book.[69] There is, however, one aspect of extradition law which should be emphasised. Extradition typically requires there to be 'dual criminality' between the requesting party and the country where the person is located. That is, the offence must be an offence under the laws of both jurisdictions, usually subject to a minimum level of penalty, commonly a maximum penalty of at least twelve months' imprisonment.[70]

The difficulties presented by this requirement are well illustrated by the case of the 'Love Bug' virus.[71] The virus, which destroyed files and stole

63 *Ibid.*, p. 105.   64 *Ibid.*, p. 87.   65 *Ibid.*, p. 106.
66 Cybercrime Convention, Explanatory Report, [237].
67 Cybercrime Convention, Art. 24.
68 Extradition Act 1988 (Cth); Extradition Act 1999 (Can); Extradition Act 2003 (UK); and 18 USC ch. 209. Some jurisdictions also make provision in relation to the transfer of criminal proceedings in order to resolve such disputes: United Nations General Assembly, Model Treaty on the Transfer of Proceedings in Criminal Matters, A/RES/45/118, 14 December 1990.
69 See generally A. Jones and A. Doobay, *Jones and Doobay on Extradition and Mutual Assistance* (London: Sweet and Maxwell, 2005); Joint Standing Committee on Treaties, *Extradition: A Review of Australia's law and policy*, Report 40 (Parliament of Australia, 2001); and US Department of Justice, *United States Attorneys' Manual*, Title 9: *Criminal Resource Manual*, 9–15.000.
70 Cybercrime Convention, Art. 24.
71 The following summary is based on Goodman and Brenner, 'Emerging consensus', 2.

passwords, first appeared in Hong Kong in 2000 and then spread rapidly throughout the world. It affected major corporations, including Ford, Siemens and Microsoft, as well as government agencies including the US Departments of Defense and State, NASA and the CIA. It was estimated to have affected over 45 million users in more than twenty countries, causing billions of dollars in damage. Although investigators were able to determine that the person responsible was a former computer-science student in the Philippines, as the Philippines had no applicable law punishing such conduct, he could not be extradited to the United States due to the lack of dual criminality.

Where dual criminality exists, however, it allows one jurisdiction to seek the surrender of a person alleged to have caused damage in the requesting jurisdiction. In a recent example, Englishman Gary McKinnon lost his appeal against extradition to the United States in respect of his unauthorised access to US federal computers.[72] It is alleged that between 2001 and 2002 he accessed ninety-seven federal computers including the Department of Defense, the US Army and Navy and NASA, causing an estimated $US700,000 worth of damage. In another recent case, an Australian national was extradited to the United States after being indicted by a Virginia Grand Jury for criminal copyright infringement.[73]

When the number of extraditable offences was relatively few, it was typical for extradition treaties to enumerate those offences which were extraditable. This tradition continued, even as the number of extraditable offences grew, so that the 1976 Treaty between Australia and the United States specified twenty-nine types of extraditable offence. This approach presents particular difficulties where novel offences arise, with very few applicable to computer-facilitated crimes, and none encompassing conduct where a computer was the target of the offence.[74] Because of such difficulties, treaties have moved away from an enumerative to an eliminative approach.[75] For example, the Australia–US Treaty was subsequently amended so that an extraditable offence was defined as an offence 'punishable under the laws in both Contracting Parties by deprivation of liberty

---

72 *McKinnon v. Government of the USA; Secretary of State for the Home Department* [2007] EWHC 762.

73 *Griffiths v. United States of America* [2005] FCAFC 34.

74 Treaty on Extradition between Australia and the United States of America, opened for signature 14 May 1974, Australian Treaty Series 1976 no. 10, Art. II(1) (entered into force 8 May 1976).

75 J. T. Soma, T. F. Muther Jr and H. M. L. Brissette, 'Transnational extradition for computer crimes: Are new treaties and laws needed?' (1997) 34 *Harvard Journal on Legislation* 317, 324–6.

of more than one year, or by a more severe penalty'.[76] This is so whether or not the contracting parties place the offence within the same category of offences or describe the offence by the same terminology.[77]

Although preferable, such an approach still requires consideration of whether an equivalent law can be found in each jurisdiction, and can still present an obstacle.[78] For example, online gambling and hate speech are just two instances of conduct that is commonly unlawful in one jurisdiction but not others. In addition, even if technically extraditable, the complexity and cost of the extradition process ensures that it is typically reserved for serious offences.[79]

---

76 Protocol Amending the Treaty on Extradition between Australia and the United States of America of 14 May 1974, Australian Treaty Series 1992 no. 43, Art. 1(1) (entered into force 21 December 1992).
77 *Ibid.*, Art. 1(3)(a).
78 See, e.g., *R* v. *Bow Street Magistrates Court and Allison, ex parte Government of the United States of America* [2000] 2 AC 216.
79 J. Paust, 'Panel: Cybercrimes and the domestication of international criminal law' (2007) 5 *Santa Clara Journal of International Law* 432, 442.

BIBLIOGRAPHY

Adler, A., 'The perverse law of child pornography' (2001) 101 *The Columbia Law Review* 209

Agence France Presse, 'Briton sentenced to 51 months prison in US for Internet piracy', *The Sydney Morning Herald*, 23 June 2007, www.smh.com.au/news/Technology/Briton-sentenced-to-51-months-prison-in-US-for-Internet-piracy/2007/06/23/1182019396798.html

'Conficker worm wiggles into millions of computers', *The Age*, 21 January 2009

Akdeniz, Y., 'Possession and Dispossession: A critical assessment of defences in cases of possession of indecent photographs of children' (2007) *Criminal Law Review* 274

Akdeniz, Y., Taylor, N. and Walker, C., 'Regulation of Investigatory Powers Act 2000 (1): BigBrother.gov.uk: State surveillance in the age of information and rights' (2001) *Criminal Law Review* 73

All Party Parliamentary Internet Group, *'Spam': Report of an Inquiry by the All Party Internet Group* (2003)

Revision of the Computer Misuse Act: Report of an Inquiry by the All Party Internet Group (2004)

'Digital Rights Management': Report of an Inquiry by the All Party Internet Group (2006)

American Psychiatric Association, *Diagnostic and Statistical Manual of Mental Disorders IV-TR* (Washington DC: APA, 2000)

Anti-Phishing Working Group, *Phishing Activity Trends Report: Q2/2008* (2008)

Origins of the Word 'Phishing' (2008), www.antiphishing.org/word_phish.html

APACS – the UK Payments Association, *Key Facts and Figures: Card fraud facts and figures* (2008), www.apacs.org.uk/resources_publications/card_fraud_facts_and_figures.html

Armagh, D. S., 'The fate of the Child Pornography Act of 1996: Virtual child pornography: Criminal conduct or protected speech?' (2002) 23 *Cardozo Law Review* 1993

Arora, V., 'The CAN-SPAM Act: An inadequate attempt to deal with a growing problem' (2006) 39 *Columbia Journal of Law and Social Problems* 299

Ashworth, A., *Principles of Criminal Law* (New York: Oxford University Press, 2006)

Attorney-General's Department, *Review of Commonwealth Criminal Law: Interim report, computer crime* (1988)

Audal, J., Lu, Q. and Roman, P., 'Computer crimes' (2008) *American Criminal Law Review* 233

AusCERT, *Australian Computer Crime and Security Survey* (2006)

Australasian Centre for Policing Research and the Australian Transaction Reports and Analysis Centre, *Standardisation of Definitions of Identity Crime Terms: A step towards consistency*, Report Series no. 145.3, Australasian Centre for Policing Research (2006)

Australian Bureau of Statistics, *Personal Fraud*, Cat. no. 4528.0 (Canberra: ABS, 2007)

  Household Use of Information Technology, Australia 2007–08, Cat. no. 8146.0 (Canberra: ABS, 2008)

Australian High Tech Crime Centre, *Malware: Viruses, worms, Trojan horses*, High Tech Crime Brief no. 10 (AIC, 2006)

  Money Mules, High Tech Crime Brief no. 16 (AIC, 2007)

Australian Institute of Criminology, *Intellectual Property Crime and Enforcement in Australia*, Research and Public Policy Series no. 94 (2008)

Australian Law Reform Commission, *Film and Literature Censorship Procedure*, Report no. 55 (1991)

  For Your Information: Australian privacy law and practice, Report 108 (2008), vol. i

Australian Payments Clearing Association, *Payment Fraud in Australia*, Media Release, 15 December 2008, www.apca.com.au/Public/apca01_live.nsf/ResourceLookup/Press_Release_Payments_Fraud_Statistics_5.pdf/$File/Press_Release_Payments_Fraud_Statistics_5.pdf

Bartholomew, M., *Cops, Robbers, and Search Engines: The role of criminal law in contributory infringement doctrine*, Buffalo Legal Studies Research Paper Series Paper no. 2008–19 (2008)

Baum, K., *Identity Theft 2004*, Bureau of Justice Statistics Bulletin (US Department of Justice, 2006)

BBC News, '"Virtual theft" leads to arrest', BBC News Online (Asia-Pacific) 14 November 2007, http://news.bbc.co.uk/2/hi/technology/7094764.stm

  'Caution for Who star Townshend', BBC News Online, 7 May 2003, http://news.bbc.co.uk/1/hi/uk/3007871.stm

  'Web paedophile given nine years', BBC News, 22 June 2006, http://news.bbc.co.uk/2/hi/uk_news/england/5106612.stm

  'Q&A: Child benefit records lost: How worried should people be by the loss of discs containing child benefit recipients' personal details?', BBC News, 22 November 2007, http://news.bbc.co.uk/2/hi/uk_news/politics/7103828.stm

  'Woman in jail over virtual murder', BBC News Online (Asia-Pacific), 24 October 2008, http://news.bbc.co.uk/2/hi/asia-pacific/7688091.stm

'Internet piracy trio sent to jail', BBC News: Technology, 6 May 2005, http://news.bbc.co.uk/1/hi/technology/4518771.stm

BC Freedom of Information and Privacy Association, *PIPEDA and Identity Theft: Solutions for protecting Canadians*' (FIPA, 2006)

Bellia, P. L., 'Spyware and the limits of surveillance law' (2005) 20 *Berkeley Technology Law Journal* 1283

Bellia, P. L. and Freiwald, S., 'Fourth Amendment protection for stored e-mail' (2008) *The University of Chicago Law Forum* 121

Biever, C., 'New hacking tool hijacks file-sharing networks', *New Scientist.com News Service*, 19 March 2004, www.newscientisttech.com/channel/tech/electronic-threats/dn4799

Binational Working Group on Cross-Border Mass Marketing Fraud, *Report on Phishing: A report to the Minister of Public Safety and Emergency Preparedness Canada and the Attorney General of the United States* (2006)

Blunn, A., *Report of the Review of the Regulation of Access to Communications* (Australian Government, Attorney-General's Department, 2005)

Bocij, P., *Cyberstalking: Harassment in the Internet age and how to protect your family* (Westport: Praeger Publishers, 2004)

Boland, M. L., 'Model Code revisited: Taking aim at the high-tech stalker' (2005) 20 *Criminal Justice* 40

Bradfield, J. L., 'Anti-stalking laws: Do they adequately protect stalking victims?' (1998) 21 *Harvard Women's Law Journal* 229

'True threats: A more appropriate standard for analyzing First Amendment protection and free speech when violence is perpetrated over the Internet' (2002) 78 *North Dakota Law Review* 753

Brenner, S. W., 'Is there such a thing as "virtual crime"?' (2001) 4 *California Criminal Law Review* 1

'Cybercrime metrics: Old wine, new bottles?' (2004) 9 *Virginia Journal of Law and Technology* 1

'Toward a criminal law for cyberspace: Distributed security' (2004) 10 *Buffalo Journal of Science and Technology* 1

'The next step: Prioritizing jurisdiction' in B. J. Koops and S. W. Brenner, *Cybercrime and Jurisdiction: A global survey* (The Hague: TMC Asser Press, 2006)

'Fantasy crime: The role of criminal law in virtual worlds' (2008) 11 *Vanderbilt Journal of Entertainment and Technology Law* 1

Brenner, S.W., Carrier, B. and Henninger, J., 'The Trojan horse defense in cybercrime cases' (2004) 21 *Santa Clara Computer and High Technology Law Journal* 1

Bronitt, S. and Gani, M., 'Shifting boundaries of cybercrime: From computer hacking to cyberterrorism' (2003) 27 *Criminal Law Journal* 303

Brown, I., 'The evolution of anti-circumvention law' (2006) 20 *International Review of Law, Computers and Technology* 271

Budd, T. and Mattinson, J., *The Extent and Nature of Stalking: Findings from the 1998 British Crime Survey*, Home Office Research Study no. 210 (2000)

Burgess, A. G., Douglas J. E. and Halloran, R., 'Stalking behaviours within domestic violence' (1997) 12 *Journal of Family Violence* 389

Butcher, S., 'Upskirt student jailed for six months', *The Age*, 25 January 2007

Calvert, C., 'Regulating sexual images on the web: Last call for Miller time, but new issues remain untapped' (2001) 23 *Hastings Communications and Entertainment Law Journal* 507

    'Opening up an academic privilege and shutting down child modeling sites: Revising child pornography laws in the United States' (2002) 107 *Dickinson Law Review* 253

Calvert, C. and Brown, J., 'Video voyeurism, privacy and the Internet: Exposing Peeping Toms in cyberspace' (2000) 18 *Cardozo Arts & Entertainment Law Journal* 469

Canada Law Reform Commission, *Electronic Surveillance*, Working Paper no. 47 (1986)

Canadian Anti-fraud Call Centre, *Phonebusters: Monthly summary report* (Competition Bureau Canada, 2008)

Canadian Internet Policy and Public Interest Clinic, *Identity Theft: Introduction and background*, CIPPIC Working Paper no. 1, ID Theft Series (2007)

    Techniques of Identity Theft, CIPPIC Working Paper no. 2, ID Theft Series (2007)

    Canadian Legislation Relevant to Identity Theft: An annotated review, CIPPIC Working Paper no. 3A, ID Theft Series (2007)

    United States Legislation Relevant to Identity Theft: An annotated review, CIPPIC Working Paper no. 3B, ID Theft Series (2007)

    Australian, French and UK Legislation Relevant to Identity Theft: An annotated review, CIPPIC Working Paper no. 3C, ID Theft Series (2007)

    Policy Approaches to Identity Theft, CIPPIC Working Paper no. 6, ID Theft Series (2007)

Carr, A., *Internet Traders of Child Pornography and Other Censorship Offenders in New Zealand* (Department of Internal Affairs, 2004)

Carr, J., *Child Abuse, Child Pornography and the Internet* (NCH, 2005)

Charlesworth, A. 'Legislating against computer misuse: The trials and tribulations of the Computer Misuse Act 1990' (1993) 4 *Journal of Law and Information Science* 80

Charlton, K. and Taylor, N., *Online Credit Card Fraud against Small Businesses*, Research and Public Policy Series no. 60 (AIC, 2004)

CIFAS, *Identity Fraud and Identity Theft*, CIFAS Online (2009)

Clarke, R., 'Human identification in information systems: Management challenges and public policy issues' (1994) *Information Technology and People* 6

Clough, J., 'Now you see it, now you don't: Digital images and the meaning of "possession"' (2008) 19 *Criminal Law Forum* 209

Cohen, L. and Felson, M., 'Social change and crime rate trends: A routine activity approach' (1979) 44 *American Sociological Review* 588

Commission on Online Child Protection, *Report to Congress* (2000)

Commonwealth of Australia, Parliamentary Debates, Senate, 30 August 2004, 26620 (Christopher Ellison, Minister for Justice and Customs)

Computer Bulletin Board Systems Task Force, *Regulation of Computer Bulletin Board Systems* (Canberra: AGPS, 1995)

Computer Crime and Intellectual Property Section, *Manual on Prosecuting Computer Crime* (US Department of Justice, 2007), www.cybercrime.gov/ccmanual/01ccma.pdf

Searching and Seizing Computers and Obtaining Electronic Evidence in Criminal Investigations (US Department of Justice, 2002)

The National Information Infrastructure Protection Act of 1996: Legislative analysis (US Department of Justice, 2003), www.cybercrime.gov/1030analysis.html

Operation Buccaneer: The investigation, US Department of Justice, www.usdoj.gov/criminal/cybercrime/ob/OBinvest.htm

Congressional Findings, Pub. L. 108–21, title V, § 501, Apr. 30, 2003, 117 Stat. 676

Congressional Findings, Section 101(a) [title I, § 121 [1]] of Pub. L. 104–208

Council of Europe, 'Convention on Cybercrime: Explanatory Report' (ETS no. 185)

Council of Europe: European Committee on Crime Problems, 'Extraterritorial criminal jurisdiction' (1992) 3 *Criminal Law Forum* 441

Craven, S., Brown, S. and Gilchrist, E., 'Sexual grooming of children: Review of literature and theoretical considerations' (2006) 12 *Journal of Sexual Aggression* 287

Cuganesan, S. and Lacey, D., *Identity Fraud in Australia: An evaluation of its nature, cost and extent* (New South Wales: SIRCA, 2003)

Deirmenjian, J. M., 'Stalking in cyberspace' (1999) 27 *Journal of the American Academy of Psychiatry and the Law* 407

Denning, D. E., *Cyberterrorism: Testimony before the Special Oversight Panel on Terrorism Committee on Armed Services*, US House of Representatives, 23 May 2000, www.cs.georgetown.edu/~denning/infosec/cyberterror.html

Department of Broadband, Communications and the Digital Economy, *Online Statistics* (Australian Government, 2008), www.archive.dbcde.gov.au/2008/01/statistical_benchmarking/online_statistics

Department of Communications, Information Technology and the Arts, *Report on the Spam Act 2003 Review* (Australian Government, Department of Communications, Information Technology and the Arts, 2006)

Department of Justice, Canada, *Lawful Access: Consultation document* (Department of Justice, Industry Canada, and Solicitor General Canada, 2002)

Voyeurism as a Criminal Offence, Consultation Paper (2002)

A Handbook for Police and Crown Prosecutors on Criminal Harassment (2004)

Department of Justice, Victoria, *Crimes Amendment (Identity Crime) Bill Exposure Draft: Discussion paper* (2008)

Dibbell, J., 'A rape in cyberspace: How an evil clown, a Haitian trickster spirit, two wizards, and a cast of dozens turned a database into a society', *The Village Voice* 23 December 1993, http://juliandibbell.com/texts/bungle_vv.html

Drugs and Crime Prevention Committee, *Inquiry into Fraud and Electronic Commerce*, Final Report, Parliament of Victoria (2004)

Dutton, W. H., di Gennaro, C. and Hargrave, A. M., *The Internet in Britain: The Oxford Internet survey* (Oxford Internet Institute, United Kingdom, 2005)

Dutton, W. H., Helsper, E. J. and Gerber M. M., *The Oxford Internet Survey: The Internet in Britain 2009* (Oxford Internet Institute, United Kingdom, 2009)

Economic and Domestic Secretariat, *Identity Fraud: A study* (Cabinet Office, 2002)

Ellison, L., 'Cyberstalking: Tackling harassment on the Internet' in D. S. Wall (ed.), *Crime and the Internet* (London: Routledge, 2001)

Ellison, L. and Akdeniz, Y., 'Cyberstalking: The regulation of harassment on the Internet' (1998) *Criminal Law Review*, Special Edition: 'Crime, Criminal Justice and the Internet' 29

Evans C. and Nguyen, K., 'Second man arrested for upskirt pics', *The Age*, 23 January 2007

Explanatory Memorandum, Law and Justice Amendment (Identity Crimes and Other Measures) Bill 2008 (Cth), Commonwealth Parliament (2008)

Explanatory Memorandum, Telecommunications (Interception and Access) Amendment Bill 2007 (Cth)

Explanatory Notes, Police and Justice Act 2006, c. 48 (UK)

Explanatory Notes, Regulation of Investigatory Powers Act (2000) c. 23 (UK)

Explanatory Notes, Sexual Offences Act 2003, c. 42 (UK)

Fafinski, S., 'Computer misuse: The implications of the Police and Justice Act 2006' (2008) 72 *Journal of Criminal Law* 53

Fallows, D., *Data Memo* (PEW Internet and American Life Project, 2007)

Farhangian, J. J., 'A problem of "virtual" proportions: The difficulties inherent in tailoring virtual child pornography laws to meet constitutional standards' (2003) 12 *Journal of Law and Policy* 241

Federal Bureau of Investigation, *Innocent Images National Initiative*, US Department of Justice, www.fbi.gov/page2/feb06/innocent_images_statistics.htm

National Incident-Based Reporting System, i: *Data collection guidelines* (US Department of Justice, 2000)

Federal Trade Commission, *2006 Identity Theft Survey Report* (2007)

'Facts for consumers: Dot cons' (2000), www.ftc.gov/bcp/edu/pubs/consumer/tech/tec09.shtm

FTC Consumer Alert: 'Free security scan' could cost time and money (Federal Trade Commission, Bureau of Consumer Protection, 2008)

Spam Summit: The next generation of threats and solutions (Federal Trade Commission, 2007)

Feldmeier, J. P., 'Close enough for government work: An examination of Congressional efforts to reduce the government's burden of proof in child pornography cases' (2003) 30 *Northern Kentucky Law Review* 205

Finch, E., *The Criminalisation of Stalking* (London: Routledge-Cavendish, 2001)

'The objective standard of reasonableness and the mentally ill stalker' (2001) 65 *The Journal of Criminal Law* 489

'Stalking the perfect stalking law: An evaluation of the efficacy of the Protection from Harassment Act 1997' (2002) *Criminal Law Review* 703

'The problem of stolen identity and the Internet' in Y. Jewkes (ed.), *Crime Online* (United Kingdom: Willan Publishing, 2007)

Fisher, B. S., Cullen, F. T. and Turner, M. G., 'Being pursued: Stalking victimization in a national study of college women' (2002) 1 *Criminology and Public Policy* 257

Foss, M. and Johnson, E., *Symantec Report on the Underground Economy July 07–June 08* (Symantec, 2008)

Fraud Prevention Expert Group, *Report on Identity Theft/Fraud* (European Commission, 2007)

Garfinkel, S. L. and Shelat, A., 'Remembrance of data passed: A study of disk sanitization practices' (2003) 1 *IEEE Security & Privacy* 17

Geltzer, J. N., 'The new pirates of the Caribbean: How data havens can provide safe harbors on the Internet beyond governmental reach' (2004) *Southwestern Journal of Law and Trade in the Americas* 433

Gilbert, D., Kerr I. R. and McGill, J., 'The medium and the message: Personal privacy and the forced marriage of police and telecommunications providers' (2007) 51 *Criminal Law Quarterly* 469

Gillespie, A. A., 'Children, chatrooms and the law' (2001) *Criminal Law Review* 435

'Child protection on the Internet: Challenges for criminal law' (2002) 14 *Child and Family Law Quarterly* 411

'The Sexual Offences Act 2003 (3): Tinkering with "child pornography"' (2004) *Criminal Law Review* 361

'Child pornography: Balancing substantive and evidential law to safeguard children effectively from abuse' (2005) 9 *The International Journal of Evidence and Proof* 29

'Cyber-bullying and harassment of teenagers: The legal response' (2006) 28 *Journal of Social Welfare & Family Law* 123

'Enticing children on the Internet: The response of the criminal law' (2006) 3 *Juridical Review* 229

'Indecent images, grooming and the law' (2006) *Criminal Law Review* 412

'"Up-skirts" and "down-blouses": Voyeurism and the law' (2008) *Criminal Law Review* 370

Goldman, E., 'A road to no warez: The No Electronic Theft Act and criminal copyright infringement' (2003) *Oregon Law Review* 369

Goldsmith, J., 'Against cyberanarchy' (1998) *University of Chicago Law Review* 1199

Goodman, M. D and Brenner, S. W., 'The emerging consensus on criminal conduct in cyberspace' (2002) *UCLA Journal of Law and Technology* 3

Goodno, N. H., 'Cyberstalking: A new crime: Evaluating the effectiveness of current state and federal laws' (2007) 72 *Missouri Law Review* 125

Grabosky, P., *Electronic Crime* (New Jersey: Pearson Prentice Hall, 2007)

Grabosky, P., Smith, R. G. and Dempsey, G., *Electronic Theft: Unlawful acquisition in cyberspace* (Cambridge: Cambridge University Press, 2001)

Grant, I., Bone, N. and Grant, K., 'Canada's criminal harassment provisions: A review of the first ten years' (2003) 29 *Queen's Law Journal* 175

Griffith, G. and Roth, L., *Protecting Children from Online Sexual Predators*, Briefing Paper no. 10/107 (NSW Parliamentary Library Research Service, 2007)

Griffith, G. and Simon, K., *Child Pornography Law*, Briefing Paper no. 9/08,(NSW Parliamentary Library Research Service, 2008)

Gross, A. V., 'Criminal liability for theft of, interference with, or unauthorized use of, computer programs, files, or systems' (2003) 51 *ALR* 4th 971

Hammack, S., 'The Internet loophole: Why threatening speech on-line requires a modification of the courts' approach to true threats and incitement' (2002) 36 *Columbia Journal of Law and Social Problems* 65

Hébert, M. and Pilon, H., *Computer Crime* (Department of Justice Canada, 1991)

Hedley, S., 'A brief history of spam' (2006) 15 *Information and Communications Technology Law* 223

Herrera-Flanigan, J. R., 'Cybercrime and jurisdiction in the United States' in B. J. Koops and S. W. Brenner, *Cybercrime and Jurisdiction: A global survey* (The Hague: TMC Asser Press, 2006)

Hirst, M., *Jurisdiction and the Ambit of the Criminal Law* (Oxford: Oxford University Press, 2003)

Hitt, J., 'Child pornography and technology: The troubling analysis of United States v Mohrbacher' (2001) 34 *University of California Davis Law Review* 1129

Holmes, N. and Valiquet, D., *Bill S-4: An Act to Amend the Criminal Code (Identity Theft and Related Misconduct)*, Legislative Summary LS-637E (Legal and Legislative Affairs Division, Canada, 2009)

Home Office, *Setting the Boundaries: Reforming the law on sex offences* (2000), vol. i

Hong, H., 'Hacking through the Computer Fraud and Abuse Act' (1997) 31 *University of California Davis Law Review* 283

Horstmann, T. J., 'Protecting traditional privacy rights in a brave new digital world: The threat posed by cellular phone-cameras and what states should do to stop it' (2007) 111 *Pennsylvania State Law Review* 739

House of Commons Standing Committee on Justice And Legal Affairs, *Computer Crime*, Final Report (1983)

Hubbard, R. W., Brauti, P. M. and Fenton, S. K., *Wiretapping and Other Electronic Surveillance: Law and procedure* (Ontario: Canada Law Book, 2008)

Hughes, D. M., 'The use of new communications and information technologies for sexual exploitation of women and children' (2002) 13 *Hastings Women's Law Journal* 127

Hyde-Bales, K., Morris, S. and Charlton, A., *The Police Recording of Computer Crime*, Development and Practice Report (Home Office, 2004)

Industry Canada, *Stopping Spam: Creating a stronger, safer Internet*, Report of the Task Force on Spam (Industry Canada, 2005)

Interac, *Consumers – Security: Fraud* (2008), www.interac.ca/consumers/security_fraud.php

Interception Legislation Team – Home Office, *Interception of Communications in the United Kingdom*, Consultation Paper, Cm. 4368 (1999)

International Federation of the Photographic Industry, *IFPI Digital Music Report 2008*, www.ifpi.org/content/section_resources/dmr2008.html

Internet Crime Complaint Center, *Internet Crime Report 2007* (Internet Crime Complaint Center, 2007)

Internet Crime Forum Legal Subgroup, *Reform of the Computer Misuse Act 1990* (2003)

Internet Crime Forum, *Chat Wise, Street Wise: Children and Internet chat services* (2001), www.internetcrimeforum.org.uk/chatwise_streetwise.pdf

Internet World Stats, *Internet Usage Statistics: The Internet big picture – world Internet users and population stats* (2009), www.internetworldstats.com/stats.htm

Jefferson, S. and Sharfritz, R., 'A survey of cyberstalking legislation' (2001) 32 *University of West Los Angeles Law Review* 323

Jenkins, P., *Beyond Tolerance: Child pornography on the Internet* (New York: New York University Press, 2001)

Johannes, R., *2006 Identity Fraud Survey Report* (Javelin Strategy and Research, 2006)

Johnson D. R. and Post, D., 'Law and borders: The rise of law in cyberspace' (1996) 48 *Stanford Law Review* 1367

Joint Standing Committee on Treaties, *Extradition: A review of Australia's law and policy*, Report 40 (Parliament of Australia, 2001)

Jones, A. and Doobay, A., *Jones and Doobay on Extradition and Mutual Assistance* (London: Sweet and Maxwell, 2005)

Karst, K. L., 'Threats and meanings: How the facts govern First Amendment doctrine' (2006) 58 *Stanford Law Review* 1337

Kaspersen, H. W. K., 'Jurisdiction in the Cybercrime Convention' in B. J. Koops and S. W. Brenner, *Cybercrime and Jurisdiction: A global survey* (The Hague: TMC Asser Press, 2006)

Kastens, A. H., 'State v Stevenson, the "Peeping Tom" case: Overbreadth or overblown?' (2001) *Wisconsin Law Review* 1371

Katyal, N. K., 'Criminal law in cyberspace' (2001) 149 *University of Pennsylvania Law Review* 1003

Keith, S., 'Fear-mongering or fact: The construction of "cyber-terrorism" in US, UK, and Canadian news media', Paper presented at Safety and Security in a Networked World: Balancing Cyber-Rights and Responsibilities sponsored by the Oxford Internet Institute, Oxford, England, 8–10 September, 2005

Kerr, O. S., 'Cybercrime's scope: Interpreting "access" and "authorization" in computer misuse statutes' (2003) 78 *New York University Law Review* 1596

'Internet surveillance law after the USA Patriot Act: The big brother that isn't' (2003) 97 *Northwestern University Law Review* 607

'Lifting the "fog" of Internet surveillance: How a suppression remedy would change computer crime law' (2003) 54 *Hastings Law Journal* 805

'The problem of perspective in Internet law' (2003) *Georgetown Law Journal* 357

'A user's guide to the Stored Communications Act – and a legislator's guide to amending it' (2004) 72 *George Washington Law Review* 1701

'Virtual crime, virtual deterrence: A skeptical view of self help, architecture and civil liability' (2005) *Journal of Law, Economics and Policy* 197

Computer Crime Law (St. Paul: Thomson West, 2006)

'Searches and seizures in a digital world' (2006) 119 *Harvard Law Review* 531

'Criminal law in virtual worlds' (2008) *University of Chicago Legal Forum* 415

'The case for the third-party doctrine' (2009) 107 *Michigan Law Review* 561

Kershaw, C., Nicholas, S. and Walker, A., *Crime in England and Wales 2007/08*, Home Office Statistical Bulletin (2008)

Kohl, U., *Jurisdiction and the Internet: Regulatory competence over online activity* (Cambridge: Cambridge University Press, 2007)

Koops, B. J. and Brenner, S. W., *Cybercrime and Jurisdiction: A global survey* (The Hague: TMC Asser Press, 2006)

Kotadia, M., 'Trojan horse found responsible for child porn', *ZDNet.co.uk*, 1 August 2003, http://news.zdnet.co.uk/security/0,1000000189,39115422,00.htm

Kowalski, M., *Cyber-Crime: Issues, data sources, and feasibility of collecting police-reported statistics*, Cat. no. 85–558, Canadian Centre for Justice Statistics (2002)

Kreston, S. S., 'Defeating the virtual defense in child pornography prosecutions' (2004) *Journal of High Technology Law* 49

Krone, T., *A Typology of Online Child Pornography Offending*, Trends and Issues in Crime and Criminal Justice (AIC, 2004)

Does Thinking Make it So? Defining online child pornography possession offences, Trends and Issues in Crime and Criminal Justice (AIC, 2005)

International Police Operations against Online Child Pornography, Trends and Issues in Crime and Criminal Justice (AIC, 2005)

LaFave, W. R., *Criminal Law*, 4th edn (St. Paul: Thomson, 2003)

Lamb, H., *Principal Current Data Types*, Internet Crime Forum (2001), found at Home Office, *Retention of Communications Data Under Part 11: Anti-Terrorism, Crime and Security Act 2001*, Voluntary Code of Practice (2001)

Lamplugh D. and Infield, P., 'Harmonizing anti-stalking laws' (2003) 34 *George Washington International Law Review* 853

Lanham, D., *Cross-Border Criminal Law* (Sydney: FT Law & Tax, 1997)

Lanning, K., *Child Molesters: A behavioural analysis* (Washington DC: National Center for Missing and Exploited Children, 1992)

Lastowka F. G. and Hunter, D., 'Virtual crimes' (2004–5) *New York Law School Law Review* 293

Law Commission, *Computer Misuse*, Working Paper no. 110 (1988)

Computer Misuse, Final Report no. 186 (1989)

Offences of Dishonesty: Money Transfers, Item 11 of the Sixth Programme of Law Reform: Criminal Law (1996)

Fraud, Final Report, Law Com no. 276 (2002)

Law Ministers from the Commonwealth, *Model Law on Computer and Computer Related Crime* (2002), www.thecommonwealth.org/shared_asp_files/uploadedfiles/%7BDA109CD2–5204–4FAB-AA77–86970A639B05%7D_Computer%20Crime.pdf

Law Reform Commission Ireland, *Report on Privacy: Surveillance and the interception of communications*, no. 57 (1998)

Lessig, L., *Code and Other Laws of Cyberspace* (New York: Basic Books, 1999)

Loren, L., 'Digitization, commodification, criminalization: The evolution of criminal copyright infringement and the importance of the willfulness requirement' (1999) 77 *Washington University Law Quarterly* 835

Lynch, J., 'Identity theft in cyberspace: Crime control methods and their effectiveness in combating phishing attacks' (2005) 20 *Berkley Technology Law Journal* 259

Madison, M. J., 'Rights of access and the shape of the Internet' (2003) *Boston College Law Review* 433

Magee, J., 'The law regulating unsolicited commercial e-mail: An international perspective' (2003) 19 *Santa Clara Computer and High Technology Law Journal* 333

McCann, A. E., 'Comment: Are courts taking Internet threats seriously enough? An analysis of true threats transmitted over the Internet, as interpreted in United States v. Carmichael' (2006) 26 *Pace Law Review* 523

McConvill, J., 'Contemporary comment: Computer trespass in Victoria' (2001) 25 *Criminal Law Journal* 220

McCusker, R., 'Spam: Nuisance or menace, prevention or cure?' Trends and Issues in Criminal Justice no. 294 (*AIC*, 2005) 3

McDonald, S., 'Wireless hotspots: The truth about their evil twins' (2006) 9 *Internet Law Bulletin* 13

McEwan, T., Mullen, P. and MacKenzie, R., 'Anti-stalking legislation in practice: Are we meeting community needs?' (2007) 14 *Psychiatry, Psychology and Law* 207

McGrath, M. and Casey, E., 'Forensic psychiatry and the Internet: Practical perspectives on sexual predators and obsessional harassers in cyberspace' (2002) 30 *Journal of the American Academy of Psychiatry and the Law* 81

McKnight, G., *Computer Crime* (London: Joseph, 1973)

Merschman, J. C., 'The dark side of the web: Cyberstalking and the need for contemporary legislation' (2001) 24 *Harvard Women's Law Journal* 255

MessageLabs, *MessageLabs Intelligence Report April 2008*, www.messagelabs.com.au/intelligence.aspx

MessageLabs Intelligence Report June 2009, www.messagelabs.com.au/resources/mlireports.

Miano, T. J., 'Formalist statutory construction and the doctrine of fair warning: An examination of United States v. Councilman' (2007) 14 *George Mason Law Review* 513

Miletic, D., '"Groomer" guilty of procuring girl, 14, for sex', *The Age*, 26 May 2006

Mishler, J. L., 'Cyberstalking: Can communication via the Internet constitute a credible threat, and should an Internet service provider be liable if it does?' (2000) 17 *Santa Clara Computer and High Technology Law Journal* 115

Mitchell, K. J., Wolak, J. and Finkelhor, D., 'Police posing as juveniles online to catch sex offenders: Is it working?' (2005) 17 *Sexual Abuse: A Journal of Research and Treatment* 241

Mnookin, J. L., 'Virtual(ly) law: The emergence of law in LambdaMOO' (1996) 2 *Journal of Computer-Mediated Communication*

Model Criminal Code Officers Committee, *Chapter 5: Sexual Offences Against the Person*, Final Report (1999)

Chapter 4: Damage and Computer Offences, Discussion Paper (2000)

Chapter 4: Damage and Computer Offences, Final Report (2001)

Chapter 3: Credit Card Skimming Offences, Final Report (2006)

Model Criminal Law Officers Committee, *Identity Crime*, Discussion Paper (2007)

Identity Crime, Final Report (2008)

Moohr, G. S., 'The crime of copyright infringement: An inquiry based on morality, harm and criminal theory' (2003) 83 *Boston University Law Review* 731

Morris, S., *The Future of Netcrime Now: Part 1 – Threats and challenges*, Home Office Online Report 62/04 (Home Office, 2004)

Muir, D., *Violence against Children in Cyberspace. A contribution to the United Nations study on violence against children* (Bangkok: ECPAT International, 2005)

Mullen, P. E., Pathé M. and Purcell, R., *Stalkers and Their Victims* (New York: Cambridge University Press, 2000)

Naraine, R., 'Computer virus "hijacks" American Express web site', Fox News, 1 May 2006, www.foxnews.com/story/0,2933,193784,00.html

Nash, V. and Peltu, M., *Rethinking Safety and Security in a Networked World: Reducing harm by increasing cooperation*, Oxford Internet Institute Forum, Discussion Paper no. 6 (2005)

Nathanson Centre on Transnational Human Rights, Crime and Security, *Organized Crime in Canada: A quarterly summary*, July to September 2003, York University, www.yorku.ca/nathanson/CurrentEvents/2003_Q3.htm

    Organized Crime in Canada: A quarterly summary, January to March 2006, York University, www.yorku.ca/nathanson/CurrentEvents/2006_Q1_.htm

National Criminal Intelligence Service, *Project Trawler: Crime on the information highways* (1999), www.cyber-rights.org/documents/trawler.htm

National Institute of Justice, *Project to Develop a Model Anti-Stalking Code for States* (Department of Justice 1993)

National Offender Management Service and Scottish Executive, *Consultation: On the possession of extreme pornographic material* (Home Office, 2005)

National Statistics, 'Value of Internet sales rises 56 per cent in 2005', News Release (National Statistics, UK 2006)

    First Release: Internet access 2007: Households and individuals (2007), www.statistics.gov.uk/pdfdir/inta0807.pdf

    Adult Mobile Phone Ownership or Use: By age, 2001 and 2003, Social Trends 34 (2009), www.statistics.gov.uk/STATBASE/ssdataset.asp?vlnk=7202>

New South Wales Law Reform Commission, *Surveillance: Final Report*, Report 108 (2005)

New Zealand Law Commission, *Intimate Covert Filming Study Paper*, no. 15 (2004)

Newman G. R. and McNally, M. M., *Identity theft literature review* (Office of Justice Programs, US Department of Justice, 2005)

Ng, K., 'Spam legislation in Canada: Federalism, freedom of expression and the regulation of the Internet' (2005) 2 *University of Ottawa Law and Technology Journal* 447

Norfolk, A., 'Computer expert faces jail over "made-up" child porn image', *Times Online*, 10 August 2006, http://technology.timesonline.co.uk/tol/news/tech_and_web/article604825.ece

O'Connell, R., *A Typology of Cybersexploitation and On-line Grooming Practices* (Cyberspace Research Unit, University of Central Lancashire, 2003)

O'Neill, M. E., 'Old crimes in new bottles: Sanctioning cybercrime' (2000) 9 *George Mason Law Review* 237

Ogilvie, E., 'Cyberstalking', Trends and Issues in Crime and Criminal Justice, no.166 (AIC, 2000)

> *Stalking: Legislative, policing and prosecution patterns in Australia*, AIC Research and Public Policy Series no. 34 (AIC, 2000)

> 'The Internet and cyberstalking', Paper Presented at the Stalking: Criminal Justice Responses Conference, *AIC*, Sydney, 7–8 December 2000

Olivenbaum, J. M., '<CTRL><ALT><DEL>: Rethinking federal computer crime legislation' (1997) 27 *Seton Hall Law Review* 574

Organisation for Economic Co-Operation and Development, *OECD Guidelines for the Security of Information Systems and Networks: Towards a culture of security* (OECD, 2002)

> *Scoping Paper on Online Identity Theft*, Ministerial Background Report (2007)

Ost, S., 'Getting to grips with sexual grooming? The new offence under the Sexual Offences Act 2003' (2004) 26 *Journal of Social Welfare and Family Law* 147

Oyama, K. A., 'E-mail privacy after United States v. Councilman: Legislative options for amending ECPA' (2006) 21 *Berkeley Technology Law Journal* 499

Packard, A., 'Does proposed federal cyberstalking legislation meet constitutional requirements?' (2000) 5 *Communication Law and Policy* 505

Paget, F., '*Identity Theft*', White Paper (McAfee, 2007)

Parker, D. B., *Crime by Computer* (New York: Scribner, 1976)

> *Fighting Computer Crime* (New York: Scribner, 1983)

Parliamentary Joint Committee on the National Crime Authority, *Organised Criminal Paedophile Activity* (Commonwealth of Australia, 1995)

> *Cybercrime* (Parliament of the Commonwealth of Australia, 2004)

Pastrikos, C., 'Identity theft statutes: Which will protect Americans the most?' (2004) 67 *Albany Law Review* 1137

Paust, J., 'Panel: Cybercrimes and the domestication of international criminal law' (2007) 5 *Santa Clara Journal of International Law* 432

Penney, S., 'Crime, copyright, and the digital age' in Law Commission of Canada, *What is a Crime? Defining criminal conduct in contemporary society* (Vancouver: UBC Press, 2004)

Peretti, K., 'Data breaches: What the underground world of "carding" reveals' (2008) 25 *Santa Clara Computer and High Technology Journal* 375

Podgor, E. S., 'International computer fraud: A paradigm for limiting national jurisdiction' (2002) 35 *University of California Davis Law Review* 267

> 'Extraterritorial criminal jurisdiction: Replacing "objective territoriality" with "defensive territoriality"' in A. Sarat and P. Ewick (eds.), *Studies in Law, Politics, and Society* (2003)

Postini Inc., *2007 Postini Communications Intelligence Report* (Postini Inc., 2007)

Potashman, M., 'International spam regulation and enforcement: Recommendations following the world summit on the information society' (2006) 29 *Boston College International & Comparative Law Review* 323

President's Working Group on Unlawful Conduct on the Internet, *The Electronic Frontier: The challenge of unlawful conduct involving the use of the Internet* (2000), www.usdoj.gov/criminal/cybercrime/unlawful.htm

Purcell, R., Pathé, M. and Mullen, P. E., 'The prevalence and nature of stalking in the Australian community' (2002) 36 *Australian and New Zealand Journal of Psychiatry* 114

'Stalking: Defining and prosecuting a new category of offending' (2004) 27 *International Journal of Law and Psychiatry* 157

Radosevich, A. C., 'Thwarting the stalker: Are anti-stalking measures keeping pace with today's stalker?' (2000) *University of Illinois Law Review* 1371

Ramasastry, A., Winn J. K. and Winn, P., 'Will wi-fi make your private network public? Wardriving, criminal and civil liability, and the security risks of wireless networks' (2005) 1 *Shidler Journal of Law, Commerce and Technology* 9

Rathmell, A., Valeri, L., Robinson N. and Servida, A., *Handbook of Legislative Procedures of Computer and Network Misuse in EU Countries*, Study for the European Commission Directorate-General Information Society (2002)

Reed, C., *Why Must You Be Mean to Me? – Crime, punishment and online personality*, School of Law Working Paper Series, Queen Mary University of London (2008)

Restatement (Third) of Foreign Relations Law of the United States

Richardson, R., *2008: CSI Computer Crime and Security Survey* (Computer Security Institute, 2008)

Ricketson, S. and Ginsburg, J.C., *Inducers and Authorisers: A comparison of the US Supreme Court's Grokster decision and the Australian Federal Court's KaZaa ruling*, Columbia Public Law and Legal Theory Working Papers, Paper no. 0698, Columbia Law School (2006)

Roach, G. and Michiels, W.J., 'Damages is the gatekeeper issue for federal computer fraud' (2006) 8 *Tulane Journal of Technology and Intellectual Property* 61

Roddy, J., 'The Federal Computer Systems Protection Act' (1979) 7 *Rutgers Journal of Computers Technology and the Law* 343

Rogers, A., 'Playing hide and seek: How to protect virtual pornographers and actual children on the Internet' (2005) *Villanova Law Review* 87

Rogers, K., 'Viagra, viruses and virgins: A pan-Atlantic comparative analysis on the vanquishing of spam' (2006) 22 *Computer Law and Security Report* 228

Rothenberg, L. E., 'Re-thinking privacy: Peeping Toms, video voyeurs, and failure of the criminal law to recognize a reasonable expectation of privacy in the public space' (2000) 49 *American University Law Review* 1127

Roundy, M. D., 'The Wiretap Act – reconcilable differences: A framework for deter-
mining the "interception" of electronic communications following United
States v. Councilman's rejection of the storage/transit dichotomy' (2006) 28
Western New England Law Review 403

Ryan, P. S., 'War, peace, or stalemate: Wargames, wardialing, wardriving, and the
emerging market for hacker ethics' (2004) 9 *Virginia Journal of Law and
Technology* 7

Schjølberg, S. and Hubbard, A. M., *Harmonizing National Legal Approaches on
Cybercrime*, Background Paper, International Telecommunications Union
(2005)

Schryen, G., 'Anti-spam legislation: An analysis of laws and their effectiveness'
(2007) 16 *Information and Communications Technology Law* 17

Scott, A. H., *Computer and Intellectual Property Crime: Federal and state law*
(Washington DC: The Bureau of National Affairs, Inc., 2001)

Scottish Law Commission, *Report on Computer Crime*, Final Report no. 106
(1987)

Senate Legal and Constitutional Legislation Committee, *Provisions of the Telecommunications Amendment Bill* 2004 (Canberra, 2004)

  Provisions of the Telecommunications (Interception) Amendment Bill 2006
  (Canberra, 2006)

Siebecker, M. R., 'Cookies and the common law: Are Internet advertisers trespassing
on our computers?' (2003) 76 *Southern California Law Review* 893

Sieber, U., *Legal Aspects of Computer-Related Crime in the Information Society*,
COMCRIME Study, European Commission (1998)

Singleton, S., 'Comment: Computer Misuse Act 1990 – recent developments' (1993)
57 *Journal of Criminal Law* 181

Sinrod E. J. and Reilly, W. P., 'Cyber-crimes: A practical approach to the application
of federal computer crime laws' (2000) 16 *Santa Clara Computer and High
Tech Law Journal* 177

Siwek, S. E., *Copyright Industries in the US Economy: The 2004 report* (International
Intellectual Property Alliance, 2004)

Smith, J. C., 'Case & comment' (1999) *Criminal Law Review* 970

Smith, R. G., Grabosky, P. and Urbas, G., *Cyber Criminals on Trial* (Cambridge:
Cambridge University Press, 2004)

Smith, R.G., Holmes, M. N. and Kaufmann, P., 'Nigerian advance fee fraud' Trends
and Issues in Criminal Justice no. 121 (AIC, 1996)

Solicitor General, Canada and US Department of Justice, *Public Advisory: Special
report for consumers on identity theft* (2003)

Solove, D. J., 'The future of the Internet surveillance law: A symposium to discuss Internet surveillance, privacy & the USA PATRIOT Act: Surveillance
law: Reshaping framework: Electronic surveillance law' (2004) 72 *George
Washington Law Review* 1264

Soma, J., Singer, P. and Hurdd, J., 'Spam still pays: The failure of the CAN-SPAM Act of 2003 and proposed legal solutions' (2008) 45 *Harvard Journal on Legislation* 165

Soma, J. T., Muther, Jr, T. F. and Brissette, H. M. L., 'Transnational extradition for computer crimes: Are new treaties and laws needed?' (1997) 34 *Harvard Journal on Legislation* 317

Sommer, P., 'Criminalising hacking tools' (2006) 3 *Digital Investigation* 68

Sophos, *Security Threat Report: 2009*, www.sophos.com/sophos/docs/eng/marketing _material/sophos-security-threat-report-jan-2009-na.pdf

Sorkin, D., 'Technical and legal approaches to unsolicited electronic mail' (2001) 35 *University of San Francisco Law Review* 325

Staff Report Prepared for the Use of the Committee on Energy and Commerce, *Sexual Exploitation of Children over the Internet*, US House of Representatives, 109th Congress, January 2007

Standing Committee of Attorney's-General, *Unauthorised Photographs on the Internet and Ancillary Privacy Issues*, Discussion Paper, Civil Law Policy (Melbourne: Department of Justice, 2005)

Standing Committee on Legal and Constitutional Affairs, *Telecommunications (Interception and Access) Amendment Bill* 2007 (Canberra, Commonwealth of Australia, 2007)

Statistics Canada, *Household Internet Use Survey-Microdata User's Guide 2003*, Cat no. 56M0002GIE (2004), http://dsp-psd.pwgsc.gc.ca/Collection/Statcan/ 56M0002G/56M0002GIE.html

    Electronic Commerce Households Spending in Canada and in Other Countries, by Region (2005), www40.statcan.ca/l01/cst01/comm07a.htm

    Residential Telephone Service Survey (2007), www.statcan.gc.ca/daily-quotidien/ 070504/dq070504a-eng.htm

Steel, A., 'Vaguely going where no-one has gone: The expansive new computer access offences' (2002) 26 *Criminal Law Journal* 72

Steiner, P., 'On the Internet, nobody knows you're a dog', *The New Yorker*, 5 July 1993

Steinhauer, J., 'Verdict in MySpace suicide case', *New York Times*, 26 November 2008

Sullivan, C., 'The response of the criminal law in Australia to computer abuse' (1988) 12 *Criminal Law Journal* 228

Symantec, *Spam Monthly Report January* 2009, http://eval.symantec.com/ mktginfo/enterprise/otherresources/b-state_of_spam_report_01-2009.en-us. pdf

Task Force on Child Protection on the Internet, *Protecting the Public*, Cm. 5668 (Home Office, 2002)

Task Force on Intellectual Property, *Progress Report of the Department of Justice's Task Force on Intellectual Property* (US Department of Justice, 2006)

Task Force on Spam, *Anti-Spam Law Enforcement* (Organisation for Economic Co-operation and Development, 2005)

  Anti-Spam Regulation (Organisation for Economic Co-operation and Development, 2005)

  Report of the OECD Task Force on Spam: Anti-spam toolkit of recommended policies and measures (Organisation for Economic Co-operation and Development, 2006)

Tasmanian Law Reform Commission, *Report on Computer Misuse*, Report no. 47 (1986)

Taylor, M. and Quayle, E., *Child Pornography: An Internet crime* (East Sussex: Brunner-Routledge, 2003)

The President's Identity Theft Task Force, *Combating Identity Theft: A strategic plan* (2007)

The White House, *The National Strategy to Secure Cyberspace* (Washington DC, 2003)

Tjaden, P. and Thoennes, J., *Prevalence, Incidence, and Consequences of Violence against Women: Findings from the national violence against women survey*, US Department of Justice, Office of Justice Programs (1998)

UK Sentencing Advisory Panel, *The Panel's Advice to the Court of Appeal on Offences Involving Child Pornography* (2002)

United Nations, *Model Treaty on the Transfer of Proceedings in Criminal Matters*, A/RES/45/118, 14 (1990)

  Manual on the Prevention and Control of Computer Related Crime, International Review of Criminal Policy Nos. 43–4 (1999)

US Attorney, District of New Jersey, 'Multi-million dollar home equity line of credit, identity theft and computer intrusion ring busted' Press Release (US Department of Justice, 2008)

US Attorney, Southern District of New York, 'U.S. announces sentencing of man in largest identity theft case in nation's history', Press Release, (US Department of Justice, 2005), www.usdoj.gov/usao/nys/pressreleases/January05/cummingssentencingpr.pdf

US Attorney General, *Report to Congress on Stalking and Domestic Violence* (US Department of Justice, Office of Justice Programs, 2001)

US Attorney's Office, District of New Jersey, '"Shadowcrew" identity theft ringleader gets 32 months in prison', News Release (2006), www.usdoj.gov/usao/nj/press/files/mant0629_r.htm

US Attorney's Office, Western District of New York and US Department of Justice Computer Crimes and Intellectual Property Section, *The Online World and Law Enforcement*, www.fpd-fln.org/online_world_and_law_enforcement.htm

US Census Bureau, *Computer and Internet Use in the United States 2003* (US Department of Commerce, 2005)

'Quarterly retail e-commerce sales 4th Quarter 2007' (US Department of Commerce, 2007), www.census.gov/mrts/www/data/pdf/07Q4.pdf

US Computer Emergency Readiness Team, *The Continuing Denial of Service Threat Posed by DNS Recursion (v 2.0)* (2006)

US Department of Justice, *Attorney General's Commission on Pornography: Final Report* (1986)

'Warez leader sentenced to 46 months' (2002), www.cybercrime.gov/sankusSent.htm

'"Shadowcrew" Internet identity and credit card thieves plead guilty' Department of Justice Press Release (2005), www.usdoj.gov/usao/nj/press/files/shad1117_r.htm

Prosecuting Intellectual Property Crimes, 3rd edn (Office of Legal Education, 2006)

'Extradited software piracy ringleader pleads guilty' Press Release, 20 April 2007, www.usdoj.gov/criminal/pr/press_releases/2007/04/2007_5117_04–20–07 rgriffiths-plea.pdf

'Alan Ralsky, ten others, indicted in international spamming and stock-fraud scheme' (2008), www.usdoj.gov/opa/pr/2008/January/08_crm_003.html

FY 2008 Performance and Accountability Report (2008)

'Retail hacking ring charged for stealing and distributing credit and debit card numbers from major US retailers: More than 40 million credit and debit card numbers stolen', Press Release (2008), www.usdoj.gov/criminal/cybercrime/gonzalezIndict.pdf

United States Attorneys' Manual, Title 9: *Criminal Resource Manual*, 9–15.000

US Department of Justice, Computer Crimes and Intellectual Property Section, *The Online World And Law Enforcement* (US Attorney's Office, Western District of New York), www.fpd-fln.org/online_world_and_law_enforcement.htm

US Department of Justice, Western District of North Carolina, 'Hacker sentenced to prison for breaking into Lowe's companies' computers with intent to steal credit card information', Press Release (2004), www.usdoj.gov/criminal/cybercrime/salcedoSent.htm

US Government Accountability Office, *Personal Information: Data breaches are frequent, but evidence of resulting identity theft is limited; however, the full extent is unknown*, Report to Congressional Requesters (Government Accountability Office, 2007)

US Securities Exchange Commission, 'Regulators launch fake scam websites to warn investors about fraud', News Release (2002), www.sec.gov/news/headlines/scamsites.htm

US Senate, *Phony Identification and Credentials Via the Internet*, Permanent Subcommittee on Investigations of the Committee on Governmental Affairs (2002)

Urbas, G. and Choo, K. R., *Resource Material on Technology-enabled Crime*, Technical and Background Paper no. 28 (AIC, 2008)

Valiquet, D., *Telecommunications and Lawful Access: I. The legislative situation in Canada* (Library of Parliament, 2006)

Virtual Global Taskforce, 'Website snares its first online grooming offender', Press Release, 22 June 2006 www.virtualglobaltaskforce.com/news/article 22062006.html

Walby, S. and Allen, J., *Domestic Violence, Sexual Assault and Stalking: Findings from the British Crime Survey*, Home Office Research Study 276 (2004)

Walden, I., *Computer Crimes and Digital Investigations* (New York: Oxford University Press, 2007)

Walker, C., 'Cyber-terrorism: Legal principle and law in the United Kingdom' (2006) *Pennsylvania State Law Review* 625

Wall, D. S., 'Digital realism and the governance of spam as cybercrime' (2005) 10 *European Journal of Criminal Policy and Research* 309

  'Surveillant Internet technologies and the growth in information capitalism: Spams and public trust in the information society' in K. Haggerty and R. Ericson (eds.), *The New Politics of Surveillance and Visibility* (Toronto: University of Toronto Press, 2005)

  Cybercrime (Cambridge: Polity, 2007)

Warren, S. D. and Brandeis, L. D., 'The right to privacy' (1890) 4 *Harvard Law Review* 193

Wasik, M., *Crime and the Computer* (Oxford: Clarendon Press, 1991)

Weimann, G., 'Cyberterrorism: The sum of all fears?' (2005) *Studies in Conflict and Terrorism* 129

Wells, C., 'Stalking: The criminal law response' (1997) *Criminal Law Review* 463

Williams, K. S., 'Child pornography law: Does it protect children?' (2004) 26 *Journal of Social Welfare and Family Law* 245

Wilson, C., *Computer Attack and Cyberterrorism: Vulnerabilities and policy issues for Congress*, Congressional Research Service Report for Congress, (Congressional Research Service, 2005)

Wilson, D. et al., *Fraud and Technology Crimes: Findings from the 2003/04 British Crime Survey, the 2004 Offending, Crime and Justice Survey and administrative sources* (Home Office Online Report, 2006)

Wolak, J., Mitchell K. and Finkelhor, D., 'Escaping or connecting? Characteristics of youth who form close online relationships' (2003) 26 *Journal of Adolescence* 105

  Internet Sex Crimes against Minors: The response of law enforcement (Crimes against Children Research Center, 2003)

  'Internet-initiated sex crimes against minors: Implications for prevention based on findings from a national study' (2004) 35 *Journal of Adolescent Health* 424e11

Wolak, J., Finkelhor, D. and Mitchell, K. J., *Child-Pornography Possessors Arrested in Internet-Related Crimes: Findings from the national juvenile online victim-ization study* (National Center for Missing and Exploited Children, 2005)

'The varieties of child pornography production' in E. Quayle and M. Taylor (eds.), *Viewing Child Pornography on The Internet: Understanding the offense, managing the offender, helping the victims* (Russell House, 2005)

Online victimization of youth: Five years later (National Center for Missing and Exploited Children, 2006)

Wood, J. R. T., *Royal Commission into the New South Wales Police Service: Final report*, v: *The paedophile inquiry* (NSW Government, 1997)

Yar, M., *Cybercrime and Society* (London: Sage Publications, 2006)

Yu, M. A., Lehrer, R. and Roland, W., 'Intellectual property crimes' (2008) 45 *American Criminal Law Review* 665

Zappen, M. J., 'How well do you know your computer? The level of scienter in 18 USC § 1462' (2003) 66 *Albany Law Review* 1161

INDEX